Outline of Course

Section A   Chapters 1, 2, 7, 5

B   15

C   11, 16

D   6, 17, 18

E   Mathematics

F   8, 21, 19, 20

G   9, 12, 13, 23

H   10, Discussion of MASS regulations for salespersons + brokers

Modern Real Estate Practice

Fillmore W. Galaty

Wellington J. Allaway

Robert C. Kyle

Tenth Edition

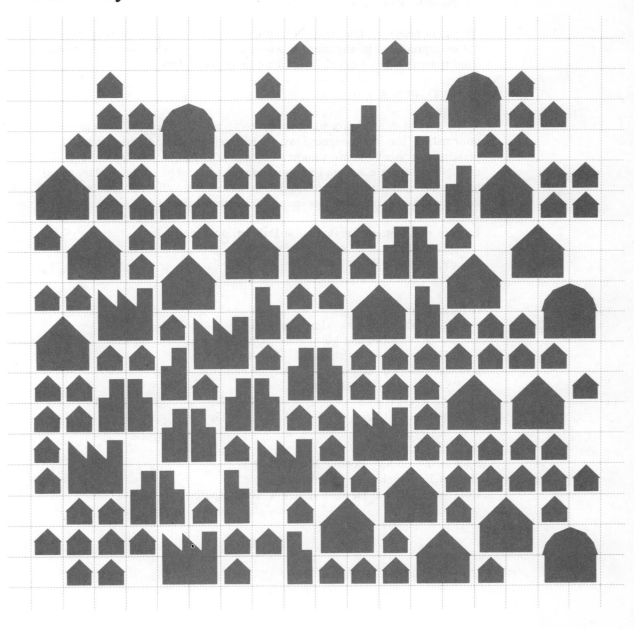

®REAL ESTATE EDUCATION COMPANY/CHICAGO
a Longman Group USA company

Published by Real Estate Education Company/Chicago
a Longman Group USA company

86 87 10 9 8 7 6

While a great deal of care has been taken to provide accurate and current information, the ideas, suggestions, general principles, and conclusions presented in this book are subject to local, state, and federal laws and regulations, court cases, and any revisions of same. The reader is thus urged to consult legal counsel regarding any points of law—this publication should not be used as a substitute for competent legal advice.

Library of Congress Cataloging in Publication Data

Galaty, Fillmore W.
    Modern real estate practice.

    Includes index.
    1. Real estate business—Law and legislation—United
States.   2. Vendors and purchasers—United States.
3. Real property—United States.   4. Real estate
business—United States.   I. Allaway, Wellington J.
II. Kyle, Robert C.   III. Title
KF2042.R4G34 1985   346.7304′37   84-22254
ISBN 0-88462-517-6   347.306437

Sponsoring Editor: Bobbye Middendorf
Project Editor: Karen Schenkenfelder
Cover and Internal Design: James A. Buddenbaum

Real Estate Education Company Series

Nevada Supplement
New Jersey Supplement, 3rd Edition
Modern Real Estate Practice in New York: For Salespersons and Brokers
   (integrated text)
North Carolina Supplement
North Dakota Supplement
Ohio Supplement, 6th Edition
Oklahoma Supplement
Modern Real Estate Practice in Pennsylvania, 3rd Edition (integrated text)
South Carolina Supplement
Tennessee Supplement
Modern Real Estate Practice in Texas, 4th Edition (integrated text)
Washington Supplement
Wisconsin Supplement, 3rd Edition

Gibson, Karp & Klayman	Real Estate Law
Greynolds & Aronofsky	Practical Real Estate Financial Analysis: Using the HP-12C Calculator
Hinds & Ordway	International Real Estate Investment
Ingleby & Boyer	Resort Timesharing Handbook
Lynge & Trowbridge	Real Estate Broker's Guide to Resort Timesharing
Kyle	Property Management, 2nd Edition
Mettling	Modern Residential Financing Methods: Tools of the Trade
Pivar	Classified Secrets
Pivar	Power Real Estate Listing
Pivar	Power Real Estate Selling
Pivar	Real Estate Ethics
Pivar	Real Estate Guide for the Licensing Exam (ASI)
Developed by Real Estate Education Company	Professional Real Estate Selling Skills
Developed by Real Estate Education Company	Straight Talk Newsletter
Developed by Real Estate Education Company in conjunction with Grubb & Ellis Company	Successful Industrial Real Estate Brokerage, 3rd Edition
Developed by Real Estate Education Company in Conjunction with Grubb & Ellis Company	Successful Leasing & Selling of Office Property, 2nd Edition

Developed by Real Estate Education Company in Conjunction with Grubb & Ellis Company	Successful Leasing & Selling of Retail Property, 2nd Edition
Reilly	Language of Real Estate, 2nd Edition
Reilly & Vitousek	Questions and Answers to Help You Pass the Real Estate Exam, 2nd Edition
Rosenauer	Effective Real Estate Sales and Marketing
Sager	Guide to Passing the Real Estate Exam (ACT)
Sirota	Essentials of Real Estate Investment, 2nd Edition
Sirota	Essentials of Real Estate Finance, 3rd Edition
Smith & Gibbons	The Real Estate Education Company Real Estate Exam Manual, 3rd Edition (ETS)
Stone	New Home Sales
Ventolo	Residential Construction
Ventolo, Allaway, & Irby	Mastering Real Estate Mathematics, 4th Edition
Ventolo & Williams	Fundamentals of Real Estate Appraisal, 3rd Edition

Contents

Part Three   **Practices**

17   **Property Management 274**

18   **Real Estate Appraisal 290**

Preface

Hundreds of thousands of professional men and women have studied *Modern Real Estate Practice* since its first printing in 1959. Although its primary use as a text has been to prepare candidates for state broker and salesperson licensing examinations, many others have studied the book as part of college and university degree programs in real estate and related fields. Still others have read it because of an interest in personal investment or because they hold positions close to the real estate profession in banks, savings and loan associations, mortgage firms, insurance companies, property management firms, or corporate real estate departments.

Through the years, the real estate industry has placed a growing emphasis on education and professionalism. State licensing examinations and educational requirements for prospective brokers and salespeople have become more sophisticated since the first edition of this book, requiring the student to demonstrate knowledge and understanding of increasingly technical information. In preparing the Tenth Edition of *Modern Real Estate Practice,* the authors have revised and updated the text to meet these requirements and to keep pace with recent trends and developments, particularly in the areas of *real estate finance and taxation.*

The Tenth Edition has been divided into three parts: Essentials, Principles, and Practices. *Essentials* consists of Chapters 1 through 4, and provides the student with an introduction to the real estate business as well as to the concepts of real property and home ownership. *Principles* encompasses Chapters 5 through 16, and represents the basic core of knowledge the real estate student must master in the topics of brokerage, ownership, legal descriptions, and real estate financing, among others. *Practices* is composed of Chapters 17 through 23, and is devoted to more practical aspects of the profession such as property management, appraisal, investment, and closing the transaction. These chapters may be taught or studied in the order suggested by the authors, or they may be adapted to any class outline or lesson plan. The review questions in each chapter have been written to apply to ETS-, ACT-, and ASI-administered real estate examinations. Also included in the Tenth Edition are a Mathematics Review, designed to help math-shy students with basic real estate computations; a Residential Construction Appendix, containing many illustrations that will assist the student in identifying important building-component terminology; and an expanded Glossary of Real Estate Terms, providing definitions of hundreds of real estate terms for easy review.

Supplements for *Modern Real Estate Practice* have been developed for over 30 states, detailing laws, principles, and practices specific to the real estate business in those particular states. A *Study Guide for Modern Real Estate Practice* contains additional review questions and study problems to further assist the student in his or her real estate education. In addition, a comprehensive Instructor's Manual and many helpful in-class transparencies are available to instructors as companions to this text. Contact Real Estate Education Company for further details about these materials.

Any comments on this text should be directed to Anita Constant, Senior Vice President, Real Estate Education Company, 500 N. Dearborn, Chicago, IL 60610.

Acknowledgments

The authors would like to thank the following reviewers for their valuable assistance in the development of the Tenth Edition of *Modern Real Estate Practice:*

Roger Cannaday, University of Illinois
John D. Ballou, Attorney-at-Law; Moraine Valley Community College
James H. Boykin, Virginia Commonwealth University
Bo Cooper, Fort Steilacoom Community College
Gardner W. Dogherty, University of Connecticut
Jerald L. Frandsen, Truckee Meadows Community College
Irene M. Hall, Foster Institute of Real Estate
Helen Marie Hartmann, Hartmann Realty Company
Dudley S. Hinds, Georgia State University
Donald L. Pietz, Central Michigan University
Lawrence Sager, Madison Area Technical College
Jules Schneider, Skills, Inc.
Arlene M. Urban, Coldwell Banker
Nancy Daggett White, Mississippi County Community College
Terrence M. Zajac, Terry Zajac Seminars

Thanks are also extended to Richard Baker, Ed Barlow, Donald Epley, Kent Huffman, Glenn Jurgens, Charlie Monroe, Henry Olivieri, William Peace, Maria Perich, Dave Schurger, Theodore D. Bell, Donald O. Bolander, Wally Davis, C. Donald Kyle, Robert Kratovil, Milton A. Morse, Jr., David Sirota, William L. Ventolo, Jr., and members of the Illinois Association of Realtors® for their contributions to earlier editions of the book.

Furthermore, special credit is extended to the following people or groups for permission to use materials or forms: American Land Title Association, Bell Federal Savings and Loan Association, Chicago Title Insurance Co., George E. Cole and Co., Financial Publishing Co., First American Title Company of Idaho, Fred B. Huebenthal, Department of Housing and Urban Development, NATIONAL ASSOCIATION OF REALTORS®, The Northern Trust Company, Northwest Suburban Board of Realtors® of Illinois, and Rand McNally and Co. Note that the George E. Cole legal forms are used through the courtesy of the Boise Cascade Corporation. These sample forms may not be applicable to all jurisdictions and are subject to pertinent changes in the law.

Finally, the authors would like to extend their appreciation to the entire staff of Real Estate Education Company for their execution of this Tenth Edition. Special assistance has been provided by Jim Gorzelany, development writer, and Karen Schenkenfelder, Project Editor in charge of editing and production. Thanks are also due to Geraldine A. Lynch, Director of Editorial and Production; Bobbye

Middendorf, Sponsoring Editor; Jeny Kucenic and Libby McGreevy, Acquisitions
Assistants.

Fillmore W. Galaty
Wellington J. Allaway
Robert C. Kyle

Part One

Essentials

1

Introduction to Modern Real Estate Practice

Key Terms

Attorney
Broker
Bundle of legal rights
Common law
Precedent
Real estate license law
Realtist
REALTOR®
REALTOR-Associate®
Salesperson
Seven sources of law

Overview

The real estate business is "big" business. Hundreds of thousands of men and women in the United States and Canada work in some aspect of the industry as brokers, salespeople, appraisers, or property managers, as well as in other areas of specialization. They aid buyers, sellers, and investors in making decisions that involve billions of dollars in property each year. In addition to people and money, real estate is a big business in terms of laws and regulations. Since real estate is one of the most heavily regulated markets, the real estate practitioner must be familiar with many sources of law on the federal, state, and local levels. This chapter will introduce you to the industry in general, as well as to the many legal considerations affecting today's real estate professional.

Real Estate Transactions

The purchase of real estate involves an entirely different type of transaction from the purchase of personal property, such as groceries, clothing, fuel, automobiles, or television sets. Although every type of sales transaction creates a change of ownership involving certain relatively simple legal problems, *even the simplest of real estate transactions brings into play a body of complex laws.*

Real estate has often been described as a **bundle of legal rights.** In other words, when a person purchases a parcel of real estate, he or she is actually buying the rights previously held by the seller. These *rights of ownership* (see figure 1.1) include the right of *possession,* the right to *control the property* within the framework of the law, the right of *enjoyment* (to use the property in any legal manner), the right of *exclusion* (to keep others from entering or occupying the property), and the right of *disposition* (to be able to sell or otherwise convey the property). Within these ownership rights are included further rights to will, devise, mortgage, encumber, cultivate, explore, lease, license, dedicate, give away, share, trade, or exchange.

**Figure 1.1
Bundle of Legal Rights**

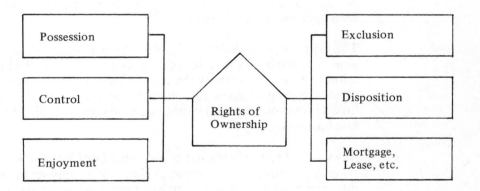

When a person acquires full ownership of real estate, however, this ownership is subject to any rights that *others* may have in the property or rights that the *owner* may reserve for him- or herself. For example, the lending institution that holds a seller's mortgage has the right to force a sale of the property if the loan is not repaid. Likewise, a person may sell real estate while retaining the rights to certain minerals or natural resources located on or beneath the surface of the land. The various rights in real estate will be discussed in detail later in the text.

Buying real estate is usually the biggest financial transaction of a person's life. The buyer pays out more cash, undertakes more debt, and has a deeper personal interest in this transaction than in any other purchase made during his or her lifetime.

When a person sells his or her real estate, the situation is similar. The real estate is likely to have been that person's biggest single investment, not only in terms of money, but also of work. Of course, there are people to whom the sale or purchase of real estate is a routine matter, but for most people, it can be a very important, complicated, and perhaps confusing affair, whether the property is located in a city (urban) or in the country (rural).

At the center of this important and sensitive transaction there is generally a middleman—the real estate **broker.** A real estate **salesperson** works on behalf of the broker. The broker and the salesperson generally represent the seller and seek a buyer for his or her property. Once they have found a prospective buyer, they bring the parties together. Then both seller and buyer look to the broker and their respective lawyers to guide and facilitate the transfer of the real estate from one party to the other.

Real Estate Law

The average citizen has very little notion of the nature of law. People generally think of laws as nothing more than rules laid down by the state to govern their conduct. However, *real estate brokers and salespeople must have a broader and better understanding of law and how various laws affect real estate.*

Sources of Real Estate Law

There are generally **seven sources of law** in the United States, all of which affect the ownership and transfer of real estate (See figure 1.2). These are: the *Constitution of the United States; laws passed by Congress; federal regulations adopted by the various agencies and commissions created by Congress; state constitutions; laws passed by state legislatures; ordinances passed by cities, towns, and other local governments; and court decisions.*

The primary purpose of the *U.S. Constitution* and the individual *state constitutions* is to establish the rights of citizens and delineate the limits of governmental authority. In a few areas of the country, municipalities are also empowered to set up local constitutions or charters with similar effects. Because they set down only broad provisions, such constitutions have only an indirect influence on the real estate business.

Laws passed by Congress and by *state and local legislative bodies* may establish specific provisions on any issue, or they may simply set broad standards of conduct and establish administrative and enforcement agencies. Generally, these agencies have the authority to adopt regulations and procedures to expand on the law and to carry out the established standards. These regulations have the effect of law.

Governmental agencies that enact rules and regulations range from the Federal Housing Administration through state real estate commissions to local zoning boards. These regulations are a means of implementing and enforcing legislative acts; they provide detailed information on legal and illegal actions and practices, and they designate penalties and violations.

Court decisions of federal, state, and municipal courts serve to clarify and interpret laws, regulations, and constitutional provisions. By applying and interpreting the laws in relation to a specific event, a court decision expands the meaning of the law. For example, an attorney draws up what he considers to be a valid contract under the provisions of state law. If the court disallows the contract, it will render an opinion as to why the contract does not fulfill the legal requirements for such a document. Future contracts in that state will then be based on the **precedent** of the requirements established by prior court decisions as well as on the statutes governing contracts.

Figure 1.2
Sources of Real
Estate Law

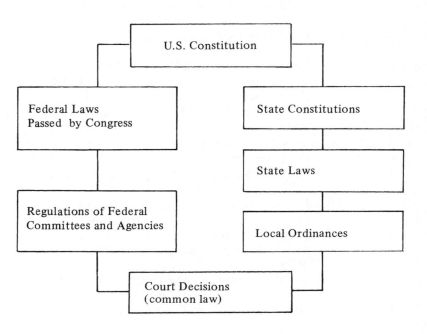

However, the courts are not always bound by the established precedent. Courts in one jurisdiction (area of authority) may not be bound by the decisions of courts in other jurisdictions. In addition, a court with superior authority in its jurisdiction may, at its discretion, reverse the ruling of a lower court.

Real estate ownership and transfer are indirectly affected by what is known as the common law. The **common law** is the body of rules and principles founded on custom, usage, and the decisions and opinions of the courts. It is derived mainly from practices developed in England and, as it applies to the United States, dates back to the practices that were in effect at the time of the American Revolution. Today the common law includes not only custom but the previous decisions of courts.

Laws Affecting Real
Estate Practice

The general sources of law encompass a number of specific areas that are important to the real estate practitioner. These include the *law of contracts,* the *general property law,* the *law of agency* (which covers the obligations of a broker to the person who engages his or her services), and the *real estate license law,* all of which will be discussed in this text.

A person engaged in the real estate business need not be an expert on real estate law, but should have a knowledge and understanding of the basic principles of the law under which he or she operates. A real estate professional must be able to recognize the technical legal problems involved in transactions that he or she will negotiate and should appreciate the necessity of referring such problems to a competent attorney. An **attorney** is a person *trained and licensed to represent another person in court, to prepare documents defining or transferring rights in property, or to give advice or counsel on matters of law.* Brokers and salespeople must be aware of their limitations in such areas.

Extreme care should be taken in handling all phases of a real estate transaction. Carelessness in handling the documents connected with a real estate sale can result in expensive legal actions. In many cases, costly court actions could have been avoided if the parties handling negotiations had exercised greater care and employed competent legal counsel.

Real estate license laws. Since real estate brokers and salespeople are engaged in the business of handling other people's real estate and money, the need for regulation of their activities has long been recognized. In an effort to protect the public from fraud, dishonesty, or incompetence in the buying and selling of real estate, all fifty states, the District of Columbia, and all Canadian provinces have passed laws that require real estate brokers and salespeople to be licensed. The first **real estate license law** was passed in California in 1917. The license laws of the various states are similar in many respects but differ in the details of their requirements.

Under these laws, a person must obtain a license in order to engage in the real estate business. In most cases, the applicant must possess certain stated personal and educational qualifications and must pass an examination to prove an adequate knowledge of the business. In addition, to qualify for license renewal and continue in business, the licensee must follow certain prescribed standards of conduct in the operation of his or her business. Some states also require licensees to complete continuing education courses. Chapter 14 describes more fully the state license laws and the required standards.

In Practice . . .	*If you do not already have a copy of the real estate broker's and salesperson's license law for your state, you should send for it* now. *Table 1.1 lists the addresses of the real estate commissions or departments for all states and Canadian provinces. When you write to your real estate commission or department, ask for the application for licensure (either the broker's or salesperson's application, depending on which license you plan to secure now), a copy of the real estate license law, a list of examination dates, and any other material normally sent to applicants. For a nominal charge, some states furnish certain study material with the application. If your state has such material, the commission will notify you.*

The Real Estate Business Is "Big" Business	Billions of dollars' worth of real estate is sold each year in the United States. In addition to this great volume of annual sales, there are rental collections by real estate management firms, appraisals of properties ranging from vacant land to modern office and apartment buildings, and the lending of money through mortgage loans on real estate.

Hundreds of thousands of people are professionally engaged in the real estate business. Full-time real estate practitioners include not only brokers, salespeople, appraisers, managers, and mortgage lenders, but also building managers and superintendents who handle real estate belonging to industrial firms, banks, trust companies, insurance firms, and other businesses, as well as state, local, and

Table 1.1
Real Estate License
Law Officials and
Commissions

Alabama—Executive Director, Alabama Real Estate Commission, State Capitol, Montgomery, 36130.

Alaska—Executive Director, Department of Commerce and Economic Development, 620 East 10th Ave., Room 203, Anchorage, 99501.

Arizona—Commissioner, Arizona Department of Real Estate, 1645 West Jefferson, Phoenix, 85007.

Arkansas—Executive Secretary, Arkansas Real Estate Commission, Number 1 Riverfront Pl., Suite 660, North Little Rock, 72114.

California—Commissioner, Department of Real Estate, 1719 24th St., Sacramento, 95816.

Colorado—Director, Colorado Real Estate Commission, 4th Floor, 1776 Logan St., Denver, 80203.

Connecticut—Real Estate Commission, 165 Capitol Ave., Hartford, 06106.

Delaware—Administrative Assistant, Delaware Real Estate Commission, P.O. Box 1401, Dover, 19901.

District of Columbia—Contact Representative, Real Estate Commission, Room 923, 614 H St. N.W., Washington, 20001.

Florida—Director, Division of Real Estate, P.O. Box 1900, 400 West Robinson St., Orlando, 32802.

Georgia—Commissioner, Real Estate Commission, 40 Pryor St., S.W., Atlanta, 30303.

Hawaii—Executive Secretary, Real Estate Commission, P.O. Box 3469, Honolulu, 96801.

Idaho—Executive Director, Idaho Real Estate Commission, State House Mail, Boise, 83702.

Illinois—Commissioner, Illinois Real Estate Administration and Disciplinary Board, 320 W. Washington St., 3rd Floor, Springfield, 62786.

Indiana—Executive Director, Real Estate Commission, 1021 State Office Building, 100 North Senate Ave., Indianapolis, 46204.

Iowa—Director, Iowa Real Estate Commission, Executive Hills, 1223 East Court, Des Moines, 50319.

Kansas—Director, Kansas Real Estate Commission, 217 E. Fourth, Topeka, 66603.

Kentucky—Executive Director, Kentucky Real Estate Commission, 222 S. First St., Suite 600, Louisville, 40202.

Louisiana—Executive Director, Real Estate Commission, P.O. Box 14785, Baton Rouge, 70898.

Maine—Director, State House Station 35, Augusta, 04333.

Maryland—Maryland Real Estate Commission, 501 St. Paul Pl., Baltimore, 21202.

Massachusetts—Executive Secretary, Board of Registration of Real Estate, Brokers and Salesmen, 100 Cambridge St., Room 1524, Boston, 02202.

Michigan—Dept. of Licensing and Regulations, P.O. Box 30018, Lansing, 48909

Minnesota—Director of Licensing, Department of Commerce, 500 Metro Square Building, St. Paul, 55101.

Mississippi—Administrator, Real Estate Commission, 1920 Dunbarton, Jackson, 39206.

Missouri—Missouri Real Estate Commission, 3523 N. Ten Mile Dr., P.O. Box 1339, Jefferson City, 65102.

Montana—Administrative Officer, Board of Realty Regulation, 1424 9th Ave., Helena, 59620–0407.

Nebraska—Director, Real Estate Commission, 301 Centennial Mall S., Lincoln, 68509.

Nevada—Administrator, Capitol Complex, 201 South Fall St., Room 128, Carson City, 89710.

New Hampshire—Executive Director, New Hampshire Real Estate Commission, 3 Capitol St., Concord, 03301.

New Jersey—Director, New Jersey Real Estate Commission, 201 E. State St., Trenton, 08625.

New Mexico—Executive Secretary, Real Estate Commission, 4000 San Pedro N.E., Suite A, Albuquerque, 87110.

New York—New York Department of State, Division of Licensing, 162 Washington Ave., Albany, 12231.

North Carolina—Executive Director, Real Estate Commission, P.O. Box 17100, Raleigh, 27619.

North Dakota—Secretary, Real Estate Commission, 314 E. Thayer Ave., Box 727, Bismarck, 58502.

Ohio—Superintendent, Department of Commerce, Division of Real Estate, Two Nationwide Plaza, Columbus, 43215.

Oklahoma—Oklahoma Real Estate Commission, 4040 N. Lincoln Blvd., Suite 100, Oklahoma City, 73105.

Oregon—Commissioner, Oregon Real Estate Division, 158 12th St., N.E., Salem, 97310.

Pennsylvania—Administrative Officer, Real Estate Commission, P.O. Box 2649, Room 611, Transportation and Safety Building, Commonwealth Ave. and Forster St., Harrisburg, 17105–2649.

Table 1.1
Real Estate License
Law Officials and
Commissions (cont.)

Rhode Island—Deputy Administrator, Real Estate Division, 100 North Main St., Providence, 02903.

South Carolina—Commissioner, P.O. Box 5917, Columbia, 29250.

South Dakota—Secretary, Real Estate Board, P.O. Box 490, Pierre, 57501.

Tennessee—Executive Director, Real Estate Commission, 706 Church St., Nashville, 37203.

Texas—Executive Secretary, Real Estate Commission, Box 12188, Austin, 78711.

Utah—Dept. of Business Regulation, Real Estate Division, 160 E. 300 South, P.O. Box 5802, Salt Lake City, 84110.

Vermont—Executive Secretary, Vermont Real Estate Commission, 7 E. State St., Montpelier, 05602.

Virgina—Assistant Director of Real Estate, Department of Commerce, 3600 W. Broad St., Richmond, 23230.

Washington—Department of Licensing, Real Estate Division, P.O. Box 247, Olympia, 98405.

West Virginia—Executive Secretary, Real Estate Commission, 1033 Quarrier Street, Suite 400, Charleston, 25301.

Wisconsin—Director, Real Estate Bureau, 1400 E. Washington Ave., P.O. Box 8936, Madison, 53708.

Wyoming—Director of Real Estate Commision, 720 W. 18th St., Cheyenne, 82002.

Canada

Alberta—Superintendent of Real Estate, Department of Consumer and Corporate Affairs, 10065 Jasper Ave., Edmonton, T5K 2B6.

British Columbia—Real Estate Council, Suite 608, 626 West Pender St., Vancouver, V6B 1V9.

Manitoba—Registrar, Real Estate Brokers Act, Room 118, 405 Broadway, Winnipeg, R3C 3L6.

New Brunswick—Department of Justice, Consumer Affairs Branch, P.O. Box 6000, Fredericton, E3B 5H1.

Newfoundland—Real Estate Division, Department of Justice, P.O. Box 999, Elizabeth Towers, St. John's, A1C 5T7.

Nova Scotia—Consumer Services Bureau, Real Estate Licensing Division, P.O. Box 998, Halifax, B3J 2X3.

Ontario—Registrar, Ministry of Consumer and Commercial Relations, Business Practices Division, 555 Yonge St., Toronto, M7A 2H6.

Prince Edward Island—Secretary, Prince Edward Island Real Estate Association and MLS, 202 Queen St., Charlottetown, C1A 4B6.

Quebec—Superintendent, 1045 de la Chevrotiere, 7e etage, Quebec, G1R 5E9.

Saskatchewan—Deputy Superintendent of Insurance, Department of Consumer and Commercial Affairs, 1871 Smith St., Regina, S4P 3V7.

federal governments. Part-time employment in the real estate business is still widespread, but the trend is toward the employment of full-time, professional men and women.

The need for trained real estate specialists is increasing. As the technical aspects of real estate activities become more complex, real estate offices require more and more people properly trained to handle and solve real estate problems. Many professional and business people and organizations, such as attorneys, banks, trust companies, abstract and title insurance companies, architects, surveyors, accountants, and tax specialists, are also highly dependent on the real estate specialist.

Professional
Organizations

The real estate business has many active, well-organized trade organizations, the largest being the NATIONAL ASSOCIATION OF REALTORS® (NAR). Founded in 1908 as the National Association of Real Estate Boards, this national organization sponsors many specialized institutes offering professional designations upon completion of required courses for brokers, salespeople, appraisers, managers, and other real estate professionals. (Such institutes and designations are listed in table 1.2.) The majority of local real estate associations throughout the U.S. and Canada are affiliated with the NAR. Active members of such affiliated local boards, having subscribed to the Association's strict Code of Ethics, are entitled to be known as REALTORS®. The term REALTOR® is a registered mark. Through its many specialized institutes, the NAR serves the interests of its members by keeping them informed of developments in their field, publicizing the services of members, improving standards and practices, and recommending or taking positions on public legislation or regulations affecting the operations of members and member firms.

	Institute	Designation(s)
Table 1.2 **NATIONAL** **ASSOCIATION OF** **REALTORS®** **Institutes and** **Professional** **Designations**	NAR—NATIONAL ASSOCIATION OF REALTORS®	GRI—Graduate, REALTORS® Institute
	AIREA—American Institute of Real Estate Appraisers	MAI—Member, Appraisal Institute RM—Residential Member
	ASREC—American Society of Real Estate Counselors	CRE—Counselor in Real Estate
	FLI—Farm and Land Institute	AFLM—Accredited Farm and Land Member
	IREF—International Real Estate Federation	*
	IREM—Institute of Real Estate Management	CPM®—Certified Property Manager AMO®—Accredited Management Organization ARM®—Accredited Resident Manager
	RESSI—Real Estate Securities and Syndication Institute	SRS—Specialist in Real Estate Securities
	RNMI—REALTORS National Marketing Institute.®	CCIM—Certified Commercial-Investment Member CRB—Certified Residential Broker CRS—Certified Residential Specialist
	SIR—Society of Industrial REALTORS®	SIR—full member
	WCR—Women's Council of REALTORS®	LTG—Leadership Training Graduate

*No specific designation offered.

A category of membership, **REALTOR-Associate®**, is available to salespeople who are affiliated with active REALTOR® members and are actively engaged in the real estate business as employees or independent contractors. All members or associates must be qualified by either a local board of REALTORS® or a state association of REALTORS®.

National Association of Real Estate Brokers. In addition to the NAR, there are also many independent real estate boards and other professional associations that were organized to set high standards for their members, promote their members' best interests, and educate the public about the real estate profession. Among them is the National Association of Real Estate Brokers, which was founded in 1947. Its membership includes individual members, as well as brokers who belong to state and local real estate boards that are affiliated with the organization. The members are known as **Realtists,** and subscribe to a code of ethics that sets professional standards for all Realtists.

Summary   Even the simplest real estate transactions involve a complex body of laws. In fact, when a person purchases real estate, he or she is, in effect, purchasing not the land itself but instead the *legal rights* to use the land in certain ways that were formerly held by the seller.

The *seven sources of law* in the United States are the U.S. Constitution, laws passed by Congress, federal regulations, state constitutions, laws passed by state legislatures, local ordinances, and court decisions.

Common law in the United States evolved predominantly from custom and usage in early England. Gradually, the basis of common law expanded to include the precedent of prior court decisions as well as custom. Much of real property law is founded in common law.

The real estate business is a dynamic industry employing hundreds of thousands of professional men and women. Every state and Canadian province has some type of *licensing requirement* for real estate brokers and salespeople. Students should become familiar with the licensing requirements of their states.

Questions

1. Rules and regulations adopted by government agencies:
   I. are used to administer and enforce legislative acts.
   II. usually outline specific illegal acts and set down penalties for violations.
   - a. I only
   - b. II only
   - c. both I and II
   - d. neither I nor II

2. Professional associations of specialists in various fields of real estate activity were organized to serve the interests of their members. Which of the following is generally a service expected of such organizations?
   - a. keeping members informed of developments in their field
   - b. improving standards and practices
   - c. providing a clearinghouse of information
   - d. all of the above

3. There are seven sources of law. Which of the following is (are) among them?
   I. court decisions
   II. local ordinances
   - a. I only
   - b. II only
   - c. both I and II
   - d. neither I nor II

4. Laws passed by the Congress and various state legislatures may:
   - a. establish specific provisions on an issue.
   - b. set precedents for future laws.
   - c. empower administrative agencies to carry out the provisions of the law.
   - d. a and c

5. Court decisions:
   I. expand the meaning of law through interpretation.
   II. form the basis for legal precedents.
   - a. I only
   - b. II only
   - c. both I and II
   - d. neither I nor II

6. Areas of law that are of particular importance to the real estate broker include:
   - a. the law of contracts.
   - b. the law of agency.
   - c. the general property law.
   - d. all of the above

7. The legal concept of precedent:
   I. grew out of the common law.
   II. must always be followed by judges when formulating court decisions.
   - a. I only
   - b. II only
   - c. both I and II
   - d. neither I nor II

8. Constitutional provisions:
   I. establish the rights of citizens and delineate government authority.
   II. are the most important laws governing the real estate broker or salesperson.
   - a. I only
   - b. II only
   - c. both I and II
   - d. neither I nor II

9. Real estate is often referred to as a *bundle of legal rights*. Which of the following is *not* among these rights?
   - a. right of exclusion
   - b. right to use the property for illegal purposes
   - c. right of enjoyment
   - d. right to sell or otherwise convey the property

10. When a person purchases real estate from a seller:
    I. he or she is actually buying the legal rights to the property that were previously held by the seller.
    II. the seller may retain one or more of his or her rights of ownership.
    - a. I only
    - b. II only
    - c. both I and II
    - d. neither I nor II

11. The purchase of real estate:

    a. is generally the largest financial investment in a person's lifetime.

    b. involves a complex body of laws.

    c. is usually facilitated by a real estate broker.

    d. all of the above

12. Real estate license laws:

    I. are in effect in all states.

    II. were passed to protect the public from the possible fraud, dishonesty, and incompetence of unscrupulous brokers and salespeople.

    a. I only   c. both I and II

    b. II only   d. neither I nor II

13. Common law:

    I. is derived from practices developed in the Spanish Empire.

    II. as it applies today, includes both customs and court decisions.

    a. I only   c. both I and II

    b. II only   d. neither I nor II

14. The designation REALTOR® refers to:

    a. a registered mark.

    b. any licensed real estate broker.

    c. an active member of a local board of the NATIONAL ASSOCIATION OF REALTORS® who subscribes to the association's Code of Ethics.

    d. a and c

15. Government agencies issue rules and regulations in order to:

    a. create control activity.

    b. implement legislative acts.

    c. expedite adherence to the laws.

    d. confuse the public action.

16. As a real estate professional, a real estate licensee should:

    I. be able to recognize the technical legal problems involved in transactions.

    II. appreciate the necessity of referring such problems to a competent attorney.

    a. I only   c. both I and II

    b. II only   d. neither I nor II

2

Real Property

Key Terms

Air rights
Chattel
Fixture
Improvement
Land
Nonhomogeneity
Parcel
Personal property
Real estate
Real property
Severance
Subsurface rights
Surface rights
Trade fixture

Overview

Will Rogers is often quoted as saying, "Buy land—they ain't making any more of the stuff !" The preamble to the NATIONAL ASSOCIATION OF REALTORS® Code of Ethics begins with the words, "Under all is the land . . . ." We see it, touch it, and refer to it every day, but what exactly is land? When we own it, do we own just the ground beneath our feet, and if so, how deep does this ownership go? What about the trees we sit under and the air we breathe—are these part of the land also? This chapter will discuss the nature and characteristics of real estate, as well as the similarities and distinctions among land, real estate, and real property. In addition, this chapter will illustrate the distinctions between real estate and personal property, and will show how an item of personal property can be converted into real estate and vice versa.

Land, Real Estate, and Real Property   You may have heard the words *land, real estate,* and *real property* used synonymously to describe the same commodity. In the broader sense they appear to be interchangeable; however there are important subtle differences in their technical meanings.

Land   The term *land* refers to more than just the surface of the earth; it includes the underlying soil and things that are permanently attached to the land by nature, such as trees and water. From a legal standpoint, land ownership also includes possession and control of the minerals and substances below the earth's surface together with the airspace above the land up to infinity.

Thus, **land** is defined as *the earth's surface extending downward to the center of the earth and upward to infinity, including things permanently attached by nature, such as trees and water* (see figure 2.1).

A specific tract of land is most commonly referred to as a **parcel.**

Figure 2.1
Land/Real Estate

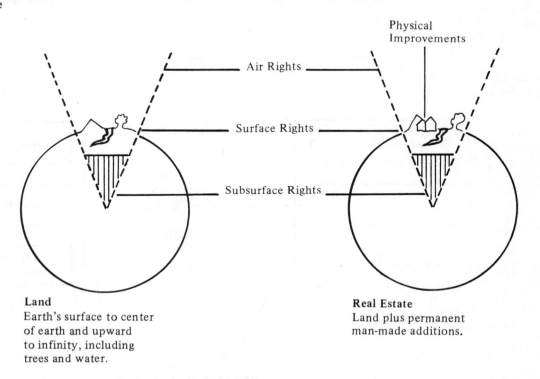

Air Rights

Physical Improvements

Surface Rights

Subsurface Rights

Land
Earth's surface to center
of earth and upward
to infinity, including
trees and water.

Real Estate
Land plus permanent
man-made additions.

Real Estate   The term *real estate* is somewhat broader than the term *land,* and includes not only the physical components of the land as provided by nature, but also all man-made permanent improvements on and to the land. In actual practice, the word **improvement** applies to the buildings erected on the land as well as to streets, utilities, sewers, and other man-made additions to the property.

Real estate, therefore, is defined as *the earth's surface extending downward to the center of the earth and upward into space, including all things permanently attached to it by nature or by people* (see figure 2.1).

Real Property

The term *real property* is broader still; it refers to the physical surface of the land, what lies below it, what lies above it, and what is permanently attached to it, as well as to the *legal rights of real estate ownership.* As discussed in Chapter 1, this *bundle of legal rights* includes the rights of possession, control, enjoyment, exclusion, and disposition, among others.

Thus, **real property** is defined as *the earth's surface extending downward to the center of the earth and upward into space, including all things permanently attached to it by nature or by man, as well as the interests, benefits, and rights inherent in the ownership of real estate* (see figure 2.2).

In Practice . . .

When people talk about buying or selling homes, office buildings, land, and the like, they usually call these things real estate. *Among those in the real estate business, the term is most often intended to refer to* real property, *as defined here. Thus, in casual usage,* real estate *generally includes the legal rights of ownership specified in the definition of real property. Sometimes the term* realty *is used instead.*

**Figure 2.2
Real Property**

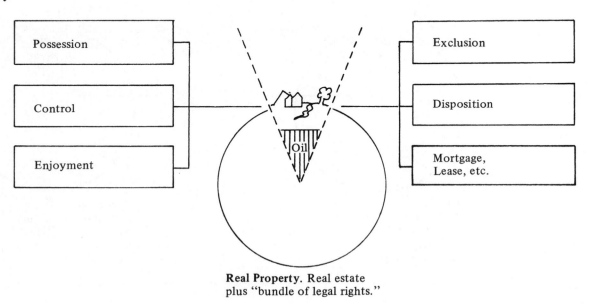

Real Property. Real estate
plus "bundle of legal rights."

Subsurface and air rights. As you can see, the concept of real property ownership involves more than **surface rights**—the rights to use the surface of the earth—it also includes subsurface rights and air rights.

Although ownership of real estate includes ownership of all minerals and other substances in the ground, the owner of a parcel of real estate does not always control the subsurface rights to the property. **Subsurface rights** are the rights to the natural resources lying below the earth's surface.

For example, a landowner may sell to an oil company his or her rights to any oil and gas found in the land. Later the same landowner can sell his or her remaining interest to a purchaser and in the sale reserve the rights to all coal that may be found in the land. After these sales, three parties have ownership interests in this real estate: (1) the oil company owns all oil and gas, (2) the seller owns all coal, and (3) the purchaser owns the rights to all the rest of the real estate.

As with the rights to minerals that lie below the surface of the land, the rights to use the air above the land may be sold or leased independently of the land itself. Such **air rights** are an increasingly important part of real estate, particularly in large cities, where air rights over railroads have been purchased to construct huge office buildings like the Pan-Am Building in New York City and the Merchandise Mart in Chicago. For the construction of such a building, the developer must purchase not only the air rights above the land but also numerous small portions of the actual land in order to construct the building's foundation supports, called *caissons.* The caisson locations are regularly spaced, and the caisson portions usually are planned to meet the lower limit of the airspace about 30 feet or so above the land so that the finished foundation supports do not interfere with the operation of trains over the surface of the railroad's remaining land ownership (see figure 2.3).

Until the development of airplanes, a property's air rights were considered to be unlimited. Today, however, the courts permit reasonable interference with these rights, such as is necessary for aircraft, as long as the owner's right to use and occupy the land is not unduly lessened. Governments and airport authorities often purchase air rights adjacent to an airport to provide glide patterns for air traffic.

With the continuing development of solar electric power, air rights—more specifically, *sun rights*—may be redefined by the courts. They may consider tall buildings that block sunlight from smaller solar-powered buildings to be interfering with the smaller buildings' sun rights.

In summary, one parcel of real property may be owned by many people, each holding a separate right to a different part of the real estate. There may be: (1) an owner of the surface rights; (2) an owner of the subsurface mineral rights; (3) an owner of the subsurface gas and oil rights; and (4) an owner of the air rights.

Real Estate Versus Personal Property

Property may be classified as either real estate or personal property. As you know, real estate is defined as a part of the earth, including the permanent additions or growing things attached to it, the air space above it, and the minerals below it.

Personal property, on the other hand, sometimes referred to as "personalty," is considered to be *all property that does not fit the definition of real estate.* Thus, per-

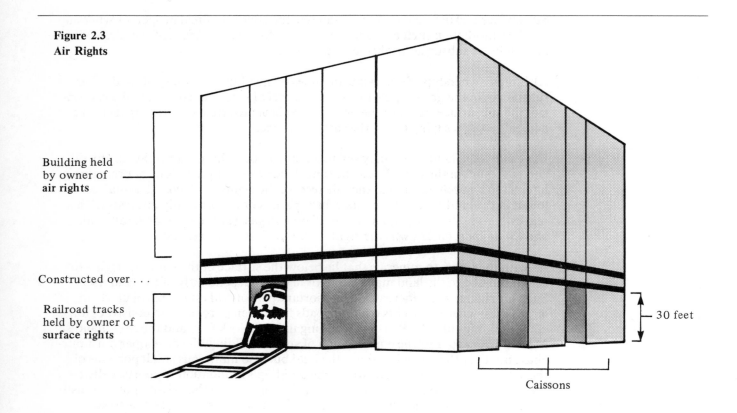

Figure 2.3
Air Rights

Building held
by owner of
air rights

Constructed over . . .

Railroad tracks
held by owner of
surface rights

30 feet

Caissons

sonal property has the unique characteristic of being *movable*. Items of personal property, also referred to as **chattels,** include such tangibles as chairs, tables, clothing, money, bonds, and bank accounts (see figure 2.4).

It is possible to change an item of real estate to personal property by **severance**. For example, a growing tree is real estate; but if the owner cuts down the tree and thereby severs it from being permanently attached to the earth, it becomes personal property. Similarly, an owner can pick an apple from a tree or cut the wheat in a field on his or her property.

Trees and crops are generally considered in two classes: (1) trees, perennial bushes, and grasses that do not require annual cultivation are considered real estate (*fructus naturales*—fruits of nature), and (2) annual crops of wheat, corn, vegetables, and fruit, known as *emblements* (*fructus industriales*—fruits of industry), are generally considered personal property. However, as long as an annual crop is growing, it is real estate if no special provisions are made in the sales contract.

As previously noted, ownership of real estate usually includes not only rights to the surface of the ground but also rights to the minerals and substances below the surface of the ground. When an owner drills into his or her land, discovers oil, and stores the oil in tanks ready for transport, the oil is converted from real estate to personal property.

The reverse situation—changing personal property into real estate—is also possible. If an owner buys cement, stones, and sand and constructs a concrete walk on

Figure 2.4
Real versus Personal
Property

Real Estate
Land and anything permanently
attached to it.

Personal Property
Movable items not attached to real
estate; items severed from real estate.

Fixture
Item of personal property converted to
real estate by permanently attaching it
to the real estate; may not be removed
by tenant.

Trade Fixture
Item of personal property attached to
real estate that is owned by a tenant
and is used in a business; legally
removable by tenant.

his or her parcel of real estate, the component parts of the concrete, which were originally personal property, are converted into real estate. They have become a permanent improvement on the land.

A mobile home is generally considered to be personal property, as it is movable and therefore not permanently affixed to the land. A mobile home may, however, be considered part of the real estate if it is sold in conjunction with a parcel of land. Real estate licensees should be familiar with local laws before attempting to market mobile homes.

Classification of Fixtures

In considering the differences between real estate and personal property, it is important to be able to distinguish between the term *fixture* and the term *trade (*or *chattel) fixture.*

Fixtures. *An article that was once personal property but has been so affixed to land or to a building that the law construes it to be a part of the real estate is a* **fixture.** Examples of fixtures are heating plants, elevator equipment in high-rise buildings, radiators, kitchen cabinets, light fixtures, and plumbing fixtures. As a matter of fact, almost any item that has been added as *a permanent part* of a building is considered a fixture.

Trade fixtures. An article owned by a tenant and attached to a rented space or building for use in conducting a business is a **trade fixture,** also called a **chattel fixture.** Examples of trade fixtures are bowling alleys, store shelves, bars, and restaurant equipment. Agricultural fixtures, such as chicken coops and tool sheds, are also included in this definition (see figure 2.4). Trade fixtures must be removed on or before the last day the property is rented. Trade fixtures that are not removed become the real property of the landlord. Acquiring the property in this way is known as *accession*.

Trade fixtures, or chattel fixtures, differ from other fixtures in the following three ways:

1. Fixtures belong to the owner of the real estate, but trade fixtures are usually owned and installed by a tenant for his or her use.

2. Fixtures are considered a permanent part of a building, but trade fixtures are removable. Trade fixtures may be affixed to a building so as to appear to be fixtures (real estate); however, due to the relationship of the parties (landlord and tenant), the law gives a tenant the right to remove his or her trade fixtures if the removal is completed before the term of the lease expires and the rented space is restored to approximately its original condition. Remember that leases usually require that at the expiration of a lease the tenant return the premises to the landlord in as good a condition as they were at the beginning of the lease, except for reasonable wear and tear and damage by the elements.

3. Fixtures are legally construed to be real estate, but trade fixtures are legally construed to be personal property. Trade fixtures (chattel fixtures) are not included in the sale or mortgage of real estate except by special agreement.

Legal tests of a fixture. Courts apply four basic tests to determine whether an article is a fixture (and therefore a part of the real estate) or a trade fixture (removable personal property). These tests are based on: (1) the intention and relationship of the parties; (2) the adaptation of the article to the real estate; (3) the method of annexation of the item; and (4) the existence of an agreement.

The *intent of the parties* at the time an article was attached is generally considered the most important factor in deciding whether or not an article is a fixture. For example, a tenant who opens a jewelry store may bolt her sale and display cases to the floor. If she wishes to remove them later, she can do so. Since these items are an integral part of her business property and it was never her intent to make them a permanent part of the structure, they would be considered trade fixtures.

The *adaptation of an article* to use in a particular building is another test of the nature of the article. For example, air conditioners installed by a landlord into wall slots specifically constructed for that purpose would be considered fixtures even though they could be readily removed.

The *permanence of the manner of annexation,* or attachment, often provides a third basis for court decisions relating to fixtures. For instance, a furnace, although it is removable, is usually attached in such a way that it cannot be taken out without causing extensive damage to the property. Moreover, the furnace is considered an essential part of the complete property and, as such, is a fixture.

Although these three tests seem simple, there is no uniformity in court decisions regarding what constitutes a fixture. Articles that appear to be permanently affixed have sometimes been held by the courts to be personal property, while items that do not appear to be permanently attached have been held to be fixtures.

In the sale of property, the one certain way to avoid confusion over the nature of an article is to make *a written agreement between the parties* establishing which items are considered part of the real estate. The real estate broker or salesperson should ensure that a sales contract includes a list of all articles that are being included in the sale, particularly if there is any doubt as to whether they are permanently attached fixtures. Articles that might cause confusion include television antennas, built-in appliances, built-in bookcases, and wall-to-wall carpeting.

Characteristics of Real Estate

Real estate possesses seven basic characteristics that affect its use both directly and indirectly. These characteristics fall into two broad categories—economic characteristics and physical characteristics (see figure 2.5).

Economic Characteristics

The basic economic characteristics of land are: (1) scarcity, (2) improvements, (3) permanence of investment, and (4) area preferences.

Scarcity. Although land as such is not rare, scarcity in an economic sense means that the total supply of land is fixed. While a considerable amount of land is still not in use, land in a given location or of a particular quality is in short supply in some areas.

Improvements. The building of an improvement on one parcel of land has an effect on the value and utilization of other neighboring tracts. Not only does an improvement affect adjoining tracts, but it often has a direct bearing on whole

**Figure 2.5
Characteristics of
Real Estate**

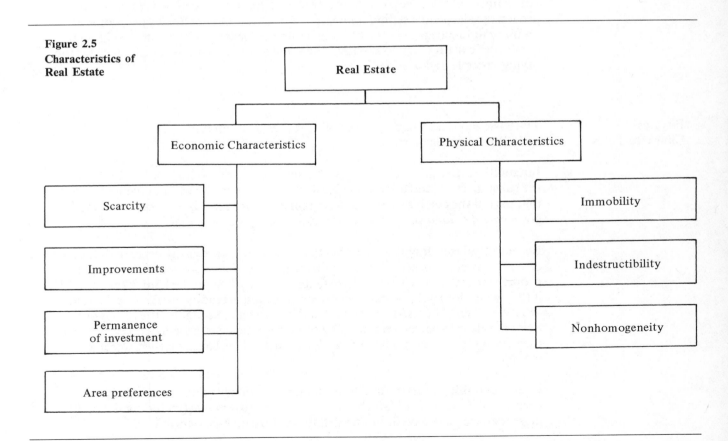

communities. For example, the improvement of a parcel of real estate by the construction of a steel plant or the selection of a site for the building of an atomic reactor can directly influence a large area. Such land improvements can influence other parcels and other communities favorably or unfavorably and may affect not only the land use itself but also the value and price of land.

Permanence of investment. Once land has been improved, the capital and labor used to build the improvement represent a large fixed investment. Although even a building can be razed to make way for a newer building or other use of the land, improvements such as drainage, electricity, water, and sewerage remain, because they generally cannot be dismantled or removed economically. The return on such investments is generally long-term and relatively stable. This permanence generally makes improved real estate unsuitable for short, rapid-turnover investing.

Area preferences. This economic characteristic, sometimes called situs, does not refer to a geographical location per se but rather to people's choices and preferences for a given area. It is the unique quality of people's preferences that results in different valuations being attributed to similar units.

Examples of likes and dislikes are numerous. Social preferences influenced the rapid movement of people to suburban areas. Some are now returning to the urban areas, however, preferring the environments and amenities offered by city living to those offered by suburbia. *Area preference is the most important economic characteristic of land.*

An example of the effect of area preference on land value can be seen in the approach of salespeople selling homes in a new development. Such salespeople attempt to influence prospects into preferring the location of the new development over other existing locations within the same general location. This illustrates the saying "people make value."

Physical Characteristics

The basic physical characteristics of land are: (1) immobility, (2) indestructibility, and (3) nonhomogeneity.

Immobility. Land, which is the earth's surface, is immobile. It is true that some of the substances of land are removable and that topography can be changed, but still that part of the earth's surface always remains. *The geographic location of any given parcel of land can never be changed.* It is rigid; it is fixed.

Because land is immobile, the rights to use land are more easily regulated than for other forms of property. For example, local governments are supported largely by property taxes on real estate. These taxes become a lien on the land. Consequently, if the owner does not pay his or her taxes, the land is readily available to be sold to satisfy the lien. The fixed amount of land in a given area enables the local government to rely on a certain amount of annual revenue from property taxes, which in turn allows the government to make long-range plans based on the projected income.

Indestructibility. Just as land is immobile, it is *durable* and *indestructible.* This permanence, not only of land but also of the improvements (including the buildings) that are placed on it, has tended to stabilize investments in land.

The fact that land is indestructible does not, of course, change the fact that the improvements on land do depreciate and can become obsolete, thereby reducing values—perhaps drastically. This gradual depreciation should not be confused with the fact that the *economic desirability* of a given location can change, thus creating "ghost towns."

Nonhomogeneity. The characteristic of **nonhomogeneity** stems from the fact that no two parcels of land are ever exactly the same. Although there may be substantial similarity, *all parcels differ geographically,* as each parcel has its own location. This may also be referred to as *heterogeneity.*

Characteristics Define Land Use

The various characteristics of a parcel of real estate affect its desirability for a specific use. Some specific physical and economic factors that would affect land use include: (1) contour and elevation of the parcel, (2) prevailing winds, (3) transportation, (4) public improvements, and (5) availability of natural resources, such as water. For example, hilly, heavily wooded land would need considerable work before it could be used for industrial purposes, but would be ideally suited for residential use. Likewise, flat land located along a major highway network would be undesirable for residential use, but would be well-located for industry.

Summary

Although most people think of *land* as the surface of the earth, the definition of this word really applies not only to the *earth's surface* but also to the *mineral deposits under the earth* and the *air above it.* The term *real estate* further expands this definition to include *all natural and man-made improvements attached to the land. Real property* is the term used to describe real estate plus the "bundle of legal rights" associated with its ownership.

The same parcel of real estate may be owned and controlled by different parties, one owning the *surface rights;* one owning the *air rights;* and another owning the *subsurface rights.*

All property that does not fit the definition of real estate is classified as *personal property,* or *chattels.* When articles of personal property are permanently affixed to land, they may become *fixtures,* and as such are considered a part of the real estate. However, personal property attached to real estate by a tenant for the purpose of his or her business is classified as a *trade,* or *chattel, fixture* and remains personal property.

The unique nature of land is apparent in both its economic and physical characteristics. The economic characteristics consist of *scarcity, improvements, permanence of investment,* and *area preferences.* The physical characteristics are *immobility, nonhomogeneity,* and *indestructibility.*

Questions

1. Which of the following is not a physical characteristic of land?
   a. indestructibility
   b. scarcity
   c. immobility
   d. nonhomogeneity

2. A construction firm builds an office center over a railroad right-of-way. This means:
   I. trains can no longer operate on the tracks under the building during business hours if the noise disturbs the occupants of the office center.
   II. the construction firm has built the office center using the subsurface rights to the property.
   a. I only
   b. II only
   c. both I and II
   d. neither I nor II

3. The term *fructus naturales* refers to which of the following?
   a. annual crops
   b. real estate
   c. personal property
   d. a and c

4. John Sexton purchases a parcel of land and sells the rights to any minerals located in the ground to an exploration company. This means that Sexton now owns all but which of the following with regard to this property?
   I. air rights
   II. surface rights
   III. subsurface rights
   a. I only
   b. I and II only
   c. III only
   d. II and III only

5. A store tenant firmly attaches appropriate appliances for his restaurant business on the leased premises. These appliances are:
   I. trade fixtures.
   II. part of the real estate once they are installed.
   a. I only
   b. II only
   c. both I and II
   d. neither I nor II

6. The definition of real estate includes many elements. Which of the following items would *not* be a part of real estate?
   a. fences
   b. permanent buildings
   c. farm equipment
   d. growing trees

7. An important characteristic of land is that it may be modified. Such modifications become a part of and tend to increase the value of real estate. Which of the following is not a modification?
   a. new access roads
   b. utilities
   c. new houses
   d. plant crops

8. Which of the following best defines real estate?
   a. land and the air above it
   b. land and all that there is above or below the surface, including all things permanently attached to it
   c. land and the buildings permanently affixed to it
   d. land and the mineral rights in the land

9. A fixture:
   I. is considered to be real estate.
   II. is an item that at one time was personal property.
   a. I only
   b. II only
   c. both I and II
   d. neither I nor II

10. The definition of *land* includes all but which of the following?
    a. minerals in the earth
    b. the air above the ground up to infinity
    c. trees
    d. buildings

11. Fred and Celia Evers are building a new enclosed front porch to their home. The lumber dealer with whom they are contracting has just unloaded a truckload of lumber in front of their house that will be used to build the porch. At this point, the lumber is considered to be:

    I. personal property.
    II. real estate.

    a. I only   c. both I and II
    b. II only   d. neither I nor II

12. When the Evers' new front porch, as described in question 11, is completed, the lumber that the dealer originally delivered will be considered to be:

    I. personal property.
    II. real estate.

    a. I only   c. both I and II
    b. II only   d. neither I nor II

13. Suppose that halfway through the construction of the Evers' new front porch, as described in question 11, work is delayed indefinitely because of unforeseen difficulties. At this point, the lumber the dealer originally delivered would be considered as:

    I. personal property if it has not been used in construction.
    II. real estate if it has been used in construction.

    a. I only   c. both I and II
    b. II only   d. neither I nor II

14. The definition of the term *real property* includes all but which of the following?

    a. items of personal property permanently affixed to the real estate
    b. legal ownership rights
    c. air and subsurface rights
    d. chattels

15. Man-made, permanent additions to land are called:

    a. chattels   c. improvements
    b. parcels   d. trade fixtures

16. Real estate may be converted into personal property:

    I. by severance.
    II. by accession.

    a. I only   c. both I and II
    b. II only   d. neither I nor II

17. Steve Jackson rents a detached, single-family home under a one-year lease. Two months into the rental period, Jackson installs awnings over the building's front windows to keep the sun away from some delicate hanging plants. Which of the following is true?

    a. Jackson must remove the awnings before the rental period is over.
    b. Because of their permanent nature, the awnings are considered to be personal property.
    c. The awnings are considered to be fixtures.
    d. a and b

18. *Area preference* refers to:

    I. relative scarcity.
    II. a physical characteristic of land.

    a. I only   c. both I and II
    b. II only   d. neither I nor II

19. Which of the following physical and economic factors would a land developer take into consideration when determining the optimum use for a parcel of land?

    a. transportation
    b. natural resources available
    c. contour and elevation
    d. all of the above

20. Which of the following would be an example of a chattel?

    I. cattle.
    II. trade fixtures.

    a. I only   c. both I and II
    b. II only   d. neither I nor II

21. The term *nonhomogeneity* refers to:
    a. a particular choice in neighborhoods.
    b. land's durability and indestructibility
    c. capital expenditures represented by a fixed investment.
    d. the fact that no two parcels of land are exactly alike.

22. Personal property may be converted to real property by:
    a. conversion.   c. accession.
    b. severance.   d. interference.

3

The Real Estate Business

Key Terms

Agricultural real estate
Business cycle
Commercial real estate
Demand
Industrial real estate
Market
Residential real estate
Special-purpose real estate
Supply
Value

Overview

The real estate business is more than just the neighborhood storefront with the sign "Realty" hanging in the window; likewise, it employs more than just brokers and salespeople. The real estate industry is composed of a variety of professionals specializing in many different fields and dealing with many different types of real estate. Whether sales, management, or appraisal, this business deals primarily with property values. This chapter will discuss the many facets of the real estate industry and will explain the concept of value, particularly how it is tested by the influences of supply and demand in the real estate market.

Real Estate—A Business of Many Specializations

Some people think of the real estate business as being made up of only brokers and salespeople. Today's real estate industry, however, employs scores of well-trained, knowledgeable individuals in areas other than real estate brokerage. Modern real estate practice provides many specializations for people who want to serve the community and earn a better-than-average income.

Real Estate Professions

The specializations that make up the real estate business include brokerage, appraisal, property management, real estate financing, property development, counseling, education, and insurance. Although each of these is a business unto itself, to be truly competent a real estate professional must possess at least a basic knowledge of all phases of the real estate business.

Brokerage. The bringing together of people interested in making a real estate transaction is *brokerage.* Typically, the broker acts as an *agent;* that is, he or she negotiates the sale, purchase, or rental of property on behalf of others for a fee or commission. The agent's commission is generally a percentage of the amount involved in the transaction. It is usually paid by the seller or, in a rental transaction, by the owner of the property. Brokerage is discussed further in Chapter 5.

Appraisal. The process of estimating the value of a parcel of real estate is *appraisal.* Although brokers must have some understanding of valuation as part of their training, qualified appraisers are generally employed when property is financed or sold by court order and large sums of money are involved. The appraiser must have sound judgment, experience, and a detailed knowledge of the methods of valuation. Appraisal is covered in Chapter 18.

Property management. A real estate agent who operates a property for its owner is involved in *property management.* The property manager may be responsible for soliciting tenants, collecting rents, altering or constructing new space for tenants, ordering repairs, and generally maintaining the property. The manager's basic responsibility is to protect the owner's investment and maximize the owner's return on the investment. Property management is discussed in Chapter 17.

Financing. The business of providing the funds necessary to complete real estate transactions is *financing.* Most transactions are financed by means of a mortgage loan, in which the property is pledged as security for the eventual payment of the loan. However, there are other forms and methods of financing real estate in addition to mortgages. Real estate financing is examined in Chapter 15.

Property development. The profession of *property development* includes the work of subdividers who purchase raw land, divide it into lots, build roads, and install sewers; the skills of land developers who improve the building lots with houses and other buildings and who sell the improved real estate, either themselves or through brokerage firms; and the work of builders and architects who plan and construct the houses and other buildings. Property development is discussed in Chapter 20.

Counseling. Providing competent, independent advice, sound guidance, and informed judgment on a variety of real estate problems, including the purchase, use, and investment of property, is *counseling.* A counselor attempts to furnish his or her client with direction in choosing among alternative courses of action. Increasing knowledge is fundamental to every counselor's ability to render his or her services.

Education. Both the real estate practitioner and the consumer can learn more about the complexities of the real estate business through *education.* Colleges, schools, real estate organizations, and continuing education programs conduct courses and seminars in all areas of the business. These courses are often taught by experienced real estate professionals.

Insurance. Among the major services of the real estate business, *insurance* is sometimes included. In some real estate offices, the real estate broker is also an insurance broker. However, note that *insurance brokerage is a separate business that requires a separate state license.* Not all real estate brokers are further licensed to sell insurance, and vice versa.

Uses of Real Property

Just as there are many areas of specialization within the real estate industry, so too are there many different types of property in which to specialize (see figure 3.1). Real estate can generally be classified into one of the following categories according to its use.

**Figure 3.1
Uses of Real Property**

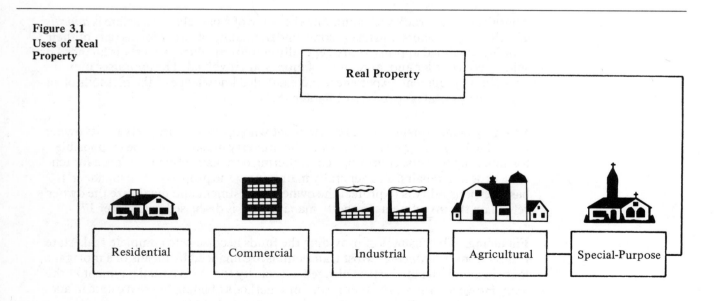

1. **Residential**—all property used for housing, from acreage to small city lots, both single- and multifamily, in urban, suburban, and rural areas.
2. **Commercial**—business property, including offices, shopping centers, stores, executive offices, theaters, hotels, and parking facilities.
3. **Industrial**—warehouses, factories, land in industrial districts, and research facilities.
4. **Agricultural**—farms, timberland, pasture land, ranches, and orchards.
5. **Special purpose**—churches, schools, cemeteries, and government-held lands.

The market for each of these types of properties can be further subdivided into: (1) the sale market, which involves the transfer of title, and (2) the rental market, which involves the transfer of space on a rental basis.

In Practice . . .

Although a real estate person or firm can, in theory, perform all the aforementioned services and handle all five classes of property, this is rarely done except in small towns. Most real estate firms tend to specialize to some degree, especially in urban areas. In some cases, a real estate person may perform only one service for one type of property. Farm brokers and appraisers of industrial property are two examples of such specialization. The vast majority of real estate firms perform two or more services for two or more types of property. One firm may provide brokerage and management services for residential property only; another firm may perform all services but specialize in industrial or commercial property.

Since the greatest number of individuals in the real estate field are involved in residential brokerage, most people tend to think of the marketing of real estate as the primary activity in the field. But many other people are also a part of the real estate business. For example, people associated with mortgage banking firms and those who negotiate mortgages for banks and savings and loan associations, people in property management firms and real estate departments of corporations, and officials and employees of such government agencies as zoning boards and assessing offices are all involved in the real estate business.

Real Estate—The Business of Value

The focus of the real estate business is the value of real estate. Value is the not the same as price. Specifically, **value** describes *a person's preferences.* Price can be defined as *the amount of goods or services that will be offered in the marketplace in exchange for any given product.*

The value of real property does not remain the same. For example, differing standards and needs can alter a personal estimate of value. The next section describes how such changes can affect price in the marketplace.

The Real Estate Market

In literal terms a **market** is a place where goods can be bought and sold, where a price can be established, and where it becomes advantageous for buyers and sellers to trade. The function of the market is to facilitate this exchange, by providing a setting in which the *supply and demand forces* of the economy can establish price levels.

Supply and Demand

The economic forces of supply and demand continually interact in the market to establish and maintain price levels. Essentially, *when supply goes up, prices will drop; when demand increases, prices will rise* (see figure 3.2).

Supply can be defined as *the amount of goods offered for sale within the market at a given price.* In real estate, this term does not apply to all existing land but rather to all the land that could readily be used for a specific purpose. To satisfy demand, land must be readily adaptable to the desired purpose at a price the market will bear. For example, land located near a city on very rocky ground could be considered part of the supply of land available for residential housing only if the market price of homes in the area were high enough to absorb the cost of removing the rocks before construction.

Demand can be defined as *the amount of goods people are willing and able to buy at a given price.* In real estate, demand is based upon the benefits that can be derived from using land for a specific purpose. For example, an investor who buys a corner lot in a business district to construct an office building does not buy the land simply for itself but rather for the benefits it offers—in this case, the rental income that it will generate.

Supply and demand in the real estate market. The characteristics of the goods in the marketplace determine how quickly the forces of supply and demand will be able to establish their price. Such characteristics are:

1. the degree of standardization of the product.
2. the mobility of the product.
3. the mobility of the parties (buyer and seller).

Real estate is not a standardized product; no two parcels can ever be exactly alike. The apparent exceptions to this are in some developments where a number of units may be built to the same specification. But even where this condition exists, each parcel of real estate is unique because it has its own geographic location.

Since real estate is fixed in nature (immobile), it cannot be moved from area to area to satisfy the pressures of supply and demand. For this reason the real estate business has local markets where offices can maintain detailed familiarity with the market conditions and available units. However, increasing mobility of the population and the growing impact of new technologies in communication and data handling have resulted in growing interest in geographic expansion of real estate firms. Computer-based market data networks have led to joint undertakings by widely dispersed real estate organizations.

Figure 3.2
Supply and Demand

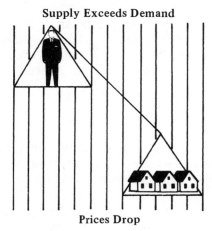

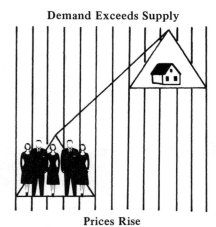

Supply Exceeds Demand

Demand Exceeds Supply

Prices Drop

Prices Rise

Where standardization and mobility are relatively great, the supply and demand forces will balance—and prices reflecting value will be established—relatively quickly. But because of its characteristics of nonhomogeneity and immobility, the real estate market is generally relatively slow to adjust. Since the product cannot be removed from the market or transferred to another market, an oversupply usually results in a lowering of price levels. Since development and construction of real estate take a considerable period of time from conception to completion, increases in demand may not be met immediately. Building and housing construction may occur in uneven spurts of activity due to factors such as these.

Factors Affecting Supply

Factors that tend to affect supply in the real estate market include the labor supply, construction costs, and government controls and financial policies (see figure 3.3).

Labor supply and construction costs. A shortage of labor in the skilled building trades, an increase in the cost of building materials, or a scarcity of materials will tend to lower the amount of housing that will be built. The impact of the labor supply and price levels depends on the extent to which higher costs can be passed on to the buyer or renter in the form of higher purchase prices or rentals. Technological advances that result in cheaper materials and more efficient means of construction may tend to counteract some price increases.

Government controls and financial policies. Government monetary policy can have a substantial impact on the real estate market. The Federal Reserve Board, as well as such government agencies as the Federal Housing Administration (FHA), the Government National Mortgage Association (GNMA), and the Federal Home Loan Mortgage Corporation (FHLMC), can affect the amount of money available to lenders for mortgage loans (see Chapter 15).

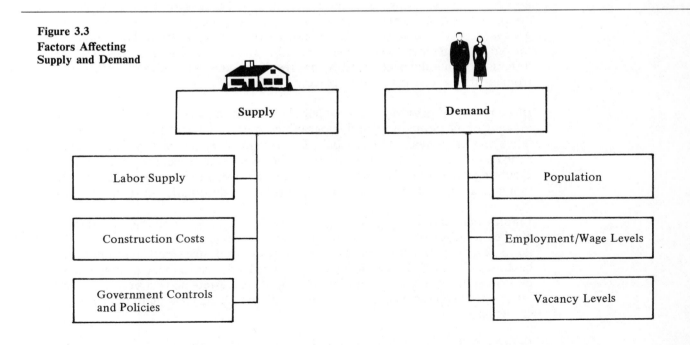

Figure 3.3
Factors Affecting Supply and Demand

In addition to acting through these agencies, the government can influence the amount of money available for real estate investment through its fiscal and/or monetary policies. Such policies include the amount of money taken out of circulation through taxation and other methods and the amount of money the government puts into circulation through spending programs ranging from welfare to farm subsidies.

At the local level, real estate taxation is one of the primary sources of revenue for government. Policies on taxation of real estate can have either positive or negative effects. Tax incentives have been one way for communities to attract new businesses and industries to their areas. And, of course, along with these enterprises come increased employment and expanded residential real estate markets. Where land is not being used to its maximum potential, some urban areas adjust the assessment and, by taxing the land and improvements at higher levels, force a more productive use of the real estate.

Local governments can also affect market operations and the development and construction of real estate by applying land-use controls. Health, fire, zoning, and building ordinances are used by communities to control and stimulate the highest potential use of land. Real estate values and markets are thereby stabilized. Community amenities such as churches, schools, and parks, and efficient governmental policies are influential factors affecting the real estate market.

Factors Affecting Demand

Factors that tend to affect demand in the real estate market include population, employment and wage levels, and vacancy levels (see figure 3.3).

Population. Population trends have a basic influence on the sale of real estate. Since shelter (whether in the form of owned or rented property) is a basic human and family need, it is obvious that the general need for housing will grow as the population grows. However, although the total population of the country is increasing, this trend is not uniform in all localities in the country. Some areas are growing faster than others. Some are not growing at all. Modern-day examples of the old western ghost towns, where the exhaustion of natural resources or the termination of an industrial operation has resulted in a mass exodus of population from an area, even exist in some places.

In a consideration of the impact of population on the real estate market, the makeup of the population, or demographics, must also be taken into account. Since residential real estate is usually for family occupancy, family size and the ratio of adults to children are important. Marriage rates affect the population mix. Doubling up—two or more families using one housing unit—is generally on the increase, an indication of an increasing shortage of affordable housing.

Employment and wage levels. These factors have an impact on the real estate market because decisions on home ownership or rental are closely related to ability to pay. Employment opportunities and wage levels in a small community can be drastically affected in a short period of time by decisions made by major employers in the area. Individuals involved in the real estate market in such communities must keep themselves well informed about the business plans of local employers.

In order to estimate how changes in wage levels will generally affect people's decisions concerning real estate, it is also important to look for trends in how individual income is likely to be used. General trends in the economy (availability of credit, the impact of inflation, and the like) will influence an individual's decision as to how income will be spent and if it will be put into savings or some other investment. *A tightening of mortgage credit may result in income being channeled into other investment areas, with a resultant lessening of real estate activity.*

Vacancy levels. Vacancy levels in a community provide a good indication of the demand for housing. A growing shortage of housing (a lower number of vacancies) will result in increasing rents and decreasing demand. Conversely, because of the immobility and permanence of investment that characterize real estate, an increase in vacancies will force rents down and demand up. As a rule of thumb in many communities, when the vacancy level goes below 5 percent, sale and rental prices tend to increase, and when the vacancy level rises above 5 percent, prices tend to weaken.

Cycles

Over the years, business has had its ups and downs. These upward and downward fluctuations in business activity are called **business cycles.** Although business cycles often seem to recur within a certain number of years, they are actually caused primarily by internal forces (such as population growth) and external forces (such as wars and oil embargoes) rather than by the passage of time.

The business cycle can generally be characterized by four stages: *expansion, recession, depression,* and *revival.* The movements of the cycle are gradual and not clearly defined.

In analyzing the patterns of business cycles, it is possible to consider a number of trends simultaneously. The long-term trend (referred to as the *secular trend*) tends to be smooth and continuous. It is most affected by such basic influences as population growth, technological advance, capital accumulation, and so on. Within this overall pattern are business cycles of varying lengths. Various segments or industries within the economy (including real estate) may have shorter cycles with different timing and different characteristics. Seasonal cycles also reflect characteristics in particular industries. Some relate to climatic conditions, consumer buying habits, vacation patterns, and the like. Some industries (such as real estate) are much more subject to seasonal fluctuations than others.

The real estate cycle. As stated earlier, the real estate market is slow in adjusting to variations in supply and demand. Because the real estate cycle is based on building activity, the time lag between the demand for units and the completion of those units causes real estate cycles to peak after the rest of the economy does and to take longer to recover from depressed periods than other economic sectors. For example, while other segments of the consumer economy made a rapid recovery from the Depression as a result of U.S. involvement in World War II, the housing market did not begin to recover sufficiently to meet growing demand until well into the 1950s. It is important to remember that the local character of the real estate market creates many local conditions that may not correspond to the general movement of the real estate cycle.

Governmental anticyclical efforts. Since the Great Depression, the federal government has attempted to establish fiscal and monetary policies to prevent extreme fluctuations in the business cycle. By increasing government spending during times of recession and taking money out of circulation through taxation and control of lending institutions during times of inflation/expansion, the government attempts to promote steady, gradual economic growth. However, the goal of a completely stable economy often seems elusive.

Summary

Although selling is the most widely recognized activity of the real estate business, the industry also involves many other services, such as *appraisal, property management, property development, counseling, property financing, education,* and *insurance.* Most real estate firms specialize in only one or two of these areas. However, the highly complex and competitive nature of our society requires that a real estate person be an expert in a number of fields.

Real property can be classified according to its general use as either *residential, commercial, industrial, agricultural,* or *special purpose.* Although many brokers deal with more than one type of real property, they usually specialize to some degree.

Real estate is the business of *value;* all real estate specializations relate directly or indirectly to it. Value is not the same as *price;* price is determined in the marketplace.

A *market* is a place where goods and services can be bought and sold and price levels established. The ideal market allows for a continual balancing of the forces of supply and demand. Because of its unique characteristics, real estate is relatively slow to adjust to the forces of supply and demand.

Supply can be defined as the amount of goods available in the market for a given price. *Demand* is defined as the amount of goods people are willing to buy at a given price. The supply of and demand for real estate are affected by many factors, including *population changes, wage and employment levels, percentage of unoccupied space, construction costs and availability of labor,* and *governmental monetary policy and controls.*

Fluctuations of business activity in this country are observed in *cycles.* Business cycles occur in four stages: *expansion, recession, depression,* and *revival.* The real estate cycle involves similar stages, but it tends to peak after the rest of the economy does, and it takes longer to recover than other sectors of the business community do.

Questions

1. Which of the following is a specialized service of the real estate business?

   a. building and development
   b. estimating value
   c. brokerage
   d. all of the above

2. The factors that influence the demand for real estate include:

   I. wage levels and employment opportunities.
   II. the number of real estate brokers.

   a. I only   c. both I and II
   b. II only   d. neither I nor II

3. Property that is part of the commercial market includes:

   a. office buildings for lease.
   b. single-family homes.
   c. churches.
   d. factories.

4. Business cycles:

   I. involve periods of expansion, recession, depression, and revival.
   II. can be regulated somewhat by government fiscal and monetary policy.

   a. I only   c. both I and II
   b. II only   d. neither I nor II

5. The forces that influence and affect supply in the real estate market include:

   a. construction costs.
   b. vacancy levels.
   c. wage levels.
   d. all of the above

6. The real estate market is considered local in character because:

   I. land is fixed, or immobile.
   II. most people are not generally mobile enough to take advantage of available real estate in distant areas.

   a. I only   c. both I and II
   b. II only   d. neither I nor II

7. In general, when the supply of a certain commodity increases:

   a. prices tend to rise.
   b. prices tend to remain level.
   c. prices tend to drop.
   d. prices can no longer be established.

8. Special-purpose properties include those used for:

   I. office buildings.
   II. private residences.

   a. I only   c. both I and II
   b. II only   d. neither I nor II

9. Peter Dickinson is a real estate broker in a large Midwestern city. Chances are his real estate firm:

   a. performs most or all of the various real estate specializations.
   b. deals only in farm property.
   c. deals only in insurance.
   d. performs two or more of the various real estate specializations for at least two types of property.

10. In an average market, certain characteristics of the goods sold will determine how quickly the forces of supply and demand will establish the goods' prices. Which of the following is *not* one of these characteristics?

    a. the product's mobility
    b. the product's cost
    c. the mobility of buyer and seller
    d. whether or not the product is standardized

11. Compared to typical markets, the real estate market:

    I. is relatively quick to adapt to the forces of supply and demand.
    II. is national in scope.

    a. I only   c. both I and II
    b. II only   d. neither I nor II

12. In general terms, a *market* refers to which of the following?
   a. a place where buyers and sellers come together
   b. the amount of goods available at a given price
   c. a forum where price levels are established
   d. both a and c

13. The demand for real estate in a particular community is affected by:
   a. population.
   b. wage levels.
   c. vacancy levels.
   d. all of the above

4

Concepts of Home Ownership

Key Terms

Adjusted sales price
Amount realized on sale
Capital gain
Coinsurance clause
Equity
Homeowner's insurance policy
Investment
Liability coverage
Replacement cost
Tax basis

Overview

To rephrase an old quotation, a home is not a house—not necessarily, anyway. While the term *home ownership* once referred mainly to detached single-family dwellings, today's homebuyer must choose among many different types of housing designed to satisfy individual needs, tastes, and financial capabilities. This chapter will discuss the various types of housing available as well as the factors a potential homeowner must consider in deciding the what, where, and how much of buying real estate. The chapter will also cover the many tax benefits available to all home-owners and the forms of property insurance designed to protect one of the biggest investments of a person's life. Note that this chapter is devoted to the ownership of a *residence;* the ownership of income-producing property will be discussed in Chapter 22, "Real Estate Investment."

Home Ownership	The desire to own one's home is a deep-rooted characteristic of American culture. To many people, home ownership represents financial stability, a psychological and emotional pride in ownership, and a sense of belonging to the community. To others, it can represent a form of investment. To all property owners, it can provide an effective shelter from a percentage of their federal income taxes.

Traditionally, the residential real estate market was composed predominantly of single-family dwellings; the typical buyer was a married couple, usually with small children. Today, however, a variety of social changes, population shifts, and economic considerations have changed the real estate market considerably. For example, many real estate buyers today are *singles,* especially unmarried women; many are *empty nesters,* married couples whose housing needs change after their children move away from home; and many are *never nesters,* married couples who choose not to have children or unmarried couples living together.

Types of Housing

As the residential market evolves, the needs of its buyers become more specialized. Thus, aside from single-family dwellings, the real estate market in any given area may include apartment complexes, condominiums and townhomes, cooperatives, planned unit developments, converted-use properties, retirement communities, singles' developments, high-rise developments, mobile homes, modular homes, timeshared occupancy, and urban homesteading.

Apartment complexes continue to be popular. A complex consists of a group of apartment buildings with any number of units in each building. The buildings may be low-rise or high-rise, and the amenities may include parking as well as club-houses, swimming pools, and in some instances, golf courses.

Condominiums and *townhouses* are a popular form of residential ownership, particularly for people who want the security of owning property but do not want the responsibilities of caring for and maintaining a house. Ownership of a condominium apartment or townhouse—which may share party walls with other units or be separated from them by airspace—involves shared ownership of common facilities, such as halls, elevators, and surrounding grounds. Management and maintenance of building exteriors and grounds are provided by agreement, with expenses paid out of monthly assessments charged to owners. The condominium form of ownership will be discussed in detail in Chapter 8.

A *cooperative* is very similar to a condominium in that it involves units within a larger building with common walls and facilities. An owner of a cooperative unit, however, owns not the unit itself but rather shares of stock in the corporation that holds title to the building. In return for stock in the corporation, the owner receives what is called a proprietary lease, which entitles him or her to occupancy of a particular unit in the building. Each unit owner must pay his or her share of the building's expenses in the same way that a condominium unit owner does. Cooperatives will be further discussed in Chapter 8.

Planned unit developments (PUDs) merge such diverse land uses as housing, recreation, and commercial units in one self-contained development. PUDs are zoned under special cluster zoning requirements that compute roads and park areas as a percentage of the square feet of land required for homes or living units.

Converted-use properties are existing structures, such as factories, office buildings, hotels, schools, and churches, that have been converted to residential use as either rental or condominium units. For economic, structural, and/or locational reasons, such buildings have been abandoned by their original owners or tenants. Rather than demolish them to make way for new structures, developers often find it both aesthetically and economically appealing to renovate the existing buildings into affordable housing. In this manner, an abandoned factory is transformed into luxury loft condominium units, a closed hotel becomes an apartment building, and an old church becomes a row of townhomes.

Retirement communities are already widely accepted in the West, Southwest, and South. They lend themselves particularly well to those areas of the country with temperate weather conditions. Retirement communities often provide stores and shops, recreational opportunities, and in some cases health-care facilities, in addition to residential units.

Single-person developments are a relatively recent concept that has been implemented throughout the country. They cater to unmarried people and often provide recreational facilities and planned social activities as well as living units. Such a development may be one apartment building, a planned unit development, or an apartment complex.

High-rise developments that combine office space, stores, theaters, and apartment units are popular across the country, particularly in metropolitan areas close to the central city. The most successful high-rise developments effectively use such natural assets as rivers, lakes, and forest preserves. These buildings usually are self-contained and include laundry facilities, restaurants, food stores, valet shops, beauty parlors, barber shops, swimming pools, and other attractive and convenient features.

Mobile homes are one of the housing industry's fastest-growing areas of development in times of high-priced housing. Mobile homes were once considered to be useful only as temporary residences or for traveling. Now many people live in them as principal residences or use them as stationary vacation homes. The lower cost of mobile homes as compared to other types of residences, coupled with the increased living space available in the newer, double-wide models and with their appreciation in value, has made mobile homes an attractive alternative to the conventionally constructed residence. The increase in mobile-home sales has resulted in growing numbers of mobile-home parks. These parks offer complete residential environments with permanent community facilities as well as semipermanent foundations and hookups for gas, water, and electricity.

Modular homes are also gaining popularity as the base price of newly constructed homes rises. Modular homes are prefabricated structures that arrive on-site preassembled from the factory. As the name implies, they are modular in construction. Each preassembled room is lowered into place on the building site by a crane; workers later finish the structure and install plumbing, wiring, and amenities. In this manner, entire developments can be built at a fraction of the time and cost of conventional types of construction.

Timeshared occupancy of vacation homes enables many people who would otherwise be unable to meet the high cost of owning a second home to enter the vacation-home market. Under this concept, several buyers purchase ownership shares in one vacation home. These shares entitle each owner to occupy the property for a definite fixed period of time each year. If this practice continues to grow, it will greatly increase the percentage of people able to afford a second home.

Urban homesteading is a government-sponsored program that encourages individuals to reclaim deteriorating inner-city property. Many people are able to purchase abandoned houses at low prices with the help of lenient government-backed financing. Such purchasers are required to complete a minimum amount of rehabilitation work on their homes within a set period of time in order to retain the property.

Factors Influencing Home Ownership

Although economists vary in their predictions of the percentage of people who will ultimately own their own homes, most believe that the peak will probably not exceed 75 percent. In fact, some economists predict that the rate of home ownership will decline over the coming decades, from 65 percent in the 1980s to under 60 percent by the year 2000. The remainder of the population will continue to rent, live in institutional housing (homes for senior citizens, retirement homes), or occupy mobile homes. In view of current land use and planning for the future, such predictions may well be proven correct.

Certainly not all individuals or families should own homes. Home ownership involves substantial commitment and responsibility, and the flexibility of renting suits some individuals' needs better than ownership does. People whose work requires frequent moves from one location to another or whose financial position or future is uncertain will particularly benefit from rental situations. Renting also gives renters more leisure time by freeing them from management and maintenance responsibilities. Table 4.1 illustrates the relative costs of owning and renting similar properties.

Table 4.1

First-Year Costs of Owning versus Renting

Rent an $80,000 home			Buy an $80,000 home	
Rent @ $600/month		$7,200	Mortgage payment @ $802/month ($70,000 @ 13.5 percent for 30 years)	$9,624
Maintenance		120		
Insurance (renter's)		150		
Utilities		1,400	Real estate taxes	1,080
Less earnings on savings:			Maintenance	800
down payment not made	$10,000		Insurance (homeowner's)	220
closing costs not incurred	2,500		Utilities	1,400
$202/month difference between rent and mortgage payment	2,424		Less income-tax savings (based on marginal rate of 30 percent) realized by deducting mortgage interest of $9,439 and real estate taxes of $1,080 ($10,519 × .30)	−3,155
	$14,924			
Assume 9 percent interest ($14,924 × .09)		−1,343		
Final cost to rent		$7,527	Appreciation on property @ 5%	−4,000
			Final cost to buy	$5,969

Note: This is a simplified analysis; many other factors affect a thorough comparison. For example, remember that the market value of a home usually appreciates. Also, after the first year, a number of those variables will change, thereby altering the final costs in subsequent years.

Those who choose to take on the responsibilities of home ownership must evaluate and make important decisions based on a variety of factors, including mortgage terms, ownership expenses, ability to pay, location, type of home, and investment considerations. It is often the responsibility of the real estate broker or salesperson to guide prospective homeowners in this process and to help them arrive at choices they can live with.

Mortgage Terms

Liberalization of mortgage terms and payment plans over the last six decades has made the dream of home ownership a reality for over 70 percent of the population. For example, the amount of a mortgage loan in relation to the value of a home (called *loan-to-value ratio*) has increased from 40 percent in 1920 to as much as 95 percent today. Payment periods of conventional mortgages have also been extended, from five years in the 1920s to 30 years or more in the '80s. Short-term fixed-rate, and longer term adjustable rate, renegotiable mortgages have gained popularity in today's unsettled financial market.

As evidenced in recent years, the *interest rates* charged by lending institutions on home mortgage loans vary greatly as changes occur in the money market. Particularly in the case of longer term mortgages (when interest charges represent a substantial amount of monthly payments in early years), the interest rate in effect when a mortgage is established may later prove to be very attractive—or unattractive—if prevailing interest rates change. As interest rates move up, an established mortgage with a lower interest rate may be a plus in selling a home if the new owner is able to assume the existing mortgage at the same interest rate. In contrast, if mortgage interest rates should fall, the homeowner may be obligated to pay the higher rate for many years, particularly if the terms of his or her mortgage include a penalty for prepayment before a new mortgage loan can be negotiated at current rates.

For years, potential homeowners have been able to receive assistance in obtaining low–down-payment mortgage loans through the federal programs of the Federal Housing Administration (FHA) and the Veterans Administration (VA). In addition, private mortgage insurance companies offer programs to assist loan applicants in receiving higher loan-to-value ratios from private lenders than they could otherwise obtain.

To buffer the effects of an unstable money market and often scarce and expensive mortgage funds, lenders offer many alternative forms of mortgages, such as variable interest rate and graduated payment mortgages. Seller financing also gains popularity in times of tight mortgage money. Mortgages and mortgage lending will be discussed in detail in Chapter 15.

Ownership Expenses

Generally, a portion of each of a homeowner's monthly mortgage payments is used to build up a reserve fund for taxes and property insurance. That portion of the loan payment that is applied to interest represents an expense to the homeowner. There are many other hidden expenses connected with home ownership, including real estate taxes, depreciation (wearing out of the building through use), insurance, maintenance and repairs, utilities, and such necessary services as garbage pickup and water supply. The owner also loses the investment return that could be realized if the money invested in a home were available for another use.

Ability to Pay

It is unwise for a person to buy a home without first examining the available cash reserves for making a down payment and determining whether his or her annual income is sufficient to meet all the costs of home ownership. Guides have been established to help determine the amount of debt a prospective homeowner should incur. Traditionally, lenders used as a rule of thumb the formula that the monthly cost of buying and maintaining a home (mortgage payments plus taxes and insurance) should not exceed 25 percent of a borrower's monthly income. Today, however, lenders have been modifying this percentage upward (sometimes to as much as 38 percent) depending on such factors as the borrower's age, potential future earnings, number of dependents, and so forth.

Location

With the exception of the physical appearance of the home itself, *location* is probably the single most important influence on a homebuyer's decision. The elements that contribute to the desirability of a community encompass far more than the geographic area and include such major factors as:

1. *Employment opportunities:* Industrial and commercial development offering vocational opportunities is essential if a community is to grow.

2. *Cultural advantages:* Schools, colleges, churches, libraries, theaters, museums, zoos, sports attractions, and parks all constitute a powerful sociological attraction to a given community.

3. *Governmental structure:* Police and fire protection, sanitation, water, and the many public utilities (gas, power, and telephone service, for instance) add to the desirability of an area, as do various quasi-municipal authorities, such as ports, public transportation, anti-pollution practices, forest preserves, and the like.

4. *Social services:* The availability and quality of hospitals, clinics, community centers, and similar facilities also attract buyers to a community.

5. *Transportation:* A community's accessibility to people and goods depends on available air, rail, and highway systems. In recent decades, the automobile and truck have dominated the transportation industry and have made it possible to open new areas for commercial and residential development. Higher energy costs and increased pollution, however, have made the development of better mass-transit facilities a greater priority, especially in urban areas. When gasoline prices were rising rapidly, the railroad systems began to attract renewed interest as an economical means of moving people and freight. Rivers, lakes, and canals were the focal points of the first towns and cities in this country, and these same water routes have regained importance, particularly along the Great Lakes and adjoining tributaries.

Types of Homes

As discussed earlier in the chapter, housing is not limited to the single-family dwelling. A buyer must choose among the various types of housing based upon considerations of financial resources and spatial requirements, present and future. Although it was once thought best for buyers to plan well ahead at the time of purchase so that their home would be large enough to accommodate a growing family, this is not always the practice today. A young buyer will frequently purchase a small condominium unit, later trading up to larger living quarters as he or she marries and later has children.

Buyers of single-family homes (and to a certain degree condominiums and townhomes) must consider the relative benefits of buying (1) a used home, (2) a ready-built new home, or (3) a new home built to specification. Building a new home to personal specifications may satisfy strong desires to plan for and create one's own lifestyle but may ultimately be too expensive for most buyers. In addition, the buyer may not be able to recoup the added costs for special features when the property is resold.

Cost benefits accrue to the builder who can construct a number of standard or semistandard models and thus capitalize on the advantage of a large-volume operation. Often the purchase of an older used home may also offer economic advantages over the buying of a new home. Some of the uncertainties concerning area development, future depreciation, and flaws in initial construction can be avoided by buying an older home, and because prices have already been discounted to reflect lack of newness, a sounder, less speculative investment results.

The feelings and preferences of buyers always influence the marketability of a particular property. No buyer can estimate exactly what specific characteristics will influence his or her ability to sell a parcel of real estate in the future. However, the more standard features with demonstrated general appeal a property has, the more likely it is to retain its value and marketability.

Investment Considerations

The purchase of a home offers financial advantages to a buyer. The monthly mortgage payments a homeowner makes represent an **investment**; that is, the purchase of an asset that has the potential for profit. The profit may be in the form of present income received, or it may be a long-term gain due to increased value when the asset is sold. In the case of a residence, as the owner reduces the mortgage debt, his or her equity in the property increases. **Equity** represents the financial interest an owner has in his or her real estate in excess of the amount outstanding on any mortgage loan. Thus, the owner establishes financial security for the future by investing and building up equity in a residence that should also increase in value. In addition, as you will see in the following section, homeowners enjoy substantial tax advantages not available to renters.

Tax Benefits for Homeowners

In order to encourage and increase the viability of home ownership, the federal government allows homeowners certain income-tax advantages. For example, a homeowner may deduct from his or her income for tax purposes the cost of mortgage interest, real estate taxes, and certain other expenses; under certain circumstances, he or she may reduce, defer, or eliminate tax liability on the profits received from the sale of a home. Such profits are called **capital gains.** (See the illustration of these benefits in table 4.2.)

Tax-Deductible Interest Payments

People who make mortgage loan payments may take that portion of each monthly payment that is applied toward interest on the loan as a deduction on their yearly income-tax returns. Homeowners may also deduct all property taxes, certain loan origination fees, and any mortgage prepayment penalties.

Capital Gains

If certain conditions are met, federal income-tax regulations give homeowners advantages in the taxation of long-term capital gains earned from the sale of their principal residence. Under tax regulations, a capital gain is the profit realized from the sale or exchange of property. If the property was held for six months or more, the gain is considered to be long term. The tax advantages to homeowners are of

Table 4.2 Homeowners' Tax Benefits	Income Tax Deductions	Capital Gains Tax Rate
	Mortgage interest Mortgage origination fees Mortgage prepayment penalties Real estate taxes	Homeowner taxed on only 40% of capital gain if property is held for longer than 6 months
	Capital Gains Deferment	**Age 55 or Older**
	Tax on some or all of gain postponed if another residence is purchased within 24 months of sale	Once in lifetime, homeowner may exclude up to $125,000 of gain on sale of home owned and used as principle residence for at least three years during last five years before sale

three kinds: reduced taxes, deferment of tax on the gain, and a once-in-a-lifetime exclusion of tax on the gain.

Reduced taxes. For tax purposes, *60 percent* of the gain a taxpayer made on the sale of a home he or she owned for *longer than six months* is excluded from the taxpayer's income. The amount of gain a taxpayer must recognize is the difference between the *amount realized on the sale* and the *tax basis*. The **amount realized** is the sale price minus the selling costs, such as the broker's commission and legal fees. The **tax basis** is the acquisition or construction cost of the home plus the cost of the lot. For example, if Roger Johnson purchased a vacant lot three years ago for $15,000 and built a house on it for $60,000, his tax basis would be $75,000 ($60,000 + $15,000 = $75,000). This year he sold the property for $120,000, eventually paying a $9,000 commission to his broker and $300 to an attorney. This means that the adjusted sales price on this transaction would be $110,700; Johnson would realize a gain of $35,700. The computations for this are as follows:

Sales price:			$120,000
	commission	$ 9,000	
	attorney	+ 300	
Less expenses:		$ 9,300	− 9,300
Amount realized:			110,700
Less tax basis:			− 75,000
Capital gain:			$ 35,700

Sixty percent of Johnson's gain can be excluded from taxable income. This means that his $35,700 capital gain would increase his taxable income by only $14,280. (Sixty percent of $35,700 is $21,420; $35,700 − $21,420 = $14,280.)

Deferment of tax on capital gain. All or part of the gain on the sale of a personal residence is exempt from immediate taxation if a new residence is bought and occupied within 24 months before or 24 months after the sale of the old residence. In this situation, the capital gains tax is not avoided but rather is *deferred* until the property is later sold in a taxable transaction (such as when another home is not purchased or when the owner dies and the property is passed on to his or her heirs).

If the new home is of value equal to or greater than that of the house sold, the entire gain may be deferred. In our example, if Johnson purchased a new home for $135,000, he would pay no capital gains tax.

The tax basis of the *new property* would be as follows:

Cost of new home:	$135,000
Less deferred gain from old home:	− 35,700
Tax basis of new home:	$ 99,300

If the new home's price is less than that of the old home, the difference between the *adjusted sales price* of the old residence and the sales price of the new residence is considered taxable gain. The *adjusted sales price* is the sales price less selling expenses *and* fix-up expenses. Thus, if Johnson incurred $3,000 in fix-up expenses, in addition to the selling expenses previously described, the adjusted sales price for his old residence would be $107,700.

If Johnson were, within the allotted time, to buy a new home for $100,000, his taxable gain, deferred gain, and new tax basis would be as follows:

Old residence's adjusted sales price:		$107,700
Less cost of new home:		− 100,000
Taxable gain:		$ 7,700
Cost of new home:		$100,000
Less:		
gain from old home:	$35,700	
minus taxable gain	− 7,700	
Deferred gain:	$28,000	− 28,000
Tax basis of new home:		$ 72,000

Over - 55 exclusion. A homeowner who sells or exchanges his or her principal residence and (1) was 55 or older before the date of sale or exchange, and (2) owned and used the property sold or exchanged as a principal residence for a period totaling at least three years within the five-year period ending on the date of the sale, may exclude from his or her gross income part or all of the capital gain on that sale or exchange. Taxpayers who meet these requirements can exclude the first *$125,000* of gain. Thus, if the homeowner in our example were over 55 and chose to take advantage of this once-in-a-lifetime exemption, his taxable gain would be zero.

Each homeowner may elect to exclude gains under the "over 55" provision *only once in a lifetime,* even if the total gain excluded is less than the $125,000 limit. When this exclusion is taken by a married couple selling a home, the tax laws hold that *both parties* have given up their once-in-a-lifetime exemption. Thus, if the over-55 exclusion is taken by a married couple and they subsequently divorce, neither one would be able to claim the exclusion in the future. Similarly, if the exclusion is taken by a married couple and one spouse dies, the survivor would not be able to claim the exclusion, even if he or she were to marry a person who has not claimed the exclusion.

In Practice . . .   *You should consult the Internal Revenue Service, a certified public accountant, or a tax lawyer for further information on and precise applications of these and other income-tax issues. IRS regulations are subject to frequent revision and official interpretation.* Never attempt to counsel clients and customers on tax issues, except in broad, general terms. *Always refer such parties to the aforementioned authorities for specific, accurate information and advice.*

Homeowners' Insurance

Because home ownership represents a large financial investment for most purchasers, homeowners usually protect their investment by taking out insurance on their property. Although it is possible for a homeowner to obtain individual policies for each type of risk (see Chapter 17 for a discussion of various kinds of available coverage), most residential property owners take out insurance in the form of a packaged **homeowner's policy.** These standardized policies insure holders against the destruction of their property by fire or windstorm, injury to others that occurs on the property, and theft of any personal property on the premises that is owned by the insured or members of his or her family.

The package homeowner's policy also includes **liability coverage** for: (1) personal injuries to others resulting from the insured's acts or negligence, (2) voluntary medical payments and funeral expenses for accidents sustained by guests or resident employees on the property of the owner, and (3) physical damage to the property of others caused by the insured. Voluntary medical payments will cover injuries to a resident employee but will not cover benefits due under any workers' compensation or occupational disease law.

Characteristics of Homeowners' Packages

Although coverage provided may vary among policies, all homeowners' policies have three common characteristics: fixed ratios of coverage, indivisible premium, and first- and third-party insurance. *Fixed ratios of coverage* require that each type of coverage in a homeowner's policy be maintained at a certain level. The amount of coverage on household contents and other items must be a fixed percentage of the amount of insurance on the building itself. While the amount of contents coverage may be increased, it cannot be reduced below the standard percentage. In addition, theft coverage may be contingent on the full amount of the contents coverage.

An *indivisible premium* combines the rates for covering each peril into a single amount. For the single rate, the insured receives coverage for all the perils included in the policy (see the lists that follow). The insured may not pick and choose the perils to be included.

As previously discussed, *first- and third-party insurance* not only provides coverage for damage or loss to the insured's property or its contents, but also covers the insured's legal liability for losses or damages to another's property or injuries suffered by another party while on the owner's property.

There are four major forms of homeowners' policies. The basic form, known as *HO-1*, provides property coverage against the following perils:

1. fire or lightning.
2. glass breakage.
3. windstorm or hail.
4. explosion.
5. riot or civil commotion.
6. damage by aircraft.
7. damage from vehicles.
8. damage from smoke.

9. vandalism and malicious mischief.
10. theft.
11. loss of property removed from the premises when endangered by fire or other perils.

Increased coverage is provided under a broad form, known as *HO-2,* which covers the following additional perils:

12. falling objects.
13. weight of ice, snow, or sleet.
14. collapse of the building or any part of it.
15. bursting, cracking, burning, or bulging of a steam or hot water heating system, or of appliances used to heat water.
16. accidental discharge, leakage, or overflow of water or steam from within a plumbing, heating, or air-conditioning system.
17. freezing of plumbing, heating, and air-conditioning systems and domestic appliances.
18. injury to electrical appliances, devices, fixtures, and wiring from short circuits or other accidentally generated currents.

Further coverage is provided by comprehensive forms *HO-3* and *HO-5*; these policies cover all possible perils except flood, earthquake, war, and nuclear attack. Other policies include *HO-4*, a form designed specifically for apartment renters, and *HO-6*, a broad-form policy for condominium owners. Apartment and condominium policies generally provide fire and windstorm, theft, and public liability coverage for injuries or losses sustained within the unit, but do not usually extend to cover losses or damages to the structure. The structure is insured by either the landlord or the condominium owners' association (except, in condominium ownership, for additions or alterations made by the unit owner, which are not covered by the association's master policy).

Claims

Most homeowners' insurance policies contain a **coinsurance clause.** This provision requires the insured to maintain fire insurance on his or her property in an amount equal to at least 80 percent of the **replacement cost** of the dwelling (not including the price of the land). If the owner carries such a policy, a claim may be made for the cost of the repair or replacement of the damaged property without deduction for depreciation.

For example, a homeowner's dwelling has a replacement cost of $100,000 and is damaged by fire. The estimated cost to repair the damaged portion of the dwelling is $71,000.

Replacement cost of dwelling	$100,000
	× 80%
Minimum coverage required on the dwelling	$ 80,000

Thus, if the homeowner carries at least $80,000 insurance on her dwelling, then her claim against the insurance company can be for the full $71,000.

If the homeowner carries coverage of less than 80 percent of the full replacement cost of the dwelling, the loss will be either settled for the actual cash value (cost of repairs less depreciation) or prorated by dividing the percentage of replacement cost actually covered by the policy by the minimum coverage requirement (usually 80 percent). For example, if the building is insured for only 60 percent of its value and there is a $71,000 loss, the insurance company will pay only $53,250 (60% ÷ 80%, or 75%, of $71,000 = $53,250).

In any event, *the total settlement cannot exceed the face value of the policy.* Because of coinsurance clauses, it is important for homeowners to periodically review all policies to be certain that the coverage is equal to at least 80 percent of the current replacement cost of their homes.

Federal Flood Insurance Program

A subsidized program authorized by Congress requires property owners in certain areas to obtain flood damage insurance on properties financed by mortgages or other loans, grants, or guarantees obtained from federal agencies and federally insured or regulated lending institutions. The program seeks to improve future management for flood-plain areas through land-use and control measures.

The Department of Housing and Urban Development (HUD), which administers the flood program, has prepared maps and identified specific flood-prone areas throughout the country. Property owners in the designated areas who do not obtain flood insurance (either because they don't want it or because they don't qualify as a result of their communities' not having properly entered the program) are unable to obtain federal and federally related financial assistance.

Flood insurance coverage is required on all types of buildings—residential, commercial, industrial, and agricultural—for either the value of the property or the amount of the mortage loan, subject to the maximum limits available. Policies are written annually and can be purchased from any licensed property insurance broker, the National Flood Insurance Program, or the designated servicing companies in each state.

Summary

One of the main goals of most Americans is the ownership of their own home.

In addition to single-family homes, current trends in *home ownership* include apartment complexes, condominiums and townhouses, cooperatives, planned unit developments, retirement communities, single-person developments, high-rise developments, converted-use properties, modular homes, and mobile homes. Other developments in home ownership include timeshared occupancy of vacation homes and government-sponsored urban homesteading programs.

In considering the purchase of a home, a prospective buyer should be aware of both the advantages and disadvantages of home ownership. While a homeowner gains financial security and pride of ownership, the costs of ownership—both the initial price and the continuing expenses—must be considered. When purchasing a home, a prospective buyer should note its specific characteristics and evaluate the desirability of the community based on the standards of its cultural activities, employment opportunities, recreational and social facilities, and transportation.

One of the *income-tax benefits* available to homeowners allows them to deduct mortgage interest payments and property taxes from their federal income tax returns. In addition, when a homeowner sells a residence he or she has owned for more than six months, the gain made on the sale will be taxed at the reduced capital gains rate if certain conditions are met. Income tax on this gain may be deferred if the homeowner purchases another residence within a set period of time. Homeowners over the age of 55 are given additional benefits.

To protect their investment in real estate, most homeowners purchase insurance. A standard *homeowner's insurance policy* covers fire, theft, and liability and can be extended to cover many types of less common risks. Another type of insurance, which covers personal property only, is available to people who live in apartments and condominiums. In addition to homeowners' insurance, the federal government makes flood insurance mandatory for people living in flood-prone areas who wish to obtain federally regulated or federally insured mortgage loans. Many homeowners' policies contain a *coinsurance clause* that requires the policyholder to maintain fire insurance in an amount equal to 80 percent of the replacement cost of the home. If this percentage is not met, the policyholder may not be reimbursed for the full repair costs if a loss occurs.

Questions

1. The real cost of owning a home includes certain costs or expenses that many people tend to overlook. Which one of the following is *not* a cost or expense of owning a home?
   a. interest paid on borrowed capital
   b. homeowner's insurance
   c. maintenance and repairs
   d. taxes on personal property

2. Federal income tax laws allow for:
   I. a tax on one-half of the capital gains realized from the sale of a residence.
   II. the deduction from a homeowner's taxable income of mortgage interest paid.

   a. I only   c. both I and II
   b. II only   d. neither I nor II

3. When a person buys a house using a mortgage loan, the difference between the amount he or she owes on the property and what it is worth represents the homeowner's:
   a. tax basis.   c. replacement cost.
   b. equity.   d. capital gain.

4. When a homebuyer chooses a location in which to live, he or she is likely to be influenced by the area's:
   I. transportation facilities.
   II. employment opportunities.

   a. I only   c. both I and II
   b. II only   d. neither I nor II

5. A homeowner's insurance policy:
   I. would cover the cost of medical expenses for a person injured in the policyholder's home.
   II. could be extended to cover theft of personal property not on the premises, civil disturbance, and glass breakage.

   a. I only   c. both I and II
   b. II only   d. neither I nor II

6. A building that is remodeled into residential units and is no longer used for the purpose for which it was originally built would be a(n):
   a. converted-use property.
   b. example of urban homesteading.
   c. planned unit development.
   d. modular home.

7. Which of the following would be likely to affect a person's decision to purchase a home?
   I. current interest rates
   II. investment considerations

   a. I only   c. both I and II
   b. II only   d. neither I nor II

8. Which of the following factors should a person consider when purchasing a home as a long-term investment?
   I. his or her ability to pay
   II. the future marketability of the real estate

   a. I only   c. both I and II
   b. II only   d. neither I nor II

9. In a homeowner's insurance policy, *coinsurance* refers to:
   a. the specific form of policy purchased by the owner.
   b. the stipulation that the homeowner must purchase fire insurance coverage equal to at least 80 percent of the replacement cost of the structure in order to be able to collect the full insured amount in the event of a loss.
   c. the stipulation that the homeowner must purchase fire insurance coverage equal to at least 70 percent of the replacement cost of the structure in order to be able to collect the full insured amount in the event of a loss.
   d. a and b

10. Federal flood insurance:
    I. is required in certain areas to insure
       properties financed by mortgage loans
       against flood damage.
    II. is a common part of a homeowner's
        insurance policy.
       a. I only   c. both I and II
       b. II only   d. neither I nor II

11. Federal income tax laws do *not* allow a
    homeowner to deduct which of the following
    expenses from his or her taxable income?
    a. mortgage interest
    b. real estate taxes
    c. all home improvements
    d. mortgage prepayment penalties

12. Under the provisions for liability coverage in
    a homeowner's insurance policy, the
    insurance company may settle a claim for:
    a. physical damage to the insured's property.
    b. funeral expenses for the insured's child.
    c. personal injury to a delivery person who is
       injured on the insured's property.
    d. a and c

13. A *townhome* is most closely associated with
    which of the following types of housing?
    a. high-rise development
    b. condominium
    c. mobile home
    d. urban homestead

14. Traditionally, mortgage lenders will not make
    a loan in which each monthly payment
    exceeds what percentage of a borrower's
    monthly income?
    a. 25 percent   c. 15 percent
    b. 20 percent   d. none of the above

15. Which of the following would probably be
    most cost-efficient to purchase for a young
    married couple living on a modest income?
    a. ready-built new home
    b. five-year-old single-family dwelling
    c. new home built to the buyers'
       specifications
    d. either a or c

16. The profit a homeowner receives from the sale
    or his or her residence:
    I. is the homeowner's tax basis.
    II. is not subject to federal income taxes.
       a. I only   c. both I and II
       b. II only   d. neither I nor II

17. A homeowner sold his house for $127,500.
    Selling expenses were $750; the house had
    been purchased new three years earlier for
    $75,000. What is the homeowner's capital
    gain on this transaction?
    a. $53,250   c. $51,750
    b. $52,500   d. $75,000

18. In question 17, how much of the capital gain
    will be subject to the homeowner's income
    tax?
    a. all of it   c. $21,300
    b. $20,700   d. $21,000

19. Brendon Wilson, age 38, sells his home and
    realizes a $25,000 gain from the sale. If certain
    conditions are met, the capital gains taxes
    levied on the profits from the sale of his home
    may be:
    a. eliminated by claiming a once-in-a-lifetime
       exclusion.
    b. deferred by purchasing another home of
       equal or greater value.
    c. reduced by the amount of mortgage
       interest paid over the life of the property's
       ownership.
    d. a and b

20. Frieda Wilson, age 62, sells her home and
    realizes a $52,000 gain from the sale. If certain
    conditions are met, the capital gains taxes on
    the profits from the sale of her home may be:
    a. eliminated by claiming a once-in-a-lifetime
       exclusion.
    b. deferred by purchasing another home of
       equal or greater value.
    c. reduced by the amount of mortgage
       interest paid over the life of the property's
       ownership.
    d. a and b

Part Two

Principles

5

Real Estate Brokerage

Key Terms

Agency coupled with an interest
Agent
Antitrust laws
Broker
COAL
Commission
Dual agency
Employee
Fiduciary relationship
Finder's agreement
Fraud
General agency

Independent contractor
Law of agency
Listing agreement
Ostensible agency
Principal
Procuring cause of sale
Puffing
Ready, willing, and able buyer
Salesperson
Special agency
Universal agency

Overview

The term *broker* can be traced back several centuries to the Norman French word *brocour,* literally meaning "wine dealer." At that time the local pub was a village's central meeting place, and it was common practice for a customer to tell the wine dealer if there was something that person wanted to buy or sell. The wine dealer would then pass the word on to other customers; if a sale was made, the *brocour* would receive a fee for his or her services. Although this is the essence of brokerage, *real estate brokerage* today is a much more complex operation involving strictly defined legal relationships with buyers and sellers. This chapter will discuss these legal relationships and will also examine the nature of the real estate brokerage business itself.

Brokerage Defined

The business of bringing buyers and sellers together in the marketplace is *brokerage.* Buyers and sellers in many fields employ the services of brokers to facilitate complex business transactions. In the real estate business, a **broker** is defined as a person who is licensed to buy, sell, exchange, or lease real property for others and to charge a fee for his or her services. Working on behalf of and licensed to represent the broker is the real estate **salesperson.**

The **principal** who employs the broker may be a seller, a prospective buyer, an owner who wishes to lease his or her property, or a person seeking property to rent. The real estate broker acts as the **agent** of the principal, who usually compensates the broker with a **commission.** This commission is contingent upon the broker's successfully performing the service for which he or she was employed, which is generally negotiating a transaction with a prospective purchaser, seller, lessor, or lessee who is ready, willing, and able to complete the contract.

Agency

A real estate broker has a unique relationship with buyers, sellers, and the entire community. The role of a broker as the agent of his or her principal is a **fiduciary relationship,** which falls within the requirements of the body of law that governs the rights and duties of the principal, agent, and third parties, known as the **law of agency.** The fiduciary relationship is one of trust and confidence in which an agent (such as a broker or an attorney) generally is responsible for the money and/or property of others.

In the typical real estate transaction, the broker is hired by a seller to market his or her real estate. In this situation, the broker is an *agent* of the seller; the seller is the broker's *client.* Unless otherwise agreed upon, a buyer who contacts the broker in order to review properties listed with his or her firm is merely the broker's *customer.* Though obligated to deal fairly with all parties to a transaction, the broker is strictly accountable *only to the principal*—in this case, the seller.

Types of Agencies

A licensed real estate broker is hired by a principal to become his or her agent. In the purest sense, an agent is someone who is authorized by another to negotiate contracts for that person. An agent may be classified as a universal agent, general agent, or special agent, based upon his or her authority.

A **universal agent** is someone who is empowered by his or her principal to represent the principal in *all matters* that can be delegated. The universal agent has the power to enter into *any* contract (such as the selling and buying of property) on behalf of the principal without his or her prior permission. This type of agency is created by a document known as a *power of attorney,* which grants the agent unlimited authority in the principal's financial and other matters.

A **general agent** is someone empowered by his or her principal to represent the principal in a *specific range of matters.* The general agent may bind the principal to any contracts within the scope of his or her authority. This type of agency is also created by a power of attorney, which stipulates the specific areas of authority in which the agent may act.

A **special agent** is authorized to represent his or her principal in *one specific transaction or business activity only.* A real estate broker is generally a special agent, hired by a seller to find a ready, willing, and able buyer for the seller's property. As a special agent, the broker is *not authorized* to sell the property or to bind the principal to any contract.

In addition to these three types of agency, all of which are created by agreement or document, there is a form of *implied agency* called an **ostensible agency.** In this case the creation of the fiduciary relationship may be implied from the acts of the parties and does not depend on the existence of a written contract. For instance, suppose real estate seller *A* implies to potential buyer *B* that *A*'s property is listed with a particular broker *C* when, in fact, it is not. *A* may be bound by *C*'s actions if *C* is approached by the buyer as the listing broker, based upon *A*'s representations to *B*.

An **agency coupled with an interest** is an agency relationship in which the agent is given an interest in the subject of the agency (the property being sold). Such an agency *cannot be revoked by the principal, nor can it be terminated upon the principal's death.* For example, a broker might supply the financing for a condominium development, provided the developer agrees to give the broker the exclusive right to sell the completed condo units. Since this is an agency coupled with an interest, the developer would not be able to revoke the listing agreement after the broker provided the financing.

Creation of Agency

An agency relationship is created by an agreement of the parties. The real estate broker-seller relationship is generally created by an employment contract, commonly referred to as a **listing agreement.**

Although a written listing agreement is usually preferred, it is not necessary in all states. Some states construe an oral agreement as binding. All that is technically necessary is that the owner either express or imply willingness to be represented in a transaction by the broker. The broker then either expresses or implies his or her willingness to carry out the owner's directions.

Because of the special nature of a real estate broker's responsibility, many states have enacted laws that require listing agreements to be in writing when a commission is to be paid for securing a person who is ready, willing, and able to buy, sell, or rent. Most real estate brokers would prefer not to rely on oral agreements with their principals; rather, they require that all agreements be in writing and signed by the principals. Listing agreements will be discussed in much greater detail in Chapter 6.

Termination of Agency

An agency between a principal and an agent may be terminated at any time, except in the case of an agency coupled with an interest. An agency may be terminated for any of the following reasons:

1. Death or incapacity of either party (notice of death is not necessary).
2. Destruction or condemnation of the property.
3. Expiration of the terms of the agency.
4. Mutual agreement to terminate the agency.
5. Renunciation by the agent or revocation by the principal.
6. Bankruptcy of the principal (since title to the property would be transferred to a court-appointed receiver).
7. Completion or fulfillment of the purpose for which the agency was created.

Buyer as Principal

Generally, a real estate broker is hired by a seller to locate a buyer for the seller's real property. In some cases, however, a broker may be hired by a potential buyer to find that person a parcel of real estate that possesses certain characteristics or is usable for specific purposes. A prospective purchaser seeking commercial or industrial property is particularly likely to hire a broker for this reason. In this situation, the broker and the buyer will usually draw up an agreement commonly referred to as a **finder's agreement,** or *buyer agency agreement.* This document sets forth in detail the nature of the property desired and the amount of the broker's compensation. Note that regardless of whether an employment agreement between the broker and his or her principal is a contract to sell or to acquire property, it usually authorizes the broker to act for the principal but does not carry with it a guarantee that the broker will be able to perform. But as an agent of the principal, the broker is obligated to make a maximum effort to carry out the assumed agency duties successfully.

Agent's Responsibilities to Principal

The broker, as an agent, owes his or her principal certain duties. These duties are clear and specific. They are not simply moral or ethical; they are the law—the *law of agency.* An agent has a *fiduciary relationship* with his or her principal; that is, a relationship of trust and confidence between employer and employee. This confidential relationship carries with it certain duties that the broker must perform— the duties of **care, obedience, accounting,** and **loyalty,** easily remembered as the word **COAL,** plus the duty of *notice* (see figure 5.1).

Figure 5.1
Agent's
Responsibilities

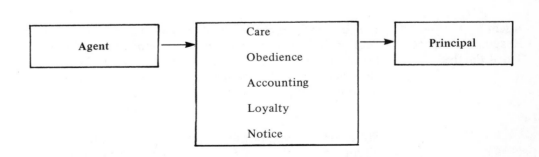

Care. The broker, as an agent, must exercise a reasonable degree of care while transacting business entrusted to him or her by the principal. Remember, the broker is liable to the principal for any loss resulting from negligence or carelessness.

Obedience. The broker is at all times obligated to act in good faith and in conformity with his or her principal's instructions and authority. Again, a broker is liable for any losses incurred by the principal due to any acts the broker performs that are not within the scope of authority granted him or her. The broker is not, however, required to obey unlawful or unethical instructions. The broker may disobey a principal or perform acts beyond his or her authority in an emergency situation as long as the broker's actions are in the principal's best interests.

Accounting. The broker must be able to report the status of all funds entrusted to him or her by the principal. Most state real estate license laws require brokers to give accurate copies of all documents to all parties affected by them and to keep copies of such documents on file for a specified period of time. In addition, the license laws generally require the broker to immediately deposit all funds entrusted to him or her in a special trust, or escrow, account; the laws make it illegal for the broker to commingle such monies with personal funds.

Loyalty. Loyalty is a must—the broker owes his or her employer 100 percent, the utmost in loyalty. An agent must always place a principal's interests above those of the other persons he or she is dealing with. Thus, an agency cannot disclose such information as the principal's financial condition, the fact that the principal (if the seller) will accept a price lower than the listing price for his or her real estate, or any similar confidential facts that might harm the principal's bargaining position.

All states forbid brokers or salespeople to buy property listed with them for their own accounts, or for accounts in which they have a personal interest, without first notifying the principal of such interest and receiving his or her consent. Likewise, by law neither brokers nor salespeople may sell property in which they have a personal interest without informing the purchaser of that interest.

Notice. Along with these four responsibilities goes the duty of notice. It is the broker's duty to keep the principal fully informed at all times of all facts or information the broker obtains that could affect the principal's business or decisions. In certain instances, the broker may be held liable for damages for failure to disclose such information.

Agent's Responsibilities to Third Parties

In dealing with a buyer a broker, as an agent of the seller, must exercise extreme caution and be aware of the laws and ethical considerations that affect this relationship. For example, brokers must be careful about the statements they or their staff members make about a parcel of real estate. Statements of opinion are permissible as long as they are offered as opinions and without any intention to deceive. Making such statements when selling real estate is called **puffing.**

Statements of fact, however, must be accurate. Brokers and salespeople must be alert to ensure that none of their statements can in any way be interpreted as involving **fraud.** Fraud is the *intentional* misrepresentation of a material fact that harms or takes advantage of another person. In addition to false statements about a property, the concept of fraud covers intentional concealment or nondisclosure of important facts. If a contract to purchase real estate is obtained as a result of fraudulent misstatements made by a broker or his or her salespeople, the contract may be disaffirmed or renounced by the purchaser. In such a case, the broker will lose a commission. If either party suffers loss because of a broker's misrepresentations, the broker can be held liable for damages. If the broker's misstatements are based upon the owner's own inaccurate statements to the broker, however, the broker may be entitled to a commission even if the buyer rescinds the sales contract.

Brokers and salespeople should be aware that the courts have ruled that a seller is responsible for revealing to a buyer any hidden, or latent, defects in a building. *A latent defect is one that is known to the seller but not to the buyer and that is not discoverable by ordinary inspection.* As an agent of the seller, a broker is likewise responsible for disclosing known latent defects. Buyers have been able to either rescind the sales contract or receive damages in such instances. Examples of such circumstances are cases in which a house was built over a ditch that was covered with decaying timber, a buried drain tile caused water to accumulate, or a driveway was built partly on adjoining property. Cases in which the seller neglected to reveal violations of zoning or building codes have also been decided in favor of the buyer.

In Practice . . .   *Because of the enormous exposure to liability that real estate licensees have under the law, some brokers purchase what is known as errors and omissions insurance policies for their firms. Operating similarly to malpractice insurance in the medical field, such policies generally cover liabilities for errors, mistakes, and negligence in the usual listing and selling activities of a real estate office or escrow company.*

Dual agency.   In dealing with buyers, the broker must be careful of any situation that might be considered a **dual,** or **double, agency.** Sometimes a broker may have the opportunity to receive compensation from both the buyer and seller in a transaction. Theoretically, however, an agent cannot be loyal to two or more distinct principals in the same transaction. Thus, state real estate license laws generally prohibit a broker from representing and collecting compensation from both parties to a transaction without their prior mutual knowledge and consent. Note, however, that although the courts tend to accept this *informed consent exception,* many indicate a reluctance to permit brokers to act as dual agents. In fact, some courts reject the consent exception altogether because of public policy considerations. Many brokers today believe in what is known as the *single agency* concept, which strictly holds that a broker can effectively be a principal to only one party at a time in a given transaction.

In Practice . . .   *Before entering into a listing agreement, a licensee should fully explain to a seller/ principal the nature of the agency relationship and the provisions of the document that creates it. Also, to avoid potential problems arising from misunderstanding under the usual agency arrangement, in which the seller is principal, a licensee should inform each buyer/customer that he or she represents the seller and owes the seller 100-percent loyalty. However, giving this information does not relieve the licensee from dealing fairly and honestly with the buyer/customer.*

Nature of the Brokerage Business

Whether or not he or she is affiliated with any national franchise or marketing organization, a real estate broker is an independent businessperson who sets the policies of his or her own office. A broker engages employees and salespeople, determines their compensation, and directs their activities. He or she is free to accept or reject agency relationships with principals. This is an important characteristic of the brokerage business: *a broker has the right to reject agency contracts that in his or her judgment violate the ethics or high standards of the office.* However, once a brokerage relationship has been established, the broker represents the person who has engaged him or her. The broker owes that person, the principal, the duty to exercise care, skill, and integrity in carrying out instructions.

Real Estate License Laws

Every state and Canadian province requires real estate brokers and salespeople to be licensed. Knowledge of your state's real estate broker's and salesperson's license law is essential to the understanding of brokers' and salespeople's legal authority and responsibilities. Basically, the license laws of the various states differ only in degree, but they are not uniform. License laws are discussed in detail in Chapter 14. In that chapter, the terms *broker* and *salesperson* are covered in greater depth. General and educational requirements and the nature of the state examinations are explained. Due to the variations of state laws affecting the licensing of real estate brokers and salespeople, a checkoff sheet is included in Chapter 14 to help you understand the requirements of your state law.

The state real estate license laws generally regulate many of the day-to-day business operations of a real estate brokerage. Such matters often include location of a definite, regular place of business for the firm, minimum size and exact placement of business signs, requirements for establishing and maintaining branch brokerage offices, proper accounting procedures, correct handling of client trust fund accounts, and specific manner of execution and retention of documents involved in the real estate transaction. Check your state law for specific regulations. The license law analysis form in Chapter 14 will help you organize your research.

Broker-Salesperson Relationship

A person licensed to perform real estate activities on behalf of a licensed real estate broker is known as a real estate salesperson. *The salesperson is responsible only to the broker under whom he or she is licensed.* A salesperson can carry out only those responsibilities assigned by that broker, since the salesperson is the agent of the broker and the sub-agent of the seller.

A broker is licensed to act as the principal's agent and can thus collect a commission for performing his or her assigned duties. A salesperson, on the other hand, has no authority to make contracts or receive compensation directly from a principal. The broker is fully responsible for the actions of all salespeople licensed under him or her. *All of a salesperson's activities must be performed in the name of his or her supervising broker.*

Independent contractor vs. employee. Salespeople are engaged by brokers as either employees or independent contractors. The agreement between a broker and a salesperson should be set down in a written contract that defines the obligations and responsibilities of the relationship. Whether a salesperson is employed by the broker or operates under the broker as an independent contractor will affect the broker's relationship with the salesperson and the broker's liability to pay and withhold taxes from that salesperson's earnings (see figure 5.2).

Figure 5.2
Employee versus Independent Contractor

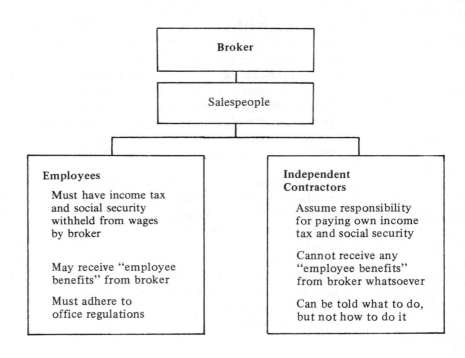

The nature of the employer-employee relationship allows a broker to exercise certain *controls* over salespeople who are employees. The broker may require an **employee** to adhere to regulations concerning such matters as working hours, office routine, and dress or language standards. As an employer, a broker is required by the federal government to withhold social security tax and income tax from wages paid to employees. He or she is also required to pay unemployment compensation tax on wages paid to one or more employees, as defined by state and federal laws. In addition, a broker may provide employees with such benefits as health insurance and profit-sharing plans.

A broker's relationship with an independent contractor is very different. The **independent contractor**-salesperson operates more independently than an employee, and the broker may not control his or her activities in the same way. Basically, the broker may control *what* the independent contractor will do but not *how* it will be done. An independent contractor assumes responsibility for paying his or her own income and social security taxes and must provide his or her own health insurance if such coverage is desired. An independent contractor receives nothing from his or her broker that could be construed as an employee benefit.

In Practice . . .

The Internal Revenue Service often investigates the independent contractor/ employee situation in many brokers' offices. The best way to ensure either status officially is for a broker to have a clearly drawn employee or independent-contractor agreement with each salesperson on the staff. The broker should have an attorney verify that such agreements are in effect and are being followed explicitly. Brokers' difficulties in this area seem to stem primarily from an overreliance on signed agreements; a signed agreement would mean little to an IRS auditor if the actions of the parties were contrary to the document's provisions.

Broker's Compensation

The broker's compensation is specified in the listing agreement, management agreement, or other contract with the principal. Compensation is usually in the form of a commission or brokerage fee computed as a *percentage of the total amount of money involved.* Such commission is usually considered to be earned when the broker has accomplished the work for which he or she was hired, and it is due at the closing. Most sales commissions are earned and payable when the sale is consummated by *delivery of the seller's deed,* and this provision is generally included in the listing agreement or in the real estate sales contract. When no time is specified in the sales or listing agreement for the payment of the broker's commission, it is generally earned when a completed sales contract has been executed by a ready, willing, and able buyer and accepted by the seller.

In order to be entitled to a sales commission, a selling broker must be able to show that he or she: (1) is a licensed broker, (2) was the procuring cause of the sale, and (3) was employed by the seller to make the sale (see figure 5.3). In order to be considered the **procuring cause of sale,** the broker must have taken action to start or cause a chain of events that resulted in the sale. A broker who causes or completes such action without a contract or promise to be paid is termed a *volunteer* and has no legal claim for compensation. In order for a broker to collect a sales commission from a seller, the broker must be able to prove that the seller agreed to pay him or her a commission for the sale. In other words, the broker must have been employed by the seller.

Figure 5.3
Broker's Compensation

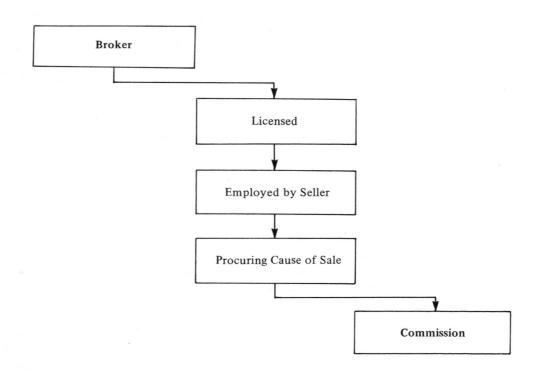

Once a seller accepts an offer from a ready, willing, and able buyer, the seller is technically liable for the broker's commission regardless of whether or not the buyer completes the purchase. **A ready, willing, and able buyer** is one who is *prepared to buy on the seller's terms and ready to take positive steps toward consummation of the transaction.* The modern courts, however, tend to prevent a broker from seeking a commission from the seller if the broker knew or should have known that the buyer was not financially able to complete the purchase.

A broker who has produced a buyer who is ready, willing, and able to meet the listing terms is usually still entitled to a commission if the transaction is *not* consummated for any of the following reasons:

1. The owner changes his or her mind and refuses to sell.
2. The owner's spouse refuses to sign the deed.
3. There are defects in the owner's title that are not corrected.
4. The owner commits fraud with respect to the transaction.
5. The owner is unable to deliver possession within a reasonable time.
6. The owner insists on terms not in the listing (for example, the right to restrict the use of the property).
7. The owner and the buyer agree to cancel the transaction.

In other words, *a broker is generally due a commission if a sale is not consummated because of the principal's default.*

The rate of a broker's commission is *negotiable in every case.* Any attempt by members of the profession, no matter how subtle, to impose uniform commission rates would be a clear violation of state and federal antitrust laws (which will be discussed later in this chapter). If no amount or percentage rate of commission is stated in the listing contract, then custom usually prevails. If such a case is taken to court, a reasonable amount of commission may be determined by evidence of the custom in a particular community.

Most license laws make it illegal for a broker to share a commission with someone who is not licensed as a salesperson or broker. This has been construed to include the giving of certain items of personal property (for instance, a broker giving a new TV to "a friend" for providing a valuable lead) and other premiums (vacations and the like) as well as finder's fees and portions of the commission.

Salesperson's Compensation

The compensation of a salesperson is set by a mutual agreement between the broker and salesperson. A broker may agree to pay a salary or a share of the commissions from transactions originated by a salesperson. A salesperson may have a drawing account against his or her earned share of commissions. Some brokers require salespeople to pay all or part of the expenses of advertising listed properties.

A recent innovation in salespeople's compensation is the *100-percent commission plan.* In a brokerage firm where this system has been adopted, all salespeople who achieve a predetermined sales quota pay a monthly service charge to their broker (to cover the costs of office space, telephones, and supervision) and receive 100 percent of the commissions from the sales they negotiate.

Legal Rights and Obligations

Every real estate transaction involves legal rights. As each contract is prepared for signature, the broker should consider securing legal counsel to protect himself and his sales force.

During the last several years, discussions (and, in some cases, court suits) have arisen between bar associations and real estate boards. These discussions are concerned with the protection of the legal rights and obligations of the parties to a real estate transaction.

While real estate brokers and salespeople do bring buyers and sellers together, they cannot offer legal advice—only a licensed attorney may do this. This matter has been brought before the supreme courts of some states. These courts uniformly recognize that a real estate broker must have the authority to secure some form of agreement between a buyer and seller, evidencing the transaction and providing for payment of the broker's commission.

In many states a special form of sales contract that must be used by real estate brokers has been approved by the bar associations and real estate boards. A broker has no authority in these states to use any other form of contract, and in some instances, if a broker were to use another form his or her license could be revoked. Other states have not adopted a specific form of contract. It is your responsibility to ascertain the rules in effect in your state by checking with your local real estate commission or board of REALTORS®.

Antitrust Laws

The real estate industry is subject to federal and state **antitrust laws.** Generally, these laws prohibit monopolies and contracts, combinations, and conspiracies that unreasonably restrain trade. The most common antitrust violations that can occur in the real estate business are price fixing and allocation of customers or markets.

Illegal *price fixing* occurs when brokers conspire to set prices for the services they perform (sales commissions, management rates) rather than let those prices be established through competition in the open market.

Allocation of customers or markets involves an agreement between brokers to divide their markets and refrain from competing for each other's business. Allocations may take place on a geographic basis, with brokers agreeing to specific territories within which they will operate exclusively. The division may also take place along other lines; for example, two brokers may agree that one will handle only residential properties under $100,000 in value, while another will handle residential properties over $100,000 in value.

The penalties for such acts are severe. For example, under the Sherman Anti-Trust Act people who fix prices or allocate markets may be found guilty of a misdemeanor, punishable by a maximum $100,000 fine and three years in prison. For corporations, the penalty may be as high as $1 million. In a civil suit, a person who has suffered a loss because of the antitrust activities of a guilty party may recover triple the value of the actual damages plus attorney's fees and costs.

Summary

Real estate brokerage is the bringing together, for a fee or commission, of people who wish to buy, sell, exchange, or lease real estate. All states and Canadian provinces require that real estate brokers and salespeople be licensed.

An important part of real estate brokerage is the *law of agency.* A real estate broker is the *agent,* generally hired by the seller, but occasionally by a buyer, to sell or find a particular parcel of real estate. The person who hires the broker is the *prin-*

cipal. The principal and the agent have a *fiduciary relationship,* under which the agent owes the principal the duties of care, obedience, accounting, loyalty, and notice.

The broker's compensation in a real estate sale generally takes the form of a *commission,* which is a percentage of the real estate's selling price. The broker is considered to have earned a commission when he or she procures a *ready, willing, and able buyer* for a seller.

A broker may hire salespeople to assist him or her in this work. The salesperson works on the broker's behalf as either an *employee* or an *independent contractor.*

Many of the general operations of a real estate brokerage are regulated by the real estate license laws. In addition, state and federal *antitrust laws* prohibit brokers from conspiring to fix prices or allocate customers or markets.

Questions

1. Under the law of agency, a real estate broker owes his or her principal the duty of:
   I. care.
   II. obedience.
      a. I only
      b. II only
      c. both I and II
      d. neither I nor II

2. A real estate broker acting as the agent of the seller:
   a. is obligated to render faithful service to the seller.
   b. can make a profit if possible in addition to his or her commission.
   c. can agree to a change in price without the seller's approval.
   d. can accept a commission from the buyer without the seller's approval.

3. To establish a firm legal contract between a broker and seller, the broker should:
   I. get an oral listing agreement from the seller.
   II. file a suit in court.
      a. I only
      b. II only
      c. both I and II
      d. neither I nor II

4. A real estate broker may lose the right to a commission in a real estate transaction if he or she:
   I. did not advertise the property.
   II. was not licensed when hired as an agent.
      a. I only
      b. II only
      c. both I and II
      d. neither I nor II

5. The statement "a broker must be employed to recover a commission for his or her services" means:
   a. the broker must work in a real estate office.
   b. the seller must have made an agreement to pay a commission to the broker for selling the property.
   c. the broker must have asked the seller the price of the property and then found a ready, willing, and able buyer.
   d. the broker must have a salesperson employed in the office.

6. A real estate broker hired by an owner to sell a parcel of real estate must comply with the:
   I. instructions of the owner.
   II. law of agency.
      a. I only
      b. II only
      c. both I and II
      d. neither I nor II

7. As an employee of a real estate broker, a real estate salesperson has the authority to:
   I. act as an agent for another person.
   II. assume responsibilities assigned by his or her employer.
      a. I only
      b. II only
      c. both I and II
      d. neither I nor II

8. A broker is entitled to collect a commission from both the seller and the buyer:
   a. when the broker holds a state license.
   b. when the buyer and the seller are related.
   c. when both parties agree to such a transaction.
   d. when both parties have attorneys.

9. Mickie Michaels, a licensed broker, learns that his neighbor, Paul Cella, wishes to sell his house. Michaels knows the property well, and while Cella is out of town for a week, Michaels is able to convince Barney Schultz to buy the property. Michaels obtains Schultz's signature on a purchase offer together with a check for an earnest money deposit. When Cella returns, Michaels obtains Cella's acceptance of Schultz's offer. In this situation:
   a. Cella is not obligated to pay Michaels a commission.
   b. Schultz is obligated to pay Michaels a commission for locating the property.
   c. Cella must pay Michaels a commission.
   d. b and c

10. A person who has the authority to enter into contracts concerning all business and legal affairs of another is called a(n):

    a. general agent.   c. special agent.
    b. universal agent.   d. attorney.

11. The document that creates the situation detailed in question 10 is a:

    I. listing agreement.
    II. power of attorney.

    a. I only   c. both I and II
    b. II only   d. neither I nor II

12. The term *fiduciary* refers to:

    a. the sale of another's property by an authorized agent.
    b. principles by which a real estate broker must conduct his or her business.
    c. one who acts as a trustee for another and has a legal authority to act on behalf of that person.
    d. the principal in a principal-agent relationship.

13. The legal relationship between broker and seller is generally a(n):

    a. special agency.   c. ostensible agency.
    b. general agency.   d. universal agency.

14. Broker Duncan Rivera lists Sam and Adele Kaufmann's house for $87,000. Adele has been transferred to another state and the couple must sell their house within three months. To expedite the sale, Rivera tells a prospective buyer that the couple will accept at least $5,000 less for the house. In this situation:

    I. Rivera has violated his agency responsibilities to the Kaufmanns.
    II. Rivera should not have disclosed this information to the prospective buyer, since it is not in the sellers' best financial interests.

    a. I only   c. both I and II
    b. II only   d. neither I nor II

15. An agency relationship may be terminated by all but which of the following means?

    a. the owner decides not to sell the house
    b. the broker discovers that the market value of the property is such that he or she will not make an adequate commission
    c. the owner dies
    d. the broker secures a ready, willing, and able buyer for the seller's property

16. A real estate broker who engages salespeople as independent contractors must:

    I. withhold income tax and social security from all commissions earned by them.
    II. require them to attend sales meetings and to participate in office insurance plans if he requires other salespeople hired as employees to do so.

    a. I only   c. both I and II
    b. II only   d. neither I nor II

17. A broker may be hired as agent by which of the following?

    a. an owner of a large apartment building, to find suitable tenants and collect rents
    b. a seller of real estate, to find a buyer who is ready, willing, and able to purchase the property
    c. a person looking for a three-flat apartment building at a certain price in a specific area of town
    d. all of the above

18. Which of the following would be considered a violation of antitrust laws?

    a. Brokers representing the Temple, ABC, and All-American Property Management Companies decide to de-escalate their current price war by charging more uniform rates.
    b. Salespeople Joe Black and Emma Marie Mitsubishi, working on behalf of two local firms, agree that Black should seek listings only from the east side of town and Mitsubishi should seek listings only from the west side of town.
    c. a and b
    d. none of the above

19. A real estate broker:
    a. who makes deliberate misstatements about real property he or she is selling is committing fraud.
    b. generally enters into a finder's agreement with a seller to find a buyer for the property.
    c. is usually the seller's universal agent.
    d. a and c

20. Which of the following types of agencies is created by a power of attorney?
    a. general agency
    b. specific agency
    c. ostensible agency
    d. agency coupled with an interest

6

Listing Agreements

Key Terms Automatic extension
Competitive market analysis
Exclusive-agency listing
Exclusive-right-to-sell listing
Listing agreement
Multiple listing
Net listing
Open listing
Special agency

Overview A retailer may employ the best salespeople in the business, maintain the most attractive shop in town, and spend thousands of dollars on public relations and advertising to further the company's image, only to go out of business because he or she does not have an adequate supply of goods on hand to sell. Such is the case in the real estate business. Without a well-stocked inventory of listed property to sell, a broker or salesperson is no more than an office clerk without an income. The listing agreement that secures the broker's inventory can take many forms, each with its own rights and responsibilities for principal and agent. This chapter will examine these forms of listing agreements as well as some of the factors a broker or salesperson must consider when "taking a listing."

| **Listing Property** | Every real estate sale involves two parties. The first is the seller. The second, of course, is the buyer. It is the seller who furnishes the real estate broker and salesperson with the necessary inventory: that is, the *listing*. How complete and accurately priced this inventory is will determine the broker's ultimate success. |

To acquire their inventories, brokers and salespeople must obtain listings. As discussed in Chapter 5, a listing agreement creates a **special agency** relationship between a broker (agent) and a seller (principal), whereby the agent is authorized to represent his or her principal's property for sale, solicit offers, and submit the offers to the principal. Listing agreements are generally written contracts of employment, although in many states oral agreements may be used under certain circumstances. Other states, however, provide that a broker cannot institute a court action to collect a commission unless he or she had a written listing agreement with the seller.

Under the provisions of the state real estate license laws, only a broker can act as agent to list, sell, or rent another person's real estate. Throughout this chapter, unless otherwise stated, the terms *broker, agent,* and *firm* are intended to include both broker and salesperson. While both have the authority to list, lease, and sell property and provide other services to a principal, state real estate license laws stipulate that these acts must be done in the name and under the supervision of the broker, never in the name of the salesperson.

Listing Agreements

The forms of listing agreements, or employment contracts, generally used are: (1) open listing, (2) exclusive-agency listing, (3) exclusive-right-to-sell listing, (4) multiple listing, and (5) net listing. The similarities and differences of the first three are examined in table 6.1.

Open listing. In an **open listing** (also known in some areas as a *general listing*), the seller retains the right to employ any number of brokers to act as his or her agents. These brokers can act simultaneously, and the seller is obligated to pay a commission only to that broker who successfully produces a ready, willing, and able buyer. If the seller personally sells the property *without the aid of any of the brokers,* he or she is not obligated to pay any of them a commission. If a broker was in any way a procuring cause in the transaction, however, he or she may be entitled to a commission. A listing contract generally creates an open listing unless wording that specifically provides otherwise is included.

**Table 6.1
Listing Agreements**

Type of Listing	Who Can Sell		
	Seller	Agent	Other Brokers
Open Listing	•	•	•
Exclusive-Agency Listing	•	•	
Exclusive-Right-to-Sell Listing		•	

Exclusive-agency listing. In an **exclusive-agency listing,** *only one broker* is specifically authorized to act as the exclusive agent of the principal. The *seller* under this form of agreement *retains the right to sell the property him- or herself* without obligation to the broker. Under such circumstances, the seller is not obligated to pay a commission to the broker unless the broker has been the procuring cause of the sale. In addition, the exclusive agent is entitled to a commission if any other broker sells the property.

Exclusive-right-to-sell listing. In an **exclusive-right-to-sell listing,** one broker is appointed as sole agent of the seller and is given the exclusive right, or *authorization,* to represent the property in question. Under this form of contract, the seller must pay the broker a commission *regardless of who sells the property* if it is sold while the listing is in effect. In other words, if the seller gives a broker an exclusive-right-to-sell listing but finds a buyer without the broker's assistance, the seller must still pay the broker a commission. This is usually the most popular form of listing agreement among brokers. (An example of this form of agreement is reproduced in figure 6.1, near the end of this chapter.)

Multiple listing. Multiple-listing contracts are used by those brokers who are members of a multiple-listing organization. Such an organization consists of a group of brokers within an area who agree to pool their listings.

The multiple-listing agreement, while not actually a separate form of listing, is, in effect, an exclusive listing with an additional authority and obligation given to the listing broker to *distribute the listing to other brokers who belong to the multiple-listing service.* The contractual obligations among the member brokers of a multiple-listing organization vary widely. Most provide that upon sale of the property *the commission is divided between the listing broker and the selling broker.* Terms for division of the commission vary from office to office.

Under most multiple-listing contracts, the broker who secures the listing is not only authorized but *obligated* to turn the listing over to his or her multiple-listing service within a definite period of time so that it can be distributed to the other member brokers. The length of time during which the listing broker can offer the property exclusively without notifying the other member brokers varies.

A multiple listing offers advantages to both the broker and the seller. Brokers develop a sizable inventory of properties to be sold and are assured of a portion of the commission if they list the property or participate in its sale. Sellers also gain under this form of listing agreement because all members of the multiple-listing organization are eligible to sell their property.

Net listing. A net listing is based on the amount of money the seller will receive if the property is sold. The seller's property is listed for this net amount, and the broker is free to offer the property for sale at any price higher than the listing price. If the property is sold, the broker pays the seller only the net amount for which the property was listed. *This type of listing is illegal in some states,* and is not recommended in most of the other states. The question of fraud is frequently raised because of uncertainty over the sales price set or received by the broker.

Termination of Listings

As discussed in Chapter 5, a listing agreement—or any agency relationship—may be terminated for any of the following reasons: (1) performance by the broker, (2) expiration of the time period stated in the agreement, (3) abandonment by the broker if he or she spends no time on the listing, (4) revocation by the owner for what the owner considers to be just cause (although the owner may be liable to the broker for damages), (5) cancellation by the broker (although the broker may be liable to the owner for damages), (6) mutual consent, (7) bankruptcy, death, or insanity of either party, (8) destruction of the property, or (9) a change in property use by outside forces (such as a change in zoning).

Expiration of listing period. All listings should specify a definite period of time during which the broker is to be employed. The use of automatic extensions of time in exclusive listings has been discouraged by the courts and outlawed in some states. Many listing contract forms specifically provide that there can be no automatic extensions of the agreement. An example of an **automatic extension** is a listing that provides for a base period of 90 days and "continues thereafter until terminated by either party hereto by 30 days' notice in writing." Some court decisions have held that such an extended period is to be considered an open listing rather than part of the original exclusive-agency listing.

Obtaining Listings

All legal owners of the listing property or their authorized agents, as well as the listing salesperson and/or broker, should sign the listing agreement. The listing salesperson can sign the contract in the broker's name if authorized by the broker.

Information needed for listing agreements. It is important to obtain as much information as possible concerning a parcel of real estate when taking a listing. This ensures that all possible contingencies can be anticipated and provided for, particularly when the listing will be shared with other brokers and salespeople in a multiple-listing arrangement. This information generally includes the following (where appropriate):

1. names and addresses of owners.
2. legal (or other sufficient) description of the property.
3. size of lot (frontage and depth).
4. number and sizes of rooms.
5. construction and age of the building.
6. information relative to the neighborhood (schools, churches, transportation, and so forth).
7. current taxes.
8. existing financing (including interest, payments, other costs, and whether the loan is assumable or not).
9. utilities and average payments.
10. appliances to be included in the transaction.
11. date of occupancy or possession.
12. possibility of seller financing.
13. zoning classification (especially important for vacant land).
14. a detailed list of exactly what will and what will not be included in the sales price.

Never forget that a real estate broker, as an agent of the seller, is responsible for the disclosure of any material information regarding the property. Getting as much initial information from the seller as possible—even if it becomes necessary to ask penetrating and possibly embarrassing questions—will pay off in the long run by saving both principal and agent from potential legal difficulties. The agent should also assume the responsibility of searching the public records for such pertinent information as legal description, lot size, and yearly taxes.

In Practice ...   *Some brokers use a separate information sheet (also known as a profile or data sheet) for recording many of the foregoing property features, including room sizes, lot sizes, and taxes. In these firms, listing agreements contain mainly the specific contract terms—listing price, duration of the agreement, signatures of the parties, and so forth.*

Pricing the Property   Once a listing is secured and all necessary information obtained, the pricing of the real estate is of primary importance. While it is the responsibility of the broker or salesperson to advise, counsel, and assist, it is ultimately the *seller* who must determine a listing price for his or her own property. However, since the average seller does not usually have the background to make an informed decision about a fair market price, the real estate agent must be prepared to offer his or her knowledge, information, and expertise in this area. A broker should reject any listing in which the price has been substantially exaggerated.

A broker or salesperson can help the seller determine a listing price for his or her property through a **competitive market analysis.** Essentially, this is a comparison of the prices of recently sold homes that are similar in location, style, and amenities to that of the listing seller. If no such comparisons can be made, or if the seller feels his or her property is unique in some way, a full-scale real estate appraisal—a professional, detailed estimate of a property's value—may be warranted.

Seller's net return. One of the main concerns of every seller is how much money he or she will make from the sale. To find the gross sales price at which a property must be listed in order for the seller to receive a given amount from the sale, the following computations can be made:

Assume that a seller wants to net $100,000 after paying the broker's commission, and that this figure is within the price range indicated by a competitive market analysis. The gross selling price, therefore, should be $100,000 *plus* the broker's commission (7 percent in this hypothetical situation).

1. The unknown gross selling price is: 100%
    Subtract the broker's commission that will be
    included in the gross selling price: $-$ 7%
    The seller's portion of the gross selling price
    will therefore be: **93**%

2. The seller wants to net $100,000, which is 93 percent of the full sales price; therefore:

    $$\frac{\$107,526.88}{.93)\overline{\$100,000}} \textbf{ gross selling price}$$

    93% = .93

3. The broker's commission will be: $107,526.88
                                         $\times$ .07
                                         $ 7,526.88

4. The seller's net is: 107,526.88
                                        $-$7,526.88
                                        $100,000.00

This, of course, does not take into consideration the various closing costs often incurred by the seller. The agent should estimate these costs and include them in his or her computations by adding them to the seller's net in step 2.

Sample Listing Agreement

Figure 6.1 is a typical listing agreement. Note that the individual specifics of a listing may vary from area to area and that state law may require additional provisions be added to such contracts. Following is a section-by-section analysis of the sample agreement; numerical references are to the specific provisions of the contract.

1. *Exclusive Right to Sell.* The title specifies that this document is an "exclusive right to sell" real property.

2. *Date.* The date of the listing contract is the date it is executed; however, this may not necessarily be the date that the contract becomes effective.

3. *Names.* The names of all persons having an interest in the property should be specified and should enter into the agreement. If the property is owned under one of the forms of co-ownership discussed in Chapter 8, that fact should be clearly established. If one or more of the owners is married, it is wise to obtain the spouse's signature to release marital rights, which will also be discussed in Chapter 8.

4. *Broker or Firm.* The name of the broker or firm entering into the listing must be clearly stated in the agreement.

5. *Contract.* This section establishes the document as a legal contract and states the promises by both parties that create and bind the agreement.

6, 7. *Commission Rate.* This paragraph establishes the broker's rate of commission. Price fixing is illegal; so a broker's commission is open to negotiation between owner and broker.

8. *Extension Clause.* This section, permitted in most states, will protect the broker if the owner or another person sells the property after the listing expires to a person with whom the original broker negotiated. In other words, the broker is guaranteed a commission for a set period of time after the agreement expires (generally 3 to 6 months) if he or she was the procuring cause of the sale, even if the broker did not actually consummate the transaction. This extension clause does not apply, however, if the owner signs a new listing agreement with another broker after the original agreement expires.

9. *Broker's Responsibilities.* This paragraph defines the rights and duties of the broker.

10. *Broker's Authority.* Here the broker is given the authority to place a sign on the property and show it to buyers, as well as the permission to supply the buyers with any and all information that may appear on the listing form. Without such permission, this information would be confidential and could not be revealed to anyone without breaching the agency doctrine of confidence.

11. *Listing Price.* The listing price is a gross sales price, and the owner should understand that any obligations such as taxes, mortgages, and assessments remain his or her responsibility and must be paid out of the proceeds of the sale.

Figure 6.1
Sample Listing
Agreement

SAMPLE FORM

EXCLUSIVE RIGHT TO SELL LISTING CONTRACT (1)

This agreement is made and entered into this _____ day of _____, 19 (2), by and between
_____(3)_____ as owner or owners (referred to herein as
"owner"), of the real estate described herein and _____ of _____(4)_____,
Indiana, as licensed real estate broker (referred to herein as "broker"). The parties, by signing this contract,
agree as follows:

1.   The broker hereby agrees to list for sale the property described herein and to use his best efforts
to find a purchaser for the property upon the terms and conditions set out in this agreement or
upon such other terms as are acceptable to the owner. Owner agrees that broker shall have the
exclusive right to sell said property for the period of this listing contract upon the terms specified
herein or any other terms accepted by owner. (5)

2.   In return for the broker's acceptance of this exclusive right to sell listing contract the owner
hereby agrees:

(a)   that, in the event the broker, owner or other person finds a purchaser who is ready, willing
and able to purchase the property described herein upon the terms specified herein or any
other terms accepted by the owner, the broker shall have completed his performance under
this contract and the owner shall pay the broker a commission for his services in an amount
equal to _____(6)_____ (_____%) percent of the gross sales price, but not
less than $ _____(7)_____;

(b)   that, in the event negotiations with a potential purchaser are begun by the broker, owner or
any other person during the period of this listing contract or if negotiations are begun after
its expiration date with a purchaser who was first contacted during the period of this listing
contract and the property is sold to such purchaser within _____ months after
the expiration date of this contract on the terms hereof or on any other terms accepted by
the owner, owner shall pay the broker a commission on the same basis as set out herein
unless the property at the time of sale is listed with another licensed broker. Owner hereby
represents that there is not now any other listing contract in force with another licensed
broker. (8)

In order to promote the purposes for which this contract is entered into and to further define the rights and
duties of the owner and the broker, it is further agreed:

1.   The broker is authorized to retain on behalf of the owner any earnest money deposit which may
be made by the potential purchaser and to retain it until the sale is completed. In the event that a
contract of sale is entered into and the purchaser defaults, the earnest money deposit shall be
applied first to the broker's advertising expenses and other expenses incurred by the broker under
this listing contract and the balance shall be divided between the owner and the broker. Both parties agree, however, to do whatever is necessary to enforce the contract made with such purchaser
to collect any sums which may be due under such contract. (9)

2.   The broker or his representatives (including other brokers or salesmen under any multiple
listing arrangement to which the broker may be a party) shall have access to the property
described below at all reasonable times for the purposes of showing to prospective purchasers.
The broker is authorized to place a "For Sale" sign on this property, to reveal any and all information which appears in this listing contract and to advertise the property for the purpose of
promoting its sale. (10)

3.   The listing price includes the balances due on all mortgages, liens, assessments for municipal
improvements, current real estate taxes and balances due on personal property or fixtures

which are a part of the property described herein and that such balances shall be paid by the owner prior to or at the time of sale of the property unless the contract of sale provides otherwise. Seller recognizes his responsibility for and agrees to advise the broker of any municipal improvements contracted for. (11)

4. The owner represents and warrants that the property is free and clear of all encumbrances except those noted above and except easements and restrictions of record and current taxes and that the present use of the property does not violate any restriction or zoning ordinance; that the owner is the sole owner of the property and that he will execute a general warranty deed or land contract (if applicable) in the event of sale and will furnish an abstract of title showing a merchantable title or a title insurance policy showing an insurable title for the amount of the sales price; that all information appearing anywhere in this contract including that on the reverse side is true and correct to the best of owner's knowledge; and that all operating equipment which is included in the sale of the property will be in good operating order at the time of closing of the sale except

_____(15)_____.

5. The property is offered for sale without regard to race, creed, color or national origin in accordance with applicable State and Federal laws. (16)

The period of this listing is from _____ A.M./P.M. of _____, 19 _____, up to and including 11:00 P.M. of _____(17)_____, 19 _____. The agreed upon listing price is $ _____, in cash or upon any other price, term, or exchange to which owner agrees. Both parties agree that this contract: is freely entered into; this writing constitutes the entire agreement; is binding upon their heirs, administrators, executors and assigns; is without relief from valuation and appraisement laws; includes the obligation to pay necessary attorney's fees of the other for its enforcement. Owner by signing below, hereby acknowledges receipt of a copy of this contract. The address and location of the listed property are: _____

_____

the legal description of which is: _____

_____

Other Conditions: _____

_____   _____
                    (Owner)   (Owner)

                                                  _____
                                                       (Real Estate Broker or Firm)

                                      by_____

                                      Title:_____

12. *Encumbrances.* This paragraph points out responsibilities of encumbrances, which are especially important to the broker because they determine whether or not the property is in fact saleable.

13. *Evidence of Ownership and Deed.* The type of deed to be executed and proof of ownership in the form of a title are stated here.

14. *Liabilities.* The owner protects both buyer and broker with this statement.

15. *Warranty of Fitness.* Although the buyer has the duty to inspect the property, exhaustive tests of all equipment are not necessary. This generally implied warranty of fitness protects the buyer against misrepresentation.

16. *Civil Rights Legislation.* This clause serves to alert the owner that both federal and state legislation exist to protect against discrimination.

17. *Termination of Agreement.* Both the exact time and the date serve to remove any ambiguity in regard to termination of the contract. A particular termination date does not necessarily include that day itself unless the phrase "up to and including" is used.

Summary

To acquire an inventory of property to sell, brokers and salespeople must obtain listings. The various kinds of listing agreements include open listings, exclusive-agency listings, exclusive-right-to-sell listings, multiple listings, and net listings.

An *open listing* is one in which the broker's commission depends upon his or her finding a buyer before the property is sold by the seller or another broker. Under an *exclusive-agency listing,* the broker is given the exclusive right to represent the seller, but the seller can avoid paying the broker a commission if he or she sells the property without the broker's help. With an *exclusive-right-to-sell listing,* the seller appoints one broker to represent him or her, and must pay that broker a commission regardless of whether it is the broker or the seller who finds a buyer for it, as long as the buyer is found within the listing period.

A *multiple listing* is an exclusive listing with the additional authority and obligation on the part of the listing broker to distribute the listing to other brokers in his or her multiple-listing organization. A *net listing,* which is outlawed in some states and considered unethical in most areas, is based on the net price the seller will receive if the property is sold. The broker under a net listing is free to offer the property for sale at the highest available price and retain as his or her commission any amount over and above the seller's net.

A listing agreement may be terminated for the same reasons as any other agency relationship.

Questions

1. A listing agreement is:
   a. the broker's employment contract with his or her salespeople.
   b. the broker's employment contract with his or her principal.
   c. generally an oral agreement.
   d. none of the above

2. Which of the following is a similarity between an exclusive-agency and an exclusive-right-to-sell listing?
   a. under both types of listing the seller retains the right to sell his or her real estate without the broker's help and not be liable to the broker for a commission
   b. both are open listings
   c. both give the responsibility of representing the seller to one broker only
   d. under both the seller authorizes only one particular salesperson to show his or her property

3. If a seller wanted a minimum return of $89,000 and the broker were to receive a 6 percent commission, what would the minimum gross selling price have to be?
   I. $90,000 plus 6 percent of $90,000
   II. $94,680.85

   a. I only   c. both I and II
   b. II only   d. neither I nor II

4. Which of the following is a similarity between an open listing and an exclusive-agency listing?
   a. under both the seller avoids paying the broker a commission if the seller sells the property him- or herself
   b. both listings grant a commission to any licensed broker who finds a buyer for the seller's property
   c. both are net listings
   d. under both the broker earns a commission regardless of who sells the property as long as it is sold within the listing period

5. A multiple listing:
   I. involves more than one parcel of real estate.
   II. is the same as an open listing.

   a. I only   c. both I and II
   b. II only   d. neither I nor II

6. A listing may be terminated by:
   I. the broker's failure to spend time on it.
   II. expiration of the time period stated in the listing.

   a. I only   c. both I and II
   b. II only   d. neither I nor II

7. A broker sold a residence for $88,000 and received $6,160 as her commission in accordance with the terms of the listing agreement. What percentage of the sales price was the broker's commission?
   a. 6 percent   c. 7 percent
   b. 6½ percent   d. 7½ percent

8. A listing agreement that runs for a set period of time and renews itself for another listing period after the initial period ends:
   I. contains an automatic extension provision.
   II. may be illegal in some states.

   a. I only   c. both I and II
   b. II only   d. neither I nor II

9. When a broker or salesperson takes a listing, who should sign the agreement?
   a. the seller
   b. the listing broker or salesperson
   c. all brokers in a multiple-listing situation
   d. a and b

10. The selling price of a parcel of real estate is determined by:
    I. the seller.
    II. the salesperson.

    a. I only   c. both I and II
    b. II only   d. neither I nor II

11. Which of the following provisions is (are) usually included in listing agreements?

    a. the rate of commission
    b. the minimum price the seller will accept
    c. the date the agreement commences and the date it terminates
    d. a and c

12. Salesperson Joseph Franks has just secured a listing to sell Joyce Randolph's home. When completing the listing agreement, Franks should:

    a. submit the completed form to his broker.
    b. obtain as much information about the property from Randolph as possible.
    c. refuse the listing if he thinks Randolph wants to price it far higher than the fair market value.
    d. all of the above

13. A competitive market analysis:

    I. can help the seller set a price for his or her real estate.
    II. is a comparison of recently sold properties similar to a seller's parcel of real estate.

        a. I only   c. both I and II
        b. II only   d. neither I nor II

14. A seller lists his residence with a broker and stipulates that he wants to receive $85,000 from the sale but that the broker can sell the residence for as much as possible and keep the difference as his commission. The broker agrees. This type of listing is:

    I. called an open listing.
    II. illegal in many states.

        a. I only   c. both I and II
        b. II only   d. neither I nor II

15. A property was listed with a broker who belonged to a multiple-listing service and was sold for $53,500 by another broker member. The total commission was 6 percent of the sales price; of this commission the selling broker received 60 percent, and the listing broker received the balance. How much was the listing broker's commission?

    a. $2,142   c. $1,464
    b. $1,926   d. $1,284

7

Interests in Real Estate

Overview

Ownership of a parcel of real estate is not necessarily absolute; this ownership is dependent upon the type of interest a person holds in the property. For example, a person may own real property forever and be able to pass it on to heirs, or this ownership may exist only as long as he or she lives. Real estate ownership may be restricted to exist as long as the owner uses it for one specific purpose; likewise, it may be restricted to exist as long as the owner refrains from using it for a specific purpose. In addition, the interest in real estate a person possesses may be reduced by the interests others possess in the property. This chapter will discuss the various interests in real estate and how they affect real estate ownership and use.

Historical Background

According to old English common law, the government or king held title to all lands under what was known as the **feudal system** of ownership. Under this system, the individual was merely a tenant whose rights of use and occupancy of real property were held at the sufferance of an overlord. Through a series of social reforms in the seventeenth century, however, the feudal system evolved into the **allodial system** of ownership. Under the allodial system, the individual was entitled to property rights without proprietary control being held by the king.

Land in the United States is held under the allodial system. The Bill of Rights of the U.S. Constitution firmly establishes the private ownership of land free from any of the overtones, obligations, or burdens of the feudal system.

Government Powers

Although an individual in the United States has maximum rights in the land he or she owns, these ownership rights are subject to certain powers, or rights, held by federal, state, and local governments. Because they are for the general welfare of the community, these limitations on the ownership of real estate supersede the rights of the individual. Such government rights include the following:

1. **Taxation:** Taxation is a charge on real estate to raise funds to meet the public needs of a government (see Chapter 10).

2. **Police power:** This is the power vested in a state to establish legislation to preserve order, protect the public health and safety, and promote the general welfare. There is no federal police power as such—it exists in this manner on a state level only. A state's police power is passed on to municipalities and counties through legislation called *enabling acts.* The use and enjoyment of property is subject to restrictions authorized by such legislation, including both environmental protection laws and zoning and building ordinances regulating the use, occupancy, size, location, construction, and rents of real estate.

3. **Eminent domain:** Through what is called a condemnation suit, a government may exercise this right to acquire privately owned real estate for public use. Three conditions must be met: (a) the proposed use must be declared by the court to be a public use, (b) just compensation must be paid to the owner, and (c) the rights of the property owner must be protected by due process of law.

   The exercise of decision-making under the right of eminent domain is generally granted by state laws to quasi-public bodies, such as land-clearance commissions and public housing or redevelopment authorities, as well as to publicly held companies such as railroads, public utilities and mining companies.

   Condemnation proceedings are instituted only when the owner's consent cannot be obtained. Otherwise, public agencies acquire real property through direct negotiation and purchase from the owner.

4. **Escheat:** While escheat is not actually a limitation on ownership, state laws provide for ownership of real estate to revert, or escheat, to the state when an owner dies and leaves no heirs and no will disposing of his or her real estate. In some states, real property will escheat to the county the land is located in,

rather than to the state. Escheat occurs only when a property becomes owner-less.

Estates in Land

The degree, quantity, nature, and extent of interest that a person has in real property is an **estate in land.** In the United States, estates in land are unique. Our present rights and interests in land are complete and free of state domination (except for the state's right to taxation, police power, and eminent domain, as previously mentioned).

Estates in land are divided into two major classifications: (1) freehold estates and (2) leasehold estates (those involving tenants). These two classifications exist for basically historical reasons. Under the common law, freehold estates were classified as real estate, while leasehold estates were considered contracts and construed to be personal property. This classification of estates was based primarily on the duration of the estate or interest. Note that there are various lesser interests or rights to real estate that are not estates in land.

Freehold estates are *estates of indeterminable length,* such as those existing for a lifetime or forever. These include (1) fee simple, (2) defeasible fee, (3) conventional life estate, and (4) legal life estate.

The first two of these estates continue for an indefinite period and are inheritable by the heirs of the owner. The third and fourth terminate upon the death of the person on whose life they are based.

Leasehold estates are *estates for a fixed term of years.* These are (1) estate for years, (2) estate from period to period, (3) estate at will, and (4) estate at sufferance. Leasehold estates will be covered in Chapter 16.

The various estates and interests in real estate are illustrated in figure 7.1.

Fee Simple Estate

An estate in **fee simple** is the *highest type of interest in real estate recognized by law.* A fee simple estate is one in which the holder is entitled to all rights incident to the property. There is no time limit on its existence—it is said to run forever. It is complete ownership. Because this estate is of unlimited duration, upon the death of its owner it passes to his or her heirs or as provided in the owner's will. The fee simple estate is, however, subject to the governmental powers previously explained. The terms *fee, fee simple,* and *fee simple absolute* are basically the same.

Defeasible Fee Estate

A **defeasible fee estate,** also called a *fee simple defeasible,* is an estate in which the holder has a fee simple title that may be divested upon the occurrence or nonoccurrence of a specified event. There are two categories of defeasible fee estates—*fee simple determinable* and *fee simple subject to a condition subsequent.*

A **determinable fee estate,** which is sometimes referred to as a *qualified fee, conditional fee,* or *base fee* estate, is an estate that may be inherited. However, this estate *will be determined* (come to an end), *immediately upon the occurrence of a designated event,* the time of such occurrence being uncertain. While the condition or event that will terminate the estate may be one that is certain to happen, the time of its happening is uncertain. Such an estate may also be based on an uncertain condition or event.

**Figure 7.1
Estates and Interests
in Real Estate**

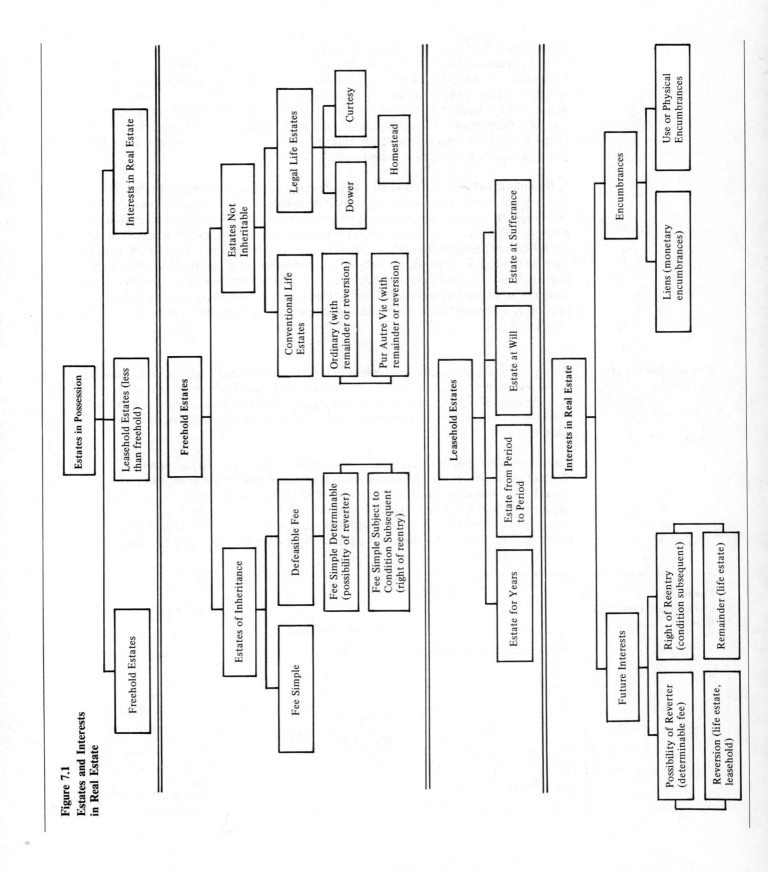

When a parcel of real estate is conveyed and the deed specifically states that the land is granted as long as it is used for certain purposes (for example, as a schoolhouse or a church), the estate conveyed is a determinable fee. The words "as long as" are the key to the creation of this estate. If the specified purpose ceases, title will revert (go back) to either the original grantor or his or her heirs or to some specified third person (or such person's heirs). The person to whom such title will revert holds a future, or contingent, interest as long as the determinable fee is in effect. This future interest is called a *possibility of reverter.*

A **fee simple subject to a condition subsequent** is similar to a determinable fee in that a grantor conveys a parcel of real estate subject to a condition of ownership, but differs in the way the estate will terminate upon violation of this condition. In a determinable fee, title to the subject property reverts back to the original owner (or his or her heirs) immediately and automatically when the condition of ownership is violated. In a fee simple subject to a condition subsequent, the estate does not automatically end upon the occurrence or nonoccurrence of a stipulated condition. The grantor reserves for him- or herself only the *right of reentry* to the property. The estate does not actually terminate until the grantor goes to court to assert this right.

Conventional Life Estates

A conventional **life estate** is an estate in land that is *limited in duration to the life of the owner or to the life or lives of some other designated person or persons.* It is not an estate of inheritance—that is, the rights cannot be passed on to the owner's heirs—because the estate terminates at the death of the owner (or designated person).

There are two types of conventional life estates—*ordinary* and *pur autre vie.* When the owner of a fee simple estate in a parcel of real estate grants an ordinary life estate to someone, the life estate is limited to the lifetime of the owner of the life estate (the life tenant); that is, it *ends with the death of the person to whom it was granted* (see figure 7.2). A life estate can, however, be created for the life of another person; that is, *A,* who owns a fee simple estate, can convey a life estate in

**Figure 7.2
Conventional Life Estate**

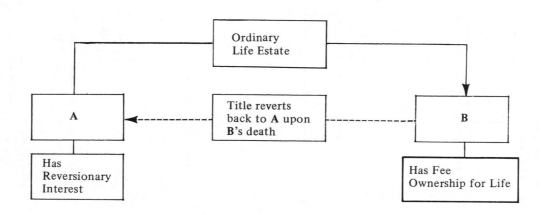

the land to *B* as long as *C* is alive. This is known as an estate pur autre vie (for the life of another), and *B* is called the life tenant. A life estate pur autre vie may be inherited by the life tenant's heirs, but only until the death of the person against whose life the estate is measured.

Remainder and reversion. When the original fee simple owner creates a life estate, he or she must also consider the future ownership of the property after the death of the life estate owner. The future interest may take one of two forms:

1. **Remainder interest:** When the deed or will that creates the life estate names a third party or parties to whom title will pass upon the death of the life estate owner, then such third party is said to own the remainder interest or estate. The remainder interest is a nonpossessory estate—a *future* interest.

2. **Reversionary interest:** When the creator of a life estate (the original fee simple owner) does not convey the remainder interest to a third party or parties, then upon the death of the life estate owner full ownership reverts to the original fee simple owner—or if he or she is deceased, to the heirs or devisees set forth in the fee simple owner's will. This interest or estate is called a *reversion.*

Thus, upon the death of the life estate owner or other designated person, the holder of the future interest, whether remainder or reversion, will be the owner of a fee simple estate.

A life tenant's interest in real property is a true ownership interest. In general, the life tenant is not answerable to the holder of the future interest, generally called the *remainderman,* who is the individual to whom the right of possession will pass upon termination of the life estate. A life tenant's rights are not absolute, however. He or she can enjoy the rights of the land but cannot encroach upon those of the remainderman. In other words, the life tenant cannot perform any acts that would permanently injure the land or property. Such injury to real estate is known in legal terms as *waste.* In such a case, those having a future interest in the property would be able to bring legal action against the life tenant for the damages or seek an injunction.

A life tenant is entitled to all income and profits arising from the property during his or her term of ownership. A life interest may be sold, leased, or mortgaged, but such interest will always terminate upon the death of the person against whose life the estate is measured.

Legal Life Estates

Curtesy, dower, and homestead are *legal life estates* created by statute in some states; they become effective automatically by operation of law upon the occurrence of certain events. Check the chart in table 7.1 to see which (if any) of these legal life estates apply in your state.

Curtesy and dower. A husband's life estate in the real estate of his deceased wife is called **curtesy.** Under the common law, a husband's curtesy interest attached, or became effective, only if a child was born of the marriage. **Dower** is the life estate that a wife has in the real estate of her deceased husband. Curtesy has been abolished in most states, and dower has been abolished in many states. In some states, a husband is given dower right in his wife's real estate, and in others, both husband and wife are given a fee simple interest in each others' real property.

Table 7.1
Legal Life Estates

State	Curtesy	Dower	Homestead
Alabama			•
Alaska			•
Arizona			•
Arkansas		•	•
California			•
Colorado			•
Connecticut			
Delaware			
District of Columbia		•[1]	
Florida			•
Georgia			•
Hawaii			•
Idaho			•
Illinois			•
Indiana			•
Iowa			•
Kansas			•
Kentucky		•[1]	•
Louisiana			•
Maine			•
Maryland			
Massachusetts	•	•	•
Michigan		•	•
Minnesota			•
Mississippi			•
Missouri			•
Montana			•
Nebraska			•
Nevada			•
New Hampshire			•
New Jersey	•	•	
New Mexico			•
New York			•
North Carolina			•
North Dakota			•
Ohio		•[1]	•
Oklahoma			•
Oregon			•
Pennsylvania			
Rhode Island	•	•	
South Carolina		•	•
South Dakota			•
Tennessee			•
Texas			•
Utah			•
Vermont	•	•	•
Virginia	•	•	•
Washington			•
West Virginia		•[1]	•
Wisconsin			•
Wyoming		•[1]	•

[1]Includes husbands' rights.

In most states a dower (or curtesy) interest means that upon the death of the owning spouse, the surviving spouse has a right to a one-third interest (one-half interest in some states) in the real property for the rest of his or her life. The purpose of dower is to give the surviving spouse a means of support when the other spouse dies. The surviving spouse has a right to demand and receive a one-third (or one-half) life estate in the real property, or its equivalent, even if the deceased spouse wills the real estate to others.

Generally, the right of dower (or curtesy) becomes effective only upon the death of a spouse. During the lifetimes of the parties, the dower right is merely the possibility of an interest. It is *inchoate,* or incomplete, until the death of the spouse who owns the property. For this reason, the right of dower cannot be assigned or transferred to another party and the owning spouse cannot cancel the right by selling the property. If, for example, a husband sells some property without his wife's release and consent, the wife can demand and receive her dower interest in that property at the time of her husband's death.

Upon the death of the owning spouse, the dower (or curtesy) right becomes *consummate* (complete). In most states, the surviving spouse can choose to take a dower interest in the deceased spouse's estate, the fee simple interest given by the deceased's will, or, if there is no will, the share of an heir as provided by the law of descent. These alternatives will be explained in Chapter 12.

As previously mentioned, many states have abolished the common-law concepts of dower and curtesy. In many cases, such rights have been repealed in favor of community property laws or the provisions of the state's law of descent or probate code. The statutes replacing dower and curtesy frequently allow the surviving spouse to take a specific portion of the estate in fee (rather than as a life estate). In addition, many such statutes limit these rights to land owned by the deceased in fee simple at the time of death rather than allowing an interest in all land owned by the deceased at any time during the marriage. Under a number of these statutes the inheritance right is inchoate, like dower; under other state laws, the inheritance right does not attach until the owning spouse dies.

In Practice . . .   *The right of dower (or curtesy) can usually be released to a purchaser of property by both spouses signing the deed of conveyance. One spouse can also release his or her interest by executing a separate quitclaim deed to the other spouse. If the dower right is not so released when property is conveyed, it can create a cloud, or imperfection, on the title to the property. It is therefore essential that both spouses sign any conveyance of one spouse's real estate. It is also a good idea for the nonowning spouse to sign any sales contract or other document involved in the transaction as well.*

Even in states where dower and curtesy have been abolished in favor of descent or community property laws, it is important that both spouses sign all instruments of conveyance. A nonowning spouse's signature on a conveyance releases any such statutory interests in the real estate being sold.

Homestead. *A tract of land that is owned and occupied as the family home is a* **homestead.** In those states that have homestead exemption laws, a portion of the area or value of such land is protected, or exempt, from judgments for unsecured debts. A family can have only one homestead at any one time.

The purpose of state homestead laws is to protect the family against eviction by general creditors and to protect the spouses by requiring that both husband and wife join in executing any deed conveying the homestead property. The homestead value that is exempt from creditors' claims is specifically defined by state law.

Homestead laws vary from state to state and are not uniform in their wording or scope. However, most generally include the following requirements: (1) In order to create a homestead, one must first *establish a family.* (In some states, a single person may establish a homestead.) (2) The family must *occupy the premises as a home.* (3) The head of the family, or householder, must *own or lease the property.* In some states the homestead interest attaches by operation of the law, but in others the family must protect its homestead interest by filing a notice as required by local statute.

As mentioned earlier, the homestead exemption protects a homeowner from the court-ordered sale of his or her home to satisfy *unsecured* debts. An unsecured debt is one in which there is no collateral—the person's home has not been given as security for payment of the loan. A charge account or personal loan would be an example of an unsecured debt. State laws usually stipulate that the homestead exemption does not apply to annual real estate taxes levied against the property or to a mortgage for purchase money or the cost of improvements, provided both spouses join in executing the mortgage.

In most cases, the homestead exemption does not actually prevent the sale of a residence to satisfy a homeowner's debts. (There are, however, a few states where the entire homestead is exempt from being sold.) Usually the homestead right merely reserves a certain amount of money for the family in the event of a court sale. For example, if the state homestead exemption is $15,000 and a court sale brings $25,000 for a property, the homeowner would receive the first $15,000 of the proceeds and the remaining $10,000 would be applied to the homeowner's debts. This basic example assumes that there are no unpaid taxes, mortgage liens, or mechanics' liens (all of which are excepted from homestead protection). If such debts were outstanding, they would be satisfied before the family received its share.

The rights to occupy the homestead and enjoy the exemption benefits generally continue for the lives of the husband and wife and their survivor(s) and also for children until they reach the age of majority. Homestead rights may be released by husband and wife joining in executing a deed. Homestead rights in property may be lost by abandonment, such as when the home is sold and the householder plans to move to a new home. Intention of the householder is a key factor.

The homestead exemption should not be confused with the frontier practice of homesteading or with the Federal Housing Administration's "Urban Homestead" program. Likewise, this right should not be confused with the homestead tax exemption, a reduction in property taxes granted to homeowners in many states (see Chapter 10).

Encumbrances

A claim, charge, or liability that attaches to and is binding on real estate is an **encumbrance.** It is a right or interest held by a party who is not the fee owner of the property. An encumbrance may lessen the value or obstruct the use of the property, but it does not necessarily prevent a transfer of title.

Encumbrances may be divided into two general classifications: (1) liens (usually monetary), which affect the title, and (2) encumbrances that affect the physical condition of the property, such as restrictions, easements, licenses, and encroachments.

Liens

A charge against property that provides security for a debt or obligation of the property owner is a **lien.** If the obligation is not repaid, the lienholder, or creditor, has the right to have it paid out of the debtor's property, usually from the proceeds of a court sale. Real estate taxes, mortgages and trust deeds, judgments, and mechanics' liens (for people who have furnished labor or materials in the construction or repair of real estate) all represent possible liens against an owner's real estate. Liens will be discussed in detail in Chapter 10.

Restrictions

Private agreements placed in the public record that affect the use of land are **deed restrictions** *and covenants.* They are usually imposed by an owner of real estate when he or she sells the property, and they are included in the seller's deed to the buyer. Deed restrictions would typically be imposed by a developer or subdivider to maintain specific standards in a subdivision, and they would be listed in the original development plans for the subdivision filed in the public record. Deed restrictions are discussed further in Chapter 19.

Easements

A right acquired by one party to use the land of another party for a special purpose is an **easement.** Although this is the common definition of an easement, a party may also have an easement right in the air above a parcel of real estate or land.

Because *an easement is a right to use land,* it is classified as an interest in real estate, but it is not an estate in land. The holder of an easement has only a right. He or she does not have an estate or ownership interest in the land over which the easement exists. An easement is sometimes referred to as an *incorporeal right* in land (a nonpossessory interest). An easement may be either appurtenant or in gross (see figure 7.3).

Easement appurtenant. An easement that is *annexed to the ownership and used for the benefit of another's parcel of land* is an **easement appurtenant.** For example, if *A* and *B* own adjacent properties in a resort community and only *A's* property borders the lake, *A* may grant *B* a right-of-way across *A's* property to the beach.

For an easement appurtenant to exist, there must be two adjacent tracts of land owned by different parties. The tract over which the easement runs is known as the *servient tenement;* the tract that is to benefit from the easement is known as the *dominant tenement.*

An easement appurtenant is considered part of the dominant tenement, and if the dominant tenement is conveyed to another party, the easement passes with the title. In legal terms it is said that *the easement runs with the land.* However, title to the land over which an easement actually runs is still retained by the servient tenement.

Easement in gross. *A mere personal interest* in or right to use the land of another is an **easement in gross.** Such an easement is not appurtenant to any ownership estate in land. Examples of easements in gross are the easement rights a railroad has in its right-of-way or the right-of-way for a pipeline or high-tension power line. Commercial easements in gross may be assigned or conveyed and may be inherited. However, personal easements in gross usually are not assignable and terminate upon the death of the easement owner. Easements in gross are often confused with the similar personal right of license, which is discussed later in this chapter.

Easement by necessity. An appurtenant easement that arises when an owner sells part of his or her land that has no access to a street or public way except over the seller's remaining land is an **easement by necessity.** An easement by necessity arises because all owners have rights of ingress to and egress from their land—they cannot be landlocked.

Easement by prescription. When the claimant has made use of another's land for a certain period of time as defined by state law, an **easement by prescription** is acquired. This *prescriptive period* is usually from 10 to 20 years, depending upon state statutes. The claimant's use must have been continuous, exclusive, and without the owner's approval. Additionally, the use must be visible, open, and notorious, so that the owner could readily learn of it.

Figure 7.3
Easements

The owner of Lot A has an **easement by necessity** across Lot B to gain access to his property from the paved road. The owner of Lot B has an **easement appurtenant** across Lot A so that she may reach the lake. The utility company has an **easement in gross** across both parcels of land for its electric power lines.

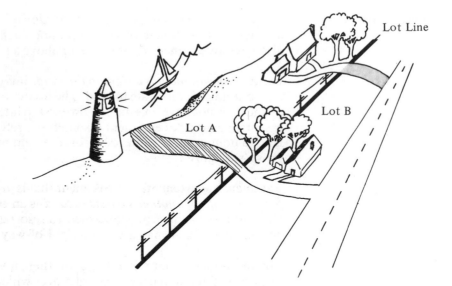

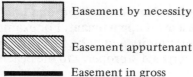

Easement by necessity

Easement appurtenant

Easement in gross

Through the concept of *tacking,* a party not in posession of real property for the entire required statutory period may successfully establish a claim of an easement by prescription. Successive periods of continuous, uninterrupted occupation by different parties may be tacked on, or combined, to reach the prescriptive period. In order to tack on one person's possession to that of another, the parties must have been *successors in interest,* such as an ancestor and his or her heir, landlord and tenant, or seller and buyer.

Party walls. A party wall is an exterior wall of a building that straddles the boundary line between two owners' lots, with half of the wall on each lot. Each lot owner owns the half of the wall on his or her lot and each has an easement right in the other half of the wall for support of his or her building. A written party-wall agreement should be used to create these easement rights. Each owner must pay a half-share of expenses to build and maintain the wall.

Creating an easement. Today, easements are commonly created by written agreement between the parties establishing the easement right. They may also be created in a number of other ways: (1) by express grant from the owner of the property over which the easement will run; (2) by the grantor in a deed of conveyance either *reserving* an easement over the sold land or *granting* the new owner an easement over the grantor's remaining land; (3) by longtime usage, as in an easement by prescription; (4) by necessity; and (5) by *implication;* that is, the situation or the parties' actions may imply that they intend to create an easement.

To create an easement there must be *two separate parties,* one of whom is the owner of the land over which the easement runs. It is impossible for the owner of a parcel of property to have an easement over his or her own land. Thus, where a valid easement exists and the dominant tenement is acquired by the owner of the servient tenement, the easement becomes dormant. The easement will not be considered terminated unless it is either the express or the implied intention of the user to terminate it.

Terminating an easement. Easements may be terminated:

1. when the purpose for which the easement was created no longer exists.
2. when the owner of either the dominant or the servient tenement becomes the owner of the other, providing there is an express intention of the parties to extinguish the easement (a situation called a *merger*).
3. by release of the right of easement to the owner of the servient tenement.
4. by abandonment of the easement (again, the intention of the parties is the determining factor).

Licenses

A personal privilege to enter the land of another for a specific purpose is a **license.** It is *not* an estate in land; it is a personal right of the party to whom it is given. A license differs from an easement in that *it can be terminated or canceled by the licensor* (the person who granted the license). If a right to use another's property is given orally or informally, it will generally be considered to be a license, rather than a personal easement in gross. A license ceases upon the death of either party and is revoked by the sale of the land by the licensor. Examples of license would include permission to park in a neighbor's driveway and the privileges that are granted by the purchase of a ticket for the theater or a sporting event.

Encroachments

When a building (or some portion of it) or a fence or driveway illegally *extends beyond the land of its owner* and covers some land of an adjoining owner or a street or alley, an **encroachment** arises. Encroachments are usually disclosed by either a physical inspection of the property or a spot survey. A spot survey shows the location of all improvements located on a property and whether any improvements extend over the lot lines. If the building on a lot encroaches on neighboring land, the neighbor may be able to either recover damages or secure removal of the portion of the building that encroaches. Encroachments of long standing (for the prescriptive period) may give rise to easements by prescription.

In Practice ...   *Since an undisclosed encroachment could render a title unmarketable, its existence should be noted in a listing agreement, and the sales contract governing the transaction should be made subject to the existence of the particular encroachment. Encroachments are not disclosed by the usual title evidence provided in a real estate sale unless a survey is submitted while the examination is being made.*

Water Rights   One of the interests that may attach to the ownership of real estate is the right to use adjacent bodies of water. Since water is essential to maintain life, the laws affecting its ownership and use are important to everyone. In the United States, the ownership of water and the land adjacent to it is determined by either the doctrines of riparian and littoral rights or the doctrine of prior appropriation.

Riparian Rights   Many states subscribe to the common-law doctrine of **riparian rights.** These rights are granted to owners of land located along the course of a river, stream, or lake. Such an owner has the unrestricted right to use the water, provided he or she does not interrupt or alter the flow of the water or contaminate the water. In addition, an owner of land that borders a nonnavigable waterway owns the land under the water to the exact center of the waterway. Land adjoining navigable rivers is usually owned to the water's edge, with the state holding title to the submerged land (see figure 7.4). Navigable waters are considered public highways in which the public has an easement or right to travel. The laws governing and defining riparian rights differ from state to state.

Figure 7.4
Riparian Rights

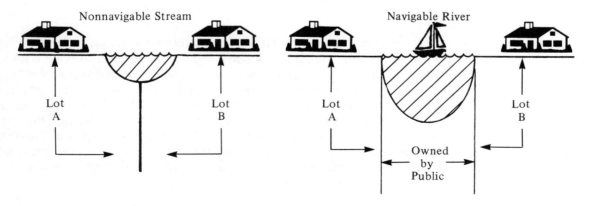

Littoral Rights   Closely related to riparian rights are the **littoral rights** of owners whose land borders on large, navigable lakes and oceans. Owners with littoral rights may enjoy unrestricted use of available waters, but own the land adjacent to the water only up to the mean high-water mark (see figure 7.5). All land below this point is owned by the government.

Riparian and littoral rights are appurtenant (attached) to the land and cannot be retained when the property is sold. This means that the right to use the water belongs to whoever owns the bordering land and cannot be retained by a former owner after the land is sold.

Where land adjoins streams or rivers, an owner is entitled to all land created through *accretion*—increases in the land resulting from the deposit of soil by the natural action of the water. (Such deposits are called *alluvion*.)

Likewise, an owner may lose land through *erosion*, the gradual and imperceptible wearing away of the land caused by flowing water (or other natural forces). This is contrasted to *avulsion*, the sudden removal of soil by an act of nature. A riparian owner generally does not lose title to land lost by avulsion—the boundary lines stay the same no matter how much soil is lost. In contrast, a riparian owner loses title to any land washed away by erosion.

Figure 7.5
Littoral Rights

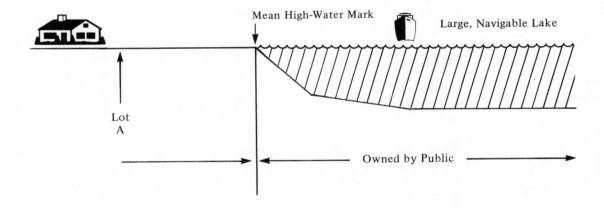

Prior Appropriation

In states where water is scarce, the ownership and use of water are often determined by the doctrine of prior appropriation. Under **prior appropriation,** *the right to use any water, with the exception of limited domestic use, is controlled by the state rather than by the adjacent landowner.* However, ownership of the land bordering bodies of water in prior appropriation states is generally determined in the same way as riparian and littoral ownership.

To secure water rights, a person must show a beneficial use for the water, such as crop irrigation, and file for and obtain a permit from the proper state department. Although statutes governing prior appropriation vary from state to state, the priority of the water right is usually determined by the oldest recorded permit date.

Once granted, water rights may be perfected through the legal processes prescribed by the individual state. When the water right is perfected, it generally becomes attached to the land of the person holding the permit. The permit holder may, if he or she chooses, sell such a water right to another party.

Issuance of a water permit does not grant access to the water source. All access rights-of-way over the land of another (easements) must be obtained from the property owner.

Summary

An *estate* is the degree, quantity, nature, and extent of interest a person holds in land. There are several types of estates, distinguished according to the degree of interest held. *Freehold estates* are estates of indeterminate length. Less than freehold estates are those for which the length can be accurately determined. These are called *leasehold estates,* and they concern tenants.

Freehold estates are further divided into estates of inheritance and life estates. Estates of inheritance include *fee simple* and *defeasible fee* estates. There are two types of life estates: (1) conventional life estates, which are created by acts of the parties; and (2) legal life estates, which are created by law. Legal life estates include *curtesy, dower,* and *homestead.*

Encumbrances against real estate may be in the form of liens, deed restrictions, easements, licenses, and encroachments.

An *easement* is the right acquired by one person to use another's real estate. Easements are classified as interests in real estate, but are not estates in land. *Easements appurtenant* involve two separately owned tracts. The tract benefited is known as the *dominant tenement;* the tract that is subject to the easement is called the *servient tenement.* An *easement in gross* is a personal right, such as that granted to utility companies to maintain poles, wires, and pipelines.

Easements may be created by agreement, express grant, grant or reservation in a deed, implication, necessity, prescription, or party-wall agreement. They can be terminated when the purpose of the easement no longer exists, by merger of both interests with an express intention to extinguish the easement, by release, or by an intention to abandon the easement.

A *license* is permission to enter another's property for a specific purpose. A license is usually created orally, is of a temporary nature, and can be revoked.

An *encroachment* is an unauthorized use of another's real estate.

Ownership of land encompasses not only the land itself but also the right to use the water on or adjacent to it. Many states subscribe to the common-law doctrine of *riparian rights,* which gives the owner of land adjacent to a nonnavigable stream ownership of the stream to its midpoint. *Littoral rights* are held by owners of land bordering large lakes and oceans and include rights to the water and ownership of the land up to the high-water mark. In states where water is scarce, water use is often decided by the doctrine of prior appropriation. Under prior appropriation, water belongs to the state, and it is allocated to users who have obtained permits.

Questions

1. The term *dower* refers to which of the following?
   a. a conventional life estate in real property
   b. ownership of a homestead
   c. a marital right
   d. none of the above

2. The right of a governmental body to take ownership of real estate for public use is called:
   a. escheat.
   b. eminent domain.
   c. condemnation.
   d. police power.

3. Peter Kelly's apple tree has been growing in the backyard for 25 years. It is a big tree, and several of its branches extend across Kelly's lot line into the backyard of a neighbor, Alice Manley. These branches are an example of an:
   a. encumbrance.
   b. encroachment.
   c. avulsion.
   d. a and b

4. A homeowner may be allowed certain protection from judgments of creditors as a result of a state's:
   I. homestead exemption.
   II. curtesy rights.
      a. I only
      b. II only
      c. both I and II
      d. neither I nor II

5. A purchaser of real estate learned that his ownership rights will continue forever and that no other person claims to be the owner or has any ownership control over the property. This person owns a:
   a. fee simple interest.
   b. life estate.
   c. determinable fee estate.
   d. fee simple estate subject to a condition subsequent.

6. Ed Roberts has the legal right to pass over the land owned by his neighbor. This is an:
   I. estate in land.
   II. easement.
      a. I only
      b. II only
      c. both I and II
      d. neither I nor II

7. A husband's life estate in property owned by his deceased wife is:
   I. curtesy.
   II. granted by statute in all states.
      a. I only
      b. II only
      c. both I and II
      d. neither I nor II

8. Janet Auden owned the fee simple title to a vacant lot adjacent to a hospital and was persuaded to make a gift of the lot. She wanted to have some control over its use, so her attorney prepared her deed to convey ownership of the lot to the hospital "as long as it is used for hospital purposes." After completion of the gift, the hospital will own:
   a. a fee simple estate.
   b. a license.
   c. a determinable fee estate.
   d. a leasehold estate.

9. After Peter Desmond had purchased his house and moved in, he discovered that his neighbor regularly used Desmond's driveway to reach a garage located on the neighbor's property. Desmond's attorney explained that ownership of the neighbor's real estate includes an easement appurtenant that gives him the driveway right. Desmond's property is properly called:
   a. the dominant tenement.
   b. a tenement.
   c. a leasehold.
   d. the servient tenement.

10. A father conveys ownership of his residence to his son but reserves for himself a life estate in the residence. The interest the son owns during the father's lifetime is:

   I. pur autre vie.
   II. a remainder.

   a. I only   c. both I and II
   b. II only   d. neither I nor II

11. If the owner of real estate does not take action to evict an encroacher before the prescriptive period has passed, then the encroacher may acquire:

   I. an easement by necessity.
   II. a license.

   a. I only   c. both I and II
   b. II only   d. neither I nor II

12. Which one of the following best describes a life estate?

   a. an estate conveyed to *A* for the life of *Z*, and upon *Z's* death to *B*
   b. an estate held by *A* and *B* in joint tenancy with right of survivorship
   c. an estate without condition
   d. a fee simple estate

13. Encumbrances on real estate:

   I. may include liens, easements, and deed restrictions.
   II. make it impossible to sell the encumbered property.

   a. I only   c. both I and II
   b. II only   d. neither I nor II

14. An estate in land that will automatically extinguish upon the occurrence of a specified event is called a:

   a. determinable fee.
   b. fee simple subject to a condition subsequent.
   c. fee simple.
   d. a and b

15. A *license* is an example of a(n):

   a. easement.   c. encumbrance.
   b. encroachment.   d. restriction.

16. A tenant in an apartment building holds a:

   I. less-than-freehold estate.
   II. license.

   a. I only   c. both I and II
   b. II only   d. neither I nor II

17. Many states determine water use by allocating water to users who hold recorded beneficial-use permits. This type of water-use privilege is called:

   a. the doctrine of riparian rights.
   b. the doctrine of highest and best use.
   c. the doctrine of prior appropriation.
   d. none of the above

18. When a homeowner who is entitled by state law to a homestead exemption is sued by his or her creditors, then the creditors:

   a. can have the court sell the home and apply the full proceeds of sale to the debts.
   b. have no right to have the debtor's home sold.
   c. can force the debtor to sell the home to pay them.
   d. can have a court sale and apply the sale proceeds, in excess of the statutory exemption, to the debts.

19. Under the allodial system, individual landowners have maximum rights, subject to certain government powers such as:

   I. police power.
   II. eminent domain.

   a. I only   c. both I and II
   b. II only   d. neither I nor II

20. During the lifetime of the parties, the right of dower (in those states that recognize it) is:

   a. incomplete.   c. inchoate.
   b. unassignable.   d. all of the above

8

How Ownership Is Held

Key Terms

Beneficiary
Common elements
Community property
Condominium
Cooperative
Co-ownership
Corporation
General partnership
Joint tenancy
Limited partnership
Partition

Partnership
Right of survivorship
Separate property
Severalty
Syndicate
Tenancy by the entirety
Tenancy in common
Trust
Trustee
Trustor
Undivided interest

Overview

There are many different forms of ownership that purchasers must consider before taking title to a parcel of real estate. The choice of ownership form will affect such matters as the owner's legal right to sell the real estate without the consent of others, the owner's right to choose who will own the property after his or her death, and the rights of creditors in the future. The choice will also in many cases have tax implications, both in terms of a possible gift tax resulting from a present transfer and in terms of future income and estate taxes. This chapter will discuss the many basic forms of real estate ownership available to individuals, as well as to business entities, and will also include a discussion of the increasingly popular cooperative and condominium forms of ownership.

Forms of Ownership	A fee simple estate in land may be held individually by one owner or by two or more co-owners under one of several forms of co-ownership: (1) in **severalty,** which means that title is held by one owner, (2) in **co-ownership,** where title is held by two or more persons, or (3) in **trust,** where title is held by a third person for the benefit of another or others, called the beneficiary or beneficiaries.

The form by which property is owned is important to the real estate broker's work for two reasons: (1) *the form of ownership existing when a property is sold determines who must sign the various documents involved* (listing contract, acceptance of offer to purchase, sales contract, and deed); and (2) *the purchaser must determine in what form he or she wishes to take title.* For example, if there is one purchaser taking title in his or her name alone, it is tenancy in severalty; if there are two or more purchasers, they may take title as tenants in common or as joint tenants. Married purchasers' choices are governed by state laws. Some states provide for married couples to own real estate as tenants by the entireties or under community property laws. Other states allow the couple to choose the form of ownership they prefer.

The forms of ownership available are controlled by the laws of the state in which the land is located. When questions about these forms are raised by the parties to a transaction, the real estate broker should recommend that the parties seek legal advice. Refer to table 8.1 to determine the forms of ownership applicable to your state. Concentrate on these as you study this chapter.

Ownership in Severalty	When title to real estate is *vested in* (presently owned by) one person or one organization, that person or organization is said to own the property *in severalty.* This person is also referred to as the *sole owner.* The various states have special laws that affect title held in severalty by either a husband or a wife. In some states, when either the husband or wife owns property in severalty (alone), it is still necessary for the spouse to join in signing documents: (1) to release dower or curtesy in states that have such rights, (2) to release homestead rights in states that provide a homestead exemption for homeowners, or (3) when the wife is a minor. In other states, only the owner's signature is needed.

Co-Ownership	When title to one parcel of real estate is vested in (owned by) two or more persons or organizations, those parties are said to be *co-owners,* or *concurrent owners,* of the property. Concurrent ownership means that two or more owners are vested in the property at the same time, each sharing in the rights of ownership, possession, and so forth. There are several forms of co-ownership, each having unique legal characteristics. The forms most commonly recognized by the various states are: (1) tenancy in common, (2) joint tenancy, (3) tenancy by the entirety, (4) community property, and (5) partnership property. Each of these forms of co-ownership will be discussed separately.

Table 8.1
Chart of Ownership

State	Sole — Individual	Tenancy in Common	Joint Tenancy	Tenancy by the Entirety	Community Property	Trust	Condominium
Alabama	•	•	•			•	•
Alaska	•	•		•		•	•
Arizona	•	•	•		•	•	•
Arkansas	•	•	•	•		•	•
California	•	•	•		•	•	•
Colorado	•	•	•			•	•
Connecticut	•	•	•			•	•
Delaware	•	•	•	•		•	•
District of Columbia	•	•	•	•		•	•
Florida	•	•	•	•		•	•
Georgia	•	•	•			•	•
Hawaii	•	•	•	•		•	•
Idaho	•	•	•	•	•	•	•
Illinois	•	•	•			•	•
Indiana	•	•	•	•		•	•
Iowa	•	•	•			•	•
Kansas	•	•	•			•	•
Kentucky	•	•	•	•		•	•
Louisiana¹					•		•
Maine	•	•	•			•	•
Maryland	•	•	•	•		•	•
Massachusetts	•	•	•	•		•	•
Michigan	•	•	•	•		•	•
Minnesota	•	•	•			•	•
Mississippi	•	•	•			•	•
Missouri	•	•	•	•		•	•
Montana	•	•	•			•	•
Nebraska	•	•	•			•	•
Nevada	•	•	•		•	•	•
New Hampshire	•	•	•			•	•
New Jersey	•	•	•	•		•	•
New Mexico	•	•	•		•	•	•
New York	•	•	•	•		•	•
North Carolina	•	•	•	•		•	•
North Dakota	•	•	•			•	•
Ohio²	•	•		•		•	•
Oklahoma	•	•		•		•	•
Oregon	•	•		•		•	•
Pennsylvania	•	•	•	•		•	•
Rhode Island	•	•	•	•		•	•
South Carolina	•	•	•			•	•
South Dakota	•	•	•			•	•
Tennessee	•	•	•	•		•	•
Texas	•	•	•		•	•	•
Utah	•	•	•			•	•
Vermont	•	•	•	•		•	•
Virginia	•	•	•	•		•	•
Washington	•	•	•		•	•	•
West Virginia	•	•	•	•		•	•
Wisconsin	•	•	•			•	•
Wyoming	•	•	•	•		•	•

¹In Louisiana, real estate can be owned by one person and by two or more persons, but these ownership interests are created by Louisiana statute. There are no estates comparable to those of joint tenancy, tenancy by the entirety, or community property, nor is there any statutory estate giving surviving co-owners the right of survivorship. Two or more persons may be co-owners under indivision, or joint, ownership.

²Ohio does not recognize joint tenancy, but permits a special form of survivorship by deed through an instrument commonly called a "joint and survivorship deed."

Tenancy in Common

When a parcel of real estate is owned by two or more people as **tenants in common,** each of the owners holds an undivided interest in severalty; that is, *each owner's fractional interest is held just as though he or she were a sole owner.* There are two important characteristics of a tenancy in common.

First, the ownership interest of a tenant in common is an **undivided interest;** there is a *unity of possession* between the co-owners. This means that although a tenant in common may hold, say, a one-half or one-third interest in a property, it is impossible to distinguish physically which specific half or third of the property he or she owns. The deed creating a tenancy in common may or may not state the fractional interest held by each co-owner: if no fractions are stated and two people hold title to the property as co-owners, each has an undivided one-half interest. Likewise, if five people held title, each would own an undivided one-fifth interest.

The second important characteristic of a tenancy in common is that *each owner holds his or her undivided interest in severalty* and can sell, convey, mortgage, or transfer that interest *without consent* of the other co-owners. Upon the death of a co-owner, his or her undivided interest passes to his heirs or devisees according to his will. The interest of a deceased tenant in common does not pass to another tenant in common unless the surviving co-owner is an heir, devisee, or purchaser (see figure 8.1). In many states, the spouse of a married tenant in common must sign a deed to a purchaser in order to release his or her dower or homestead rights.

When two or more people acquire title to a parcel of real estate and the deed of conveyance does not stipulate the character of the tenancy created, then by operation of law the grantees usually acquire title as tenants in common. However, if the conveyance is made to a husband and wife with no further explanation, this assumption may not apply. In some states, a conveyance made to a husband and wife creates tenancy by the entirety, in others, community property, and in at least one state, a joint tenancy. It is therefore important to know the legal interpretation of such a situation under your state law.

Figure 8.1
Tenancy in Common

A and B are tenants in common.

A	B
½	½

B dies and wills his interest to C and D equally.

A	C	D
½	¼	¼

Joint Tenancy

Most states recognize some form of **joint tenancy,** which is an estate, or unit of interest, in land owned by two or more people. The basis of joint tenancy is *unity of ownership.* Only one title exists, and it is vested in a unit made up of two or more people. The death of one of the joint tenants does not destroy the unit; it only reduces by one the number of people who make up the owning unit. The remaining joint tenants receive the interest of the deceased tenant by **right of survivorship** (see figure 8.2).

**Figure 8.2
Joint Tenancy with
Right of Survivorship**

1. **A, B,** and **C** are joint tenants.

> **A, B, C**

3. **B** dies, then **A** holds title in severalty.

> **A**

2. **C** dies, then **A** and **B** remain as joint tenants.

> **A + B**

4. **A** dies and wills his interest to **D** and **E.**

D	E
½	½

5. **D** and **E** are tenants in common.

This right of survivorship is generally one of the distinguishing characteristics of joint tenancy. As each successive joint tenant dies, the surviving joint tenants acquire the interest of the deceased joint tenant. The last survivor takes title in severalty; upon this person's death, the property goes to his or her heirs.

In Practice . . .   *Married couples often find it advantageous to take title to property as joint tenants. The reason is that if one spouse dies, the surviving spouse automatically becomes sole owner of the property. The surviving spouse can therefore enjoy the benefits of ownership without waiting for the conclusion of probate proceedings. This benefit of rights of survivorship also applies to property held in a tenancy by the entirety, discussed later in this chapter.*

Creating joint tenancies. A joint tenancy can be created only by grant or purchase (through a deed of conveyance), or by devise (giving the property by will). It cannot be implied or created by operation of law. The conveyance must specifically state the intention to create a joint tenancy, and the grantees or devisees must be explicitly identified as joint tenants. For example, typical wording in a conveyance creating a joint tenancy would be "to *A* and *B* as joint tenants and not as tenants in common." Some states, however, have abolished the right of survivorship as a distinguishing characteristic of joint tenancy. In these states, the conveyance must also explicitly indicate the intention to create the right of survivorship in order for that right to exist. In such cases, appropriate wording might be "to *A* and *B* and to the survivor of them, his or her heirs and assigns, as joint tenants."

Four unities are required to create a joint tenancy:

1. unity of *time*—all joint tenants acquire their interest at the same time.
2. unity of *title*—all joint tenants acquire their interest by the same instrument of conveyance.
3. unity of *interest*—all joint tenants hold equal ownership interests.
4. unity of *possession*—all joint tenants hold an undivided right to possession.

These four unities are present when title is acquired by *one deed, executed and delivered at one time, and conveying equal interests to all the grantees who hold undivided possession of the property as joint tenants.*

In many states, if real estate is owned in severalty by a person who wishes to create a joint tenancy between him- or herself and others, the owner will have to convey the property to an intermediary (usually called a *nominee,* or *straw man*), and the nominee must convey it back, naming all the parties as joint tenants in the conveyance.

Some states have eliminated this "legal fiction" by allowing an owner in severalty to execute a deed to him- or herself and others "as joint tenants and not as tenants in common" and thereby create a valid joint tenancy without the actual presence of the four unities. In some states that have tried to accomplish this same result, the courts have held that such a conveyance creates a wholly new estate, usually referred to as an *estate of survivorship*.

Most state laws hold that there is no dower in joint tenancy. Thus, business associates can hold title to a parcel of real estate as joint tenants, and their spouses, if any, are not required to join in a conveyance in order to waive dower rights.

Terminating joint tenancies. A joint tenancy is destroyed when any one of the essential unities of joint tenancy is terminated. Thus, while a joint tenant is free to convey his or her interest in the jointly held property, doing so will destroy the unity of interest and, in turn, the joint tenancy. For example, if *A, B,* and *C* hold title as joint tenants and *A* conveys her interest to *D,* then *D* will own an undivided one-third interest in severalty as a tenant in common with *B* and *C,* who will continue to own their undivided two-thirds interest as joint tenants (see figure 8.3).

**Figure 8.3
Combination of
Tenancies**

A, B, and C are joint tenants.

A, B, C

A sells her interest to **D**.

D 1/3	**B + C** 2/3

D becomes a tenant in common with **B** and **C** as joint tenants.

Joint tenancies may also be terminated by operation of law, such as in bankruptcy or foreclosure sale proceedings. In addition, in states where a mortgage on real property is held to be a conveyance of land, a joint tenant who mortgages his or her property without the other tenants joining in the mortgage will also destroy the joint tenancy.

**Termination of
Co-Ownership by
Partition Suit**

Tenants in common or joint tenants who wish to terminate their co-ownership of real estate may file in court a suit to **partition** the land. The right of partition is a legal way to dissolve a co-ownership when the parties do not voluntarily agree to its termination. If the court determines that the land cannot actually be divided into parts, it will order the real estate sold and divide the proceeds of the sale among the co-owners according to their fractional interests.

Tenancy by the Entirety

Some states allow **tenancy by the entirety,** which is a special form of tenancy in which the owners are husband and wife. Both spouses have an equal, undivided interest in the whole property, with each spouse, in essence, owning the entire estate. Upon the death of one spouse, the tenancy operates like a joint tenancy—full title automatically passes to the surviving spouse.

The distinguishing characteristics of tenancy by the entirety are: (1) the owners must be husband and wife; (2) the owners have rights of survivorship; (3) during the owners' lives, title can be conveyed *only by a deed signed by both parties* (one party cannot convey a one-half interest); and (4) there is generally no right to partition. Under early common law, a husband and wife were held to be one person in the eyes of the law—the wife's legal personality was merged with that of her husband's. As a result, real estate owned by a husband and wife as tenants by the entireties is considered to be held by one indivisible legal unit.

Like a joint tenancy, *a tenancy by the entirety cannot be created by operation of law, but must be created by grant, purchase, or devise.* Most states that recognize it now require that the intention to create a tenancy by the entirety be specifically stated. Unless the specific intention to create a tenancy by the entirety is stated in the original document, a tenancy in common usually results.

Community Property Rights

The concept of community property originated in Spanish law rather than English common law and was adopted by eight of the western and southwestern states (Arizona, California, Idaho, Louisiana, Nevada, New Mexico, Texas, and Washington). There are many variations among the community property laws of these states.

Community property laws are based on the concept that a husband and wife, rather than merging into one entity, are equal partners. Thus, any property acquired during a marriage is considered to be obtained by mutual effort. Community property states recognize two kinds of property. **Separate property** is that which is owned solely by either spouse before the marriage or is acquired by gift or inheritance after the marriage. Such separate, or exempted, property also includes any property purchased with separate funds after the marriage. Any income earned from a person's separate property generally remains part of his or her separate property. Property classified as sole and separate can be mortgaged or conveyed by the owning spouse without the signature of the nonowning spouse.

Community property consists of all other property, real and personal, acquired by either spouse during the marriage. Any conveyance or encumbrance of community property requires the signatures of both spouses. Upon the death of one spouse, the survivor automatically owns one-half of the community property. The other half is distributed according to the deceased's will. If the deceased died without a will, the other half is inherited by the surviving spouse or by the deceased's other heirs, depending upon state law.

Examples of Co-Ownership

To clarify the concepts of co-ownership further, note the following four examples of co-ownership arrangements:

1. A deed conveys title to *A* and *B.* The intention of the parties is not stated, so generally ownership as tenants in common is created. If *A* dies, her one-half interest will pass to her heirs or according to her will.

2. A deed conveying title one-third to C and two-thirds to D creates a tenancy in common, with each owner having the fractional interest specified.

3. A deed to H and W as husband and wife may create a tenancy by the entirety, community property, or other interests between the husband and wife as provided by state law.

4. A conveyance of real estate to two people (not husband and wife) by such wording as "to Y and Z, as joint tenants and not as tenants in common" may create a joint tenancy ownership. Upon the death of Y, the title to the property usually passes to Z by right of survivorship. However, in those states that do not recognize the right of survivorship, additional provisions are required (such as "and to the survivor and his or her heirs and assigns").

Note also that *a combination of interests can exist in one parcel of real estate.* For example, when M and spouse hold title to an undivided one-half as joint tenants, and S and spouse hold title to the other undivided one-half as joint tenants, the relationship among the owners of the two half interests is that of tenants in common.

Trusts

In most states, title to real estate can be held in a trust. In order for a trust to be created, the title to the real estate involved must be conveyed by the **trustor** (also known as a *settlor*), the person originating the trust, to a **trustee,** who will own the property for one or more people or legal entities, called **beneficiaries.** The trustee is a *fiduciary,* one who acts in confidence or trust, and has a special legal relationship with the beneficiary or beneficiaries. The trustee can be either an individual or a corporation, such as a trust company. The trustee has only as much power and authority as is given by the instrument that creates the trust. Such an instrument may be a trust agreement, will, trust deed, or deed in trust (see figure 8.4). Real estate ownership can generally be held under either: (1) living and testamentary trusts or (2) land trusts. In addition, real estate may be held by a number of people in a *real estate investment trust,* which will be discussed in Chapter 22.

Figure 8.4
Trust Ownership

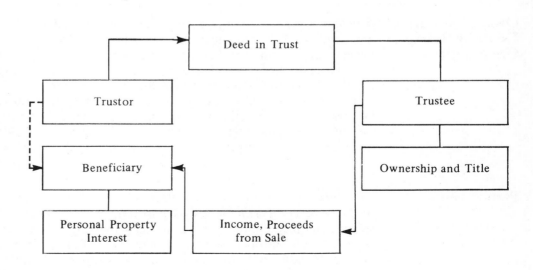

Living and Testamentary Trusts

Property owners may provide for their own financial care and/or that of their families by establishing a trust. Such trusts may be created by agreement during a property owner's lifetime (living) or established by will after his or her death (testamentary).

The individual creating a trust makes an agreement with a trustee (usually a corporate trustee) by which the individual conveys his or her assets (real and/or personal), or a certain portion of them, to the trustee with the understanding that the trustee will assume certain duties. These duties include the care and investment of the trust assets to produce an income. After payment of operating expenses and trustee's fees, this income is paid to or used for the benefit of the beneficiaries. These trusts may continue for the lifetimes of the beneficiaries, or the assets can be distributed when the property owner's children reach certain predetermined ages.

Land Trusts

A few states permit the establishment of land trusts in which real estate is the only asset. As in all trusts, the legal title to the property is conveyed to a trustee, and the beneficial interest is in the beneficiary, who, in the case of land trusts, is usually the trustor.

One of the distinguishing characteristics of a land trust is that the *public records do not indicate the beneficiary's identity.* A land trust agreement is executed by the trustor and the trustee. Under this agreement, the trustee has a *real property* interest, yet deals with the property only upon the beneficiary's written direction. While the beneficial interest in the trust real estate is considered to be *personal property,* the beneficiary retains management and control of the property and has the right of possession as well as the right to any income or proceeds from its sale.

Usually only individuals create land trusts, but corporations as well as individuals can be beneficiaries. A land trust generally continues for a definite term, such as 20 years. If the beneficiaries do not extend the trust term when it expires, the trustee is usually obligated to sell the real estate and distribute the net proceeds to the beneficiaries.

Ownership of Real Estate by Business Organizations

A business entity is an organization that exists independently of the people who are members of the organization—for example, a corporation. Ownership by a business organization makes it possible for many people to hold an interest in the same parcel of real estate. There are various ways in which investors may be organized to finance a real estate project. Some provide for the real estate to be owned by the entity itself; others provide for direct ownership of the real estate by the investors. Business organizations may be categorized as: (1) partnerships, (2) corporations, or (3) syndicates. The purchase or sale of real estate by any business organization involves complex legal questions, and legal counsel is usually required.

Partnerships

An association of two or more people to carry on a business as co-owners and share in the business's profits and losses is a **partnership.** There are two kinds of partnerships, general and limited. In a **general partnership,** all partners participate to some extent in the operation and management of the business and may be held personally liable for business losses and obligations. A **limited partnership** includes general partners as well as limited, or silent, partners. The business is run by the general partner or partners. The limited partners do not participate, and each can be held liable for the business's losses *only* to the extent of his or her investment. The limited partnership is a popular method of organizing investors in a real estate project.

A partnership is not usually a legal entity, and technically, under common law, a partnership cannot own real estate. Title must be vested in the partners as individuals in a tenancy in common or joint tenancy, not in the partnership. Most states, however, have adopted the *Uniform Partnership Act,* under which realty may be held in the partnership name, and the *Uniform Limited Partnership Act,* which establishes the legality of the limited partnership form and also provides that realty may be held in the partnership name.

General partnerships are dissolved and must be reorganized if one partner dies, withdraws, or goes bankrupt. In a limited partnership, the agreement creating the partnership may provide for the continuation of the organization upon the death or withdrawal of one of the partners.

Corporations

A **corporation** is an artificial person, or legal entity, created under the authority of the laws of the state from which it receives its charter. Because the corporation is a legal entity, real estate ownership by a corporation is an *ownership in severalty.* A corporation is managed and operated by its *board of directors.* A corporation's charter sets forth the powers of the corporation, including its right to buy and sell real estate after passage of a resolution to that effect by its board of directors. Some charters permit a corporation to purchase real estate for any purpose; others limit such purchases to land that is needed to fulfill the entity's corporate purpose.

As a legal entity, a corporation exists in perpetuity until it is formally dissolved. The death of one of the officers or directors does not affect title to property that is owned by the corporation.

Individuals participate, or invest, in a corporation by purchasing stock. Since stock is *personal property,* stockholders do not have a direct ownership interest in real estate owned by a corporation. Each stockholder's liability for the corporation's losses is usually limited to the amount of his or her investment.

One of the main disadvantages of corporate ownership of income property is that the profits are subject to double taxation. As a legal entity, a corporation must file an income-tax return and pay tax on its profits. In addition, the portions of the remaining profits distributed to stockholders as dividends are taxed again as part of the stockholders' individual incomes.

Syndicates

Generally speaking, a **syndicate** is a *joining together of two or more people or firms in order to make and operate a real estate investment.* A syndicate is not in itself a legal entity; however, it may be organized into a number of ownership forms, including co-ownership (tenancy in common, joint tenancy), partnership, trust, or corporation. A *joint venture* is a form of partnership in which two or more people or firms carry out a *single business project.* Joint ventures are characterized by a time limitation resulting from the fact that the joint venturers do not intend to establish a permanent relationship. More will be said about these organizations in Chapter 22.

Cooperative and Condominium Ownership

During the first half of this century, the nation's population grew rapidly and concentrated in the large urban areas. This population concentration led to multiple-unit housing—high-rise apartment buildings in the center city and low-rise apartment complexes in adjoining suburbs. Initially these buildings were occupied by "tenants" under the traditional rental system. But the urge to "own a part of the land," together with certain tax advantages that accrue to such ownership, gave rise at first to *cooperative* ownership and, more recently, to the *condominium* form of ownership of multiple-unit buildings.

Cooperative Ownership

Under the usual **cooperative** arrangement, title to land and building is held by a *corporation* (or land trust). The building management sets a price for each apartment in the building. Each purchaser of an apartment in the building receives stock in the corporation when he or she pays the agreed-upon price for the apartment. The purchaser then becomes a stockholder of the corporation and, *by virtue of that stock ownership, receives a proprietary lease* to his or her apartment for the life of the corporation.

The cooperative building's real estate taxes are assessed against the corporation as owner. The mortgage is signed by the corporation, creating one lien on the entire parcel of real estate. Taxes, mortgage interest and principal, and operating and maintenance expenses on the property are shared by the tenant-shareholders in the form of monthly assessments similar to rent.

Thus, while the cooperative tenant-owners do not actually own an interest in real estate (they own stock, which is *personal property*), for all practical purposes they control the property through their stock ownership and their voice in the management of the corporation. For example, the bylaws of the corporation generally provide that each prospective purchaser of an apartment lease must be approved by an administrative board.

One disadvantage of cooperative ownership became particularly evident during the Depression years and must still be considered. This is the possibility that if enough owner-occupants became financially unable to make prompt payment of their monthly assessments, the corporation might be forced to allow mortgage and tax payments to go unpaid. Through such defaults, the entire property could be ordered sold by court order in a foreclosure suit. Such a sale would usually destroy the interests of all occupant-shareholders, even those who have paid their assessments. Another disadvantage is that some cooperatives provide that a tenant-owner can sell his or her interest back to the cooperative only at the original purchase price, so that the cooperative gains any profits made on the resale. These limitations have diminished the appeal of this form of ownership and resulted in greater preference for the condominium form of ownership.

Condominium Ownership

The **condominium** form of occupant ownership of apartment buildings has gained increasing popularity in recent years. Condominium laws, often called horizontal property acts, have been enacted in every state. Under these laws, the occupant-owner of each apartment holds a *fee simple title* to his or her apartment and also a specified share of the indivisible parts of the building and land, known as the **common elements** (see figure 8.5). The individual unit owners in a condominium own these common elements together as *tenants in common.* State law usually limits this relationship among unit owners in that there is *no right to partition.*

**Figure 8.5
Condominium
Ownership**

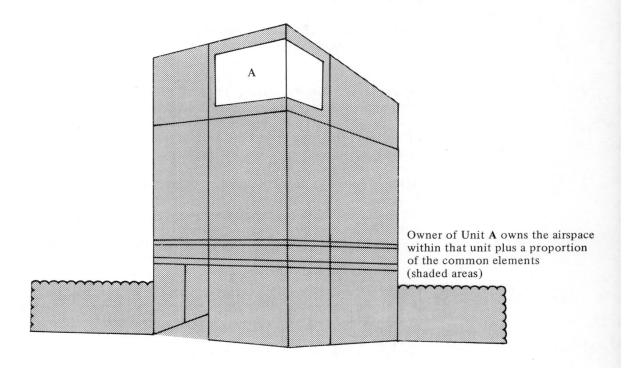

Owner of Unit **A** owns the airspace within that unit plus a proportion of the common elements (shaded areas)

The condominium form of ownership is usually used for apartment buildings. These may range from freestanding high-rise buildings to townhouse arrangements. The common elements include such items as the land, walls, hallways, elevators, stairways, and roof. In some instances (particularly with townhouse developments) lawns and recreational facilities such as swimming pools, clubhouses, tennis courts, and golf courses, may also be considered common elements. In addition, the condominium form of ownership is used for such other types of properties as commercial property, office buildings, or multi-use buildings that contain offices and shops as well as residential units.

Creation of a condominium. State laws usually specify that a condominium is created and established when the owners or developers of the property execute and record a *declaration* of its creation in the county where the property is located. The various state laws require many items to be contained in or attached to the declaration. Generally these items include: (1) a legal description of the land, (2) a plat map illustrating and identifying each unit, (3) a list of the value of the land and of each unit, (4) a list of the percentage of undivided interest in all common areas and facilities assigned to each unit, (5) a copy of the condominium's by-laws, and (6) provisions for the establishment of a condominium owners' association.

Ownership. Once the property is established as a condominium, each unit becomes a separate parcel of real estate that may be dealt with like any other parcel of real property. A condominium unit is *owned in fee simple and may be held by one or more people in any type of ownership or tenancy that is recognized by state law.*

Real estate taxes are assessed and collected on each unit as an individual property. Default in the payment of taxes or a mortgage loan by one unit owner may result in a foreclosure sale of that owner's unit, but does not affect the ownership of the other unit owners.

Operation and administration. The condominium property is generally administered by an association of unit owners according to the bylaws set forth in the declaration. The association may be governed by a board of directors or other official entity, it may manage the property on its own, or it may engage a professional property manager to perform this function.

Acting through its board of directors or other officers, the association must enforce any rules it adopts regarding the operation and use of the property. The association is responsible for the maintenance, repair, cleaning, and sanitation of the common elements and structural portions of the property. It must also maintain fire and extended-coverage insurance as well as liability insurance for these portions of the property.

Expenses incurred in fulfilling these responsibilities are paid for by the unit owners in the form of monthly *assessments,* collected by the owners' association. Such fees are assessed each unit owner. They are due monthly, quarterly, semi-annually, or annually, depending on the provisions of the bylaws. If such assessments are not paid, the association usually has the option to seek a court-ordered judgment to have the property sold to cover the outstanding amount.

Termination. State laws usually stipulate that a building can be removed from condominium ownership under certain circumstances. In such cases, most or all of the unit owners must be party to a revocation agreement filed in the public record in the county where the property is located. All unit owners would then become tenants in common, each owning an undivided interest in the entire property that is equal to the percentage of ownership in the common elements he or she previously held.

Timeshared ownership. *Timesharing* is a variation of condominium ownership that permits multiple purchasers to buy undivided interests in real estate—usually a unit of a resort hotel or development—with a right to use the facility for a fixed or variable time period. Some timesharing programs allow for a rotation system in which the tenant in common can occupy his or her unit at different times of the year in different years. Other programs sell only specific months or weeks of the year. For example, 12 individuals could own equal, undivided interests in one condominium unit, with each owner entitled to use the premises for a specified month of each year.

Timesharing enables a person to own a share in a vacation home in a desirable location for a fraction of the cost of full ownership and year-round maintenance. Maintenance and other common expenses are prorated among the unit owners.

The laws regarding the origination and sale of timeshared units are generally complex and vary from state to state. You should be familiar with the provisions of the relevant statutes before dealing with such properties.

Summary

Sole ownership, or *ownership in severalty,* indicates that title is held by one person or entity. There are several ways in which title to real estate can be held concurrently by more than one person, called *co-ownership.*

Under *tenancy in common,* each party holds an undivided interest in severalty. An individual owner may sell his or her interest. Upon the death of an owner, his or her interest passes to the heirs or according to the will. There are no special requirements to create this interest. When two or more parties hold title to real estate, they will hold title as tenants in common unless there is an expressed intention otherwise. *Joint tenancy* indicates two or more owners with the right of survivorship. The intention of the parties to establish a joint tenancy with right of survivorship must be clearly stated. In some states the four unities of *time, title, interest,* and *possession* must be present; other states by statute eliminate this legal requirement.

Tenancy by the entirety, in those states where it is recognized, is actually a joint tenancy between husband and wife. It gives the husband and wife the right of survivorship in all lands acquired by them *jointly* during marriage. During their lives, both must sign the deed for any title to pass to a purchaser. *Community property* rights exist only in certain states and pertain only to land owned by husband and wife. Usually the property acquired by joint efforts during the marriage is community property and one-half is owned by each spouse. Properties acquired by a spouse before the marriage and through bequests, inheritance, or gifts after the marriage are termed *separate property.* Community property is a statutory right, and as a result, each state that has established the right of community property has also defined the rights it encompasses.

Real estate ownership may also be held in *trust.* In creating a trust, title to the property involved is conveyed to a *trustee* under a living or testamentary trust or a land trust.

Various types of business organizations may own real estate. A *corporation* is a legal entity and holds title to real estate in severalty. While a *partnership* is technically not a legal entity, the *Uniform Partnership Act* and the *Uniform Limited Partnership Act,* adopted by most states, enable a partnership to own property in the partnership's name. A *syndicate* is an association of two or more people or firms to make an investment in real estate. Many syndicates are *joint ventures* and are organized for only a single project. A syndicate may be organized as a co-ownership, trust, corporation, or partnership.

Cooperative ownership of apartment buildings indicates title in one entity (corporation or trust) that must pay taxes, mortgage interest and principal, and all operating expenses. Reimbursement comes from shareholders or beneficiaries through monthly assessments. Shareholders have proprietary, long-term leases entitling them to occupy their apartments. Under *condominium ownership,* each occupant-owner holds fee simple title to his or her apartment unit plus a share of the common elements. Each owner receives an individual tax bill and may mortage his or her unit as desired. Expenses for operating the building are collected by an owners' association through monthly assessments. A variation of condominium ownership called *timesharing* enables multiple purchasers to own a share in real estate, with the right to use it for a part of each year.

Questions

1. The *unities* necessary to create a joint tenancy include which of the following?
   a. interest
   b. time
   c. possession
   d. all of the above

2. A parcel of real estate was purchased by Howard Evers and Tinker Chance. The seller's deed received at the closing conveyed the property "to Howard Evers and Tinker Chance," without further explanation. Thus:
   a. Evers and Chance are joint tenants.
   b. Evers and Chance are tenants in common.
   c. Evers and Chance each own an undivided one-half interest in the property.
   d. b and c

3. Martin, Barton, and Fargo are joint tenants owning a tract of land. Fargo conveys her interest to Vonder. This means that:
   I. Martin and Barton are still joint tenants.
   II. Vonder is a tenant in common with Martin and Barton.
     a. I only
     b. II only
     c. both I and II
     d. neither I nor II

4. In most states, a conveyance made "to Cranshaw and Steinberg" without further wording creates a:
   a. joint tenancy.
   b. tenancy in common.
   c. trust.
   d. partnership.

5. A purchaser under the cooperative form of ownership receives:
   I. a deed to his or her unit.
   II. a proprietary lease and the right to use the common elements.
     a. I only
     b. II only
     c. both I and II
     d. neither I nor II

6. Ownership of real property by one person without the ownership participation of others is called:
   a. trust.
   b. severalty.
   c. solety.
   d. condominium.

7. The *right of survivorship* is closely associated with a:
   a. corporation.
   b. cooperative.
   c. trust.
   d. joint tenancy.

8. Peterson and Kelley have purchased a block of apartment buildings in a large city and have decided, for business reasons, to take ownership to the real estate under a land trust, as permitted in their state. Under this ownership arrangement:
   I. the beneficiaries' identities will not appear in the public records.
   II. the beneficiaries will be unable to control the property or personally participate in the buildings' management.
     a. I only
     b. II only
     c. both I and II
     d. neither I nor II

9. In a trust, the person in whom title is vested is called the:
   a. trustee.
   b. trustor.
   c. beneficiary.
   d. straw man.

10. Which of the following forms of ownership may be created by operation of law?
    I. joint tenancy
    II. tenancy by the entirety
      a. I only
      b. II only
      c. both I and II
      d. neither I nor II

11. If property is held by two or more owners as tenants in common, upon the death of one owner the ownership of his or her interest will pass:
    a. to the remaining owner or owners.
    b. to the heirs or whomever is designated under the deceased owner's will.
    c. to the surviving owner and/or his or her heirs.
    d. to the deceased owner's surviving spouse.

12. Riley has organized a group of investors to finance the development of a shopping center. This group of investors:
    I. is called a syndicate.
    II. may be organized as a limited partnership.
       a. I only   c. both I and II
       b. II only   d. neither I nor II

13. Real estate owned by a corporation:
    I. may be sold upon a stockholder's request.
    II. is held in severalty.
       a. I only   c. both I and II
       b. II only   d. neither I nor II

14. Alma Johnson bought an apartment in a large building for her personal use and received a deed conveying to her a fee simple estate. Each year Johnson receives a tax bill on her apartment. Her form of apartment ownership is called a:
    a. real estate investment trust.
    b. cooperative.
    c. corporation.
    d. condominium.

15. Gayle Dickins and Sam Swenson are getting married. Under the laws of the state in which they live, any real estate that either owns at the time of their marriage will remain that spouse's property in severalty. Any property acquired by either after the wedding belongs to both of them equally. This form of ownership is called:
    a. general partnership property.
    b. joint tenancy.
    c. tenancy by the entireties.
    d. community property.

16. Harold Albertson owns a fee simple title to unit 12 and 4½ percent of the common elements. Albertson:
    I. owns a life estate.
    II. may mortgage unit 12 without placing a lien on the title of the other unit owners.
       a. I only   c. both I and II
       b. II only   d. neither I nor II

17. A legal arrangement whereby title to property is held for the benefit of a beneficiary is a:
    I. trust.
    II. limited partnership.
       a. I only   c. both I and II
       b. II only   d. neither I nor II

18. Which of the following statements applies equally to joint tenants and tenants by the entireties?
    a. There is no right to file a partition suit.
    b. The survivor becomes owner.
    c. A deed signed by one will convey a fractional interest.
    d. A deed will not convey any interest unless signed by both spouses.

19. **A, B,** and **C** were co-owners of a parcel of real estate. **B** died and his interest passed, according to his will, to become part of his estate. **B** was a:
    a. tenant by the entirety.
    b. joint tenant.
    c. tenant in common.
    d. corporate officer.

20. In a tenancy by the entirety:
    I. the co-owners are husband and wife.
    II. the co-owners have the right to partition.
       a. I only   c. both I and II
       b. II only   d. neither I nor II

21. A condominium is created:
    a. when construction is completed on the structure.
    b. when the owner or developer files a declaration of condominium in the public record.
    c. when a condominium owners' association is established.
    d. when all unit owners file documents in the public records asserting their decision.

22. A *straw man* is most often associated with which of the following forms of ownership?
    a. corporation   c. partnership
    b. joint tenancy   d. cooperative

23. A married couple are selling their home, owned under a tenancy by the entirety. In order for the deed conveying the property to be valid, who must sign it?

  I. the husband
 II. the wife

    a. I only   c. both I and II
    b. II only   d. neither I nor II

24. The term *separate property* is most closely associated with which of the following?

    a. joint tenancy
    b. tenancy by the entirety
    c. community property
    d. partnership

25. Generally, a condominium building:

  I. is managed under the supervision of an association of unit owners.
 II. may not be converted back to apartment status once it has been declared a condominium.

    a. I only   c. both I and II
    b. II only   d. neither I nor II

26. Which of the following best describes ownership of a cooperative?

    a. The purchaser is a stockholder.
    b. The purchaser holds a fee simple title.
    c. The purchaser holds a reverter.
    d. a and c

9

Legal Descriptions

Overview

In everyday life, we often describe real estate casually, perhaps as "the lot on 1546 East Main Street," or "the big house on the corner of Main and Oak." In real estate practice, however, parcels of land cannot always be referred to in such an imprecise manner. Deeds, sales contracts, and other documents must state the exact size and location of real estate according to an established system of land description. This chapter will explain how land is identified and measured and will include discussions of each of the three forms of legal description used in the United States.

Describing Land	One of the essential elements of a valid deed is an accurate description of the land being conveyed. The real estate involved must be identifiable from the wording of the deed and with reference to only the documents named in the deed. The courts have usually held that a description of land is legally sufficient if a competent surveyor can locate the real estate in question.

The courts of most states have accepted a street address as being sufficient to locate or identify a parcel of real estate, but not to serve as a legal description. However, the legal description in a deed or mortgage may be followed by the words "commonly known as" and the street address. A **legal description** is an *exact way of describing real estate in a contract, deed, mortgage, or other document that will be accepted by a court of law.*

The average parcel of land has been conveyed and transferred many times in the past. The description of the land in a deed, mortgage, or other instrument should be the same as that used in the previous instrument of conveyance. Discrepancies, errors, and legal problems can be avoided or reduced if this practice is followed in drawing subsequent conveyances.

Methods of Describing Real Estate	There are three basic methods of describing real estate: (1) metes and bounds, (2) rectangular survey, and (3) recorded plat of subdivision. Consult figure 9.1 to determine the system of land description commonly used in your state.
Metes and Bounds	A **metes-and-bounds description** makes use of the boundaries and measurements of the land in question. Such a description starts at a definitely designated point called the **point or place of beginning** (abbreviated POB) and proceeds around the boundaries of the tract by reference to linear measurements and directions. A metes-and-bounds description always ends at the point where it began (the POB), so that the tract being descibed is fully enclosed.

In a metes-and-bounds description, the actual distance between monuments takes precedence over linear measurements set forth in the description if the two measurements differ. **Monuments** are fixed objects used to establish real estate boundaries. Natural objects such as stones, large trees, lakes, streams, and intersections of major streets or highways, as well as man-made markers placed by surveyors, are commonly used as monuments. (Under the rectangular survey system, as discussed later, section lines, quarter-section lines, township lines, and similar points of reference are used in the same way as monuments in the description and location of property.) Measurements often include the words "more or less"; the location of the monuments is more important than the distance stated in the wording.

An example of a metes-and-bounds description of a parcel of land (pictured in figure 9.2) follows:

"A tract of land located in Red Skull, Virginia, described as follows: Beginning at the intersection of the east line of Jones Road and the south line of Skull Drive;

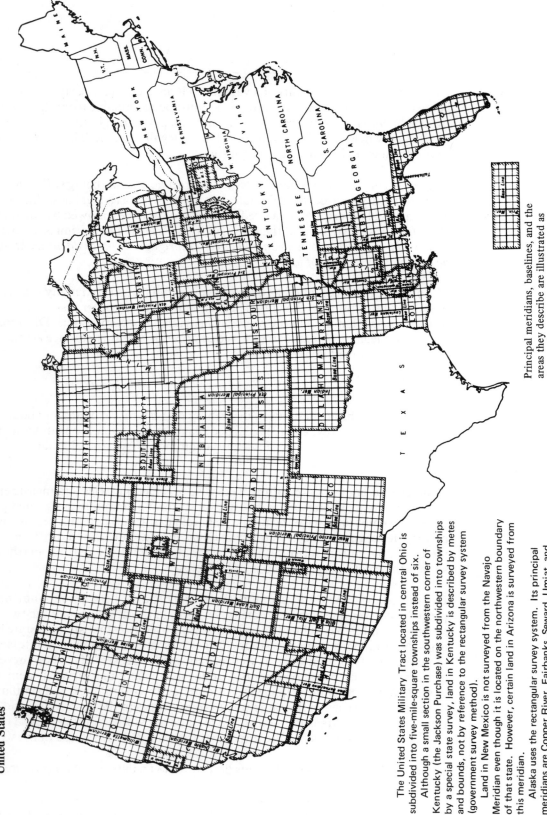

**Figure 9.1
Public Land Survey
Systems of the
United States**

The United States Military Tract located in central Ohio is subdivided into five-mile-square townships instead of six.

Although a small section in the southwestern corner of Kentucky (the Jackson Purchase) was subdivided into townships by a special state survey, land in Kentucky is described by metes and bounds, not by reference to the rectangular survey system (government survey method).

Land in New Mexico is not surveyed from the Navajo Meridian even though it is located on the northwestern boundary of that state. However, certain land in Arizona is surveyed from this meridian.

Alaska uses the rectangular survey system. Its principal meridians are Copper River, Fairbanks, Seward, Umiat, and Kateel River.

Land in Hawaii is surveyed through the metes and bounds method.

Principal meridians, baselines, and the areas they describe are illustrated as shown above.

Areas in which metes and bounds descriptions are used are left blank.

thence east along the south line of Skull Drive 200 feet; thence south 15° east 216.5 feet, more or less, to the center thread of Red Skull Creek; thence northwesterly along the center line of said creek to its intersection with the east line of Jones Road; thence north 105 feet, more or less, along the east line of Jones Road to the place of beginning."

**Figure 9.2
Metes-and-Bounds
Tract**

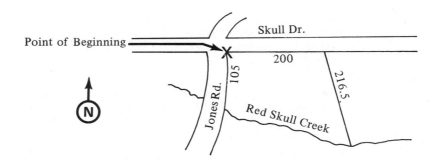

When used to describe property within a town or city, a metes-and-bounds description may begin as follows:

"Beginning at a point on the southerly side of Kent Street, 100 feet easterly from the corner formed by the intersection of the southerly side of Kent Street and the easterly side of Broadway; thence. . . ."

In this description, the point of beginning (POB) is given by reference to the corner intersection. *The description must close by returning to the POB.* The reference point of the street intersection is not included in the land described, but is the point of beginning, sometimes called the point of commencement (POC), of this description.

Metes-and-bounds descriptions are highly complicated and should be handled with extreme care. When they include compass directions of the various lines and concave or convex curved lines, they can be difficult to understand. In such cases, the advice and counsel of a surveyor should be sought.

**Rectangular
(Government)
Survey System**

The **rectangular survey system,** sometimes called the *government survey method,* was established by Congress in 1785, soon after the federal government was organized. The system was developed as a standard method of describing all lands conveyed to or acquired by the federal government, including the extensive area of the Northwest Territory.

The rectangular survey system is based on sets of two intersecting lines: principal meridians and base lines. The **principal meridians** are north and south lines, and the **base lines** are east and west lines. Both are exactly located by reference to degrees of longitude and latitude. Each principal meridian has a name or number and is crossed by its own base line. These lines are pictured in figure 9.1. Each principal meridian and its corresponding base line are used to survey a definite area of land, indicated on the map by boundary lines.

Each principal meridian affects or controls *only* the specific area of land shown by the boundaries on the chart. No parcel of land is described by reference to more than one principal meridian, and the meridian used may not necessarily be the nearest one.

Ranges. The land on either side of a principal meridian is divided into *six-mile-wide strips* by lines that run north and south, parallel to the meridian. These north- south strips of land are called **ranges** (see figure 9.3). They are designated by consecutive numbers east or west of the principal meridian. For example, Range 3 East would be a strip of land between 12 and 18 miles east of its principal meridian.

Townships. Lines running east and west parallel with the base line and six miles apart are referred to as **township lines,** and form *strips* of land (or *tiers*) called *townships* (see figure 9.3). These tiers of townships are designated by consecutive numbers north or south of the base line. For instance, the strip of land between 6 and 12 miles north of a base line is Township 2 North.

The **township squares** formed by the intersecting township and range lines are the basic units of the rectangular survey system. Theoretically, townships are six miles square and contain 36 square miles (23,040 acres). Note that *although a township square is part of a township strip, the two terms do not refer to the same thing.* In this discussion, the word *township* used by itself refers to the township square.

Figure 9.3
Principal Meridian
and Base Line

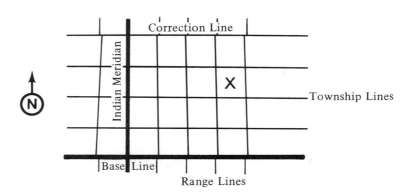

Each township is given a legal description by using: (1) the designation of the township strip in which the township is located, (2) the designation of the range strip, and (3) the name or number of the principal meridian for that area. For example, in figure 9.3, the township marked *X* is described as Township 3 North, Range 4 East of the Indian Meridian because the township is in the third strip, or tier, north of the base line. This strip (or tier) designates the township number and direction. The township is also located in the fourth range strip (those running north and south) east of the Indian Meridian. Finally, reference is made to the Indian Meridian because the land being described is within the boundary of land surveyed from that meridian. This description is abbreviated as *T3N, R4E Indian Meridian.*

Sections. Each township contains 36 **sections.** Sections are numbered 1 through 36, as shown in figure 9.4. Section 1 is always in the northeast, or upper right-hand, corner. By law, each section number 16 has been set aside for school purposes and is referred to as a *school section.* The sale or rental proceeds from this land were originally available for township school use.

Figure 9.4
Sections in a Township

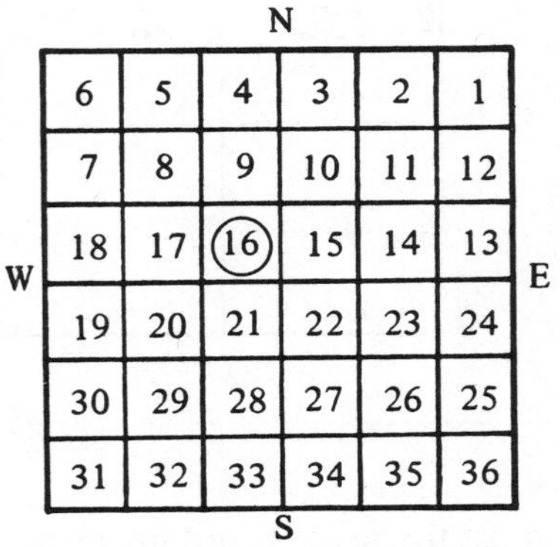

16 = School Section

As illustrated in figure 9.5, each section contains one square mile, or *640 acres,* and is divided into *quarters* for reference purposes. One could refer to the southeast quarter, which is a 160-acre tract; this would be abbreviated as SE¼. Quarter sections can be divided into quarters or halves, and such parts can be further divided by quarters. The SE¼ of SE¼ of SE¼ of Section 1 would be a ten-acre square in the lower right-hand corner of Section 1. Sometimes this description is written without the word *of*: SE¼, SE¼, SE¼ Section 1. It is possible to combine portions of a section, as: NE¼ of SW¼ and N½ of NW¼ of SE¼ of Section 1. Notice that because of the word *and* in this description, the area is 60 acres.

Correction lines. Due to the curvature of the earth, the convergence of the north and south lines (range lines) must be compensated for. All range lines continually approach each other and, if extended northward, would eventually meet at the North Pole. An accurate survey of a township would show its north line to be about 50 feet shorter than its south line. Thus, in the case of the fourth township north of the base line the difference is four times as great, or about 200 feet. The rectangular survey system compensates for the resulting shortages with **correction lines** (see figure 9.3). Every fourth township line (east and west lines parallel with the base lines) is designated a correction line, and on each correction line the range lines are measured to the full distance of six miles apart. However, because of the curvature of the earth and the crude instruments used in early days, few townships are exactly six-mile squares or contain exactly 36 square miles.

Figure 9.5
A Section

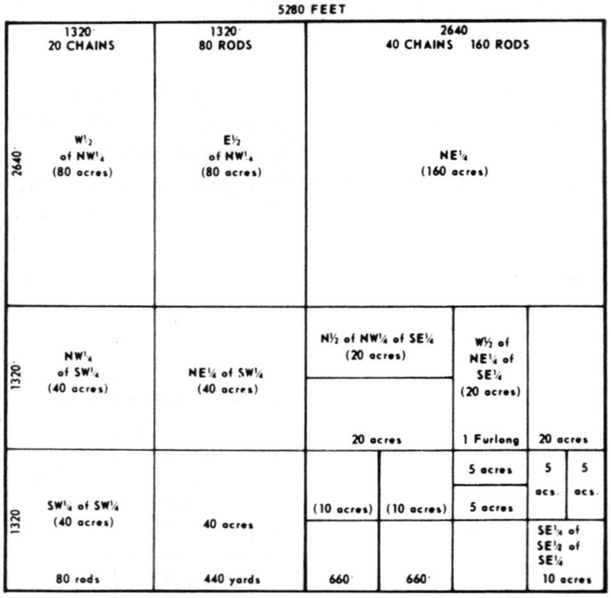

Since most townships contain a smaller area than required, surveyors follow well-established, uniform rules in adjusting such errors. These rules provide that any overage or shortage in the 36-square-mile area of a township be adjusted in those sections adjacent to its north and west boundaries. All other sections are to be one square mile. These correction provisions explain some of the variations of acreage in sections and townships under the rectangular survey system of land descriptions.

Government lots. Undersized or oversized sections are classified as *fractional sections* and may occur for a number of reasons. For example, part of the section may be submerged under water. In some areas, the rectangular survey was made by separate crews and may have resulted in gaps less than a section wide being left when the surveys met. Other errors resulted from the difficulties encountered in the actual survey.

Areas smaller than full quarter sections were designated as **government lots** by government surveyors. Fractional sections were divided into as many full-sized quarter sections as possible, and the remaining area was divided into numbered government lots. The overage or shortage was corrected whenever possible by placing the government lots in the north or west portions of the fractional sections. For example, a government lot might be described as Government Lot 2 in the northwest quarter of fractional section 18, Township 2 North, Range 4 East of the Salt Lake Meridian.

In Practice . . .

When reading a government survey description of land, it is helpful to read from the end of the description to the beginning to determine the location and size of the property. For example, consider the following description:

"The S ½ of the NW ¼ of the SE ¼ of Section 11, Township 8 North, Range 6 West of the Fourth Principal Meridian."

To locate this tract of land from this citation alone, read the description from end to beginning. First search for the Fourth Principal Meridian on a map of the United States. Then, on a regional map, find the township in which the property is located by counting six range strips west of the Fourth Principal Meridian, and eight townships north of its corresponding base line. After locating Section 11 on the map, you would then divide the section into quarters, the SE ¼ into quarters, and then the NW ¼ into halves. The S ½ of the NW ¼ contains the property in question.

This technique also works in computing the size of a tract of land from its government survey description. Working backward, first determine that the SE ¼ of the section contains 160 acres (640 acres divided by 4). The NW ¼ of that quarter section contains 40 acres (160 acres divided by 4), and the S ½ of that quarter section—the property in question—contains 20 acres (40 acres divided by 2). In general, the longer *the government survey description, the* smaller *the tract of land it describes.*

Metes-and-bounds descriptions with rectangular survey system. Land within states using the rectangular survey system may also require a metes-and-bounds description. This usually occurs in describing an irregular tract, a tract too small to be described by quarter sections, or a tract that does not follow either the lot or block lines of a recorded subdivision or section, quarter section, or other fractional section lines. An example of a combined metes-and-bounds and rectangular survey system description is as follows (see figure 9.6):

"That part of the northwest quarter of Section 12, Township 10 North, Range 7 West of the Third Principal Meridian, bounded by a line described as follows: Commencing at the southeast corner of the northwest quarter of said Section 12, thence north 500 feet; thence west parallel with the south line of said section 1,000 feet; thence south parallel with the east line of said section 500 feet to the south line of said northwest quarter; thence east along said south line to the point of beginning."

Figure 9.6
Metes and Bounds
with Rectangular
Survey

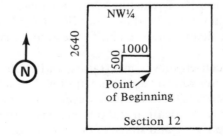

Recorded Plat of Subdivision

The third method of land description is by *lot and block number* referring to a **plat of subdivision** placed in the public records of the county where the land is located.

The first step in subdividing land is the preparation of a *plat of survey* by a licensed surveyor or engineer, as illustrated in figure 9.7. On this plat the land is divided into blocks and lots, and streets or access roads for public use are indicated. The blocks and lots are assigned numbers or letters. Lot sizes and street details must be indicated completely and must comply with all local ordinances and requirements. When properly signed and approved, the subdivision plat may be recorded in the county in which the land is located; it thereby becomes part of the legal description. In describing a lot from a recorded subdivision plat, the lot and block number, name or number of the subdivision plat, and name of the county and state are used. For example:

Lots 2, 3, and 4 in Block 5 of L. Robinson's Subdivision of the northwest quarter of Section 9, Township 4 North, Range 3 East of the Seward Principal Meridian in _____ county, _____ (state).

Some subdivided lands are further divided by a later resubdivision. For example, if Alan Roswell bought two full blocks of John Welch's subdivision and resubdivided this land into different-sized lots, then Roswell might convey:

Lot 1 in Block A of Roswell's resubdivision of Blocks 2 and 3 and John Welch's Hometown Subdivision of the west one-half of Section 19, Township 10 North, Range 13 East of the Black Hills Principal Meridian in _____ county, _____ (state).

This method of land description is used in all states, whether under the rectangular survey system or not. Some states have passed *plat acts* that specify the smallest tract that may be conveyed without a subdivision plat being prepared, approved, and recorded. In some states, for example, the minimum size is five acres.

Preparation and Use of a Survey

Legal descriptions should not be changed, altered, or combined without adequate information from a competent authority, such as a surveyor or title attorney. Legal descriptions should *always* include the name of the county and state in which the land is located. Meridians often relate to more than one state and occasionally relate to two base lines, so a description cannot be certain unless the county and state are given. For example, the description "the southwest quarter of Section 10, Township 4 North, Range 1 West of the Fourth Principal Meridian" could refer to land in either Illinois or Wisconsin. The county and state must be specified in order to clarify the ambiguity.

A licensed surveyor is trained and authorized to locate a given parcel of land and to determine its legal description. The surveyor does this by preparing a *survey,* which sets forth the legal description of the property, and a *survey sketch,* which shows the location and dimensions of the parcel. When a survey also shows the location, size, and shape of buildings located on the lot, it is referred to as a *spot survey.* Surveys are required in many real estate transactions, such as when: (1) conveying a portion of a given tract of land, (2) conveying real estate as security for a mortgage loan, (3) showing the location of new construction, (4) locating roads and highways, and (5) determining the legal description of the land on which a particular building is located.

**Figure 9.7
Subdivision Plat
Map**

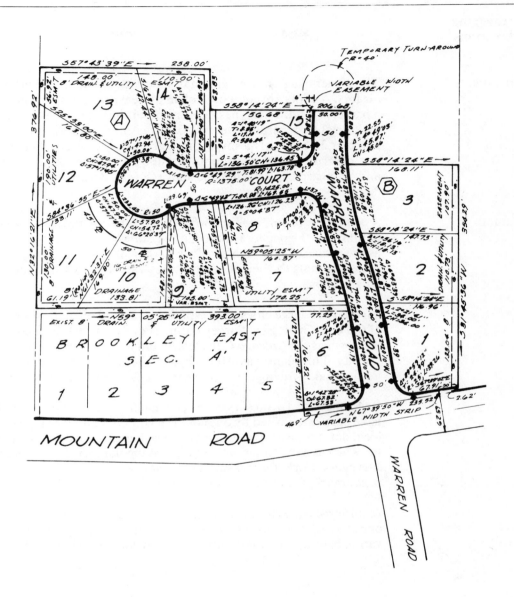

In Practice . . .

Because legal descriptions, once recorded, affect title to real estate, they should be prepared only *by a surveyor or attorney. Real estate licensees who attempt to draft legal descriptions create potential risks for themselves and their clients and customers. Further, when entered on a document of conveyance, legal descriptions should be copied with care. For example, an incorrectly worded legal description in a sales contract may obligate the seller to convey or the buyer to purchase more or less land than intended. Title problems can arise for the buyer when he or she seeks to convey the property at a future date. Even if the contract can be corrected by the parties involved before the sale is closed, the licensee runs the risk of losing a commission. In addition, he or she may be held liable for damages suffered by an injured party because of an improperly worded legal description.*

Measuring Elevations

Air Lots

The owner of a parcel of land may subdivide the air above his or her land into **air lots.** Air lots are composed of airspace within specific boundaries located over a parcel of land. This type of description is found in titles to tall buildings located on air rights, generally over railroad tracks. (See the discussion of air rights in Chapter 2.) Similarly a surveyor, in preparing a subdivision plat for condominium use, describes each condominium unit by reference to the elevation of the floors and ceilings on a vertical plane above the city datum.

Datum

A point, line, or surface from which elevations are measured or indicated is a **datum.** For the purpose of the United States Geological Survey, datum is defined as the mean sea level at New York harbor. It is of special significance to surveyors in determining the height of structures, establishing the grade of streets, and similar situations.

Virtually all large cities have established a local official datum that is used in place of the U.S. Geological Survey datum. For instance, the official datum for Chicago is known as the *Chicago City Datum* and is a horizontal plane below the surface of the city. This plane was established in 1847 as corresponding to the low water level of Lake Michigan in that year, and is considered to be zero elevation.

Benchmarks. To aid surveyors, permanent reference points called **benchmarks** have been established throughout the United States (see figure 9.8). Cities with local datums also have designated local benchmarks, which are given official status when assigned a permanent identifying number. Local benchmarks simplify surveyors' work, for measurements may be based on them rather than on the basic benchmark, which may be miles away.

A surveyor's measurement of elevation based on the USGS datum will differ from one computed according to a local datum. A surveyor can always translate an elevation based on a local datum to the elevation based on the USGS.

Figure 9.8
Benchmark

Legal Description of a Condominium Interest

With the enactment of *condominium property acts* in all states, there is an increased demand for determination of elevations of horizontal planes. As discussed in Chapter 8, among other things these acts require that a registered land surveyor prepare a plat of survey showing the elevations of floor and ceiling surfaces and the boundaries of a condominium apartment with reference to an official datum. Typically, a separate plat will be prepared for each floor in the condominium building.

The following is an example of the legal description of a condominium apartment unit that includes a fractional share of the common elements of the building and land:

"UNIT _____ as delineated on survey of the following described parcel of real estate (hereinafter referred to as Development Parcel): The north 99 feet of the west ½ of Block 4 (except that part, if any, taken and used for street), in Sutton's Division Number 5 in the east ½ of the southeast ¼ of Section 24, Township 3 South, Range 68 West of the Sixth Principal Meridian, in Denver County, Colorado, which survey is attached as Exhibit A to Declaration made by Colorado National Bank as Trustee under Trust No. 1250, recorded in the Recorder's Office of Denver County, Colorado, as Document No. 475637; together with an undivided ____ % interest in said Development Parcel (excepting from said Development Parcel all the property and space comprising all the units thereof as defined and set forth in said Declaration and Survey)."

Land Units and Measurements

It is important to know and understand land units and measurements—they are an integral part of legal descriptions. Some commonly used measurements follow:

1. A *rod* is 16½ feet.
2. A *chain* is 66 feet, or 100 links.
3. A *mile* is 5,280 feet.
4. An *acre* contains 43,560 square feet, or 160 square rods.
5. A *section* of land is one square mile and contains 640 acres; a *quarter section* contains 160 acres; a *quarter of a quarter section* contains 40 acres.
6. A *circle* contains 360 degrees; a *quarter segment* of a circle contains 90 degrees; a *half segment* of a circle contains 180 degrees. One *degree* (1°) can be subdivided into 60 minutes (60′), each of which contains 60 seconds (60″). One and a half degrees would be written 1°30′0″.

Table 9.1 lists further land measurement units and their metric equivalents.

Summary

Documents affecting or conveying interests in real estate must contain an accurate description of the property involved. There are three methods of *legal description* of land in the United States: (1) metes and bounds, (2) rectangular (government) survey, and (3) recorded plat of subdivision. A legal description is a precise method of identifying a parcel of land. A property's description should always be the same as the one used in previous documents.

Nineteen states (and parts of Ohio) have always used only metes-and-bounds descriptions of land and continue to do so. In a *metes-and-bounds description,* the actual location of monuments takes precedence over the written linear measurement in a document. When property is being described by metes and bounds, the

Table 9.1	Unit	Measurement	Metric Equivalent
Units of Land Measurement	mile	5,280 feet; 320 rods; 1,760 yards	1.609 kilometers
	rod	5.50 yards; 16.5 feet	5.029 meters
	sq. mile	640 acres	2.590 sq. kilometers
	acre	4,840 sq. yards; 160 sq. rods; 43,560 sq. feet	4,047 sq. meters
	sq. yard	9 sq. feet	0.836 sq. meters
	sq. foot	144 sq. inches	0.093 sq. meters
	chain	66 feet or 100 links	20.117 meters
	kilometer	0.62 mile	1,000 meters
	hectare	2.47 acres	10,000 sq. meters

description must always enclose a tract of land; that is, the boundary line must end at the point at which it started.

The *rectangular survey system* is used in 30 states. It involves surveys based on 35 principal meridians. Under this government survey system, each principal meridian and its corresponding base line are specifically located. Any particular parcel of land is surveyed from only one principal meridian and its base line. The area surveyed from each meridian is also outlined by boundaries as shown in figure 9.1.

East and west lines parallel with the base line form six-mile-wide strips called *township tiers.* North and south lines parallel with the principal meridian form *ranges.* The resulting squares are each 36 square miles in area and are called *townships.* Townships are designated by their township tier and range numbers and their principal meridian—for example, Township 3 North, Range 4 East of the _____ Meridian. Townships are divided into 36 *sections* of one square mile each.

By reference to quarter sections, half sections, and quarter of quarter sections, it is possible to describe a small tract of land within a given section without the formality of subdividing the land into lots and blocks.

When a tract is irregular or its boundaries do not coincide with a section, regular fractions of a section, or a boundary of a lot or block in a subdivision, a surveyor can prepare a combination rectangular survey and metes-and-bounds description. The principal difference between metes-and-bounds descriptions in the 30 states that use the rectangular survey system and the 20 states that do not is that in those that do, every legal description refers to a section, township, range, and principal meridian.

Land in every state can be subdivided into lots and blocks by means of a *recorded plat of subdivision.* An approved plat of survey showing the division into blocks, giving the size, location, and designation of lots, and specifying the location and size of streets to be dedicated for public use is filed for record in the recorder's office of the county in which the land is located. *It is possible to resubdivide portions of a previously recorded subdivision.* By referring to a subdivision plat, the legal description of a building site in a town or city can be given by lot, block, and subdivision in a section, township, and range of a principal meridian in a county and state.

The services of licensed surveyors are necessary in the conduct of the real estate business. A plat of survey prepared by a surveyor is the usual method of certifying the legal description of a certain parcel of land. When a survey also shows the location, size, and shape of the buildings located on the lot, it is referred to as a *spot survey.* Spot surveys are customarily required in purchases of real estate when a mortgage or new construction is involved.

Air lots, condominium descriptions, and other measurements of vertical elevations may be computed from the United States Geological Survey *datum,* which is the mean sea level in New York harbor. Most large cities have established local survey datums for surveying within the area. The elevations from these datums are further supplemented by reference points, called *benchmarks,* placed at fixed intervals from the datums.

Questions

1. A *monument* is used in which of the following types of legal descriptions?
    I.   recorded plat of subdivision
    II. metes and bounds
    III. rectangular survey

    a. I only   c. I and II
    b. II only   d. I, II, and III

2. What is the proper description of the following shaded area?

    a. SW¼ of the NE¼ and the N½ of the SE¼ of the SW¼
    b. N½ of the NE¼ of the SW¼ and the SE¼ of the NW¼
    c. SW¼ of the SE¼ of the NW¼ and the N½ of the NE¼ of the SW¼
    d. S½ of the SW¼ of the NE¼ and the NE¼ of the NW¼ of the SE¼

3. When surveying land, a surveyor refers to the principal meridian that is:
    a. nearest the land being surveyed.
    b. in the same state as the land being surveyed.
    c. not more than 40 townships or 15 ranges distant from the land being surveyed.
    d. within the area boundary of the land being surveyed.

4. The N½ of the SW¼ of a section contains:
    a. 40 acres.   c. 160 acres.
    b. 20 acres.   d. 80 acres.

5. A street address identifying a parcel of real estate:
    I. is often used in conjunction with a metes-and-bounds legal description.
    II. is generally by itself an adequate legal description.

    a. I only   c. both I and II
    b. II only   d. neither I nor II

6. A system of describing real estate that uses feet, degrees, and natural markers as monuments is:
    a. rectangular survey.
    b. metes and bounds.
    c. government survey.
    d. recorded plat of subdivision.

7. Government lots:
    I. are generally irregular in size.
    II. are owned by the federal government.

    a. I only   c. both I and II
    b. II only   d. neither I nor II

8. A *school section:*
    I. contains 640 acres.
    II. is section 16 within a township.

    a. I only   c. both I and II
    b. II only   d. neither I nor II

Questions 9 through 12 refer to the following illustration of a township:

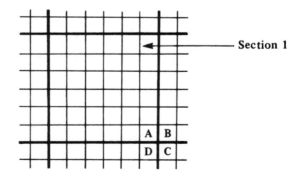

9. The section marked *A* is which of the following?
    a. school section   c. section 31
    b. section 36   d. government lot

10. Which of the following is section 6?
    a. D   c. B
    b. C   d. A

11. The section directly below *C* is which of the following?
    a. section 12   c. section 30
    b. section 25   d. section 7

12. Which of the following is lot *D*?
    a. section 36   c. section 1
    b. section 31   d. section 6

13. An acre contains:
    a. 160 square feet.   c. 640 square feet.
    b. 43,560 square feet.   d. 360 degrees.

14. How many acres are there in the following tract?
    Beginning at the NW corner of the SW¼, thence south along the west line to the SW corner of the section, then east along the south line of the section 2,640 feet, more or less, to the SE corner of the said SW¼, then in a straight line to the POB.
    a. 100 acres   c. 90 acres
    b. 160 acres   d. 80 acres

15. A legal description for a parcel of real estate to be conveyed should be prepared by which of the following persons?
    a. attorney   c. surveyor
    b. real estate broker   d. a or c

16. *A datum* is:
    I. used in the description of an air lot.
    II. indicated through the use of benchmarks.
    a. I only   c. both I and II
    b. II only   d. neither I nor II

17. Which of these shaded areas depicts the NE¼ of the SE¼ of the SW¼?

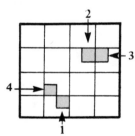

    a. area 1   c. area 3
    b. area 2   d. area 4

18. The proper description of the shaded township area in this illustration is:

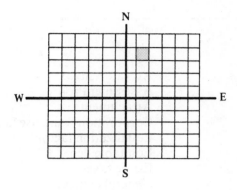

    a. T4N R2W.   c. T4N R2E.
    b. T2W R4N.   d. T2E R4N.

19. If a farm described as "the NW¼ of the SE¼ of Section 10, Township 2 North, Range 3 West of the 6th. P.M." sold for $1,500 an acre, what would the sale price be?
    a. $30,000   c. $45,000
    b. $15,000   d. $60,000

20. A *rod* is:
    I. a point of reference in a metes-and-bounds description.
    II. 16.5 feet.
    a. I only   c. both I and II
    b. II only   d. neither I nor II

10

Real Estate Taxes and Other Liens

Key Terms

Ad valorem tax
Assessment roll
Attachment
Corporation franchise tax
Equalization factor
Equitable lien
Estate taxes
General contractor
General lien
Inheritance taxes
Internal Revenue Service tax lien
Involuntary lien
Judgment
Lien
Mechanic's lien
Mill

Mortgage lien
Priority
Redemption
Special assessment
Specific lien
Statutory lien
Subcontractor
Subordination agreement
Surety bail bond
Tax foreclosure
Tax lien
Tax sale
Vendee's lien
Vendor's lien
Voluntary lien

Overview

As discussed in previous chapters, the ownership interest a person has in real estate can be diminished by the interests of others. Specifically, taxing bodies, creditors, and courts can lessen an ownership interest by making a claim—called a *lien*—against a person's property to secure payment of taxes, debts, and other obligations. This chapter will discuss the nature of liens, specifically focusing on real estate tax liens, which affect every owner of real estate. In addition, the chapter will describe liens other than taxes that involve real and personal property.

Liens

A **lien** is defined as a charge against property that provides security for a debt or obligation of the property owner. A lien allows a creditor (lienor) to force the sale of property that has been given as security by the debtor (lienee) to satisfy the lienee's debt in case of default. A lien does not constitute ownership; it is a type of *encumbrance*—a charge or burden on a property that may diminish its value. Note, however, that while all liens are encumbrances, not all encumbrances are necessarily liens. As discussed in Chapter 7, encumbrances that are not liens (such as easements and deed restrictions) are *incorporeal rights* in real estate and give the parties in question certain rights, or interests, in the real estate. The right of easement is an example of such an incorporeal right.

Generally, liens are enforced by court order. A creditor must institute a legal action for the court to sell the real estate in question for full or partial satisfaction of the debt.

A lien may be voluntary or involuntary. A **voluntary lien** is created by the lienee's action, such as taking out a mortgage loan. An **involuntary lien** is created by law. Involuntary liens are either statutory or equitable. A **statutory lien** is created by statute. An **equitable lien** arises out of common law. A real estate tax lien, for example, is an involuntary, statutory lien; that is, it is created by statute without any action by the property owner. A court-ordered judgment requiring payment of the balance on a delinquent charge account would be an involuntary, equitable lien on the debtor's property.

Liens may be further classified into two other categories: general and specific. As illustrated in figure 10.1, **general liens** usually affect all the property of a debtor, both real and personal, and include judgments, estate and inheritance taxes, debts

Figure 10.1
General Liens

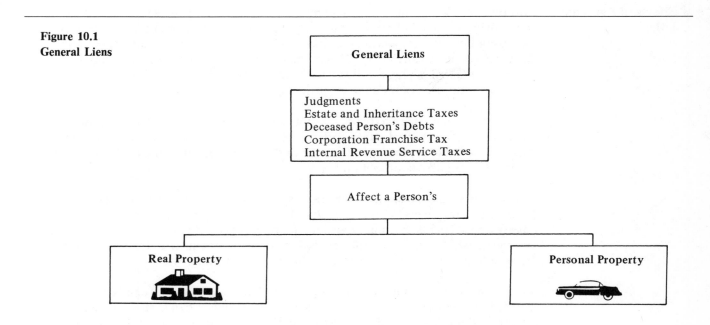

of a deceased person, corporation franchise taxes, and Internal Revenue Service taxes. **Specific liens,** on the other hand, are usually secured by a specific parcel of real estate and affect only that particular property. As illustrated in figure 10.2, these include mechanics' liens, mortgages, taxes, special assessments, liens for public utilities, vendors' liens, vendees' liens, surety bail bond liens, and attachments.

Figure 10.2
Specific Liens

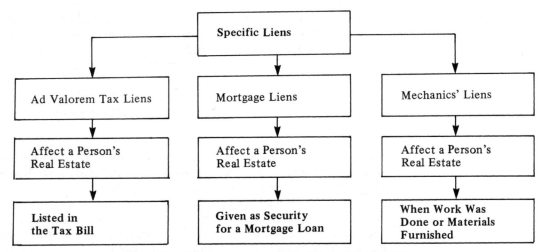

Also: Special Assessments, Utility Liens, Vendors' Liens, Vendees' Liens, Surety Bail Bond Liens, and Attachments

Effects of Liens on Title

Although the fee simple estate held by a typical real estate owner can be reduced in value by the lien and encumbrance rights of others, the owner is still free to convey his or her title to a willing purchaser. This purchaser will, however, buy the property subject to any liens and encumbrances of the seller. This is because, once properly established, liens will *run with the land;* that is, they will bind successive owners if steps are not taken to clear the lien.

Remember, liens attach to property, not to the property owner. Thus, although a purchaser who buys real estate under a delinquent lien is not responsible for payment of the debt secured by the lien, he or she faces a possible loss of the property if the creditors take court action to enforce payment of their liens.

Priority of Liens. Real estate taxes and special assessments generally take **priority** over all other liens. This means that if the property goes through a court sale to satisfy unpaid debts or obligations, outstanding real estate taxes and special assessments will be paid from the proceeds *first.* The remainder of the proceeds will be used to pay other outstanding liens in the order of their priority.

For example, if the courts ordered a parcel of land sold to satisfy a judgment lien entered in the public record on February 7, 1985, subject to a first mortgage lien recorded January 22, 1983, and to this year's as-yet unpaid real estate taxes, the proceeds of the sale would be distributed in the following order:

1. to the taxing bodies for this year's real estate taxes.
2. to the mortgage lender for the entire amount of the mortgage loan outstanding as of the date of the sale.
3. to the creditor named in the judgment lien (if any proceeds remain after paying the first two items).
4. to the foreclosed-upon landowner (if any proceeds remain after paying the first three items).

Liens other than general taxes and special assessments take priority from the date of recording in the public records of the county where the property is located (see figure 10.3). Exceptions to this rule include mechanics' liens (discussed later in this chapter), which take priority as provided by state law but never take priority over tax and general assessment liens.

Figure 10.3
Priority of Liens

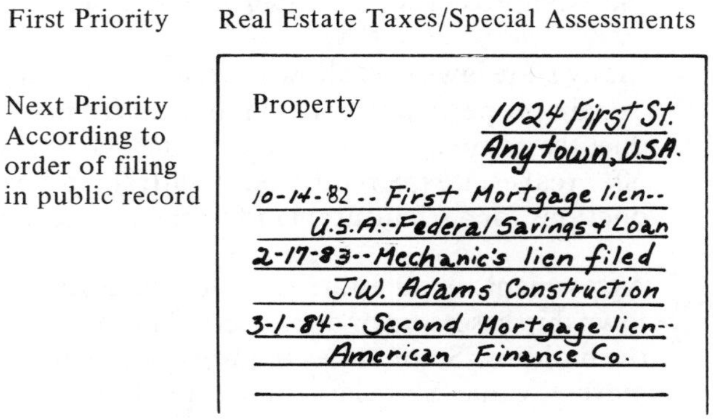

First Priority   Real Estate Taxes/Special Assessments

Next Priority   Property   1024 First St.
According to   Anytown, USA.
order of filing   10-14-82 -- First Mortgage lien--
in public record   U.S.A.--Federal Savings & Loan
                      2-17-83--Mechanic's lien filed
                               J.W. Adams Construction
                      3-1-84-- Second Mortgage lien--
                               American Finance Co.

Subordination agreements are written agreements between lienholders to change the priority of mortgage, judgment, and other liens under certain circumstances. Priority and recording of liens will be discussed in detail in Chapter 13, "Title Records."

Tax Liens

As discussed in Chapter 7, the ownership of real estate is subject to certain government powers. One of these powers is the right of state and local governments to impose **tax liens** for the support of their governmental functions. Because the location of real estate is permanently fixed, the government can levy taxes with a rather high degree of certainty that the taxes will be collected. Since the annual taxes levied on real estate usually have priority over other previously recorded liens, they may be enforced by the court sale of the real estate free of such other liens.

Real estate taxes can be divided into two types: (1) *general real estate tax,* or **ad valorem tax,** and (2) **special assessment,** or *improvement tax.* Both of these taxes are levied against specific parcels of property and automatically become liens on those properties.

**General Tax
(Ad Valorem Tax)**

The general real estate tax is made up of the taxes levied on real estate by various governmental agencies and municipalities. These include cities, towns, villages, and counties. Other taxing bodies are school districts or boards (including local elementary and high schools, junior colleges, and community colleges), drainage districts, water districts, and sanitary districts. Municipal authorities operating recreational preserves such as forest preserves and parks are also authorized by the legislatures of the various states to levy real estate taxes.

General real estate taxes are levied for the *general support or operation* of the governmental agency authorized to impose the levy. These taxes are known as *ad valorem* taxes because the amount of the tax varies in accordance with the *value of the property being taxed.*

Exemptions from general taxes. Under most state laws, certain real estate is exempt from real estate taxation. For example, property owned by cities, various municipal organizations (such as schools, parks, and playgrounds), the state and federal governments, and religious corporations, hospitals, or educational institutions is tax exempt. Usually the property must be used for tax-exempt purposes by the exempted group or organization. If it is not so used, it will be subject to tax.

Many state laws also allow special exemptions to reduce real estate tax bills for certain property owners or land uses. *Homeowners* and *senior citizens* are frequently granted set reductions in the assessed value of their homes. Some states offer real estate tax reductions to attract industries, and many states offer tax reductions for agricultural land to encourage the continuation of agricultural uses.

Assessment. Real estate is valued, or assessed, for tax purposes by county or township assessors or appraisers. The land is usually appraised separately from the building. Some states require assessments to be a certain percentage of true, or market, value. State laws may provide for property to be reassessed periodically.

Property owners who claim that errors were made in determining the assessed value of their property may present their objections, usually to a local board of appeal or board of review. Protests or appeals regarding tax assessments may ultimately be taken to court. Such cases generally involve a proceeding whereby the court reviews the certified assessment records of the tax assessment official.

Equalization. In some jurisdictions, when it is necessary to correct general inequalities in state-wide tax assessments, uniformity may be achieved by use of an **equalization factor.** Such a factor may be provided for use in counties or districts where the assessments are to be raised or lowered. The assessed value of each property is multiplied by the equalization factor, and the tax rate is then applied to the equalized assessment. For example, the assessments in one county are determined to be 20 percent lower than the average assessments throughout the rest of the state. This underassessment can be corrected by decreeing the application of an equalization factor of 120 percent to each assessment in that county. Thus, a parcel of land, assessed for tax purposes at $98,000 would be taxed, based upon an equalized assessment of $117,600 in this county ($98,000 × 1.20 = $117,600).

Tax rates. The process of arriving at a real estate tax rate begins with the *adoption of a budget* by each county, city, school board, or other taxing district (see figure 10.4). Each budget covers the financial requirements of the taxing body for the coming fiscal year, which may be the January to December calendar year or some other 12-month period designated by statute. The budget must include an estimate of all expenditures for the year and indicate the amount of income expected from all fees, revenue sharing, and other sources. The net amount remaining to be raised from real estate taxes is then determined from these figures.

The next step is *appropriation,* the action taken by each taxing body that authorizes the expenditure of funds and provides for the sources of such monies. Appropriation generally involves the adoption of an ordinance or the passage of a law setting forth the specifics of the proposed taxation.

The amount to be raised from the general real estate tax is then imposed on property owners through a *tax levy,* the formal action taken to impose the tax, by a vote of the taxing district's governing body.

Figure 10.4
Determining a Real
Estate Tax Rate

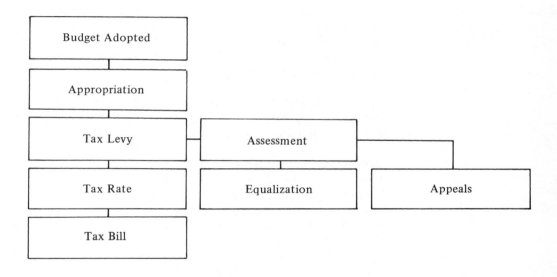

The *tax rate* for each individual taxing body is computed separately. To arrive at a tax rate, the total monies needed for the coming fiscal year are divided by the total assessments of all real estate located within the jurisdiction of the taxing body. For example, a taxing district's budget indicates that $300,000 must be raised from real estate tax revenues, and the assessment roll (assessor's record) of all taxable real estate within this district equals $10,000,000. The tax rate is computed thus:

$$\$300,000 \div \$10,000,000 = .03, \; or \; 3\%$$

The tax rate may be expressed in a number of different ways. In many areas it is expressed in mills. A **mill** is *1/1,000 of a dollar, or $.001.* The tax rate computed in the foregoing example could be expressed as follows:

$3 per $100 of assessed value
or
30 mills ($30 per $1,000 of assessed value)

Tax bills. A property owner's tax bill is computed by applying the tax rate to the assessed valuation of the property. For example, on a property assessed for tax purposes at $90,000 at a tax rate of 3 percent, or 30 mills, the tax will be $2,700 ($90,000 × .030 = $2,700). If an equalization factor is used, the computation on a property with an assessed value of $120,000 and a tax rate of 4 percent with an equalization factor of 120 percent would be as follows:

$$\$120,000 \times 1.20 = \$144,000$$
$$\$144,000 \times .040 = \$5,760 \text{ tax}$$

Generally, one tax bill that incorporates all real estate taxes levied by the various taxing districts is prepared for each property. In some areas, however, separate bills are prepared for select taxing bodies. Sometimes the real estate taxing bodies may operate on different budget years, so that the taxpayer receives separate bills for various taxes at different times during the year.

Due dates for payment of taxes are usually set by statute. In many areas, taxes are payable in two installments. Collection procedures vary: in some areas, taxes become due during the current tax year; in others, they are payable in arrears during the year after the taxes are levied; and in still others, a partial payment is due in the year of the tax, with the balance due the following year. Knowledge of local tax-payment schedules is especially important in computing the proration of current taxes when a property is sold.

Some states offer discounts to encourage prompt payment of real estate taxes. Penalties in the form of monthly interest charges are added to all taxes that are not paid when due. The due date is also called the *penalty date.*

Enforcement of tax liens. To be enforceable, real estate taxes must be valid, which means they must be: (1) properly levied, (2) used for a legal purpose, and (3) applied equitably to all affected property. Tax liens are generally given priority over all other liens against a property. Real estate taxes that have remained delinquent for the period of time specified by state law can be collected by the tax-collecting officer through either **tax foreclosure** (similar to mortgage foreclosure) or **tax sale.** While there are substantial differences in the methods and details of the various states' tax-sale procedures, the results are the same.

Tax sales are usually held pursuant to a published notice after a court has rendered a judgment for the tax and penalties and ordered that the property be sold. The sale is usually conducted by the tax collector as an annual public sale. Since there is a definite amount of delinquent tax and penalty to be collected, the purchaser must pay at least this amount. Since a defaulted owner has the right of **redemption** (the right to buy back the real estate), in many areas bidding takes place on the percentage of interest the bidder may receive from the defaulted owner if and when the property is redeemed. In this type of bidding, *the person bidding the lowest interest rate becomes the successful purchaser.* A *certificate of sale* is usually given to the successful bidder when he or she pays the delinquent tax amount.

Generally, the delinquent taxpayer can redeem the property at any time before the tax sale by paying the delinquent taxes plus interest and charges (any court costs or attorney's fees); this is known as an *equitable right of redemption.* Most state laws also grant a period of redemption *after the tax sale* during which the defaulted owner or lienholders (creditors of the defaulted owner) may redeem the property by paying the amount paid at the tax sale plus interest and charges (including any taxes levied since the sale); this is known as the *statutory right of redemption*. If no redemption is made within this statutory redemption period, the certificate holder can apply for a *tax deed*. The quality of the title conveyed by a tax deed varies from state to state according to statutory provisions.

In some states, titles to tax-delinquent land are sold or conveyed to the state or a taxing authority. At the expiration of the redemption period, titles to these lands are then sold at auction to the highest bidder. The tax deeds issued to purchasers in such cases are regarded as conveying good title, since they are considered conveyances by the state of state-owned land. In some jurisdictions, tax-delinquent land that is not sold at a tax sale due to lack of buyers is forfeited to the state. The state may then either use the land for its own purposes or sell it to the highest bidder.

Special Assessments (Improvement Taxes)

Special assessments are *special taxes levied on real estate that require property owners to pay for improvements that benefit the real estate they own.* These taxes are often levied to pay for such improvements as streets, alleys, street lighting, curbs, and similar items, and are enforced in the same manner as general real estate taxes. The procedures for making a special assessment vary widely from state to state, but usually include the following steps.

The authority to recommend or initiate the *specific improvement* is vested either in the property owners, who may petition for an improvement, or in a proper legislative authority, such as the city council or board of trustees, who may initiate the proposal for an improvement. Hearings are held, and notices are given to the owners of the property affected.

After the preliminary legal steps have been taken, the legislative authority authorized by statute to act in such cases adopts an *ordinance* that sets out the nature of the improvement, its cost, and a description of the area to be assessed.

The proper authority spreads the assessment (called the **assessment roll**) over the various parcels of real estate that will benefit. The amount of the assessment for each parcel is usually determined by one of the following criteria: (1) estimated benefit each tract will receive by reason of the assessment, and (2) front footage. Regardless of the basis used, the assessment will usually vary from parcel to parcel, as all will not benefit equally from the improvement.

After hearing the benefits and nature of improvements to be made, and after hearing any objections from members of the local community affected by the improvements, the local authority, usually a court of record, will either approve or reject the proposal. This is usually referred to as *confirming the assessment roll.*

After all of these steps have been taken, the assessment becomes a lien on the land assessed. When the improvement has been completed, a *warrant* is issued by the proper authority, often the clerk of the court that approved the roll. This warrant gives the local collector the authority to issue special assessment bills and begin collection.

In most states, an assessment becomes a *lien* following the confirmation of the roll. Special assessments are usually due and payable in equal annual installments over a period of five to ten years. Interest is also charged each property owner on the total amount of his or her assessment. The first installment generally becomes due during the year following confirmation. The bill will include yearly interest on the entire assessment. As subsequent installments are billed in following years, each bill will include a year's interest on the unpaid balance. Property owners usually have the right to prepay any or all installments and thus stop the interest charges.

In Practice . . .

While real property taxes are deductible items for income-tax purposes, note that special assessment taxes are not. Annual interest charged in connection with special assessments is *deductible, however.*

Liens Other than Taxes

Aside from real estate tax and special assessment liens, the following types of liens may also be charged against real property either voluntarily or involuntarily: mortgage liens, mechanics' liens, judgments, estate and inheritance tax liens, vendors' liens, vendees' liens, liens for municipal utilities, surety bail bond liens, corporation franchise tax liens, and Internal Revenue Service tax liens.

Mortgage Liens

In general, a **mortgage lien** is a voluntary lien on real estate given to a lender by a borrower as security for a mortgage loan. It becomes a lien on real property when the mortgage funds are disbursed and when the lender files or records the mortgage in the office of the proper official of the county where the property is located. Mortgage lenders generally require a preferred lien, referred to as a *first mortgage lien;* this means that (aside from real estate taxes), there are no other major liens against the property that would take priority over the mortgage lien.

Mortgages and mortgage liens will be discussed in detail in Chapter 15, "Real Estate Financing."

Mechanics' Liens

A mechanic's lien is a right *granted by statute.* No such lien existed under common law. The purpose of the **mechanic's lien** is to *give security to those who perform labor or furnish material in the improvement of real property.* In general, the mechanic's lien right is based on the *enhancement of value theory.* Because of the labor performed and material furnished, the real estate has been enhanced in value. Therefore, the parties who performed the work or supplied materials are given a right of lien on the real estate on which they worked as security for the payment of their proper charges. A mechanic's lien is a specific, involuntary lien.

In order for a person to be entitled to a mechanic's lien, the work that was done must have been by contract (express or implied consent) with the owner or owner's authorized representative. Such a lien is relied on to cover situations in which the owner has not fully paid for the work, or when the general contractor has been paid but has not paid the subcontractors or suppliers of materials. Generally, a person claiming a mechanic's lien must file a notice of lien in the public record of the county where the property is located within a statutory period of time after the work has been completed.

The time at which a mechanic's lien attaches to the real estate varies according to state law. For example, priority may be established as of the date: (1) the construction began or materials were first furnished; (2) the work was completed; (3) the individual subcontractor's work was either commenced or completed; (4) the contract was signed or work ordered; or, (5) a notice of the lien was recorded, filed, posted, or served.

In most states, while a mechanic's lien takes priority from the time it attaches, a claimant's notice of lien will not be filed in the public records until some time after that. A purchaser of property that has been recently constructed, altered, or repaired should therefore be cautious about possible unrecorded mechanics' liens against the property.

In some states, mechanics' liens may be given priority over previously recorded liens (such as mortgages). Inasmuch as the rights of a claimant are statutory, they are controlled by the requirements of the laws of the state in which the real estate is located. It is usually provided that a claimant must take steps to enforce his or her lien within a certain time, usually one or two years after the filing of the lien claim, or the lien will expire. Enforcement usually requires a court action to foreclose the lien through the sale of the subject real estate in order to obtain the money to satisfy the lien.

If improvements have been ordered by a third party, such as a tenant, a property owner should execute a document called a *notice of nonresponsibility* to relieve him- or herself from possible mechanics' liens. By posting this notice in some conspicuous place on the property and recording a verified copy of it in the public record, the owner gives notice that he or she will not be responsible for the work done.

Subcontractors' liens. A landowner usually hires a **general contractor** to perform a particular construction job, and it is this person to whom the owner pays all fees and expenses. The general contractor, in turn, hires a number of **subcontractors** to actually furnish the materials and perform the labor. Both the general contractors and subcontractors are entitled to mechanics' liens if they are not paid in full. Payment in full to the general contractor will not necessarily free a landowner from the lien rights of unknown, unpaid suppliers and laborers. Thus, an owner must protect him- or herself against known, as well as unknown, mechanics and materialmen. Since an owner does not actually hire these subcontractors (they are said not to be "in privity with the owner"), he or she would not be aware of them or the extent of the work or materials they provide. Subcontractors, therefore, are generally required to serve a landowner with personal notice of their individual lien claims. In some states, however, such personal notice may not be required if a general contractor furnishes an owner with a sworn statement listing all subcontractors and materialmen and the extent of labor or materials furnished by each.

Judgments

A **judgment** is a *decree issued by a court.* When the decree provides for the awarding of money and sets forth the amount of money owed by the debtor to the creditor, the judgment is referred to as a *money judgment.*

A judgment becomes a *general, involuntary lien on both real and personal property* owned by the debtor. Usually, a lien covers only property located within the county in which the judgment is issued. Therefore, notices of the lien must be filed in other counties when a creditor wishes to extend the lien coverage. The court will issue a legal document called a *writ of execution* directing the sheriff to seize and sell as much of the debtor's property as is necessary to pay the debt and the expenses of the sale. A judgment differs from a mortgage in that a *specific* parcel of real estate was not given as security at the time that the debtor-creditor relationship was created.

A judgment takes its priority as a lien on the debtor's property from one or a combination of the following (as provided or required by the law of the state in which the real estate is located): (1) the date the judgment was entered by the court, (2) the date the judgment was filed for record in the recorder's office, or (3) the date an execution was issued. Judgments are enforced through the issuance of an execution and the ultimate sale of the debtor's real or personal property by a sheriff. When the property is sold to satisfy the debt, the debtor should demand a legal document known as a *satisfaction of judgment,* or *satisfaction piece,* which should be filed with either the clerk of the court or, in some states, the recorder of deeds, so that the record will be cleared of the judgment.

Attachments. To prevent a debtor from conveying title to his or her unsecured real estate (realty that is not mortgaged or is similarly unencumbered) while a court suit is being decided, a creditor may seek a writ of **attachment.** By this writ, the court retains custody of the property until the suit is concluded. In order to obtain an attachment, a creditor must first post with the court a surety bond or deposit sufficient to cover any possible loss or damage the debtor may sustain during the period the court has custody of the property, in case the judgment is not awarded to the creditor.

Lis pendens. A judgment or other decree affecting real estate is rendered at the conclusion of a lawsuit. Generally, there is a considerable time lag between the filing of a lawsuit and the rendering of a judgment. When any suit is filed that affects title to a specific parcel of real estate (such as a foreclosure suit), a notice known as a *lis pendens* (Latin for "litigation pending") is recorded, or registered. A lis pendens is not a lien, but rather a *notice of a possible future lien.* Recording of the lis pendens gives notice to all interested parties, such as prospective purchasers and lenders, and establishes a priority for the later lien, which is dated back to the date the lis pendens was filed for record.

Estate and Inheritance Tax Liens

Federal **estate taxes** and state **inheritance taxes** (as well as the debts of deceased persons) are *general, statutory, involuntary liens* that encumber a deceased person's real and personal property. These are normally paid or cleared in probate court proceedings. Probate and issues of inheritance will be discussed in Chapter 12, "Transfer of Title."

Vendors' Liens

A **vendor's lien** is a *seller's claim* against the title of property he or she conveyed to a buyer; it occurs in cases where the seller did not receive the full, agreed-upon purchase price. This is a *specific, equitable, involuntary lien* for the amount of the unpaid balance due the seller.

Vendees' Liens

A **vendee's lien** is a *buyer's claim* against a seller's property in cases where the seller failed to deliver title. This usually occurs when property is purchased under an installment contract (contract for deed, agreement of sale), and the seller fails to deliver title after all other terms of the contract have been satisfied. A vendee's lien is a *specific, equitable, involuntary lien* for any money paid plus the value of any improvements made to the property by the buyer.

Liens for Municipal Utilities

Municipalities that furnish water to property owners are generally given the right to a *specific, equitable, involuntary lien* on the property of an owner who refuses to pay bills for water or any other such municipal utility services.

Surety Bail Bond Lien

A real estate owner charged with a crime for which he or she must face trial may choose to put up real estate instead of cash as surety for bail. The execution and recording of such a **surety bail bond** creates a *specific, voluntary lien* against the owner's real estate. This lien is enforceable by the sheriff or other court officer if the accused person does not appear in court as required.

Corporation Franchise Tax Lien

State governments generally levy a **corporation franchise tax** on corporations as a condition of allowing them to do business in the state. Such a tax is a *general, statutory, involuntary* lien on all property, real and personal, owned by the corporation.

IRS Tax Lien

An **Internal Revenue Service (IRS) tax lien** results from a person's failure to pay any portion of his or her federal IRS taxes, such as income and withholding taxes. A federal tax lien is a *general, statutory, involuntary lien* on all real and personal property held by the delinquent taxpayer.

Summary

Liens are claims, or charges, of creditors or tax officials against the real and personal property of a debtor. A lien is a type of encumbrance. All liens are encumbrances, but not all encumbrances are necessarily liens. Liens are either *general,* covering all real and personal property of a debtor-owner, or *specific,* covering only the specific parcel of real estate described in the mortgage, tax bill, or building or repair contract or other document.

With the exception of real estate tax liens and mechanics' liens, the priority of liens is generally determined by the order in which they are placed in the public record of the county in which the debtor's property is located.

Real estate taxes are levied annually by local taxing authorities. Tax liens are generally given priority over other liens. Payments are required before stated dates, after which penalties accrue. An owner may lose title to his or her property for nonpayment of taxes, since such tax-delinquent property can be sold at an annual tax sale. Some states allow a time period during which a defaulted owner can redeem his or her real estate from a tax sale.

Special assessments are levied to allocate the cost of improvements, such as new sidewalks, curbs, or paving, to the real estate that benefits from them. Assessments are usually payable annually over a five- or ten-year period, together with interest due on the balance of the assessment.

Mortgage liens are voluntary, specific liens given to lenders to secure payment for mortgage loans.

Mechanics' liens protect general contractors, subcontractors, and material suppliers whose work enhances the value of real estate.

A *judgment* is a court decree obtained by a creditor, usually for a monetary award from a debtor. The lien of a judgment can be enforced by issuance of a *writ of execution* and sale by the sheriff to pay the judgment amount and costs.

Attachment is a means of preventing a defendant from conveying his or her real estate before completion of a suit in which a judgment is sought.

Lis pendens is a recorded notice of a lawsuit that is awaiting trial in court and may result in a judgment that will affect title to a parcel of real estate.

Federal estate taxes and *state inheritance taxes* are general liens against a deceased owner's property.

Vendors' liens and *vendees' liens* are liens against a specific parcel of real estate. A vendor's lien is a seller's claim against a purchaser who has not paid the entire purchase price, and a vendee's lien is a purchaser's claim against a seller under an installment contract who has not conveyed title.

Liens for *water charges or other municipal utilities* and *surety bail bond liens* are specific liens, while *corporation franchise tax liens* are general liens against a corporation's assets.

Internal Revenue Service tax liens are general liens against the property of a person who is delinquent in payment of IRS taxes.

Questions

1. Which of the following best refers to the type of lien that affects all real and personal property of a debtor?
   a. specific lien
   b. voluntary lien
   c. involuntary lien
   d. general lien

2. General contractor Ralph Hammond was hired to build a room addition to Thom and Harriet Elkin's home. Hammond completed the work several weeks ago, but still has not been paid. In this situation, Hammond is entitled to a mechanic's lien; which of the following is correct concerning his lien?
   a. It is a general lien.
   b. It is a specific lien.
   c. Hammond must file a notice of his lien in the public records.
   d. b and c

3. After real estate has been sold by the state or county to satisfy a delinquent real estate tax lien, the owner usually has a right to:
   a. buy another parcel of land.
   b. remain in possession indefinitely.
   c. redeem the property from sale within the time specified by state law.
   d. have the sale canceled.

4. *Priority of liens* refers to which of the following?
   a. the order in which a debtor assumes responsibility for payment of obligations
   b. the order in which liens will be paid if property is sold by court order to satisfy a debt
   c. the dates liens are filed for record; the lien with the earliest recording date will always take priority over other liens
   d. the fact that specific liens have greater priority than general liens

5. A lien on real estate made to secure payment for specific municipal improvements made to a parcel of real estate is which of the following?
   a. mechanic's lien
   b. special assessment
   c. ad valorem
   d. utility lien

6. When real estate is assessed for tax purposes:
   I. the homeowner may usually appeal the assessment.
   II. an equalization factor may be used.
   a. I only
   b. II only
   c. both I and II
   d. neither I nor II

7. Which of the following municipalities or agencies usually make levies for general real estate taxes?
   I. school districts
   II. counties
   a. I only
   b. II only
   c. both I and II
   d. neither I nor II

8. A specific parcel of real estate has a market value of $80,000 and is assessed for tax purposes at 25 percent of market value. The tax rate for the county in which the property is located is 30 mills. The tax bill will be:
   a. $500.
   b. $550.
   c. $600.
   d. $700.

9. Which of the following taxes is (are) used to distribute the cost of civic services among real estate owners?
   I. personal property tax
   II. inheritance tax
   a. I only
   b. II only
   c. both I and II
   d. neither I nor II

10. A mechanic's lien claim arises when a general contractor has performed work or provided material to improve a parcel of real estate on the owner's order and the work has not been paid for. Such a contractor has a right to:
    a. tear out his or her work.
    b. record a notice of the lien.
    c. record a notice of the lien and file a court suit within the time required by state law.
    d. have personal property of the owner sold to satisfy the lien.

11. Which of the following is (are) considered liens on real estate?
    I. easements running with the land
    II. unpaid mortgage loans
    a. I only
    b. II only
    c. both I and II
    d. neither I nor II

12. A mortgage lien and a judgment lien have which of the following characteristics in common?

    I. Both may involve a debtor-creditor relationship.
    II. Both are general liens.

        a. I only   c. both I and II
        b. II only   d. neither I nor II

13. Which of the following is classified as a general lien?

    a. vendor's lien
    b. surety bail bond lien
    c. debts of a deceased person
    d. general real estate taxes

14. Which of the following liens would usually be given higher priority?

    a. a mortgage dated last year
    b. the current real estate tax
    c. a mechanic's lien for work started before the mortgage was made
    d. a judgment rendered yesterday

15. Which of the following steps is usually required *before* a special assessment becomes a lien against a specific parcel of real estate?

    I. An ordinance is passed.
    II. The improvement is completed.

        a. I only   c. both I and II
        b. II only   d. neither I nor II

16. Special assessment liens:

    a. take priority over all other liens.
    b. are voluntary liens.
    c. are not tax-deductible items.
    d. a and c

17. What is the annual real estate tax on a property that is valued at $135,000 and assessed for tax purposes at $47,250 with an equalization factor of 125 percent, when the tax rate is 25 mills?

    a. $1,417.50   c. $4,050.00
    b. $1,476.56   d. none of the above

18. Which of the following is a voluntary, specific lien?

    a. IRS tax lien   c. mortgage lien
    b. mechanic's lien   d. vendor's lien

19. Donny Prelate sold Ernest Tully a parcel of real estate; title has passed, but to date, Tully has not paid the purchase price in full as originally agreed upon. If Prelate does not receive payment, which of the following would he be entitled to enforce?

    a. attachment   c. lis pendens
    b. vendee's lien   d. vendor's lien

20. General contractor Kim Kelly is suing homeowner Bob Baker for nonpayment for services; suit will be filed in the next few weeks. Recently Kelly learned that the homeowner has listed his property with a local real estate broker for sale. In this instance, which of the following will probably be used by Kelly and her attorneys to protect her interest?

    a. lis pendens   c. vendee's lien
    b. attachment   d. a and b

11

Real Estate Contracts

Key Terms

Agreement in writing
Assignment
Bilateral contract
Breach
Competent parties
Consideration
Contract
Counteroffer
Earnest money
Equitable title
Escrow agreement
Executed contract
Executory contract
Expressed contract
Implied contract

Installment contract
Legality of object
Novation
Offer and acceptance
Option
Real estate sales contract
Specific performance suit
Statute of frauds
Statute of limitations
Unenforceable contract
Unilateral contract
Valid contract
Void contract
Voidable contract

Overview

"Get it in writing," is a phrase commonly used to warn one party to an agreement to protect his or her interests by entering into a written *contract* with the other party, outlining the rights and obligations of both. The real estate business makes use of many different types of contracts, including listing agreements, leases, and sales contracts. Brokers and salespeople must understand the content and uses of such agreements and must be able to explain them to buyers and sellers. This chapter will first deal with the legal principles governing contracts in general, and will then examine the types of contracts used in the real estate business in particular.

Contracts	Brokers and salespeople use many types of contracts and agreements in the course of their business in order to successfully carry out their responsibilities to sellers, buyers, and the general public. Among these are listing agreements, sales contracts, option agreements, installment contracts, leases, and escrow agreements.
	Before studying these specific types of contracts, you must first understand the general body of law that governs the operation of such agreements, known as *contract law.*
Contract Law	A **contract** is a legally enforceable promise or set of promises that must be performed and for which, if a breach of promise occurs, the law provides a remedy. Depending on the situation and the nature or language of the agreement, a contract may be: (1) expressed or implied; (2) unilateral or bilateral; (3) executory or executed; and (4) valid, unenforceable, voidable, or void. These terms are used to describe the type, status, and legal effect of a contract, and are discussed in the sections that follow.
Expressed and Implied Contracts	Depending upon how a contract is created, it may be expressed or implied. In an **expressed contract,** the parties state the terms and show their intentions in words. An expressed contract may be either oral or written. In an **implied contract,** the agreement of the parties is demonstrated by their acts and conduct.
In Practice . . .	*In the usual agency relationship, a listing agreement is an expressed contract between the seller and the broker that names the broker as the fiduciary representative of the seller. However, the courts have held that a broker may, under certain situations, also have an implied contract to represent a buyer. For example, a broker took a listing for a residence and showed it to several potential purchasers, one of whom requested that a physical inspection of the property be made. The broker complied, but mistakenly hired an unqualified person to make the inspection. The interested party bought the property, discovered a serious physical defect, and sued the broker. The court ruled that, although the broker was the agent of the seller, in complying with the buyer's request he had by implication accepted an agency agreement to represent the purchaser. By hiring an inspector who was not competent to do the job, the broker violated his duty to the purchaser under this implied agreement.*
Bilateral and Unilateral Contracts	According to the nature of the agreement made, contracts may also be classified as either bilateral or unilateral. In a **bilateral contract,** both parties promise to do something; one promise is given in exchange for another. A real estate sales contract is a bilateral contract because the seller promises to sell a parcel of real estate and deliver title to the property to the buyer, who promises to pay a certain sum of money for the property. Today, most contracts are interpreted by the courts to be bilateral, that is, an exchange of promises.
	A **unilateral contract** is one-sided agreement whereby one party makes a promise in order to induce a second party to do something. The second party is not legally

obligated to act; however, if the second party does comply, the first party is obligated to keep the promise. An offer of a reward would be an example of a unilateral contract. For example, if a person runs a newspaper ad offering a reward for the return of a lost pet, that person is promising to pay if the act of returning the pet is fulfilled.

Executed and Executory Contracts

A contract may be classified as either executed or executory, depending on whether or not the agreement is completely performed. A fully **executed contract** is one in which both parties have fulfilled their promises and thus performed the contract. An **executory contract** exists when something remains to be done by one or both parties.

Validity of Contracts

A contract can be described as either valid, void, voidable, or unenforceable (see table 11.1), depending on the circumstances.

Table 11.1 Legal Effects of Contracts	Type of Contract	Legal Effect	Example
	Valid	Binding and Enforceable on Both Parties	Agreement Complying with Essentials of a Valid Contract
	Void	No Legal Effect	Contract for an Illegal Purpose
	Voidable	One or Both Parties May Disaffirm	Contract with a Minor (Minor May Disaffirm)
	Unenforceable	Neither Party May Sue to Force Performance	Certain Oral Agreements

A **valid contract** complies with all the essential elements (which will be discussed later in this chapter), and is binding and enforceable on both parties.

A **void contract** is one that has no legal force or effect because it does not meet the essential elements of a contract. For example, one of the essential conditions in order for a contract to be valid is that it be for a legal purpose; thus, a contract to commit a crime is void.

A **voidable contract** is one that seems on the surface to be valid but may be rescinded, or disaffirmed, by the party who might be injured if the contract were to be enforced. (In some cases, this may be both parties.) For example, a contract entered into with a minor is usually voidable; a minor is generally permitted to disaffirm a real estate contract at any time while he or she is under age or within a reasonable time after reaching legal age. A voidable contract will be considered by the courts to be a valid contract if the party who has the option to disaffirm the agreement does not do so within a prescribed period of time.

An **unenforceable contract** has all the elements of a valid contract; however, neither party can sue the other to force performance. For example, in many states an oral listing agreement is unenforceable. In these states a broker taking an oral listing runs the risk of being unable to sue a seller if the broker sells the seller's property but is not paid a commission as promised. Unenforceable contracts are said to be "valid as between the parties," because once the agreement is fully executed and both parties are satisfied, neither would have reason to initiate a lawsuit to force performance.

Elements Essential to a Valid Contract

In general, the essentials of a valid contract include the following:

1. **Offer and acceptance:** This requirement, also called *mutual assent,* means that there must be a "meeting of the minds." Offer and acceptance are technical legal terms. Courts look to the objective intent of the parties to determine if they intended to enter into a binding agreement. The terms of the agreement must be fairly definite and understood by both parties.

2. **Consideration:** Courts will not enforce gratuitous (free) promises. This means that a promise will not be legally enforced against a person making a promise unless the person to whom the promise was made has given up something in exchange for the promise. So, if Bob promises to pay Alice $75,000 for her house, the promise would not be enforceable, since Alice has promised to do nothing in return. However, if Alice promises to tender the deed to her house in exchange for the $75,000, her promise serves as consideration, and Bob's promise would be enforceable against him by Alice. Consideration is something of legal value (usally one party suffering a legal detriment), bargained for and given in exchange for a promise or an act. The phrase "good and valuable consideration" is sometimes used in contracts. This is redundant, however, since any return promise to perform that has been bargained for and exchanged is legally sufficient to satisfy the consideration element. Consideration is a complex legal concept; thus, a complete understanding of it is beyond the scope of this text.

3. **Legally competent parties:** Both parties to the contract must be of legal age and have sufficient mental capacity. In most states, 18 is the age of contrauctal capacity for men and women. A party has sufficient mental capacity if he or she understands the nature and effect of the contract. Mental capacity is not the same as medical sanity.

4. **Legality of object:** To be valid, a contract must not contemplate a purpose that is illegal or against public policy.

Misrepresentation, fraud, undue influence, and duress. To be valid, every contract must be entered into as the free and voluntary act of each party. Misrepresentation, fraud, undue influence, or duress would deprive a person of the ability to enter into a contract freely using reasonable judgment and caution. If these detriments are present, the injured party may void (rescind) the contract. If the uninjured party were to sue for breach, the injured party could use lack of voluntary assent as a defense.

Agreement in writing and signed. Not all contracts need to be in writing to be enforceable. Every state has enacted a statute of frauds which requires certain types of contracts to be in writing. The statute of frauds is designed to prevent fraudulent oral testimony regarding contracts where the possibility and consequences of fictitious evidence are great.

Contracts for the transfer of an interest in land must be in writing to be enforceable. Real estate contracts generally require the signatures of the buyers and sellers and the seller's spouse's signature to release potential marital rights such as dower and homestead. An agent may sign for a principal if he or she has the proper authority, such as a power of attorney. When sellers are co-owners, all co-owners must sign if the entire ownership is being transferred.

Accurate description of the property.   A real estate sales contract must contain an accurate description of the property being conveyed. The test that most courts use is whether the subject property can be identified with reasonable certainty. This may require a legal description, but in many cases a street address is sufficient.

In Practice . . .

If there is any ambiguity in a contract, the courts will generally interpret the agreement against the party who prepared it. For example, a broker is responsible for preparing all listing agreements for his or her firm. If there were any doubt whether a listing agreement was an exclusive agency or an exclusive right to sell, the courts would probably construe it to be an exclusive agency, thus ruling against the broker who was responsible for preparing the document.

Performance of Contract

Under any contract, each party has certain rights and duties to fulfill. The question of when a contract must be performed is an important factor. Many contracts call for a specific time at or by which the agreed-upon acts must be completely performed. In addition, many contracts provide that "time is of the essence." This means that the contract should be performed within the time limit specified, and any party who has not performed on time is probably liable for breach of contract.

When a contract does not specify a date for performance, the acts it requires should be performed within a reasonable time. The interpretation of what constitutes a reasonable time will depend upon the situation. Generally, if the act can be done immediately—such as a payment of money—it should be performed immediately, unless the parties agree otherwise.

Assignment and Novation

Often after a contract has been entered into, one party may want to withdraw without actually terminating the agreement. This may be accomplished through either assignment or novation.

Assignment refers to a transfer of rights and/or duties under a contract. Generally speaking, rights may be assigned to a third party unless the agreement forbids such an assignment. Duties may also be assigned (delegated), but the original obligor remains secondarily liable for them (after the new obligor), unless he or she is specifically released from this responsibility. A contract that requires some personal quality or unique ability of one of the parties may not be assigned. Most contracts include a clause that either permits or forbids assignment.

A contract may also be performed by **novation,** or the substitution of a new contract for an existing agreement with the intent of extinguishing the old contract. The new agreement may be between the same parties, or a new party may be substituted for either (this is *novation of the parties*). The parties' intent must be to discharge the old obligation. The new agreement must be supported by consideration and must conform with all the essential elements of a valid contract. For example, when a real estate purchaser assumes the seller's existing mortgage loan (see Chapter 15), the lender may choose to release the seller and substitute the buyer as the party primarily liable for the mortgage debt.

Discharge of Contract

A contract may be completely performed, with all terms carried out, or it may be breached (broken) if one of the parties defaults. In addition, there are various other methods by which a contract may be discharged (canceled). These include:

1. *Partial performance of the terms along with a written acceptance* by the person for whom acts have not been done or to whom money has not been paid.

2. *Substantial performance,* in which one party has substantially performed the contract but does not complete all the details exactly as the contract requires. Such performance—for example, under construction contracts—may be sufficient to force payment, with certain adjustments for any damages suffered by the other party.

3. *Impossibility of performance,* in which an act required by the contract cannot be legally accomplished.

4. *Mutual agreement* of the parties to cancel.

5. *Operation of law,* as in the voiding of a contract by a minor, or as a result of fraud or the expiration of the statute of limitations, or as a result of a contract being altered without the written consent of all parties involved.

Default—Breach of Contract

A **breach** of contract is a violation of any of the terms or conditions of a contract without legal excuse, such as when a seller breaches a sales contract by not delivering title to the buyer under the conditions stated in the agreement. If either party to a contract intends to breach the contract, or default, the defaulting party assumes certain burdens, and the nondefaulting party has certain rights.

With real estate contracts, if the *seller defaults,* the buyer has three alternatives:

1. The buyer may *rescind, or cancel, the contract* and recover his or her earnest money.
2. The buyer may file a court suit, known as a **suit for specific performance,** to force the seller to perform the contract.
3. The buyer may *sue the seller for compensatory damages* (a personal judgment).

A suit for damages is seldom used in this instance, however, because in most cases the buyer would be able to collect only a minimal amount in damages.

If the *buyer defaults,* the seller may pursue one of the following courses:

1. The seller may *declare the contract forfeited.* The right to forfeit is usually provided in the terms of the contract, and the seller is usually entitled to retain the earnest money and all payments received from the buyer.
2. The seller may *rescind the contract;* that is, he or she may cancel, or terminate, the contract as if it had never been made. This requires the seller to return all payments the buyer has made.
3. The seller may *sue for specific performance.* In some cases this may require the seller to offer, or tender, a valid deed to the buyer to show the seller's compliance with the contract terms.
4. The seller may *sue for compensatory damages.*

Statute of limitations. The law of every state allows a specific time limit during which parties to a contract may bring legal suit to enforce their rights. Any party who does not take steps to enforce his or her rights within this **statute of limitations** may lose them. (Compare this with the principle of *laches,* discussed in Chapter 19).

Contracts Used in the Real Estate Business

As mentioned earlier, the types of written agreements most commonly used by brokers and salespeople are listing agreements, real estate sales contracts, option agreements, contracts for deed, leases, and escrow agreements.

Broker's Authority to Prepare Documents

In many states, specific guidelines have been drawn, either by agreement between lawyer and broker associations, by court decision, or by statute, regarding the authority of real estate licensees to prepare contracts for their clients and customers. As a rule, a licensed real estate broker is not authorized to practice law—that is, to prepare legal documents such as deeds and mortgages. A broker or salesperson may, however, be permitted to fill in the blanks on certain preprinted documents (such as sales contracts and leases) approved by the state bar association and/or real estate commission or association, provided he or she does not charge a separate fee for completing such forms. You should determine the current legal authority of licensed real estate brokers in your state by questioning your state license officials or local real estate board.

Contract forms. *Printed forms* are used for all kinds of contracts because most transactions are basically similar in nature. The use of printed forms raises three problems: (1) what to *fill in the blanks,* (2) what printed matter is not applicable to a particular sale and is to be *ruled out* by drawing lines through the unwanted words, and (3) what additional clauses or agreements (called *riders* or *addendums*) are to be *added.* All changes and additions are usually initialed in the margin or on the rider by both parties when the contract is executed. The newer forms provide more alternative provisions, which may be used or ruled out depending upon what the parties wish to express in their agreement.

In Practice . . .

It is essential that both parties to a contract understand exactly what they are agreeing to. Poorly drafted documents, especially those containing extensive legal language, may be subject to various interpretations and lead to litigation. The parties to a real estate transaction should be advised to have sales contracts and other legal documents examined by their attorneys before signing them, to ensure that such agreements accurately reflect their intentions. Where preprinted forms do not sufficiently cover special provisions in a transaction, the parties should be encouraged to have an attorney draft a sales contract that properly covers such provisions.

Listing Agreements

Listing agreements are *instruments used by the real estate broker in order to represent a principal legally.* They are contracts that establish the rights of the broker as agent and of the buyer or seller as principal. There are many forms of listing agreements: (1) open listing, (2) net listing, (3) exclusive-agency listing, (4) exclusive-right-to-sell listing, and (5) multiple listing. Review the explanations of the types of listing agreements presented in Chapter 6.

Sales Contracts   A **real estate sales contract** sets forth all details of the agreement between a buyer and a seller for the purchase and sale of a parcel of real estate. Depending on the state or locality, this agreement may be known as an *offer to purchase, contract of purchase and sale, earnest money agreement, deposit receipt,* or other variation of these titles. But whatever the contract is called, when it has been prepared and signed by the purchaser it is an offer to purchase the subject real estate. Later, if the document is accepted and signed by the seller, it then becomes, or ripens into, a contract of sale. An example of a real estate sales contract is figure 11.1.

In a few localities, it is customary to prepare a shorter document, known as a *binder,* for the purchaser to sign. This document states the essential terms of the purchaser's offer and acknowledges receipt of his or her deposit. It also provides that the parties agree to have a more formal and complete contract of sale drawn up by an attorney upon the seller's acceptance and signing of the binder. Throughout the country, a binder receipt might be used in any situation where the details of the transaction are too complex for the standard sales contract form.

Every sales contract requires at least two parties, a seller and a buyer. The same person cannot be both buyer and seller, as a person cannot legally contract with him- or herself. The contract of sale is the most important document in the sale of real estate, since it sets out in detail the agreement between the buyer and the seller and establishes their legal rights and obligations. It is more important than the deed itself, because *the contract, in effect, dictates the contents of the deed.*

Details to be included in a real estate sales contract are the price, terms, legal description of the land, kind and condition of the title, form of deed the seller will deliver, kind of title evidence required, who will provide title evidence, and how defects in the title, if any, are to be eliminated. The contract must state all the terms and conditions of the agreement and spell out all contingencies. In situations where a contract is vague in its terms and one party sues the other based on one of these terms, the courts may refuse to make a contract for the parties. The real estate broker must be aware of the responsibilities and legal rights of the parties to a sale and must see that an adequate contract is prepared.

Contracts in writing. Every state has adopted the common-law doctrine known as the **statute of frauds,** which provides that certain oral agreements are not enforceable in a court of law. Thus, no action may be brought on any contract for the sale of real estate unless the contract is in writing and signed by the parties to be bound by the agreement. A written agreement establishes the interest of the purchaser and his or her rights to enforce that interest by court action. It thus prevents the seller from selling the property to another person who might offer a higher price. The signed contract agreement also obligates the buyer to complete the transaction according to the terms agreed upon in the contract.

Offer and acceptance. One of the essential elements of a valid contract of sale is a *meeting of the minds* whereby the buyer and seller agree on the terms of the sale. This is usually accomplished through the process of **offer and acceptance.**

A broker lists an owner's real estate for sale at the price and conditions set by the owner. This is considered to be an invitation for prospective buyers to make offers to buy. A prospective buyer who wants to purchase the property, at those terms or some other terms, is found. A contract of sale is drawn up, signed by the prospective buyer, and presented by the broker to the seller. This is an *offer* to buy. If the

Figure 11.1
Real Estate Sales
Contract

DuPAGE BOARD OF REALTORS
STANDARD RESIDENTIAL SALES CONTRACT

1. BUYER, _Mary L. Barton_

Address _2121 Greenside Avenue, Sheffield_ ; County, _Brown_ ; State _Indiana_ agrees to purchase, and

SELLER, _Steven and Martha Smithson_

Address _647 Briar Lane, Oak Brook_ ; County, _DuPage_ ; State _Illinois_ agrees to sell to Buyer.

at the **PRICE** of _One Hundred Sixty Five Thousand and xx/100---_ Dollars ($ _165,000_)

PROPERTY commonly known as _647 Briar Lane, Oak Brook, Illinois_
and legally described as follows:

(hereinafter referred to as "the premises")
with approximate lot dimension of _70 feet x 160 feet_
together with all improvements and fixtures, if any, including, but not limited to: All central heating, plumbing and electrical systems and equipment; the hot water heater; central cooling, humidifying and filtering equipment; fixed carpeting; built-in kitchen appliances, equipment and cabinets; water softener (except rental units); existing storm and screen windows and doors; attached shutters, shelving systems, fireplace screen; roof or attic T.V. antenna; all planted vegetation; garage door openers and car units; and the following items of personal property:
Refrigerator located in kitchen

All of the foregoing items shall be left on the premises, are included in the sale price, and shall be transferred to the Buyer by a Bill of Sale at the time of closing.

2. THE EARNEST MONEY: Buyer has paid $ _10,000 by check_
(Indicate check and/or note and due date) (and will pay within _five_ days the additional sum of $ _7,000_) as earnest money to be applied on the purchase price. The earnest money shall be held by the Listing Broker for the mutual benefit of the parties concerned and upon the closing of the sale, shall be applied first to the payment of any expenses incurred by broker for the Seller in said matter, and second to payment of the broker's sales commission, rendering the overplus, if any, to the Seller.

3. THE CLOSING DATE: _September 14_ , 19 _85_ (or on the date, if any, to which said date is extended by reason of paragraphs 12 & 6) at _office of seller's attorney_ , or at Buyer's lending institution, if any.

4. POSSESSION: Possession shall be granted to Buyer at closing or as otherwise agreed providing this transaction shall have been closed.

5. THE DEED: Seller shall convey or cause to be conveyed to Buyer (in joint tenancy) or his nominee, by a recordable, stamped general warranty deed with release of homestead rights, good title to the premises subject only to the following "permitted exceptions" if any: (a) General real estate taxes for 19 _85_ and subsequent years; (b) Special Assessments confirmed after this contract date; (c) Building, building line and use or occupancy restrictions, conditions and covenants of record; (d) Zoning laws and Ordinances; (e) Easements for public utilities; (f) Drainage ditches, feeders, laterals and drain tile, pipe or other conduit; (g) If the property is other than detached, single-family homes, party walls, party wall rights and agreements; covenants, conditions and restrictions of record; terms, provisions, covenants, and conditions of the declaration of condominium, if any, and all amendments thereto; any easements established by or implied from the said declaration of condominium or amendments thereto, if any; limitations and conditions imposed by the Illinois Condominium Property Act, if applicable; installments of assessments due after the date of closing and easements established pursuant to the declaration of condominium.

6. FINANCING CONDITION: This Contract is subject to the condition that on or before _____**August 20, 1985**_____ , the Buyer shall secure, or there shall be made available to the Buyer, a written commitment for a loan to be secured by a mortgage or trust deed on the property in the amount of $ **130,000**_____ , or such lesser sum as Buyer accepts, with initial interest not to exceed ____**14**____ % per annum, said loan to be amortized over a period of ____**30**____ years with a loan service charge not to exceed ____**4**____ %, plus any other usual and customary processing fees or closing costs charged or required by the lender where application has been made. (If the loan is to be other than a variable-rate mortgage, fill in the blank space immediately following, stating the type of loan to be acquired: ___**Conventional Fully Amortized Loan**_____) If after the Buyer has submitted a true loan application and otherwise made every reasonable effort to procure a loan commitment from any source made available to him and has been unable to do so, and after serving written notice thereof upon the Seller or his agent within the time specified herein for securing such commitment, then this Contract shall become null and void, and all monies paid by the Buyer hereunder shall be refunded; however, **if Seller, at his option, notifies Buyer within 5 days of Buyer's notice, that Seller intends to procure for Buyer such a commitment within 30 days, then this Contract shall remain in full force and effect.** Buyer shall, at his expense, execute all documents necessary to procure a mortgage loan from any one reasonable source suggested by Seller. IN THE EVENT THE BUYER DOES NOT SERVE NOTICE OF FAILURE TO PROCURE SAID LOAN COMMITMENT UPON SELLER AS HEREIN PROVIDED, THEN THIS CONTRACT SHALL CONTINUE IN FULL FORCE AND EFFECT WITHOUT ANY LOAN CONTINGENCIES. Buyer shall be allowed a reasonable time prior to closing to have a mortgage or trust deed placed of record and to arrange for access to the proceeds thereof, and any delays caused by Buyer's lending institution in ordering a Commitment for Title Insurance required under paragraph 12 hereof shall not constitute a default by the Seller. Seller shall allow reasonable inspection of the premises by the Buyer's lender and furnish any pertinent information requested by lender's representative.

7. SELLER'S REPRESENTATIONS: Seller represents: (a) that he has received no notice of any ordinance or building code violation or pending special assessment from any governmental body in connection with the premises; and (b) that all equipment and appliances to be conveyed, including but not limited to, the following are in operating condition on the date of closing: all mechanical equipment, heating and cooling equipment, water heaters and softeners, septic and plumbing systems, electrical systems, kitchen equipment remaining with the premises, and any miscellaneous mechanical personal property to be transferred to the Buyer. Upon the Buyer's request, Buyer or his representative shall have the right to inspect all said equipment, appliances and systems prior to closing. The Buyer is requested to make a preliminary inspection at least ten (10) days prior to closing and thereafter promptly serve notice to Seller of any deficiencies discovered; which deficiencies Seller shall promptly, and at his expense, remedy. IN THE ABSENCE OF WRITTEN NOTICE OF ANY DEFICIENCY FROM THE BUYER PRIOR TO CLOSING, IT SHALL BE CONCLUDED THAT THE CONDITION OF THE ABOVE EQUIPMENT IS SATISFACTORY TO THE BUYER AND THE SELLER SHALL HAVE NO FURTHER RESPONSIBILITY WITH REFERENCE THERETO.

8. COMMISSION: Seller agrees that ____**Fresh Aire Realty, Inc.**_____ Listing Broker, brought about this sale and agrees to pay them a Broker's commission as agreed.

9. COOPERATING BROKER: _____**Red Arrow Real Estate, Inc.**_____

10. OTHER TERMS AND CONDITIONS: This contract is subject to the Terms and Conditions set forth on the reverse side hereof, which are expressly understood to be a part of this contract.

THE PRINTED MATTER OF THIS CONTRACT HAS BEEN PREPARED UNDER THE SUPERVISION OF THE DUPAGE BOARD OF REALTORS AND THE DUPAGE COUNTY BAR ASSOCIATION. HOWEVER, THE PARTIES ARE CAUTIONED THAT THIS IS A LEGALLY BINDING CONTRACT. IF THE TERMS ARE NOT UNDERSTOOD PLEASE SEEK LEGAL COUNSEL BEFORE SIGNING IT.

Date of Acceptance _____
(The date shall be inserted only after the parties have agreed to all the terms and conditions of this Contract.)

Buyer _____*Mary L. Barton*_____   Seller _____*Steven Smithson*_____

Buyer _____   Seller _____*Martha Smithson*_____

Form #100 Copyright 1959 Rev. 2/82

This form was developed for use by, and is reproduced with the permission of, the DuPage Board of Realtors®.

seller agrees to the offer *exactly as it was made* and signs the contract, the offer has been *accepted* and the contract is *valid.* The broker must then advise the buyer of the seller's acceptance, or, preferably, deliver a signed copy of the contract to the buyer.

Any attempt by the seller to change the terms proposed by the buyer creates a **counteroffer.** The buyer is relieved of his or her original offer because the seller has, in effect, rejected it. The buyer can accept the seller's counteroffer or can reject it and, if he or she wishes, make another counteroffer. Any change in the last offer made results in a counteroffer, until one party finally agrees to the other party's last offer and both parties sign the final contract (see figure 11.2).

Figure 11.2
Offer and Acceptance

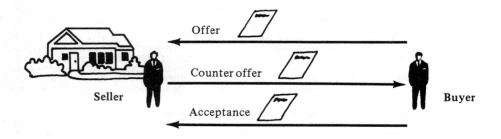

An offer or counteroffer *may be withdrawn at any time before it has been accepted* (even if the person making the offer or counteroffer agreed to keep the offer open for a set period of time). In addition, an offer is not considered to be accepted until the person making the offer has been *notified of the other party's acceptance.* When the parties are communicating through an agent or at a distance, questions may arise regarding whether an acceptance, rejection, or counteroffer has effectively taken place. The real estate broker or salesperson should transmit all offers, acceptances, or other responses as soon as possible in order to avoid such problems.

Equitable title. When a buyer signs a contract to purchase real estate, he or she does not receive title to the land; only a deed can actually convey title. However, after both buyer and seller have executed a sales contract, the buyer acquires an interest in the land known as **equitable title.** Acquisition of equitable title may give the buyer an insurable interest in the property. If the parties decide not to go through with the purchase and sale, the buyer may be required to give the seller a quitclaim deed to release the buyer's equitable interest in the land. (Quitclaim deeds will be discussed in Chapter 12, "Transfer of Title.")

Destruction of premises. In many states, once the sales contract is signed by both parties and unless the contract provides otherwise, the buyer must bear the loss of any damage to or destruction of the property by fire or other casualty. Through laws and court decisions, however, a growing number of states have placed the risk of any loss that occurs before the deed is delivered on the seller. Quite a few of these states have adopted the *Uniform Vendor and Purchaser Risk Act,* which specifically provides that the seller (vendor) bears any loss that occurs before the title passes or the buyer (vendee) takes possession. In any case, the seller may be made to assume the risk of loss when he or she has been negligent, is unable to deliver good title, or has delayed the closing of the transaction.

Earnest money deposits. It is customary for a purchaser to put down a cash deposit when making an offer to purchase real estate. This cash deposit, commonly referred to as **earnest money,** *generally gives evidence of the purchaser's intention to carry out the terms of the contract.* This deposit is paid to the broker, and the sales contract typically provides that the broker will hold the deposit for the parties.

The amount of the deposit is a matter to be agreed upon by the parties. Under the terms of most listing agreements, a real estate broker is required to accept a reasonable amount as earnest money. Generally, the deposit should be sufficient to discourage the buyer from defaulting, compensate the seller for taking the property off the market, and cover any expenses the seller and broker might incur if the buyer defaults. Most contracts provide that the deposit (less any previously agreed-upon commission that may be owed the broker) becomes the seller's property if the buyer defaults.

Under the laws of most states, earnest money must be held by a broker in a special *trust,* or *escrow, account.* This money cannot be *commingled,* or mixed, with a broker's personal funds. (However, in many states a broker is permitted to place a minimal amount of his or her own money into the trust account in order to keep it open.) Likewise, a broker may not use such funds for his or her own personal use; this illegal act is known as *conversion.* A broker need not open a special escrow account for each earnest money deposit received: one such account into which all such funds are deposited is sufficient. A broker should maintain full, complete, and accurate records of all earnest money deposits. State license laws usually have strict provisions covering these deposits.

There is some uncertainty as to exactly who owns the earnest money once it is put on deposit. Until the offer is officially accepted, the money is, in a sense, the buyer's. Once the seller accepts the offer, however, the buyer may not demand the money, even though the seller is not entitled to it until the transaction has been completed. Under no circumstances does the money belong to the broker, who must maintain it in his or her trust account. This uncertain nature of earnest money deposits makes it absolutely necessary that such funds be properly protected pending a final decision on their disbursement.

Parts of a sales contract. All real estate sales contracts can be divided into a number of general parts. Although each form of contract will contain these divisions, their location in the contract may vary. Study the sample contract in figure 11.1 to determine the exact terms of the agreement. This contract is divided into the following main sections:

1. Identification of the buyer and the buyer's statement, or obligation.
2. Legal description of the property involved.
3. Identification of the seller and statement of the type of deed the seller agrees to give, including the conditions and provisions (interests of others) to which the deed will be made subject; this is sometimes known as the "subject to" section of the contract.

4. Financial statement of the purchase price and how the purchaser intends to pay for the property, including provision for an earnest money deposit and the conditions of any mortgage financing the purchaser intends to obtain.
5. Provisions for the closing and the purchaser's possession of the property.
6. Provisions for title evidence.
7. Provisions for prorations, which are adjustments for taxes, insurance, fuel, and the like.
8. Provisions in the event of destruction or damage to premises.
9. Provisions of default.
10. Provisions for contingencies
11. Miscellaneous provisions.
12. Dates and signatures.

Option Agreements

An **option** is a *contract by which an* optionor *(generally an owner) gives an* optionee *(a prospective purchaser or lessee) the right to buy or lease the owner's property at a fixed price within a stated period of time.* The optionee pays a fee (the agreed-upon consideration) for this option right and assumes no obligation to make any other payment until deciding, within the specified time, either to: (1) exercise his or her option right (to buy or lease the property), or (2) allow the option right to expire.

For example, for a consideration of a specified amount of money, a present owner (optionor) agrees to give an optionee an irrevocable right to buy his or her real estate at a certain price for a limited period of time. At the time the option is signed by the parties, the owner does not sell, nor does the optionee buy. They merely agree that the optionee will have the right to buy and the owner will be obligated to sell *if* the optionee decides to exercise his or her right of option.

The option agreement requires the optionor to act only after the optionee gives notice that he or she elects to execute the option and buy. If the option is not exercised within the time specified, then the optionor's obligation and the optionee's right will expire. The optionee cannot recover the consideration paid for the option right. However, the owner could, if he or she wished, agree to apply the money paid for the option on the purchase price of the real estate.

A common application of an option is a lease that includes an option for the tenant to purchase the property. Options on commercial real estate are frequently made dependent upon the fulfillment of specific conditions, such as the obtaining of a zoning change or a building permit. The optionee is usually obligated to exercise his or her option if the conditions are met. Similar terms could also be included in a sales contract.

Installment Contracts (Contracts for Deed)

A real estate sale can be made under an **installment contract,** sometimes called a *contract for deed, land contract of sale,* or *articles of agreement for warranty deed.* In other words, the real estate is sold under contract. Basically, an installment contract is a means of financing a buyer's purchase of land whereby *the seller receives a nominal down payment and regular periodic payments (usually monthly) over a number of years,* in accordance with the contract terms. An example of an installment contract is figure 11.3.

Under an installment contract, the seller, also known as the *vendor,* retains fee ownership while the buyer, known as the *vendee,* secures possession and an equitable interest in the property. The buyer agrees to give the seller a down payment and pay regular monthly installments of principal and interest over a number of years. The buyer also agrees to pay real estate taxes, insurance premiums, repairs, and upkeep on the property. While the buyer obtains possession when the contract is signed by both parties, *the seller is not obligated to execute and deliver a deed to the buyer until the terms of the contract have been satisfied.* Under most installment contracts, the buyer is entitled to a deed as soon as he or she is able to complete the terms of the contract.

Real estate is occasionally sold with the new buyer assuming an existing installment contract from the original buyer/vendee. Generally, when a buyer assumes an existing contract, the original buyer/vendee must assign or convey his or her interest to the new buyer, and the original seller/vendor must approve the new purchaser.

Default—termination of contract. Installment contracts usually include a provision that a default by the buyer permits the seller to forfeit the contract, retain all payments already made, and evict the buyer. In some states, however, laws have been enacted that require the seller to refund to the buyer any payments received in excess of a reasonable rental or use value of the property. In other states, a defaulted installment contract must be foreclosed in the same manner as a mortgage.

Leases

A lease is a contract in which the owner agrees to give possession of all or a part of the real estate to another person in exchange for a rental fee. Leases are discussed in detail in Chapter 16.

Escrow Agreements

An escrow is *a means by which the parties to a contract carry out the terms of their agreement.* The parties appoint a disinterested third party to act as the *escrowee,* or *escrow agent.* This escrow agent must be someone who is not a party to the contract and will not benefit in any way from the contract.

Any real estate transaction can be closed through an escrow. The parties to the transaction enter into an **escrow agreement** (usually a separate agreement from the contract) that sets forth the duties of the escrow agent and the obligations and requirements of the parties to the transaction. An escrow agreement may be used in closing such real estate transactions as a sale, mortgage loan, exchange of property, installment contract (contract for deed), or lease.

An escrow agreement requires the seller to deposit with the escrow agent the deed and other pertinent documents, such as leases, insurance policies, and a mortgage payment letter, if the existing mortgage is to be paid in full and released of record. It also provides for the buyer to deposit the purchase price and an executed mortgage and note if he or she is securing mortgage funds to purchase the property. The escrow agent is authorized to have the title examined, and if it is found to meet the conditions of the escrow agreement, the sale is concluded. Title then passes to the buyer, and the seller receives payment. The escrow procedure will be more fully detailed in Chapter 23, "Real Estate Closing."

Local Forms

To gain familiarity with the forms used in your area, go to brokers or real estate companies in your area and ask if they will give (or sell) you copies of the sales contract, listing agreement, and other forms they use. Usually such forms can also

Figure 11.3
Real Estate
Installment Contract

REAL ESTATE CONTRACT—MONTHLY PAYMENTS   NO. 127   **GEORGE E. COLE®**
Improved Property, Cook County.   **September, 1975**   **LEGAL FORMS**

THIS AGREEMENT, made this __5th.__ day of __October__ 19__85__, between_____
__Donald Hollinger__ of the __City of Chicago__
County of Cook and the State of Illinois, Seller, and__Celia Watson__
of the__City of Chicago_____County of Cook and State of Illinois, Purchaser: Witnesseth, that,
if Purchaser shall first make the payments and perform the covenants hereinafter mentioned on the part of
Purchaser to be made and performed Seller hereby covenants and agrees to convey or cause to be conveyed
to Purchaser, in fee simple, clear of all encumbrances whatever, except as herein stated, by a good and suf-
ficient_____recordable Warranty Deed, with release of dower and homestead rights, good title
to the real estate situated in the County of Cook and State of Illinois, known and described as follows:

Lot 4, Block 7 of the City Subdivision, Township 5 North, Range Three East
of the Third Principal Meridian, also known as 257 Windsor, Chicago, Ill.

subject to zoning and building laws or ordinances, building, building line, and use or occupancy restrictions,
conditions and covenants of record, and party wall rights or agreements, if any, roads, highways, streets and
alleys, if any, and to general taxes for the year__1985_____and subsequent years, and to any unpaid installments of special assessments or special taxes which fall due after this date and to a mortgage securing an unpaid principal balance of $_____, which Purchaser hereby assumes and agrees to pay as a part of
the purchase price hereof.

    And in addition to paying the mortgage above mentioned, Purchaser hereby covenants and agrees to
pay to Seller at the office of __City Title and Trust, 230 North La Salle, Chicago__
_____or at such place as Seller may from time to time, in writing, designate and appoint, the
sum of__$89,500_____DOLLARS,
with interest at__14_____per centum per annum, payable monthly, as follows: $__15,000__
cash, receipt of which is hereby acknowledged, $__15,000_____on __November 1__
and $__855.55__on the__1st._____day of each month thereafter until said sum and said
interest are fully paid; said monthly installments to be applied first on interest on the principal sum remaining
from time to time unpaid, and the remainder on principal. As soon as Purchaser has paid said purchase
price down to the amount of the unpaid balance payable on account of the mortgage at that time on said
premises, Seller shall convey said premises to Purchaser subject to said mortgage, to the matters and things
hereinabove referred to, and to

Purchaser further agrees to pay general taxes for the year___1985___and subsequent years, and all special assessments or special taxes and installments thereof falling due after this date, heretofore or here-after levied or imposed upon said real estate, when they become due and payable and to exhibit the tax or assessment receipts to Seller.

Purchaser further agrees to keep said premises fully insured in companies acceptable to Seller and de-posit the policies with Seller or with the holder of said mortgage. And upon the expiration of any policy or policies on said premises Seller shall have the right as the agent of Purchaser to place new insurance on said premises for such period not exceeding five years as Seller may elect.

Purchaser further agrees to keep the buildings on said premises in good repair and neither to suffer nor commit any waste on or to said premises, and if Purchaser fails to keep said premises in repair then Seller may, if he so elects, cause said premises to be put in repair and Purchaser agrees immediately to pay for the cost thereof.

And if Purchaser fails to pay taxes, assessments, insurance or any other items which, under the terms of this agreement it is the obligation of Purchaser to pay, then Seller may, if he so elects, pay the same and the amount thereof shall become so much additional purchase price and immediately due and payable to Sell-er in addition to said monthly payments and shall bear interest at eight per centum per annum until paid.

And if Purchaser fails to make any of the payments, or any part thereof, or fails to perform any of the covenants on the part of Purchaser hereby made and entered into, (a) this contract shall, at the option of Seller, be forfeited and determined, and Purchaser shall forfeit all payments made on this contract, and such pay-ments shall be retained by Seller in full satisfaction and in liquidation of all damages sustained, and Seller shall have the right to re-enter and take possession of the premises aforesaid; and written notice of such forfeiture filed in the office of the recorder of deeds of Cook County, Illinois shall be sufficient evidence of such for-feiture; or (b) all of the deferred payments hereunder shall, at the option of Seller, become immediately due and payable.

Evidence of title has been submitted to and approved by Purchaser and on delivery of a deed hereunder shall become the property of Purchaser, subject to the rights of mortgage holders.

Seller warrants to Purchaser that no notice from any city, village or other governmental authority of a dwelling code violation which existed in the dwelling structure before the execution of this contract has been received by the Seller, his principal or his agent within 10 years of the date of execution of this con-tract.

Time is of the essence of this contract. The covenants and agreements herein contained shall extend to and be obligatory upon the heirs, executors, administrators and assigns of the respective parties.

IN WITNESS WHEREOF, the parties have hereunto set their hands and seals, the day and year first above written.

SIGNED AND DELIVERED IN PRESENCE OF _____(SEAL)

Donald Hollinger   *Donald Hollinger*   (SEAL)

Celia Watson   *Celia Watson*   (SEAL)

be obtained at a title or abstract company and some banks and savings and loan associations, or they may be purchased at your local office supply and stationery stores. *Study the forms and compare them to the real estate sales contract printed in this chapter.*

Summary

A *contract* is defined as a legally enforceable promise or set of promises that must be performed and, if a breach occurs, for which the law provides a remedy.

Contracts may be classified according to whether the parties' intentions are *expressed* or are *implied* by their actions. They may also be classified as *bilateral,* when both parties have obligated themselves to act, or *unilateral,* when one party is obligated to perform only if the other party acts. In addition, contracts may be classified according to their legal enforceability as either *valid, void, voidable,* or *unenforceable.*

Many contracts specify a time for performance. In any case, all contracts must be performed within a reasonable time. An *executed* contract is one that has been fully performed. An *executory* contract is one in which some act remains to be performed.

The *essentials of a valid contract* are: (1) offer and acceptance; (2) consideration; (3) legally competent parties; and (4) legality of object. A valid *real estate contract* must include a description of the property, and it should be in writing and signed by both parties.

In a number of circumstances, a contract may be canceled before it is fully performed. Furthermore, in many types of contracts, either of the parties may transfer his or her rights and obligations under the agreement by *assignment* of the contract or *novation* (substitution of a new contract).

If either party to a real estate sales contract defaults, several alternative actions are available. Contracts usually provide that the seller has the right to declare a sale canceled through forfeiture if the buyer defaults. In general, if either party has suffered a loss because of the other's default, he or she may sue for damages to cover the loss. If one party insists on completing the transaction, he or she may sue the defaulter for *specific performance* of the terms of the contract; in this way, a court can order the other parties to comply with the agreement.

Contracts frequently used in the real estate business include listings, sales contracts, options, installment contracts (contracts for deed), leases, and escrow agreements.

A *real estate sales contract* binds a buyer and a seller to a definite transaction, as described in detail in the contract. The buyer is bound to purchase the property for the amount stated in the agreement. The seller is bound to deliver a good and marketable title, free from liens and encumbrances (except those allowed by the "subject to" clause of the contract).

Under an *option* agreement, the optionee purchases from the optionor, for a limited time period, the exclusive right to purchase or lease the optionor's property. For a potential purchaser or lessee, an option is a means of buying time to consider or complete arrangements for a transaction. An *installment contract,* or *contract for deed,* is a sales/financing agreement under which a buyer purchases a seller's real estate on time. The buyer may take possession of and responsibility for the property but does not receive the deed until the terms of the contract are complete.

Any real estate transaction may be completed through an *escrow,* a means by which the parties to a contract carry out the terms of their agreement. The parties appoint a third party to act as the *escrowee,* or *escrow agent.* In the sale of real estate, the seller's deed and the buyer's money are deposited with an escrow agent under an escrow agreement that sets forth the conditions to be met before the sale will be consummated. The escrow agent records the deed, and when the title conditions and any other requirements of the escrow agreement have been met, the title passes and the sale is completed.

Questions

1. A contract is said to be *bilateral* if:
   a. one of the parties is a minor.
   b. the contract has yet to be fully performed.
   c. only one party to the agreement is bound to act.
   d. all parties to the contract are bound to act.

2. Timothy Smith makes an offer to purchase certain property listed with Olaf Real Estate and leaves a deposit with broker Janice Olaf. Regarding this deposit, Olaf should:
   a. hold on to it until the sales contract is signed.
   b. deposit it in a trust account.
   c. give it to the seller along with the offer.
   d. deposit it in her checking account.

3. A contract for the sale of real estate that does not state the consideration to be paid for the property and is not signed by the parties is considered to be:
   I. voidable.
   II. executory.
   a. I only   c. both I and II
   b. II only   d. neither I nor II

4. A real estate purchaser is said to have *equitable title:*
   I. when the sales contract is signed by both buyer and seller.
   II. when the transaction goes through escrow.
   a. I only   c. both I and II
   b. II only   d. neither I nor II

5. A seller gave an open listing to several brokers, specifically promising that if one of the brokers found a buyer for the seller's real estate, the seller would then be obligated to pay a commission to that broker. This offer by the seller is a(n):
   a. executed agreement.
   b. discharged agreement.
   c. implied agreement.
   d. unilateral agreement.

6. In the completion of a printed form of sales contract, several words were crossed out and others inserted. In order to eliminate future controversy as to whether the changes were made before or after the contract was signed, the broker should:
   a. write a letter to each party listing the changes.
   b. have each party write a letter to the other approving the changes.
   c. redraw the entire contract.
   d. have both parties initial or sign on the margin near each change.

7. The essential elements of a valid real estate contract include:
   I. duress.
   II. the signatures of the parties involved.
   a. I only   c. both I and II
   b. II only   d. neither I nor II

8. If, after the sales contract is signed, the seller decides not to sell:
   I. the seller may cancel the contract and retain the buyer's earnest money deposit.
   II. the buyer may institute a suit for specific performance of the contract or for money damages.
   a. I only   c. both I and II
   b. II only   d. neither I nor II

9. Under the statute of frauds of every state, all contracts for the sale of real estate must be in writing. The principal reason for this statute is to:
   a. prevent the buyer from defrauding the seller.
   b. protect the broker.
   c. prevent fraudulent proof of a fictitious oral contract.
   d. protect the buyer from the broker.

10. During the period of time after a real estate sales contract is signed but before title actually passes, the status of the contract is:
    a. voidable.   c. executed.
    b. executory.   d. implied.

11. Which of the following is *not* one of the elements essential to a valid contract?

    a. offer and acceptance
    b. duress
    c. legality of object
    d. consideration

12. A party may withdraw from the terms of a contract through which of the following legal concepts?

    I. assignment
    II. novation

    a. I only   c. both I and II
    b. II only   d. neither I nor II

13. The earnest money deposit:

    I. is made by the buyer upon signing the sales contract and evidences his or her intention to carry out the contract terms.
    II. is generally held by the seller under the terms of the typical real estate sales contract.

    a. I only   c. both I and II
    b. II only   d. neither I nor II

14. Which one of the following best describes a land installment contract, or contract for deed?

    a. a contract to buy land only
    b. a mortgage on land
    c. a means of conveying title immediately while the purchaser pays for the property in installments
    d. a method of selling real estate whereby the purchaser pays for the property in regular installments while the seller retains title to the property

15. When a real estate sales transaction is to be closed in escrow:

    a. the seller and escrow agent execute a separate escrow agreement.
    b. the buyer's purchase money, mortgage, and mortgage note are deposited with the escrow agent.
    c. a person who is a party to the contract is usually appointed as the escrow agent.
    d. the escrow agreement sets forth only the obligations of the escrow agent.

16. Which of the following provisions covers the kind and condition of the seller's title and may be found under the "subject to" part of the sales contract?

    I. ". . . agree to buy at the price of sixty-five thousand dollars. . . ."
    II. "General taxes for the current year are to be prorated from January 1 to the date of closing."

    a. I only   c. both I and II
    b. II only   d. neither I nor II

17. A contract may be discharged by which of the following means?

    a. impossibility of performance
    b. operation of law
    c. agreement of the parties
    d. all of the above

18. When a real estate broker or salesperson completes a real estate sales contract, he or she should be careful to include all pertinent information in the document because:

    I. it establishes the legal rights and obligations of buyer and seller.
    II. it establishes what the contents of the deed of conveyance will be.

    a. I only   c. both I and II
    b. II only   d. neither I nor II

19. Broker Sam Manella has found a buyer for Joe Taylor's home. The buyer has entered into a real estate sales contract for the property for $1,000 less than the asking price and has deposited $5,000 earnest money with broker Manella. Taylor is out of town for the weekend and Manella has been unable to inform him of the signed agreement. At this point, the real estate sales contract is a(n):

    a. voidable contract.
    b. offer.
    c. executory agreement.
    d. implied contract.

20. If, in question 19, seller Taylor does not agree to the terms of the real estate sales contract as presented to him by broker Manella, he may:

    I. refuse to sign it and ask that Manella return the buyer's earnest money.
    II. present the buyer with a counteroffer.

    a. I only   c. both I and II
    b. II only   d. neither I nor II

21. Caz Krys is selling his home to Burton Timmins. After the sales contract has been signed by both parties, but before the title has passed to the buyer, the home is destroyed in a fire. Generally, who must bear the loss?

    I. Caz Krys, the seller
    II. Burton Timmins, the buyer

    a. I only   c. both I and II
    b. II only   d. neither I nor II

22. When a broker uses a client's earnest money deposit for his or her own personal use, the broker is guilty of:

    I. commingling.
    II. conversion.

    a. I only   c. both I and II
    b. II only   d. neither I nor II

23. An option agreement:

    I. is generally limited to a specified time period.
    II. must recite a set amount of consideration for purchase of the property.

    a. I only   c. both I and II
    b. II only   d. neither I nor II

24. The purchaser of real estate under an installment contract:

    a. generally pays no interest charge.
    b. is called a vendor.
    c. is not required to pay property taxes for the duration of the contract.
    d. is called a vendee.

25. By local law or court decision, who is usually authorized to draft deeds and other legal contracts?

    a. a licensed real estate broker
    b. an attorney licensed to practice law
    c. a licensed real estate salesperson
    d. all of the above

Transfer of Title

Key Terms

Adverse possession
Bargain and sale deed
Deed
Deed in trust
Delivery and acceptance
Descent
Escheat
Grantee
Granting clause
Grantor
Habendum clause
Heir
Intestate

Involuntary alienation
Last will and testament
Probate
Quitclaim deed
Special warranty deed
"Subject to" clause
Testate
Testator
Title
Transfer tax
Trustee's deed
Voluntary alienation
Warranty deed

Overview

A parcel of real estate may be transferred from one owner to another in a number of different ways. It may be given *voluntarily,* such as by sale or gift, or it may be taken *involuntarily,* by operation of law. In addition, it may be transferred by the living, or it may be transferred by will or descent after a person has died. In every instance, however, a transfer of title to a parcel of real estate is a complex legal procedure involving a number of laws and documents. This chapter will discuss the four methods of title transfer, as well as the various legal documents of conveyance that the real estate broker or salesperson must be familiar with.

Title

Title to real estate means the right to or ownership of the land; in addition, it represents the *evidence* of ownership. So the term *title* has two functions: it represents the "bundle of rights" the owner possesses in the real estate, and it also denotes the facts that, if proven, would enable a person to recover or retain ownership or possession of a parcel of real estate.

Titles are either *original* or *derivative*. Original title to real property can be vested only in the state, and is usually obtained through discovery, occupancy, conquest, or cession to the state. All other titles are derivative and are vested in individuals (or corporations, partnerships, and the like).

The laws of each state govern real estate transactions for land located within its boundaries. Each state has the authority to pass legislative acts that affect the methods of transferring title or other interests in real estate. Title to real estate may be transferred in most states by the following methods: (1) voluntary alienation; (2) involuntary alienation; (3) will; and (4) descent.

Voluntary Alienation

Voluntary alienation (transfer) of title may be made by either gift or sale. To transfer title by voluntary alienation during his or her lifetime, an owner must use some form of deed of conveyance.

A **deed** is a *written instrument by which an owner of real estate intentionally conveys to a purchaser his or her right, title, or interest in a parcel of real estate.* All deeds must be in writing in accordance with the requirements of the statute of frauds. The owner (who sells or gives the land) is referred to as the **grantor,** and the purchaser (who acquires the title) is called the **grantee.** A deed is executed (or signed) by the grantor.

Requirements for a Valid Conveyance

Although the formal requirements for a valid deed are not uniform in all states, certain requirements are basic (see figure 12.1). These are:

1. a *grantor* having the legal capacity to execute (sign) the deed.
2. a *grantee* named with reasonable certainty, so that he or she can be identified.
3. a recital of *consideration.*
4. a *granting clause* (words of conveyance).
5. a habendum clause (to define ownership taken by the grantee).
6. designation of any *limitations* on the conveyance of a full fee simple estate.
7. an accurate *legal description* of the property conveyed.
8. *exceptions and reservations* affecting the title **("subject to" clause).**
9. the *signature of the grantor,* sometimes with a seal.
10. *delivery* of the deed and *acceptance* by the grantee to pass title.

Grantor. A grantor must have a legal existence, be of lawful age, and be legally competent in order to convey title to real estate. The laws of the state where the real estate is located will control the precise legal requirements to convey title. However, rules governing contracts (discussed in Chapter 11) usually apply to determine if a grantor is competent to convey real property.

Figure 12.1
Elements of a Valid
Conveyance

```
┌─────────────────────────────────────┐
│                DEED                  │
│   1. Grantor                         │
│   2. Grantee                         │
│   3. Consideration                   │
│   4. Granting Clause                 │
│   5. Habendum Clause                 │
│   6. Limitations                     │
│   7. Legal Description               │
│   8. Exceptions and Reservations     │
│   9. Grantor's Signature             │
│  10. Delivery and Acceptance         │
└─────────────────────────────────────┘
```

A grantor must be of sound mind and of lawful age, generally at least 18 years old. As is the case with most documents, a deed executed by an *infant* (one who has not reached majority) is considered to be *voidable,* not void. Generally, the rule is that an infant can disaffirm, or repudiate, his or her conveyance of real estate after reaching majority, at which time he or she has a reasonable period in which to disaffirm. What constitutes a reasonable time varies with the particular case.

A grantor is generally held to have sufficient mental capacity to execute a deed if he or she is capable of understanding the action. A deed executed by a person considered to be mentally incompetent is only *voidable*—it is not void. However, in some states, a deed executed by a person who has been judged legally incompetent is considered to be void. In such instances, court authority must be secured before real estate owned by a legally incompetent person can be conveyed.

In most states, the grantor's spouse is required to join in and sign any deed of conveyance in order to waive any marital and/or homestead rights. This varies according to state law and the manner in which the title to real estate is held by the conveying parties, as discussed in Chapters 7 and 8.

It is important that a grantor's name be spelled correctly and that there be no variation in its spelling throughout the deed. If for any reason a grantor's name has been changed from that by which title was originally acquired, he or she must show both names. It is customary for such a grantor to be described as, for example, "John Smith, now known as John White." It is best for a grantor to first state the name under which the title was acquired and then indicate his or her current name.

When title to property has been acquired under a woman's unmarried name and she subsequently marries, the conveyance must show both names. In many states her spouse, if living, must join in the deed to release marital and/or homestead rights.

Grantee. To be valid, a deed must name a grantee and do so in such a way that he or she is readily identifiable. A deed naming as the grantee a wholly fictitious person, a company that does not legally exist, or a society or club that is not properly incorporated is considered void.

Consideration. In order to be valid, all deeds must contain a clause acknowledging the grantor's receipt of a consideration. In most states, the amount of consideration must be stated in dollars. When a deed conveys real estate as a gift to a relative, "love and affection" may be sufficient consideration. However, in deeds conveying property as a gift, it is customary in most states to recite a *nominal* consideration, such as "$10.00 and other good and valuable consideration." The full dollar amount of consideration is seldom set forth in the deed, except when the instrument is executed by a corporation or trustee, or pursuant to court order.

Granting clause (words of conveyance). A deed of conveyance transfers a present interest in real estate. Therefore, it must contain words of grant that state the grantor's intention to convey the property at this time; an expression of intent to convey at some future time is inadequate. Such words of grant, or conveyance, are contained in the **granting clause.** Depending on the type of deed and the obligations agreed to by the grantor, the wording is generally either "convey and warrant," "grant," "grant, bargain, and sell," or "remise, release, and quit-claim."

If more than one grantee is involved, the granting clause should cover the creation of their specific rights in the property. The clause might state, for example, that the grantees will take title as joint tenants or tenants in common. The wording is especially important in states where specific wording is necessary to create a joint tenancy.

The granting clause should also indicate what interest in the property is being conveyed by the grantor. Deeds that convey the entire fee simple interest of the grantor usually contain such wordings as "to Jacqueline Smith and to her heirs and assigns forever." If the grantor is conveying less than his or her complete interest, such as a life estate to property, the wording must indicate this limitation on the grantee's interest. For example, a deed creating a life estate would convey property "to Jacqueline Smith for the duration of her natural life."

Habendum clause. When it is necessary to define or explain the ownership to be enjoyed by the grantee, a **habendum clause** follows the granting clause. The habendum clause begins with the words "to have and to hold." Its provisions must agree with those set down in the granting clause. When there is a discrepancy between the two clauses, the provisions in the granting clause are usually followed.

Description of real estate. For a deed to be valid, it must contain an accurate description of the real estate conveyed. Land is considered adequately described if a competent surveyor can locate the property from the description used. The rules relative to describing real estate were discussed in Chapter 9.

Exceptions and reservations ("subject to" clauses). As mentioned in the discussion of warranties, a deed should specifically note any encumbrances, reservations, or limitations that affect the title being conveyed. Such exceptions to clear title may include mortgage liens, taxes, restrictions, and easements that run with the land. For example, a deed may grant title to a grantee "subject to general real estate taxes for the year 1982 and subsequent years."

In addition to existing encumbrances, a grantor may reserve some right in the land for his or her own use (an easement, for instance). A grantor may also place certain restrictions on a grantee's use of the property. For example, a developer may restrict the number of houses that may be built on a one-acre lot in a subdivision. A deed must clearly indicate such restrictions. They may be stated in the deed or contained in a previously recorded document (such as the subdivider's master deed) that is expressly cited in the deed. Many of these deed restrictions have time limits, often including renewal clauses.

Signature of grantor. To be valid, a deed must be signed by *all grantors* named in the deed. As discussed previously, when a grantor's spouse has been named as a grantor in order to release marital or other rights, the spouse also must sign the deed. This requirement will vary according to state law and the manner in which title is held by the conveying parties. In some states there must be witnesses to the grantor's signature, but this requirement is not uniform from state to state.

Most states permit a grantor's signature to be signed by an attorney-in-fact acting under a power of attorney. An *attorney-in-fact* is any person who has been given power of attorney (specific written authority) to execute and sign legal instruments for a grantor. In such cases, it is usually necessary for an authorizing document known as a *power of attorney* to be recorded in the county where the property is located. Since the power of attorney terminates upon the death of the person granting such authority, adequate evidence must be submitted that the grantor was alive at the time the attorney-in-fact signed the deed.

A grantor who is unable to write is permitted to sign his or her name by *mark* in most states. With this type of signature, two persons other than the notary public taking the acknowledgment usually must witness the grantor's execution of the deed and sign as witnesses.

In some states, it is still necessary for a seal or the word *seal* to be written or printed after an individual grantor's signature. The use of a corporate seal by corporations is always required.

Acknowledgment. An acknowledgment is a form of declaration made voluntarily by a person who is signing a formal, written document before a notary public or authorized public officer. This acknowledgment usually states that the person signing the deed or other document is known to the officer or has produced sufficient identification and that the person signing is doing so as his or her own *free and voluntary act.* The acknowledgment provides evidence that the signature is genuine.

Usually an acknowledgment is made before a *notary public;* however, it can also be taken by a judge, justice of the peace, or commanding officer in the military, as prescribed by state law. The form of a *certificate of acknowledgment* varies from state to state. The certificate form authorized by the state where the property is located should be used even if the party signing is a resident of another ("foreign") state. In other words, the laws of the state where the land is located govern the procedure.

Although it is customary to acknowledge the execution of a deed to real estate, such acknowledgment is not essential to the *validity* of the deed unless state statutes require it. However, in some states, an unacknowledged instrument is not admissible as evidence in court without proof of the genuineness of the signature. The acknowledgment is accepted as such proof.

From a purely practical point of view, a deed that is not acknowledged is not a satisfactory instrument. In some states, an unacknowledged deed is not eligible for recording (see Chapter 13). And although an unrecorded deed is valid between the grantor and the grantee, it is often not a valid conveyance against subsequent innocent purchasers. For this reason a grantee would not, in effect, secure good title to the property. To help assure good title, a grantee should always require acknowledgment of the grantor's signature on a deed.

Delivery and acceptance. Before a transfer of title by conveyance can take effect, there must be an actual **delivery** of the deed by the grantor and either actual or implied **acceptance** by the grantee. Delivery may be made by the grantor to the grantee personally or to a third party, commonly known as an *escrowee,* for ultimate delivery to the grantee upon the completion of certain requirements. *Title is said to pass when a deed is delivered.* The effective date of the transfer of title from the grantor and to the grantee is the date of delivery of the deed itself. When a deed is delivered in escrow, the date of delivery of the conveyance is generally ("relates back" to) the date that it was deposited with the escrow agent. (However, when the real estate is registered under the Torrens system, as discussed in Chapter 13, title does not pass until the deed has been examined and accepted for registration.)

Delivery is a very technical aspect of the validity of a deed and is usually strictly construed by the courts. Brokers should consult legal counsel with questions regarding delivery.

Execution of Corporate Deeds

Under the law, a corporation is considered to be a legal entity. The laws affecting corporations' rights to convey real estate vary from state to state. Some basic rules must be followed:

1. A corporation can convey real estate only by authority granted in its *bylaws* or upon a proper resolution passed by its *board of directors.* If all or a substantial portion of a corporation's real estate is being conveyed, it is usually required that a resolution authorizing the sale be secured from the *stockholders.*

2. Deeds to real estate can be *signed only by an authorized officer,* and in most states the officer's signature is required.

3. The corporate *seal* must be affixed to the conveyance.

Rules pertaining to religious corporations and not-for-profit corporations vary widely. Since the legal requirements must be followed explicitly, it is advisable to consult an attorney for all corporate conveyances.

Types of Deeds

There are several forms of deeds. The most common are:

1. warranty deed.
2. special warranty deed.
3. quitclaim deed.
4. deed of bargain and sale.
5. deed in trust.
6. trustee's deed.
7. deed executed pursuant to a court order.

There are other instruments that affect title to property but do not convey title. These include *mortgages* and *trust deeds (deeds of trust)*. These documents are not intended to convey title but are financing instruments that establish real estate as security for the payment of a debt. A complete discussion of these instruments can be found in Chapter 15, "Real Estate Financing."

Warranty deeds. For a purchaser of real estate, a **warranty deed** (shown in figure 12.2) provides the *greatest protection* of any deed. It is referred to as a warranty deed or general warranty deed because the grantor is legally bound by certain covenants or warranties. In most states, the warranties are usually implied by the use of certain words specified in the state statutes. Each state law should be examined, but some of the specific words include: "convey and warrant," "warrant generally," and, in some states, "grant, bargain, and sell." In some localities, the grantor's warranties are expressly written into the deed itself. The basic warranties are:

1. *Covenant of seisin:* The grantor warrants that he or she is the owner of the property and has the right to convey title to it. The grantee may recover damages up to the full purchase price if this covenant is broken.

2. *Covenant against encumbrances:* The grantor warrants that the property is free from any liens or encumbrances except those specifically stated in the deed. Encumbrances would generally include such items as mortgages, mechanics' liens, and easements. If this covenant is breached, the grantee may sue for expenses to remove the encumbrance.

3. *Covenant of quiet enjoyment:* The grantor guarantees that the grantee's title is good against third parties who might bring court actions to establish superior title to the property. If the grantee's title is found to be inferior, the grantor is liable for damages.

4. *Covenant of further assurance:* The grantor promises to obtain and deliver any instrument needed in order to make the title good. For example, if the grantor's spouse has failed to sign away dower rights, the grantor must deliver a quitclaim deed executed by the spouse to clear the title.

5. *Covenant of warranty forever:* The grantor guarantees that if at any time in the future the title fails, he or she will compensate the grantee for the loss sustained.

These covenants in a general warranty deed are not limited to matters that occurred during the time the grantor owned the property; they extend back to its origins. (The differences among a warranty deed, a bargain and sale deed, and a quitclaim deed are illustrated in figure 12.3.)

Special warranty deeds. A conveyance that carries only one covenant is a **special warranty deed.** The grantor warrants *only* that the property was not encumbered during the time he or she held title except as noted in the deed. Special warranty deeds generally contain the words "remise, release, alienate, and convey" in the granting clause. Any additional warranties to be included must be specifically stated in the deed. The full consideration for the property is also stated in the deed.

A special warranty deed is usually used by fiduciaries, such as trustees, executors, and corporations, and sometimes by grantors who have acquired title at tax sales. It is based on the theory that a fiduciary or corporation has no authority to warrant against acts of its predecessors in title. Such unauthorized warranties by a

Figure 12.2
Warranty Deed

GEORGE E. COLE·
LEGAL FORMS

NO. 808
April, 1980

WARRANTY DEED
Statutory (ILLINOIS)
(Individual to Individual)

CAUTION: Consult a lawyer before using or acting under this form.
All warranties, including merchantability and fitness, are excluded.

THE GRANTOR

Walter J. Anderson, a widower

of the __Village__ of __Rockvale__ County of __Cook__
State of __Illinois__ for and in consideration of

__Ten and xx/100----------------__ DOLLARS,
_____ in hand paid,

CONVEY s__ and WARRANT s__ to
Brian L. Johnson and Susan R. Johnson of
303 W. Maple, Rolling Hills, Wisconsin,
as joint tenants to have and to hold
(NAME AND ADDRESS OF GRANTEE)

(The Above Space For Recorder's Use Only)

the following described Real Estate situated in the County of __Cook__ in the
State of Illinois, to wit:

Lot 47 and the South half of Lot 48 in Block 5 in the Sunset Subdivision,
a subdivision in the West 1/2 of the East 1/2 of Section 8, Township 23
North, Range 12 East of the Third Principal Meridian, in Cook County,
Illinois.

Subject to: General real estate taxes for 1985 and subsequent years
including special assessments (if any); building, use,
and occupancy restrictions, conditions, and covenants of
record; zoning laws and public and private easements
of record.

hereby releasing and waiving all rights under and by virtue of the Homestead Exemption Laws of the State of
Illinois.

DATED this __24th__ day of __March__ 19__85__

PLEASE
PRINT OR
TYPE NAME(S)
BELOW
SIGNATURE(S)

Walter J. Anderson (SEAL) _____ (SEAL)
Walter J. Anderson

_____ (SEAL) _____ (SEAL)

State of Illinois, County of _____ ss. I, the undersigned, a Notary Public in and for
said County, in the State aforesaid, DO HEREBY CERTIFY that

IMPRESS
SEAL
HERE

personally known to me to be the same person ___ whose name _____ subscribed
to the foregoing instrument, appeared before me this day in person, and acknowledged that ___h___ signed, sealed and delivered the said instrument as _____
free and voluntary act, for the uses and purposes therein set forth, including the
release and waiver of the right of homestead.

Given under my hand and official seal, this _____ day of _____ 19___

Commission expires _____ 19___ _____
NOTARY PUBLIC

This instrument was prepared by _____
(NAME AND ADDRESS)

MAIL TO:
(Name)
(Address)
(City, State and Zip)

OR   RECORDER'S OFFICE BOX NO. _____

ADDRESS OF PROPERTY:
_____
_____
THE ABOVE ADDRESS IS FOR STATISTICAL PURPOSES
ONLY AND IS NOT A PART OF THIS DEED.
SEND SUBSEQUENT TAX BILLS TO:
_____
(Name)
_____
(Address)

Figure 12.3
Types of Deeds

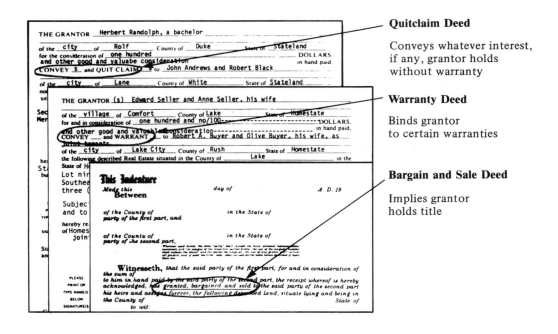

Quitclaim Deed

Conveys whatever interest, if any, grantor holds without warranty

Warranty Deed

Binds grantor to certain warranties

Bargain and Sale Deed

Implies grantor holds title

corporation are considered to be beyond the scope and authority of the corporate powers and are referred to as *ultra vires.* Fiduciaries may hold title for a limited time without having a personal interest in the proceeds.

Bargain and sale deeds. Deeds using the words "grant and release" or "grant, bargain, and sell" in the granting clause are usually **bargain and sale deeds.** A bargain and sale deed contains no real warranties against encumbrances; however, it does *imply* that the grantor holds title and possession of the property. Because the warranty is not specifically stated, the grantee has little legal recourse if defects later appear in the title. In some areas, a covenant against encumbrances initiated by the grantor may be added to a standard bargain and sale deed to create a *bargain and sale deed with covenant against the grantor's acts.* This deed is roughly equivalent to a special warranty deed. In other areas, warranties used in general warranty deeds may be inserted into a bargain and sale deed to give the grantee similar protection.

Quitclaim deeds. A **quitclaim deed** provides the grantee with the least protection of any deed. It carries no covenant or warranties and, in most states, usually conveys only such interest, if any, that the grantor may have when the deed is delivered. By a quitclaim deed, the grantor only "remises, releases, and quitclaims" his or her interest in the property to the grantee. In most states, a quitclaim deed is the only type of deed that may be used to convey less than a fee simple title. For example, it might convey an easement or it might reconvey equitable title back to a seller.

In some states, a quitclaim deed does not necessarily convey property: rather, it conveys only the grantor's right, title, or interest, whatever that may be. Thus, if the grantor has no interest in the property, the grantee will acquire nothing by virtue of the quitclaim deed, nor will he or she acquire any right of warranty claim against the grantor. A quitclaim deed can convey title as effectively as a warranty deed if the grantor has good title when he or she delivers the deed, but it provides none of the guarantees that a warranty deed does.

A quitclaim deed is frequently used to cure a defect, called a "cloud on the title," in the recorded history of a real estate title. For example, if the name of the grantee is misspelled on a warranty deed placed in the public record, a quitclaim deed with the correct spelling may be executed to the grantee in order to perfect the title. When a deed is to be used for the special purpose of clearing a cloud on the title or releasing an interest in property of which the grantor never had possession, caution should be used in selecting the form of the deed. A grantor who "grants and releases" will probably be bound by a covenant of possession, but if the grantor "releases and quitclaims all interest, if any," then the quitclaim deed will pass, without warranty, any title the grantor may have.

A quitclaim deed is also used when a grantor allegedly has *inherited* property but is not certain of the validity of the title of the decedent from whom the property was inherited. The use of a warranty deed in such an instance could carry with it obligations of warranty, while a quitclaim deed would convey only the grantor's interest.

Deeds in trust. To convey real estate to a trustee, usually in order to establish a land trust, a **deed in trust** is used. Under the terms of such an instrument, full powers to sell, mortgage, subdivide, and the like are granted to the trustee. The trustee's use of these powers, however, is controlled by the beneficiary under the provisions of the trust agreement (see Chapter 8).

Trustee's deed. A deed of conveyance executed by a trustee is a **trustee's deed.** It is usually used when a trustee named in a will, agreement, or deed in trust sells or conveys the trust real estate's title out of the trust. The trustee's deed sets forth the fact that the trustee executes the instrument in accordance with the powers and authority granted to him or her by the trust instrument or the deed in trust.

Deeds executed pursuant to court order. This classification covers such deed forms as executors' deeds, masters' deeds, administrators' deeds, sheriffs' deeds, and many others. These statutory deed forms are used to convey title to property that is transferred by court order or by will. The forms of such deeds must conform to the laws of the state where the property is located.

One characteristic of such instruments is that the *full consideration* is usually stated in the deed. This is done because the deed is executed pursuant to a court order, and since the court has authorized the sale of the property for a given amount of consideration, this amount should be *exactly* stated in the document.

Transfer Tax Stamps

Most states have enacted laws providing for a tax on conveyances of real estate, usually referred to as the state **transfer tax.** In these states, the tax is usually payable when the deed is recorded, through the purchase of *stamps* from the county recorder of the county in which the deed is recorded. The stamps are then affixed to deeds and conveyances before the document can be recorded.

The transfer tax is usually paid by the seller. A *tax rate* of 50 or 55 cents for each $500 or fraction thereof of taxable consideration is common in many states. Often, when real estate is transferred subject to the unpaid balance of an existing mortgage that was made by the seller before the time of transfer and that is being assumed by the buyer, the amount of the assumed mortgage may be deducted from the full consideration to determine the taxable consideration. However, *this is not true in all states.*

In many states, a *transfer declaration form* must be signed by both the buyer and the seller or their agents. This form usually requires such information as the full sales price of the property; the legal description of the property; the address, date, and type of deed; and the type of improvement. If the transfer is between relatives or is a compulsory transaction in accordance with a court order, this must also be specified in the transfer declaration form.

Certain deeds may be *exempted* from the tax, such as gifts of real estate; deeds not made in connection with a sale (such as a change of joint tenants); conveyances to or from or between governmental bodies; deeds by charitable, religious, or educational institutions; deeds securing debts or releasing property as security for a debt; partitions; tax deeds; deeds pursuant to mergers of corporations; and deeds from subsidiary to parent corporations for cancellation of stock.

See your state supplement for *Modern Real Estate Practice* or check with local officials to determine the conditions and cost of the transfer tax in your area.

Involuntary Alienation	Title to property can be transferred by **involuntary alienation;** that is, without the owner's consent (see figure 12.4). Such transfers are usually carried out by operations of law ranging from government condemnation of land for public use to the sale of property to satisfy delinquent tax or mortgage liens. When a person dies intestate and leaves no heirs, the title to his or her real estate passes to the state by operation of law based on the principle of **escheat.**

Federal, state, and local governments, school boards, some government agencies, and certain public and quasi-public corporations and utilities (railroads and gas and electric companies) have the power of *eminent domain.* Under this power, private property may be taken for public use through a *suit for condemnation.* The exercise of eminent domain is subject to a court's determination of three necessary conditions: (1) that the use is for the benefit of the public; (2) that an equitable amount of compensation, as set by the court, will be paid to the owner; and (3) that the rights of the property owner will be protected by due process of law.

Land may also be transferred without an owner's consent in order to satisfy debts contracted by the owner. In such cases the debt is foreclosed, the property is sold, and the proceeds of the sale are applied to pay off the debt. Debts that could be foreclosed include mortgage loans, real estate taxes, mechanics' liens, or general judgments against the property owner. (See Chapters 10 and 15.)

In addition to the involuntary transfer of land by legal processes, land may be transferred by natural forces. As discussed in Chapter 7, owners of land bordering on rivers, lakes, and other bodies of water may acquire additional land through the process of *accretion,* the slow accumulation of soil, rock, or other matter deposited by the movement of water on an owner's property. The opposite of accretion is *erosion,* the gradual wearing away of land by the action of water and wind.

Figure 12.4
Involuntary
Alienation

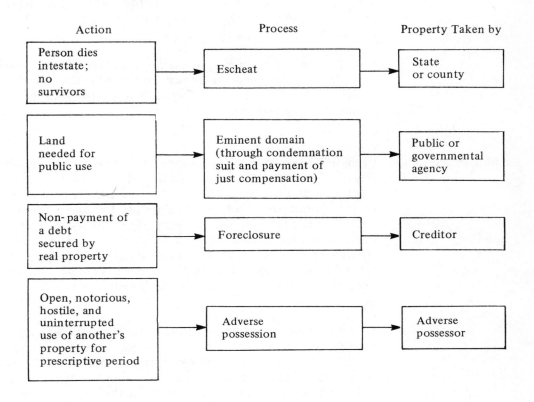

	Action	Process	Property Taken by
	Person dies intestate; no survivors	Escheat	State or county
	Land needed for public use	Eminent domain (through condemnation suit and payment of just compensation)	Public or governmental agency
	Non-payment of a debt secured by real property	Foreclosure	Creditor
	Open, notorious, hostile, and uninterrupted use of another's property for prescriptive period	Adverse possession	Adverse possessor

In addition, property may be lost through *avulsion,* the sudden tearing away of land by such natural means as earthquakes or tidal waves.

Adverse possession is another means of involuntary transfer. An owner who does not use his or her land or does not inspect it for a number of years may lose title to another person who has some claim to the land, takes possession, and, most importantly, uses the land. Usually the possession of the claimant must be open, notorious, hostile, and uninterrupted for the number of years set by state law (as long as 20 years in some states). Through the principal of *tacking*, successive periods of adverse possession can be combined by successive adverse possessors, thus enabling a person who is not in possession for the entire required time to establish a claim of adverse possession.

Through adverse possession, the law recognizes that the use of land is an important function of its ownership. In many cases, an adverse user's rights may supersede those of a fee owner. The subject of adverse possession is extremely technical because the right is statutory, and state requirements must be carefully followed in order to establish ownership. A claimant who does not receive title may acquire an easement by prescription (see Chapter 7). When a transaction involves the possibility of title by adverse possession, the parties should seek legal counsel.

Transfer of a Deceased Person's Property	Every state has a law known as the *statute of descent and distribution.* When a person dies **intestate** (without having left a will), the decedent's real estate and personal property pass to his or her heirs according to this statute. In effect, the state makes a will for such decedents. In contrast, a person who dies **testate** has prepared a will indicating the way that person's property will be disposed after his or her death.

Legally, when a person dies, title to his or her real estate immediately passes either to the heirs by descent or to the persons named in the will. However, before the heirs can take possession of the property, the estate must be probated, and all claims against it must be satisfied. |
| **Probate Proceedings** | **Probate** is a legal process by which a court determines who will inherit the property of a deceased person and what the assets of the estate are. Probate court proceedings must take place in the county where the real estate in question is located. In the case of a person who has died testate, the court also rules on the validity of the will. If the will is upheld, the property is distributed according to its provisions. If a person has died without a will, the court determines who inherits by reviewing a *proof of heirship.* This statement, usually prepared by an attorney, gives personal information regarding the decedent's spouse, children, and relatives. From this document the court decides which parties will receive what portion of the estate.

To initiate probate proceedings, the custodian of the will, an heir, or another interested party must petition the court. The court then holds a hearing to determine the validity of the will and/or the order of descent, should no valid will exist. If for any reason a will is declared invalid by the court, any property owned by the decedent will pass by the laws of descent. Once the heirs are established, the court will appoint an administrator to oversee the administration and distribution of the estate (usually the executor named in the will). Probate proceedings vary from state to state, and local procedures must be followed.

The court gives the administrator or executor the authority to appraise the assets of the estate and satisfy all debts that were owed by the decedent. He or she is also responsible for paying federal estate taxes and, in most states, state inheritance taxes. Once all these liens against the property have been satisfied, the executor distributes the remaining assets of the estate according to the provisions of the will or the state law of descent. |
| **In Practice ...** | *A broker entering into a listing agreement with the executor or administrator of an estate in probate should be aware that the amount of commission will be fixed by the court and that such commission is payable only from the proceeds of the sale. The broker will not be able to collect a commission unless the court approves the sale.* |
| **Transfer of Title by Will** | A **last will and testament** is an instrument made by an owner to voluntarily convey title to the owner's property after his or her death. A will takes effect only after the death of the decedent; until that time, any property covered by the will can be conveyed by the owner and thus removed from the owner's estate. |

A person who has died and left a will is said to have died *testate*. A party who makes a will is known as a **testator,** the gift of real property by will is known as a *devise,* and a person who receives property by will is known as a *devisee.* In addition, a gift of personal property is known as a *legacy* or *bequest;* the person receiving the personal property is known as a *legatee.*

The privilege of disposing of property by will is statutory. So to be effective, a will must conform to all the statutory requirements of the state in which the real estate is located. In addition, a will cannot supersede the state laws of dower and curtesy, which were enacted to protect the inheritance rights of the surviving spouse. In a case where a will does not provide the minimum statutory inheritance, the surviving spouse has the option of informing the court that he or she will take the minimum statutory share rather than the lesser share provided in the will. This practice, called *renouncing the will,* is a right reserved only to a surviving spouse. In states with community property laws, a surviving spouse automatically owns one-half of the couple's community property acquired during the marriage. Therefore, no statutory inheritance rights are necessary to protect the surviving spouse's interest in the community property.

A will differs from a deed in that a deed conveys a present interest in real estate during the lifetime of the grantor, while a will conveys no interest in the property until after the death of the testator. To be valid, a deed *must* be delivered during the lifetime of the grantor. The parties named in a will have no rights or interests as long as the party who has made the will is still alive; they acquire interest or title only after the owner's death. State laws usually require that upon the death of a testator, his or her will must be filed with the court and *probated* in order for title to pass to the devisees.

Legal requirements for making a will. The legal capacity to make a will varies widely from state to state (see figure 12.5). Usually, a person must be of *legal age* and of *sound mind* when he or she executes the will. There are no rigid tests to determine the capacity to make a will. Usually, the courts hold that, to make a valid will, the testator must have sufficient mental capacity to understand the nature and extent of his or her property, the identity of natural heirs, and that execution of the will means that at his death his property goes to those named in the will. The courts also hold that the drawing of a will must be a voluntary act, free of any undue influence by other people.

**Figure 12.5
Requirements for a
Valid Will**

```
                    WILL

        1. Legal Age
        2. Sound Mind
        3. Proper Wording
        4. No Undue Influence
        5. Witnesses
```

Because a will must be valid and admitted to probate in order to convey title to real estate effectively, it must be executed and prepared in accordance with the laws of the state where the real estate is located. In most states, a written will must be signed by its testator before two or more witnesses, who must also sign the document. Usually the witnesses should not be people who are named as devisees in the will.

The testator may modify his or her will. A modification or amendment of, or addition to, a previously executed will is called a *codicil*.

Certain states do not permit the use of holographic and/or nuncupative wills to convey title to property. A *holographic will* is one that is in the testator's handwriting but is not witnessed or acknowledged. A *nuncupative will* is one that is given orally by a testator and put into writing by witnesses.

Transfer of Title by Descent

By law, the title to real estate and personal property of a person who dies intestate passes to his or her heirs. Under the **descent** statutes, the primary **heirs** of the deceased are his or her spouse and close blood relatives, such as children, parents, brothers, sisters, aunts, uncles, and, in some cases, first and second cousins. The closeness of the relationship to the decedent determines the specific rights of the heirs. As previously discussed, the relative's right to inherit must be established by proof of heirship during the probate process.

The right to inherit under descent laws varies from state to state, and intestate property is distributed according to the laws of the state in which the property is located. When a husband dies leaving a wife and one child, the wife and child usually take the entire estate between them, some states dividing it equally and some allowing one-third to the surviving spouse. If, however, a wife and two or more children survive, it is customary for the wife to take one-third and the children to divide the remaining two-thirds equally among them. If a wife but no children or descendants of the children exists, some state laws give the wife one-half of the estate and divide the other half equally among collateral heirs, such as parents and brothers and sisters of the decedent; in other states the wife receives all the property.

When children have been legally adopted, most states consider them to be heirs of the adopting parents but not heirs of ancestors of the adopting parents.

In most states, illegitimate children inherit from the mother but do not inherit from the father unless he has admitted parentage in writing or parentage has been established legally. Of course if he legally adopts such a child, that child will inherit as an adopted child.

Summary

Title to real estate is the right to and evidence of ownership of the land. It may be transferred in four ways: (1) voluntary alienation, (2) involuntary alienation, (3) will, and (4) descent.

The voluntary transfer of an owner's title is made by a *deed,* executed (signed) by the owner as *grantor* to the purchaser or donee as *grantee.* The form and execution of a deed must comply with the statutory requirements of the state in which the land is located.

Among the most common of these requirements are: a grantor with legal capacity to contract, a readily identifiable grantee, a granting clause, a legal description of the property, a recital of consideration, exceptions and reservations on the title ("subject to" clause), and the signature of the grantor, properly witnessed if necessary. In addition, the deed should be acknowledged before a notary public or other officer in order to provide evidence that the signature is genuine and to allow recording. If required by state law, deeds are subject to state transfer taxes when they are recorded. Title to the property passes when the grantor delivers a deed to the grantee and it is accepted.

The obligation of a grantor is determined by the form of the deed; that is, whether it is a general warranty deed, special warranty deed, bargain and sale deed, or quitclaim deed. The words of conveyance in the granting clause are important in determining the form of deed.

A *general warranty deed* provides the greatest protection of any deed by binding the grantor to certain convenants or warranties. A *special warranty deed* warrants only that the real estate is not encumbered except as stated in the deed. A *bargain and sale deed* carries with it no warranties, but implies that the grantor holds title to the property. A *quitclaim deed* carries with it no warranties whatsoever, and conveys only the interest, *if any,* the grantor possesses in the property.

An owner's title may be transferred without his or her permission by a court action, such as a *foreclosure* or judgment sale, a tax sale, *condemnation* under the right of eminent domain, *adverse possession,* or *escheat.* Land may be also transferred by the natural forces of water and wind, which either increase property by *accretion* or decrease it through *erosion* or *avulsion.*

The real estate of an owner who makes a valid *will* (who dies testate) passes to the devisees through the probating of the will. The title of an owner who dies without a will (intestate) passes according to the provisions of the *law of descent* of the state in which the real estate is located.

Questions

1. Title to real estate may be transferred during a person's lifetime by which of the following means?

    a. voluntary alienation
    b. descent
    c. involuntary alienation
    d. a and c

2. Who is required to sign a deed in order to make it valid?

    I. grantor
    II. grantee

        a. I only   c. both I and II
        b. II only   d. neither I nor II

3. Harry Hughes, age 15, recently inherited many parcels of real estate from his late father and has decided to sell one of them in order to pay inheritance taxes. If Hughes entered into a deed conveying his interest in the property to a purchaser without the signature of his legal guardian, such a conveyance would be:

    a. valid.   c. invalid.
    b. void.   d. voidable.

4. The various deeds of conveyance an owner of real estate may use to voluntarily transfer his or her right, title, or interest in real estate include:

    I. sheriffs' deeds.
    II. warranty deeds.

        a. I only   c. both I and II
        b. II only   d. neither I nor II

5. Title to an owner's real estate can be transferred at the death of owner by which one of the following documents?

    a. warranty deed
    b. special warranty deed
    c. trustee's deed
    d. last will and testament

6. The determination of the type of deed used in conveying title can be made by examining:

    a. the grantor's name.
    b. the grantee's name.
    c. the granting clause.
    d. the acknowledgment.

7. Matilda Fairbanks bought acreage in a distant county, never went to see the acreage, and did not use the ground. Harold Sampson moved his mobile home onto the land, had a water well drilled, and lived there for many years. Sampson may become the owner of the land if he has complied with the state law regarding:

    I. requirements for a valid conveyance.
    II. adverse possession.

        a. I only   c. both I and II
        b. II only   d. neither I nor II

8. All deeds should be:

    I. recorded.
    II. signed by the grantee.

        a. I only   c. both I and II
        b. II only   d. neither I nor II

9. Alvin Rosewell executes a deed to Sylvia Plat as grantee, has it acknowledged, and receives payment from the buyer. Rosewell holds the deed, however, and arranges to meet Plat the next morning at the courthouse to deliver the deed to her. In this situation at this time:

    a. Plat owns the property since she has paid for it.
    b. title to the property will not officially pass until Plat has been given the deed the next morning.
    c. title to the property will not pass until Plat has received the deed and recorded it the next morning.
    d. Plat will own the property when she has signed the deed the next morning.

10. Claude Johnson, a bachelor, died owning real estate that he devised by his will to his niece, Annette. In essence, at what point does title pass to his niece?

    a. immediately upon Johnson's death
    b. after his will has been probated
    c. after Annette has paid all inheritance taxes
    d. when Annette executes a new deed to the property

11. A person who pays for and receives a quitclaim deed:

    I. will receive whatever title the grantor possessed in the property.
    II. can force the grantor to make the title good by a suit in court.
       a. I only   c. both I and II
       b. II only   d. neither I nor II

12. Which of the following types of deeds most usually recites the full, actual consideration paid for the property?

    a. warranty deed
    b. trustee's deed
    c. deed in trust
    d. deed executed pursuant to court order

13. A grantor in a special warranty deed is bound by which of the following warranties?

    I. warranty of quiet enjoyment
    II. warranty against encumbrances
       a. I only   c. both I and II
       b. II only   d. neither I nor II

14. The basic requirements for a valid conveyance are governed by:

    I. state law.
    II. local custom.
       a. I only   c. both I and II
       b. II only   d. neither I nor II

15. An owner of real estate who was adjudged legally incompetent made a will during his stay at a nursing home. He later died and was survived by a wife and three children. His real estate will pass:

    a. to his wife.
    b. to the heirs mentioned in his will.
    c. according to the state law of descent.
    d. to the state.

16. A warranty deed usually obligates the grantor to the covenants of:

    a. seisin.
    b. quiet enjoyment.
    c. escheat.
    d. a and b

17. Which of the following types of deeds merely implies but does not specifically warrant that the grantor holds good title to the property?

    a. special warranty deed
    b. bargain and sale deed
    c. quitclaim deed
    d. trustee's deed

18. Local transfer taxes on real estate conveyances are usually paid:

    I. by the grantee.
    II. to the state real estate commission.
       a. I only   c. both I and II
       b. II only   d. neither I nor II

19. Entrepreneur Harley Wilcox is purchasing a large apartment building in a choice urban location. For financial and professional reasons, Wilcox wants to hold the property as beneficiary under a land trust. Which of the following instruments would be used to create this trust?

    a. trust deed   c. trustee's deed
    b. deed in trust   d. a or c

20. Which of the following is not one of the manners in which title to real estate may be transferred by involuntary alienation?

    a. eminent domain   c. erosion
    b. escheat   d. seisin

21. A person who has died leaving a valid will is called a(n):

    a. devisee.   c. legatee.
    b. testator.   d. intestate.

22. The statute or act that creates the need for a deed to be in writing is:

    I. the law of descent and distribution.
    II. in effect in all states.
       a. I only   c. both I and II
       b. II only   d. neither I nor II

23. Which of the following best describes the covenant of quiet enjoyment?

   a. The grantor promises to obtain and deliver any instrument needed to make the title good.
   b. The grantor guarantees that if the title fails in the future, he or she will compensate the grantee.
   c. The grantor warrants that he or she is the owner and has the right to convey title to it.
   d. The grantor assures that the title is good against the title claims of third parties.

24. Which of the following instruments would *not* be given to convey title to property?

   I. executor's deed
   II. trust deed

   a. I only   c. both I and II
   b. II only   d. neither I nor II

25. An instrument authorizing one person to act for another is called a(n):

   a. power of attorney.
   b. release deed.
   c. deed in trust.
   d. acknowledgment.

13

Title Records

Key Terms   Abstract of title
Actual notice
Attorney's opinion of title
Bulk transfer
Certificate of title
Chain of title
Constructive notice
Evidence of title
Financing statement
Marketable title
Priority
Recording
Security agreement
Subrogation
Suit to quiet title
Title insurance
Torrens system
Uniform Commercial Code

Overview   For the protection of real estate owners, taxing bodies, creditors, and the general public, public records are maintained in every city, county, parish, or borough in the United States. Such records help to establish official ownership, give notice of encumbrances, and establish priority of liens. The placing of documents in the public record is known as **recording.** This chapter will discuss the necessity for recording and the various types of title evidence that may be determined by an examination of the public records.

Public Records and Recording

In all states, public records are maintained by designated officials as required by the state's laws. These include records maintained by the recorder of deeds, county clerk, county treasurer, city clerk and collector, and clerks of various courts of record. Records involving taxes, special assessments, ordinances, and zoning and building records also fall into this category.

The principle expressed by the original statute of frauds has long been enacted into all state laws, so no transfer of real estate should be enforceable unless it is in writing. Written instruments are required for all transfers of title or interest, whether by deed, mortgage, or lease.

In addition to the statute of frauds, which requires that instruments affecting interests in real estate must be in writing, many state legislatures have also passed laws that require owners or parties interested in real estate to record, or file, in the public records all documents affecting their interest in real estate in order to give *legal, public, and constructive notice* to the world of their interest. These statutory enactments are commonly referred to as *recording acts.*

Necessity for Recording

Before an individual purchases a fee simple estate to a parcel of real estate, he or she wants to be sure that the seller will be able to convey a good title to the property. The present owner of the real estate undoubtedly purchased his or her interest from a previous owner, so the same question of *kind and condition* of title has been inquired into many times in the past. As long as taxes are paid and liens do not become delinquent, it is expected that a fee simple title will remain a marketable title.

All states have laws that provide that a *deed or mortgage may not be effective as far as later purchasers* are concerned unless such documents have been *recorded.* Thus the public records should reveal the condition of the title, and a purchaser should be able to rely on a search of such public records.

Recording Acts

Under the recording acts, in order to give constructive notice (discussed in the next section of this chapter), all instruments in writing affecting any estate, right, title, or interest in land *must be recorded in the county where the land is located.* The purpose of this requirement is to give to everyone interested in the title to a parcel of property notice of the various interests of all other parties. From a practical point of view, the recording acts give legal **priority** to those interests that are recorded first.

To be *eligible for recording,* an instrument must be drawn and executed in conformity with the provisions of the recording statutes of the state in which the real estate is located. The prerequisites for recording are not uniform. For example, many states require that the names be typed below the signatures on a document and that the instrument be acknowledged before a notary public or other officer.

In a few states, the instrument must also be witnessed. A number of states require that the name of the attorney who prepared the document must also appear on it.

Notice

Through the legal maxim of *caveat emptor,* the courts charge a prospective real estate buyer or mortgagee (lender) with the responsibility of inspecting the property and searching the public records to ascertain the interests of other parties. **Constructive notice** is a presumption of law that charges a buyer with the responsibility of learning this information. The information is available; therefore the buyer or lender is responsible for learning it. Failure to do so is no defense for not knowing of a right or interest, since the recording of that interest in the public records or possession of the real estate gives notice to the world, or constructive notice, of an individual's rights in the property.

Constructive notice, or what a buyer is charged with knowing, is distinguished from **actual notice,** or what the person actually knows (see figure 13.1). Once an individual has searched the public records and inspected the property, he or she has actual notice, or knowledge, of the information learned. An individual is said to have actual notice of any information of which he or she has *direct knowledge.* If it can be proved an individual has actual knowledge of information concerning a parcel of real estate, he or she cannot rely on a lack of constructive notice, such as an unrecorded deed or an owner who is not in possession. For example, Bill Wilson mortgaged his land to Jane Fry, and she failed to record the mortgage. Wilson later mortgaged the same land to Edgar Morse, who *knew* of the existence of the earlier mortgage. In this case, Morse is charged with actual knowledge of the existing mortgage, so his mortgage is a second mortgage, with Fry's mortgage having a prior claim on the property.

Figure 13.1
Notice

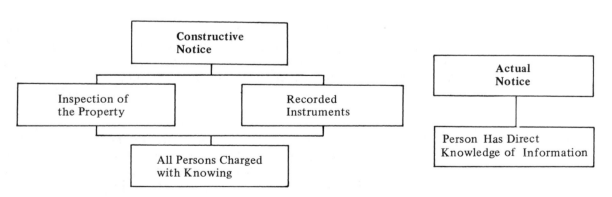

Real estate taxes and special assessments are direct liens on specific parcels of real estate and need not be recorded in the recorder's office. Other liens, such as inheritance taxes and franchise taxes, are placed by statutory authority against all real estate owned either by a decedent at the time of death or by a corporation at the time the franchise tax became a lien; these liens are not recorded either.

Priorities. Many complicated situations can arise that affect the priority of rights in a parcel of real estate. For example, a purchaser may receive a deed and take possession of the property but not record the deed. By taking possession, a purchaser gives constructive notice that he or she has an interest in the land. Such a purchaser's rights would be considered superior to the rights of a subsequent purchaser who acquired a deed from the original owner at a later date and recorded the deed but did not inspect the property to determine who was in possession. How the courts rule in any situation depends, of course, on the specific facts of the case. These are strictly legal questions that should be referred by the parties to their lawyers.

Foreign Language Documents

Deeds or mortgages written in a foreign language, although valid between the parties to a transaction, usually do not impart constructive notice when recorded. Recorded documents must be in the English language. An official translation by a consulate of the country in which the language is used, when attached to a foreign language document, may meet state recording requirements. Both the original document and the translation are then recorded and become part of the public record.

Chain of Title

State statutes generally require that recorded instruments must be within the **chain of title,** so that a search of the grantor-grantee indexes will reveal the document and the interest. Thus, when a mortgage executed by a purchaser is recorded prior to the recording of the deed of conveyance to the purchaser (who becomes the mortgagor), there is no notice to the world that the mortgagor had an interest to convey because the mortgage is not within the chain of title. However, the mortgage could become constructive notice if the deed were dated *on or before* the date of the mortgage. Then when the mortgage was recorded, it would be properly indexed by date to show that the purchaser obtained title on or before the date when he or she executed the mortgage.

The chain of title shows the record of ownership of the property over a period of time, depending on the length of the title search. An **abstract of title** is a condensed history of all the instruments affecting a particular parcel of land. In the United States, chains of title in colonial states frequently date back to a grant from the king of England. In those states admitted to the Union after the formation of the United States, the deeds of conveyance in the chain of title generally stem from the *patent* issued by the U. S. government. In a few states, such as Louisiana and Texas, the chains of title date back to a point prior to acquisition of the land by the federal government.

Through the chain of title, the ownership of the property can be traced from its origin to its present owner. If this cannot be done, it is said that there is a *gap* in the chain. In such cases, it is usually necessary to establish ownership by a court action called a **suit to quiet title.**

Evidence of Title

When dealing with an owner of real estate, a purchaser or lender requires satisfactory proof that the seller is the owner and has good title to the property. The owner is generally required to produce documentary proof called **evidence of title.** There are four forms of title evidence: (1) abstract of title and lawyer's opinion, (2) title insurance policy, (3) Torrens certificate, and (4) certificate of title.

Sometimes the question is raised as to whether a recorded warranty deed or other form of conveyance is evidence of title. A deed is not considered an evidence of title; while it conveys the interest of the grantor, even a warranty deed contains no proof of the kind or condition of the grantor's title. The only effective proof must be one of the evidences of title, based upon an adequate search of the public records to *ascertain the ownership interests and condition of the title.*

Abstract of Title and Lawyer's Opinion

An abstract of title is a brief history (in abstract, or brief, form) of the instruments appearing in the county record that affect title to the parcel in question. The legal description of the property is in the abstract's caption. Abstracts usually commence with the government's ownership of the land. They usually consist of several sections, or continuations, and each section covers a specific period of time. It is therefore necessary for each succeeding section of the abstract to begin with a search of the public record from a date immediately following the date of the previous section. If this were not done, there would be a gap in the abstract.

When an abstract is first prepared or is continued, the abstractor lists and summarizes each instrument in chronological order along with information relative to taxes, judgments, special assessments, and the like. The abstractor concludes with a certificate indicating which records were examined and when, and he or she signs the abstract. Abstractors must exercise due care, since they can be liable for negligence for any failure to include or accurately record all pertinent data. Note, however, that an *abstractor does not pass judgment on or guarantee the condition of the title.*

In a sale of land, the seller's attorney usually orders the abstract continued to cover the current date. When the abstractor has completed the abstract, it is submitted to the buyer's attorney, who must *examine the entire abstract.* This means that the lawyer must examine each section from the origin of that title. Following his or her detailed examination, the attorney must evaluate all the facts and material in order to prepare a written report for the purchaser on the condition of the ownership; this report is called an **attorney's opinion of title.**

As transfers of title have accumulated through the years, each abstract of title to individual property has become more and more voluminous, and the time needed by an attorney to examine an abstract has therefore increased. Because of the need for careful examination of the record and the number of errors or potential errors involved, many attorneys have filed court suits to protect their clients' claims to title. These *suits to quiet title* are filed to secure court decrees to clear up actual or potential defects in the abstracts.

In many ways, the title evidence system of abstract examination and opinion and the certification of title by attorneys (discussed later in this chapter) were imperfect and open to objection. For example, it is difficult to detect forged deeds or false statements, including incorrect marital information and transfers involving incompetent parties or minors. Or an honest mistake could be made against which the owner of real estate had no recourse. To provide purchasers with protection against this type of error and to give insurance along with defense of the title, title insurance became available.

Title Insurance

A **title insurance** policy is a contract by which a title insurance company agrees, subject to the terms of its policy, to indemnify (that is, to compensate or reimburse) the insured (the owner, mortgagee, or other interest holder) against any losses sustained as a result of defects in the title other than those exceptions listed in the policy. The title company agrees to defend, at its own expense, any lawsuit attacking the title if the lawsuit is based on a defect in title against which the policy insures. (See figure 13.2 for a typical owner's title insurance policy.)

A seller seeking to obtain a title insurance policy as evidence of his or her ownership makes an application to the title insurance company. The person agrees to pay a certain fee, and the title company examines the title records and agrees to insure against certain undiscovered defects. Exactly which defects the title company will insure against depends on the type of policy it issues (see table 13.1). A *standard coverage* policy usually insures against defects that may be found in the public records plus such items as forged documents, documents of incompetent grantors, incorrect marital statements, and improperly delivered deeds. An *extended coverage* policy generally includes all the protection of a standard policy plus additional protection to cover risks that may be discovered only through inspection of the property, inquiries of persons in actual possession of the land, or examination of an accurate survey. The company does not agree to insure against any defects in or liens against the title that are found by the title examination and listed in the policy.

Table 13.1 Owner's Title Insurance Policy	Standard Coverage	Extended Coverage	Not Covered by Either Policy
	1. Defects found in public records 2. Forged documents 3. Incompetent grantors 4. Incorrect marital statements 5. Improperly delivered deeds	Standard coverage plus defects discoverable through: 1. Property inspection 2. Inquiries of persons in possession 3. Examination of survey 4. Unrecorded liens not known of by policyholder	1. Defects and liens listed in policy 2. Unrecorded defects 3. Rights of parties in possession 4. Questions of survey

Upon completion of the examination, the title company usually issues a report of title, or a commitment to issue a title policy. This describes the policy that will be issued and includes the following: (1) the name of the insured party, (2) the legal description of the real estate, (3) the estate or interest covered, (4) a schedule of all exceptions, consisting of encumbrances and defects found in the public records, and (5) conditions and stipulations under which the policy is issued. An *owner's policy will usually exclude coverage* against the following exceptions: unrecorded documents, unrecorded defects of which the policyholder has knowledge, rights of parties in possession, and questions of survey. Under the contract, the title insurance company provides to defend the title at its own expense as well as to pay any claims against the property if the title proves to be defective. This is subject, of course, to the conditions and stipulations of the policy itself.

Like any other contract of insurance, a title insurance policy contains the names of the insured parties and the consideration (the premium, which in the case of title insurance is paid once for the life of the policy). The maximum loss for which the

Figure 13.2
Owner's Title
Insurance Policy

AMERICAN LAND TITLE ASSOCIATION
OWNER'S POLICY FORM B-1970
(Amended 10-17-70)

———————— T I T L E   I N S U R A N C E   C O M P A N Y

SUBJECT TO THE EXCLUSIONS FROM COVERAGE, THE EXCEPTIONS CONTAINED IN SCHEDULE B AND THE PROVISIONS OF THE CONDITIONS AND STIPULATIONS HEREOF, ———————— TITLE INSURANCE COMPANY, a ———————— corporation, herein called the Company, insures, as of Date of Policy shown in Schedule A, against loss or damage, not exceeding the amount of insurance stated in Schedule A, and costs, attorneys' fees and expenses which the Company may become obligated to pay hereunder, sustained or incurred by the insured by reason of:

1. Title to the estate or interest described in Schedule A being vested otherwise than as stated therein;

2. Any defect in or lien or encumbrance on such title;

3. Lack of a right of access to and from the land; or

4. Unmarketability of such title.

In Witness Whereof, ———————— TITLE INSURANCE COMPANY has caused this policy to be signed and sealed as of the date of policy shown in Schedule A, the policy to become valid when countersigned by an authorized signatory.

———————— TITLE INSURANCE COMPANY

By·

President.

ATTEST:

Secretary.

IMPORTANT

This policy necessarily relates solely to the title as of the date of the policy. In order that a purchaser of the real estate described herein may be insured against defects, liens or encumbrances, this policy should be reissued in the name of such purchaser.

Reproduced by permission of the American Land Title Association, Washington, DC, and the Chicago Title Insurance Company, Chicago, Illinois.

SCHEDULE A

Number	Date of Policy	Amount of Insurance

1. Name of Insured.

2. The estate or interest in the land described herein and which is covered by this policy is:

   Fee Simple

3. The estate or interest referred to herein is at Date of Policy vested in the Insured.

4. The land herein described is encumbered by the following mortgage or trust deed, and assignments:

   and the mortgages or trust deeds, if any, shown in Schedule B hereof.

5. The land referred to in this policy is described as follows:

SCHEDULE B

This policy does not insure against loss or damage by reason of the following exceptions:

General Exceptions:

(1) Rights or claims of parties in possession not shown by the public records.
(2) Encroachments, overlaps, boundary line disputes, and any matters which would be disclosed by an accurate survey and inspection of the premises.
(3) Easements, or claims of easements, not shown by the public records.
(4) Any lien, or right to a lien, for services, labor, or material heretofore or hereafter furnished, imposed by law and not shown by the public records.
(5) Taxes or special assessments which are not shown as existing liens by the public records.

Special Exceptions: The mortgage, if any, referred to in Schedule A.

Countersigned

_____

Authorized Signatory

Schedule B of this Policy consists of   pages

EXCLUSIONS FROM COVERAGE

The following matters are expressly excluded from the coverage of this policy:

1. Any law, ordinance or governmental regulation (including but not limited to building and zoning ordinances) restricting or regulating or prohibiting the occupancy, use or enjoyment of the land, or regulating the character, dimensions or location of any improvement now or hereafter erected on the land, or prohibiting a separation in ownership or a reduction in the dimensions or area of the land, or the effect of any violation of any such law, ordinance or governmental regulation.

2. Rights of eminent domain or governmental rights of police power unless notice of the exercise of such rights appears in the public records at Date of Policy.

3. Defects, liens, encumbrances, adverse claims, or other matters (a) created, suffered, assumed or agreed to by the insured claimant; (b) not known to the Company and not shown by the public records but known to the insured claimant either at Date of Policy or at the date such claimant acquired an estate or interest insured by this policy and not disclosed in writing by the insured claimant to the Company prior to the date such insured claimant became an insured hereunder; (c) resulting in no loss or damage to the insured claimant; (d) attaching or created subsequent to Date of Policy; or (e) resulting in loss or damage which would not have been sustained if the insured claimant had paid value for the estate or interest insured by this policy.

Figure 13.2 (cont.)

CONDITIONS AND STIPULATIONS

1. Definition of Terms

The following terms when used in this policy mean:

(a) "insured": the insured named in Schedule A, and, subject to any rights or defenses the Company may have had against the named insured, those who succeed to the interest of such insured by operation of law as distinguished from purchase including, but not limited to, heirs, distributees, devisees, survivors, personal representatives, next of kin, or corporate or fiduciary successors.

(b) "insured claimant": an insured claiming loss or damage hereunder.

(c) "knowledge": actual knowledge, not constructive knowledge or notice which may be imputed to an insured by reason of any public records.

(d) "land": the land described, specifically or by reference in Schedule A, and improvements affixed thereto which by law constitute real property; provided, however, the term "land" does not include any property beyond the lines of the area specifically described or referred to in Schedule A, nor any right, title, interest, estate or easemen. in abutting streets, roads, avenues, alleys, lanes, ways or waterways, but nothing herein shall modify or limit the extent to which a right of access to and from the land is insured by this policy.

(e) "mortgage": mortgage, deed of trust, trust deed, or other security instrument.

(f) "public records": those records which by law impart constructive notice of matters relating to said land.

2. Continuation of Insurance after Conveyance of Title

The coverage of this policy shall continue in force as of Date of Policy in favor of an insured so long as such insured retains an estate or interest in the land, or holds an indebtedness secured by a purchase money mortgage given by a purchaser from such insured, or so long as such insured shall have liability by reason of covenants of warranty made by such insured in any transfer or conveyance of such estate or interest; provided, however, this policy shall not continue in force in favor of any purchaser from such insured of either said estate or interest or the indebtedness secured by a purchase money mortgage given to such insured.

3. Defense and Prosecution of Actions—Notice of Claim to be given by an Insured Claimant

(a) The Company, at its own cost and without undue delay, shall provide for the defense of an insured in all litigation consisting of actions or proceedings commenced against such insured, or a defense interposed against an insured in an action to enforce a contract for a sale of the estate or interest in said land, to the extent that such litigation is founded upon an alleged defect, lien, encumbrance, or other matter insured against by this policy.

(b) The insured shall notify the Company promptly in writing (i) in case any action or proceeding is begun or defense is interposed as set forth in (a) above, (ii) in case knowledge shall come to an insured hereunder of any claim of title or interest which is adverse to the title to the estate or interest, as insured, and which might cause loss or damage for which the Company may be liable by virtue of this policy, or (iii) if title to the estate or interest, as insured, is rejected as unmarketable. If such prompt notice shall not be given to the Company, then as to such insured all liability of the Company shall cease and terminate in regard to the matter or matters for which such prompt notice is required; provided, however, that failure to notify shall in no case prejudice the rights of any such insured under this policy unless the Company shall be prejudiced by such failure and then only to the extent of such prejudice.

(c) The Company shall have the right at its own cost to institute and without undue delay prosecute any action or proceeding or to do any other act which in its opinion may be necessary or desirable to establish the title to the estate or interest as insured, and the Company may take any appropriate action under the terms of this policy, whether or not it shall be liable thereunder, and shall not thereby concede liability or waive any provision of this policy.

(d) Whenever the Company shall have brought any action or interposed a defense as required or permitted by the provisions of this

policy, the Company may pursue any such litigation to final determination by a court of competent jurisdiction and expressly reserves the right, in its sole discretion, to appeal from any adverse judgment or order.

(e) In all cases where this policy permits or requires the Company to prosecute or provide for the defense of any action or proceeding, the insured hereunder shall secure to the Company the right to so prosecute or provide defense in such action or proceeding, and all appeals therein, and permit the Company to use, at its option, the name of such insured for such purpose. Whenever requested by the Company, such insured shall give the Company all reasonable aid in any such action or proceeding, in effecting settlement, securing evidence, obtaining witnesses, or prosecuting or defending such action or proceeding, and the Company shall reimburse such insured for any expense so incurred.

4. Notice of Loss—Limitation of Action

In addition to the notices required under paragraph 3(b) of these Conditions and Stipulations, a statement in writing of any loss or damage for which it is claimed the Company is liable under this policy shall be furnished to the Company within 90 days after such loss or damage shall have been determined and no right of action shall accrue to an insured claimant until 30 days after such statement shall have been furnished. Failure to furnish such statement of loss or damage shall terminate any liability of the Company under this policy as to such loss or damage.

5. Options to Pay or Otherwise Settle Claims

The Company shall have the option to pay or otherwise settle for or in the name of an insured claimant any claim insured against or to terminate all liability and obligations of the Company hereunder by paying or tendering payment of the amount of insurance under this policy together with any costs, attorneys' fees and expenses incurred up to the time of such payment or tender of payment, by the insured claimant and authorized by the Company.

6. Determination and Payment of Loss

(a) The liability of the Company under this policy shall in no case exceed the least of:

(i) the actual loss of the insured claimant; or

(ii) the amount of insurance stated in Schedule A.

(b) The Company will pay, in addition to any loss insured against by this policy, all costs imposed upon an insured in litigation carried on by the Company for such insured, and all costs, attorneys' fees and expenses in litigation carried on by such insured with the written authorization of the Company.

(c) When liability has been definitely fixed in accordance with the conditions of this policy, the loss or damage shall be payable within 30 days thereafter.

7. Limitation of Liability

No claim shall arise or be maintainable under this policy (a) if the Company, after having received notice of an alleged defect, lien or encumbrance insured against hereunder, by litigation or otherwise, removes such defect, lien or encumbrance or establishes the title, as insured, within a reasonable time after receipt of such notice; (b) in the event of litigation until there has been a final determination by a court of competent jurisdiction, and disposition of all appeals therefrom, adverse to the title, as insured, as provided in paragraph 3 hereof; or (c) for liability voluntarily assumed by an insured in settling any claim or suit without prior written consent of the Company.

8. Reduction of Liability

All payments under this policy, except payments made for costs, attorneys' fees and expenses, shall reduce the amount of the insurance pro tanto. No payment shall be made without producing this policy for endorsement of such payment unless the policy be lost or destroyed, in which case proof of such loss or destruction shall be furnished to the satisfaction of the Company.

9. Liability Noncumulative

It is expressly understood that the amount of insurance under this policy shall be reduced by any amount the Company may pay under

CONDITIONS AND STIPULATIONS (Continued)

any policy insuring either (a) a mortgage shown or referred to in Schedule B hereof which is a lien on the estate or interest covered by this policy, or (b) a mortgage hereafter executed by an insured which is a charge or lien on the estate or interest described or referred to in Schedule A, and the amount so paid shall be deemed a payment under this policy. The Company shall have the option to apply to the payment of any such mortgages any amount that otherwise would be payable hereunder to the insured owner of the estate or interest covered by this policy and the amount so paid shall be deemed a payment under this policy to said insured owner.

10. Apportionment

If the land described in Schedule A consists of two or more parcels which are not used as a single site, and a loss is established affecting one or more of said parcels but not all, the loss shall be computed and settled on a pro rata basis as if the amount of insurance under this policy was divided pro rata as to the value on Date of Policy of each separate parcel to the whole, exclusive of any improvements made subsequent to Date of Policy, unless a liability or value has otherwise been agreed upon as to each such parcel by the Company and the insured at the time of the issuance of this policy and shown by an express statement herein or by an endorsement attached hereto.

11. Subrogation Upon Payment or Settlement

Whenever the Company shall have settled a claim under this policy, all right of subrogation shall vest in the Company unaffected by any act of the insured claimant. The Company shall be subrogated to and be entitled to all rights and remedies which such insured claimant would have had against any person or property in respect to such claim had this policy not been issued, and if requested by the Company, such insured claimant shall transfer to the Company all rights

and remedies against any person or property necessary in order to perfect such right of subrogation and shall permit the Company to use the name of such insured claimant in any transaction or litigation involving such rights or remedies. If the payment does not cover the loss of such insured claimant, the Company shall be subrogated to such rights and remedies in the proportion which said payment bears to the amount of said loss. If loss should result from any act of such insured claimant, such act shall not void this policy, but the Company, in that event, shall be required to pay only that part of any losses insured against hereunder which shall exceed the amount, if any, lost to the Company by reason of the impairment of the right of subrogation.

12. Liability Limited to this Policy

This instrument together with all endorsements and other instruments, if any, attached hereto by the Company is the entire policy and contract between the insured and the Company.

Any claim of loss or damage, whether or not based on negligence, and which arises out of the status of the title to the estate or interest covered hereby or any action asserting such claim, shall be restricted to the provisions and conditions and stipulations of this policy.

No amendment of or endorsement to this policy can be made except by writing endorsed hereon or attached hereto signed by either the President, a Vice President, the Secretary, an Assistant Secretary, or validating officer or authorized signatory of the Company.

13. Notices, Where Sent

All notices required to be given the Company and any statement in writing required to be furnished the Company shall be addressed to its principal office at _____
or at any branch office of the Company.

company may be liable cannot exceed the face amount of the policy (unless the amount of coverage has been extended by use of what is called an *inflation rider*). When a title company makes a payment to settle a claim covered by a policy, the company acquires by the right of **subrogation** all the remedies and rights of the insured party against anyone responsible for the settled claim.

Title companies issue various forms of title insurance policies, the most common of which are the *owner's* title insurance policy, the *mortgage* title insurance policy, the *leasehold* title insurance policy, and the *certificate of sale* title insurance policy. As the names indicate, each of these policies is issued to insure specific interests. For example, a mortgage title insurance policy insures a mortgage company or lender that it has a valid first lien against the property. A leasehold title insurance policy insures a lessee that he or she has a valid lease. A certificate of sale policy is issued to a purchaser in a court sale and insures the purchaser's interest in property sold under a court order.

Title search. The examination undertaken by an abstractor or title insurance company to determine what, if any, defects there are in a property's chain of title is called a *title search*. Generally, the title searcher begins the examination with the original source of title, which often dates from a government patent grant or award of title. If this is not possible, the search may begin with title records dating back 40 to 60 years, depending on local custom. After examining the original source of title, the searcher then checks the title in the recorder's office and searches the records in other governmental offices such as the tax offices and assessment offices (for sewer or special assessment liens that may be in effect).

In Practice . . .

A title search is not normally ordered until major contingencies in the sales contract, such as financing, have been cleared (for example, after a loan commitment has been secured from a lender). Before a lender will forward money on a loan secured by real estate, it will generally order a title search at the expense of a borrower to assure itself that there are no liens superior in priority to its mortgage on the property.

In addition, in some states a preliminary title report is ordered upon acceptance of an offer to purchase, and copies are given to the buyers, agents, and sellers. In fact, the entire contract may depend upon the buyers' written approval of this document within a given number of days after receiving it. Sellers usually are given a copy first, to ensure that the correct property has been researched.

The Torrens System

The **Torrens system** of land title registration was developed in 1857 by an Australian, Sir Robert Torrens, who took the idea from the system of registering title to shipping vessels. Approximately 10 states have adopted the Torrens system; it is also popular in Canada. In the states that have adopted the Torrens system, the established recording system is also still in use. Registration of land titles is not compulsory. The owner of real estate may continue under the standard recording system or may register his or her title under the Torrens system.

Although the provisions of the Torrens system are not uniform, the procedures to be followed in registering land titles in the various states are substantially the same. A written application to register a title to real estate is made with the county court of the county in which the real estate is located. The application lists all facts regarding the title and liens against the real estate. A court hearing is held, and all persons known to have an interest in the real estate are given notice. Any interested person may appear to present a claim. If the applicant proves that he or she is the owner, the court enters an order for the registration of the real estate, and the *registrar of titles,* also known as the *title examiner,* is directed to register the title.

Transferring title under the Torrens system. Once real estate is registered under the Torrens system, a **certificate of title** is prepared by the registrar, who keeps the original and issues a duplicate to the owners of the property (see figure 13.3). At the same time, signature cards are signed by the owners in order to protect them from forgery.

When a title to registered property is conveyed, mortgaged, or encumbered in any way, the owner delivers the deed, mortgage, or other instrument to the grantee, mortgagee, or encumbrancer, together with the owner's duplicate certificate of title. When these documents are presented to the registrar for examination and approval, he or she checks the signatures with the signature cards. When everything is in order, the registrar registers the transfer or document. A deed to Torrens registered land does not pass ownership. It is the *registration* that transfers title to the grantee. If such property is mortgaged, the registrar of titles issues a mortgagee's duplicate certificate of title to the lender. Torrens registrars usually retain all original documents delivered to them for registration.

At any time, the Torrens original certificate of title in the registrar's office reveals the owner of the land and all mortgages, judgments, and similar liens. This record exists because a mortgage judgment or other *lien is not valid until it has been entered on the original title certificate* by the registrar.

Under most state land registration acts, title to Torrens registered property *can never be acquired through a claim of adverse possession.* This gives an owner of registered land protection against such claims.

Under the Torrens system, it may be necessary to verify the payment of taxes and special assessments, since the county treasurer and county collector are not usually required to register their tax liens on the Torrens records. Usually judgments or decrees of the federal courts are not required to be registered, so a separate federal court search is required. Searches for unpaid taxes, special assessments, and federal liens can be obtained from the registrar of titles.

Under the Torrens system, a certificate of title is issued instead of a title insurance policy. The certificate does not set forth a dollar amount. If a claim or suit regarding title arises, the holder of a Torrens certificate must defend the suit at his or her own expense and prove loss in order to gain a right to any compensation from the registrar. The registrar of titles is not required to go to court to defend a certificate holder. State laws generally provide that a certificate holder who has suffered a loss as a result of a registrar's mistake may file a claim against an indemnity fund established to compensate people financially for bona fide losses.

Some state laws permit an owner to remove the title to his or her land from Torrens registration. In other states, land once registered must remain under the Torrens system.

Figure 13.3
Torrens Certificate
of Title

RT-13

Certificate of Title

DISTRICT COURT N°

STATE OF
COUNTY OF }S.S.

REGISTRATION

This is to certify, that

now the owner of an estate, to wit: in fee simple
of and in the following described land, situated in the County of   and State of   , to wit:

Subject to the incumbrances, liens and interest noted by the memorial underwritten or indorsed hereon:
and subject to the following rights or incumbrances subsisting, as provided in the twenty-fourth section of
An act concerning the registration of land and the title thereto of the General laws of the State of
for the year 1905, and the amendments thereof, namely:
1. Liens, claims or rights arising under the laws or the constitution of the United States, which the statutes
of this state cannot require to appear of record.
2. Any tax or special assessment for which a sale of the land has not been had at the date of the certificate of title.
3. Any lease for a period not exceeding three years when there is actual occupation of the premises under the lease.
4. All public highways embraced in the description of the lands included in the certificates shall be deemed to be
excluded.
5. Such right of appeal or right to appear and contest the application as is allowed by law.
6. The rights of any person in possession under deed or contract for deed from the owner of the certificate of title.
That the said

In Witness Whereof, I have hereunto subscribed my name and affixed the seal
of my office this   day of   19

Registrar of Titles,
In and for the County of   and State of
By
DEPUTY

MEMORIAL

OF ESTATES, EASEMENTS OR CHARGES ON THE LAND DESCRIBED IN THE CERTIFICATE OF TITLE HERETO ATTACHED.

DOCUMENT NUMBER	KIND OF INSTRUMENT	DATE OF INSTRUMENT			DATE OF REGISTRATION					AMOUNT	RUNNING IN FAVOR OF	SIGNATURE OF REGISTRAR
		MONTH	DAY	YEAR	MONTH	DAY	YEAR	HOUR				
								A.M.	P.M.			

Certificate of Title   In some localities, a *certificate of title prepared by an attorney* is used, and no abstract is prepared. The attorney examines the public records and issues a certificate of title that expresses his or her opinion of the title's status. The certificate states who the title owner is and gives the details of all liens and encumbrances against the title. It is an opinion of the validity of the grantor's or mortgagor's title and the existence of liens and encumbrances. However, it is not a title insurance policy and does not carry the full protection of such a policy.

Marketable Title   Under the terms of the usual real estate sales contract, the seller is required to deliver marketable title to the buyer at the closing. Generally, a **marketable title** is one that is so free from significant defects (other than those specified in the sales contract) that the purchaser can be assured against having to defend the title. Proper evidence of title is proof that the title is, in fact, marketable. Specifically, in order for title to be marketable it must: (1) be free from any significant liens and encumbrances; (2) disclose no serious defects and not be dependent on doubtful questions of law or fact to prove its validity; (3) not expose a purchaser to the hazard of litigation or threaten the quiet enjoyment of the property; and (4) convince a reasonably well-informed and prudent person, acting upon business principles and willful knowledge of the facts and their legal significance, that he or she could, in turn, sell or mortgage the property at a fair market value.

Although an unmarketable title (one that does not meet these requirements) does not mean that the property cannot be transferred under any circumstances, it does mean that there are *certain defects in the title that may limit or restrict its ownership.* A buyer cannot be forced to accept a conveyance that is materially different from the one bargained for in the sales contract; he or she cannot be forced to buy a lawsuit. Note that questions of marketable title must be raised by a purchaser (or his or her broker or attorney) prior to acceptance of the deed. Once a buyer has accepted a deed with unmarketable title, the only available legal recourse is to sue the seller under the covenants of warranty (if any) contained in the deed.

Uniform Commercial Code   The **Uniform Commercial Code** (UCC) is a codification of commercial law that has been adopted, wholly or in part, in all states. While this code generally does not apply directly to real estate, it has replaced state laws relating to chattel mortgages, conditional sales agreements, and liens on chattels, crops, or items that are to become fixtures. In many areas, UCC filings have replaced chattel mortgages as financing instruments for personal property.

To create a security interest in a chattel, including chattels that will become fixtures, Article 9 of the UCC requires the use of a **security agreement,** which must contain a complete description of the items against which the lien applies. A short notice of this agreement, called a **financing statement,** which includes the legal description of the real estate involved, must be filed in the recorder's office where mortgages are recorded. The recording of the financing statement constitutes notice to subsequent purchasers and mortgagees of the security interest in chattels and fixtures on the real estate. Many mortgagees require the signing and recording of a financing statement when the mortgaged premises include chattels or readily removable fixtures (washers, dryers, and the like) as part of the security for the mortgage debt. If the financing statement has been properly recorded, upon the borrower's default the creditor could repossess the chattels and remove them from the property.

Article 6 of the UCC covers **bulk transfers,** which are defined as the sale of the major part of the materials, supplies, merchandise, or other inventory of an enterprise *not* made in the ordinary course of the transferor's business. The purpose of this article is to outlaw the fraud perpetrated when a business person who is in debt sells all stock in trade (personal property) and disappears without having paid his or her creditors. Under Article 6, a bulk sale does not give the purchaser of such goods a clear title unless the purchaser complies with the article's requirements, which include giving notice of the sale to the seller's creditors. Some sales of business property involve the sale of the business and all of the owner's stock in trade, which may constitute a bulk sale.

Summary

The purpose of the recording acts is to give legal, public, and *constructive notice* to the world of parties' interests in real estate. The recording provisions have been adopted to create system and order in the transfer of real estate. Without them, it would be virtually impossible to transfer real estate from one party to another. The interests and rights of the various parties in a particular parcel of land must be recorded so that such rights will be legally effective against third parties who do not have knowledge or notice of the rights.

Possession of real estate is generally interpreted as notice of the rights of the person in possession. *Actual notice* is knowledge acquired directly and personally by a person.

There are four forms of *title evidence* commonly in use throughout the United States: (1) abstract of title and lawyer's opinion, (2) owner's title insurance policy, (3) Torrens certificate, and (4) certificate of title.

A deed of conveyance is evidence that a grantor has conveyed his or her interest in land, but it is not evidence of the kind or condition of the title. The purpose of a deed is to transfer a grantor's interest in real estate to a grantee. It does not *prove* that the grantor has any interest at all, even if he or she conveys the interest by means of a warranty deed that carries with it the implied covenants of warranty.

Each of the forms of title evidence bears a date and is evidence up to and including that date. All forms of title evidence show the previous actions that affect the title. A Torrens certificate, title insurance policy, certificate of title, and abstract of title reveal the history of a title. Each must be *later dated,* or continued or reissued, to cover a more recent date.

Title evidence shows whether or not a seller is conveying *marketable title.* Marketable title is generally one that is so free from significant defects that the purchaser can be assured against having to defend the title.

Under the Uniform Commercial Code, security interests in chattels must be recorded using a *security agreement* and *financing statement.* The recording of a financing statement gives notice to purchasers and mortgagees of the security interests in chattels and fixtures on the specific parcel of real estate.

Questions

1. Jim Anderson bought Ward Cleaver's home, and Cleaver delivered his deed to Anderson. Because it was a warranty deed, Anderson can assume which of the following?

    I. He has evidence of title.
    II. There are no outstanding mortgages or liens on the property.

    a. I only   c. both I and II
    b. II only   d. neither I nor II

2. An owner's title insurance policy with standard coverage generally covers all but which of the following?

    a. forged documents
    b. incorrect marital statements
    c. rights of parties in possession
    d. incompetent grantors

3. Actual notice refers to:

    I. the facts a person may ascertain by examining the public records.
    II. what a person has actual knowledge of.

    a. I only   c. both I and II
    b. II only   d. neither I nor II

4. Phil Simpson bought Larry Fine's house, received a deed, and moved into the residence, but neglected to record the document. One week later, Fine died, and his heirs in another city, unaware that the property had been sold, conveyed title to Melvin Howard, who recorded the deed. Who owns the property?

    a. Phil Simpson
    b. Melvin Howard
    c. Larry Fine's heirs
    d. both Simpson and Howard

5. Marketable title refers to:

    a. a property that can command a fair market value.
    b. a property that is free from significant title defects.
    c. the certificate issued under the Torrens system.
    d. a and b

6. The Torrens system of property registration:

    a. is used in all states.
    b. is mandatory where it is in effect.
    c. is a voluntary system.
    d. registers only titles—liens and encumbrances are not noted on the certificate of title.

7. A purchaser went to the county building to check the recorder's records. She found that the seller was the grantee in the last recorded deed and that no mortgage was on record against the property. Thus, the purchaser may assume which of the following?

    I. All taxes are paid and no judgments are outstanding.
    II. The seller has good title.

    a. I only   c. both I and II
    b. II only   d. neither I nor II

8. When a title insurance policy is being issued, the public records are searched, and the title company's record of title is continued to date. When the title examination is completed, the title company notifies the parties in writing of the condition of the title. This notification is referred to as:

    a. a chain of title.
    b. a report of title or commitment for title insurance.
    c. a Torrens certificate.
    d. an abstract.

9. In locations where the abstract system is used, an abstract is usually examined by the:

    a. broker.
    b. abstract company.
    c. purchaser.
    d. attorney for the purchaser.

10. The person who prepares an abstract of title for a parcel of real estate:

    I. writes a brief history of the title after inspecting the county records for documents affecting the title.
    II. insures the condition of the title.

    a. I only   c. both I and II
    b. II only   d. neither I nor II

11. A purchaser of real estate is charged with knowledge of all recorded documents, so he or she must have current title evidence to indicate the rights and interests revealed by public records. The purchaser is also charged with the responsibility to:

    I. make improvements on the property.
    II. learn the rights of the parties in possession.
    - a. I only
    - b. II only
    - c. both I and II
    - d. neither I nor II

12. Which *one* of the following statements *best* explains why instruments affecting real estate are recorded with the recorder of deeds of the county where the property is located?

    - a. Recording gives constructive notice to the world of the rights and interests in a particular parcel of real estate.
    - b. The law requires that such instruments be recorded.
    - c. The instruments must be recorded to comply with the terms of the statute of frauds.
    - d. Recording proves the execution of the instrument.

13. When a claim is settled by a title insurance company, the company acquires all rights and claims of the insured against any other person who is responsible for the loss. This is called:

    - a. escrow.
    - b. abstract of title.
    - c. subordination.
    - d. subrogation.

14. The documents referred to as title evidence include:

    - a. title insurance.
    - b. warranty deeds.
    - c. security agreements.
    - d. all of the above

15. Evidence of the kind of estate and all liens against an interest in a parcel of real estate can usually be proved by:

    - a. a recorded deed.
    - b. a court suit for specific performance.
    - c. one of the four evidences of title.
    - d. a foreclosure suit.

16. Written instruments affecting real estate should be recorded:

    - a. in the county where the real estate is located.
    - b. to give actual notice of the owner's interest in the property.
    - c. to give constructive notice of the owner's interest in the property.
    - d. a and c

17. A title insurance policy usually includes:

    I. a legal description of the insured parcel of real estate.
    II. the exceptions that are not covered by the policy.
    - a. I only
    - b. II only
    - c. both I and II
    - d. neither I nor II

18. To give notice of a security interest in personal property items, a lienholder must record which of the following?

    - a. security agreement
    - b. financing statement
    - c. bulk transfer
    - d. quitclaim deed

19. *Chain of title* refers to which of the following?

    - a. a summary or history of all instruments and legal proceedings affecting a specific parcel of land
    - b. a series of links measuring 7.92 inches each
    - c. an instrument or document that protects the insured parties (subject to specific exceptions) against defects in the examination of the record and hidden risks such as forgeries, undisclosed heirs, errors in the public records, and so forth
    - d. the succession of conveyances from some starting point whereby the present owner derives his or her title

20. The date and time a document was recorded establish which of the following?

    - a. priority
    - b. chain of title
    - c. subrogation
    - d. marketable title

14

Real Estate License Laws

Key Terms

Branch office
Broker
Broker-salesperson
Denial, suspension, or revocation of license
Irrevocable consent
NARELLO
Real estate commission
Real estate education
Real estate license law
Real estate recovery fund
Rules and regulations
Salesperson

Overview

Generally, broker and salesperson license applicants are required to pass an examination designed to test their knowledge of real estate principles and laws. Foremost among these laws is each state's *real estate license law,* which sets forth strict operating restrictions for licensees and penalties for noncompliance. This chapter will introduce you to some of the provisions that are basic to most state license laws. It is recommended that you read through this chapter, then study your state law and the license law chapter in your state supplement for *Modern Real Estate Practice* (where available). In addition, you should complete the license law analysis form that takes the place of end-of-chapter questions; this will help you to identify and learn key provisions in your state law.

Real Estate License Laws in All States

All states, the District of Columbia, and Canadian provinces have enacted **real estate license laws** that provide the state with the authority to license and regulate the activities of real estate brokers and salespeople. Certain details of the law vary from state to state, but the main provisions of many state laws are similar and are based on the so-called *pattern law* recommended by the License Law Committee of the NATIONAL ASSOCIATION OF REALTORS®. In addition, uniform policies and standards in the fields of license law administration and enforcement are promoted by an organization of state license law officials known as **NARELLO**—the National Association of Real Estate License Law Officials.

Purposes of License Laws

Although a yearly fee is charged for real estate licenses, it is not the primary purpose of license laws to raise revenue. The purposes of the laws are: (1) to protect the public from dishonest or incompetent brokers or salespeople, (2) to prescribe certain standards and qualifications for licensing brokers and salespeople, (3) to maintain high standards in the real estate profession, and (4) to protect licensed brokers and salespeople from unfair or improper competition.

Basic Provisions of License Laws

The authority that controls the licenses of real estate brokers and salespeople is generally the state **real estate commission.** The commission generally has the power to issue licenses, make real estate information available to licensees and the public, and enforce the real estate license law. The law is usually enforced through the **denial, suspension, or revocation of licenses,** although certain officials may be able to bring civil and/or criminal court actions against violators in serious cases.

Generally, each state's real estate commission has adopted a series of administrative **rules and regulations** that further define the basic law, provide for its administration, and set forth additional operating guidelines for brokers and salespeople. These rules and regulations usually have the *same force and effect as the law* itself. Throughout this chapter, all discussions of the license law also include the typical provisions of state real estate commissions' rules and regulations.

Who Must Be Licensed

Generally, the state license laws stipulate that any person who, for another and for compensation or promise of compensation, performs any of the following acts with regard to real estate (and in some states, business opportunities) must be licensed as a real estate **broker:**

1. sells.
2. lists.
3. buys.
4. rents or leases.
5. collects rents.
6. deals in options.

7. exchanges.
8. offers to perform or negotiate one of these activities.
9. represents that he or she engages in any of these activities.

The specific provisions vary from state to state, and many states cite additional activities that a person must be licensed to perform. In some states, for example, a person who, for others and for a fee, auctions real estate, negotiates a mortgage loan, or deals in cemetery lots may be required to have a broker's license. It is important to identify the specific requirements for your state.

Any person who performs any of the previously listed activities while employed by or associated with a real estate broker must be licensed as a real estate **salesperson.** In addition, some states have a special name or issue a special license for an individual who has qualified as a real estate broker and passed the broker's exam but is currently acting as a salesperson associated with and responsible to another licensed broker. Such person may be known as a **broker-salesperson** or an *associate broker.* To summarize, a broker is authorized to operate his or her own real estate business; a salesperson can operate only in the name of and under the supervision of a licensed broker.

Exceptions. In certain situations, the real estate license laws *do not generally apply* to individuals even though they perform the previously mentioned activities. Such persons and situations usually include:

1. a person or firm who sells his, her, or its own property when this is not the person's or firm's principal vocation.
2. a person acting under a power of attorney.
3. a salaried employee of a property owner who acts on behalf of the property owner, when dealing in real estate is not the owner's principal vocation.
4. an attorney-at-law performing his or her regular duties.
5. a receiver, trustee, guardian, administrator, executor, or other person acting under court order.
6. an auctioneer performing his or her regular duties (although, as previously mentioned, such person must be licensed in some states).
7. a public official or employee performing his or her regular duties.

Licensing Procedure   All states vary in their specific requirements for licensing. However, most require that an applicant be of legal age, a high school graduate, and a state resident for a certain period of time. In addition, he or she must not have had a real estate license revoked for a certain period of time in any state, not have been convicted of a serious crime for a certain period of time, and so forth. Some states may also require credit reports, fingerprint cards or FBI clearance, and/or personal references. In addition, most states require a salesperson applicant to be sponsored by a licensed broker who operates within the state and for whom the salesperson will work.

Educational requirements. Many states require license applicants to complete a certain number of hours of **real estate education** as a prerequisite to obtaining a license. These requirements vary from state to state, but generally broker applicants are required to complete more hours of classroom time than salesperson applicants. In addition, a number of states have enacted *continuing education* requirements that stipulate that in order to qualify for license renewal, licensees must complete a set number of real estate classes *after* they have been licensed.

Examinations. All states require license applicants to pass a written real estate examination prior to licensing. State requirements vary as to the length, manner, and passing grade for such exams, but generally the broker's exam is more inclusive than the salesperson's exam. The states also vary in their regulations regarding retests and appeals for applicants who have failed the exams.

Licensing of nonresidents. Most state licensing agencies have reciprocity agreements with the licensing agencies of certain other states. These agreements provide that out-of-state brokers will be allowed to operate within the state upon meeting certain requirements. Generally, reciprocity agreements are made between states that have similar licensing requirements or states that adjoin each other. Some states require out-of-state brokers to take the local state real estate licensing exam; others do not. In addition, most states require nonresident brokers to file an **irrevocable consent** agreement with the state licensing agency. This document states that suits and actions may be brought against the out-of-state broker within the state in which the agreement is filed and that the outcome of such suits will be valid and binding.

Licensing of corporations and partnerships. Generally, a corporation or partnership may be licensed as a real estate broker if at least one partner or officer of the organization is a licensed real estate broker. Any other officer or partner who intends to engage in real estate activities on behalf of the firm, however, must be individually licensed as a broker. Some states require that all officers or partners who are not participating in the business be registered as nonactive brokers. The license laws usually provide that no officer or partner may be registered as a real estate salesperson.

Real Estate Recovery Fund

Many states have instituted a special **real estate recovery fund** from which members of the general public may collect if they have suffered financial loss as a result of the actions of a real estate licensee. The fund is usually maintained with special fees that licensees must pay when they register. Generally people who seek reimbursement from the fund can do so only after they have filed a court suit and won a money judgment against the licensee. If the aggrieved individual cannot collect the judgment from the licensee in any other way, he or she can apply for payment from the recovery fund. The registrant's license is usually suspended until he or she repays the recovery fund for the amount paid to the injured party.

General Operation of a Real Estate Business

The state license laws regulate many of the everyday operations of real estate brokers and salespeople. Generally, every resident real estate broker must maintain a definite place of business within the state and may operate one or more branch offices. **Branch offices** usually are managed by licensed real estate brokers under the supervision of the principal broker. Generally, all licenses are issued to the principal broker rather than to the individual associate brokers and salespeople.

Brokers must usually keep detailed accounting records and retain copies of the documents used in all listings and transactions for a specified period of time. In addition, many license laws include specific provisions regarding the contents of contracts and documents used in transactions. Each broker must also maintain a special trust account for the deposit of funds belonging to clients and customers.

Brokers must never *commingle* a client's funds with their own money, except in those states where a broker is permitted to deposit a small amount of personal cash in a trust account in order to keep it open.

Brokers cannot use any misleading or fraudulent advertising in the course of business, and they cannot generally use blind ads (that is, advertising that does not specifically indicate that the advertiser of the property is a real estate broker). In addition, salespeople usually cannot advertise in their own names, but only in the name of their supervising broker.

Suspension or Revocation of a Real Estate License

The state license laws usually detail the various violations of the license law and other reasons for which a real estate license may be suspended or revoked. You should study the rules for your state and know them thoroughly.

Summary

The *real estate license laws* were enacted by the various states to protect the public from dishonest brokers and salespeople, prescribe certain licensing standards, maintain high standards in the real estate profession, and protect licensed brokers from unfair or improper competition.

Each state law stipulates who must be licensed and who is exempt from licensing, sets forth certain operating standards that brokers and salespersons must adhere to, and creates certain licensing procedures and requirements.

Note, however, that each state law is different. *You must know your own state license law.* If you do not have a copy of your state real estate license law, secure one immediately.

The analysis form that takes the place of questions in this chapter will help you to determine and learn the requirements of your state law. Use it as a study device while you read through your state law and state supplement (where available), or use it as a testing device *after* studying the license law. (Be sure to check your answers against the provisions of the law.)

Remember, you will be operating and working under your state real estate license law—*you must know it well.*

Analysis Form: Real Estate Broker's and Salesperson's Law
State (or province) of

Instructions: After studying your state law, answer the questions and fill in the information indicated. If the question or point does not apply in your state, indicate this fact by some statement such as *no, none, not required,* or *does not apply.* If you complete this form carefully, the information will be invaluable when you prepare for your state license examination and for future use.

1. When was your state law originally passed?_____

2. Has it been amended? _____ If so, when was the last amendment passed?

3. What are the requirements for licensure in your state?

	For Broker's License	For Salesperson's License
Minimum age	_____	_____
Apprenticeship (years)	_____	_____
Education	_____	_____
Examination required?	_____	_____
Bond required (if any)	_____	_____
Number and type of recommendations required	_____	_____
Photograph required?	_____	_____

4. Copy exactly the definition of a *broker* as given by your law. Know this definition and be able to list the activites that it includes.

_____

_____

_____

5. Copy exactly the definition of a *salesperson* as given by your law. Learn this definition.

_____

_____

_____

6. What persons or groups are *exempt* from licensure in your state?

_____

_____

_____

7. What fees are required in your state?

	For Broker	For Salesperson
For original license application	_____	_____
Additional fee for examination	_____	_____
Periodic renewal fee	_____	_____
Recovery fund	_____	_____

8. For what period is the license certificate issued?   _____   _____

On what date does it expire?   _____   _____

During what month or by what date must the certificate be renewed?   _____   _____

9. Following are some of the reasons why a state may discipline a broker or salesperson, refuse to issue a license, or revoke or suspend a license. Place a check mark in front of the reasons given in your state law. Cross out reasons that do not apply and add other reasons that are not listed here. When you have compiled your list, memorize the reasons. *Almost every state examination will require you to know these grounds for discipline.* Be absolutely sure you know them.

_____ Filing for record any papers to cloud title as claim for commission

_____ Making false affidavits or committing perjury in any court proceeding

_____ Pursuing a continued and flagrant course of misrepresentation

_____ Making false promises through salespeople, advertising, and the like

_____ Acting for more than one party without approval of all parties

_____ Failing to remit or account for funds belonging to others

_____ Misleading advertising or an ad without the broker's name

_____ Misusing the term REALTOR® or other insignia of membership

_____ Procuring license by fraud, filing fradulent application

_____ Willfully disregarding or violating provisions of the licensing act or regulations

_____ Paying a commission to any unlicensed person in violation of the act

_____ Representing a broker other than one's employer

_____ Being convicted of embezzlement, fraud, and similar crimes, or state or federal felonies

_____ Displaying For Sale signs without proper authorization from a seller

_____ Not clearly explaining to a principal the duration of an exclusive listing agreement

_____ Engaging in conduct that constitutes bad faith or improper, incompetent, fraudulent, or dishonest dealing

_____ Employing unlicensed salespeople

_____ Accepting a commission in violation of the licensing act

_____ Operating an office or branch office from an unregistered location

_____ Commingling funds or property of a principal with a broker's personal funds

_____ Failing to deposit the money of others in an escrow or trustee account

_____ Other:

10. What penalties are provided in your state law for operating without a license?

	Individuals		Corporations	
	1st Offense	2nd Offense	1st Offense	2nd Offense
Fine	_____	_____	_____	_____
Imprisonment	_____	_____	_____	_____

Are other penalties or fines provided and, if so, for what offenses?

11. What is the name of the state department, board, commission, or office that is responsible for administering of the real estate law in your state?

12. If there is a real estate commission or advisory committe, how many members are there? What is their term of office?

13. What are the requirements in regard to a broker's maintaining an office and/or a sign?

14. What provisions and/or requirements are made for the discharge or termination of employment of a real estate salesperson by a broker?

15. List the main requirements for issuance of a certificate to a nonresident broker.

16. Does your state provide for a real estate recovery fund?

15

Real Estate Financing

Key Terms

Acceleration clause
Alienation clause
Amortized loan
Balloon payment
Conventional loan
Defeasance clause
Deficiency judgment
Fannie Mae (FNMA)
FHA loan
Foreclosure
Freddie Mac (FHLMC)
Ginnie Mae (GNMA)
Interest
Lien theory
Mortgage
Negotiable instrument

Note
Points
Prepayment penalty
Primary market
Regulation Z
Release deed
Right of redemption
Satisfaction of mortgage
Secondary market
Straight (term) loan
Title theory
Trust deed
Usury
VA loan
Warehousing agency

Overview

Rarely is a parcel of real estate purchased on a cash basis; almost every real estate transaction involves some type of financing. Thus, an understanding of real estate financing is of prime importance to the real estate licensee. Usually the buyer in a real estate transaction borrows the major portion of the purchase price by securing a loan and pledging the real property involved as security (collateral) for the loan. This is generally known as a *mortgage loan.* The mortgage loan, though the most popular method of financing a real estate purchase, is only one of many financing techniques. This chapter will fully discuss the basic mortgage loan, as well as alternative types of financing and payment plans. In addition, the chapter will examine the various sources of mortgage money and the role of the federal government in real estate financing.

Mortgage Theory	The concept of mortgage lending originated in England under Anglo-Saxon law. Originally, a borrower who needed to finance the purchase of land (the *mortgagor*) was forced to convey title to the property to the lender (the *mortgagee*), to ensure payment of the debt. If the obligation was not paid, the mortgagor automatically forfeited the land to the creditor, who was already the legal owner of the property.

Through the years, English courts began to acknowledge that a mortgage was only a *security device* and the mortgagor was the true owner of the mortgaged real estate. Under this concept, real estate was merely given as *security* for the payment of a debt, which was represented by a *note*. |
| **United States Mortgage Law** | Upon gaining independence from England, the original 13 colonies adopted the English laws as their own basic body of law. From their inception, American courts of equity considered a mortgage as a voluntary lien on real estate, given to secure the payment of a debt or the performance of an obligation.

Even so, some of the states recognized—and still do recognize—a lender as the owner of mortgaged land. This ownership is subject to defeat upon full payment of the debt or performance of the obligation. These states are called **title theory** states. Under title theory, a mortgagee has the right to possession of and rents from the mortgaged property upon default by the mortgagor.

Those states that interpret a mortgage purely as a lien on real property are called **lien theory** states. In such states, if a mortgagor defaults, the lender is required to foreclose the lien (generally through a court action), offer the property for sale, and apply the funds received from the sale to reduce or extinguish the obligation. As protection to the borrower, these states generally allow a statutory redemption period during which a defaulted mortgagor can redeem his or her property. Failure to redeem within this time period will result in the borrower's loss of the property.

Today, a number of states have modified the strict interpretation of title and lien theories. These *intermediary,* or *modified lien theory,* states allow a lender to take possession of the mortgaged real estate upon default.

Regardless of whether a state follows the title or lien theory of mortgages, the security interest that the mortgagee has in the real estate is legally considered *personal property.* This interest can be transferred *only* with a transfer of the debt that the mortgage secures. In reality, *the differences between the rights of the parties to a mortgage loan in a lien theory state and a title theory state are more technical than actual.* |
| **Security and Debt** | Generally, any interest in real estate that may be sold may be pledged as security for a debt. The basic principle of property law, that a person cannot convey greater rights in property than he or she actually has, applies equally to the right |

to mortgage. So the owner of a fee simple estate can mortgage the fee, and the owner of a leasehold or subleasehold can mortgage that leasehold interest. For example, a large retail corporation renting space in a shopping center may mortgage its leasehold interest in order to finance some remodeling work.

As discussed in Chapter 8, the owner of a cooperative interest holds a personal property interest, not an interest in real estate. Although a cooperative owner has a leasehold interest, the nature of that leasehold is not generally acceptable to lenders as collateral. The owner of a condominium unit, however, can mortgage his or her fee interest in the condominium apartment.

Mortgage Loan Instruments

There are two parts to a mortgage loan—the security for the debt and the debt itself. Therefore, when a property is to be mortgaged, the owner must execute, or sign, two separate instruments:

1. The **mortgage** is the document that creates the lien, or conveys the property to the mortgagee as *security* for the debt.

**Figure 15.1
Mortgage and Trust
Deed**

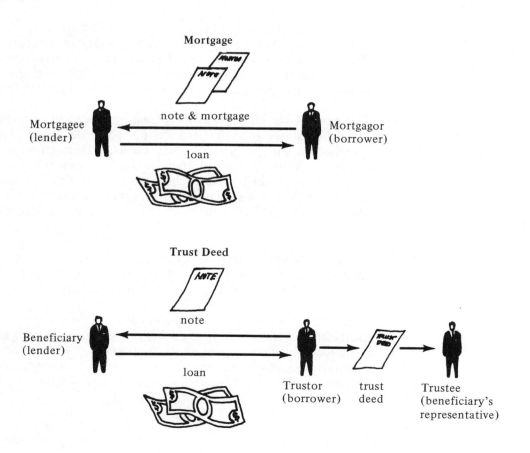

2. The **note** is the promise, or agreement, to repay the debt in definite installments with interest. The mortgagor executes one or more promissory notes to total the amount of the debt.

By itself, a mortgage document is basically a pledge of property given by a borrower to a lender to secure a loan. Since a pledge of security is not legally effective unless there is a debt to secure, a note is also required. *Both documents must be executed in order to create an enforceable mortgage loan.*

Trust deeds. In some areas of the country, and in certain situations, lenders prefer to use a three-party instrument known as a **trust deed,** or *deed of trust,* rather than a mortgage document. A trust deed conveys the real estate as security for the loan to a third party, called the *trustee.* The trustee then holds title on behalf of the lender, known as the *beneficiary,* who is the legal owner and holder of the note. The wording of the conveyance sets forth actions that the trustee may take if the borrower, usually known as the *trustor,* defaults under any of the trust deed terms. (See figure 15.1 for a comparison of mortgages and trust deeds.) In states where trust deeds are generally preferred, foreclosure procedures for defaulted trust deeds are usually simpler and faster than those for mortgage loans.

Usually the lender chooses the trustee and reserves the right to substitute trustees in the event of death or dismissal. Although the trust deed is particularly popular in certain states, it is used all over the country. For example, in the financing of a commercial or industrial real estate venture that involves a large loan and several lenders, the borrower generally executes a trust deed rather than a mortgage. This is because a trust deed can be used to secure several notes, one note held by each lender.

Provisions of the Note	In general, the promissory note (or notes) executed by a borrower (known as the *maker* or *payor*) states the amount of the debt, the time and method of payment, and the rate of interest. If the note is used with a mortgage, it names the mortgagee as the payee; if it is used with a trust deed, the note may be made payable to the bearer. It may also refer to or repeat several of the clauses that appear in the mortgage document or trust deed. The note, like the mortgage or trust deed, should be signed by all parties who have an interest in the property. In states where dower and curtesy are in effect or where homestead or community property is involved, both spouses have an interest in the property and must sign the note. Figure 15.2 is an example of a note commonly used with a mortgage.

A note is a **negotiable instrument;** that is, a written promise or order to pay a specific sum of money. An instrument is said to be negotiable when its holder, known as the *payee,* may transfer his or her right to payment to a third party. This may be accomplished by signing the instrument over to the third party or, in some cases, by merely delivering the instrument to that person. The transferee, or new holder of the note, is known as a *holder in due course.* Other examples of negotiable instruments include checks and bank drafts.

To be negotiable, or freely transferable, an instrument must meet certain requirements of Article 3 of the Uniform Commercial Code. The instrument must be in writing, made by one person to another, and signed by the maker. It must contain an unconditional promise to pay a sum of money on demand or at a set date in the future. In addition, the instrument must be payable to the order of a specifically

Figure 15.2
Note (Used with Mortgage)

NOTE

.........April 12................, 19..85...   ....Chicago........, ...Illinois.........
                                                            [City]   [State]

.........222 Kelly Street, Chicago, Illinois 60601.........
                          [Property Address]

1. BORROWER'S PROMISE TO PAY

In return for a loan that I have received, I promise to pay U.S. $..79,000.00.............. (this amount is called "principal"), plus interest, to the order of the Lender. The Lender is ..First City Savings and Loan ....Association of Chicago, Illinois... I understand that the Lender may transfer this Note. The Lender or anyone who takes this Note by transfer and who is entitled to receive payments under this Note is called the "Note Holder."

2. INTEREST

Interest will be charged on unpaid principal until the full amount of principal has been paid. I will pay interest at a yearly rate of ....14......%.

The interest rate required by this Section 2 is the rate I will pay both before and after any default described in Section 6(B) of this Note.

3. PAYMENTS

(A) Time and Place of Payments

I will pay principal and interest by making payments every month.

I will make my monthly payments on the ......1st.. day of each month beginning on ...May 1........................, 19..85.... I will make these payments every month until I have paid all of the principal and interest and any other charges described below that I may owe under this Note. My monthly payments will be applied to interest before principal. If, on ....April 1, 2015..............., I still owe amounts under this Note, I will pay those amounts in full on that date, which is called the "maturity date."

I will make my monthly payments at ....130 North LaSalle Street, Chicago, Illinois.........
.... or at a different place if required by the Note Holder.

(B) Amount of Monthly Payments

My monthly payment will be in the amount of U.S. $..936.15..............................

4. BORROWER'S RIGHT TO PREPAY

I have the right to make payments of principal at any time before they are due. A payment of principal only is known as a "prepayment." When I make a prepayment, I will tell the Note Holder in writing that I am doing so.

I may make a full prepayment or partial prepayments without paying any prepayment charge. The Note Holder will use all of my prepayments to reduce the amount of principal that I owe under this Note. If I make a partial prepayment, there will be no changes in the due date or in the amount of my monthly payment unless the Note Holder agrees in writing to those changes.

5. LOAN CHARGES

If a law, which applies to this loan and which sets maximum loan charges, is finally interpreted so that the interest or other loan charges collected or to be collected in connection with this loan exceed the permitted limits, then: (i) any such loan charge shall be reduced by the amount necessary to reduce the charge to the permitted limit; and (ii) any sums already collected from me which exceeded permitted limits will be refunded to me. The Note Holder may choose to make this refund by reducing the principal I owe under this Note or by making a direct payment to me. If a refund reduces principal, the reduction will be treated as a partial prepayment.

6. BORROWER'S FAILURE TO PAY AS REQUIRED

(A) Late Charge for Overdue Payments

If the Note Holder has not received the full amount of any monthly payment by the end of .....fifteen.... calendar days after the date it is due, I will pay a late charge to the Note Holder. The amount of the charge will be ....5..% of my overdue payment of principal and interest. I will pay this late charge promptly but only once on each late payment.

(B) Default

If I do not pay the full amount of each monthly payment on the date it is due, I will be in default.

(C) Notice of Default

If I am in default, the Note Holder may send me a written notice telling me that if I do not pay the overdue amount by a certain date, the Note Holder may require me to pay immediately the full amount of principal which has not been paid and all the interest that I owe on that amount. That date must be at least 30 days after the date on which the notice is delivered or mailed to me.

(D) No Waiver By Note Holder

Even if, at a time when I am in default, the Note Holder does not require me to pay immediately in full as described above, the Note Holder will still have the right to do so if I am in default at a later time.

(E) Payment of Note Holder's Costs and Expenses

If the Note Holder has required me to pay immediately in full as described above, the Note Holder will have the right to be paid back by me for all of its costs and expenses in enforcing this Note to the extent not prohibited by applicable law. Those expenses include, for example, reasonable attorneys' fees.

7. GIVING OF NOTICES

Unless applicable law requires a different method, any notice that must be given to me under this Note will be given by delivering it or by mailing it by first class mail to me at the Property Address above or at a different address if I give the Note Holder a notice of my different address.

Any notice that must be given to the Note Holder under this Note will be given by mailing it by first class mail to the Note Holder at the address stated in Section 3(A) above or at a different address if I am given a notice of that different address.

MULTISTATE FIXED RATE NOTE—Single Family—**FNMA/FHLMC UNIFORM INSTRUMENT**   Form 3200 12/83 named person or to the bearer (whoever has possession of the note). Instruments that are payable *to order* must be transferred by endorsement; those payable *to bearer* may be transferred by delivery.

Payment Plans   Most mortgage and trust deed loans are **amortized loans.** That is, regular payments are applied, first to the interest owed and the balance to the principal amount, over a term of perhaps 20 to 40 years. (Most loans are based on a 30-year term.) At the end of the term, the full amount of the principal and all interest due will be reduced to zero. Such loans are also called *direct reduction loans.*

Most amortized mortgage and trust deed loans are paid in monthly installments; some, however, are payable quarterly or semiannually. These payments may be computed based on a number of payment plans, which tend to alternately gain and lose favor with lenders and borrowers as the cost and availability of mortgage money fluctuates. Such payment plans include the following (illustrated in figure 15.3):

1. The most frequently used plan requires the mortgagor to pay a *constant amount,* usually monthly. The mortgagee credits each payment first to the interest due and then applies the balance to reduce the principal of the loan. Thus, while each payment is the same, the portion applied towards repayment of the principal grows and the interest due declines as the unpaid balance of the loan is reduced. This is known as a *fully amortized loan.*

2. The mortgagor may pay a *different amount for each installment,* with each payment consisting of a fixed amount credited toward the principal plus an additional amount for the interest due on the balance of the principal outstanding since the last payment was made. This is known as *straight-line amortization.*

3. A mortgagor may choose a *straight payment plan* that calls for periodic payments of interest, with the principal to be *paid in full at the end of the loan term.* This is known as a **straight,** or **term, loan.** Such plans are generally used for home-improvement loans and second mortgages rather than for residential first mortgage loans.

4. The mortgagor may elect to take advantage of a *flexible payment plan,* such as a graduated payment mortgage, generally used to enable younger buyers and buyers in times of high interest rates to purchase real estate. Under this plan, a mortgagor makes lower monthly payments for the first few years of the loan (typically the first five years), and larger payments for the remainder of the term, when the mortgagor's income is expected to have increased.

5. When a mortgage or trust deed loan requires periodic payments that will not fully amortize the amount of the loan by the time the final payment is due, the final payment is a larger amount than the others. This is called a **balloon payment,** and this type of loan is a *partially amortized loan.* For example, a loan made for $80,000 at 11½ percent interest may be computed on a 30-year amortization schedule but paid over a 20-year term with a final balloon payment due at the end of the twentieth year. In this case, each monthly payment would be $792.24 (the amount taken from a 30-year amortization schedule), with a final balloon payment of $56,340 (the amount of principal still owing after 20 years). It is frequently assumed that if the payments are promptly made, the lender will extend the balloon payment for another limited term. The lender, however, is in no way legally obligated to grant this extension and can require payment in full when the note is due.

Figure 15.3
Payment Plans

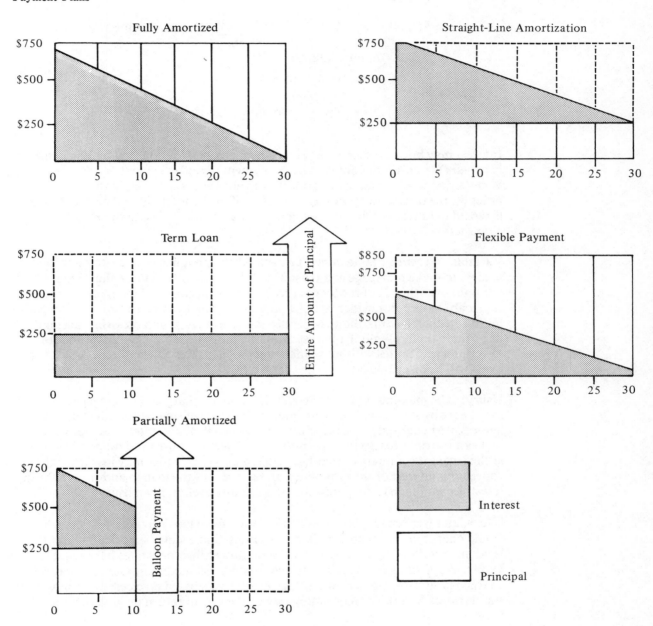

Interest

A charge for the use of money is called **interest**. A lender charges a borrower a certain percentage of the principal as interest for each year the debt is outstanding. The amount of interest due on any one installment payment date is calculated by computing the total yearly interest, based on the unpaid balance, and dividing that figure by the number of payments made each year. For example, if the current outstanding loan balance is $50,000 with interest at the rate of 12 percent per annum and constant monthly payments of $617.40, the interest and principal due on the next payment would be computed as follows:

$$
\begin{array}{ll}
\$50,000 & \underline{\hspace{1.2em}\$500.00}\text{ month's interest} \\
\underline{\times\quad .12} & 12)\$6,000.00 \\
\$\ \ 6,000\text{ annual interest} &
\end{array}
$$

$$
\begin{array}{l}
\$617.40 \\
\underline{-500.00} \\
\$117.40\text{ month's principal}
\end{array}
$$

Interest may be due either at the end of each payment period (known as payment *in arrears*) or at the beginning of each payment period (payment *in advance*). Whether interest is charged in arrears or in advance is specified in the note. In practice, the distinction becomes important if the property is sold before the debt is repaid in full, as will become evident in Chapter 23, "Closing the Real Estate Transaction."

Variable and renegotiable interest rates. Although it has been customary for lenders to make mortgage and trust deed loans at an interest rate that remains constant over the life of the loan, in recent years variable and renegotiable interest rate loans have become increasingly popular among lenders. In times of rising interest rates, such loans allow the lender to keep a loan profitable over the length of its term; in times of falling interest rates, the mortgagor can take advantage of lower mortgage rates without refinancing the loan. Variable and renegotiable rate loans will be discussed later in the chapter.

Usury. The maximum rate of interest that may be charged on mortgage loans may be set by state law. Charging interest in excess of this rate is called **usury,** and lenders are penalized for making usurious loans. In some states, a lender who makes a usurious loan will be permitted to collect the borrowed money, but only at the legal rate of interest. In other states, a usurious lender may lose the right to collect any interest or may lose the entire amount of the loan in addition to the interest. Loans made to corporations are generally exempt from usury laws.

Usury laws were enacted to protect borrowers from unscrupulous lenders who would charge unreasonably high interest rates. Some states specifically limit the legal maximum interest rate to a fixed amount, while other states have what is known as a *floating interest rate.* In such states, the maximum rate that may be charged is adjusted up or down at specific intervals based on a certain economic standard, such as the prime lending rate or the rate of return on government bonds.

With a fluctuating, or floating, usury ceiling, the maximum legal rate that may be charged on a loan originated one month may be different from the maximum rate that could have been charged the previous month. *The rate of interest charged on any one loan, however, remains constant throughout the term of the loan* (except for variable interest loans).

Money available for borrowing is a commodity, subject to the economic laws of supply and demand, and lenders are in business to make money by lending money and charging interest. When there is plenty of money available, interest rates become fairly low. When money is scarce, interest rates go up. Lenders, who want to earn a fair return on the loans they make, invest their money in loans that will yield the highest rate of interest. Mortgage loans then become harder to obtain, because lenders prefer to invest their money at rates that are not limited by usury laws.

Service-charge points. When a mortgage or trust deed is originated, the mortgage company's commission fee or service charge is computed as a percentage of the loan amount. This *loan origination fee* is commonly referred to as **points;** one point equals one percentage point of the loan amount. For example, a service charge of two points on an $80,000 mortgage loan would be 2 percent of $80,000, or $1,600. Some usury laws specifically limit the number of points a lender may charge for originating or assuming a mortgage or trust deed loan.

In Practice . . .	*Interest payments made under a mortgage loan are deductible for federal income-tax purposes. This deduction, in effect, reduces the borrower's total cost of housing for the year. Since under most types of amortized loans the borrower pays mostly interest in the early years of the loan, his or her tax liability for these years will be more greatly reduced than in later years of the loan. In addition, service-charge points paid by the borrower are tax deductible.*

Prepayment

When a loan is amortized over a long term, the total interest paid by the borrower can be a larger amount of money than the principal of the loan. If an amortized loan is paid off ahead of its full term, the lender will collect less interest from the borrower. For this reason, some mortgage and trust deed notes require the borrower to pay a **prepayment premium,** or **penalty,** against the unearned portion of the interest for any payments made ahead of schedule. A loan may not be prepaid under any circumstances unless the note contains a provision allowing for it.

The premium charged may run from one percent of the balance due at the time of prepayment to all interest due for the first ten years of the loan. Some lenders allow the borrower to pay off 20 percent of the original loan in any one year without paying a premium; but if the loan is paid off in full, the borrower may be charged a percentage of the principal paid in excess of that allowance. Some states either limit or do not permit a lender to charge a penalty on prepaid residential mortgage or trust deed loans; other states allow a lender to charge a prepayment penalty *only* if the loan is paid off with funds borrowed from another source.

Provisions of the Mortgage Document or Trust Deed

The mortgage document or trust deed refers to the terms of the note and clearly establishes that the conveyance of land is security for the debt. It identifies the lender as well as the borrower, and it includes an accurate legal description of the property. It should be signed by all parties who have an interest in the real estate. The instrument also sets forth the obligations of the borrower and the rights of the lender. (Figure 15.4 is a sample mortgage; figure 15.5, a trust deed.)

Duties of the Mortgagor or Trustor

The borrower is required to fulfill many obligations. These usually include the following:

1. payment of the debt in accordance with the terms of the note.
2. payment of all real estate taxes on the property given as security.

**Figure 15.4
Mortgage**

———————————————— [Space Above This Line For Recording Data] ————————————————

MORTGAGE

THIS MORTGAGE ("Security Instrument") is given on ...... April 12 ....,
19 85 ..... The mortgagor is ..Thomas..Perkins..and..Celia..Perkins,..husband..and..wife..................
.... ("Borrower"). This Security Instrument is given to ....
.. First City Savings and Loan Association ...., which is organized and existing
under the laws of ...Illinois..and..the..United..States....., and whose address is ..130..North..La..Salle.........
..Chicago, Illinois .... ("Lender").
Borrower owes Lender the principal sum of .....Seventy..Nine..Thousand..and..xx/100————————————
————————————————————————————.... Dollars (U.S. $..79,000.00...........). This debt is evidenced by Borrower's note
dated the same date as this Security Instrument ("Note"), which provides for monthly payments, with the full debt, if not
paid earlier, due and payable on ....April 1, 2015.. This Security Instrument
secures to Lender: (a) the repayment of the debt evidenced by the Note, with interest, and all renewals, extensions and
modifications; (b) the payment of all other sums, with interest, advanced under paragraph 7 to protect the security of this
Security Instrument; and (c) the performance of Borrower's covenants and agreements under this Security Instrument and
the Note. For this purpose, Borrower does hereby mortgage, grant and convey to Lender the following described property
located in ....Cook.. County, Illinois:

> Lot 4 in Block 5 of the Daley Subdivision, a subdivision located in
> the Southeast 1/4 of Section 17, Township 5 North, Range 12 East of
> the Third Principal Meridian.
> Permanent Tax Index No. 17-09-788-971

which has the address of ....222..Kelly..Street.., ...Chicago..........................,
                                    [Street]   [City]
Illinois ....60601................................... ("Property Address");
                    [Zip Code]

TOGETHER WITH all the improvements now or hereafter erected on the property, and all easements, rights,
appurtenances, rents, royalties, mineral, oil and gas rights and profits, water rights and stock and all fixtures now or
hereafter a part of the property. All replacements and additions shall also be covered by this Security Instrument. All of the
foregoing is referred to in this Security Instrument as the "Property."

BORROWER COVENANTS that Borrower is lawfully seised of the estate hereby conveyed and has the right to
mortgage, grant and convey the Property and that the Property is unencumbered, except for encumbrances of record.
Borrower warrants and will defend generally the title to the Property against all claims and demands, subject to any
encumbrances of record.

THIS SECURITY INSTRUMENT combines uniform covenants for national use and non-uniform covenants with
limited variations by jurisdiction to constitute a uniform security instrument covering real property.

UNIFORM COVENANTS. Borrower and Lender covenant and agree as follows:
   1. Payment of Principal and Interest; Prepayment and Late Charges. Borrower shall promptly pay when due
the principal of and interest on the debt evidenced by the Note and any prepayment and late charges due under the Note.
   2. Funds for Taxes and Insurance. Subject to applicable law or to a written waiver by Lender, Borrower shall pay
to Lender on the day monthly payments are due under the Note, until the Note is paid in full, a sum ("Funds") equal to
one-twelfth of: (a) yearly taxes and assessments which may attain priority over this Security Instrument; (b) yearly
leasehold payments or ground rents on the Property, if any; (c) yearly hazard insurance premiums; and (d) yearly
mortgage insurance premiums, if any. These items are called "escrow items." Lender may estimate the Funds due on the
basis of current data and reasonable estimates of future escrow items.
   The Funds shall be held in an institution the deposits or accounts of which are insured or guaranteed by a federal or
state agency (including Lender if Lender is such an institution). Lender shall apply the Funds to pay the escrow items.
Lender may not charge for holding and applying the Funds, analyzing the account or verifying the escrow items, unless
Lender pays Borrower interest on the Funds and applicable law permits Lender to make such a charge. Borrower and
Lender may agree in writing that interest shall be paid on the Funds. Unless an agreement is made or applicable law
requires interest to be paid, Lender shall not be required to pay Borrower any interest or earnings on the Funds. Lender
shall give to Borrower, without charge, an annual accounting of the Funds showing credits and debits to the Funds and the
purpose for which each debit to the Funds was made. The Funds are pledged as additional security for the sums secured by
this Security Instrument.
   If the amount of the Funds held by Lender, together with the future monthly payments of Funds payable prior to
the due dates of the escrow items, shall exceed the amount required to pay the escrow items when due, the excess shall be,
at Borrower's option, either promptly repaid to Borrower or credited to Borrower on monthly payments of Funds. If the
amount of the Funds held by Lender is not sufficient to pay the escrow items when due, Borrower shall pay to Lender any
amount necessary to make up the deficiency in one or more payments as required by Lender.
   Upon payment in full of all sums secured by this Security Instrument, Lender shall promptly refund to Borrower
any Funds held by Lender. If under paragraph 19 the Property is sold or acquired by Lender, Lender shall apply, no later
than immediately prior to the sale of the Property or its acquisition by Lender, any Funds held by Lender at the time of
application as a credit against the sums secured by this Security Instrument.

ILLINOIS—Single Family—**FNMA/FHLMC UNIFORM INSTRUMENT**   Form 3014 12/83
                                                                                          44713 SAF SYSTEMS AND FORMS
                                                                                                CHICAGO, IL

3. Application of Payments. Unless applicable law provides otherwise, all payments received by Lender under paragraphs 1 and 2 shall be applied: first, to late charges due under the Note; second, to prepayment charges due under the Note; third, to amounts payable under paragraph 2; fourth, to interest due; and last, to principal due.

4. Charges; Liens. Borrower shall pay all taxes, assessments, charges, fines and impositions attributable to the Property which may attain priority over this Security Instrument, and leasehold payments or ground rents, if any. Borrower shall pay these obligations in the manner provided in paragraph 2, or if not paid in that manner, Borrower shall pay them on time directly to the person owed payment. Borrower shall promptly furnish to Lender all notices of amounts to be paid under this paragraph. If Borrower makes these payments directly, Borrower shall promptly furnish to Lender receipts evidencing the payments.

Borrower shall promptly discharge any lien which has priority over this Security Instrument unless Borrower: (a) agrees in writing to the payment of the obligation secured by the lien in a manner acceptable to Lender; (b) contests in good faith the lien by, or defends against enforcement of the lien in, legal proceedings which in the Lender's opinion operate to prevent the enforcement of the lien or forfeiture of any part of the Property; or (c) secures from the holder of the lien an agreement satisfactory to Lender subordinating the lien to this Security Instrument. If Lender determines that any part of the Property is subject to a lien which may attain priority over this Security Instrument, Lender may give Borrower a notice identifying the lien. Borrower shall satisfy the lien or take one or more of the actions set forth above within 10 days of the giving of notice.

5. Hazard Insurance. Borrower shall keep the improvements now existing or hereafter erected on the Property insured against loss by fire, hazards included within the term "extended coverage" and any other hazards for which Lender requires insurance. This insurance shall be maintained in the amounts and for the periods that Lender requires. The insurance carrier providing the insurance shall be chosen by Borrower subject to Lender's approval which shall not be unreasonably withheld.

All insurance policies and renewals shall be acceptable to Lender and shall include a standard mortgage clause. Lender shall have the right to hold the policies and renewals. If Lender requires, Borrower shall promptly give to Lender all receipts of paid premiums and renewal notices. In the event of loss, Borrower shall give prompt notice to the insurance carrier and Lender. Lender may make proof of loss if not made promptly by Borrower.

Unless Lender and Borrower otherwise agree in writing, insurance proceeds shall be applied to restoration or repair of the Property damaged, if the restoration or repair is economically feasible and Lender's security is not lessened. If the restoration or repair is not economically feasible or Lender's security would be lessened, the insurance proceeds shall be applied to the sums secured by this Security Instrument, whether or not then due, with any excess paid to Borrower. If Borrower abandons the Property, or does not answer within 30 days a notice from Lender that the insurance carrier has offered to settle a claim, then Lender may collect the insurance proceeds. Lender may use the proceeds to repair or restore the Property or to pay sums secured by this Security Instrument, whether or not then due. The 30-day period will begin when the notice is given.

Unless Lender and Borrower otherwise agree in writing, any application of proceeds to principal shall not extend or postpone the due date of the monthly payments referred to in paragraphs 1 and 2 or change the amount of the payments. If under paragraph 19 the Property is acquired by Lender, Borrower's right to any insurance policies and proceeds resulting from damage to the Property prior to the acquisition shall pass to Lender to the extent of the sums secured by this Security Instrument immediately prior to the acquisition.

6. Preservation and Maintenance of Property; Leaseholds. Borrower shall not destroy, damage or substantially change the Property, allow the Property to deteriorate or commit waste. If this Security Instrument is on a leasehold, Borrower shall comply with the provisions of the lease, and if Borrower acquires fee title to the Property, the leasehold and fee title shall not merge unless Lender agrees to the merger in writing.

7. Protection of Lender's Rights in the Property; Mortgage Insurance. If Borrower fails to perform the covenants and agreements contained in this Security Instrument, or there is a legal proceeding that may significantly affect Lender's rights in the Property (such as a proceeding in bankruptcy, probate, for condemnation or to enforce laws or regulations), then Lender may do and pay for whatever is necessary to protect the value of the Property and Lender's rights in the Property. Lender's actions may include paying any sums secured by a lien which has priority over this Security Instrument, appearing in court, paying reasonable attorneys' fees and entering on the Property to make repairs. Although Lender may take action under this paragraph 7, Lender does not have to do so.

Any amounts disbursed by Lender under this paragraph 7 shall become additional debt of Borrower secured by this Security Instrument. Unless Borrower and Lender agree to other terms of payment, these amounts shall bear interest from the date of disbursement at the Note rate and shall be payable, with interest, upon notice from Lender to Borrower requesting payment.

If Lender required mortgage insurance as a condition of making the loan secured by this Security Instrument, Borrower shall pay the premiums required to maintain the insurance in effect until such time as the requirement for the insurance terminates in accordance with Borrower's and Lender's written agreement or applicable law.

8. Inspection. Lender or its agent may make reasonable entries upon and inspections of the Property. Lender shall give Borrower notice at the time of or prior to an inspection specifying reasonable cause for the inspection.

9. Condemnation. The proceeds of any award or claim for damages, direct or consequential, in connection with any condemnation or other taking of any part of the Property, or for conveyance in lieu of condemnation, are hereby assigned and shall be paid to Lender.

In the event of a total taking of the Property, the proceeds shall be applied to the sums secured by this Security Instrument, whether or not then due, with any excess paid to Borrower. In the event of a partial taking of the Property, unless Borrower and Lender otherwise agree in writing, the sums secured by this Security Instrument shall be reduced by the amount of the proceeds multiplied by the following fraction: (a) the total amount of the sums secured immediately before the taking, divided by (b) the fair market value of the Property immediately before the taking. Any balance shall be paid to Borrower.

If the Property is abandoned by Borrower, or if, after notice by Lender to Borrower that the condemnor offers to make an award or settle a claim for damages, Borrower fails to respond to Lender within 30 days after the date the notice is given, Lender is authorized to collect and apply the proceeds, at its option, either to restoration or repair of the Property or to the sums secured by this Security Instrument, whether or not then due.

Unless Lender and Borrower otherwise agree in writing, any application of proceeds to principal shall not extend or postpone the due date of the monthly payments referred to in paragraphs 1 and 2 or change the amount of such payments.

Figure 15.4 (cont.)

10. Borrower Not Released; Forbearance By Lender Not a Waiver. Extension of the time for payment or modification of amortization of the sums secured by this Security Instrument granted by Lender to any successor in interest of Borrower shall not operate to release the liability of the original Borrower or Borrower's successors in interest. Lender shall not be required to commence proceedings against any successor in interest or refuse to extend time for payment or otherwise modify amortization of the sums secured by this Security Instrument by reason of any demand made by the original Borrower or Borrower's successors in interest. Any forbearance by Lender in exercising any right or remedy shall not be a waiver of or preclude the exercise of any right or remedy.

11. Successors and Assigns Bound; Joint and Several Liability; Co-signers. The covenants and agreements of this Security Instrument shall bind and benefit the successors and assigns of Lender and Borrower, subject to the provisions of paragraph 17. Borrower's covenants and agreements shall be joint and several. Any Borrower who co-signs this Security Instrument but does not execute the Note: (a) is co-signing this Security Instrument only to mortgage, grant and convey that Borrower's interest in the Property under the terms of this Security Instrument; (b) is not personally obligated to pay the sums secured by this Security Instrument; and (c) agrees that Lender and any other Borrower may agree to extend, modify, forbear or make any accommodations with regard to the terms of this Security Instrument or the Note without that Borrower's consent.

12. Loan Charges. If the loan secured by this Security Instrument is subject to a law which sets maximum loan charges, and that law is finally interpreted so that the interest or other loan charges collected or to be collected in connection with the loan exceed the permitted limits, then: (a) any such loan charge shall be reduced by the amount necessary to reduce the charge to the permitted limit; and (b) any sums already collected from Borrower which exceeded permitted limits will be refunded to Borrower. Lender may choose to make this refund by reducing the principal owed under the Note or by making a direct payment to Borrower. If a refund reduces principal, the reduction will be treated as a partial prepayment without any prepayment charge under the Note.

13. Legislation Affecting Lender's Rights. If enactment or expiration of applicable laws has the effect of rendering any provision of the Note or this Security Instrument unenforceable according to its terms, Lender, at its option, may require immediate payment in full of all sums secured by this Security Instrument and may invoke any remedies permitted by paragraph 19. If Lender exercises this option, Lender shall take the steps specified in the second paragraph of paragraph 17.

14. Notices. Any notice to Borrower provided for in this Security Instrument shall be given by delivering it or by mailing it by first class mail unless applicable law requires use of another method. The notice shall be directed to the Property Address or any other address Borrower designates by notice to Lender. Any notice to Lender shall be given by first class mail to Lender's address stated herein or any other address Lender designates by notice to Borrower. Any notice provided for in this Security Instrument shall be deemed to have been given to Borrower or Lender when given as provided in this paragraph.

15. Governing Law; Severability. This Security Instrument shall be governed by federal law and the law of the jurisdiction in which the Property is located. In the event that any provision or clause of this Security Instrument or the Note conflicts with applicable law, such conflict shall not affect other provisions of this Security Instrument or the Note which can be given effect without the conflicting provision. To this end the provisions of this Security Instrument and the Note are declared to be severable.

16. Borrower's Copy. Borrower shall be given one conformed copy of the Note and of this Security Instrument.

17. Transfer of the Property or a Beneficial Interest in Borrower. If all or any part of the Property or any interest in it is sold or transferred (or if a beneficial interest in Borrower is sold or transferred and Borrower is not a natural person) without Lender's prior written consent, Lender may, at its option, require immediate payment in full of all sums secured by this Security Instrument. However, this option shall not be exercised by Lender if exercise is prohibited by federal law as of the date of this Security Instrument.

If Lender exercises this option, Lender shall give Borrower notice of acceleration. The notice shall provide a period of not less than 30 days from the date the notice is delivered or mailed within which Borrower must pay all sums secured by this Security Instrument. If Borrower fails to pay these sums prior to the expiration of this period, Lender may invoke any remedies permitted by this Security Instrument without further notice or demand on Borrower.

18. Borrower's Right to Reinstate. If Borrower meets certain conditions, Borrower shall have the right to have enforcement of this Security Instrument discontinued at any time prior to the earlier of: (a) 5 days (or such other period as applicable law may specify for reinstatement) before sale of the Property pursuant to any power of sale contained in this Security Instrument; or (b) entry of a judgment enforcing this Security Instrument. Those conditions are that Borrower: (a) pays Lender all sums which then would be due under this Security Instrument and the Note had no acceleration occurred; (b) cures any default of any other covenants or agreements; (c) pays all expenses incurred in enforcing this Security Instrument, including, but not limited to, reasonable attorneys' fees; and (d) takes such action as Lender may reasonably require to assure that the lien of this Security Instrument, Lender's rights in the Property and Borrower's obligation to pay the sums secured by this Security Instrument shall continue unchanged. Upon reinstatement by Borrower, this Security Instrument and the obligations secured hereby shall remain fully effective as if no acceleration had occurred. However, this right to reinstate shall not apply in the case of acceleration under paragraphs 13 or 17.

BY SIGNING BELOW, Borrower accepts and agrees to the terms and covenants contained in this Security Instrument and in any rider(s) executed by Borrower and recorded with it.

Thomas Perkins ....(Seal)
　　　　　　　　　　　　　　　　　　　　　—Borrower

Alia Perkins ....(Seal)
　　　　　　　　　　　　　　　　　　　　　—Borrower

Figure 15.5
Trust Deed

TRUST DEED AND NOTE   NO. 2604   GEORGE E. COLE®
                     September, 1975   LEGAL FORMS

THIS INDENTURE WITNESSETH, That the undersigned as grantors, of __Chicago__,
County of __Cook__ and State of __Illinois__, for and in consideration of the sum of
One Dollar and other good and valuable considerations, in hand paid, convey and warrant to __First Security Title and Trust__, of __Chicago__, County of __Cook__
and State of __Illinois__, as trustee, the following described Real Estate, with all improvements
thereon, situated in the County of __Cook__ in the State of __Illinois__ to wit:

Lot 7, Block 23, Uptown Subdivision of the Northwest quarter of Section 14,
Township 9 North, Range 3 East of the Third Principal Meridian in Cook County,
Illinois.

hereby releasing and waiving all rights under and by virtue of the homestead exemption laws of the State of
__Illinois__

GRANTORS AGREE to pay all taxes and assessments upon said propery when due, to keep the buildings thereon insured to their full insurable value, to pay all prior incumbrances and the interest thereon and to keep the property tenantable and in good repair and free of liens. In the event of failure of grantors to comply with any of the above covenants, then grantee is authorized to attend to the same and pay the bills therefor, which shall, with 8% interest thereon, become due immediately, without demand. On default in any payments hereunder, grantee may declare the whole indebtedness due and proceed accordingly.

AS FURTHER SECURITY grantors hereby assign, transfer and set over to grantee all the rents, issues and profits of said premises, from and after this date, and authorize him to sue for, collect and receipt for the same, to serve all necessary notices and demands, to bring forcible detainer proceedings to recover possession thereof, to rent the said premises as he may deem proper and to apply the money so arising to the payment of this indebtedness, or to any advancements made as aforesaid, and it shall not be the duty of grantee to inquire into the validity of any such taxes, assessments, liens, incumbrances, interest or advancements.

In trust, nevertheless, for the purpose of securing performance of the following obligation, to-wit:
$ __87,500__   __June 26__   19 __85__
_____ after date for value received I (we) promise to pay to the order of
__One City Savings and Loan Association__ the sum of
__Eighty-seven thousand__ Dollars
at the office of the legal holder of this instrument with interest at __14__ per cent per annum after date hereof until paid.

And to secure the payment of said amount I (we) hereby authorize, irrevocably any attorney of any court of record in any County or State in the United States to appear for us in such court, in term time or vacation, at any time after maturity hereof, and confess a judgment without process in favor of the holder of this instrument for such amount as may appear to be unpaid thereon, together with costs, and reasonable attorney's fees, and to waive and release all errors which may intervene in any such proceedings, and to consent to immediate execution upon such judgment, hereby ratifying and confirming all that my (our) said attorney may do by virtue hereof.

IN THE EVENT of the trustee's death, inability, or removal from said __Cook__
County, or of his resignation, refusal or failure to act, then _____,
of said County, is hereby appointed to be the first successor in this trust; and if for any like cause first successor fails or refuses to act, the person who shall then be the acting Recorder of Deeds of said County is hereby appointed to be second successor in this trust. And when all the aforesaid covenants and agreements are performed the trustee, or his successor in trust, shall release the premises to the party entitled thereto on receiving his reasonable charges.

Witness our hands and seals this __26th.__ day of __June__ 19 __85__.

                                   John William Baker   (SEAL)
                                   John William Baker
                                   Rebecca Anne Taylor-Baker (SEAL)
                                   Rebecca Anne Taylor-Baker

This instrument was prepared by _____
                                        (NAME AND ADDRESS)

3. maintenance of adequate insurance to protect the lender if the property is destroyed or damaged by fire, windstorm, or other hazard.
4. maintenance of the property in good repair at all times.
5. obtainment of the lender's authorization before placing a second mortgage (junior lien) against the property.
6. obtainment of the lender's authorization before making any major alterations on the property.

Failure to meet any of these obligations can result in a borrower's default on the note. When this happens, the mortgage or trust deed usually provides for a grace period (30 days, for example) during which the borrower can meet the obligation and cure the default. If he or she does not do so, the lender has the right to foreclose the mortgage or trust deed and collect on the note. The most frequent cause of default is the borrower's failure to meet monthly installments.

Provisions for Default

The provisions of a mortgage or trust deed include an **acceleration clause** to assist the lender in foreclosure. If a borrower defaults, the lender has the right to accelerate the maturity of the debt—to declare the *entire* debt due and payable *immediately*—even though the terms of the mortgage or trust deed allow the borrower to amortize the debt in regular payments over a period of years. Without the acceleration clause, the lender would have to sue the borrower every time a payment became due and in default.

Other clauses in a mortgage or trust deed enable the lender to take care of the property in the event of the borrower's negligence or default. If the borrower does not pay taxes or insurance premiums or make necessary repairs on the property, the lender may step in and do so to protect his or her security (the real estate). Any money advanced by the lender to cure such defaults is either added to the unpaid debt or declared immediately due and owing from the borrower.

Assignment of the Mortgage

As mentioned earlier, a note is a negotiable instrument; as such, it may be sold to a third party, or holder in due course. If the holder of the note wishes to sell and the third party also wishes to have the real estate as security, the mortgagee must execute an *assignment of mortgage* document, which is a separate form. Under its terms, the present owner of the mortgage note (the mortgagee) becomes the assignor and executes the assignment to the assignee, who becomes the new owner of the mortgage and the debt. This assignment must be recorded. Upon payment in full, or satisfaction of the debt, the assignee who holds the mortgage and note is required to execute the satisfaction, or release, of mortgage as discussed in the following section. In the event of a foreclosure, the assignee (not the original mortgagee) is required to file the suit.

Release of the Mortgage Lien

When all mortgage loan payments have been made and the note paid in full, the mortgagor wants the public record to show that the debt has been paid and the mortgage released. By the provisions of the **defeasance clause** in the usual mortgage, when the note has been fully paid the mortgagee is required to execute a **satisfaction of mortgage**, also known as a *release of mortgage* or *mortgage discharge.* This document reconveys to the mortgagor all interest in the real estate that was conveyed to the mortgagee by the original recorded mortgage document. By having this release entered in the public record, the owner shows that the mortgage lien has been removed from his or her property.

If a mortgage has been assigned by a recorded assignment, the release must be executed by the assignee mortgagee.

When a real estate loan secured by a trust deed has been completely repaid, the beneficiary requests in writing that the trustee convey the property back to the grantor. The trustee then executes and delivers a **release deed,** sometimes called a *deed of reconveyance,* to the grantor conveying the same rights and powers that the trustee was given under the trust deed. The release deed should be acknowledged and recorded in the public records of the county where the property is located.

Tax and Insurance Reserves

Many lenders require borrowers to provide a reserve fund to meet future real estate taxes and insurance premiums. When the mortgage or trust deed loan is made, the borrower starts the reserve by depositing funds to cover the amount of unpaid real estate taxes prorated from the lien date to the end of the current month. If a new insurance policy has just been purchased, the insurance premium reserve will be started with the deposit of one-twelfth of the annual tax and insurance premium liability. Thereafter the monthly loan payments required of the borrower will include interest, principal, and tax and insurance reserves.

RESPA, the federal Real Estate Settlement Procedures Act (discussed in Chapter 23), limits the amount of tax and insurance reserves that a lender may require.

Federal flood insurance program. As described in Chapter 4, this subsidized plan authorized by Congress requires property owners in certain areas to obtain flood-damage insurance on properties financed by mortgages or other loans, grants, or guarantees obtained from federal agencies and federally insured or regulated lending institutions. The program seeks to improve future management and planning of flood-plain areas through land-use and control measures.

Assignment of Rents

When a mortgage or trust deed is executed, the borrower may make an assignment of rents to the lender. The assignment becomes effective upon the borrower's default. The rent assignment may be included in the mortgage or trust deed, or it may be made as a separate document. In either case, the rent assignment should be drafted in language that clearly indicates that the parties intend to assign the rents, not merely pledge them as security for the loan. In title theory states, the lender is generally automatically entitled to any rents if the borrower defaults.

Buying Subject to or Assuming a Seller's Mortgage or Trust Deed

A person who purchases real estate that has an outstanding mortgage or trust deed on it may take the property subject to the mortgage or may assume it and agree to pay the debt. This technical distinction becomes important if the buyer defaults and the mortgage or trust deed is foreclosed.

When the property is sold *subject to* the mortgage, the courts frequently hold that the purchaser is not personally obligated to pay the debt in full. The purchaser has bought the real estate knowing that he or she must make the loan payments and that, upon default, the lender will foreclose and the property will be sold by court order to pay the debt. If the sale does not pay off the entire debt, the purchaser is not liable for the difference; however, the original seller might still have some liability for that difference. In contrast, when the grantee not only purchases the property subject to the mortgage, but *assumes and agrees to pay* the debt, then the grantee becomes personally obligated for the payment of the *entire debt.* If the mortgage is foreclosed in such a case and the court sale does not bring enough money to pay the debt in full, a deficiency judgment against both the assumer and the original borrower may be obtained for the unpaid balance of the note. Not all states recognize this distinction, but most observe it.

When a mortgage is assumed, most lending institutions charge a transfer fee to cover the costs of changing their records. This charge is customarily borne by the purchaser.

Alienation clause. Frequently, when a real estate loan is made, the lender wishes to prevent some future purchaser of the property from being able to assume that loan, particularly at its old rate of interest. For this reason, some lenders include an **alienation clause** (also known as a *resale clause* or *due-on-sale clause*) in the note. An alienation clause provides that upon the sale of the property by the borrower to a buyer who wants to assume the loan, the lender has the choice of either declaring the entire debt to be immediately due and owing or permitting the buyer to assume the loan at current market interest rates.

Recording Mortgages and Trust Deeds	The mortgage document or trust deed must be recorded in the recorder's office of the county in which the real estate is located. The recordation gives constructive notice to the world of the borrower's obligations and establishes the lien's priority. If the property is registered in Torrens, notice of the lien must be entered on the original certificate of title on file at the registrar's office.
First and Second Mortgages or Trust Deeds	Mortgages and other liens normally have priority in the order in which they have been recorded. A mortgage or trust deed on land that has no prior mortgage lien on it is a *first mortgage* or *first trust deed.* When the owner of this land later executes another loan for additional funds, the new loan becomes a *second mortgage or trust deed,* or *a junior lien,* when recorded. The second lien is subject to the first lien; the first has prior claim to the value of the land pledged as security. Because second loans represent a greater risk to the lender, they are usually issued at higher interest rates.

The priority of mortgage or trust deed liens may be changed by the execution of a *subordination agreement,* in which the first lender subordinates his or her lien to that of the second lender. To be valid, such an agreement must be signed by both lenders.

Foreclosure	When a borrower defaults in making payments or fulfilling any of the obligations set forth in the mortgage or trust deed, the lender can enforce his or her rights through a foreclosure. A **foreclosure** is a legal procedure whereby the property that is pledged as security in the mortgage document or trust deed is sold to satisfy the debt. The foreclosure procedure brings the rights of all parties to a conclusion and passes title in the subject property either to the person holding the mortgage document or trust deed or to a third party who purchases the realty at a *foreclosure sale.* Property thus sold is *free of the mortgage and all junior liens.*

Methods of Foreclosure

There are three general types of foreclosure proceedings—judicial, nonjudicial, and strict foreclosure. The specific provisions of these vary from state to state.

Judicial foreclosure. A judicial foreclosure proceeding provides that the property pledged as security may be sold by court order after the mortgagee gives sufficient public notice. Upon a borrower's default, the lender may *accelerate* the due date of all remaining monthly payments. The lender's attorney can then file a suit to foreclose the lien. Upon presentation of the facts in court, the property is ordered sold. A public sale is advertised and held, and the real estate is sold to the highest bidder.

Nonjudicial foreclosure. Some states allow nonjudicial foreclosure procedures to be used when a *power-of-sale clause* is contained in the loan document. In those states that recognize trust deed loans, the trustee is generally given the power of sale, although nonjudicial foreclosure is not allowed in a few states that permit trust deeds. Some states allow a similar power of sale to be used with a mortgage loan.

To institute a nonjudicial foreclosure, the trustee (or mortgagee) must record a notice of default at the county recorder's office within a designated time period in order to give notice to the public of the intended auction. This official notice is generally accompanied by advertisements published in local newspapers that state the total amount due and the date of the public sale. The purpose of this notice is not to notify the defaulting debtor but rather to publicize the sale. After selling the property, the trustee (or mortgagee) may be required to file a copy of a notice of sale or affidavit of foreclosure.

Strict foreclosure. Although the judicial and nonjudicial foreclosure procedures are the prevalent practices today, in some states it is still possible for a lender to acquire the mortgaged property by a strict foreclosure process. After appropriate notice has been given to the delinquent borrower and the proper papers have been prepared and filed, the court establishes a specific time period during which the balance of the defaulted debt must be paid in full. If this is not done, the court usually awards full legal title to the lender.

Deed in Lieu of Foreclosure

An alternative to foreclosure would be for the lender to accept, or "buy," a *deed in lieu of foreclosure* from the borrower. This is sometimes known as a *friendly foreclosure,* since it is by agreement rather than by civil action. The major disadvantage to this manner of default settlement is that the mortgagee takes the real estate subject to all junior liens, while foreclosure eliminates all such liens.

Redemption

Most states give a defaulting borrower a chance to redeem his or her property. Redemption generally takes one of two forms—equitable redemption and statutory redemption.

Historically, the **right of redemption** is inherited from the old common-law proceedings in which the court sale ended the *equitable right of redemption.* Carried over to statutory law, this concept provides that if, during the course of a foreclosure proceeding but *before the foreclosure sale,* the borrower or any other person who has an interest in the real estate (such as another creditor) pays the lender the amount currently due, plus costs, the debt will be reinstated as before. In some cases, the person who redeems may be required to repay the accelerated loan in full. If some person other than the mortgagor or trustor redeems the real estate, the borrower becomes responsible to that person for the amount of the redemption.

As discussed earlier, many states also allow a defaulted borrower a period in which to redeem his or her real estate *after the sale.* During this *statutory redemption* period (which may be as long as one year) the court may appoint a receiver to take charge of the property, collect rents, pay operating expenses, and so forth. If the mortgagor or trustor can raise the necessary funds to redeem the property within the statutory period, he or she pays the redemption money to the court. Since the debt was paid from the proceeds of the sale, the borrower can take possession free and clear of the former defaulted loan.

Deed to Purchaser at Sale

If redemption is not made or if no redemption period is allowed by state law, then the successful bidder at the sale receives a deed to the real estate. This is a statutory form of deed that may be executed by a sheriff or master-in-chancery to *convey such title as the borrower had* to the purchaser at the sale. There are no warranties with such a deed; the title passes as is, but free of the former defaulted debt.

Deficiency Judgment

If the foreclosure sale of the real estate secured by a mortgage or trust deed does not produce a sufficient sales price to pay the loan balance in full after deducting expenses and accrued unpaid interest, the mortgagee may be entitled to a *personal judgment* against the maker of the note for the unpaid balance. Such a judgment is called a **deficiency judgment.** It may also be obtained against any endorsers or guarantors of the note and any owners of the mortgaged property who may have assumed the debt by written agreement. If there are any surplus proceeds from the foreclosure sale after the debt and all junior liens are paid off and expenses and interest are deducted, these proceeds are paid to the borrower.

Conventional, Insured, and Guaranteed Loans

Mortgage and trust deed loans are generally classified as conventional, insured, or guaranteed loans. Loans are classified as **conventional** when the payment of the debt rests solely upon the ability of the borrower to pay, with security provided by the mortgage or trust deed. Repayment of insured and guaranteed loans is additionally secured through insurance issued by the Federal Housing Administration (FHA) or a private mortgage insurance company, or by a guarantee made by the Veterans Administration (VA).

Conventional Loans

In making conventional loans, lenders rely primarily on their own appraisal of the security and their own credit reports and information concerning the credit reliability of the prospective borrower. Many lending institutions, such as savings and loans, banks, and insurance companies, are restricted by law to mortgage investments that are first mortgages or trust deeds. However, a number of second mortgage institutions are in business for the purpose of lending funds based upon junior liens. When money is tight, there is greater activity in this second mortgage market than there is when there are ample first mortgage funds available.

In addition, the ratio of the debt to the value of the property in conventional loans (known as the *loan-to-value ratio*) is generally lower than with insured and guaranteed loans. (The VA allows up to 100 percent loans; FHA usually allows up to 97 percent loans.) The lower the loan-to-value ratio is, the lower the lender's risk is.

FHA-Insured Loans The Federal Housing Administration (FHA) was created in 1934 under the National Housing Act to encourage improvement in housing standards and conditions, provide an adequate home-financing system through insurance of housing credit, and exert a stabilizing influence on the mortgage market. The FHA was the government's response to the lack of housing, excessive foreclosures, and collapsed building industry that occurred during the Depression.

The FHA, which operates under the Department of Housing and Urban Development (HUD), neither builds homes nor lends money itself. Rather, *it insures loans on real property made by approved lending institutions.* It does not insure the property, but it does insure the lender against loss. The common term **FHA loan,** then, refers to a loan that is not made by the agency but insured by it.

The most popular FHA program is Title II, Section 203(b), which applies to loans on one- to four-family residences. While interest rates on these loans are no longer fixed by the FHA, such rates are generally ½ percent less than those charged under conventional loans. These rates are generally lower because the protection of the FHA mortgage insurance makes them a lesser risk to the lender. Technical requirements established under congressional authority must be met before the FHA will issue the insurance. Three of these requirements are:

1. In addition to paying interest, the *borrower is charged between 2.9 and 3.8 percent* of the outstanding loan amount as a *premium for the FHA insurance.* This amount is payable at the closing, or it may be financed for the term of the loan.

2. The mortgaged real estate must be appraised by an *approved FHA appraiser,* and the ratio of possible mortgage debt to the appraised value of the property decreases as the appraised value of the property increases. The ratio cannot exceed 97 percent on the first $25,000 of appraised value and 95 percent on any amount greater than $25,000. This means that a family using an FHA-insured loan to purchase a home appraised at $75,000 must make a down payment of $3,250, or 3 percent of $25,000 ($750) and 5 percent of $50,000 ($2,500). For houses less than one year old that were not built to FHA standards, the loan ratio is 90 percent of the appraised value or selling price, whichever is less. Note that if the purchase price exceeds the FHA-appraised value, the buyer must pay the difference in cash as part of the down payment. In addition, the FHA has set maximum loan amounts for various regions of the country. Contact your local FHA office for such amounts in your area. FHA regulations require that both buyer and seller sign a statement indicating that they have examined the FHA appraisal.

3. The FHA regulations set *standards* for type and construction of buildings, quality of neighborhood, and credit requirements for borrowers.

Prepayment privileges. When a mortgage or trust deed loan is insured by the FHA and the real estate given as security is a single-family dwelling or an apartment building with no more than four units, the borrower retains the privilege of prepaying the debt without penalty. On the first day of any month before the loan matures, the borrower may pay the entire debt or an amount equal to one or more monthly payments on the principal. The borrower must give the lender written notice of intention to exercise this privilege at least 30 days beforehand, or the lender has the option of charging up to 30 days' interest in lieu of such notification.

Other FHA loan programs.   In addition to loans made under Title II, Section 203(b), as previously discussed, FHA loans are also granted under the folllowing programs:

1. Title I: Home improvement loans are covered under this title; such loans are for relatively low amounts with a repayment term of no longer than seven years and 32 days.

2. Title II, Section 234: Loans made to purchase condominiums are covered under this program, which in most respects is similar to the basic 203(b) program.

3. Title II, Section 245: Graduated payment mortgages, as discussed in this chapter, are allowed under this program; depending on interest rates, the loan-to-value ratio of such loans might range from 87 to 93 percent.

Private Mortgage Insurance

Aside from the FHA, mortgage insurance may also be obtained through private sources. Under the provisions of such privately insured lending programs, home purchasers can obtain conventional mortgage or trust deed loans of up to 95 percent of the appraised property value at prevailing interest rates and reasonable insurance premium costs. The leader in this field is the *Mortgage Guaranty Insurance Corporation (MGIC)* of Milwaukee, Wisconsin, which instituted the program in 1957.

VA-Guaranteed (GI) Loans

Under the Servicemen's Readjustment Act of 1944 and subsequent federal legislation, the Veterans Administration is authorized to guarantee loans to purchase or construct homes for eligible veterans—those who have served a minimum of 181 days' active service since September 16, 1940 (90 days for veterans of World War II, the Korean War, and the Viet Nam conflict; two full years for those enlisting for the first time after September 7, 1980). The VA also guarantees loans to purchase mobile homes and plots on which to place them. GI loans assist veterans in financing the purchase of homes with little or no down payments, at comparatively low interest rates. Rules and regulations are issued from time to time by the VA, setting forth the qualifications, limitations, and conditions under which a loan may be guaranteed. (Table 15.1 is a comparison of VA and FHA loan programs.)

Like the term *FHA loan,* **VA loan** is something of a misnomer. The VA does not normally lend money itself; it guarantees loans made by lending institutions approved by the agency. The term *VA loan,* then refers to a loan that is not made by the agency but guaranteed by it.

There is no VA limit on the amount of the loan a veteran can obtain; this is determined by the lender. The VA does, however, set a limit on the amount of the loan that it will guarantee, currently 60 percent of the loan amount or $27,500, whichever is less, in the purchase, construction, repair, or alteration of a house, condominium, or farm residence.

Note that the $27,500 figure (or 60 percent) is the amount of the guarantee and refers to the amount the lender would receive from the VA in the case of a default and foreclosure if the sale did not bring enough to cover the outstanding balance. For example, if a $60,000 loan were in default, the property could sell at foreclosure for as little as $32,500 ($60,000 — $27,500), and the lender would recoup the full value of the loan.

To determine what portion of a mortgage loan the VA will guarantee, the veteran must apply for a *certificate of eligibility*. This certificate does not mean that the veteran will automatically receive a mortgage. It merely sets forth the maximum guarantee the veteran is entitled to.

The VA will also issue a *certificate of reasonable value* (CRV) for the property being purchased, stating its current market value based on a VA-approved appraisal. The CRV places a ceiling on the amount of a VA loan allowed for the property; if the purchase price is greater than the amount cited in the CRV, the veteran must pay the difference in cash.

Only in certain situations (such as in isolated rural areas) where financing is not reasonably available does the VA lend money itself; otherwise, a veteran obtains a loan from a VA-approved lending institution. The VA does not require a down payment. Although the VA guarantee is never more than $27,500, in practice the veteran may be able to obtain a 100 percent loan if the appraised valuation of the property is $110,000 or less and the veteran is entitled to a full $27,500 (the usual 25 percent down payment) guarantee.

Table 15.1 Comparison of FHA and VA Loan Programs	Federal Housing Administration	Veterans Administration
	1. Financing is available to veterans and nonveterans alike	1. Financing available only to veterans and certain unremarried widows and widowers
	2. Financing programs for owner-occupied, rental, and other types of construction; owner-occupied has greater loan-to-value ratio	2. VA financing limited to owner-occupied residential (1- to 4-family) dwellings—must sign occupancy certificate on two separate occasions
	3. Requires a larger down payment than VA	3. Does not normally require down payment, though lender may require small down payment
	4. Different evaluation methods; like VA, there are prescribed valuation procedures for the approved appraisers to follow	4. Methods of valuation differ—VA issues a certificate of reasonable value
	5. FHA valuation sets the maximum loan FHA will insure but does not limit the sales price	5. With regard to home loans, the VA loan may not exceed the appraised value of the home
	6. No prepayment penalty	6. No prepayment penalty
	7. On default, foreclosure, and claim, the FHA lender usually gets U.S. debentures	7. Following default, foreclosure, and claim, the lender usually receives cash
	8. Insures the loan by way of mutual mortgage insurance; premiums paid by borrower	8. Guarantees up to 60 percent of the loan or $27,500, whichever is less
	9. No secondary financing permitted till after closing	9. Secondary financing permitted in exceptional cases
	10. Borrower is subject to 1 percent loan origination fee	10. Borrower prohibited from paying discount points (except in refinancing and certain defined circumstances); he or she can pay a 1 percent loan origination fee
	11. FHA loan can be assumed without FHA approval	11. Borrower must pay a 1 percent funding fee to VA in addition to any other fees
		12. VA loan can be assumed by nonveteran without VA approval

Maximum loan terms are 30 years for one- to four-family dwellings and 40 years for farm loans. The interest rate cannot exceed the rate set periodically by the VA Administrator. Residential property purchased with a VA loan must be owner-occupied.

VA loans can be assumed by purchasers who do not qualify as veterans. The original veteran borrower remains liable for the loan unless he or she obtains a release of the liability, which must be approved by the VA.

Prepayment. As with an FHA loan, the borrower under a VA loan can prepay the debt at any time without penalty. Also, the veteran may not be required to pay more than a one percent origination fee.

Discount points on VA loans. From a borrower's point of view, a mortgage or trust deed loan is a means of financing an expenditure; from a lender's point of view, it is an investment. VA loans are made by approved lending institutions, such as mortgage companies, and then sold to investors, such as insurance companies. By selling the loans instead of collecting the principal and interest over the long term, lending institutions can continuously replenish their supplies of funds.

Discounts, or discount points, are usually charged by a lending institution *when the VA interest rate is less than the market rate.* As with service-charge points, one point equals one percentage point (1%) of the loan amount. VA regulations prohibit charging discount points to the buyer; they are *charged to the seller.* (Note: In FHA and conventional loans, points are usually negotiated between the seller and the buyer.)

If a mortgage loan made at a fixed VA interest rate of 12 percent is compared to a similar mortgage loan made in the conventional mortgage market at 12½ percent interest, the VA loan yields one-half percentage point less in interest. If both loans were offered to an investor at the same price, he or she would choose to buy the 12½ percent loan. The only way to sell the 12 percent loan is to reduce the price, or discount it to bring up its yield.

Generally, one point of the mortgage principal is deducted for each one-eighth percent difference in the interest yield. In the case of the 12 percent and 12½ percent loans, there is one-half percentage point difference in yield, which equals four-eighths; therefore, a difference of four percentage points would be discounted. For example, if the mortgage amount were $50,000, then a four-point discount would represent four percent of $50,000, or $2,000. The discounted value of the loan would be $50,000 minus $2,000, or $48,000. The investor who pays $48,000 for a $50,000, 12 percent mortgage note will receive $6,000 per year interest, which would be nearly 12½ percent return, or yield, on the $48,000 investment. Discount points, then, represent the percentage by which the face amount of a VA mortgage loan is discounted, or reduced, when it is sold to an investor in order to make its fixed interest rate yield competitive in the current money market. Without this discount, an investor would not be interested in a VA loan and would rather make conventional loans in order to earn the higher market rate of interest on the investment.

At the closing of a purchase financed by a VA loan, the seller is charged the discount amount, which is paid to the lending company. This discount charge makes up the difference between the lender's cost of the loan and the expected selling price of the loan.

In Practice ...   *Regulations and requirements regarding FHA and VA loans change frequently. Check with local lenders, as well as with your local FHA and VA offices, from time to time for current information regarding these government-backed loan programs.*

Other Financing Techniques

By altering the terms of the basic mortgage or trust deed and note, a borrower and a lender can tailor financing instruments to best suit the type of transaction and the financial needs of both parties. Especially in times of tight, expensive mortgage money, such "creative financing" gains prominence. In addition, real estate may be financed using instruments other than mortgages and trust deeds, as will be discussed in the following section.

Purchase-Money Mortgages or Trust Deeds

A purchase-money mortgage is a note and mortgage or trust deed created at the time of purchase to facilitate the sale. It is often *given by the purchaser to the seller* to finance the property. A purchase-money mortgage is usually given to cover a portion of the purchase price, such as the down payment; it may even be given to finance the entire purchase price (especially in times of tight money). This may be a first or second mortgage, and it becomes a lien on the property when the title passes. In the event of the foreclosure of a purchase-money mortgage or trust deed, the lien takes priority over judgment liens against the borrower, homestead exemptions of the borrower and spouse, and (in some states) dower rights of the spouse.

Adjustable Rate Mortgages or Trust Deeds

Adjustable rate loans are generally originated at one rate of interest, with the rate fluctuating up or down during the loan term based on a certain economic indicator, such as the cost-of-funds index for federally chartered savings and loan associations. Details of how and when the rate of interest on the loan will change are included in the provisions of the note. Generally, interest rate adjustments are limited to one each year, and there is a set maximum number of increases that may be made over the life of the loan. Certain regulations may enable a lender to adjust the interest rate on a monthly basis. The borrower is usually given the right to prepay the loan in full without penalty (see the discussion on prepayment penalties in this chapter) whenever the interest rate is changed.

Renegotiable Rate Mortgages or Trust Deeds

Renegotiable rate loans are long-term loans that are renewable every three, four, or five years, at which time the interest rate is increased or decreased. These adjustments are based on a national index—for instance, the interest rates on previously occupied homes as compiled by the Federal Home Loan Bank Board. Interest rates may generally change at a maximum rate of one-half percent per year, with a five percent maximum over the life of the loan; specifics are included in the provisions of the note. Often such limitations are self-imposed by lenders. Borrowers must usually be notified of any rate change at least 90 days in advance of the change. Downward interest adjustments are mandatory, while upward adjustments are optional. Borrowers are usually allowed to prepay without penalty within a reasonable time after receiving notice of a rate change.

Shared-Appreciation Mortgages or Trust Deeds

A shared-appreciation loan is one in which the lender originates a mortgage or trust deed loan at a favorable interest rate (several points below the going rate) in return for a guaranteed share of the gain (if any) the borrower will realize when the property is eventually sold. This type of loan was originally made to developers of large real estate projects, but in times of expensive mortgage money it has appeared in the residential financing market. The specific details of the shared-appreciation agreement are set forth in the mortgage or trust deed and note documents.

Reverse Annuity Mortgages or Trust Deeds

A reverse annuity loan is one in which regular monthly payments are made *to the borrower,* based on the equity the homeowner has invested in the property given as security for the loan. A reverse loan allows senior citizens on fixed incomes to realize the equity buildup in their homes without having to sell. The borrower is charged a fixed rate of interest, and the loan is eventually paid from the sale of the property or from the borrower's estate upon his or her death.

Package Mortgages or Trust Deeds

A package loan not only includes the real estate, but also *expressly includes all fixtures and appliances installed on the premises.* In recent years, this kind of loan has been used extensively in financing furnished condominium units. Such loans usually include the kitchen range, refrigerator, dishwasher, garbage disposal unit, washer and dryer, food freezer, and other appliances, as well as furniture, drapes, and carpets, as part of the real estate in the sales price of the home.

Not all state courts agree that personal property (such as a washer and dryer) becomes real estate under these circumstances and is subject to the package mortgage. You must determine whether or not the package mortgage is used in your state. The rights of a person who acquires a security interest in fixtures or in personal property that will become attached to real estate and thus become a fixture, are usually defined in the *Uniform Commercial Code* (see Chapter 13).

Blanket Mortgages or Trust Deeds

A blanket loan covers *more than one parcel or lot,* and is usually used to finance subdivision developments (though it can be used to finance the purchase of improved properties as well). These loans usually include a provision, known as a *partial release clause,* that the borrower may obtain the release of any one lot or parcel from the lien by repaying a definite amount of the loan. The lender issues a partial release for each parcel released from the mortgage lien; this release form includes a provision that the lien will continue to cover all other, unreleased lots.

Wraparound Encumbrances

A wraparound mortgage, also known as an *all-inclusive trust deed,* enables a borrower who is paying off an existing mortgage or trust deed loan to obtain additional financing from a second lender. *The new lender assumes payment of the existing loan and gives the borrower a new, increased loan at a higher interest rate.* The total amount of the new loan includes the existing loan as well as the additional funds needed by the borrower. The borrower makes payments to the new lender on the larger loan, and the new lender makes the payments on the original loan.

A wraparound mortgage is frequently used as a method of refinancing real property or financing the purchase of real property when an existing mortgage cannot be prepaid. It is also used to finance the sale of real estate when the buyer wishes to put up a minimum of initial cash for the sale. The buyer executes a wraparound document to the seller, who will collect payments on the new loan and continue to make payments on the old loan. The buyer should require a protective clause in the document granting him or her the right to make payments directly to the original lender in the event of a potential default on the old loan by the seller.

Open-End Mortgages or Trust Deeds

An open-end loan, which is being used with increasing frequency, secures a *note* executed by the borrower to the lender, as well as any future *advances* of funds made by the lender to the borrower or his or her successors in title.

The mortgage or trust deed usually includes a statement of the maximum amount to be secured. Any sums the lender may have to pay to protect his or her security due to the borrower's neglect for such items as taxes, assessments, or insurance premiums are added to this maximum amount.

An open-end mortgage is frequently used by borrowers to obtain additional funds in order to improve their property. The borrower "opens" the mortgage or trust deed to increase the debt to its original amount after the debt has been reduced by payments over a period of time. The terms of an open-end mortgage usually restrict the increase in debt to a limit of either the original amount of the debt or a stipulated amount set forth in the mortgage or trust deed. The lender is not obligated to advance the additional funds.

Construction Loans

A construction loan is made to *finance the construction of improvements* on real estate (homes, apartments, office buildings, and so forth). Under a construction loan, the lender disburses the loan proceeds while the building is being constructed.

Payments are made from time to time to the *general contractor* for that part of the construction work that has been completed since the previous payment. Prior to each payment, the lender inspects the work; the general contractor must provide the lender with adequate waivers of lien releasing all mechanics' lien rights (see Chapter 10) for the work covered by the payment. This kind of loan generally bears a higher interest rate because of the risks assumed by the lender. These risks include the inadequate releasing of mechanics' liens just referred to, possible delays in completing the building, or the financial failure of the contractor or subcontractors. This type of financing is generally short-term, or *interim, financing*. The borrower is expected to arrange for a permanent loan (also known as an *end loan* or *take-out loan*) that will repay or "take out" the construction financing lender when the work is completed.

Sale and Leaseback

Sale-and-leaseback arrangements are used rather extensively as a means of financing large commercial or industrial plants. The land and building, usually used by the seller for business purposes, are sold to an investor, such as an insurance company. The real estate is then leased back by the buyer (the investor) to the seller, who continues to conduct business on the property as a tenant. The buyer becomes the lessor, and the original owner becomes the lessee. This enables a business firm that has money invested in a plant to free that money so it can be used as working capital.

Sale-and-leaseback arrangements are very complex. They involve complicated legal procedures, and their success is usually related to the effects the transaction has on the firm's tax situation. A real estate broker should consult with legal and tax experts when involved in this type of transaction.

Installment Contracts (Contracts for Deed)

As discussed in Chapter 11, real estate can be purchased under an *installment contract,* also known as a contract for deed, land contract of sale, agreement of sale, or articles of agreement for warranty deed. Real estate is often sold on contract in one of two situations: (1) when mortgage financing is unavailable or too expensive and (2) when the purchaser does not have a sufficient down payment to cover the difference between a mortgage or trust deed loan and the selling price of the real estate.

Investment Group Financing

Large real estate projects, such as high-rise apartment buildings, office complexes, and shopping centers, are often financed as a joint venture through group financing arrangements, such as syndicates, limited partnerships, and real estate investment trusts. These complex investment agreements are discussed in Chapter 22, "Real Estate Investment."

Sources of Real Estate Financing

Most loans to finance real estate purchases are obtained from financial institutions designed to hold individuals' savings. These institutions lend out and invest these deposits to earn interest, some of which is directed back to the savers, some of which is retained as income. Mortgage loans are generally made by institutional lenders, such as savings and loan associations, commercial banks, mutual savings banks, life insurance companies, mortgage banking companies, mortgage brokers, and credit unions.

Savings and Loan Associations

Savings and loan associations are traditionally the most active participants in the home-loan mortgage market, specializing in long-term residential loans. The principal function of a savings and loan is to promote thrift and home ownership. Generally, real estate mortgages are the main source of investment for savings and loan associations—over 85 percent of their assets are annually fed into the mortgage market. Traditionally, they are the most flexible of all the lending institutions with regard to their mortgage lending procedures, and they are generally local in nature. In addition, savings and loans participate in FHA-insured and VA-guaranteed loans, though only to a limited extent.

All savings and loan associations must be chartered, either by the federal government or by the state in which they are located. Savings and loans are regulated on a national level by the Federal Home Loan Bank system (FHLB). The FHLB sets up mandatory guidelines for member associations and provides depositors with savings insurance through the Federal Savings and Loan Insurance Corporation (FSLIC).

Commercial Banks

Traditionally, commercial banks have not been considered a prime source of real estate financing, since they are not specifically set up to finance long-term loans. This is because most of a bank's assets are tied up in demand (checking) accounts rather than long-term savings accounts. Primarily, bank loan departments handle such short-term loans as construction, home-improvement, and mobile-home loans. In some areas, however, commercial banks are originating an increasing number of home mortgages. Commercial banks usually issue a larger proportion of VA and FHA loans than do savings and loan associations. Like the savings and loan associations, banks must be chartered by the state or federal government;

bank deposits are insured by the Federal Deposit Insurance Corporation (FDIC).

Mutual Savings Banks

These institutions, which operate like savings and loan associations, are located primarily in the northeastern section of the United States. They issue no stock and are mutually owned by their investors. Although mutual savings banks do offer limited checking account privileges, they are primarily savings institutions and are highly active in the mortgage market, investing in loans secured by income property as well as residential real estate. In addition, since mutual savings banks usually seek low-risk loan investments, they often prefer to originate FHA-insured or VA-guaranteed loans.

Life Insurance Companies

Insurance companies amass large sums of money from the premiums paid by their policyholders. While a certain portion of this money is held in reserve to satisfy claims and cover operating expenses, much of it is invested in profit-earning enterprises, such as long-term real estate loans.

Most insurance companies like to invest their money in large, long-term loans that finance commercial and industrial properties. They also invest in residential mortgage and trust deed loans by purchasing large blocks of government-backed loans (FHA-insured and VA-guaranteed loans) from the Federal National Mortgage Association and other agencies that warehouse such loans for resale in the secondary mortgage market (as discussed later in this chapter).

In addition, many life insurance companies seek to further ensure the safety of their investments by insisting on equity positions (known as *equity kickers*) in many projects they finance. This means that the company requires a partnership arrangement with, for example, a project developer or subdivider as a condition of making a loan. This is called *participation financing*.

Mortgage Banking Companies

Mortgage banking companies operate primarily as loan correspondents. They originate mortgage loans with money belonging to such other institutions as insurance companies and pension funds or to individuals, and they act as the liaison between borrower and lender. In addition, many mortgage banking companies have sufficient funds of their own to make real estate loans that may later be sold to investors (with the mortgage company receiving a fee for servicing the loans). Mortgage banking companies are often involved in all types of real estate loan activities.

Mortgage banking companies are generally organized as stock companies. As a source of real estate financing, they are subject to considerably fewer lending restrictions and limitations than commercial banks or savings and loans.

Mortgage Brokers

Mortgage brokers are individuals who are licensed to act as intermediaries in bringing borrowers and lenders together. They locate potential borrowers, process preliminary loan applications, and submit the applications to lenders for final approval. Frequently, they work with or for mortgage banking companies in these activities. Many mortgage brokers are also real estate brokers who offer these financing services in addition to their regular brokerage activities.

Credit Unions

Credit unions are cooperative organizations in which members place money in savings accounts, usually at higher interest rates than other savings institutions offer. In the past, most credit unions made only short-term consumer and home-improvement loans, but in recent years they have been branching out into originating longer-term first and second mortgage and trust deed loans.

Application for Credit

All mortgage lenders require prospective borrowers to file an application for credit that provides the lender with the basic information needed to evaluate the acceptability of the proposed loan. The application includes information regarding the purpose of the loan, the amount, rate of interest, and the proposed terms of repayment. This is considered a preliminary offer of a loan agreement; final terms may require lengthy negotiations.

A prospective borrower must submit personal information to the lender, including employment, earnings, assets, and financial obligations. Details of the real estate that will be the security for the loan must be provided, including legal description, improvements, title, survey, and taxes. For loans on income property or those made to corporations, additional information is required, such as financial and operating statements, schedules of leases and tenants, and balance sheets.

The lender carefully investigates the application information, studying credit reports and an appraisal of the property before deciding whether or not to grant the loan. The lender's acceptance of the application is written in the form of a *loan commitment,* which creates a contract to make a loan and sets forth the details. With borderline cases, a commitment may be made based on the lender's current financial position.

In Practice . . .

Since interest rates and loan terms change frequently, you should check with local sources of real estate financing on a regular basis to learn of specific loan rates and terms. As a licensee, you can better serve your customers—and thus more effectively sell your clients' properties—if you can knowledgeably refer buyers to local lenders offering the most favorable terms.

Government Influence in Mortgage Lending

Aside from FHA-insured and VA-guaranteed loan programs, the federal government influences mortgage lending through the Federal Reserve System as well as through various federal agencies, such as the Farmers' Home Administration. It also deals in the secondary mortgage market through the Government National Mortgage Association, the Federal Home Loan Mortgage Corporation, and the Federal National Mortgage Association.

Federal Reserve System

Established in 1913 under President Woodrow Wilson, the Federal Reserve System (also known as "the Fed") operates to maintain sound credit conditions, help counteract inflationary and deflationary trends, and create a favorable economic climate. The Federal Reserve System divides the country into 12 federal reserve districts, each served by a federal reserve bank. All nationally chartered banks must join the Federal Reserve and purchase stock in its district reserve banks.

The Federal Reserve regulates the flow of money and interest rates in the marketplace indirectly, through its member banks, by controlling their *reserve requirements* and *discount rates.*

Reserve controls. The Federal Reserve requires each member bank to keep a certain amount of its assets on hand as reserve funds unavailable for loans or any other use. This requirement was designed primarily to protect customer deposits, but more importantly, it provides a means of manipulating the flow of cash in the money market. By increasing its reserve requirements, the Federal Reserve, in effect, limits the amount of money that member banks can use to make loans, causing interest rates to increase.

In this manner, the government can slow down an overactive economy by limiting the number of loans that would have been directed toward major purchases of goods and services. The opposite is also true—by decreasing the reserve requirements, the Federal Reserve can allow more loans to be made, thus increasing the amount of money circulated in the marketplace and causing interest rates to decline.

Discount rates. Federal Reserve member banks are permitted to borrow money from the district reserve banks to expand their lending operations. The interest rate that the district banks charge for the use of this money is called the discount rate. This rate is the basis on which the banks determine the percentage rate of interest that they, in turn, charge their loan customers. Theoretically, when the Federal Reserve discount rate is high, bank interest rates are high; therefore, fewer loans will be made and less money will circulate in the marketplace. Conversely, a lower discount rate results in lower interest rates, more bank loans, and more money in circulation.

Government Influence in the Secondary Market

Mortgage lending takes place in both the primary and secondary mortgage markets. The **primary market,** which this chapter has principally dealt with thus far, includes: (1) lenders who supply funds to borrowers as an investment and (2) lenders who also originate loans for the purpose of selling them to investors. Loans are bought and sold in the **secondary mortgage market** after they have been originated. For example, a lender may wish to sell a number of loans in order to raise immediate funds when it needs more money to meet the mortgage demands in its area. Secondary market activity is especially desirable when money is in short supply, because it provides a great stimulant to the housing construction market as well as to the mortgage market.

Generally, when a loan has been sold the original lender continues to collect the payments from the borrower. The lender then passes the payments along to the investor who has purchased the loan and charges the investor a fee for servicing the loan.

A major source of secondary mortgage market activity is a **warehousing agency,** which purchases a number of mortgage loans and assembles them into one or more packages of loans for resale to investors. The major warehousing agencies are the Federal National Mortgage Association (FNMA), the Government National Mortgage Association (GNMA), and the Federal Home Loan Mortgage Corporation (FHLMC).

Federal National Mortgage Association. The Federal National Mortgage Association (FNMA), often referred to as **Fannie Mae,** is a quasi-governmental agency, organized as a privately owned corporation, that provides a secondary market for mortgage loans—primarily FHA and VA loans. The corporation raises funds to purchase loans by selling government-guaranteed FNMA bonds at market interest rates. These bonds are secured by blocks, or pools, of mortgages acquired through FNMA's loan commitment program.

Mortgage banking firms are generally actively involved with FNMA, originating loans and selling them to FNMA while retaining the servicing functions.

Government National Mortgage Association. The common name for the Government National Mortgage Association (GNMA) is **Ginnie Mae.** It exists as a corporation without capital stock and is a division of the Department of Housing and Urban Development (HUD). GNMA is designed to administer special assistance programs and work with FNMA in secondary market activities. Fannie Mae and Ginnie Mae can join forces in times of tight money and high interest rates through their tandem plan. Basically, the *tandem plan* provides that FNMA can purchase high-risk, low-yield (usually FHA) loans at full market rates, with GNMA guaranteeing payment and absorbing the difference between the low yield and current market prices.

Ginnie Mae also guarantees investment securities issued by private offerors, such as banks, mortgage companies, and savings and loan associations, that are backed by pools of FHA and VA mortgage loans. The *Ginnie Mae pass-through certificate* is a security interest in a pool of mortgages that provides for a monthly "pass-through" of principal and interest payments directly to the certificate holder. Such certificates are guaranteed by Ginnie Mae.

Federal Home Loan Mortgage Corporation. The Federal Home Loan Mortgage Corporation (FHLMC), or **Freddie Mac,** provides a secondary market for mortgage loans, primarily conventional loans. Freddie Mac has the authority to purchase mortgages, pool them, and sell bonds in the open market with the mortgages as security. Note, however, that FHLMC does not guarantee payment of Freddie Mac mortgages.

Many lenders use the standardized forms and follow the guidelines issued by Freddie Mac, since use of FHLMC forms is mandatory for lenders who wish to sell mortgages in the agency's secondary mortgage market. The standardized documents include loan applications, credit reports, and appraisal forms.

Farmer's Home Administration

The Farmer's Home Administration (FmHA) is a federal agency of the Department of Agriculture that was originally designed to handle emergency farm financing and that channels credit to farmers and rural residents, as well as to certain small communities. FmHA loan programs fall into two categories: (1) guaranteed loans, made and serviced by a private lender and guaranteed for a specific percentage by the FmHA; and (2) insured loans that are originated, made, and serviced by the agency.

Financing Legislation

The federal government regulates the lending practices of mortgage lenders through the Truth-in-Lending Act, Equal Credit Opportunity Act, and the Real Estate Settlement Procedures Act.

Regulation Z

Commonly referred to as the *Truth-in-Lending Act,* **Regulation Z** requires credit institutions to inform borrowers of the true cost of obtaining credit so that the borrower can compare the costs of various lenders and avoid the uninformed use of credit. When credit is extended to individuals for personal, family, or household uses, and the amount of credit is $25,000 or less, Regulation Z applies. If a credit transaction is secured by a residence, Regulation Z always applies, regardless of the amount. The regulation does not apply to business or commercial loans, nor to agricultural loans over $25,000.

The regulation requires that the customer be fully informed of all finance charges, as well as the true annual interest rate, before a transaction is consummated. The finance charges must include any loan fees, finders' fees, service charges, and points, as well as interest. In the case of a mortgage loan made to finance the purchase of a dwelling, the lender must compute and disclose the annual percentage rate (APR) but does not have to indicate the total interest payable during the term of the loan. Also, the lender does not have to include as part of the finance charge such actual costs as title fees, legal fees, and closing expenses.

Advertising. Regulation Z provides strict regulation of real estate advertisements that include mortgage financing terms. General phrases like "liberal terms available" may be used, but if details are given they must comply with this act. By the provisions of the act, the *annual percentage rate*—which includes all charges—rather than the interest rate alone *must be stated.* The total finance charge must be specified as well.

Specific credit terms, such as the down payment, monthly payment, dollar amount of the finance charge, or term of the loan, may not be advertised unless the following information is set forth as well: cash price; required down payment; number, amount, and due dates of all payments; and annual percentage rate. The total of all payments to be made over the term of the mortgage must also be specified unless the advertised credit refers to a first mortgage or trust deed to finance acquisition of a dwelling.

Three-day right of rescission. In the case of most consumer credit transactions covered by Regulation Z, the borrower has three days in which to rescind the transaction by merely notifying the lender. However, this right of rescission does not apply to residential first mortgage or trust deed loans.

Penalties. Regulation Z provides penalties for noncompliance. The penalty for violation of Regulation Z is twice the amount of the finance charge, for a minimum of $100 and a maximum of $1,000, plus court costs, attorney's fees, and any actual damages. Willful violation is a misdemeanor punishable by a fine of up to $5,000 or one year's imprisonment, or both.

Federal Equal Credit Opportunity Act

The federal Equal Credit Opportunity Act (ECOA) prohibits lenders and others who grant or arrange credit to consumers from discriminating against credit applicants on the basis of race, color, religion, national origin, sex, marital status, age (provided the applicant is of legal age), or dependency upon public assistance. In addition, lenders and other creditors must inform all rejected credit applicants, in writing, of the principal reasons why credit was denied or terminated.

Real Estate Settlement Procedures Act

The federal Real Estate Settlement Procedures Act (RESPA) was created to ensure that the buyer and seller in a residential real estate transaction involving a new first mortgage loan have knowledge of all settlement costs. This important federal law will be discussed in detail in Chapter 23.

Summary

Mortgage and trust deed loans provide the principal sources of financing for real estate operations. Mortgage loans involve a borrower, called the *mortgagor,* and a lender, the *mortgagee.* Trust deed loans involve a third party, called the *trustee,* in addition to the borrower (the *trustor*) and the lender (the *beneficiary*).

Some states recognize the lender as the owner of mortgaged property; these are known as *title theory states.* Others recognize the borrower as the owner of mortgaged property and are known as *lien theory states.* A few *intermediary states* recognize modified versions of these theories.

After a lending institution has received, investigated, and approved a loan application, it issues a commitment to make the mortgage loan. The borrower is required to execute a *note,* agreeing to repay the debt, and a *mortgage* or *trust deed,* placing a lien on the real estate to secure his or her note. This is recorded in the public record in order to give notice to the world of the lender's interest.

The note for the amount of the loan usually provides for *amortization* of the loan. The note also sets the rate of *interest* at which the loan is made and that the mortgagor or trustor must pay as a charge for borrowing the money. Charging more than the maximum interest rate allowed by state statute is called *usury* and is illegal. The mortgage document or trust deed secures the debt and sets forth the obligations of the borrower and the rights of the lender. Payment in full of the note by its terms entitles the borrower to a satisfaction, or *release,* which is recorded to clear the lien from the public records. Default by the borrower may result in *acceleration* of payments, a *foreclosure* sale, and, after the *redemption period* (if provided by state law), *loss of title.*

There are many types of mortgage and trust deed loans, including *conventional loans* and those *insured by the FHA or an independent mortgage insurance company or guaranteed by the VA.* FHA and VA loans must meet certain requirements in order for the borrower to obtain the benefits of the government backing, which induces the lender to lend its funds. The interest rates for these loans may be less than those charged for conventional loans. In order to be able to sell VA loans to investors, lenders may charge *discount points,* which are paid by the seller.

Other types of real estate financing include purchase-money mortgages or trust deeds, adjustable rate mortgages, renegotiable rate mortgages, shared-appreciation mortgages, reverse annuity mortgages, blanket mortgages, package mortgages, wraparound mortgages, open-end mortgages, construction loans, sale-and-leaseback agreements, contracts for deed, and investment group financing.

The federal government affects real estate financing money and interest rates through the Federal Reserve Board's *discount rate* and *reserve requirements;* it also participates in the *secondary mortgage market.* The secondary market is generally composed of the investors who ultimately purchase and hold the loans as investments. These include insurance companies, investment funds, and pension plans. *Fannie Mae* (Federal National Mortgage Association), *Ginnie Mae* (Government National Mortgage Association), and *Freddie Mac* (Federal Home Loan Mortgage Corporation) take an active role in creating a secondary market by regularly purchasing mortgage and trust deed loans from originators and retaining, or *warehousing,* them until investment purchasers are available.

Regulation Z, the federal Truth-in-Lending Act, requires lenders to inform prospective borrowers who use their homes as security for credit of *all finance charges* involved in such a loan. Severe penalties are provided for noncompliance. The federal *Equal Credit Opportunity Act* prohibits creditors from discriminating against credit applicants on the basis of race, color, religion, national origin, sex, marital status, age, or dependency upon public assistance. The *Real Estate Settlement Procedures Act* requires lenders to inform both buyers and sellers in advance of all fees and charges required for the settlement or closing of a residential real estate transaction.

Questions

1. The McBains are purchasing a lakefront summer home in a new resort development. The house is completely equipped, and the McBains have obtained a trust deed loan that covers the purchase price of the residence, including the furnishings and appliances. This kind of financing is called:

   a. a wraparound trust deed.
   b. a package trust deed.
   c. a blanket trust deed.
   d. an unconventional loan.

2. In general, a promissory note:

   I. is a negotiable instrument.
   II. may be sold by the lender to a third party.

   a. I only   c. both I and II
   b. II only   d. neither I nor II

3. With a fully amortized mortgage or trust deed loan:

   I. interest may be charged in arrears, meaning at the end of each period for which interest is due.
   II. the interest portion of each payment remains the same throughout the entire term of the loan.

   a. I only   c. both I and II
   b. II only   d. neither I nor II

4. Freddie Mac:

   a. mortgages are guaranteed by the full faith and credit of the federal government.
   b. buys and pools blocks of conventional mortgages, selling bonds with such mortgages as security.
   c. can tandem with GNMA to provide special assistance in times of tight money.
   d. buys and sells VA and FHA mortgages.

5. Discount points on a VA loan:

   I. represent the percentage by which the face amount of a VA loan is reduced when it is sold to an investor in order to make its rate of return competitive with that of other loan investments.
   II. are charged to the seller.

   a. I only   c. both I and II
   b. II only   d. neither I nor II

6. A developer has obtained a large loan in order to finance the construction of a planned unit development.

   I. This is a short-term loan, and the developer has arranged for long-term financing in order to repay it when the construction is completed.
   II. The borrowed money is disbursed in installments, and the lender inspects the construction that has been completed to date and ensures that all subcontractors and laborers have been properly paid before disbursing each installment of the loan.

   a. I only   c. both I and II
   b. II only   d. neither I nor II

7. The Carters purchased a residence for $75,000. They made a down payment of $15,000 and agreed to assume the seller's existing mortgage, which had a current balance of $23,000. The Carters financed the remaining $37,000 of the purchase price by executing a mortgage and note to the seller. This type of loan, by which the seller becomes the mortgagee, is called a:

   a. wraparound mortgage.
   b. package mortgage.
   c. balloon note.
   d. purchase-money mortgage.

8. In a sale and leaseback:
   I. the seller/vendor retains title to the real estate.
   II. the buyer/vendee gets possession of the property.
   a. I only   c. both I and II
   b. II only   d. neither I nor II

9. In theory, when the Federal Reserve Board raises its discount rate, which of the following should happen?
   I. Interest rates will rise.
   II. Interest rates will fall.
   III. Mortgage money will become scarce.
   a. I only   c. I and III
   b. II only   d. II and III

10. Which of the following best defines the *secondary market?*
    a. lenders who exclusively deal in second mortgages
    b. where loans are bought and sold after they have been originated
    c. the major lender of residential mortgages and trust deeds
    d. the major lender of FHA and VA loans

11. Generally, the most active participant in the residential-loan market is which of the following?
    a. commercial bank
    b. credit union
    c. savings and loan association
    d. mortgage banker

12. Which of the following is a participant in the secondary market?
    I. FNMA
    II. GNMA
    a. I only   c. both I and II
    b. II only   d. neither I nor II

13. The person who obtains a real estate loan by signing a note and a mortgage is called the:
    I. mortgagor.
    II. beneficiary.
    a. I only   c. both I and II
    b. II only   d. neither I nor II

14. A borrower obtains a mortgage loan in order to make repairs on her home. The loan is not insured or guaranteed by a government agency, and the mortgage document secures the amount of the loan as well as any future funds advanced to the borrower by the lender. This borrower has obtained:
    I. a wraparound mortgage.
    II. a conventional loan.
    a. I only   c. both I and II
    b. II only   d. neither I nor II

15. The Stevensons sold their farmland to the Crawfords, but retained the rights to and ownership of all coal and other minerals in the land. The Crawfords obtained a mortgage loan from their bank and executed a mortgage to the bank as security. Which of the following statements is true regarding this transaction?
    a. The Crawfords' mortgage covers the land and the minerals.
    b. The Crawfords' mortgage covers the land but not the minerals.
    c. The Crawfords' mortgage covers only the minerals.
    d. If the Crawfords default, the bank automatically acquires the mineral rights.

16. A graduated payment mortgage:
    I. allows for smaller payments to be made in the early years of the loan.
    II. allows for the debt's interest rate to increase or decrease from time to time, depending on certain economic factors.
    a. I only   c. both I and II
    b. II only   d. neither I nor II

17. If a lender originates a VA loan at 11½ percent while the going mortgage interest rate is 13 percent, approximately how many discount points must the lender charge in order to bring his or her effective yield on the loan up to 13 percent?
    a. 1½ points   c. 8 points
    b. 6 points   d. 12 points

18. The borrower under a trust deed is known as the:
    a. trustor.   c. beneficiary.
    b. trustee.   d. vendee.

19. FHA-insured loans are made from funds furnished by:
    a. the FHA.
    b. private lenders approved by the FHA.
    c. the Fed.
    d. a and b

20. A borrower obtains a $76,000 mortgage loan at 11½ percent interest. If the monthly payments of $785 are credited first on interest and then on principal, what will the balance of the principal be after the borrower makes the first payment?

    a. $75,215.00   c. $75,543.66
    b. $75,943.33   d. $75,305.28

21. Regulation Z requires lenders to:
    I. properly inform buyers and sellers of commercial property of all settlement costs in a real estate transaction.
    II. inform prospective borrowers of all charges, fees, and interest involved in making a home mortgage or trust deed loan.

    a. I only   c. both I and II
    b. II only   d. neither I nor II

22. The federal Equal Credit Opportunity Act prohibits lenders from discriminating against potential borrowers on the basis of which of the following?

    a. race   c. national origin
    b. sex   d. all of the above

23. Which of the following is an example of a conventional loan?

    a. a mortgage loan insured by the Federal Housing Administration
    b. a second loan for home improvements secured through a credit union
    c. a trust deed obtained through a private lender with a VA guarantee
    d. all of the above

24. A renegotiable rate mortgage is one in which:
    I. the lender profits from the property's appreciation when it is sold.
    II. the interest rate is lower in the early years of the loan and higher in later years, when the mortgagor's salary is expected to rise.

    a. I only   c. both I and II
    b. II only   d. neither I nor II

25. Which of the following is *not* a necessary element of a mortgage?

    a. signature of grantor
    b. date
    c. legal capacity of parties
    d. document in writing

26. Which of the following is true of a second mortgage?

    a. It has priority over a first mortgage.
    b. It cannot be used as a security instrument.
    c. It is not negotiable.
    d. It is usually issued at a higher rate of interest than a first mortgage.

16

Leases

Overview

When an owner of real property does not wish to use the property personally or wants to derive some measure of income from its ownership, he or she can allow it to be used by another person in exchange for consideration. The person who makes periodic payments for the use of the property *leases* it from the owner. Generally, any type of real property may be leased; the apartment dweller as well as the commercial or industrial tenant may find it advantageous to lease real estate for a given period of time rather than purchase it. This chapter will examine the various leasehold estates a landlord and a tenant may enter into and the types and specific provisions of lease agreements commonly used in the real estate business.

Leasing Real Estate

A **lease** is a contract between an owner of real estate (known as the *lessor*) and a tenant (the *lessee*) that transfers the right to exclusive possession and use of the owner's property to the tenant for a specified period of time. This agreement generally sets forth the length of time the contract is to run, the amount to be paid by the lessee for the right to use the property, and other rights and obligations of the parties.

In effect, the lease agreement is a combination of a conveyance (of an interest in the real estate) and a contract (to pay rent and assume other obligations). The landlord (lessor) grants the tenant (lessee) the right to occupy the premises and use them for purposes stated in the lease. In return, the landlord retains the right to receive payment for the use of the premises as well as a **reversionary right** to retake possession after the lease term has expired. The lessor's interest in leased property is called a *leased fee estate plus reversionary right.*

The statute of frauds in most states requires that an agreement to lease real estate be in writing if it will not be performed within one year of the date of making. In other words, a *lease for a term of more than one year must be written.* It should also be signed by both lessor and lessee. A lease for one year or less is usually enforceable if it is entered into orally.

Leasehold Estates

When a landowner leases his or her real estate to a tenant, the tenant's right to occupy the land for the duration of the lease is called a **leasehold estate.** A leasehold estate is an estate in land that is generally considered personal property. However, when the contract is a lease for life or for 99 years, under which the tenant assumes many of the landowner's obligations, certain states give the tenant some of the benefits and privileges of a property owner.

In the discussion of interests and estates in Chapter 7, freehold estates were differentiated from leasehold estates. Just as there are several types of freehold (ownership) estates, there are also various leasehold estates. The four most important are: (1) estate for years, (2) periodic estate, or estate from period to period, (3) tenancy at will, and (4) tenancy at sufferance (see table 16.1).

Estate for Years

A leasehold estate that continues for a *definite period of time* is an **estate for years.** An estate for years always has a specific starting and ending time and does not automatically renew itself at the end of the lease period. When a definite term is specified in a written or oral lease and that period of time expires, the lessee is required to vacate the premises and surrender possession to the lessor. No notice is required to terminate such a lease at the end of the lease period. A lease for years may be terminated prior to the expiration date by the mutual consent of both parties, but otherwise neither party may terminate without showing that the lease agreement has been breached. As is characteristic of all leases, a lease, or estate, for years gives the lessee the right to occupy and use the leased property—subject, of course, to the terms and covenants contained in the lease agreement itself, which is generally a written document.

Table 16.1	Type of Estate	Distinguishing Characteristics
Leasehold Estates	Estate for Years	For Definite Period of Time
	Estate from Period to Period	Automatically Renews
	Tenancy at Will	For Indefinite Period of Time
	Tenancy at Sufferance	Without Landlord's Consent

Periodic Estates

Periodic estates, sometimes called **estates from period to period,** or from year to year, are created when the landlord and tenant enter into an agreement that continues for an *indefinite length of time without a specific expiration date;* rent, however, is payable at definite intervals. These tenancies are generally created by agreement or operation of law to run for a certain amount of time; for instance, month to month, week to week, or year to year. The agreement is automatically renewed for similar succeeding periods until one of the parties gives notice to terminate. In effect, the payment and acceptance of rent extend the lease for another period.

A tenancy from period to period is usually created when a tenant with an estate for years remains in possession, or holds over, after the expiration of the lease term. When no new lease agreement has been made, a **holdover tenancy** is created, and the landlord may evict the tenant if he or she chooses or may acquiesce to the holdover tenancy. Acceptance of rent is usually considered conclusive proof of the landlord's acquiescence. The courts customarily hold that a tenant who holds over can do so for a term equal to the term of the original lease, providing the period is for one year or less. The courts have usually ruled that a holdover tenancy cannot exist for longer than one year. Thus, if the original lease were for six months and the tenancy were held over, the courts would usually consider the holdover to be for a like period, that is, six months. However, if the original lease were for five years, the holdover tenancy could not exceed one year.

A **month-to-month tenancy** is generally created when a tenant takes possession with no definite termination date and pays rent on a monthly basis. Some leases stipulate that in the absence of a renewal agreement, a tenant who holds over does so as a month-to-month tenant. This is usually a valid agreement. In a few states, a holdover tenancy is considered a tenancy at will. (See the following discussion.)

In order to *terminate* a periodic estate, either the landlord or the tenant must give *proper notice.* The form of the notice and the time at which it must be given are usually set out in detail in the statutes of the various states. Normally, to terminate an estate from week to week, one week's notice is required; to terminate an estate from month to month, one month's notice is required. Notices of termination for an estate from year to year vary widely and usually require a minimum of two months' and a maximum of six months' notice.

Tenancy at Will

An estate that gives the tenant the right to possess with the *consent of the landlord* is a **tenancy at will.** It may be created by express agreement or by operation of law, and during its existence the tenant has all the rights and obligations of a lessor-lessee relationship, including the payment of rent at regular intervals.

For example, at the end of a lease period, a landlord informs a tenant that in a few months the city is going to demolish the apartment building to make way for an expressway. The landlord gives the tenant the option to occupy the premises until demolition begins. If the tenant agrees to stay, a tenancy at will is created.

The term of an estate at will is indefinite, but the estate may be terminated by giving proper notice in accordance with the statutes of the state where the land is located. An estate at will is automatically terminated by the death of either the landlord or the tenant.

Tenancy at Sufferance

A **tenancy at sufferance** arises when a tenant who lawfully came into possession of real property continues, after his or her rights have expired, to hold possession of the premises *without the consent of the landlord.* Two examples of estates at sufferance are: (1) when a tenant for years *fails to surrender* possession at the expiration of the lease and (2) when a mortgagor, without consent of the purchaser, continues in possession after the foreclosure sale and expiration of the redemption period. The latter example is a tenancy at sufferance *by operation of law.* In some states, a tenant may be charged up to double rent for the period while he or she was in possession as a tenant at sufferance.

Standard Lease Provisions

In determining the validity of a lease, the courts apply the rules governing contracts. If the intention to convey temporary possession of a certain parcel of real estate from one person to another is expressed, the courts generally hold that a lease has been created. Most states require no special wording to establish the landlord-tenant relationship. The lease may be written, oral, or implied, depending on the circumstances. However, the provisions of the statutes of the state where the real estate is located must be followed to assure the validity of the lease. An example of a typical residential lease is figure 16.1.

Once a valid lease has been executed, the lessor, as the owner of the real estate, is usually bound by the *implied covenant of quiet possession.* Under this covenant, the lessor guarantees that the lessee may take possession of the leased premises and that he or she will not be evicted from these premises by any person who successfully claims to have a title superior to that of the lessor.

The requirements for a valid lease are essentially the same as those for any other contract. Generally, the essentials of a valid lease are:

1. *Offer and acceptance:* The parties must reach a mutual agreement on all the terms of the contract.

2. *Consideration:* As discussed earlier, the law of contracts controls the creation of a landlord-tenant relationship. All contracts must be supported by a valid consideration. In leasing real estate, *rent* is the normal consideration granted for the right to occupy the leased premises; however, the payment of rent is not essential as long as consideration was granted in creation of the lease itself. Some courts have construed rent as being any consideration that supports the lease, thus not limiting its definition to the payment of monthly rent (as will be illustrated later in discussions of gross, net, and percentage leases). The courts consider a lease to be a contract and not subject to subsequent changes in the

**Figure 16.1
Residential Lease
Agreement**

APARTMENT LEASE — UNFURNISHED
(For Use In Illinois)

GEORGE E. COLE®
LEGAL FORMS

NO. L-17
APRIL 1982
CAUTION: Consult a lawyer before using or acting under this form.
All warranties, including merchantability and fitness, are excluded.

IF UNHEATED, CHECK HERE: ____
(SEE PARAGRAPH 11)

APARTMENT LEASE
UNFURNISHED

DATE OF LEASE	TERM OF LEASE		MONTHLY RENT	SECURITY DEPOSIT*
	BEGINNING	ENDING		
April 1, 1985	May 1, 1985	April 30, 1986	$500	$500

* *IF NONE, WRITE "NONE". Paragraph 2 of this Lease then INAPPLICABLE.*

LESSEE

NAME • J.P. Smithers

APT. NO. • 305

ADDRESS OF PREMISES • 248 West Windsor
Chicago, Illinois

LESSOR

NAME • Maddox Management

BUSINESS ADDRESS • 1309 45th. Street
Chicago, Illinois

In consideration of the mutual covenants and agreements herein stated, Lessor hereby leases to Lessee and Lessee hereby leases from Lessor for a private dwelling the apartment designated above (the "Premises"), together with the appurtenances thereto, for the above Term.

ADDITIONAL COVENANTS AND AGREEMENTS *(if any)*

Lessee will maintain smoke detector.

LEASE COVENANTS AND AGREEMENTS

RENT

1. Lessee shall pay Lessor or Lessor's agent as rent for the Premises the sum stated above, monthly in advance, until termination of this lease, at Lessor's address stated above or such other address as Lessor may designate in writing.

SECURITY DEPOSIT

2. Lessee has deposited with Lessor the Security Deposit stated above for the performance of all covenants and agreements of Lessee hereunder. Lessor may apply all or any portion thereof in payment of any amounts due Lessor from Lessee, and upon Lessor's demand Lessee shall in such case during the term of the lease promptly deposit with Lessor such additional amounts as may then be required to bring the Security Deposit up to the full amount stated above. Upon termination of the lease and full performance of all matters and payment of all amounts due by Lessee, so much of the Security Deposit as remains unapplied shall be returned to Lessee. This deposit does not bear interest unless and except as required by law. Where all or a portion of the Security Deposit is applied by Lessor as compensation for property damage, Lessor when and as required by law shall provide to Lessee an itemized statement of such damage and of the estimated or actual cost of repairing same. If the building in which Premises are located (the "Building") is sold or otherwise transferred, Lessor may transfer or assign the Security Deposit to the purchaser or transferee of the Building, who shall thereupon be liable to Lessee for all of Lessor's obligations hereunder, and Lessee shall look thereafter solely to such purchaser or transferee for return of the Security Deposit and for other matters (including any interest or accounting) relating thereto.

CONDITION OF PREMISES; REDELIVERY TO LESSOR

3. Lessee has examined and knows the condition of Premises and has received the same in good order and repair except as herein otherwise specified, and no representations as to the condition or repair thereof have been made by Lessor or his agent prior to, or at the execution of this lease, that are not herein expressed or endorsed hereon; and upon the termination of this lease in any way, Lessee will immediately yield up Premises to Lessor in as good condition as when the same were entered upon by Lessee, ordinary wear and tear only excepted, and shall then return all keys to Lessor.

LIMITATION OF LIABILITY

4. Except as provided by Illinois statute, Lessor shall not be liable for any damage occasioned by failure to keep Premises in repair, and shall not be liable for any damage done or occasioned by or from plumbing, gas, water, steam or other pipes, or sewerage, or the bursting, leaking or running of any cistern, tank, wash-stand, water-closet, or waste-pipe, in, above, upon or about the Building or Premises, nor for damage occasioned by water, snow or ice being upon or coming through the roof, skylight, trap-door or otherwise, nor for damages to Lessee or others claiming through Lessee for any loss or damage of or to property wherever located in or about the Building or Premises, nor for any damage arising from acts or neglect of co-tenants or other occupants of the Building, or of any owners or occupants of adjacent or contiguous property.

USE; SUBLET; ASSIGNMENT

5. Lessee will not allow Premises to be used for any purpose that will increase the rate of insurance thereon, nor for any purpose other than that hereinbefore specified, nor to be occupied in whole or in part by any other persons, and will not sublet the same, nor any part thereof, nor assign this lease, without in each case the written consent of the Lessor first had, and will not permit any transfer, by operation of law, of the interest in Premises acquired through this lease, and will not permit Premises to be used for any unlawful purpose or purpose that will injure the reputation of the same or of the Building or disturb the tenants of the Building or the neighborhood.

USE AND REPAIR

6. Lessee will take good care of the apartment demised and the fixtures therein, and will commit and suffer no waste therein; no changes or alterations of the Premises shall be made, nor partitions erected, nor walls papered, nor locks on doors installed or changed, without the consent in writing of Lessor; Lessee will make all repairs required to the walls, ceilings, paint, plastering, plumbing work, pipes and fixtures belonging to Premises, whenever damage or injury to the same shall have resulted from misuse or neglect; no furniture filled or to be filled wholly or partially with liquids shall be placed in the Premises without the consent in writing of Lessor; the Premises shall not be used as a ''boarding'' or ''lodging'' house, nor for a school, nor to give instructions in music, dancing or singing, and none of the rooms shall be offered for lease by placing notices on any door, window or wall of the Building, nor by advertising the same directly or indirectly, in any newspaper or otherwise, nor shall any signs be exhibited on or at any windows or exterior portions of the Premises or of the Building without the consent in writing of Lessor; there shall be no lounging, sitting upon, or unnecessary tarrying in or upon the front steps, the sidewalk, railing, stairways, halls, landing or other public places of the Building by Lessee, members of the family or others persons connected with the occupancy of Premises; no provisions, milk, ice, marketing, groceries, furniture, packages or merchandise shall be taken into the Premises through the front door of the Building except where there is no rear or service entrance; cooking shall be done only in the kitchen and in no event on porches or other exterior appurtenances; Lessee, and those occupying under Lessee, shall not interfere with the heating apparatus, or with the lights, electricity, gas, water or other utilities of the Building which are not within the apartment hereby demised, nor with the control of any of the public portions of the Building; use of any master television antenna hookup shall be strictly in accordance with regulations of Lessor or Lessor's agent; Lessee and those occupying under Lessee shall comply with and conform to all reasonable rules and regulations that Lessor or Lessor's agent may make for the protection of the Building or the general welfare and the comfort of the occupants thereof, and shall also comply with and conform to all applicable laws and governmental rules and regulations affecting the Premises and the use and occupancy thereof.

ACCESS

7. Lessee will allow Lessor free access to the Premises at all reasonable hours for the purpose of examining or exhibiting the same or to make any needful repairs which Lessor may deem fit to make for the benefit of or related to any part of the Building; also Lessee will allow Lessor to have placed upon the Premises, at all times, notice of "For Sale" and "To Rent," and will not interfere with the same.

RIGHT TO RELET

8. If Lessee shall abandon or vacate the Premises, the same may be re-let by Lessor for such rent and upon such terms as Lessor may see fit; and if a sufficient sum shall not thus be realized, after paying the expenses of such reletting and collecting, to satisfy the rent hereby reserved, Lessee agrees to satisfy and pay all deficiency.

HOLDING OVER

9. If the Lessee retains possession of the Premises or any part thereof after the termination of the term by lapse of time or otherwise, then the Lessor may at Lessor's option within thirty days after the termination of the term serve written notice upon Lessee that such holding over constitutes either (a) renewal of this lease for one year, and from year to year thereafter, at double the rental specified under Section 1 for such period, or (b) creation of a month to month tenancy, upon the terms of this lease except at double the monthly rental specified under Section 1, or (c) creation of a tenancy at sufferance, at a rental of _____ dollars per day for the time Lessee remains in possession. If no such written notice is served then a tenancy at sufferance with rental as stated at (c) shall have been created, and in such case if specific per diem rental shall not have been inserted herein at (c), such per diem rental shall be one-fifteenth of the monthly rental specified under Section 1 of this lease. Lessee shall also pay to Lessor all damages sustained by Lessor resulting from retention of possession by Lessee.

RESTRICTIONS ON USE

10. Lessee will not permit anything to be thrown out of the windows, or down the courts or light shafts in the Building; nothing shall be hung from the outside of the windows or placed on the outside window sills of any window in the Building; no parrot, dog or other animal shall be kept within or about the Premises; the front halls and stairways and the back porches shall not be used for the storage of carriages, furniture or other articles.

WATER AND HEAT

11. The provisions of subsection (a) only hereof shall be applicable and shall form a part of this lease unless this lease is made on an unheated basis and that fact is so indicated on the first page of this lease, in which case the provisions of subsection (b) only hereof shall be applicable and form a part of this lease.

(a) Lessor will supply hot and cold water to the Premises for the use of Lessee at all faucets and fixtures provided by Lessor therefor. Lessor will also supply heat, by means of the heating system and fixtures provided by Lessor, in reasonable amounts and at reasonable hours, when necessary, from October 1 to April 30, or otherwise as required by applicable municipal ordinance. Lessor shall not be liable or responsible to Lessee for failure to furnish water or heat when such failure shall result from causes beyond Lessor's control, nor during periods when the water and heating systems in the Building or any portion thereof are under repair.

(b) Lessor will supply cold water to the Premises for the use of Lessee at all faucets and fixtures provided by Lessor therefor. Lessor shall not be liable or responsible to Lessee for failure to furnish water when such failure shall result from causes beyond Lessor's control, nor during periods when the water system in the Building or any portion thereof is under repair. All water heating and all heating of the Premises shall be at the sole expense of Lessee. Any equipment provided by Lessee therefor shall comply with applicable municipal ordinances.

Figure 16.1 (cont.)

STORE ROOM	12. Lessor shall not be liable for any loss or damage of or to any property placed in any store room or any storage place in the Building, such store room or storage place being furnished gratuitously and not as part of the obligations of this lease.
DEFAULT BY LESSEE	13. If default be made in the payment of the above rent, or any part thereof, or in any of the covenants herein contained to be kept by the Lessee, Lessor may at any time thereafter at his election declare said term ended and reenter the Premises or any part thereof, with or (to the extent permitted by law) without notice or process of law, and remove Lessee or any persons occupying the same, without prejudice to any remedies which might otherwise be used for arrears of rent, and Lessor shall have at all times the right to distrain for rent due, and shall have a valid and first lien upon all personal property which Lessee now owns, or may hereafter acquire or have an interest in, which is by law subject to such distraint, as security for payment of the rent herein reserved.
NO RENT DEDUCTION OR SET OFF	14. Lessee's covenant to pay rent is and shall be independent of each and every other covenant of this lease. Lessee agrees that any claim by Lessee against Lessor shall not be deducted from rent nor set off against any claim for rent in any action.
RENT AFTER NOTICE OR SUIT	15. It is further agreed, by the parties hereto, that after the service of notice or the commencement of a suit or after final judgment for possession of the Premises, Lessor may receive and collect any rent due, and the payment of said rent shall not waive or affect said notice, said suit, or said judgment.
PAYMENT OF COSTS	16. Lessee will pay and discharge all reasonable costs, attorney's fees and expenses that shall be made and incurred by Lessor in enforcing the covenants and agreements of this lease.
RIGHTS CUMULATIVE	17. The rights and remedies of Lessor under this lease are cumulative. The exercise or use of any one or more thereof shall not bar Lessor from exercise or use of any other right or remedy provided herein or otherwise provided by law, nor shall exercise nor use of any right or remedy by Lessor waive any other right or remedy.
FIRE AND CASUALTY	18. In case the Premises shall be rendered untenantable during the term of this lease by fire or other casualty, Lessor at his option may terminate the lease or repair the Premises within 60 days thereafter. If Lessor elects to repair, this lease shall remain in effect provided such repairs are completed within said time. If Lessor shall not have repaired the Premises within said time, then at the end of such time the term hereby created shall terminate. If this lease is terminated by reason of fire or casualty as herein specified, rent shall be apportioned and paid to the day of such fire or other casualty.
SUBORDINATION	19. This lease is subordinate to all mortgages which may now or hereafter affect the real property of which Premises form a part.
PLURALS; SUCCESSORS	20. The words "Lessor" and "Lessee" wherever herein occurring and used shall be construed to mean "Lessors" and "Lessees" in case more than one person constitutes either party to this lease; and all the covenants and agreements herein contained shall be binding upon, and inure to, their respective successors, heirs, executors, administrators and assigns and be exercised by his or their attorney or agent.
SEVERABILITY	21. Wherever possible each provision of this lease shall be interpreted in such manner as to be effective and valid under applicable law, but if any provision of this lease shall be prohibited by or invalid under applicable law, such provision shall be ineffective to the extent of such prohibition or invalidity, without invalidating the remainder of such provision or the remaining provisions of this lease.

WITNESS the hands and seals of the parties hereto, as of the Date of Lease stated above.

LESSEE: _____ (seal)   LESSOR: _____ (seal)

_____ (seal)   _____ (seal)

ASSIGNMENT BY LESSOR

On this _____, 19 _____, for value received. Lessor hereby transfers. assigns and sets over to

_____ all right, title and interest in and to the above lease and the rent thereby reserved.

except rent due and payable prior to _____, 19 _____.

_____ (seal)

_____ (seal)

GUARANTEE

On this _____, 19 _____, in consideration of Ten Dollars ($10.00) and other good and valuable consideration. the receipt and sufficiency of which is hereby acknowledged, the undersigned Guarantor hereby guarantees the payment of rent and performance by Lessee. Lessee's heirs. executors. administrators. successors or assigns of all covenants and agreements of the above lease.

_____ (seal)

_____ (seal)

rent or other terms unless these changes are in writing and executed in the same manner as the original lease.

3. *Capacity to contract:* The parties must have the legal capacity to contract.

4. *Legal objectives:* The objectives of the lease must be legal.

As discussed earlier in this chapter, the statute of frauds usually requires that leases that will not be fully performed within one year of the date of making must be in writing. When the statute of frauds applies and the provisions of the lease do not comply with its terms, the lease is considered to be *unenforceable.* In addition, a description of the leased premises should be clearly stated. If the lease covers land, the legal description of the real estate should be used. If, on the other hand, the lease is for a part of the building, such as office space or an apartment, the space itself or the apartment designation should be clearly and carefully described. If supplemental space is to be included, the lease should clearly identify it.

To be valid, a lease for more than a year's duration must be signed by the landlord, since the courts consider a lease to be a conveyance of an interest in real estate. The tenant's signature is usually *not essential if the tenant has actually taken possession.* Of course, it is preferable for both parties to sign the lease.

Use of Premises

A lessor may restrict a lessee's use of the premises through provisions included in the lease. This is most important in leases for stores or commercial space. For example, a lease may provide that the leased premises are to be used *only* for the purpose of a real estate office *and for no other.* In the absence of such limitations, a lessee may use the premises for any lawful purpose.

Term of Lease

The term of a lease is the period for which the lease will run, and it should be set out precisely. The date of the beginning of the term and the date of its ending should be stated together with a statement of the total period of the lease: for example, "for a term of thirty years beginning June 1, 1986 and ending May 31, 2016." Courts do not favor leases with an indefinite term and will hold that such perpetual leases are not valid unless the language of the lease and the surrounding circumstances clearly indicate that such is the intention of the parties. Leases are controlled by the statutes of the various states and must be in accordance with those provisions. In some states, terms of agricultural leases are limited by statute. Also, the laws of some states prohibit leases that run for 100 years or more.

Security Deposits

Most leases require the tenant to provide some form of security. This security, which guarantees payment of rent and safeguards against a tenant's destruction of the premises, may be established by: (1) contracting for a lien on the tenant's property, (2) requiring the tenant to pay a portion of the rent in advance, (3) requiring the tenant to post security, and/or (4) requiring the tenant to have some third person guarantee the payment of the rent. Many states have laws that set maximum amounts for security deposits and specify how they must be handled. Some require that lessees receive annual interest on their security deposits.

In Practice . . .

A lease should specify whether a payment is a security deposit or an advance rental. If it is a security deposit, the tenant is generally not entitled to apply it to the final month's rent. If it is an advance rental, the landlord must treat it as income for tax purposes.

**Confession of
Judgment Clauses**

Confession of judgment clauses are included in many leases to assist the landlord in forcing *collection of rent.* In such clauses, the tenant authorizes any attorney of record to appear in court in the tenant's name and to confess judgment, or agree that a judgment be entered against the tenant in favor of the landlord for the delinquent rent, court costs, and attorney's fees. Such a clause may be called a *cognovit.* Many states have now declared confession of judgment clauses illegal when used in residential leases.

**Legal Principles of
Leases**

Most states provide that leases can be filed for record in the county in which the property is located. But unless the lease is for a relatively long term, it *usually is not recorded.* Possession of the property by the lessee is notice to the world of his or her rights, and an inspection of the property will result in *actual notice* of the lessee's leasehold interest.

When a lease runs for a period of *three years* or longer, recordation is more common. The recording of a *long-term lease* places the world on notice of the long-term rights of the lessee. The recordation of such a lease is usually required if the lessee intends to mortgage his or her leasehold interest.

In some states, only a *memorandum of lease* is filed for record. The terms of the lease are not disclosed to the public by the filing of a memorandum of lease; however, the objective of giving public notice of the rights of the lessee is still accomplished. The memorandum of lease must set forth the names of the parties and a description of the property being leased.

**Possession of
Leased Premises**

As noted earlier, leases carry the implied covenant that the landlord will give the tenant possession of the premises. In most states, the landlord must give the tenant *actual* occupancy, or possession, of the leased premises. Thus, if the premises are occupied by a holdover tenant, or adverse claimant, at the beginning of the new lease period, it is the landlord's duty to bring whatever action is necessary to recover possession and to bear the expense of this action. In a few states, however, the landlord is bound only to give the tenant the right of possession; it is the tenant's obligation to bring any court action necessary to secure actual possession.

Improvements

Neither the landlord nor the tenant is required to make any improvements to the leased property. In the absence of an agreement to the contrary, the tenant may make improvements with the landlord's permission. Any such alterations generally become the property of the landlord; that is, they become fixtures. However, as discussed in Chapter 2, a tenant may be given the right to install trade fixtures or chattel fixtures by the terms of the lease. It is customary to provide that such trade fixtures may be removed by the tenant before the lease expires, provided the tenant restores the premises to the condition they were in when he or she took possession.

**Maintenance of
Premises**

Under the principle of caveat emptor, a landlord is not obligated to make any repairs to leased premises. However, many states now require a residential lessor to maintain dwelling units in a habitable condition and to make any necessary repairs to common elements, such as hallways, stairs, or elevators. The tenant does not have to make any repairs, but he or she must return the premises in the same condition they were received, with allowances for ordinary use.

Assignment and Subleasing

The lessee may assign the lease or may sublease if the lease terms do not prohibit it. A tenant who transfers all of his or her leasehold interests *assigns* the lease. One who transfers less than all of his or her leasehold interests by leasing them to a new tenant **subleases** (see figure 16.2). In most cases, the sublease or assignment of a lease does not relieve the original lessee of the obligation to make rental payments unless the landlord agrees to waive such liability. Most leases prohibit the lessee from assigning or subletting without the lessor's consent; this allows the lessor to retain control over the occupancy of the leased premises. The sublessor's (original lessee's) interest in the real estate is known as a *sandwich lease.*

Figure 16.2
Assignment versus Subletting

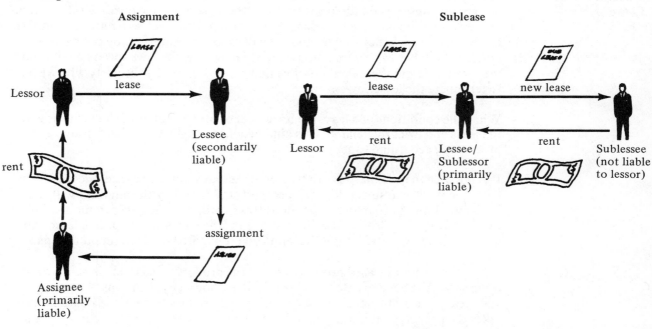

Options

Many leases contain an *option* that grants the lessee the privilege of *renewing* the lease but requires that the lessee give *notice* on or before a specific date of his or her intention to exercise the option. Some leases grant to the lessee the option to purchase the leased premises; the provisions for the option to purchase vary widely. Options to purchase are becoming more common (see Chapter 11).

Destruction of Premises

In land leases involving *agricultural land,* the courts have held that damage to or destruction of the improvements, even if it is not the tenant's fault, does not relieve the tenant from the obligation to pay rent to the end of the term. This ruling has been extended in most states to include *ground leases* upon which the tenant has constructed a building and, in many instances, leases that give possession of an entire building to the tenant. When the tenant leases an entire building, the courts have held that he or she is also leasing the land upon which that building is located.

In those cases where the leased premises are only a part of the building (such as office or commercial space or an apartment in an apartment building), the tenant is *not* required to continue to pay rent upon destruction of the leased premises. In some states, if the property was destroyed as a result of the landlord's negligence, the tenant can recover damages from the landlord.

In Practice . . .   *All of these general statements concerning destruction of leased premises are controlled largely by the terms of the lease. Printed lease forms and all carefully prepared leases generally include a provision covering the subject of destruction of the premises. Great care must be exercised in reading the entire lease document before signing it.*

Termination of Lease

A written lease for a definite period of time expires at the end of that time period; no separate notice is required to terminate the lease when it expires. Oral and written leases that do not specify a definite expiration date (such as a month-to-month or year-to-year tenancy or a tenancy at will) may be terminated by giving proper notice in advance as required by state law. Generally, the laws specify a minimum time period or number of days' notice that must be given by the party who wishes to terminate the lease.

When the conditions of a lease are breached, or broken, a landlord may terminate the lease and evict the tenant. This kind of action must be handled through a court proceeding according to state law.

It is possible that the parties to a lease will mutually agree to cancel the lease. The tenant may offer to surrender the lease, and acceptance by the landlord will result in termination. A tenant who abandons leased property, however, remains liable for the terms of the lease—including the rent. The terms of the specific lease will usually dictate whether or not the landlord is obligated to try to rerent the space.

When the owner of leased property dies or the property is sold, *the lease does not terminate.* The heirs of a deceased landlord are bound by the terms of existing valid leases. In addition, if a landlord conveys leased real estate, the new landlord takes the property subject to the rights of the tenants. If a tenant under an estate for years or from year to year dies, the lease will remain in effect; the deceased lessee's heirs will be bound by the terms of his or her lease agreement.

Breach of Lease

When a tenant breaches any lease provision, the landlord may sue the tenant to obtain a judgment to cover rent past due, damages to the premises, or other defaults. Likewise, when a landlord breaches any lease provision, the tenant is entitled to similar remedies.

Suit for possession—actual eviction.   When a tenant breaches a lease or improperly retains possession of leased premises, the landlord may regain possession through a **suit for possession.** This process is known as **actual eviction.** Law requires the landlord to serve *notice* on the tenant before commencing the suit. Usually at least a ten-day notice is required in case of a *default* in most lease terms, but in many states, only a five-day notice must be given before filing a suit for possession based on a default in payment of rent. When a court issues a judgment for possession to a landlord, the tenant must peaceably remove him- or herself and all belongings, or the landlord can have the judgment enforced by a *bailiff* or other court officer, who will *forcibly remove* the tenant and his or her possessions.

Tenants' remedies—constructive eviction. If a landlord breaches any clause of a lease agreement, the tenant has the right to sue, claiming a judgment for damages against the landlord. If an action or omission on the landlord's part results in the leased premises becoming uninhabitable for the purpose intended in the lease, the tenant may have the right to abandon the premises. This action, called **constructive eviction,** terminates the lease agreement if the tenant can prove that the premises have become uninhabitable because of the conscious neglect of the landlord. In order to claim constructive eviction, *the tenant must actually remove him- or herself from the premises* while the uninhabitable condition exists.

For example, a lease requires the landlord to furnish steam heat; because of the landlord's failure to repair a defective heating plant, the heat is not provided. If this results in the leased premises becoming uninhabitable, the tenant may abandon them. It should be noted that some leases provide that if the failure to furnish heat is accidental and not the landlord's fault, it is not grounds for constructive eviction.

Pro-Tenant Legislation

For the most part, leases are drawn up primarily for the benefit of the landlord. However, consumer awareness has fostered the belief that a valid lease is dependent on both parties' fulfillment of certain obligations. To provide laws outlining such obligations, several states have adopted some variation of the *Uniform Residential Landlord and Tenant Act.* This model law addresses such issues as the landlord's right of entry, maintenance of premises, the tenant's protection against retaliation by the landlord for complaints, and the disclosure of the property owners' names and addresses to the tenants. The act further sets down specific remedies available to both the landlord and the tenant if a breach of the lease agreement occurs.

The federal government also took steps to increase tenants' protection with the implementation of the Tenants' Eviction Procedures Act in 1976. This act establishes standardized eviction procedures for people living in *government-subsidized housing.* It requires that the landlord have a valid reason for evicting the tenant and that the landlord give the tenant proper notice of eviction. This act does not supersede state laws in this area; however, it does provide recourse for tenants in states that have no such laws. The act applies only to multiunit residential buildings that are owned or subsidized by the Department of Housing and Urban Development and to buildings that have government-insured mortgages.

Types of Leases

The manner in which rent is determined indicates the type of lease that is in force. The three primary types of leases are based upon rentals. They are: (1) the gross lease, (2) the net lease, and (3) the percentage lease (see table 16.2).

Gross Lease

In a **gross lease,** the tenant's obligation is to pay a *fixed rental,* and the landlord pays all taxes, insurance, mortgage payments, repairs, and the like connected with the property (usually called *property charges*). This type of lease is most often used for residential apartment rentals.

Table 16.2 Types of Leases	Type of Lease	Lessee Pays	Lessor Pays
	Gross Lease Residential (also small commercial)	Basic Rent	Property Charges (taxes, repairs, insurance, etc.)
	Net Lease Commercial/Industrial	Basic Rent Plus Most or All Property Charges	May Pay Some Property Charges
	Percentage Lease Commercial/Industrial	Basic Rent Plus Percent of Gross Sales (may pay property costs)	May Pay Some or All Property Charges

Net Lease

The **net lease** provides that in addition to the rent, the *tenant pays most or all of the property charges.* The monthly rental paid to the landlord is in addition to these charges and so is net income for the landlord after operating costs have been paid. Leases for entire commercial or industrial buildings and the land on which they are located, ground leases, and long-term leases are usually net leases.

Percentage Lease

Either a gross lease or a net lease may be a **percentage lease.** A percentage lease provides that the rental is based on a *percentage of the gross or net income* received by the tenant doing business on the leased property. This type of lease is usually used in the rental of retail business locations.

The percentage lease usually provides for a minimum fixed rental fee plus a percentage of that portion of the tenant's business income that exceeds a stated minimum. For example, a lease might provide for a minimum monthly rental of $1,200, with the further agreement that the tenant pay an additional amount each month equivalent to 4 percent of all gross sales in excess of $30,000. (Note that while the $1,200 rental represents 4 percent of $30,000 gross, the percentage feature of this lease will not actually begin to apply until after the tenant has grossed in excess of $30,000.) The percentage charged in such leases varies widely with the nature of the business, and it is negotiable between landlord and tenant. A tenant's bargaining power is determined by the volume of his or her business. Of course, percentages vary with the location of the property and general economic conditions.

Other Lease Types

Variable leases. There are several types of leases that allow for increases in the fixed rental charge during the lease period. Two of the more common ones are the *graduated lease,* which provides for increases in rent at set future dates, and the *index lease,* which allows rent to be increased or decreased periodically based on changes in the government cost-of-living index.

Ground leases. When a landowner leases his or her land to a tenant who agrees to *erect a building* on it, the lease is usually referred to as a **ground lease.** Such a lease must be for a long enough term to make the transaction desirable to the tenant making the investment in the building. These leases are generally *net leases* that require the lessee to pay rent as well as real estate taxes, insurance, upkeep, and repairs. Such leases often run for terms of 50 years or longer, and a lease for 999 years is not impossible. Although such leases are considered to be personal property, certain states' laws may give leaseholders some of the rights and obligations of real property owners.

Oil and gas leases. When oil companies lease land to explore for oil and gas, a special lease agreement must be negotiated. Usually, the landowner receives a cash payment for executing the lease. If no well is drilled within a year or other period stated in the lease, the lease expires; however, most oil and gas leases provide that the oil company may continue its rights for another year by paying another flat rental fee. Such rentals may be paid annually until a well is produced. If oil and/or gas is found, the landowner usually receives one-eighth of its value as a royalty. In this case, the lease will continue for as long as oil or gas is obtained in significant quantities.

Summary	A *lease* is an agreement that grants one person the right to use the property of another for a certain period in return for consideration. The lease agreement is a combination of a conveyance creating a leasehold interest in the property and a contract outlining the rights and obligations of the landlord and the tenant.

A leasehold estate that runs for a specific length of time creates an *estate for years,* while one that runs for an indefinite period creates a *periodic tenancy* (year to year, month to month) or a *tenancy at will.* A leasehold estate is generally classified as personal property.

The requirements of a valid lease include offer and acceptance, consideration, capacity to contract, and legal objectives. In addition, the state statute of frauds generally requires that any lease that will not be executed within one year must be in writing. Leases also generally include clauses relating to such rights and obligations of the landlord and tenant as the use of the premises, subletting, judgments, maintenance of the premises, and termination of the lease period.

Leases may be terminated by the expiration of the lease period, the mutual agreement of the parties, or a breach of the lease by either landlord or tenant. It is important to note that neither the death of the tenant nor the landlord's sale of the rental property terminates a lease.

Upon a tenant's default on any of the lease provisions, a landlord may sue for a money judgment or for *actual eviction* in a case where a tenant has improperly retained possession of the premises. If the premises have become uninhabitable due to the landlord's negligence, the tenant may have the right of *constructive eviction;* that is, the right to abandon the premises and refuse to pay rent until the premises are repaired.

There are several basic types of leases, including *net leases, gross leases,* and *percentage leases.* These leases are classified according to the method used in determining the rental rate of the property.

Questions

1. Alvin Yates's lease will expire in two weeks. At that time, he will move to larger quarters on the other side of town. In order to terminate this lease agreement:

    I. Yates must give the landlord prior notice.
    II. the landlord must give Yates prior notice.

    a. I only   c. both I and II
    b. II only   d. neither I nor II

2. A tenant's right to occupy, or take possession of, leased premises is:

    a. a reversionary interest.
    b. an estate in land.
    c. a leasehold interest.
    d. b and c

3. A ground lease is usually:

    a. short term.
    b. for 100 years or longer.
    c. long term.
    d. a gross lease.

4. A percentage lease is a lease that provides for:

    a. a rental of a percentage of the value of a building.
    b. a definite periodic rent not exceeding a stated percentage.
    c. a definite monthly rent plus a percentage of the tenant's gross receipts in excess of a certain amount.
    d. a graduated amount due monthly and not exceeding a stated percentage.

5. If a store building rented to several tenants collapsed, and the tenants moved out:

    I. this would be called actual eviction.
    II. the tenants would be liable for the rent until the expiration date of their leases.

    a. I only   c. both I and II
    b. II only   d. neither I nor II

6. Under the terms of a net lease:

    I. the tenant is usually responsible for paying the real estate taxes for the leased property.
    II. the tenant has an option to buy the leased property within a specified length of time.

    a. I only   c. both I and II
    b. II only   d. neither I nor II

7. A lease for more than one year must be in writing because:

    a. the landlord or tenant may forget the terms.
    b. the tenant must sign the agreement to pay rent.
    c. the statute of frauds requires it.
    d. it is the customary procedure to protect the tenant.

8. A lease calls for a minimum rent of $300 per month plus 4 percent of the annual gross business over $150,000. If the total rent paid at the end of the year was $4,800, how much business did the tenant do during the year?

    a. $150,000   c. $180,000
    b. $75,000   d. $160,000

9. Paul Robinson occupies a building under a written lease for a five-year term with monthly rental payments. The lease expired last month, but Roberts has remained in possession and the landlord has accepted his most recent rent payment without comment. At this point:

    a. Robinson is a holdover tenant.
    b. Robinson's lease has been renewed for another five years.
    c. Robinson's lease has been renewed for another month.
    d. Robinson is a tenant at sufferance.

10. Albert Franzen rented a studio apartment to Wilbur Post under a one-year written lease. Three and one-half months into the lease term, Franzen died. With regard to the written lease between Post and his late landlord:

   I. Post continues to be bound by its terms.
  II. Franzen's heirs are now bound by its terms.

    a. I only   c. both I and II
    b. II only   d. neither I nor II

11. Which of the following terms refers to a tenant's legal right to possession of leased property against the ownership claims of third parties?

    a. tenancy at will
    b. cognovit
    c. covenant of quiet possession
    d. constructive eviction

12. A tenant's lease has expired, the tenant has neither vacated nor negotiated a renewal lease, and the landlord has declared that she does not want the tenant to remain in the building. The tenancy is called:

    a. estate for years.
    b. periodic estate.
    c. tenancy at will.
    d. tenancy at sufferance.

13. The requirements of a valid lease include:

    a. offer and acceptance.
    b. consideration.
    c. capacity to contract.
    d. all of the above

14. When a tenant holds possession of a landlord's property without a current lease agreement and without the landlord's approval:

   I. the tenant is maintaining a gross lease.
   II. the landlord may file suit for possession.

    a. I only   c. both I and II
    b. II only   d. neither I nor II

15. Which of the following best describes a *net lease?*

    a. an agreement in which the tenant pays a fixed rent and the landlord pays all taxes, insurance, and so forth on the property
    b. a lease in which the tenant pays rent in addition to some or all property charges
    c. a lease in which the tenant pays the landlord a percentage of the monthly income derived from the property
    d. an agreement granting an individual a leasehold interest in fishing rights to shoreline properties

16. If no special provision is included in the lease regarding permanent improvements made by a tenant on leased property, such improvements:

   I. are called fixtures.
   II. remain the property of the tenant after the lease expires.

    a. I only   c. both I and II
    b. II only   d. neither I nor II

17. Most residential leases contain a provision in which the landlord agrees to furnish hot water for the tenant. If a tenant with such a lease is unable to receive hot water because of a faulty hot-water heater, which of the following remedies may the tenant take if the landlord refuses to fix the equipment?

    a. The tenant may sue the landlord for damages.
    b. The tenant may abandon the premises.
    c. The tenant may terminate the lease agreement.
    d. all of the above

18. Actual eviction occurs when:

    a. a tenant peaceably vacates a property upon termination of a lease.
    b. a landlord regains possession through a legal action.
    c. a court officer removes a tenant from the premises.
    d. b and c

19. A tenant who transfers the entire remaining term of his or her lease to a third party is:

    a. a sublettor.
    b. assigning the lease.
    c. automatically relieved of any further obligation under it.
    d. giving the third party a sandwich lease.

20. Which of the following leases would probably be recorded?

    I. a two-year residential lease
    II. a five-year net lease for commercial property with provisions for yearly rental increases and an option to purchase the property at the end of the lease term

    a. I only   c. both I and II
    b. II only   d. neither I nor II

Part Three

Practices

17

Property Management

Key Terms

Business interruption insurance
Casualty insurance
Contents and personal property insurance
Fire and hazard insurance
Liability insurance
Management agreement
Multiperil policies
Property manager
Replacement cost
Surety bond
Workers' compensation acts

Overview

A real estate owner who rents the upstairs apartment in the building where he or she resides generally has no problem with property management—setting and collecting rents, maintenance, and repairs are easy enough with only one tenant. But the owners of large, multiunit developments often lack the time and/or expertise to successfully manage their properties. Enter the *property manager,* a real estate professional hired to maintain the property and ensure the profitability of the owner's investment. This chapter will examine the growing property management profession and will include discussions of the types of property insurance available to further protect an owner's real estate investment.

Property Management	The need for specialized property managers began to emerge during the 1930s as lending institutions found themselves owning numerous foreclosed income properties. Since lenders often lacked the expertise to administer these properties, they looked to the real estate industry for expert management assistance. In recent years the increased size of buildings; the technical complexities of construction, maintenance, and repair; and the trend toward absentee ownership by individual investors and investment groups have led to the expanded use of professional property managers for both residential and commercial properties.
	Property management has become so important that many brokerage firms maintain separate management departments staffed by carefully selected, well-trained people. Many corporate and institutional owners of real estate have also established property management departments. However, many real estate investors still manage their own property and thus must acquire the knowledge and skills of a property manager. In some states, property managers must be licensed real estate brokers.
Functions of the Property Manager	In the simplest terms, a **property manager** is someone who *preserves the value of an investment property while generating income as an agent for the owners.* More specifically, a property manager is expected to merchandise the property and control operating expenses so as to maximize income. In addition, a manager should maintain and modernize the property to preserve and enhance the owner's capital investment. The manager carries out these objectives by: (1) securing suitable tenants, (2) collecting the rents, (3) caring for the premises, (4) budgeting and controlling expenses, (5) hiring and supervising employees, and (6) keeping proper accounts and making periodic reports to the owner.
Securing Management Business	In today's market, property managers may look to corporate owners, apartments and condominiums, investment syndicates, trusts, and absentee owners as possible sources of management business. In securing business from any of these sources, word of mouth is often the best advertising. A manager who consistently demonstrates that he or she can increase property income over previous levels should have no difficulty finding new business.
	Before contracting to manage any property, the professional property manager should be certain that the building owner has realistic income expectations and is willing to spend money on necessary maintenance. Attempting to meet impossible owner demands by dubious methods can endanger the manager's reputation and prove detrimental to obtaining future business.
The Management Agreement	The first step in taking over the management of any property is to enter into a **management agreement** with the owner (see figure 17.1). This agreement creates an agency relationship between the owner and the property manager, just as a listing agreement creates an agency relationship between selling owner and listing broker. A property manager is usually considered to be a *general agent*, whereas a

Figure 17.1
Property
Management
Agreement

Between

OWNER___Elinore Q. Franks_____

and

AGENT___Don Silver Management_____

for Property located at___312 West East Street, Clinton_____

Beginning _January 1,_____ 19_83_____

Ending_____June 1,_____ 19_84_____

MANAGEMENT
AGREEMENT

In consideration of the covenants herein contained._____

___Elinore Q. Franks_____(hereinafter called

"OWNER"), and___Don Silver Mgt._____(hereinafter called "AGENT"),
agree as follows:

1. The OWNER   hereby employs the AGENT exclusively to rent and
manage the property (hereinafter called the "Premises") known as_____

___312 West East Street_____

___Clinton, Astate, 10010_____

upon the terms hereinafter set forth. for a period of____1½____years beginning

on the__1st____day of__January_____, 19_83_____, and ending on

the____1st_____day of__June_____,19_84_____, and there-
after for yearly periods from time to time, unless on or before _____90___ days
prior to the date last above mentioned or on or before _____90 days prior
to the expiration of any such renewal period, either party hereto shall notify
the other in writing that it elects to terminate this Agreement, in which case
this Agreement shall be thereby terminated on said last mentioned date.
(See also Paragraph 6(c) below.)

2. THE AGENT AGREES:

(a) To accept the management of the Premises, to the extent, for the period, and upon the terms herein provided and agrees to furnish the services of its organization for the rental operation and management of the Premises.

(b) To render a monthly statement of receipts, disbursements and charges to the following person at the address shown:

Name	Address
Regina Stump, CPA	211 North Blvd. Suite 601
on behalf of owner	Burton, Astate, 10014

and to remit each month the net proceeds (provided Agent is not required to make any mortgage, escrow or tax payment on the first day of the following month). Agent will remit the net proceeds or the balance thereof after making allowance for such payments to the following persons, in the percentages specified and at the addresses shown:

Name	Percentage	Address
Elinore Q. Franks	100	912 Knowles, Suite 900
		Burton, Astate, 10015

In case the disbursements and charges shall be in excess of the receipts, the OWNER agrees to pay such excess promptly, but nothing herein contained shall obligate the AGENT to advance its own funds on behalf of the OWNER.

(c) To cause all employees of the AGENT who handle or are responsible for the safekeeping of any monies of the OWNER to be covered by a fidelity bond in an amount and with a company determined by the AGENT at no cost to the OWNER.

3. THE OWNER AGREES:

To give the AGENT the following authority and powers (all or any of which may be exercised in the name of the OWNER) and agrees to assume all expenses in connection therewith:

(a) To advertise the Premises or any part thereof, to display signs thereon and to rent the same; to cause references of prospective tenants to be investigated; to sign leases for terms not in excess of____2____years and to renew and or cancel the existing leases and prepare and execute the new lease without additional charge to the OWNER; provided, however, that the AGENT may collect from tenants all or any of the following: a late rent administrative charge, a non-negotiable check charge, credit report fee, a subleasing administrative charge and/or broker's commission and need not account for such charges and/or commission to the OWNER; to terminate tenancies and to sign and serve such notices as are deemed needful by the AGENT; to institute and prosecute actions to oust tenants and to recover possession of the Premises; to sue for and recover rent; and, when expedient, to settle, compromise and release such actions or suits, or reinstate such tenancies.

Figure 17.1 (cont.)

(b) To hire, discharge and pay all engineers, janitors and other employees; to make or cause to be made all ordinary repairs and replacements necessary to preserve the Premises in its present condition and for the operating efficiency thereof and all alterations required to comply with lease requirements, and to do decorating on the Premises; to negotiate contracts for non-recurring items not exceeding $ __5.000__ and to enter into agreements for all necessary repairs, maintenance, minor alterations and utility services; and to purchase supplies and pay all bills.

(c) To collect rents and/or assessments and other items due or to become due and give receipts therefor and to deposit all funds collected hereunder in the Agent's custodial account.

(d) To refund tenants' security deposits at the expiration of leases and, only if required to do so by law, to pay interest upon such security deposits.

(e) To execute and file all returns and other instruments and do and perform all acts required of the OWNER as an employer with respect to the Premises under the Federal Insurance Contributions Acts, the Federal Unemployment Tax Act and Subtitle C of the Internal Revenue Code of 1954 with respect to wages paid by the AGENT on behalf of the OWNER and under any similar Federal or State law now or hereafter in force (and in connection therewith the OWNER agrees upon request to promptly execute and deliver to the AGENT all necessary powers of attorney, notices of appointment and the like).

4. THE OWNER FURTHER AGREES:

(a) To indemnify, defend and save the AGENT harmless from all suits in connection with the Premises and from liability for damage to property and injuries to or death of any employee or other person whomsoever, and to carry at his (its) own expense public liability, elevator liability (if elevators are part of the equipment of the Premises), and workmen's compensation insurance naming the OWNER and the AGENT and adequate to protect their interests and in form, substance and amounts reasonably satisfactory to the AGENT, and to furnish to the AGENT certificates evidencing the existence of such insurance. Unless the OWNER shall provide such insurance and furnish such certificate within ___30___ days from the date of this Agreement, the AGENT may, but shall not be obligated to, place said insurance and charge the cost thereof to the account of the OWNER.

(b) To pay all expenses incurred by the AGENT, including, without limitation, attorney's fees for counsel employed to represent the AGENT or the OWNER in any proceeding or suit involving an alleged violation by the AGENT or the OWNER, or both, of any constitutional provision, statute, ordinance, law or regulation of any governmental body pertaining to fair employment, Federal Fair Credit Reporting Act, environmental protection, or fair housing, including, without limitation, those prohibiting or making illegal discrimination on the basis of race, creed, color, religion or national origin in the sale, rental or other disposition of housing or any services rendered in connection therewith (unless the AGENT is finally adjudicated to have personally and not in a representative capacity violated such constitutional provision, statute, ordinance, law or regulation), but nothing herein contained shall require the AGENT to employ counsel to represent the OWNER in any such proceeding or suit.

(c) To indemnify, defend and save the AGENT harmless from all claims, investigations and suits with respect to any alleged or actual violation of state or federal labor laws, it being expressly agreed and understood that as between the OWNER and the AGENT, all persons employed in connection with the Premises are employees of the OWNER not the AGENT. The OWNER's obligation under this paragraph 4(c) shall include the payment of all settlements, judgments, damages, liquidated damages, penalties, forfeitures, back pay awards, court costs, litigation expense and attorneys' fees.

(d) To give adequate advance written notice to the AGENT if payment of mortgage indebtedness, general taxes or special assessments or the placing of fire, steam boiler or any other insurance is desired.

5. TO PAY THE AGENT EACH MONTH:

(a) FOR MANAGEMENT:_____per month or_seven____

percent (_7____%) of the monthly gross receipts from the operation of the Premises during the period this Agreement remains in full force and effect, whichever is the greater amount.

(b) APARTMENT LEASING_$100 per unit for each new rental or lease renewal____

_____

_____

(c) FOR MODERNIZATION (REHABILITATION/CONSTRUCTION)

2½% of total costs_____

_____

(d) FIRE RESTORATION_____

4% of total costs_____

_____

_____

(e) OTHER ITEMS OF MUTUAL AGREEMENT_____

_____

_____

_____

_____

6. IT IS MUTUALLY AGREED THAT:

(a) The OWNER expressly withholds from the AGENT any power or authority to make any structural changes in any building or to make any other major alterations or additions in or to any such building or equipment therein, or to incur any expense chargeable to the OWNER other than expenses related to exercising the express powers above vested in the AGENT without the prior written direction of the following person:

Name	Address
Elinore Q. Franks	912 Knowles, Suite 100, Burton, Astate, 10015

real estate broker is usually considered to be a *special agent* (see Chapter 5). As agent, the property manager is charged with the same agency responsibilities as the listing broker—care, obedience, accounting, loyalty, and notice (COAL-N). (Agency responsibilities were discussed at length in Chapter 5.)

The management agreement should be in writing and should cover the following points:

1. *Description* of the property.

2. *Time period* the agreement will cover.

3. *Definition of management's responsibilities:* All of the manager's duties should be stated in the contract; exceptions should be noted.

4. *Statement of owner's purpose:* This statement should indicate what the owner desires the manager to accomplish with the property. One owner may wish to maximize net income and therefore instruct the manager to cut expenses and minimize reinvestment. Another owner may want to increase the capital value of the investment, in which case the manager should initiate a program for improving the property's physical condition.

5. *Extent of manager's authority:* This provision should state what authority the manager is to have in such matters as hiring, firing, and supervising employees, fixing rental rates for space, making expenditures, and authorizing repairs within the limits established previously with the owner. (Repairs that exceed a certain expense limit may require the owner's written approval.)

6. *Reporting:* Agreement should be reached on the frequency and detail of the manager's periodic reports on operations and financial position. These reports serve as a means for the owner to monitor the manager's work and as a basis for both the owner and the manager to assess trends that can be used in shaping future management policy.

7. *Management fee:* The fee can be based on a percentage of gross or net income, a commission on new rentals, a fixed fee, or a combination of these.

8. *Allocation of costs:* The agreement should state which of the property manager's expenses, such as office rent, office help, telephone, advertising, association fees, and social security, will be paid by the manager and which will be charged to the property's expenses and paid by the owner.

After entering into an agreement with a property owner, a manager must handle the property as if it were his or her own. In all activities, the manager must be aware that his or her first responsibility is to *realize the highest return on the property that is consistent with the owner's instructions.*

Management Considerations

A property manager must protect the interest of the property owner by: (1) constantly *improving the reputation* as well as the *physical condition* of the property, (2) protecting the owner from *insurable losses,* (3) protecting the owner by helping the neighborhood and the community to offer the best possible *residential and business environments,* (4) keeping constant *check on all expenditures* to be sure that costs are kept as low as possible for the results that must be accomplished, and (5) *adjusting the rental rate* as necessary to produce the highest total income.

A property manager must live up to his or her side of the management agreement in both the letter and the spirit of the contract. The owner must be kept well informed on all matters of policy, as well as on the financial condition of the property and its operation. Finally, a manager must keep in contact with others in the field, improving his or her knowledge of the subject and keeping informed on current policies pertaining to the profession.

Budgeting Expenses

Before attempting to rent any property, a property manager should develop an operating budget based on anticipated revenues and expenses and reflecting the long-term goals of the owner. In preparing a budget, a manager should begin by allocating money for such continuous, fixed expenses as employees' salaries, real estate taxes, property taxes, and insurance premiums.

Next, the manager should establish a cash reserve fund for such variable expenses as repairs, decorating, and supplies. The amount allocated for the reserve funds can be computed from the previous yearly costs of the variable expenses.

Capital expenditures. If an owner and a property manager decide that modernization or renovation of the property would enhance its value, the manager should budget money to cover the costs of remodeling. In the case of large-scale construction, the expenses charged against the property's income should be spread over several years. Although budgets should be as accurate an estimate of cost as possible, adjustments may sometimes be necessary, especially in the case of new properties.

Renting the Property

Effective rental of the property is essential to the success of a property manager. However, the role of the manager in managing a property should not be confused with that of a broker or rental agency solely concerned with renting space. The property manager may use the services of a rental agency to solicit prospective tenants or collect rents, but the rental agency does not undertake the full responsibility of maintenance and management of the properties.

Setting rental rates. In establishing rental rates for a property, a basic concern must be that, in the long term, the income from the rentable space cover the fixed charges and operating expenses and also provide a fair return on the investment. However, consideration must also be given to the prevailing rates in comparable buildings and the current level of vacancy in the property to be rented. In the short term, rental rates are primarily a result of supply and demand. Decisions about rental rates should start with a detailed survey of the competitive space available in the neighborhood. Prices should be noted and judgment should be applied to adjust for differences between neighboring properties and the properties the manager will manage.

Note that while apartment rental rates are stated in monthly amounts, office and commercial space rentals are usually stated according to either the annual or the monthly rate per square foot of space.

If a high level of vacancy exists, an immediate effort should be made to determine what is wrong with the property or what is out of line in the rental rates. *A high level of vacancy does not necessarily indicate that rents are too high.* The trouble may be inept management or defects in the property. The manager should attempt to identify and correct the problems rather than lower the rent. Conversely, *while a high percentage of occupancy may appear to indicate an effective rental program, it could also mean that rental rates are too low.* With an apartment house or office building, any time the occupancy level exceeds 95 percent serious consideration should be given to raising the rents.

Tenant selection. Generally, the highest rents can be secured from satisfied tenants. While a broker may sell a property and then have no further dealings with the purchaser, a building manager must continue to deal with each tenant, and his or her success is greatly dependent on retaining sound, long-term relationships. In selecting prospective commercial or industrial tenants, a manager should be sure that each person will "fit the space." The manager should be certain that: (1) the *size of the space* meets the tenant's requirements, (2) the tenant will have the *ability to pay* for the space for which he or she contracts, (3) the *tenant's business will be compatible* with the building and the other tenants, and (4) if the tenant is likely to expand in the future, there will be *expansion space available.* After a prospect becomes a tenant, *the manager must be sure that the tenant remains satisfied in all respects commensurate with fair business dealing.*

Note that in selecting residential tenants, the property manager must comply with all federal and local fair housing laws (see Chapter 21).

Collecting rents. A building will not be a profitable operation unless the property manager can collect all rents when they are due. Any substantial loss resulting from nonpayment of rent will quickly eliminate the margin of profitability in an operation.

The best way to minimize problems with rent collection is to make a *careful selection* of tenants in the first place. A property manager's desire to have a high level of occupancy should not override good judgment in accepting only those tenants who can be expected to meet their financial obligations to the property owner. A property manager should investigate financial references given by the prospect, local credit bureaus, and, when possible, the prospective tenant's former landlord.

The terms of rental payment should be spelled out in detail in the lease agreement. These details include the time and place of payment, provisions and penalties for late payment, and provisions for cancellation and damages in case of nonpayment. A *firm and consistent collection plan* with a sufficient system of notices and records should be established by the property manager. In cases of delinquency, every attempt must be made to make collections without resorting to legal action. However, for those cases in which it is required, a property manager must be prepared to initiate and follow through with the necessary steps in conjunction with the property owner's or management firm's legal counsel.

Maintaining the Property

One of the most important functions of a property manager is the supervision of property maintenance. A manager must learn to balance services provided with the costs they entail so as to satisfy the tenants' needs while minimizing operating expenses.

The broad term *maintenance* actually covers several types of activities. First, the manager must *protect the physical integrity of the property* to ensure that the condition of the building and its grounds are kept at present levels. Over the long term, preserving the property by repainting the exterior or replacing the heating plant will help to keep the building functional and decrease routine maintenance costs.

A property manager must also *supervise the routine cleaning and repairs* of the building. Such day-to-day duties as cleaning common areas, minor carpentry and plumbing, and regularly scheduled upkeep of heating, air conditioning, and landscaping are generally handled by regular building employees or by outside firms that have contracted with the manager to provide certain services.

In addition, especially when dealing with commercial or industrial space, a property manager will be called on to *alter the interior of the building to meet the functional demands of the tenant.* These alterations range from repainting to completely gutting the interior and redesigning the space.

Designing interior space is especially important when renting new buildings, since the interior is usually left incomplete so that it can be adapted to the needs of the individual tenants. Another portion of a manager's responsibility is the supervision of modernization or renovation of buildings that have become functionally obsolete and thus unsuited to today's building needs. (See Chapter 18 for a definition of *functional obsolescence.*) The renovation of a building often increases the building's marketability and thus its possible income.

Employees versus contracted services. One of the major decisions a property manager faces is whether to contract for maintenance services from an outside firm or hire on-site employees to perform such tasks. This decision should be based on a number of factors, including size of the building, complexity of tenants' requirements, and availability of suitable labor. In a large building or one where the tenants have sophisticated needs, a property manager may find that it is necessary to keep a large on-site crew to deal with the day-to-day operations of the property; in a small apartment building, one full-time janitor can handle most of the everyday problems.

The Management Profession

For those interested in pursuing a career in property management, most large cities have local associations of building and property owners and managers that are affiliates of regional and national associations. The Institute of Real Estate Management was founded in 1933 and is part of the NATIONAL ASSOCIATION OF REALTORS®. The Institute awards the designation of *Certified Property Manager* (CPM) to persons who have met certain requirements. The Building Owners and Managers Association International (BOMA International) is a federation of local associations of owners and managers, primarily of office buildings. Participation in groups like these allows property managers to gain valuable professional knowledge and to discuss their problems with other managers facing similar issues.

Insurance

One of the most important responsibilities of a property manager is to protect the property owner against all major insurable risks. In some cases, a property manager or a member of his or her firm may be a licensed insurance broker. In any case, a competent, reliable insurance agent who is well-versed in all areas of insurance pertaining to property should be selected to survey the property and make recommendations. If the manager is not completely satisfied with these recommendations, additional insurance surveys should be obtained. Final decisions, however, must be made by the property owner. Note that *in most states, an insurance broker must pass a state examination to secure a special license to sell insurance.*

Types of Coverage

There are many kinds of insurance coverage available to income-property owners and managers. Some of the more common types are:

1. **Fire and hazard:** Fire insurance policies provide coverage against direct loss or damage to property from a fire on the premises. Standard fire coverage can be extended to cover hazards such as windstorm, hail, smoke damage, or civil insurrection.

2. **Business interruption:** Most hazard policies insure against the actual loss of property but do not cover loss of revenues from income property. Interruption insurance covers the loss of income that occurs if the property cannot be used to produce income.

3. **Contents and personal property:** *Inland marine insurance* covers building contents and personal property during periods when they are not actually located on the business premises.

4. **Liability:** Public liability insurance covers the risks an owner assumes when the public enters the building. Claims are used to pay medical expenses for a person injured in the building as a result of the landlord's negligence. Another liability risk is that of medical or hospital payments for injuries sustained by building employees hurt in the course of their employment. These claims are covered by state laws known as **Workers' Compensation Acts.** These laws require a building owner who is an employer to obtain a workers' compensation policy from a private insurance company.

5. **Casualty:** Casualty insurance policies include coverage against theft, burglary, vandalism, machinery damage, and health and accident insurance. Casualty policies are usually written on specific risks, such as theft, rather than being all-inclusive.

6. **Surety bonds:** Surety bonds cover an owner against financial losses resulting from an employee's criminal acts or negligence while carrying out his or her duties.

Today, many insurance companies offer **multiperil policies** for apartment and business buildings. These policies offer the property manager an insurance package that includes such standard types of commercial coverage as fire, hazard, public liability, and casualty.

Claims

When a claim is made under a policy insuring a building or other physical object, there are two possible methods of determining the amount of the claim. One is the *depreciated,* or actual, cash value of the damaged property, and the other is replacement cost. If a 30-year-old building is damaged, the timbers and materials are 30 years old and therefore do not have the same value as new material. Thus, in determining the amount of the loss under what is called *actual cash value,* the cost of new material would be reduced by the estimated depreciation the item had suffered during the time it had been in the building.

The alternate method is to cover **replacement cost.** This would represent the actual amount a builder would charge to replace the damaged property, including materials, at the time of the loss.

When purchasing insurance, a manager must assess whether the property should be insured at full replacement cost or at a depreciated cost. As with the homeowners' policies discussed in Chapter 4, commercial policies include *coinsurance clauses* that require the insured to carry fire coverage, usually in an amount equal to 80 percent of the building's replacement value.

In Practice ...   *Often, a property owner will pay for repairing or replacing small casualty losses out of pocket and attempt to deduct the cost on his or her tax return instead of filing a claim with the company that insures the building. The intent of this is to avoid rate increases or cancellation of a policy. However, the IRS will not allow such deductions, because the taxpayer voluntarily elected not to claim reimbursement from the insurance company. Since the IRS will allow a property owner to deduct all losses suffered, up to the deductible portion of the insurance policy, some owners/ managers might consider obtaining policies with a higher deductible, which should also result in a lower insurance premium.*

Summary   *Property management* is a specialized service to owners of income-producing properties in which the managerial function may be delegated to an individual or a firm with particular expertise in the field. The manager, as agent of the owner, becomes the administrator of the project and assumes the executive functions required for the care and operation of the property.

A *management agreement* must be carefully prepared to define and authorize the manager's duties and responsibilities. This agreement establishes the agency relationship between owner and manager.

The first step a property manager should take when managing a building is to draw up a budget of estimated variable and fixed expenses. The budget should also allow for any proposed expenditures for major renovations or modernizations agreed on by the manager and the owner. These projected expenses, combined with the manager's analysis of the condition of the building and the rent patterns in the neighborhood, will form the basis on which rental rates for the property are determined.

Once a rent schedule is established, the property manager is responsible for soliciting tenants whose needs are suited to the available space and who are financially capable of meeting the proposed rents. The manager is generally obligated to collect rents, maintain the building, hire necessary employees, pay taxes for the building, and deal with tenant problems.

Once the property is rented, one of the manager's primary responsibilities is supervising its maintenance. Maintenance includes safeguarding the physical integrity of the property and performing routine cleaning and repairs as well as adapting the interior space and overall design of the property to suit the tenants' needs and meet the demands of the market.

In addition, the manager is expected to secure adequate insurance coverage for the premises. The basic types of coverage applicable to commercial structures include *fire and hazard insurance* on the property and fixtures, *business interruption insurance* to protect the owner against income losses, and *casualty insurance* to provide coverage against such losses as theft, vandalism, and destruction of machinery. The manager should also secure *public liability insurance* to insure the owner against claims made by people injured on the premises and *workers' compensation policies* to cover the claims of employees injured on the job.

Questions

1. Which of the following types of insurance coverage insures the property owner against the claims of employees injured while on the job?
   a. business interruption
   b. workers' compensation
   c. casualty
   d. surety bond

2. In renting units in an apartment building, a property manager must comply with which of the following?
   a. the terms of the management agreement
   b. the owner
   c. fair housing laws
   d. all of the above

3. From a management point of view, apartment building occupancy that reaches as high as 98 percent would tend to indicate that:
   a. the building is poorly managed.
   b. the building is well-managed.
   c. the building is a desirable place to live.
   d. rents should be raised.

4. A deliveryman slips on a defective stair in an apartment building and is hospitalized. A claim against the building owner for medical expenses will be made under which of the following policies held by the owner?
   a. workers' compensation
   b. casualty
   c. liability
   d. fire and hazard

5. The relationship between a building owner and a property manager is:
   I. an agency relationship.
   II. established in the management agreement.
      a. I only   c. both I and II
      b. II only   d. neither I nor II

6. Which of the following should *not* be a consideration in selecting a tenant?
   a. the size of the space versus the tenant's requirements
   b. the tenant's ability to pay
   c. the racial and ethnic backgrounds of the tenants
   d. the compatibility of the tenant's business to other tenants' businesses

7. The need for property management specialists has been created by:
   I. the increased size of buildings.
   II. the technical complexities of maintenance and repair.
      a. I only   c. both I and II
      b. II only   d. neither I nor II

8. An owner-manager agreement should include:
   a. a statement of the owner's purpose for the building.
   b. a clear definition of the manager's authority.
   c. what portion of the property manager's personal operating expenses will be paid by the owner.
   d. all of the above

9. In drawing up an operating budget for the property, the manager should consider:
   I. the variable expenses.
   II. the long-range desires of the owner.
      a. I only   c. both I and II
      b. II only   d. neither I nor II

10. Generally, the provisions of the manager-owner agreement should include:
    I. a definition of the manager's responsibilities.
    II. a listing of previous owners of the property.
       a. I only   c. both I and II
       b. II only   d. neither I nor II

11. Rents should be determined on the basis of:
    a. prevailing rental rates in the area.
    b. operating expenses, fixed charges, and a proper net profit to the owner.
    c. current level of vacancy.
    d. all of the above

12. Property manager Frieda Jacobs hires Albert Weston as the full-time janitor for one of the buildings she manages. While repairing a faucet in one of the apartments, Weston steals a television set. Jacobs could protect the owner against liability for this type of loss by purchasing:
    a. liability insurance.
    b. workers' compensation insurance.
    c. a surety bond.
    d. casualty insurance.

13. Before accepting a tenant, the property manager should:
    a. determine if the available space fits the tenant's needs.
    b. check the tenant's ability to pay.
    c. check whether the tenant is compatible with other tenants.
    d. all of the above

14. The possible methods of determining the amount of a claim under an insurance policy covering damage to a building include the:
    I. replacement cost method.
    II. actual cash value method.

    a. I only   c. both I and II
    b. II only   d. neither I nor II

15. In assuming responsibility for the maintenance of a property, the manager is expected to:
    I. directly or indirectly supervise the routine cleaning and repair work of the building.
    II. adapt the interior space of the building to meet the requirements of individual tenants.

    a. I only   c. both I and II
    b. II only   d. neither I nor II

18

Real Estate Appraisal

Key Terms

Appraisal
Capitalization rate
Cost approach
Cubic-foot method
Depreciation
Functional obsolescence
Gross rent multiplier
Highest and best use
Income approach
Locational obsolescence
Market comparison approach
Physical deterioration

Plottage
Quantity-survey method
Reconciliation
Regression
Replacement cost
Reproduction cost
Square-foot method
Substitution
Unit-in-place method
Value

Overview

As stated earlier in the text, real estate is the business of value. Members of the general public informally estimate this value when they buy, sell, or invest in real estate. A formal estimate of value is generally conducted by a professional real estate appraiser and serves as a basis for the pricing, financing, insuring, or leasing of real property. This chapter will examine value—what determines it, adds to it, and detracts from it. It will also discuss in detail the various methods professional appraisers use to estimate the value of residential as well as commercial and industrial real estate.

Appraising	An **appraisal** is an estimate or opinion of value. In the real estate business, the highest level of appraisal activity is conducted by professional real estate appraisers who are recognized for their knowledge, training, skill, and integrity in this field. Formal appraisal reports are relied upon in important decisions made by mortgage lenders, investors, public utilities, governmental agencies, businesses, and individuals. In most states, a person does not have to be licensed to appraise real estate. Some states require an appraiser to be a licensed broker or salesperson, and a handful of states require an appraisal license.

Not all estimates of real estate value are made by professional appraisers; often the real estate agent must help a seller arrive at a market value for his or her property without the aid of a formal appraisal report. Thus, it is necessary for everyone engaged in the real estate business, even those who are not experts in appraisal, to possess at least a fundamental knowledge of real estate valuation. |
| **Value** | Value is an abstract word with many acceptable definitions. In a broad sense, **value** may be defined as the relationship between an object desired and a potential purchaser. It is the power of a good or service to command other goods or services in exchange. In terms of real estate appraisal, value may be described as the *present worth of future benefits arising from the ownership of real property.*

For a property to have value in the real estate market, it must have four characteristics:

1. *Utility:* The capacity to satisfy human needs and desires.
2. *Scarcity:* A finite supply.
3. *Effective demand:* The need or desire for possession or ownership backed up by the financial means to satisfy that need. (Note: When the word *demand* is used in economics, *effective demand* is usually assumed.)
4. *Transferability:* The transfer of ownership rights from one person to another with relative ease. |
| **Market Value** | While a given parcel of real estate may have many different kinds of value at the same time (as illustrated in figure 18.1), generally the goal of an appraiser is an estimate of *market value.* The market value of real estate is the highest price, in terms of money, that a property will bring in a competitive and open market, allowing a reasonable time to find a purchaser who buys the property with knowledge of all the uses to which it is adapted and for which it is capable of being used. Included in this definition are the following key points:

1. Market value is the *highest* price a property will bring—not the average price or the lowest price.
2. Payment must be made in *cash* or its equivalent.
3. Both buyer and seller must act without *undue pressure.*
4. A *reasonable length of time* must be allowed for the property to be exposed in the *open market.* |

Figure 18.1
Kinds of Value

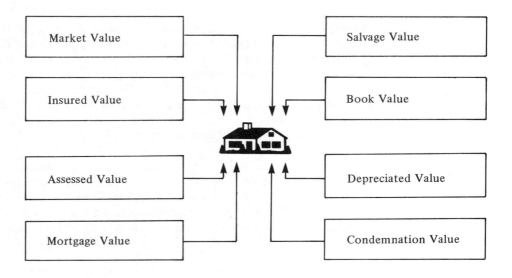

5. Both buyer and seller must be *well informed* or *well advised.*
6. The *present use* of the property as well as its *potential use* must be recognized.

Market value versus market price. Market value is an estimated price based on an analysis of comparable sales and other pertinent market data. *Market price,* on the other hand, is what a property *actually* sells for—its selling price. Theoretically, the ideal market price would be the same as the market value; however, there are circumstances under which a property may be sold at below market value, such as when a seller is forced to sell quickly or when a sale is arranged between relatives. Thus, the market price can be taken as accurate evidence of current market value only after considering the relationship of the buyer and the seller, the terms and conditions of the market, and the effect of the passage of time since the sale was made.

Market value versus cost. It is also important to distinguish between market value and *cost.* One of the most common errors made in valuing property is the assumption that cost represents market value. Cost and market value *may* be equal, and often are when the improvements on a property are new and represent the highest and best use of the land.

But more often, cost does not equal market value. For example, two homes are identical in every respect except that one is located on a street with heavy traffic and the other is on a quiet, residential street. The value of the former may be less than that of the latter, although the cost of each may be exactly the same. Another example would be a situation in which the demand for homes greatly exceeds the available supply to such an extent that buyers actually pay more than it would cost to construct such homes in order to secure housing without long delay. In this instance, market value could easily exceed cost.

Basic Principles of Value

Whether an appraiser observes them or not, there are always a number of economic principles at work that affect the value of real estate. The most important of these principles are defined in the following paragraphs.

Highest and best use. The most profitable use to which the property is adapted and needed or the use that is likely to be in demand in the reasonably near future is the **highest and best use.** For example, a highest-and-best-use study may show that a parking lot in a busy downtown area should, in fact, be replaced by an office building. To place a value on the property based on its present use would be erroneous, since a parking lot is not the highest and best use of the land. In appraising a residential location, the determination of highest and best use will not involve just the income available in money. Amenities or owner satisfaction—an unusual view of the mountains, for instance—may be a key factor.

Substitution. The principle of **substitution** states that the maximum value of a property tends to be set by the cost of purchasing an equally desirable and valuable substitute property, assuming that no costly delay is encountered in making the substitution. For example, if there are two similar houses for sale in an area, the one with the lower asking price would normally be purchased first.

Supply and demand. This principle states that the value of a property will increase if the supply decreases and the demand either increases or remains constant—and vice versa. For example, the last lot to be sold in a residential area where the demand for homes is high would probably be worth more than the first lot sold in that area.

Conformity. This means that maximum value is realized if the use of land conforms to existing neighborhood standards. There should also be a reasonable degree of conformity along social and economic lines. In residential areas of single-family houses, for example, buildings should be similar in design, construction, size, and age to other buildings in the neighborhood, and they will usually house families of similar social and economic status.

Anticipation. This principle holds that value can increase or decrease in anticipation of some future benefit or detriment affecting the property. For example, the value of a house may be affected if there are rumors that the block on which the house is located may be converted to commercial use in the near future.

Increasing and diminishing returns. Improvements to land and structures will eventually reach a point at which they will no longer have an effect on property values. As long as money spent on improvements produces an increase in income or value, the *law of increasing returns* is applicable. But at the point where additional improvements will not produce a proportionate increase in income or value, the *law of diminishing returns* applies.

Regression. The principle that, between dissimilar properties, the worth of the better property is adversely affected by the presence of the lesser-quality property is known as **regression.** Thus, in a neighborhood where the homes average in the $75,000 range, a structure that would be worth at least $90,000 in another neighborhood would tend to be valued closer to $75,000. Conversely, the principle of *progression* states that the worth of a lesser property tends to increase if it is located among better properties.

Plottage. The principle of **plottage** holds that the merging or consolidation of adjacent lots held by separate land owners into one larger lot under a single land use tends to produce a higher total land value than the sum of the two sites valued separately. For example, if two adjacent lots are valued at $35,000 each, their total value if consolidated into one larger lot under a single use might be $90,000. The process of merging the two lots under one owner is known as *assemblage.*

Contribution. The value of any component of a property consists of what its addition contributes to the value of the whole or what its absence detracts from that value. For example, the cost of installing an air-conditioning system and remodeling an older office building may be greater than is justified by the rental increase that may result from the improvement to the property.

Competition. This principle states that excess profits tend to attract competition. For example, the success of a retail store may attract investors to open similar stores in the area. This tends to mean less profit for all stores concerned unless the purchasing power in the area increases substantially.

Change. No physical or economic condition remains constant. Real estate is subject to natural phenomena, such as tornadoes, fires, and routine wear and tear of the elements. The real estate business is also subject to the demands of its market, just as is any business. It is an appraiser's job to be knowledgeable about the past and, perhaps, predictable effects of natural phenomena and the behavior of the marketplace.

The Three Approaches to Value

In order to arrive at an accurate estimate of value, three basic approaches, or techniques, are traditionally used by appraisers: the market comparison approach, the cost approach, and the income approach. Each method serves as a check against the others and narrows the range within which the final estimate of value will fall. Each method is generally considered most reliable for specific types of property.

The Market Comparison Approach

In the **market comparison approach,** an estimate of value is obtained by comparing the subject property (the property under appraisal) with recently sold comparable properties (properties similar to the subject). This approach is most often used by brokers and salespeople when helping a seller to set a price for his or her residential real estate in an active market. Since no two parcels of real estate are exactly alike, each comparable property must be compared to the subject property, and the sales prices must be adjusted for any dissimilar features. The principal factors for which adjustments must be made fall into four basic categories:

1. *Date of sale:* An adjustment must be made if economic changes occur between the date of sale of the comparable property and the date of the appraisal.

2. *Location:* An adjustment may be necessary to compensate for locational differences. For example, similar properties might differ in price from neighborhood to neighborhood, or even in more desirable locations within the same neighborhood.

3. *Physical features:* Physical features that may cause adjustments include age of building, size of lot, landscaping, construction, number of rooms, square feet of living space, interior and exterior condition, presence or absence of a garage, fireplace, or air conditioner, and so forth.

4. *Terms and conditions of sale:* This consideration becomes important if a sale is not financed by a standard mortgage procedure.

After a careful analysis of the differences between comparable properties and the subject property, the appraiser assigns a dollar value to each of these differences. On the basis of their knowledge and experience, appraisers estimate dollar adjustments that reflect actual values assigned in the marketplace. The value of a feature present in the subject property but not in the comparable property is *added* to the total sales price. This presumes that, all other comparables being equal, a property having a feature (such as a fireplace or wet bar) not present in the comparable property would tend to have a higher market value solely because of this feature. (The feature need not be a physical amenity; it may be a locational or aesthetic feature.) Likewise, the value of a feature present in the comparable but not the subject property is *subtracted*. The adjusted sales price represents the probable value range of the subject property. From this range, a single market value estimate can be selected.

The market comparison approach is essential in almost every appraisal of real estate. It is considered the most reliable of the three approaches in appraising residential property, where the amenities (intangible benefits) are so difficult to measure. An example of the market data approach is shown in table 18.1.

The Cost Approach

The **cost approach** to value is based on the principle of substitution, which states that the maximum value of a property tends to be set by the cost of acquiring an equally desirable and valuable substitute property, assuming that no costly delay is encountered in making the substitution. The cost approach is sometimes called appraisal by summation.

The cost approach consists of five steps:

1. Estimate the value of the land as if it were vacant and available to be put to its highest and best use.
2. Estimate the current cost of constructing the building(s) and site improvements.
3. Estimate the amount of accrued depreciation resulting from physical deterioration, functional obsolescence, and/or locational obsolescence.
4. Deduct accrued depreciation from the estimated construction cost of new building(s) and site improvements.
5. Add the estimated land value to the depreciated cost of the building(s) and site improvements to arrive at the total property value.

Land value (step 1) is estimated by using the market comparison approach; that is, the location and improvements of the subject site are compared to those of similar nearby sites, and adjustments are made for significant differences.

There are two ways to look at the construction cost of a building for appraisal purposes (step 2): reproduction cost and replacement cost. **Reproduction cost** is the

Table 18.1
Market Comparison Approach to Value

	Subject Property	Comparables				
		A	**B**	**C**	**D**	**E**
Sale Price		$68,000	$67,500	$69,500	$68,000	$65,000
Location	good	same	poorer +1500	same	same	same
Age	6 years	same	same	same	same	same
Size of Lot	60' × 135'	same	same	larger −1500	same	larger −1500
Landscaping	good	same	same	same	same	same
Construction	brick	same	same	same	same	same
Style	ranch	same	same	same	same	same
No. of Rooms	6	same	same	same	same	same
No. of Bedrooms	3	same	same	same	same	same
No. of Baths	1½	same	same	same	same	same
Sq. Ft. of Living Space	1500	same	same	same	same	same
Other Space (basement)	full basement	same	same	same	same	same
Condition— Exterior	average	better −500	poorer +1000	better −500	same	poorer +500
Condition— Interior	good	same	same	better −500	same	same
Garage	2-car attached	same	same	same	same	none +2500
Other Improvements						
Financing						
Date of Sale	current	current	1 yr. ago +2500	current	current	current
Net Adjustments		−500	+5000	−2500	-0-	+1500
Adjusted Value		$67,500	$72,500	$67,000	$68,000	$66,500

Note: Since the value range of the properties in the comparison chart (excluding comparable B) is close, and comparable D required no adjustment, an appraiser would conclude that the indicated market value of the subject is $68,000.

dollar amount required to construct an *exact duplicate* of the subject building at current prices. **Replacement cost** of the subject property would be the construction cost at current prices of a property that is not necessarily an exact duplicate, but serves the same purpose or function as the original. Replacement cost is most often used in appraising, since it eliminates obsolete features and takes advantage of current construction materials and techniques.

An example of the cost approach to value is shown in table 18.2.

Determining reproduction or replacement cost. An appraiser using the cost approach computes the reproduction or replacement cost of a building using one of the following methods:

1. **Square-foot method:** The cost per square foot of a recently built comparable structure is multiplied by the number of square feet in the subject building; this

**Table 18.2
Cost Approach to
Value**

Land Valuation: Size 60 × 135 @ $450 per front foot = $27,000
Plus site improvements: driveway, walks, landscaping, etc. = 4,000
Total Land Valuation $31,000

Building Valuation: Replacement Cost
1,500 sq. ft. @ $65 per sq. ft. = $97,500

Less Depreciation:
Physical depreciation,
  curable
    (items of deferred maintenance)
    exterior painting $4,000
  incurable (structural deterioration) 5,200
Functional obsolescence 2,000
Locational obsolescence -0-
    Total Depreciation −11,200

Depreciated Value of Building $ 86,300
Indicated Value by Cost Approach $117,300

is the most common method of cost estimation. Table 18.2 is an example of the square-foot method.

2. **Cubic-foot method:** The cost per *cubic* foot of a recently built comparable structure is multiplied by the number of cubic feet in the subject structure.

3. **Unit-in-place method:** The replacement cost of a structure is estimated based on the cost of individual building components, as installed, per individual unit of use, such as square or cubic footage. Such computations include the costs of labor, and also include indirect costs such as overhead, building permits, and the builder's profits.

4. **Quantity-survey method:** An estimate is made of the quantities of raw materials needed to replace the subject structure (lumber, plaster, brick, and so on), as well as of the current price of such materials and their installation costs. For example, reproduction might be stated as: 10,000 concrete slabs at $3.50 per slab, 1,500 doorknobs at $7.00 each, and so forth. These factors are added together to arrive at the total replacement cost of the structure.

Depreciation. In a real estate appraisal, **depreciation** refers to any condition that adversely affects the value of an *improvement* to real property. Land, however, does not depreciate—it retains its value indefinitely, except in such rare cases as misused farmland. For appraisal purposes (as opposed to depreciation for tax purposes, which will be discussed in Chapter 22), depreciation is divided into three classes according to its cause:

1. **Physical deterioration—*curable:*** Repairs that are economically feasible, considering the remaining years of life of the building. A new roof would be a warranted expense on a 40-year-old brick building otherwise in good condition.

    Physical deterioration—incurable: Repairs that would not contribute a comparable value to the building. Near the end of a building's useful life, major repair work, such as replacement of weatherworn siding, may not warrant the financial investment.

2. **Functional obsolescence**—*curable:* Physical or design features that are no longer considered desirable by property buyers, but could be replaced or redesigned at low cost. Outmoded fixtures, such as plumbing, are usually easily replaced. Room function might be redefined at no cost if the basic room layout allows for it. A bedroom adjacent to a kitchen, for instance, may be converted to a family room.

   Functional obsolescence—incurable: Currently undesirable physical or design features that could not be easily remedied. Many older multistory industrial buildings are considered less suitable than one-story buildings. An office building that cannot be air-conditioned suffers from functional obsolescence.

3. **Locational (economic) obsolescence**—*incurable only:* Caused by factors not on the subject property, such as environmental, social, or economic forces, this type of obsolescence cannot usually be considered curable. Proximity to a nuisance, such as a polluting factory or a deteriorating neighborhood, would be an unchangeable factor that could not be cured by the owner of the subject property.

In determining a property's depreciation, most appraisers use the *breakdown method,* in which depreciation is broken down into all three classes, with separate estimates for curable and incurable factors in each class. Depreciation, however, is difficult to measure, and the older the building, the more difficult it is to estimate. Much of functional obsolescence and all of locational obsolescence can be evaluated only by considering the actions of buyers in the marketplace.

In Practice ...   *The cost approach is most helpful in the appraisal of special-purpose buildings such as schools, churches, and post offices. Such properties are difficult to appraise using other methods because there are seldom many local sales to use as comparables, and the properties do not usually generate income.*

The Income Approach   The **income approach** to value is based on the present worth of the future rights to income. It assumes that the income derived from a property will, to a large extent, control the value of that property. The income approach is used for valuation of income-producing properties—apartment buildings, central business districts, shopping centers, and the like. In estimating value using the income approach, an appraiser must go through the following steps:

1. Estimate annual potential *gross income.*

2. Based on market experience, deduct an appropriate allowance for vacancy and rent loss in order to arrive at the *effective gross income.*

3. Based on appropriate operating standards, deduct the annual *operating expenses* of the real estate from the effective gross income in order to arrive at the annual *net income.* Management costs are always included as operating expenses, even if the current owner manages the property him- or herself. Mortgage payments, however (including principal and interest), are *not* considered operating expenses.

4. Estimate the price a typical investor would pay for the income produced by this particular type and class of property. This is done by estimating the rate of return (or yield) that an investor will demand for the investment of his or her capital in this type of building. This rate of return is called the **capitalization**

(or "cap") **rate** and is determined by comparing the relationship of net income to the sales prices of similar properties that have sold in the current market. For example, a comparable property that is producing an annual net income of $15,000 is sold for $100,000. The capitalization rate is $15,000 ÷ $100,000, or 15 percent. If other comparable properties sold at prices that yield substantially the same rate, it may be assumed that 15 percent is the rate that the appraiser should apply to the subject property.

5. Finally, the capitalization rate is applied to the property's annual net income, resulting in the appraiser's estimate of the property's value.

With the appropriate capitalization rate and the projected annual net income, the appraiser can obtain an indication of value by the income approach in the following manner:

$$\text{Net Income} \div \text{Capitalization Rate} = \text{Value}$$

$$\text{Example: } \$15,000 \text{ income} \div 10\% \text{ cap rate} = \$150,000 \text{ value}$$

This formula and its variations are important in dealing with income property.

$$\frac{\text{Income}}{\text{Rate}} = \text{Value} \qquad \frac{\text{Income}}{\text{Value}} = \text{Rate} \qquad \text{Value} \times \text{Rate} = \text{Income}$$

A very simplified version of the computations used in applying the income approach is illustrated in table 18.3.

Table 18.3		
Income Approach to Value	**Gross Annual Income Estimate** (potential rent income) =	$60,000
	Less vacancy and loss of rent (estimated) @ 5% =	−3,000
	Effective Gross Income	$57,000
	Expenses:	
	Real estate taxes $9,000	
	Insurance 1,000	
	Heat 2,800	
	Janitor 5,200	
	Utilities, electricity, water, gas 800	
	Repairs 1,200	
	Decorating 1,400	
	Replacements of equipment 800	
	Maintenance 1,200	
	Legal and accounting 600	
	Management 3,000	
	Total Expenses	$27,000
	Annual Net Income	$30,000
	Capitalization Rate = 10%	
	Capitalization of annual net income: $\dfrac{\$30,000}{.10}$	
	Indicated Value by Income Approach = $300,000	

In Practice ...   *The most difficult step in the income approach to value is determining the appropriate capitalization rate for the property. This rate must be selected to accurately reflect the recapture of the original investment over the building's economic life, give the owner an acceptable rate of return on his or her investment, and provide for the repayment of borrowed capital. Note that an income property that carries with it a great deal of risk as an investment generally requires a higher rate of return than would a property considered a safe investment.*

Gross rent or income multipliers. Certain properties, such as single-family homes or two-flat buildings, are not purchased primarily for income. As a substitute for the income approach, the **gross rent multiplier** (GRM) method is often used in appraising such properties. The GRM relates the sales price of a property to its rental income. (Gross *monthly* income is used for residential property; gross *annual* income is used for commercial and industrial property.) The formula is as follows:

$$\frac{\text{Sale Price}}{\text{Rental Income}} = \text{Gross Rent Multiplier}$$

For example, if a home recently sold for $82,000 and its monthly rental income was $650, the GRM for the property would be computed thus:

$$\frac{\$82,000}{\$650} = 126.2 \text{ GRM}$$

To establish an accurate GRM, an appraiser must have recent sales and rental data from at least four properties that are similar to the subject property. The resulting GRM can then be applied to the estimated fair market rental of the subject property in order to arrive at its market value. The formula would then be:

$$\text{Rental Income} \times \text{GRM} = \text{Estimated Market Value}$$

Table 18.4 shows some examples of GRM comparisons.

Table 18.4	Comparable No.	Sale Price	Monthly Rent	GRM
Gross Rent Multiplier	1	$70,000	$500	140.0
	2	68,500	490	139.8
	3	70,500	505	139.6
	4	67,900	485	140.0
	Subject	?	495	?

Note: Based on an analysis of these comparisons, a GRM of 140 seems reasonable for homes in this area. In the opinion of an appraiser, then, the estimated value of the subject property would be $495 × 140, or $69,300.

Generally, gross *annual* income is used in appraising industrial and commercial properties. The ratio used to convert annual income into market value is called a gross income multiplier (GIM). The formula to determine a GIM would be as follows:

$$\frac{\text{Sale Price}}{\text{Annual Gross Income}} = \text{Gross Income Multiplier}$$

In Practice . . . *Much skill is required to use multipliers accurately, because there is no fixed multiplier for all areas or all types of properties. Therefore, many appraisers view the technique simply as a quick, informal way to check the validity of a property value obtained by the three accepted appraisal methods: market comparison, cost, and income. In fact, GRMs and GIMs have been used less in recent years because this technique fails to take into consideration the tax situations of different possible investors, and it does not recognize alternative methods of financing.*

Reconciliation

If the three approaches to value are applied to the same property, they will normally produce three separate indications of value. **Reconciliation** is the art of analyzing and effectively weighing the findings from the three approaches.

Although each approach may serve as an independent guide to value, whenever possible all three approaches should be used as a check on the final estimate of value. The process of reconciliation is more complicated than simply taking the average of the three value estimates. An average implies that the data and logic applied in each of the approaches are equally valid and reliable, and should therefore be given equal weight. In fact, however, certain approaches are more valid and reliable with some kinds of properties than with others.

For example, in appraising a home the income approach is rarely used, and the cost approach is of limited value unless the home is relatively new; therefore, the market data approach is usually given greatest weight in valuing single-family residences. In the appraisal of income or investment property, the income approach would normally be given the greatest weight. In the appraisal of churches, libraries, museums, schools, and other special-use properties where there is little or no income or sales revenue, the cost approach would usually be assigned the greatest weight. From this analysis, or reconciliation, a single estimate of market value is produced.

The Appraisal Process

The key to an accurate appraisal lies in the methodical collection of data. The appraisal process is an orderly set of procedures used to collect and analyze data in order to arrive at an ultimate value conclusion. The data are divided into two basic classes:

1. *Specific data,* covering details of the subject property as well as comparative data relating to costs, sales, and income and expenses of properties similar to and competitive with the subject property.

2. *General data,* covering the nation, region, city, and neighborhood. Of particular importance is the neighborhood, where an appraiser finds the physical, economic, social, and political influences that directly affect the value and potential of the subject property.

Figure 18.2 outlines the steps an appraiser takes in carrying out an appraisal assignment. The numbers in the following list correspond to the numbers on the flowchart.

1. *State the problem:* The kind of value to be estimated must be specified, and the valuation approach(es) most valid and reliable for the kind of property under appraisal must be selected.

2. *List the data needed and their sources:* Based on the approach(es) the appraiser will be using, the types of data needed and the sources to be consulted are listed.

3. *Gather, record, and verify the general data:* Detailed information concerning the economic, political, and social conditions of the region and/or city and comments on the effects of these data on the subject property must be obtained.

4. *Gather, record, and verify the specific data on the subject property:* Specific data include information about the subject site and improvements.

5. *Gather, record, and verify the data for the valuation approach used:* Depending upon the approach(es) used, comparative information relating to sales, income and expenses, and construction costs of comparable properties must be collected. As with steps 3 and 4, all data should be verified, usually by checking the same information against two different sources. In the case of sales data, one source should be a person directly involved in the transaction.

6. *Analyze and interpret the data:* All information collected must be reviewed to ensure that all relevant facts have been considered and handled properly and that no errors have been made in calculations.

7. *Reconcile data for final value estimate:* The appraiser finally makes a definite statement of conclusions reached. This is usually in the form of a value estimate of the property.

8. *Prepare appraisal report:* After the three approaches have been reconciled and an opinion of value reached, the appraiser prepares a formal written report for his or her client. The statement may be a completed *form,* a *letter,* a short *summary,* or a lengthy written *narrative.* It should contain the following information:
   a. the estimate of value and the date to which it applies.
   b. the purpose for which the appraisal was made.
   c. a description of the neighborhood and the subject property.
   d. factual data covering costs, sales, and income and expenses of similar, recently sold properties.
   e. an analysis and interpretation of the data collected.
   f. a presentation of one or more of the three approaches to value in enough detail to support the appraiser's final value conclusion.
   g. any qualifying conditions.
   h. supportive material, such as charts, maps, photographs, floor plans, leases, and contracts.
   i. the certification and signature of the appraiser.

Figure 18.2
The Appraisal
Process

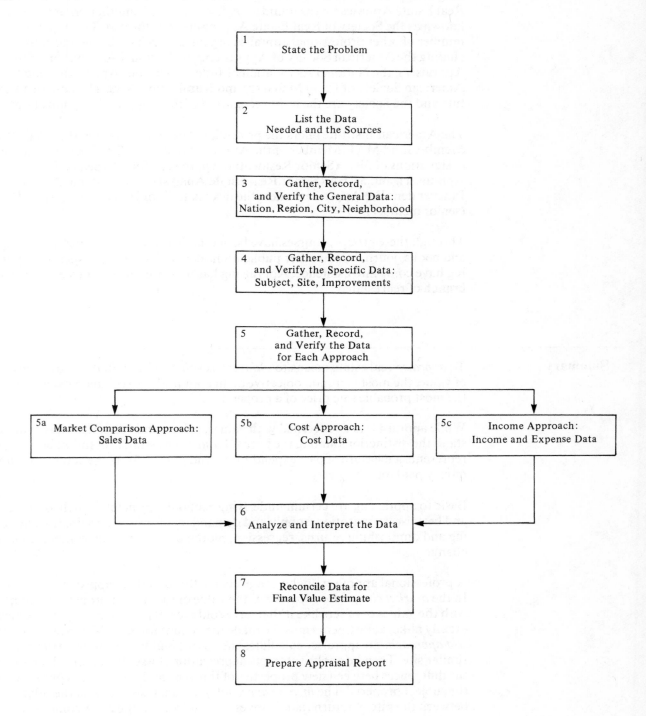

The Profession of Appraising

While appraising has existed since the origin of the concept of property, the huge number of foreclosures during the depression of the 1930s resulted in the beginning of appraising as an organized profession. In 1932 the American Institute of Real Estate Appraisers was founded. A few years later another organization, now known as the Society of Real Estate Appraisers, was formed. Through the years a number of other professional appraisal organizations have come into existence, including the American Society of Appraisers, the National Association of Review Appraisers, the National Association of Independent Fee Appraisers, and the American Society of Farm Managers and Rural Appraisers. The American Institute and the Society are the most recognized of these appraisal organizations.

The American Institute offers the professional designations of RM (Residential Member) and MAI (Member of the Appraisal Institute). The Society offers the designations of SRA (Senior Residential Appraiser), SRPA (Senior Real Property Appraiser), and SREA (Senior Real Estate Analyst). The National Association of Independent Fee Appraisers offers the designations of IFA (member) and IFAS (senior member).

Through these groups, courses have been established in universities and colleges, and books, journals, and other publications devoted to various aspects of appraising have come into existence. Appraising has now become the most specialized branch of real estate.

Summary

To *appraise* real estate means to *estimate its value.* Although there are many types of value, the most common objective of an appraisal is to estimate *market value* — the most probable sale price of a property.

While appraisals are concerned with values, prices, and costs, it is vital to understand the distinctions among the terms. *Value* is an estimate of future benefits, *cost* represents a measure of past expenditures, and *price* reflects the actual amount of money paid for a property.

Basic to appraising are certain underlying economic principles, such as highest and best use, substitution, supply and demand, conformity, anticipation, increasing and diminishing returns, regression, plottage, contribution, competition, and change.

A professional appraiser analyzes a property through three approaches to value. In the *market comparison approach,* the value of the subject property is compared with the values of others like it that have sold recently. Since no two properties are exactly alike, adjustments must be made to account for any differences. With the *cost approach,* an appraiser calculates the cost of building a similar structure on a similar site. Then he or she subtracts depreciation (losses in value), which reflects the differences between new properties of this type and the present condition of the subject property. The *income approach* is an analysis based on the relationship between the rate of return that an investor requires and the net income that a property produces.

A special, informal version of the income approach, called the *gross rent multiplier* (GRM), is often used to estimate the value of single-family residential properties that are not usually rented but could be. The GRM is computed by dividing the sales price of a property by its gross monthly rent.

Normally, the application of the three approaches will result in three different estimates of value. In the process of *reconciliation,* the validity and reliability of each approach are weighed objectively to arrive at the single best and most supportable conclusion of value.

Questions

1. Which of the following approaches to value makes use of comparables?

   a. market comparison   c. income
   b. cost   d. all of the above

2. The elements of value include which of the following?

   I. utility
   II. scarcity

      a. I only   c. both I and II
      b. II only   d. neither I nor II

3. The principle of value that states that two adjacent parcels of land combined into one larger parcel would have a greater value than the two parcels valued separately is called:

   a. substitution.
   b. plottage.
   c. highest and best use.
   d. contribution.

4. The amount of money a property commands in the marketplace is its:

   I. market price.
   II. market value.

      a. I only   c. both I and II
      b. II only   d. neither I nor II

5. Joe Hamel has his "dream house" constructed for $100,000 in an area where most newly constructed homes are not as well-equipped as his and typically sell for only $80,000. The value of Hamel's house is likely to be affected by the principle of:

   a. progression.   c. change.
   b. assemblage.   d. regression.

6. In question 5, the owners of the lesser-valued homes in Hamel's immediate area are likely to be affected by the principle of:

   a. progression.   c. competition.
   b. increasing returns.   d. regression.

7. Depreciation, as used in real estate appraisals, can be caused by which of the following?

   a. functional obsolescence
   b. physical deterioration
   c. locational obsolescence
   d. all of the above

8. *Reconciliation* refers to which of the following?

   a. loss of value due to any cause
   b. separating the value of the land from the total value of the property in order to compute depreciation
   c. analyzing the results obtained by the three approaches to value to determine a final estimate of value
   d. the process by which an appraiser determines the highest and best use for a parcel of land

9. One method an appraiser uses to determine a building's replacement cost involves an estimate of the raw materials needed to build the structure, plus the cost of such materials, labor, and other expenses. This is called the:

   a. square-foot method.
   b. quantity-survey method.
   c. cubic-foot method.
   d. unit-in-place method.

10. If a property's annual net income is $37,500 and it is valued at $300,000, what is its capitalization rate?

    a. 12.5 percent   c. 15 percent
    b. 10.5 percent   d. 18 percent

11. Certain data must be determined by an appraiser before value can be computed by the income approach. Which one of the following is *not* required for this process?

    a. annual net income
    b. proper capitalization rate
    c. accrued depreciation
    d. annual gross income

12. The ceiling, or top limit, of value of an improved parcel of real estate usually is:

    a. the sales price paid for a similar property.
    b. the cost of buying a lot and erecting a similar building on it.
    c. the capitalized value of present net rents.
    d. the depreciated value of the building plus the cost of land.

13. The income approach would be given the most weight in the valuation of:

    I. homes.
    II. noninvestment-type property.
        a. I only   c. both I and II
        b. II only   d. neither I nor II

14. The value of a parcel of real estate is:

    I. an estimate of its future benefits.
    II. the amount of money paid for the property.
        a. I only   c. both I and II
        b. II only   d. neither I nor II

15. Capitalization is the process by which the estimated future annual net income is used as the basis to:

    a. determine cost.
    b. estimate value.
    c. establish depreciation.
    d. determine potential tax value.

16. From the reproduction or replacement cost of the building, an appraiser deducts depreciation, which represents:

    a. the remaining economic life of the building.
    b. remodeling costs to increase rentals.
    c. loss of value due to any cause.
    d. costs to modernize the building.

17. In the market comparison approach to value, the probable sales price of a building may be estimated by:

    I. capitalizing net income.
    II. considering sales of similar properties.
        a. I only   c. both I and II
        b. II only   d. neither I nor II

18. Which of the following factors would *not* be important in comparing properties under the market comparison approach to value?

    a. difference in dates of sale
    b. difference in real estate taxes
    c. difference in appearance and condition
    d. difference in original cost

19. In the income approach to value:

    I. the reproduction or replacement cost of the building must be computed.
    II. the capitalization rate must be estimated.
        a. I only   c. both I and II
        b. II only   d. neither I nor II

20. In the cost approach to value, it is necessary to:

    a. determine a dollar value for depreciation.
    b. estimate future expenses and operating costs.
    c. check sales prices of recently sold homes in the area.
    d. a and b

21. Which of the following formulas would be used to determine the capitalization rate of an office building?

    a. Income = Rate $\times$ Value
    b. $\dfrac{\text{Income}}{\text{Rate}} = \text{Value}$
    c. $\dfrac{\text{Income}}{\text{Value}} = \text{Rate}$
    d. a and b

22. The appraised value of a residence with five bedrooms and one bathroom would probably be reduced because of:

    a. economic obsolescence.
    b. functional obsolescence.
    c. physical deterioration—curable.
    d. physical deterioration—incurable.

19

Control of Land Use

Key Terms
Buffer zone
Building code
Building permit
Conditional-use permit
Covenant
Deed restriction
Direct public ownership
Enabling acts
Laches
Master plan
Nonconforming use
Spot zoning
Subdivision regulations
Variance
Zoning board of appeal
Zoning ordinances

Overview
The various ownership rights a person possesses in a parcel of real estate are subject to certain public and private land-use controls, such as zoning ordinances, building codes, and deed restrictions. The purpose of these controls is to ensure that our limited supply of land is being put to its highest and best use, for the benefit of the general public as well as private owners. This chapter will discuss the three types of land-use controls and how they help shape and preserve the physical surface of our nation.

Land-Use Controls	The control and regulation of land use is accomplished in both the public and private sectors through: (1) public land-use controls, (2) private land-use controls through deed restrictions, and (3) public ownership of land—including parks, schools, and expressways—by the federal and local governments.

Public Controls

Under the *police powers,* granted by the Fourteenth Amendment to the U.S. Constitution, each state, and in turn its municipalities, has the inherent authority to adopt regulations necessary to protect the public health, safety, and general welfare. This includes limitations, or controls, on the use of privately owned real estate. Although the courts have traditionally been conservative in extending the scope of police power, changing social and economic conditions, along with greater concern for the general welfare of the people, have influenced the courts toward making broader interpretations of this power in recent years—and the trend is likely to continue.

Our growing urban populations, the many new types of industry, and the increasing complexity of our civilization make it necessary for cities, towns, and villages to increase their controls over the private use of real estate. Police power in many areas has been increased to include controls over noise, air, and water pollution, as well as population density. New problems that must be dealt with arise every day.

The police powers of governmental authority that regulate privately owned real estate have been extended to include the following:

1. city planning
2. zoning
3. subdivision regulations
4. codes that regulate building construction, safety, and public health
5. environmental protection legislation

City Planning

Some concerned individuals were dissatisfied with the manner in which metropolitan areas were haphazardly developing in the late nineteenth and early twentieth centuries. During this period, unofficial citizens' groups in cities like New York, Boston, and Chicago adopted city plans. One of the first such plans was the McMillan Improvement Plan for Washington, D.C. Adopted in 1901, it set forth the overall strategy for the development of the famous park system of our nation's capital.

A few years later the Burnham Plan for the city of Chicago was published. The Burnham Plan was probably the most influential force in urban planning throughout the country. The subject matter of this plan encompassed rapid transit and suburban growth, a comprehensive park system, forest preserves, transportation and terminals, streets and subdivision control, and problems of the central city.

Today, the country is witnessing a much broader approach to urban planning and development than that submitted under early city plans. The decentralization of the American city in the post–World War II years, coupled with the increasing popularity of the suburban shopping center, has created many satellite communities, often referred to as *bedroom communities,* or *dormitory suburbs.* These references were based on the fact that most of the populace of such communities originally worked in the central city but slept in the suburbs. Today, whole communities, known as *New Towns,* are being created and developed in accordance with well-developed, overall city plans.

It is predicted that by the end of this century, some large urban areas will consolidate into a larger configuration, known as a *megalopolis.* These large, continuous metropolitan areas may exist in many places around the country where major cities are being interconnected with other communities developed under well-defined city plans. The urban growth along the eastern seaboard from New York to Boston is an example of this.

Implementing urban planning. City planning includes devising a **master plan,** giving advice on planning and scheduling public works programs (especially those concerning traffic facilities and public buildings), controlling subdivision developments, and preparing, modifying, and administering zoning ordinances and regulations. In most cases a city, county, or regional *planning commission* is created for these purposes. A combination of residential, commercial, and industrial property is usually included in master plans. This is done in order to spread the tax load and provide employment for local residents.

City planning and zoning serve as means to meet the social and economic needs of our ever-changing communities. Economic and physical surveys are both essential in preparing a master plan. Such plans must also include the coordination of numerous civic plans and developments to ensure orderly city growth with stabilized property values.

Zoning

Zoning ordinances are laws of local government authorities (such as cities and counties) that regulate and control the use of land and structures within designated districts or zones. Zoning regulates and affects such things as use of the land, lot sizes, types of structures permitted, building heights, setbacks (the minimum distance away from streets or sidewalks that structures may be built), and density (the ratio of land area to structure area or population). Often, the purpose of zoning is to implement a local master plan.

Zoning powers are conferred on municipal governments by state **enabling acts.** There are no nationwide zoning ordinances; with the exception of Hawaii, no states have statewide zoning ordinances. (State and federal governments may, however, regulate land use through special legislation, such as scenic easement and coastal management laws).

Zoning ordinances generally divide land use into three use classifications: (1) residential, (2) commercial, and (3) industrial. A fourth use now included by many communities is *cluster zoning,* or *multiple-use zoning,* which permits planned unit developments.

To ensure adequate control, land-use areas are further divided into subclasses. For example, residential areas may be subdivided to provide for detached single-family dwellings, semidetached structures containing not more than four dwelling units, walk-up apartments, high-rise apartments, and so forth. In addition, some communities require the use of **buffer zones**—such as landscaped parks and playgrounds —to separate and screen residential areas from nonresidential areas. Some special types of zoning are listed in table 19.1.

Table 19.1 Special Types of Zoning	Type of Zoning	Primary Purpose
	Bulk Zoning	To control density and avoid overcrowding through restrictions on setback, building height, and percentage of open areas
	Aesthetic Zoning	To require that new buildings conform to specific types of architecture
	Incentive Zoning	To require that street floors of office buildings be used for retail establishments
	Directive Zoning	To use zoning as a planning tool to encourage use of land for its highest and best use

Adoption of zoning ordinances. Today, approximately 98 percent of all cities with populations in excess of 10,000 have enacted comprehensive zoning ordinances governing the utilization of land located *within corporate limits*. Many states have enacted legislation that provides that the use of land located *within one to three miles* of an incorporated area must receive the approval and consent of the incorporated area, even if the property is not contiguous to the village, town, or city.

Zoning ordinances must not violate the rights of individuals and property holders (as provided under the due process provisions of the Fourteenth Amendment of the U.S. Constitution) or the various provisions of the state constitution of the state in which the real estate is located. If the means used to regulate the use of property are destructive, unreasonable, arbitrary, or confiscatory, the legislation is usually considered void. *Tests* usually applied in determining the validity of ordinances require that:

1. The power must be exercised in a reasonable manner.
2. The provisions must be clear and specific.
3. The ordinance must be free from discrimination.
4. The ordinance must promote public health, safety, and general welfare under the police power concept.
5. The ordinance must apply to all property in a similar manner.

When *down zoning* occurs in an area—for instance, when land zoned for residential construction is rezoned for conservation or recreational purposes only—the state is not usually responsible for compensating property owners for any resulting loss of value. However, if the courts find that a "taking" has occurred, then the down zoning will be held to be an unconstitutional attempt to use the power of eminent domain without providing fair compensation to the property owner.

Zoning laws are generally enforced through local requirements that building permits must be obtained before property owners can build on their land. A permit will not be issued unless a proposed structure conforms to the permitted zoning, among other requirements.

Nonconforming use. In the enforcement of a zoning ordinance, a frequent problem is the situation in which a building does not conform to the zoning use because it was erected prior to the enactment of the zoning law. Such a building is not a violation, because when it was built there was no zoning ordinance; it is referred to as a **nonconforming use.** Nonconforming uses are dealt with in various ways by local zoning authorities. For example, the uses may be allowed to continue until: (1) the improvements are destroyed or torn down; (2) the current use is discontinued; or (3) the ownership of the property is transferred. If the building is destroyed or torn down, then any new structure must comply with the terms of the zoning ordinance.

Zoning boards of appeal. Frequently, the comprehensive plan that establishes zoning ordinances can have the detrimental effect of *overzoning.* **Zoning appeal boards** have been established in most communities for the specific purpose of hearing complaints about the effects of zoning ordinances on specific parcels of property. Petitions may be presented to the appeal board for variances or exceptions in the zoning law. The board of appeals has great power, and it is important to the community that the members of the board be free of personal or political influence.

Zoning variations. Each time a plan is created or a zoning ordinance enacted, some owners are inconvenienced and want to change the use of a property. Generally, such owners may appeal for either a conditional-use permit or a variance to allow a use that does not meet zoning requirements.

A **conditional-use permit** is generally granted a property owner to allow a special use of property that is in the public interest. For example, a restaurant may be built in an industrially zoned area if it is deemed necessary to provide meal services for area workers.

A **variance** may be sought by a property owner who has suffered hardship as a result of a zoning ordinance. For example, if an owner's lot is level next to a road, but slopes steeply 30 feet away from the road, the zoning board may be willing to allow a variance so the owner can build closer to the road than would normally be allowed. However, the board might refuse to allow a change if there were another possible building site on the same parcel and the only hardship that would result from using the alternate site was a longer driveway that would cost more money.

In addition, a property owner can change the zoning classification of a parcel of real estate by obtaining an *amendment* to the official *zoning map*, which is a part of the original zoning ordinance for the area. The proposed amendment must be brought before a public hearing on the matter and approved by the governing body of the community.

If proposed zoning variations result in small areas that differ significantly from adjoining parcels in a way that is not in harmony with the general plan for the area, such variations might by considered to be **spot zoning.** An example would be a variance that allows a store in a residential area. In such cases, and when spot zoning appears to be arbitrary and unreasonable, spot zoning is usually not permitted by the courts.

In Practice . . .   *Purchasers of property must be aware of zoning requirements—zoning regulations do not render the title unmarketable if they differ from what the purchaser thought they were. Licensees, too, should determine whether or not a buyer's proposed use for the property conforms to existing zoning ordinances. However, existing violations of zoning regulations do render the title unmarketable. If either the seller or a licensee misrepresents the actual permitted zoning use, the buyer may be able to rescind the transaction on the basis of the misrepresentation.*

Subdivision Regulations

Most communities have adopted **subdivision regulations,** often as part of a master plan. These will be covered in detail in Chapter 20. Subdivision regulations usually provide for the following:

1. location, grading, alignment, surfacing, and widths of streets, highways, and other rights of way.
2. installation of sewers and water mains.
3. minimum dimensions of lots and length of blocks.
4. building and setback lines.
5. areas to be reserved or dedicated for public use, such as parks or schools.
6. easements for public utilities.

Subdivision regulations, like all other forms of zoning or building regulations, cannot be static. They must remain flexible to meet the ever-changing needs of society.

Building Codes

Most cities and towns have enacted ordinances to *specify construction standards* that must be met when repairing or erecting buildings. These are called **building codes,** and they set the requirements for kinds of materials, sanitary equipment, electrical wiring, fire prevention standards, and the like.

Most communities require the issuance of a **building permit** by the city clerk or other official before a person can build a structure or alter or repair an existing building on property within the corporate limits of the municipality. Through the permit requirement, city officials are made aware of new construction or alterations and can verify compliance with building codes and zoning ordinances by examining the plans and inspecting the work. Once the completed structure has been inspected and found satisfactory, the city inspector issues a *certificate of occupancy.*

If the construction of a building or an alteration violates a deed restriction (discussed later in this chapter), the issuance of a building permit will *not* cure this violation. A building permit is merely evidence of the applicant's compliance with municipal regulations. Rights of adjoining owners in a subdivision to enforce subdivision restrictions usually prevail over the police power legislation of the community when there is a conflict if the restrictions are more limiting.

The subject of city planning, zoning, and restriction of the use of real estate is extremely technical, and the interpretation of the law is not altogether clear. Questions concerning any of these subjects in relation to real estate transactions should be referred to legal counsel.

Environmental Protection Legislation

Federal and state legislators have passed a number of environmental protection laws in an attempt to respond to the growing public concern over the improvement and preservation of America's natural resources. Table 19.2 contains a brief summary of significant federal environmental legislation.

The various states have responded to the environmental issue by passing a variety of localized environmental protection laws regarding all manners of pollution—air, water, noise, and solid waste disposal. For example, many states have enacted laws that prevent builders or private individuals from constructing septic tanks or other effluence-disposal systems in certain areas, particularly where public bodies of water—streams, lakes, and rivers—are concerned.

In addition to the states and the federal government, cities and counties also frequently pass environmental legislation of their own.

Private Land-Use Controls

A real estate owner can create a **deed restriction** by including a provision for it in the deed when the property is conveyed.

There is a distinction between restrictions on the owner's right to *sell* and restrictions on his or her right to *use*. In general, provisions in a deed conveying a fee simple estate with restrictions that the grantee will not sell, mortgage, or convey it are usually considered void. Such restrictions attempt to limit the basic principle of the *free alienation (transfer) of property;* the courts usually consider them against public policy and therefore unenforceable. There are exceptions to this, of course, but they are very technical.

Table 19.2	Legislation	Major purpose
Federal Environmental Legislation	National Environmental Policy Act—1970	To establish a Council for Environmental Quality for land-use planning; in addition, created the Environmental Protection Agency (EPA) to enforce federal environmental legislation
	Clean Air Amendment—1970	To create more stringent standards for automotive, aircraft, and factory emission
	Water Quality Improvement Act—1970	To strengthen water pollution standards
	Resource Recovery Act—1970	To expand the solid waste disposal program
	Water Pollution Control Act Amendment—1972	To create standards for cleaning navigable streams and lakes by the mid-'80s
	Clean Water Act—1974	To establish standards for water suppliers
	Resource Conservation & Recovery Act—1976	To regulate potentially dangerous solid waste disposal
	Clean Water Act Amendment—1977	To update the list of potentially dangerous water pollutants under the 1974 act

A subdivider may establish restrictions on the right to *use* land through a **covenant** in a deed or by a separate recorded declaration. These use restrictions are usually considered valid if they are reasonable restraints and are for the benefit of all property owners in the subdivision. If, however, such restrictions are too broad in their terms, they prevent the free transfer of property. If they are "repugnant" to the estate granted, such restrictions will probably not be enforceable. If any restrictive covenant or condition is considered void by a court, it will not affect the validity of the deed or divest the grantee of his or her estate. The estate will then stand freed from the invalid covenant or condition.

Plats of new subdivisions will frequently set forth on the face of the plat, or on a declaration attached thereto, restrictive covenants concerning the use of the land. When a lot in that subdivision is conveyed by an owner's deed, the deed refers to the plat or declaration of restrictions and incorporates these restrictions as limitations on the title conveyed by the deed. In this manner, the restrictive covenants are included in the deed by reference and become binding on all grantees. Such covenants or restrictions usually relate to: (1) type of building; (2) use to which the land may be put; (3) type of construction, height, setbacks, and square footage; and (4) cost.

Most restrictions have a *time limitation,* for example, "effective for a period of 25 years from this date." After that time, the restrictions become inoperative unless they are extended by majority agreement of the people who own the property at that time. Frequently it is also provided that the effective term of the restrictions may be extended with the consent of a majority (or sometimes two-thirds) of the owners in a subdivision.

In most states, *deed restrictions take precedence over zoning ordinances.* Deed restrictions may be more restrictive of an owner's use, so if there is a conflict between a zoning ordinance and the restrictions in a deed or plat of subdivision, the latter will prevail.

Enforcement of deed restrictions. Subdividers usually place restrictions on the use of all lots in a subdivision as a *general plan* for the benefit of all lot owners. Such restrictions give each lot owner the right to apply to the court for an *injunction* to prevent a neighboring lot owner from violating the recorded restrictions. If granted, the court injunction will direct the violator to stop or remove the violation upon penalty of being in contempt of court. The court retains the power to punish the violator for failure to obey the court order. If adjoining lot owners stand idly by while a violation is being committed, they can *lose the right* to the court's injunction by their inaction; the court might claim their right was lost through **laches,** that is, loss of a right through undue delay or failure to assert it.

Conditions in a deed are different from restrictions or covenants. A grantor's deed of conveyance of land can be subject to certain stated conditions whereby the buyer's title may *revert* (go back) to the seller. (This was discussed in Chapter 7 as a determinable fee estate.) For example, Bill Potter conveys a lot to Jane Knish by a deed that includes a condition forbidding the sale, manufacture, or giving away of intoxicating liquor on the lot and provides that in case of violation the title (ownership) reverts to Potter. If Knish operates a tavern on the lot, Potter can file suit and obtain title to the property. Such a condition in the title is enforced by a *reverter,* or *reversion* clause.

Direct Public Ownership

Over the years, the government's general policy has been to encourage private ownership of land. It is necessary, however, for a certain amount of land to be owned by the government for such uses as municipal buildings, state legislative houses, schools, and military stations. Such **direct public ownership** is a means of land control.

There are other examples of necessary public ownership. Urban renewal efforts, especially government-owned housing, are one way that public ownership serves the public interest. Publicly owned streets and highways serve a necessary function for the entire population. In addition, public land is often used for such recreational purposes as parks. National and state parks and forest preserves create areas for public use and recreation, and at the same time help to conserve our natural resources.

At present, the federal government owns approximately 775 million acres of land, nearly one-third of the total area of the United States. At times the federal government has held title to as much as 80 percent of the nation's total land area.

Summary

The control of land use is exercised in two ways: through public controls and private (or nongovernment) controls.

Public controls are ordinances based upon the states' *police power* to protect the public health, safety, and welfare. Through power conferred by state enabling acts, cities and municipalities enact city plans and zoning ordinances.

Any effective control of land requires an overall *city plan* to be developed based upon a local economic survey of the community. *Zoning ordinances* segregate residential areas from business and industrial zones and control not only land use, but height and bulk of buildings and density of populations. Zoning enforcement problems involve boards of appeal, conditional-use permits, variances, and exceptions, as well as nonconforming uses. *Subdivision regulations* are required to maintain control of the development of expanding community areas so that growth will be harmonious with community standards.

Building codes are different from zoning ordinances. Zoning ordinances control use; building codes control construction of buildings by specifying standards for construction, plumbing, sewers, electrical wiring, and equipment.

In addition to land-use control on the local level, the state and federal governments have occasionally intervened when necessary to preserve natural resources through *environmental legislation*.

Private controls are exercised by owners, generally subdividers, who control use of subdivision lots by carefully planned *deed restrictions* that are made to apply to all lot owners. The usual recorded restrictions may be enforced by adjoining lot owners obtaining a court *injunction* to stop a violator. Reverter-type restrictions are called *conditions,* and the grantors or their heirs exercise the *right of reverter* (when such right was reserved as a part of the original conveyance) to enforce the conditions.

Public ownership is a means of land-use control that provides land for such public benefits as parks, highways, schools, and municipal buildings.

Questions

1. A clause put in a deed as a means of forcing the grantee to live up to the condition under which he or she holds title to the land is a:
   a. restriction.
   b. reverter.
   c. laches.
   d. conditional-use clause.

2. For a zoning ordinance to be valid, the courts have decided that the ordinance must:
   I. not violate the due process provisions of the Fourteenth Amendment of the U.S. Constitution.
   II. be free from discrimination.
   III. not result in a loss of property values.

   a. I and II   c. I and III
   b. II and III   d. I, II, and III

3. If a land owner wants to use his or her property in a manner that is prohibited by a local zoning ordinance but would be of benefit to the community, the property owner can request permission to use the property in this way by asking for which of the following?
   a. variance
   b. down zoning
   c. conditional-use permit
   d. spot zoning

4. A new building is erected that does not conform to local zoning ordinances and the builder did not seek prior permission to construct the building in this manner. This building is an example of a:
   I. nonconforming use.
   II. variance.

   a. I only   c. both I and II
   b. II only   d. neither I nor II

5. Public land-use controls include all but which of the following?
   a. subdivision regulations
   b. deed restrictions
   c. environmental protection laws
   d. city plan specifications

6. Generally, a strict deed restriction takes legal priority over which of the following?
   I. zoning ordinance
   II. environmental protection law

   a. I only   c. both I and II
   b. II only   d. neither I nor II

7. To determine whether or not a location can be used for a retail store, one would examine:
   I. the city building code.
   II. the city's list of permitted nonconforming uses.

   a. I only   c. both I and II
   b. II only   d. neither I nor II

8. The purpose of a building permit is:
   a. to override a deed restriction.
   b. to maintain municipal control over the volume of building.
   c. to provide evidence of compliance with municipal regulations.
   d. all of the above

9. Which of the following would probably be included in a list of deed restrictions?
   I. types of buildings that may be constructed on the property
   II. minimum requirements for setbacks and square footage

   a. I only   c. both I and II
   b. II only   d. neither I nor II

10. The aim of a city planning commission includes:
    I. the coordination of civic developments.
    II. the stabilization of property values by orderly city growth.

    a. I only   c. both I and II
    b. II only   d. neither I nor II

11. The grantor of a deed may place restrictions on the:
    I. right to sell the land.
    II. use of the land.

    a. I only   c. both I and II
    b. II only   d. neither I nor II

12. Zoning powers are conferred on municipal governments:

    I. by state enabling acts.
    II. through police power.

        a. I only   c. both I and II
        b. II only   d. neither I nor II

13. A restriction in a seller's deed may be enforced by which of the following?

    I. court injunction
    II. zoning board of appeals

        a. I only   c. both I and II
        b. II only   d. neither I nor II

14. Zoning ordinances control the use of privately owned land by establishing land-use districts. Which one of the following is *not* a usual zoning district?

        a. residential   c. industrial
        b. commercial   d. rental

15. Zoning laws are generally enforced by:

    a. zoning boards of appeal.
    b. ordinances stipulating that building permits will not be issued unless the proposed structure conforms to the zoning ordinance.
    c. deed restrictions.
    d. a and b

16. Zoning boards of appeal are established to hear complaints about:

    a. restrictive covenants.
    b. the effects of a zoning ordinance.
    c. building codes.
    d. a and c

20

Subdividing and Property Development

Key Terms

Clustering
Curvilinear system
Dedication
Density zoning
Developer
Gridiron pattern
Interstate Land Sales Full Disclosure Act
Loop streets
Minimum standards
Plat of subdivision
Property report
Radburn plan
Subdivider
Subdivision

Overview

As our country's population grows and shifts to new locations, the demand for housing grows and shifts. To meet new demand, subdividers and property developers convert raw land or property that is no longer serving its highest and best use into subdivisions for residential and other uses. These subdividers and developers, working with local officials, are largely responsible for the orderly growth of such communities. This chapter will deal with the process of developing and subdividing property and will also discuss some of the legal aspects of selling subdivided land.

Developing and Subdividing Land

Subdividing and developing land for community use are important activities that can assist the orderly growth of cities and towns. Poorly designed and located subdivisions may result in developments that are detrimental to the growth of a town or community. "Wildcat" subdividing and development practices were common during the 1920s and early 1930s. In those years, city, town, village, and county officials were not knowledgeable about good city planning methods. This resulted in the approval of scattered subdivisions without provision of proper safeguards for water, septic fields, sewage disposal, and other health and safety factors. Today subdividers, with the help of real estate specialists, are applying the economic rules of land value by determining the highest and best use of acreage before the land is actually subdivided.

Subdividers and Developers

Land in large tracts must receive special attention before it can be converted into sites for homes, stores, or other uses. As our cities and towns grow in size, additional land will be required for their expansion. In order for such new areas to develop soundly, the services of competent subdividers and land developers working closely with city planners are required. A **subdivider** is someone who buys undeveloped acreage, divides it into smaller, usable lots, and sells the lots to potential users. A land **developer,** on the other hand, builds homes or other buildings on the lots and sells them. Developing is generally a much more extensive activity than is subdividing. A developer may use his or her own sales organization or may act through local real estate brokerage firms. City planners, working with land developers, plan whole communities that are later incorporated into cities, towns, or villages.

Regulation of Land Development

As discussed in Chapter 19, *no uniform city planning and land development legislation exists that affects the entire country.* Laws governing subdividing and land planning are controlled by the state and local governmental bodies (county, city, town, or village) where the land is located. However, through the rules and regulations that have been developed by governmental agencies such as the Federal Housing Administration, we do have a set of **minimum standards** as usable guides. These minimum standards are not mandatory except for those developers who are seeking FHA approval of their subdivided area in anticipation of making FHA mortgage financing available to purchasers. These regulations are not uniform throughout the entire country. They are flexible, and subject to review by regional officers, who have the authority to modify the regulations to meet customs and local climate, health, and hazard conditions. Some of the major FHA minimum standards will be discussed later in this chapter. Although many governmental authorities have adopted some of these FHA minimum standards, a large number have established higher standards for subdividers of land under their jurisdiction.

Land Planning

Although the recording of a plat of subdivision of land prior to public sale for residential or commercial use is usually required, land planning precedes the actual subdividing process. The land development plan must comply with the overall local plan if a *master land plan* has been adopted by the county, city, village, or town. In complying with this local plan, the developer must take into consideration the zoning laws and land-use restrictions that have been adopted for health and safety purposes. The basic city plan and zoning requirements are not inflexible, but long, expensive, and frequently complicated hearings are usually required before alterations can be authorized.

As discussed in Chapter 19, most villages, cities, and other areas that are incorporated under state laws have *planning committees* or *planning commissioners.* Depending upon how the particular group was organized, such committees or commissions may have only an advisory status to the aldermen or trustees of the community. In other instances, the commission can have authority to approve or disapprove plans. Communities establish strict criteria before approving new subdivisions. The following are frequently included: (1) *dedication* of land for streets, schools, parks, (2) assurance by *bonding* that sewer and street costs will be paid, and (3) *compliance with zoning ordinances* governing use and lot size, along with fire and safety ordinances.

Because of the fear that they may pollute streams, rivers, lakes, and underground water sources, septic systems are usually no longer authorized in most areas, and an approved sewage-disposal arrangement must be included in a land development plan. The shortage of water has caused great concern, and local authorities usually require land planners to submit information on how they intend to satisfy sewage-disposal and water-supply requirements. Frequently a planner will also have to submit some sort of environmental impact statement.

When property to be subdivided is located outside the limits of cities, villages, and incorporated towns, most state laws require that the proposed land plan be submitted to county authorities (county, borough, or parish) for approval, and also to all incorporated communities (cities, towns, or villages) located within a radius of one to three miles. If there is more than one such incorporated area, each must review and approve the plan.

Local officials are not quick to approve such plans unless they comply with their community's ordinances and requirements. This is the main reason that developers now have less freedom in planning an outlying suburban development than one located in a city, town, or village.

Subdividing

The process of **subdivision** generally involves three distinct stages of development: (1) the initial planning stage, (2) the final planning stage, and (3) the disposition, or start-up.

During the *initial planning stage,* the subdivider seeks out raw land in a suitable area that he or she can profitably subdivide. Once the land is located, the property is analyzed for its highest and best use, and preliminary subdivision plans are drawn up accordingly. As previously discussed, close contact is initiated between the subdivider and local planning and zoning officials: if the project requires zoning variances, negotiations begin along these lines. The subdivider also locates financial backers and initiates marketing strategies at this point in the process.

The final planning stage is basically a follow-up of the initial stage. Final plans are prepared, approval is sought from local officials, permanent financing is obtained, the land is purchased, final budgets are prepared, and marketing programs are designed.

The *disposition,* or *start-up,* carries the subdividing process to a conclusion. Subdivision plans are recorded with local officials, and streets, sewers, and utilities are installed. Buildings, open parks, and recreational areas are constructed and landscaped if they are part of the subdivision plan. Marketing programs are then initiated, and title to the individual parcels of subdivided land is transferred as the lots are sold.

Subdivision Plans

In plotting out a subdivision according to local planning and zoning controls, a subdivider usually determines the size as well as the location of the individual lots. The size of the lots, both in front footage and in depth, together with the total amount of square footage, is generally regulated by local ordinances; this must be taken into careful consideration. Frequently ordinances regulate both the minimum and the maximum size of a lot.

The land itself must be studied, usually in cooperation with a surveyor, so that the subdivision can be laid out with consideration of natural drainage and land contours.

In laying out a subdivision, a subdivider should provide for *utility easements,* as well as easements for water and sewer mains. Usually the water and sewer mains will be laid in the street, with connecting junction boxes available for each building site. When the city, town, or village installs the water or sewer mains connecting a new building with the junction box in the street, a tie-in, or connection, fee is frequently charged to help the authority defray the cost of such installation.

Most subdivisions are laid out by use of *lots and blocks.* An area of land is designated as a block, and the area making up this block is divided into lots. Usually, lots and blocks are both numbered consecutively. However, if a developer does not intend to subdivide an entire tract of land at one time (and he or she may not if the site is of any substantial size), some variation from consecutive numbering may be granted.

Although subdividers customarily designate areas reserved for schools, parks, and future church sites, this is usually not considered good subdividing. Once a subdivision has been recorded, the purchasers of the lots have a vested interest in those areas reserved for schools, parks, and churches. If for any reason in the future, any such purpose is not appropriate, it will become difficult for the developer to abandon the original plan and use that property for residential purposes. To get around this situation, many developers designate such areas as *out-lot A, out-lot B,* and so forth. Such a designation does not vest any rights in these out-lots in the purchasers of the homesites. Then, for example, if one of these areas is to be used for church purposes, it can be so conveyed and so used. If, on the other hand, the out-lot is not to be used for such a purpose, it can be resubdivided into residential properties without the burden of securing the consent of the lot owners in the area.

Plat of subdivision. The subdivider's completed **plat of subdivision,** a map of the development indicating the location and boundaries of individual properties, must contain all necessary approvals of public officials and must be recorded in the county where the land is located.

Once the plat has been filed for record, all areas that have been set aside for street purposes are considered to be **dedicated.** This usually means that the land shown as streets now belongs to the city or town. If this is not the subdivider's intention, the plat should specify that the streets are private.

Since the plat will be the basis for future conveyances, the subdivided land should be carefully measured, with all lot sizes and streets noted by the surveyor and accurately entered on the document. Survey monuments should be established, and measurements should be made from these monuments, with the location of all lots carefully marked.

Covenants and restrictions. Deed restrictions, discussed in Chapters 7 and 19, are originated and recorded by the subdivider as a means of *controlling and maintaining the desirable quality and character of the subdivision.* The subdivider should provide for some form of restrictions. If the subdivision plan is to be submitted for FHA approval, such restrictive covenants must comply with FHA standards. These restrictions can be included in the subdivision plat, or they may be set forth in a separate recorded instrument, commonly referred to as a *declaration of restrictions.*

Subdividers usually place restrictions upon the use of all lots in a subdivision as a general plan for the benefit of all lot owners. Such restrictions give each lot owner the right to apply to the court for an *injunction* to prevent the violation of the recorded restrictions by a neighboring lot owner.

FHA standards. FHA minimum standards have been established for subdivisions in residential areas that are to be submitted for approval for FHA loan insurance. The primary minimum standards established by the FHA are the following:

1. Streets must comply with approved widths and must be paved.
2. The area must be free from hazards, such as airplane landing fields, heavy through traffic, and excessive noise or air pollution.
3. Each lot must have access to all utilities.
4. Provisions for shopping, schools, churches, recreation, and transportation must be available.
5. Lots must comply with minimum, and in some cases maximum, size requirements.
6. Plans for construction must be approved and must meet minimum standards.
7. Uniform building setbacks and lot lines are usually required.
8. Minimum landscaping is usually required.

Trained personnel are available in each FHA regional office to meet with subdividers, developers, and builders to assist them in meeting the minimum FHA standards.

Development costs. Most homeowners do not understand the costs of developing land. The subdivider, developer, and builder frequently invest many hundreds of thousands of dollars (and in larger developments, several million dollars) before the subdivision is even announced to the public.

The difference between the raw land cost, usually on a per acre basis, and the asking price per front foot of subdivided lot surprises the average homeowner. An analysis of these development costs will substantiate the sales price for a typical building lot of four to six times the cost of the raw land, if the development is a financial success. These costs, of course, vary from area to area and according to the nature of the development itself.

In most areas, an acre of land will yield between two and three subdivided lots, assuming that each lot does not contain more than 10,000 square feet. (A lot 100 × 100 feet would contain 10,000 square feet.) An acre contains 43,560 square feet. The apparent shrinkage is due to roads, streets, parkways, and public sidewalks.

In the subdivision of a typical parcel of raw land, a lot's sales price will generally reflect such expenses as cost of land; installation of sewers, water mains, storm drains, landscaping, and street lights; earthworks (mass dirt removal, site grading, and similar operations); paving; engineering and surveying fees; brokers' commissions; inspections; bonding costs; filing and legal fees; sales costs; and overhead. In certain areas, a subdivider may also be required to give financial assistance to school districts, park districts, and the like, either in the form of donated school or park sites or in the form of a fixed subsidy per subdivision lot. Should such further costs be incurred, they must, of course, be added proportionately to the sales price of each building site.

Subdivision Density

Zoning ordinances generally restrict land use. Such restrictions often include covenants that control minimum lot sizes and population density for subdivisions and land developments. For example, a typical zoning restriction may set the minimum lot area on which a subdivider can build a single-family housing unit at 15,000 square feet. This means that the subdivider will be able to build approximately 2½ houses per acre. However, many zoning authorities now establish special density zoning standards for certain subdivisions. **Density zoning** ordinances restrict the *average maximum number of houses per acre* that may be built within a particular subdivision. For example, in the previous explanation, a 15,000-square-foot–lot minimum meant that the developer could build only 2.5 houses per acre. On the other hand, if the area is density zoned at an average maximum of 2.5 houses per acre, the developer is free to achieve an open, clustered effect. Regardless of lot size or the number of clustered units, the subdivider will be consistent with the ordinance as long as the average number of units in the development remains at or below the maximum density. This average is called *gross density.*

Street patterns. By varying street patterns and clustering housing units, a subdivider can dramatically increase the amount of open and/or recreational space in a development. Most subdivisions are structured around one, a combination, or a modification of the following basic street patterns: gridiron, curvilinear, loop streets, and Radburn Plan streets. These patterns are illustrated in figure 20.1.

The **gridiron pattern** evolved out of the government rectangular survey system. Featuring large lots, wide streets, and limited-use service alleys, the system works reasonably well up to a point. However, an overabundance of grid-patterned streets often results in monotonous neighborhoods, with all lots facing busy streets. In addition, sidewalks are usually located adjacent to the streets, and the system provides for little or no open, park, or recreational space.

Figure 20.1
Street Patterns

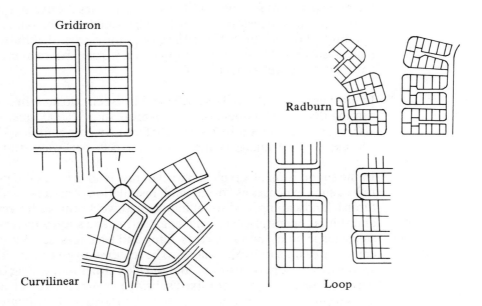

Gridiron

Radburn

Curvilinear

Loop

The **curvilinear system** integrates major arteries of travel with smaller secondary and cul-de-sac streets carrying minor traffic. In addition, small open parks are often provided for at intersections.

By utilizing **loop streets** rather than a traditional grid pattern, a developer can provide residents with convenient pedestrian and auto access and attractive open space. Although the main streets are loosely patterned after the grid system, residential streets all have limited access, with few lots facing the busier thoroughfares.

The **Radburn Plan** originated in the New Jersey town of the same name and features clusters of housing units grouped into large cul-de-sac blocks, often called "superblocks." Pedestrian access and open space are provided for between each cluster, and pedestrian travel is well separated from auto traffic.

Clustering for open space. By slightly reducing lot sizes and **clustering** them around varying street patterns, a developer can house as many people in the same area as could be done using traditional subdividing plans, but with substantially increased tracts of open space.

For example, compare the two illustrations in Figure 20.2. The first is a plan for a conventionally designed subdivision containing 368 housing units. It uses 23,200 linear feet of street and leaves only 1.6 acres open for park areas. Contrast this with the second subdivision pictured. Both subdivisions are equal in size and terrain. But when lots are minimally reduced in size and clustered around limited-access, cul-de-sac streets, the number of housing units remains nearly the same (366), with less street area (17,000 linear feet), and drastically increased open space (23.5 acres). In addition, with modern building designs this clustered plan could be modified to accommodate 550 patio homes or 1,100 townhouses.

Figure 20.2
Clustered Subdivision
Plan

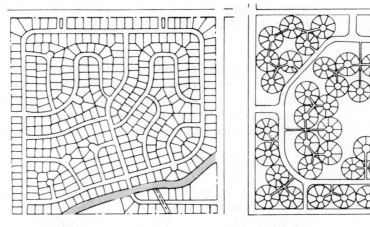

Conventional Plan
12,500-square-foot lots
368 housing units
1.6 acres of parkland
23,200 linear feet of street

Cluster Plan
7,500-square-foot lots
366 housing units
23.5 acres of parkland
17,700 linear feet of street

Subdivided Land Sales

Mass housing development, limited to the construction of single-family dwellings during the post–World War II years, greatly expanded in the 1950s. This expansion occurred as a result of population growth, new production techniques, and an increasing public interest in land use for future development, retirement, and recreation. As the industry grew, so did the number of fraudulent acts and practices perpetrated by unscrupulous dealers and developers against the unsuspecting public.

Interstate Land Sales Full Disclosure Act

To protect the masses from such "overenthusiastic sales promotions" in interstate land sales, Congress passed a federal law, the **Interstate Land Sales Full Disclosure Act.** Basically a consumer protection act, the law requires those engaged in the interstate sale or leasing of 100 or more lots to file a *statement of record* and *register* the details of the land with the U.S. Department of Housing and Urban Development (HUD).

The seller is also required to furnish prospective buyers a **property report** containing all essential information about the property, such as distance over paved roads to nearby communities, number of homes currently occupied, soil conditions affecting foundations and septic systems, type of title a buyer will receive, and existence of liens. The property report must be given to a prospective purchaser at least three business days before any sales contract is signed.

Any contract to purchase a lot covered by this act may be revoked at the purchaser's option until midnight of the seventh day following the signing of the contract. If a contract is signed for the purchase of a lot covered by the act and a property report is not given to the purchaser, he or she may revoke the contract within two years.

If the seller misrepresents the property in any sales promotion, a buyer induced by such a promotion is entitled to sue the seller for civil damages under federal law. Failure to comply with the law may also subject a seller to criminal penalties of up to five years' imprisonment and a $10,000 fine for each violation.

State Subdivided Land Sales Laws

Many state legislatures have enacted their own subdivided land sales laws. Some affect only the sale of land located outside of the state to state residents, while others affect sales of land located both inside and outside the state. Generally, these state land sales laws tend to be stricter and more detailed than the federal law. As a real estate salesperson or broker, you must know the specifics of your state's law.

Summary

A *subdivider* is someone who buys undeveloped acreage, divides it into smaller parcels, and sells it. A *land developer* builds homes on the lots and sells them, either through his or her own sales organization or through local real estate brokerage firms. City planners and land developers, working together, plan whole communities that are later incorporated into cities, towns, or villages.

Land development must generally comply with master land plans adopted by counties, cities, villages, or towns. This may entail approval of land-use plans by local *planning committees* or *commissioners*.

The process of subdivision includes dividing the tract of land into *lots and blocks* and providing for *utility easements,* as well as laying out street patterns and widths. A subdivider must generally record a completed *plat of subdivision,* with all necessary approvals of public officials, in the county where the land is located. Subdividers usually place *restrictions* upon the use of all lots in a subdivision as a general plan for the benefit of all lot owners.

Subdivisions that are to be submitted for approval for FHA loan insurance must meet certain *FHA minimum standards.*

By *varying street patterns and housing density,* and *clustering housing units,* a subdivider can dramatically increase the amount of open and recreational space within a development.

Subdivided land sales are regulated on the federal level by the *Interstate Land Sales Full Disclosure Act.* This law requires developers engaged in interstate land sales or the leasing of 100 or more units to register the details of the land with HUD. At least three business days before any sales contract is signed, such developers must also provide prospective purchasers with a property report containing all essential information about the property. Subdivided land sales are also regulated by many states' laws.

Questions

1. To control and maintain the quality and character of a subdivision, a developer will establish which of the following?

    a. out-lots
    b. deed restrictions
    c. buffer zones
    d. b and c

2. An owner of a large tract of land who, after adequate study of all facts, legally divides the land into lots of suitable size and location for the construction of residences, is known as a:

    I. subdivider.
    II. land developer.

        a. I only   c. both I and II
        b. II only   d. neither I nor II

3. A map illustrating the sizes and locations of streets and lots in a subdivision is called a:

    a. gridiron pattern.
    b. survey.
    c. plat of subdivision.
    d. property report.

4. Which of the following is *not* included in the FHA minimum standards for subdivisions?

    a. provisions for shopping must be available
    b. lots must be of uniform size
    c. streets must be of approved width and be paved
    d. the area must be free from hazards

5. *Gross density* refers to which of the following?

    a. the maximum number of residents that may, by law, occupy a subdivision
    b. the average maximum number of houses per acre that may, by law, be built in a subdivision
    c. the maximum size lot that may, by law, be built in a subdivision
    d. the minimum number of houses that may, by law, be built in a subdivision

6. The type of street pattern that is based on the rectangular survey system is called the:

    a. Radburn plan.   c. loop streets plan.
    b. gridiron system.   d. cul-de-sac system.

7. FHA minimum standards for land development:

    I. must be complied with by all subdividers.
    II. concern only the design and construction of buildings.

        a. I only   c. both I and II
        b. II only   d. neither I nor II

8. Legal restrictions established by a recorded deed or subdivision plat that are permitted by public policy and are not in violation of constitutional or statutory rights are enforceable through:

    I. zoning ordinances.
    II. court injunctions.

        a. I only   c. both I and II
        b. II only   d. neither I nor II

9. Which of the following would *not* be a part of the development cost of land?

    a. curbs and gutters
    b. installation of telephone lines
    c. raw land cost
    d. developer's overhead

10. Which of the following items are *not* usually designated on the plat for a new subdivision?

    a. easements for sewer and water mains
    b. land to be used for streets, schools, and civic facilities
    c. numbered lots and blocks
    d. prices of residential and commercial lots

11. The possibility of pollution has led to:

    I. elimination of the general use of the septic system as a means of sewage disposal.
    II. strict compliance with local zoning laws in drawing up a plan for sewage disposal.

        a. I only   c. both I and II
        b. II only   d. neither I nor II

12. A street pattern featuring clusters of housing units grouped into large, cul-de-sac blocks is generally called a:

    a. Radburn Plan.
    b. curvilinear system.
    c. loop street system.
    d. gridiron system.

13. Which of the following kinds of information need *not* be included in a property report given to a land buyer in compliance with the Interstate Land Sales Full Disclosure Act?
    a. soil conditions affecting foundations
    b. financial condition of the seller
    c. number of homes currently occupied
    d. existence of liens

14. Many real estate brokers serve as agents for developers in:
    I. instructing the developers in their legal responsibilities.
    II. finding property for subdivision purposes.
    a. I only
    b. II only
    c. both I and II
    d. neither I nor II

15. To protect the public from fraudulent interstate land sales, a developer involved in interstate land sales of 100 or more lots must:
    I. provide each purchaser with a report of the details of the land, as registered with the Department of Housing and Urban Development.
    II. pay the prospective buyer's expenses to see the property involved.
    a. I only
    b. II only
    c. both I and II
    d. neither I nor II

16. A subdivider can increase the amount of open and/or recreational space in a development by:
    a. varying street patterns.
    b. meeting FHA standards.
    c. clustering housing units.
    d. a and c

21

Fair Housing Laws and Ethical Practices

Key Terms
Blockbusting
Civil Rights Act of 1866
Code for Equal Opportunity
Code of Ethics
Department of Housing and Urban Development
Federal Fair Housing Act of 1968
Office of Equal Opportunity
Redlining
Steering

Overview
In order to achieve and maintain a favorable reputation in the community, a real estate licensee must be able to demonstrate more than good business ability. It is crucial that his or her *ethics,* or business principles, be above reproach as well. The various state license laws require licensees to adhere to certain ethical practices, as do the codes of ethics subscribed to by members of professional real estate organizations. Further, the federal and state governments have enacted laws that require licensees to follow ethical practices when dealing with the public, in order to ensure equal opportunity in housing for everyone. This chapter will deal with such fair housing laws, and will examine the codes of ethical practices to which most brokers and salespeople adhere.

Equal Opportunity in Housing

Brokers and salespeople who offer residential property for sale anywhere in the United States must be aware of the federal, state, and local laws pertaining to human rights and nondiscrimination. These laws, under such titles as open housing, fair housing, or equal opportunity housing, generally prohibit undesirable and discriminatory activities. Their provisions affect every phase of the real estate sales process from listing to closing, and *all brokers and salespeople must comply with them.*

The goal of legislators who have enacted fair housing laws and regulations is to create a single, unbiased housing market—one in which every homeseeker has the opportunity to buy any home in the area he or she chooses, providing that the home is within the homeseeker's financial means. Since most of the housing in the United States is produced and marketed through the private real estate market, owners, real estate brokers, apartment management companies, real estate boards, lending agencies, builders, and developers must all take a part in creating this single housing market.

As a potential licensee, the student of real estate must be aware of undesirable and illegal housing practices in order to avoid them. The licensee must realize that failure to comply with fair housing practices is not only a criminal act, but also grounds for license revocation.

Federal Fair Housing Laws

The efforts of the federal government to guarantee equal housing opportunities to all U.S. citizens began over one hundred years ago with the passage of the **Civil Rights Act of 1866.** This law, an outgrowth of the Fourteenth Amendment, prohibits any type of discrimination based on race. "All citizens of the United States shall have the same right in every state and territory as is enjoyed by white citizens thereof to inherit, purchase, lease, sell, hold, and convey real and personal property." A summary of federal fair housing laws appears in table 21.1.

Table 21.1
Summary of Federal Fair Housing Laws

Law	Purpose
Civil Rights Act of 1866	Prohibits discrimination in housing based on race without exception
Executive Order No. 11063	Prohibits discrimination in housing funded by FHA or VA loans
Civil Rights Act of 1964	Prohibits discrimination in federally funded housing programs
Fair Housing Act of 1968	Prohibits discrimination in housing based on race, color, religion, sex, or national origin with certain exceptions

Aside from a few isolated court decisions, there was little effort to enforce the
principles of fair housing until 1962, when President John Kennedy issued *Executive Order No. 11063*. This order guaranteed nondiscrimination in all housing financed by FHA and VA loans. Because of the relatively small percentage of housing affected by Executive Order No. 11063, however, it had limited impact.

The scope of the federal government's fair housing regulation was expanded by
the *Civil Rights Act of 1964,* which prohibited discrimination in any housing program that receives whole or partial federal funding. However, since only a very
small percentage of housing in the United States is government-funded, this law
also had little impact on the housing industry.

Fair Housing Act of 1968. In 1968, two major events occurred that greatly encouraged the progress of fair housing. The first of these was the passage of the
Federal Fair Housing Act, which is contained in *Title VIII of the Civil Rights Act
of 1968*. This law provides that it is unlawful to discriminate on the basis of race,
color, religion, sex, or national origin when selling or leasing residential property.
It covers dwellings and apartments, as well as vacant land acquired for the construction of residential buildings, and prohibits the following discriminatory acts:

1. refusing to sell, rent, or negotiate with any person, or otherwise making a
   dwelling unavailable to any person.
2. changing terms, conditions, or services for different individuals as a means of
   discrimination.
3. practicing discrimination through any statement or advertisement that restricts the sale or rental of residential property.
4. representing to any person, as a means of discrimination, that a dwelling is not
   available for sale or rental.
5. making a profit by inducing owners of housing to sell or rent because of the
   prospective entry into the neighborhood of persons of a particular race, color,
   religion, or national origin.
6. altering the terms or conditions for a home loan to any person who wishes to
   purchase or repair a dwelling, or otherwise denying such a loan, as a means of
   discrimination.
7. denying people membership or limiting their participation in any multiple-
   listing service, real estate brokers' organization, or other facility related to the
   sale or rental of dwellings, as a means of discrimination.

The following exemptions to the Federal Fair Housing Act are also provided:

1. The sale or rental of a single-family home is exempted when the home is owned
   by an individual who does not own more than three such homes at one time
   and when the following conditions exist: (a) a broker, salesperson, or agent is
   not used, and (b) discriminatory advertising is not used. If the owner is not living in the dwelling at the time of the transaction or was not the most recent occupant, only one such sale by an individual is exempt from the law within any
   24-month period.

2. The rental of rooms or units is exempted in an owner-occupied one- to four-
   family dwelling.

3. Dwelling units owned by religious organizations may be restricted to people of
   the same religion if membership in the organization is not restricted on the
   basis of race, color, or national origin.

4. A private club that is not in fact open to the public may restrict the rental or occupancy of lodgings that it owns to its members, as long as the lodgings are not operated commercially.

In addition to the general provisions of the Federal Fair Housing Law, the Department of Housing and Urban Development has issued numerous rules and regulations that establish guidelines for the real estate industry in such specific areas as advertising and marketing procedures.

Jones **v.** *Mayer.*   The second significant fair housing development of 1968 was the Supreme Court decision in the case of *Jones* v. *Alfred H. Mayer Company,* 392, U. S. 409 (1968). In its ruling, the Court upheld the previously discussed Civil Rights Act of 1866, which "prohibits all racial discrimination, private or public, in the sale and rental of property."

The importance of this decision rests in the fact that while the 1968 federal law exempts individual homeowners and certain groups, the 1866 law *prohibits all racial discrimination without exception.* So despite any exemptions in the 1968 law, an aggrieved person may seek a remedy for racial discrimination under the 1866 law against *any* homeowner, regardless of whether or not the owner employed a real estate broker and/or advertised the property.

Amendment to Fair Housing Law.   A 1972 amendment to the Federal Fair Housing Act of 1968 instituted the use of an equal housing opportunity poster. This poster, which can be obtained from HUD (illustrated in figure 21.1), features the equal housing opportunity slogan, an equal housing statement pledging adherence to the fair housing act and support of affirmative marketing and advertising programs, and the equal housing opportunity logo shown in figure 21.2.

When HUD investigates a broker for discriminatory practices, it considers failure to display the poster evidence of discrimination.

Blockbusting and Steering

Blockbusting and steering are undesirable housing practices frequently discussed in connection with fair housing. While they are not mentioned by name in the Federal Fair Housing Act of 1968, both are prohibited by that law.

It is a common misconception that blockbusting is the purchase of a home in a homogeneous neighborhood by a member of a minority group. In fact, **blockbusting** means *inducing homeowners to sell by making representations regarding the entry or prospective entry of minority persons into the neighborhood.* The blockbuster frightens homeowners into selling, and makes a profit by buying the homes cheaply and selling them at considerably higher prices to minority persons. The Federal Fair Housing Act specifically prohibits this practice.

Steering is the channeling of homeseekers to particular areas, either to maintain the homogeneity of an area or to change the character of an area in order to create a speculative situation. This practice makes certain homes unavailable to homeseekers on the basis of race or national origin; on these grounds it is prohibited by the provisions of the Federal Fair Housing Act. Steering is often difficult to detect, however, because the steering tactics can be so subtle that the homeseeker is unaware that his or her choice has been limited.

Figure 21.1
Equal Housing
Opportunity Poster

EQUAL HOUSING OPPORTUNITY

We Do Business in Accordance With the Federal Fair Housing Law

(Title VIII of the Civil Rights Act of 1968, as Amended by the Housing and Community Development Act of 1974)

IT IS ILLEGAL TO DISCRIMINATE AGAINST ANY PERSON BECAUSE OF RACE, COLOR, RELIGION, SEX, OR NATIONAL ORIGIN

- In the sale or rental of housing or residential lots
- In advertising the sale or rental of housing
- In the financing of housing
- In the provision of real estate brokerage services

Blockbusting is also illegal

An aggrieved person may file a complaint of a housing discrimination act with the:

U.S. DEPARTMENT OF HOUSING AND URBAN DEVELOPMENT
Assistant Secretary for Fair Housing and Equal Opportunity
Washington, D.C. 20410

HUD–928.1 (7-75) Previous editions are obsolete

Figure 21.2
Equal Housing
Opportunity Symbol

EQUAL HOUSING
OPPORTUNITY

Redlining

The practice of refusing to make mortgage loans or issue insurance policies in specific areas without regard to the economic qualifications of the applicant is known as **redlining.** This practice, which often contributes to the deterioration of older, transitional neighborhoods, is frequently based on racial grounds rather than on any real objections to the applicant. It is important to note that a lending institution that refuses a loan solely on sound economic grounds cannot be accused of redlining.

In an effort to counteract redlining, the federal government passed the *Home Mortgage Disclosure Act* in 1975. This act requires all institutional mortgage lenders with assets in excess of $10 million and one or more offices in a given geographic area to make annual reports by census tracts of all mortgage loans the institution makes or purchases. This law enables the government to detect lending or insuring patterns that might constitute redlining.

Enforcement

The Federal Fair Housing Act is administered by the **Office of Equal Opportunity** (OEO) under the direction of the Secretary of the **Department of Housing and Urban Development** (HUD). Any aggrieved person may file a complaint with the secretary or his or her delegate within 180 days after a discriminatory action occurs. Complaints may be reported to: Fair Housing, Dept. of Housing and Urban Development, Washington, DC 20410, or to Fair Housing c/o the nearest HUD regional office.

After investigating a complaint, HUD will decide whether or not to attempt to resolve the dispute and will notify the complainant of the decision within 30 days after the complaint is filed. The secretary's efforts to resolve the dispute are limited to conference, conciliation, and persuasion. If HUD decides to attempt conciliation, the complainant should wait to see if the matter can be settled out of court before filing suit; HUD will terminate all efforts at conciliation when the case actually comes to trial in court. An aggrieved person always has the option to take the alleged violator to court, whether or not a complaint has been filed with HUD.

If the agency is investigating the incident, however, the courts generally wait until it has completed its efforts before going ahead with the case.

If HUD is unable to obtain voluntary compliance from the accused violator within 30 days after the complaint is filed, the complainant then has another 30 days in which to file suit in the appropriate court if he or she chooses to do so. In states with fair housing laws that are substantially equivalent to federal statutes, such suits must be brought in state court within the time period specified by state law. If no such law exists, the complaint may be taken to a U.S. district court if a suit is filed within 180 days after the discriminatory action occurs.

In addition, court actions may be brought by the attorney general in cases where accused violators of the Federal Fair Housing Act of 1968 are engaged in practices that show a pattern of discrimination.

Complaints brought under the Civil Rights Act of 1866 must be taken directly to a federal court.

Substantially Equivalent State Laws

Whenever a state or municipality has a fair housing law that has been ruled *substantially equivalent* to the federal law, all complaints in that state or locality, including those filed with HUD, are referred to and handled by the state enforcement agencies. To be considered substantially equivalent, the local law and its related regulations must contain prohibitions comparable to the federal law. In addition, the state or locality must show that its local enforcement agency is taking sufficient affirmative action in processing and investigating complaints and in finding remedies for discriminatory practices. Contact your nearest HUD regional office to find out if the law in your state or municipality has been ruled substantially equivalent to the federal law.

Threats or Acts of Violence

The Federal Fair Housing Act of 1968 contains criminal provisions protecting the rights of those who seek the benefits of the open housing law, as well as owners, brokers, or salespeople who aid or encourage the enjoyment of open housing rights. Unlawful actions involving threats, coercion, and intimidation are punishable by appropriate civil action. In such cases, the victim should report the incident immediately to the local police and to the nearest office of the Federal Bureau of Investigation.

Implications for Brokers and Salespeople

To a large extent, the laws place the burden of responsibility for effecting and maintaining fair housing on real estate licensees—brokers and salespeople. And brokers and salespeople *must* comply with the laws; it's as simple as that. The laws are explicit and widely known. Anyone who violates them, whether intentionally or unintentionally, should be aware of the legal ramifications. In such cases, the complainant does not have to prove guilty knowledge or specific intent—only the fact that discrimination occurred.

How does a broker go about complying with the laws and making that policy known? As mentioned earlier, HUD regulations require that a public statement in the form of an approved fair housing poster must be displayed by a broker in any place of business where housing is offered for sale or rent (including model homes). HUD also offers guidelines for nondiscriminatory language and illustrations for use in real estate advertising. The agency further requires every broker to take affirmative marketing action in the choice of advertising media and in individual canvassing in order to assure that all interested individuals have the same range of housing options.

In addition, the NATIONAL ASSOCIATION OF REALTORS® suggests that a broker's position can be emphasized and problems can be avoided by the prominent display of a sign stating that it is against company policy as well as state and federal laws to offer any information on the racial, ethnic, or religious composition of a neighborhood or to place restrictions on listing, showing, or providing information on the availability of homes for any of these reasons. If a prospect still expresses a locational preference for housing based upon race, the association's guidelines suggest the following response: "I cannot give you that kind of advice. I will show you several homes that meet your specifications. You will have to decide which one you want."

Compliance with the fair housing laws involves knowing the regulations and doing as the law demands. It is, however, often hard to distinguish practices that are discriminatory in intent from those that are discriminatory in effect. A good test of whether or not an action is discriminatory is the answer to the question: Are we doing this for everyone? If the act is not done for everyone, it could be construed as discriminatory.

There's more to fair housing practices than just following the letter of the law. Discrimination involves a sensitive area, human emotions—specifically, fear and self-preservation based on considerable prejudice and misconception. The broker or salesperson who keeps his or her own actions in check by complying with the law still has to deal, in many cases, with a general public whose attitudes cannot be altered by legislation alone. Therefore, a licensee who wishes to comply with the fair housing laws and also succeed in the real estate business must work to educate the public.

In some communities, the public is working to change the attitudes and practices of real estate licensees. After determining that undesirable actions were in fact being practiced in their areas, some citizens have mobilized community support by boycotting brokerages, advertising and selling local residential property through citizen-run neighborhood associations, and even establishing and supporting actual real estate firms (both profit and nonprofit) whose purpose is to promote a single housing market. Similar measures, which in effect hurt the local broker's business, have been taken in communities all over the United States—an added reason why licensees should comply with the fair housing laws.

For every broker and salesperson, a sincere, positive attitude toward fair housing laws is a good start in dealing with this sensitive issue. It provides effective models for all who come in contact with the licensee. Active cooperation with local real estate board programs and community committees is also an excellent idea. This evidences the licensee's willingness to serve the community and observe the laws, and it helps to change public attitudes. Both factors can result in good public relations and, ultimately, more business for the licensee.

Standards of Professional Practice

Professional Organizations

Years ago, real estate brokers realized the need for an organization to assist them in improving their business abilities and to educate the public to the value of qualified real estate brokers. The NATIONAL ASSOCIATION OF REALTORS® (NAR) was organized in 1908 (as the National Association of Real Estate Boards) to meet this need. This association has grown with the business and today is one of the leading trade organizations in the country. It is the parent organization of most local real estate boards that operate throughout the United States, and the professional activities of all REALTORS®—brokers and salespeople who are active members of local boards that are affiliated with the national association—are governed by the association's Code of Ethics. (Note that a licensed broker or salesperson is not required to become a REALTOR®.)

There are also many independent real estate boards and other professional associations that were organized to set high standards for their members, promote their members' best interests, and educate the public about the real estate profession. The National Association of Real Estate Brokers (Realtists) was founded in 1947. Its membership includes individual members, as well as brokers, who belong to state and local real estate boards affiliated with the organization. The members also subscribe to a code of ethics that sets professional standards for all Realtists.

Code of Ethics

The importance of adhering to a set of ethical business standards cannot be overemphasized. At least one state real estate commission has adopted a code of ethics as part of its real estate license law, and others may follow this example.

The NAR adopted its **Code of Ethics** in 1913. Through the years it has proved helpful to everyone in the real estate business because it contains practical applications of business ethics and statements of good practices that everyone in the business should know and carefully follow. A real estate business is only as good as its reputation, and reputations are built on sound business practices and fair dealings with clients, other real estate brokers, and the general public. In addition, the NAR publishes records of interpretations of the Code known as Standards of Practice. Similar to case law, the interpretations establish precedents for local boards to follow in hearings that involve violations of the Code. The REALTORS® Code of Ethics is reproduced in figure 21.3.

Code for Equal Opportunity

In order to better support fair housing opportunities in its members' communities, the NAR has adopted a **Code for Equal Opportunity.** The Code basically sets forth suggested standards of conduct for REALTORS® so that they may comply with the letter as well as the spirit of the fair housing laws. The Code provides that:

1. In the sale, purchase, exchange, rental, or lease of real property, REALTORS® and their REALTOR-Associates® have the responsibility to offer equal service to all clients and prospects without regard to race, color, religion, sex, or national origin. This encompasses:
   a. standing ready to enter broker-client relationships or to show property equally to members of all races, creeds, or ethnic groups.

b. receiving all formal written offers and communicating them to the owner.

c. exerting their best efforts to conclude all transactions.

d. maintaining equal opportunity employment practices.

2. Members, individually and collectively, in performing their agency functions, have no right or responsibility to volunteer information regarding the racial, creedal, or ethnic composition of any neighborhood or any part thereof.

3. Members shall not engage in any activity that has the purpose of inducing panic selling.

4. Members shall not print, display, or circulate any statement or advertisement with respect to the sale or rental of a dwelling that indicates any preference, limitations, or discrimination based on race, color, religion, sex, or ethnic background.

5. Members who violate the spirit or any provision of this Code of Equal Opportunity shall be subject to disciplinary action.

The Code of Ethics and the Code for Equal Opportunity are two segments of the NAR's overall equal opportunity program, which is designed to ensure that no person is denied equal professional real estate services. The national association has also developed an Affirmative Marketing Agreement through which participating members inform the minority community of available real estate services and encourage the participation of minorities in the housing industry.

Summary

The federal regulations regarding equal opportunity in housing are principally contained in two laws. The *Civil Rights Act of 1866* prohibits all racial discrimination, and the *Federal Fair Housing Act* (Title VIII of the Civil Rights Act of 1968) prohibits discrimination on the basis of race, color, religion, sex, or national origin in the sale or rental of residential property. Discriminatory actions include refusing to deal with an individual or a specific group, changing any terms of a real estate or loan transaction, changing the services offered for any individual or group, making statements or advertisements that indicate discriminatory restrictions, or otherwise attempting to make a dwelling unavailable to any person or group because of race, color, religion, sex, or national origin.

Complaints under the Federal Fair Housing Act may be reported to and investigated by the *Department of Housing and Urban Development.* Such complaints may also be taken directly to a U.S. district court. In states and localities that have enacted fair housing legislation that is "substantially equivalent to the federal law," complaints are handled by state and local agencies and state courts. Complaints under the Civil Rights Act of 1866 must be taken to a federal court.

A real estate business is only as good as its reputation. Real estate licensees can maintain good reputations by demonstrating good business ability and adhering to an ethical standard of business practices. Many licensees subscribe to a code of ethics as members of professional real estate organizations. The *Code of Ethics* of the NATIONAL ASSOCIATION OF REALTORS® is reprinted in this chapter. The provisions of this and the *Code for Equal Opportunity* suggest an excellent set of standards for all licensees to follow.

Figure 21.3
REALTORS® Code of Ethics

Code of Ethics[1]
of the
National Association of Realtors®

Revised and Approved by the
Delegate Body of the Association
at its 75th Annual Convention
November 15, 1982

Preamble . . .

Under all is the land. Upon its wise utilization and widely allocated ownership depend the survival and growth of free institutions and of our civilization. The REALTOR® should recognize that the interests of the nation and its citizens require the highest and best use of the land and the widest distribution of land ownership. They require the creation of adequate housing, the building of functioning cities, the development of productive industries and farms, and the preservation of a healthful environment.

Such interests impose obligations beyond those of ordinary commerce. They impose grave social responsibility and a patriotic duty to which the REALTOR® should dedicate himself, and for which he should be diligent in preparing himself. The REALTOR®, therefore, is zealous to maintain and improve the standards of his calling and shares with his fellow REALTORS® a common responsibility for its integrity and honor. The term REALTOR® has come to connote competency, fairness, and high integrity resulting from adherence to a lofty ideal of moral conduct in business relations. No inducement of profit and no instruction from clients ever can justify departure from this ideal.

In the interpretation of this obligation, a REALTOR® can take no safer guide than that which has been handed down through the centuries, embodied in the Golden Rule, "Whatsoever ye would that men should do to you, do ye even so to them."

Accepting this standard as his own, every REALTOR® pledges himself to observe its spirit in all of his activities and to conduct his business in accordance with the tenets set forth below.

Article 1

The REALTOR® should keep himself informed on matters affecting real estate in his community, the state, and nation so that he may be able to contribute responsibly to public thinking on such matters.

Article 2

In justice to those who place their interests in his care, the REALTOR® should endeavor always to be informed regarding laws, proposed legislation, governmental regulations, public policies, and current market conditions in order to be in a position to advise his clients properly.

Article 3

It is the duty of the REALTOR® to protect the public against fraud, misrepresentation, and unethical practices in real estate transactions. He should endeavor to eliminate in his community any practices which could be damaging to the public or bring discredit to the real estate profession. The REALTOR® should assist the governmental agency charged with regulating the practices of brokers and salesmen in his state.

Article 4

The REALTOR® should seek no unfair advantage over other REALTORS® and should conduct his business so as to avoid controversies with other REALTORS®.

Article 5

In the best interests of society, of his associates, and his own business, the REALTOR® should willingly share with other REALTORS® the lessons of his experience and study for the benefit of the public, and should be loyal to the Board of REALTORS® of his community and active in its work.

1. Published with the consent of the NATIONAL ASSOCIATION OF REALTORS®, author of and owner of all rights in the Code of Ethics of the NATIONAL ASSOCIATION OF REALTORS®, © NATIONAL ASSOCIATION OF REALTORS® 1982— All Rights Reserved. The NATIONAL ASSOCIATION OF REALTORS® reserves exclusively unto itself the right to comment on and interpret the CODE and particular provisions thereof. For the NATIONAL ASSOCIATION's official interpretations of the CODE, see INTERPRETATIONS OF THE CODE OF ETHICS; NATIONAL ASSOCIATION OF REALTORS®.

Article 6

To prevent dissension and misunderstanding and to assure better service to the owner, the REALTOR® should urge the exclusive listing of property unless contrary to the best interest of the owner.

Article 7

In accepting employment as an agent, the REALTOR® pledges himself to protect and promote the interests of the client. This obligation of absolute fidelity to the client's interests is primary, but it does not relieve the REALTOR® of the obligation to treat fairly all parties to the transaction.

Article 8

The REALTOR® shall not accept compensation from more than one party, even if permitted by law, without the full knowledge of all parties to the transaction.

Article 9

The REALTOR® shall avoid exaggeration, misrepresentation, or concealment of pertinent facts. He has an affirmative obligation to discover adverse factors that a reasonably competent and diligent investigation would disclose.

Article 10

The REALTOR® shall not deny equal professional services to any person for reasons of race, creed, sex, or country of national origin. The REALTOR® shall not be party to any plan or agreement to discriminate against a person or persons on the basis of race, creed, sex, or country of national origin.

Article 11

A REALTOR® is expected to provide a level of competent service in keeping with the standards of practice in those fields in which the REALTOR® customarily engages.

The REALTOR® shall not undertake to provide specialized professional services concerning a type of property or service that is outside his field of competence unless he engages the assistance of one who is competent on such types of property or service, or unless the facts are fully disclosed to the client. Any person engaged to provide such assistance shall be so identified to the client and his contribution to the assignment should be set forth.

The REALTOR® shall refer to the Standards of Practice of the National Association as to the degree of competence that a client has a right to expect the REALTOR® to possess, taking into consideration the complexity of the problem, the availability of expert assistance, and the opportunities for experience available to the REALTOR®.

Article 12

The REALTOR® shall not undertake to provide professional services concerning a property or its value where he has a present or contemplated interest unless such interest is specifically disclosed to all affected parties.

Article 13

The REALTOR® shall not acquire an interest in or buy for himself, any member of his immediate family, his firm or any member thereof, or any entity in which he has a substantial ownership interest, property listed with him, without making the true position known to the listing owner. In selling property owned by himself, or in which he has any interest, the REALTOR® shall reveal the facts of his ownership or interest to the purchaser.

Article 14

In the event of a controversy between REALTORS® associated with different firms, arising out of their relationship as REALTORS®, the REALTORS® shall submit the dispute to arbitration in accordance with the regulations of their board or boards rather than litigate the matter.

Article 15

If a REALTOR® is charged with unethical practice or is asked to present evidence in any disciplinary proceeding or investigation, he shall place all pertinent facts before the proper tribunal of the member board or affiliated institute, society, or council of which he is a member.

Article 16

When acting as agent, the REALTOR® shall not accept any commission, rebate, or profit on expenditures made for his principal-owner, without the principal's knowledge and consent.

Figure 21.3 (cont.)

Article 17

The REALTOR® shall not engage in activities that constitute the unauthorized practice of law and shall recommend that legal counsel be obtained when the interest of any party to the transaction requires it.

Article 18

The REALTOR® shall keep in a special account in an appropriate financial institution, separated from his own funds, monies coming into his possession in trust for other persons, such as escrows, trust funds, clients' monies, and other like items.

Article 19

The REALTOR® shall be careful at all times to present a true picture in his advertising and representations to the public. He shall neither advertise without disclosing his name nor permit any person associated with him to use individual names or telephone numbers, unless such person's connection with the REALTOR® is obvious in the advertisement.

Article 20

The REALTOR®, for the protection of all parties, shall see that financial obligations and commitments regarding real estate transactions are in writing, expressing the exact agreement of the parties. A copy of each agreement shall be furnished to each party upon his signing such agreement.

Article 21

The REALTOR® shall not engage in any practice or take any action inconsistent with the agency of another REALTOR®.

Article 22

In the sale of property which is exclusively listed with a REALTOR®, the REALTOR® shall utilize the services of other brokers upon mutually agreed upon terms when it is in the best interests of the client.

Negotiations concerning property which is listed exclusively shall be carried on with the listing broker, not with the owner, except with the consent of the listing broker.

Article 23

The REALTOR® shall not publicly disparage the business practice of a competitor nor volunteer an opinion of a competitor's transaction. If his opinion is sought and if the REALTOR® deems it appropriate to respond, such opinion shall be rendered with strict professional integrity and courtesy.

Note: Where the word REALTOR® is used in this Code and Preamble, it shall be deemed to include REALTOR-ASSOCIATE®. Pronouns shall be considered to include REALTORS® and REALTOR-ASSOCIATES® of both genders.

The Code of Ethics was adopted in 1913. Amended at the Annual Convention in 1924, 1928, 1950, 1951, 1952, 1955, 1956, 1961, 1962, 1974, and 1982.

Questions

1. Which of the following acts is permitted under the Federal Fair Housing Act?

   a. advertising property for sale only to a special group
   b. altering the terms of a loan for a member of a minority group
   c. refusing to sell a home to an individual because he or she has a poor credit history
   d. telling an individual that an apartment has been rented when in fact it has not

2. Complaints relating to the Civil Rights Act of 1866:

   a. must be taken directly to a federal court.
   b. are no longer reviewed in the courts.
   c. are handled by HUD.
   d. are handled by state enforcement agencies.

3. In his or her business relations, a broker should:

   I. utilize the services of other brokers when it is in the best interests of his or her clients.
   II. not publicly criticize the business practices of a competitor.
      a. I only   c. both I and II
      b. II only   d. neither I nor II

4. Under the Federal Fair Housing Act, complaints may be:

   I. filed with the Department of Housing and Urban Development.
   II. handled by the local U.S. district court.
      a. I only   c. both I and II
      b. II only   d. neither I nor II

5. Which of the following situations is (are) considered to be discriminatory under the Federal Fair Housing Act?

   a. The Penford Club of Metropole City will rent lodging only to graduates of Penford University who are members of this private club.
   b. Martin McBain, who as owner is personally selling a house that he inherited from his uncle and does not live in, refuses to show the property to an Oriental family.
   c. The owner of a 20-unit apartment building refuses to rent apartments to women.
   d. All of the above are discriminatory.

6. Broker Beth Silverman informs homeowner James Albert of the prospective entry of a minority group into homeowner Albert's neighborhood. Broker Silverman, seeing that Albert is very upset, offers to buy Albert's house at a low price. Silverman is:

   I. guilty of steering.
   II. protecting the best interests of the homeowner.
      a. I only   c. both I and II
      b. II only   d. neither I nor II

7. After broker Harold Gorman takes a sale listing of a residence, the owner specifies that he will not sell his home to a black person. The broker should:

   I. say nothing and show the property to anyone who is interested, including blacks.
   II. explain to the owner that this violates federal law and he cannot do it.
      a. I only   c. both I and II
      b. II only   d. neither I nor II

8. The REALTORS® Code of Ethics suggests a set of standards for all brokers and salespeople to follow. Which of the following provisions is *not* contained in the Code?

   a. A REALTOR® should not engage in the practice of law.
   b. A REALTOR® must protect the public against fraud and unethical practices in the real estate field.
   c. A REALTOR® should not accept compensation from more than one party without the full knowledge of all parties to the transaction.
   d. In the event of a REALTOR®'s controversy with another REALTOR®, the matter should be settled through litigation.

9. Under the Supreme Court decision in the case of *Jones* v. *Alfred H. Mayer Company:*

   I. racial discrimination is prohibited by any party in the sale or rental of real estate.
   II. sales by individual residential homeowners are exempted provided the owner does not employ a broker.

      a. I only   c. both I and II
      b. II only   d. neither I nor II

10. Which of the following laws prohibit(s) discrimination in housing based on race, without exceptions?

    I. Civil Rights Act of 1866
    II. Fair Housing Act of 1968

       a. I only   c. both I and II
       b. II only   d. neither I nor II

11. The act of channeling home seekers to a particular area either to maintain or to change the character of a neighborhood is:

    a. blockbusting.
    b. redlining.
    c. steering.
    d. permitted under the Fair Housing Act of 1968.

12. The EZ-Go Mortgage Co. makes it a practice not to lend money to potential homeowners attempting to purchase property located in predominantly black neighborhoods. This practice is:

    a. blockbusting.   c. illegal.
    b. redlining.   d. b and c

13. A REALTOR® is prohibited from discriminating on the basis of race in his or her business practices by the:

    I. Fair Housing Act of 1968.
    II. REALTORS® Code of Ethics.

       a. I only   c. both I and II
       b. II only   d. neither I nor II

14. If a state or local law has been declared substantially equivalent to the federal Fair Housing Act, violations of the fair housing laws are referred to and handled by:

    a. federal courts.
    b. local boards of REALTORS®.
    c. state enforcement agencies.
    d. HUD.

15. An exception that allows the rental of rooms or units in an owner-occupied building with no more than four units is provided in:

    a. the Civil Rights Act of 1964.
    b. the Civil Rights Act of 1866.
    c. *Jones* v. *Mayer.*
    d. the Fair Housing Act of 1968.

22

Real Estate Investment

Key Terms

Adjusted basis
Appreciation
Basis
Boot
Cash flow
Cost recovery
Depreciation
Exchange
General partnership

Installment sale
Leverage
Limited partnership
Long-term capital gain
Pyramiding
Real estate investment syndicate
Real estate investment trust
Recapture
Tax shelter

Overview

The market for real estate investment is one of the most active in the country. Besides generating income and building up equity, real estate investment can aid in sheltering an owner's income against increasing taxes and the effects of inflation and deflation. This chapter will present a basic introduction to real estate investment; major emphasis is placed on investment opportunities open to small or beginning investors, as well as the various tax shelters available to all real estate investors. Note that the examples and computations given in this chapter are symbolic and used for *illustrative purposes only.* Such examples are included in the discussion in order to explain a particular feature or concept of investment, *not to teach the reader how, when, or what amount of money to invest.*

Investing in Real Estate

Often, customers ask a real estate broker or salesperson to act as an investment counselor; too often, the licensee is placed in that role by eager, inexperienced investors with high hopes for quick profits. While it may be the real estate licensee's responsibility to analyze and discuss with the potential investor his or her financial status, future goals, and investment motivations, the broker or salesperson should always *refer a potential real estate investor to a competent tax accountant, attorney, or investment specialist* who can give expert advice regarding the investor's specific interest.

Real estate practitioners should possess an essential knowledge of real estate investment so they can counsel customers on a basic level. Any such discussion should begin with an examination of the traditional advantages and disadvantages of investing in real estate as opposed to other commodities.

Advantages of Real Estate Investment

Traditionally, real estate investments have shown a *high rate of return,* generally higher than the prevailing interest rate charged by mortgage lenders. Theoretically, this means that an investor can use borrowed money to finance a real estate purchase and feel relatively sure that the asset will yield more money than it costs to finance the purchase.

In addition, real estate entrepreneurs enjoy many **tax shelters** that are unavailable to investors in other money-making activities. These shelters may allow an investor to reduce or defer payment of large portions of his or her federal and state income taxes. The various tax advantages—capital gains, exchanges, depreciation, and installment sales—will be discussed later in this chapter.

Also, real estate values usually rise in keeping with the ever-increasing rate of inflation. This concept, known as *inflation hedge,* provides the real estate investor with relative assurance that as the purchasing power of the dollar decreases, the value of his or her assets will increase to offset the inflationary effects. Inflation will also be discussed in detail later in this chapter.

Finally, a distinct advantage of real estate investment is that an investor can use borrowed money to finance his or her assets, which significantly increases the investor's buying power. This concept of *leverage* will be discussed later. In addition to the advantage of using borrowed money, the portion of an investor's mortgage payments applied to the principal represents *equity buildup* and increases the value of the investor's ownership interest in the asset with each remittance. This means the investor can refinance the property, receiving a certain amount of cash, should the need arise.

Disadvantages of Real Estate Investment

Unlike stocks and bonds, *real estate is not highly liquid* over a short period of time. This means that an investor cannot usually sell his or her real estate quickly without taking some sort of loss. An investor in listed stocks need only call a stockbroker in order to liquidate a certain portion of his or her assets quickly when funds are needed. In contrast, even though a real estate investor may be able to raise a limited amount of cash by refinancing the property, he or she lists his or her property with a real estate broker and may often have to sell the property at a substantially lower price than its market value in order to facilitate a quick sale.

In addition, *it is difficult to invest in real estate without some degree of expert advice.* Investment decisions must be made based on a careful study of all the facts in a given situation, reinforced by a broad and thorough knowledge of real estate and the manner in which it affects and is affected by the human element. As mentioned earlier, *all investors should seek legal and tax counsel before making any real estate investments.*

Also, a certain amount of *physical and mental effort is usually required* to maintain a real estate investment. Rarely can a real estate investor sit idly by and watch his or her money grow; management decisions must be made. For example, can the investor effectively manage the property personally, or would it be preferable to hire a professional property manager? How much rent should be charged? How should repairs and tenant grievances be handled? "Sweat equity" (physical and mental energy) must usually be invested to make the asset potentially profitable.

Finally, and most important, *a high degree of risk* is often involved in real estate investment. There is always the possibility that an investor's property will decrease in value during the period it is held or that it will not generate an income sufficient to make it profitable.

The Investment

The most important form of real estate investment is *direct ownership.* Both individuals and corporations may own real estate directly and manage it for appreciation, cash flow (income), and tax shelter purposes. Property held for **appreciation** is generally expected to increase in value and show a profit when sold at some future date. Income property is just that—property held for current income and, one hopes, a profit upon its sale.

Appreciation

Among the avenues of investment open to those interested in holding property primarily for appreciation are purchases of agricultural and undeveloped land. Recent developments in many areas of the country indicate that even purchases of residential property will appreciate substantially.

Agricultural and undeveloped land. Quite often an investor speculates in purchases of either agricultural (farm) land or undeveloped (raw) land, located in what he or she expects will be a major path of growth. This type of investment carries with it many inherent risks. The investor must consider such questions as: How fast will the area develop? Will it grow sufficiently for the investor to make a good profit? Will the expected growth even occur? More importantly, will the profits eventually realized from the property be great enough to offset the costs of holding the land?

Despite these risks, land is traditionally a good inflation hedge. In addition, it can be a source of income to offset some of the holding costs. For example, agricultural land can be leased out to tenant farmers for crops, timber, or grazing. Since land cannot technically wear out, the Internal Revenue Service does not allow the tax shelter of depreciation (cost recovery). Also, such land may not be liquid at certain times under certain circumstances, because few people are willing to purchase raw or agricultural land on short notice.

The value of land purchased for appreciation must appreciate at a rate great enough to compensate the owner for the cost of holding it. For example, imagine that an investor purchased raw land for $2,000 per acre with annual real estate taxes of $80 per acre and miscellaneous expenses of approximately 10 percent per year. For the investor just to break even, the land must appreciate by an average of $280 per acre each year the investor holds the property—an appreciation rate of *14 percent per year* (10% of $2,000 = $200 + $80 = $280 ÷ $2,000 = 14 percent). (This of course is a simplistic problem, used for illustrative purposes only.)

Two main factors affect appreciation: inflation and intrinsic value.

Inflation. Historically, *inflation* has been a dominant factor in the growth of our economy. Inflation is defined as the *increase in the amount of money in circulation, which results in a decline in its value coupled with a rise in wholesale and retail prices.*

Intrinsic value. Intrinsic value is the result of a person's individual choices and preferences for a given geographical area, based on the features and amenities that the area has to offer. For example, property located in a well-kept suburb near a shopping center would have a greater intrinsic value to most people than similar property located near a sewage treatment plant. As a rule, the greater the intrinsic value, the more money a property can command upon its sale.

Most land speculation is based on the principle of present versus future intrinsic value. What was farmland a few years ago could very well be a booming community today. It is the wise investor who knows how to advantageously identify, buy, and sell such speculative properties.

Income

Generally, the wisest initial investment a person who wishes to buy and personally manage real estate can make is the purchase of rental income property.

Cash flow. The object of an investor's directing funds into income property is to generate spendable income, usually called cash flow. The **cash flow** is the total amount of money remaining after all expenditures have been paid, including taxes, operating costs, and mortgage payments. The cash flow produced by any given parcel of real estate is determined by at least three factors: amount of rent received, operating expenses, and method of debt repayment.

Generally, the amount of *rent* (income) that a property may command depends on a number of factors, including location, physical appearance, and amenities. If the cash flow from rents is not enough to cover all expenses, a *negative cash flow* will result.

To keep cash flow high, an investor should *keep operating expenses low.* Such operating expenses include general maintenance of the building, repairs, utilities, taxes, and tenant services (switchboard facilities, security systems, and so forth). Like inadequate rental income, poor or overly expensive management can result in negative cash flow.

An investor often stands to make more money by investing borrowed money, usually obtained through a mortgage loan or deed of trust loan. *Low mortgage payments* spread over a long period of time result in a higher cash flow because they allow the investor to retain more income each month; conversely, higher mortgage payments would contribute to a lower cash flow.

Cash flow management. Cash flow may be manipulated either as a means of enhancing the attractiveness of a particular investment in order to command a higher selling price or as a means of producing higher or lower income levels in order to take advantage of high- and low-income years for tax purposes. Cash flow may be controlled through the use of various management techniques, such as obtaining high temporary rents through short-term leases or postponing minor repairs to generate a higher cash flow for any given period of time.

Investment opportunities. Traditional income-producing property investments include apartment buildings, hotels, motels, commercial properties, shopping centers, office buildings, and industrial properties. Investors in recent years have found single-family dwellings, townhouses, and condominium units to be favorable investments in certain situations.

Leverage

Real estate is expensive—even the most run-down property can cost tens of thousands of dollars. Regardless of cost, however, people with modest incomes are able to invest in real estate by using leverage. Essentially, **leverage** is the use of *borrowed money to finance the bulk of an investment.* As a rule, an investor can receive a maximum return from his or her initial investment (the down payment) by:

1. Making a small down payment.
2. Paying low interest rates.
3. Spreading mortgage payments over as long a period as possible.

For example, assume an investor purchases a property with a selling price of $200,000, for $20,000 down and a long-term mortgage at 12 percent interest with no prepayment penalty. One year later the investor is able to sell the property for $240,000. Disregarding ownership expenses, the return based on the purchase price (if the investor had paid cash) is 20 percent. *But by using leverage,* the investor actually received a *92 percent* return on the initial $20,000 investment (before depreciation and income tax). The computations for this example are as follows:

Gross profit:
$ 240,000 selling price
− 200,000 purchase price
$ 40,000 gross profit

Less mortgage interest:
$200,000 purchase price
− 20,000 down payment
$180,000 mortgage

$180,000 mortgage
×   .12 interest
$ 21,600 mortgage interest (first and only year)

Return on investment:
$ 40,000 gross profit
− 21,600 mortgage interest
$ 18,400 net profit

$$\frac{.92}{\$20,000\ )\$18,400.00} = 92\ percent\ return\ on\ investment$$
down payment   net profit

Risks are generally proportionate to leverage. A high degree of leverage gives the investor and lender a high degree of risk; lower leverage results in a lower risk.

Equity buildup. In the example using leverage, all computations were made based on interest payments rather than full mortgage loan installments. This is because the equity buildup in the property is like money in the bank to the real estate investor. Equity buildup is that portion of the payment directed toward the principal rather than the interest, *plus* any gain in property value due to appreciation. Although this accumulated equity is not as liquid as money in the bank, it may be sold, exchanged, or even refinanced to be used as leverage for other investments. Note that this equity is not physically available to the investor until the property is sold. In addition, that portion of the buildup that is due to appreciation will be subject to capital-gains taxes at the time of sale.

Pyramiding through refinancing. By holding and refinancing using equity and appreciation buildup, rather than selling or exchanging already-owned properties, an investor can increase his or her holdings substantially without investing any additional capital. This practice is known as **pyramiding.** By reinvesting and doubling his or her holdings periodically, it is conceivable that an investor who started out with a small initial cash down payment could own (heavily mortgaged) properties worth hundreds of thousands or millions of dollars. Eventually, the income derived from such assets could pay off the various mortgage debts and show a handsome profit.

Tax Benefits

One of the main reasons real estate investments are so popular—and profitable—is that federal law allows investors to shelter certain portions of their incomes from taxation. Four of the more common methods of sheltering real estate profits are capital gains, exchanges, depreciation, and installment sales.

The discussions and examples used in this section are designed to introduce the reader to general tax concepts—a tax attorney or CPA should be consulted for further details on specific regulations. Internal Revenue Service regulations are subject to frequent change; again, consult a tax expert for up-to-date information.

Capital Gains

Income earned from the sale of assets (such as real estate) that are held for a specific period of time—currently more than six months—is called a **long-term capital gain** and is subject to less tax than is ordinary income. Investors may exclude *60 percent* of their long-term capital gains from their income, meaning that *only 40 percent of a capital gain is taxed as income.*

Capital gain on real estate is determined by two factors, the adjusted basis and the net selling price. **Basis** usually refers to the initial cost an investor pays for a parcel of real estate. Generally, the **adjusted basis** represents the basis plus the cost of any physical improvements to the property minus depreciation. Basically then, the gain is the *difference between the adjusted basis and the net selling price.* (A property's net selling price is the sale price less the broker's commission and other selling costs.)

For example, assume an investor purchased a one-family dwelling for rental purposes ten years ago for $45,000. The value of the land was set at $10,000; the value of the improvements totaled $35,000. The investor is now selling the home for

$100,000; of this sum, $20,000 represents the new value of the land. Shortly before selling the property, the investor made $3,000 worth of capital improvements to the structure. Depreciation has been taken on a straight-line 35-year basis. (Depreciation, now called "cost recovery," will be discussed later in this section.) The investor paid the selling broker a 7-percent commission and also paid $600 in closing costs. So the investor's capital gain would be computed as follows:

Selling price:		$ 100,000
Less:		
7% commission	$ 7,000	
closing costs	+ 600	
	$ 7,600	− 7,600
Net sales price:		$ 92,400
Less value of land:		− 20,000
		$ 72,400
Basis:		
building	$ 35,000	
improvements	+ 3,000	
	$ 38,000	
Less depreciation:		
($35,000 ÷ 35 years =		
$1,000; $1,000 × 10		
years' ownership)	− 10,000	
Adjusted basis:	$ 28,000	− 28,000
Capital gain on improvements:		$ 44,400
Plus capital gain on land:		
value at sale	$ 20,000	
less original value	− 10,000	
	$ 10,000	+ 10,000
Total capital gain:		$ 54,400
		× .40
Capital gain taxable as income:		$ 21,760

Exchanges

By **exchanging** one property for another, a real estate investor can further reduce, defer, or even eliminate capital-gains tax. Tax laws generally provide that an investor's capital gains are not taxed when he or she exchanges income-producing properties of like kind. Note, however, that *the tax is deferred, not eliminated.* If the investor ever sells the property, he or she will be required to pay tax on the total capital gain. Or an investor can keep exchanging upward in value, adding to his assets as long as he lives without ever personally having to pay any capital-gains tax.

To qualify as a tax-deferred exchange, the properties involved must be of *like kind*—for example, real estate for real estate. Any additional capital or personal property included with the transaction to even out the exchange is considered **boot,** and the party receiving it is taxed at the time of the exchange. The value of the boot is added to the basis of the property with which it is given.

For example, investor Smith owns an apartment building with a market value of $200,000 and an adjusted basis of $90,000. He wants to exchange it for a different apartment building owned by Jones, which has a market value of $250,000 and an adjusted basis of $150,000. For Jones's building, investor Smith exchanges his building plus a cash boot of $50,000. After the exchange, investor Smith's new basis in his new building is $140,000 (the $90,000 basis of the building he exchanged plus the $50,000 cash boot he paid).

Investor Jones, on the other hand, exchanged a building worth $250,000 with an adjusted basis of $150,000 for a building worth only $200,000 plus $50,000 cash. She must pay capital-gains tax on the $50,000 boot, but her basis in the new building remains the same as for the building she exchanged—$150,000. If investor Jones had received all cash for her first building, her capital-gains tax liability would increase to $100,000 ($250,000 minus the $150,000 basis).

Similar deferred tax benefits for homeowners are discussed in Chapter 4.

Depreciation (Cost Recovery)

Depreciation is an accounting concept. The Internal Revenue Service Code now calls depreciation **cost recovery.** Depreciation allows an investor to recover the cost of an income-producing asset by way of tax deductions over the period of the asset's useful life.

Depreciation may have very little relationship to the actual physical deterioration of the asset. In fact, *when the cost recovery deductions exceed the amount of income received from an asset, an investor may apply these excess deductions against income from other sources.* Cost recovery deductions may be taken only on personal property and improvements to land, and only if they are used in a trade or business or for the production of income. Thus, an individual cannot claim a cost recovery deduction on his or her own personal residence. *Land cannot be depreciated*—technically it never wears out or becomes obsolete.

If depreciation is taken in equal amounts over an asset's useful life, the method used is called *straight-line depreciation.* It is also possible to use an accelerated method, that is, to claim greater deductions in the early years of ownership, gradually reducing the amount deducted in each year of the useful life. For example, the IRS permits an accelerated depreciation method called the *accelerated cost recovery system* (ACRS). Many investors use accelerated depreciation as a way of receiving the tax benefits of depreciation as quickly as possible.

Normally, in the initial years of a real estate investment, the taxable loss exceeds cash outlays. This happens because depreciation (especially accelerated depreciation) usually exceeds the gross income generated by the investment. It is thus possible for an investor to have a positive cash flow from an investment and still report a loss on his or her tax return. Because the investor/taxpayer can use the reported loss to offset taxable income from other sources, the loss is sometimes referred to as a *tax shelter.*

Recapture. The main disadvantage of using an accelerated method of depreciation is that while an investor can take greater tax reductions, he or she cannot take full advantage of capital-gains tax benefits. When an investor sells a property that was depreciated using an accelerated recovery method, that portion of the gain in excess of what would have been earned using straight-line recovery will be taxed as ordinary income rather than as capital gains, if the property has not been held for a statutorily required period of time. This is called **recapture.**

Installment Sales

An investor may defer federal income tax on a capital gain, provided he or she does not receive all cash for the asset at the time of sale but instead receives payments in two or more periods. This transaction is an **installment sale.** This method of reporting is now automatic, unless the taxpayer elects not to use it. As the name implies, the seller receives payment in installments and pays income tax each year based only on the amount received during that year. (This can be accomplished by selling through a contract for deed or similar instrument.) Besides avoiding tax payments on money not yet collected, the installment method often saves an investor money by spreading out the gain over a number of years. The gain may be subject to a lower tax rate than if it were received in one lump sum.

The three steps used in determining tax liability under an installment sale are:

1. Determine the total taxable gain on the transaction.
2. Determine the seller's total proceeds from the sale (often called the *contract price*).
3. Determine the amount of gain to be realized each year (the ratio of the total taxable gain to the total proceeds, multiplied by the amount of cash received in that year).

For example, an investor selling a property for $135,000 accepts a down payment of $40,500 and an installment mortgage from the buyer of $94,500, to be paid over 20 years beginning in the following year. Assume that the seller's total taxable gain from the sale is $30,375. The investor must claim 22.5 percent of the down payment as a capital gain, 22.5 percent being the ratio between the $30,375 gain and the $135,000 contract price ($30,375 \div 135,000 = 22.5\%$). The investor then reports an initial capital gain of $9,112.50, which is 22.5% of the original down payment: $40,500 down payment $\times$ .225 = $9,112.50 *initial capital gain.*

The investor's capital gains for the next 20 years (the mortgage loan period) would be as follows: $94,500 \div 20 = $4,725 principal paid to the seller each year; $4,725 $\times$ .225 = $1,063.13 *capital gain each year.*

In Practice ...

Because the seller under an installment sale can defer all or a substantial part of his or her gain, the seller can accept a small cash down payment and thus expand the market of potential buyers. This may also put the seller in a position to negotiate for a higher sales price. Note, however, that IRS regulations prohibit a seller from reporting a loss for tax purposes when selling by means of an installment sale.

Real Estate Investment Syndicates

A **real estate investment syndicate** is a form of business venture in which a group of people pool their resources to own and/or develop a particular piece of property. In this manner, people with only modest capital can invest in large-scale, high-profit operations, such as high-rise apartment buildings and shopping centers. A certain amount of profit is realized from rents collected on the investment, but the main return usually comes when the syndicate sells the property after sufficient appreciation.

A syndicate investor enjoys the same federal and state income-tax advantages as a direct-ownership real estate investor, because no matter how small his or her interest in the syndicate properties, the investor owns a certain percentage of a particular parcel of real estate. As a real estate owner, the syndicate investor is as much entitled to preferred tax treatment as is a sole owner of a similar property. However, syndicate interests may be more difficult to sell on the open market than real estate. In addition, approval by the syndicate's management may be required before an investor can sell his or her interest in the project. Some partnership agreements may even require that such interest be sold only to another member of the syndicate.

Syndicate participation can take many different legal forms, from tenancy in common and joint tenancy to various kinds of partnerships, corporations, and trusts. *Private syndication,* which generally involves a small group of closely associated and/or widely experienced investors, is distinguished from *public syndication,* which generally involves a much larger group of investors who may or may not be knowledgeable about real estate as an investment. The distinction between the two, however, is usually based on the nature of the arrangement between syndicator and investors, not on the type of syndicate. For this reason, any pooling of individuals' funds raises questions of registration of securities under federal securities laws and state securities laws, commonly referred to as *blue-sky laws.*

Securities laws include provisions to control and regulate the offering and sale of securities. This is to protect members of the public who are not sophisticated investors but may be solicited to participate. Real estate securities must be registered with state officials and/or with the Federal Securities and Exchange Commission (SEC) when they meet the defined conditions of a public offering. The number of prospects solicited, the total number of investors or participants, the financial background and sophistication of the investors, and the value or price per unit of investment are pertinent facts. Salespeople of such real estate securities may be required to obtain special licenses.

Forms of Syndicates   Real estate investment syndicates are usually organized as either general or limited partnerships.

A **general partnership** is organized so that *all members of the group share equally in the managerial decisions, profits, and losses involved with the investment.* A certain member (or members) of the syndicate is designated to act as trustee for the group and holds title to the property and maintains it in the syndicate's name.

Under a **limited partnership** agreement, *one party* (or parties), usually a property developer or real estate broker, *organizes, operates, and is responsible for the entire syndicate.* This person is called the *general partner.* The other members of the partnership are merely investors; they have no voice in the organization and direction of the operation. These *passive investors are called limited partners.* The limited partners share in the profits and compensate the general partner for his or her efforts out of such profits. Unlike a general partnership, in which each member is responsible for the total losses (if any) of the syndicate, the limited partners stand to lose only as much as they invest—nothing more. The general partner(s) is totally responsible for any excess losses incurred by the investment. The sale of a limited partnership interest involves the sale of an *investment security,* as defined by the SEC. Therefore, such sales are subject to state and federal laws concerning the sale of securities. Unless exempt, the securities must be registered with the federal Securities and Exchange Commission and the appropriate state authorities.

**Real Estate
Investment Trusts**

By directing their funds into **real estate investment trusts** (REITs), real estate investors can take advantage of the same tax benefits as mutual fund investors. A real estate investment trust does not have to pay corporate income tax as long as 95 percent of its income is distributed to its shareholders and certain other conditions are met. There are three types of investment trusts: equity trusts, mortgage trusts, and combination trusts. In order to form an REIT legally, a group of 100 or more members must hold shares in the trust.

Equity trusts. Much like mutual fund operations, equity REITs pool an assortment of large-scale income properties and sell shares to investors. This is in contrast to a real estate syndicate, through which several investors pool their funds in order to purchase *one* particular property. An equity trust also differs from a syndicate in that the trust realizes and directs its main profits through the *income* derived from the various properties it owns rather than from the sale of those properties.

Mortgage trusts. Mortgage trusts operate similarly to equity trusts, except that the mortgage trusts buy and sell real estate mortgages (usually short-term, junior instruments) rather than real property. A mortgage trust's major sources of income are mortgage interest and origination fees. Mortgage trusts may also make construction loans and finance land acquisitions.

Combination trusts. Combination trusts invest shareholders' funds in both real estate assets and mortgage loans. It has been predicted that these types of trusts are best able to withstand economic slumps because they can balance their investments and liabilities more efficiently than the other types of trusts.

Summary

Traditionally, real estate investments command a *high rate of return,* while at the same time allowing an investor to take advantage of many *tax shelters* unavailable to other types of investors. In addition, real estate is an effective *inflation hedge,* and an investor can make use of other people's money to make investments through *leverage.* On the other hand, real estate is *not a highly liquid investment* and often carries with it a *high degree of risk.* Also, it is difficult to invest in real estate without *expert advice,* and a certain amount of *mental and physical effort* is required to establish and maintain the investment.

Investment property held for *appreciation* purposes is generally expected to increase in value to a point where its selling price is enough to cover holding costs and show a profit as well. The two main factors affecting appreciation are *inflation* and the property's present and future *intrinsic value.* Real estate held for *income* purposes is generally expected to generate a steady flow of income, usually called *cash flow,* and to show a profit upon its sale.

In order for an investor to take advantage of maximum *leverage* in financing an investment, he or she should attempt to make a small down payment, pay low interest rates, and spread mortgage payments over as long a period as possible. By holding and refinancing properties, known as *pyramiding,* an investor can substantially increase his or her holdings without investing additional capital.

An investor can take advantage of special *capital-gains* tax rates, based on only 40 percent of the total gain of a real estate sale, by holding investment property for longer than six months.

By *exchanging* one property for another with an equal or greater selling value, an investor can *defer* paying tax on the gain realized until a sale is made. A total tax deferment is possible only if the investor receives no cash or other incentive to even out the exchange. If received, such cash or property is called *boot* and is taxed at the taxpayer's regular income-tax rate.

Depreciation (cost recovery) is a concept that allows an investor to recover in tax deductions the basis of an asset over the period of its useful life. Only costs of improvements to land may be recovered, not costs for the land itself. A taxpayer who uses an accelerated method of depreciation is subject to *recapture*.

An investor may defer federal income taxes on gain realized from the sale of an investment property through an *installment sale*. In this situation the investor pays income tax only on the portion of the total gain he or she receives in any year.

Individuals may also invest in real estate through an *investment syndicate;* these generally include *general and limited partnerships.* Another form of real estate investment is the *real estate investment trust* (REIT). REITs can be *equity trusts, real estate mortgage trusts,* or *combination trusts.*

Questions

1. Wilma Carver is considering investing in real estate. Her tax accountant informed her of many general advantages and disadvantages to this form of investment. Which of the following was probably among the *advantages?*

   I. tax shelters
   II. ease of sale at a top price at any given time

      a. I only   c. both I and II
      b. II only   d. neither I nor II

2. Which of the following was probably among the *disadvantages* to real estate investment the accountant mentioned to Ms. Carver?

   I. difficult to invest without expert advice
   II. physical efforts may be necessary

      a. I only   c. both I and II
      b. II only   d. neither I nor II

3. Capital gains taxes are based on:

   a. 40 percent of an investment's sales price.
   b. 40 percent of an investment's sales price less its basis.
   c. 40 percent of an investment's sales price less its adjusted basis.
   d. 40 percent of an investment's sales price less depreciation.

4. A portion of the gain on a sale of real estate may generally be recaptured when which of the following cost recovery methods is used?

   I. accelerated method
   II. straight-line method

      a. I only   c. both I and II
      b. II only   d. neither nor II

5. When an investor attempts to purchase a parcel of real estate through the use of borrowed funds, he or she is taking advantage of:

   a. leverage.   c. capital gains.
   b. depreciation. d. exchanging.

6. An investment syndicate in which all members share equally in the managerial decisions, profits, and losses involved in the venture would be an example of which of the following?

   a. real estate investment trust
   b. limited partnership
   c. real estate mortgage trust
   d. general partnership

7. The increase of money in circulation coupled with a rise in prices, resulting in a decline in the value of money, is called:

   a. appreciation.   c. negative cash flow.
   b. inflation.   d. recapture.

8. If an investor holding an income property wishes to maintain a high degree of cash flow, he or she should:

   I. keep operating expenses low.
   II. charge low rents so there will be few vacancies.

      a. I only   c. both I and II
      b. II only   d. neither I nor II

9. Investor Mary Clark is contemplating purchasing an apartment building for both income and appreciation purposes for $150,000. All else being equal, which of the following choices should yield Clark the largest percentage of return on her initial investment after the first year?

   a. Clark pays $150,000 cash for the property.
   b. Clark gives the seller a $75,000 down payment and seller a 15-year purchase-money mortgage for the balance at 11.5 percent interest.
   c. Clark gives the seller $15,000 down and obtains a 30-year mortgage for the balance at 12 percent interest.
   d. Clark gives the seller $20,000 down and agrees to pay the seller 10 percent of the unpaid balance each year for ten years, plus 11 percent interest.

10. For tax purposes, the initial cost of an investment property plus the cost of any subsequent improvements to the property, less recovery deductions, represents the investment's:

   a. adjusted basis.
   b. capital gains.
   c. basis.
   d. salvage value.

11. Julia Kinder is exchanging her apartment building for an apartment building of greater market value and must include a $10,000 boot to even out the exchange. Which of the following may she use as a boot?

   a. $10,000 cash
   b. common stock with a current market value of $10,000
   c. an auto with a current market value of $10,000
   d. any of the above if acceptable to the exchangers

12. Capital gains:

   I. may be realized only from the sale of improvements to real estate, not from the sale of land itself.
   II. are limited to 25 percent of an income property's gross income for the year of sale.

   a. I only
   b. II only
   c. both I and II
   d. neither I nor II

13. Toward which of the following might an investor direct his or her funds in order to hold real estate primarily for appreciation purposes?

   I. farmland
   II. shopping center

   a. I only
   b. II only
   c. both I and II
   d. neither I nor II

14. A property's equity represents its current value less which of the following?

   a. recovery deductions
   b. mortgage indebtedness
   c. physical improvements
   d. selling costs and recovery deductions

15. Barney Rudolph is exchanging his four-unit apartment building for a six-unit building of the same market value. His gain on the transaction is $28,000. This gain:

   a. will not be taxed, because Rudolph exchanged properties.
   b. represents the exchange's cash boot.
   c. will be taxed at the 40 percent capital-gains rate.
   d. b and c

16. In an installment sale, taxable gain is received and must be reported as income by the seller:

   a. in the year the sale is initiated.
   b. in the year the final installment payment is made.
   c. in each year that installment payments are received.
   d. at any one time during the period installment payments are received.

17. An investor in a real estate investment syndicate:

   I. is likely to obtain his or her main return on investment when the property is sold after appreciating sufficiently.
   II. receives the same tax advantages as a sole owner of investment property.

   a. I only
   b. II only
   c. both I and II
   d. neither I nor II

18. When an investor holds and refinances investment properties, using their equities as leverage, he or she is taking advantage of which of the following concepts?
    a. pyramiding
    b. negative cash flow
    c. recapture
    d. useful life

19. For which of the following can an individual claim a cost recovery deduction?
    I. carpeting included in the sale of real estate
    II. a five-acre parcel of land
    a. I only
    b. II only
    c. both I and II
    d. neither I nor II

23

Closing the Real Estate Transaction

Key Terms   Accrued item
Closing agent
Closing statement
Credit
Debit
Doctrine of relation back
Escrow
Prepaid item
Proration
Real Estate Settlement Procedures Act (RESPA)
Uniform Settlement Statement

Overview   After securing and servicing a listing, advertising the property, finding and qualifying potential buyers, and negotiating for and obtaining a signed sales contract on the seller's property, a real estate licensee is one step away from receiving his or her commission. That last step is the real estate closing, a procedure that includes both title and financial considerations. This chapter will discuss both aspects of real estate closing, focusing on the licensee's role in this concluding phase of a real estate transaction. Special emphasis will be placed on the computations necessary to settle all necessary expenses between buyer and seller, and between seller and broker; the chapter also includes a detailed example of a real estate closing to illustrate these computations.

Closing the Transaction

The preceding chapters discuss the various elements involved in and leading up to the completion, consummation, or closing of a real estate transaction. Every real estate professional needs this broad knowledge in order to carry out his or her legal responsibilities to the seller, the buyer, the community, and the public at large.

The knowledge and ability to prepare for the closing of a sale are equally important. Such knowledge is absolutely necessary to real estate brokers; and although salespeople are not usually burdened with the technicalities of closing, they must clearly understand what takes place. A real estate professional should be able to assist in preclosing arrangements and advise the parties in estimating their expenses and the approximate amounts the buyer will need and the seller will actually receive at the closing. The closing represents the culmination of the service the broker's firm provides. The sale, which the broker has negotiated, is completed, and the broker's commission (and thus the salesperson's commission) is generally paid out of the proceeds at the closing.

License Examination Closing Problems

In some states, a closing statement problem is part of the broker's licensing examination. Although the salesperson's examination does not usually include completion of a closing statement problem, most require an applicant to compute prorations, and many include the completion of a sales contract and listing agreement from the description of a sample transaction.

At the Closing

Generally speaking, the closing of a real estate transaction involves a gathering of interested parties at which the promises made in the *real estate sales contract* are kept, or *executed;* that is, the seller's deed is delivered in exchange for the purchase price. In many sales transactions, two closings actually take place at this time: (1) the closing of the buyer's loan—the disbursal of mortgage funds by the lender—and (2) the closing of the sale. A closing involving all interested parties is often called a "round table close."

As discussed in Chapter 11, a sales contract is the blueprint for the completion of a real estate transaction. A contract should be complete and should provide for all possibilities in order to avoid misunderstandings that could delay or even prevent the closing of the sale. Before going ahead with this exchange, the parties should assure themselves that the various conditions and stipulations of their sales contract have been met.

The buyer will want to be sure that the seller is delivering good title and that the property is in the promised condition. This involves inspecting the title evidence, the deed the seller will give, any documents representing the removal of undesired liens and encumbrances, the survey, the termite report, and any leases, if there are tenants on the premises. The seller will want to be sure that the buyer has obtained the stipulated financing and has sufficient funds to complete the sale. Both parties will wish to inspect the closing statement to make sure that all monies involved in the transaction have been properly accounted for. In doing this, the parties will most likely be represented by attorneys.

When the parties are satisfied that everything is in order, the exchange is made, and all pertinent documents are then recorded. The documents must be recorded in the correct order to avoid creating a defect in the title. For example, if the seller is paying off an existing loan and the buyer is obtaining a new loan, the seller's satisfaction of mortgage must be recorded before the seller's deed to the buyer. The buyer's new mortgage must then be recorded after the deed, since the lender cannot have a security interest in the buyer's property until it belongs to the buyer.

Where Closings Are Held and Who Attends

Closings may be held at a number of locations, including the offices of the title company, the lending institution, the office of one of the parties' attorneys, the broker, the county recorder (or other local recording official), or the escrow company. Those attending a closing may include any of the following interested parties:

1. buyer.
2. seller.
3. real estate agent (broker and/or salesperson).
4. attorney(s) for the seller and/or buyer.
5. representatives and/or attorneys for lending institutions involved with the buyer's new mortgage loan, the buyer's assumption of the seller's existing loan, or the seller's payoff of an existing loan.
6. representative of the title insurance company.

Closing agent. One person usually conducts the proceedings at a closing and calculates the official settlement, or division of charges and expenses between the parties. In some areas, real estate brokers preside; but more commonly, the **closing agent** is the buyer's or seller's attorney, a representative of the lender, or a representative of a title company. Some title companies and law firms employ paralegal assistants, called *closers,* who conduct all closings for their firms. The closer is the person in such offices who arranges the closing with the parties involved, prepares the closing statements, compares figures with lenders, and orders title evidence, surveys, and other miscellaneous items needed.

Broker's Role at Closing

Depending on the locality, the broker's role at a closing can vary from simply collecting his or her commission to conducting the proceedings. As discussed earlier in the text, a real estate broker is not authorized to give legal advice or otherwise engage in the practice of law. In some areas of the country, principally in some of the eastern states, this means that a broker's job is essentially over when the sales contract is signed; at that point, the attorneys take over. Even so, a broker's service generally continues after the contract is signed in that he or she advises the parties in practical matters and makes sure all the details are taken care of so that the closing can proceed smoothly. In this capacity the broker might make arrangements for such items as title evidence, surveys, appraisals, termite inspections, and repairs, or he or she might recommend sources of these services to the parties.

Lender's Interest in Closing

Whether a buyer is obtaining new financing or assuming the seller's existing loan, the lender wants to protect its security interest in the property—to make sure that the buyer is getting good, marketable title and that tax and insurance payments are maintained—so that there will be no liens with greater priority than the mortgage lien and the insurance will be paid up if the property is damaged or destroyed. For this reason, the lender will frequently require the following items: (1) a title insurance policy; (2) a fire and hazard insurance policy, with receipt for the premium; (3) additional information, such as a survey, a termite or other inspection report, or a certificate of occupancy (for newly constructed buildings); (4) establishment of a reserve, or escrow, account for tax and insurance payments; and possibly (5) representation by its own attorney at the closing.

RESPA Requirements

The federal **Real Estate Settlement Procedures Act (RESPA),** enacted in 1974 and revised in 1975, was created to ensure that the buyer and seller in a residential real estate sale or transfer have knowledge of all settlement costs. In this context, residential real estate includes one- to four-family homes, cooperatives, and condominiums. *RESPA requirements apply when the purchase is financed by a federally related mortgage loan.* Federally related loans include those (1) made by banks, savings and loan associations, or other lenders whose deposits are insured by federal agencies (FDIC or FSLIC); (2) insured by the FHA or guaranteed by the VA; (3) administered by the U.S. Department of Housing and Urban Development; or (4) intended to be sold by the lender to Fannie Mae, Ginnie Mae, or Freddie Mac.

RESPA regulations apply only to transactions involving new first mortgage loans. A transaction financed solely by a purchase-money mortgage taken back by the seller, an installment contract (land contract of sale, contract for deed), or the buyer's assumption of the seller's existing loan would not be covered by RESPA, unless the terms of the assumed loan are modified or the lender imposes charges of over $50 for the assumption. As of June 20, 1976, when a transaction is covered by RESPA, the following requirements must be complied with:

1. *Special information booklet:* Lenders must give a copy of the HUD booklet *Settlement Costs and You* to every person from whom they receive or for whom they prepare a loan application. This booklet provides the borrower with general information about settlement (closing) costs and explains the various RESPA provisions, including a line-by-line discussion of the Uniform Settlement Statement (see item 3).

2. *Good faith estimate of settlement costs:* At the time of the loan application, or within three business days, the lender must provide the borrower with a good faith estimate of the settlement costs the borrower is likely to incur. This estimate may be a specific figure or a range of costs based upon comparable past transactions in the area. In addition, if the lender requires use of a particular attorney or title company to conduct the closing, the lender must state whether it has any business relationship with that firm and must estimate the charges for this service.

3. *Uniform Settlement Statement (HUD Form 1):* RESPA provides that loan closing information must be prepared on a special HUD form, the **Uniform Settlement Statement,** designed to detail all financial particulars of a transaction. A copy of this form is illustrated in figure 23.3. The completed statement must itemize all charges imposed by the lender. Charges incurred by the buyer and seller, contracted for separately and outside the closing, do not have to be disclosed. Items paid for prior to the closing must be clearly marked as such on the statement and are omitted from the totals. This statement must be made available for inspection by the borrower *at or before* the closing. Upon the borrower's request, the closing agent must permit the borrower to inspect the settlement statement, to the extent that the figures are available, one business day

before the closing. Lenders must retain these statements for two years after the date of closing unless the loan (and its servicing) is sold or otherwise disposed of. The Uniform Settlement Statement may be altered to allow for local custom, and certain lines may be deleted if they do not apply in the area.

4. *Prohibition against kickbacks:* RESPA explicitly prohibits the payment of kickbacks, or unearned fees, such as when an insurance agency pays a kickback to a lender for referring one of the lender's recent customers to the agency. This prohibition does *not* include fee splitting between cooperating brokers or members of multiple-listing services, brokerage referral arrangements, or the division of a commission between a broker and his or her salespeople.

RESPA is administered by the U.S. Department of Housing and Urban Development (HUD).

The Title Procedure

As discussed earlier, the principle of caveat emptor requires the purchaser and the purchaser's lender to assure themselves that the seller's property and title comply with the contract requirements. The sales contract usually includes time limitations for the parties to obtain and present title evidence and remove any objections to the title. A contract that includes the provision "time is of the essence" expresses the agreement of the parties that all *time limitations are to be met exactly as stated.*

The seller usually is required to show that he or she owns the property by producing a current *abstract* or *title commitment* from the title insurance company. When an abstract of title is used, the purchaser's attorney examines it and issues an opinion of title. This opinion, like the title commitment, sets forth the status of the seller's title, showing liens, encumbrances, easements, conditions, or restrictions that appear on the record and to which the seller's title is subject.

On the date when the sale is actually completed, that is, the date of delivery of the deed, the buyer has a title commitment or an abstract that was issued several days or weeks before the closing. For this reason, the title or abstract company is usually required to make two searches of the public records. The first, as discussed, shows the status of the seller's title on the date of the sales contract; the seller usually pays the charges for this report (depending on local custom). The second search is made after the closing and covers the date when the deed is recorded to the purchaser; the purchaser generally pays to "bring the title down" to the closing date.

In this later search, the seller is usually required to execute an *affidavit of title.* This is a sworn statement in which the seller assures the title company (and the buyer) that since the date of the title examination there have been no judgments, bankruptcies, or divorces involving the seller, no unrecorded deeds or contracts made, no repairs or improvements that have not been paid for, and no defects in the title that the seller knows of, and that he or she is in possession of the premises. This form is always required by the title insurance company before it will issue an owner's policy, particularly an extended-coverage policy, to the buyer. Through this affidavit, the title company obtains the right to sue the seller if his or her statements in the affidavit prove incorrect.

In some areas where real estate sales transactions are customarily closed through an escrow, the escrow agreement generally includes provision for an extended-coverage policy to be issued to the buyer as of the date of closing. In such cases, there is no gap between the date of commitment and the closing, so there is no need for the seller to execute an affidavit of title.

In certain areas of the country, primarily in the eastern states, it is strictly the buyer's responsibility to assure him- or herself that the seller's title is good. In such cases, the *buyer* generally orders and pays for the title evidence.

Checking the Premises

In general, it is important for the buyer to inspect the property to determine the interests of any parties in possession or other interests that cannot be determined from inspecting the public record. A *survey* is frequently required so that the purchaser will know the location and size of the property he or she intends to purchase. The contract will specify whether the seller is to pay for this. It is usual for the survey to "spot" the location of all buildings, driveways, fences, and other improvements located primarily on the premises being purchased, as well as any such improvements located on adjoining property that may encroach upon the premises being bought. The survey also sets out, in full, any existing easements and encroachments. So that the survey will clearly identify the location of the property, the house number, if any, should be stated.

Releasing Existing Liens

When the purchaser is paying cash or is obtaining a new mortgage in order to purchase the property, the seller's existing mortgage usually is paid in full and released of record. In order to know the exact amount required to pay the existing mortgage, the seller secures a current *payoff statement* from the mortgagee. This payoff statement sets forth the unpaid amount of principal, interest due through the date of payment, the fee for issuing the release deed, credits, if any, for tax and insurance reserves, and any penalties that may be due because the loan is being prepaid before its maturity. The same procedure would be followed for any other liens that must be released before the buyer takes title.

For transactions in which the buyer is assuming the seller's existing mortgage loan, the buyer will want to know the exact balance of the loan as of the closing date. In some areas it is customary for the buyer to obtain an *estoppel certificate* from the seller, stating the exact balance due and the last interest payment made.

Closing in Escrow

As discussed in Chapter 11, a real estate transaction may be closed through an escrow. Although there are a few states where transactions are never closed in escrow, escrow closings are used to some extent in most states; in the western section of the country, the majority of transactions are closed in escrow.

An **escrow** is a method of closing a real estate transaction in which a disinterested third party is authorized to act as escrow agent and is given the responsibility to coordinate the closing activities. The escrow agent may also be called the *escrowee* or *escrow holder.* The escrow agent may be an attorney, a title company, a trust company, an escrow company, or the escrow department of a lending institution. While many brokerages do offer escrow services, a broker cannot be a disinterested party in a transaction from which he or she expects to collect a commission. Because the escrow agent is placed in a position of great trust, many states have laws regulating escrow agents and limiting who may serve in this capacity.

The Escrow Procedure   When a transaction will be closed in escrow, the buyer and seller choose an escrow agent and execute an escrow agreement after the sales contract is signed. This agreement sets forth the details of the transaction and the instructions to the escrow agent. Once the contract is signed, the broker turns over the earnest money to the escrow agent, who deposits it in a special trust, or escrow, account.

The escrow agreement requires the buyer and seller to deposit all pertinent documents and other items with the escrow agent before the specified date of closing. The seller will usually deposit:

1. the *deed* conveying the property to the buyer.
2. title *evidence* (abstract, title insurance policy, or Torrens certificate).
3. existing fire and hazard *insurance* policies.
4. letter from the mortgagee of the existing mortgage, setting forth the *amount* needed to pay the loan in full, or the exact amount the buyer will assume.
5. *affidavits of title* (if required).
6. *payoff letter* (estoppel certificate) if the seller's mortgage is to be paid off.
7. other instruments or documents necessary to clear the title or to complete the transaction.

The buyer will deposit:

1. the balance of the *cash needed* to complete the purchase.
2. *mortgage papers,* if the buyer is securing a new mortgage.
3. other documents needed to complete the transaction.

The escrow agent is given the authority to examine the title evidence. When clear title is shown in the name of the buyer and all other conditions of the escrow agreement have been met, the agent is authorized to disburse the purchase price—minus all charges and expenses—to the seller and record the deed and mortgage or trust deed (if a new mortgage has been executed by the purchaser) as provided by the escrow agreement.

If the escrow agent's examination of the title discloses liens against the seller or a lien for which the seller is responsible, the escrow agreement generally provides that a portion of the purchase price can be withheld from the seller and used to pay such liens as are necessary to clear the title so the transaction can be closed.

If the seller cannot clear his or her title, or if for any reason the sale cannot be consummated and the buyer will not accept the title as it is, then the escrow agreement generally provides that the parties be returned to their former status. To accomplish this, the purchaser reconveys title to the seller and the escrow agent restores all purchase money to the buyer. Because the escrow is dependent upon specific conditions being met before the transfer becomes binding on the parties, the courts have held that the parties can be reinstated to their former status.

Some advantages of closing a sale through an escrow are: (1) the buyer's money will not be paid to the seller until the seller's title is acceptable under the terms of the contract, (2) the seller knows that the buyer's money must actually be received (the check must clear) before title passes, so the seller is assured of getting the purchase price, and (3) neither party need be present when title is passed. Because the escrow agent will run a final inspection of the title before the closing date, *the buyer is protected from the risk of judgments and other liens originating against the seller's title prior to the date of closing.*

| **In Practice . . .** | *Fees charged by the escrow agent are typically split between buyer and seller. However, a purchaser under new VA financing is not allowed to pay any escrow fees, so all such costs are the sole responsibility of the seller. In addition, FHA regulations stipulate that the buyer may pay up to one-half of fees charged by the escrow agent.* |

Doctrine of Relation Back

If a seller deposits his or her deed with an escrow agent under the terms of a valid escrow agreement and then dies, but thereafter the conditions of the escrow are satisfied, the *deed passes title to the purchaser as of the date it was delivered to the escrow agent.* This is called the **doctrine of relation back**—the title relates back to the date on which the deed was deposited in escrow. When the conditions of the escrow agreement have not been met, however, the deed is not considered as having been delivered and title does not pass to the purchaser.

Preparation of Closing Statements

A typical real estate sales transaction involves numerous expenses for both parties in addition to the purchase price. Furthermore, there are a number of property expenses that the seller will have already paid in advance for a set period of time or that the buyer will pay in the future. The financial responsibility for these items must be *prorated,* or divided, between the buyer and the seller. In closing a transaction, it is customary to account for all these items by preparing a written statement to determine how much money the buyer needs and how much the seller will net after the broker's commission and expenses. While there are many different formats of closing statements, or settlement statements, all are designed to achieve the same results.

How the Closing Statement Works

The completion of a **closing statement** involves an accounting of the parties' debits and credits. A **debit** is a charge, an amount that the party being debited owes and must pay at the closing. A **credit** is an amount entered in a person's favor—either an amount that the party being credited has already paid, an amount that he or she must be reimbursed for, or an amount the buyer promises to pay in the form of a loan.

To determine the amount the buyer needs at the closing, the buyer's debits are totaled—any expenses and prorated amounts for items prepaid by the seller are added to the purchase price. Then the buyer's credits are totaled. These would include the earnest money (already paid), the balance of the loan the buyer is obtaining or assuming, and the seller's share of any prorated items that the buyer will pay in the future. Finally, the total of the buyer's credits is subtracted from the total amount the buyer owes (debits) to arrive at the actual amount of cash the buyer must bring to the closing. Usually the buyer brings a bank cashier's check or a certified personal check.

A similar procedure is followed to determine how much money the seller will actually receive. The seller's debits and credits are each totaled. The credits would include the purchase price, plus the buyer's share of any prorated items that the seller has prepaid.

The seller's debits would include expenses, the seller's share of prorated items to be paid later by the buyer, and the balance of any mortgage loan or other lien that the seller is paying off. Finally, the total of the seller's charges is subtracted from the total credits to arrive at the amount the seller will receive.

Expenses   In addition to the payment of the sales price and the proration of taxes, interest, and the like, a number of other expenses and charges may be involved in a real estate transaction. These may include the following items.

Broker's commission. The broker's commission is usually paid by the seller, since the broker is usually the seller's agent. When the buyer has employed the broker, the buyer pays the commission. As discussed in Chapter 5, it is important that the broker's rate of commission be negotiated between the broker and the principal for each transaction and be specifically stated in the listing agreement.

Attorney's fees. If either of the parties' attorneys will be paid from the closing proceeds, that party will be charged with the expense in the closing statement.

Recording expenses. The charges for recording different types of documents vary widely among states and sections of a state. In one county, for example, the charge for recording a single-page deed may be $10, and a four-page mortgage might be about $15. These charges are established by law and are based upon the number of words and pages included in the instrument. You should verify recording charges in your area.

The *seller* usually pays for recording charges (filing fees), which are necessary in order to clear all defects and furnish the purchaser with a clear title in accordance with the terms of the contract. Items usually charged to the seller would include the recording of release deeds or satisfaction of mortgages, quitclaim deeds, affidavits, and satisfaction of mechanic's lien claims. The *purchaser* pays for recording charges incident to the actual transfer of title. Items usually charged to the purchaser include recording the deed that conveys title to the purchaser and a mortgage or trust deed executed by the purchaser.

Transfer tax. As discussed in Chapter 12, most states and/or counties require some form of transfer tax, conveyance fee, or tax stamps on real estate conveyances. This expense is usually borne by the seller, although customs may vary.

Title expenses. The responsibility for title expenses varies according to local custom. As discussed earlier, in most areas the seller is required to furnish evidence of good title and pay for the title search. If the buyer's attorney inspects the evidence or if the buyer purchases title insurance policies, the buyer is charged for these expenses. In some situations the title or abstract company is required to make two searches of the public records; the first showing the status of the seller's title on the date of the sales contract, and the second continuing after the closing and through the date the purchaser's deed is recorded. In such cases, the seller pays for the initial search and the purchaser pays for the "later date" charge.

A title or abstract company will normally furnish an estimate, usually without charge, of the customary charges for these services in your area.

Loan fees. When the purchaser is securing a mortgage to finance the purchase, the lender (mortgage company) will usually charge a service charge, loan origination fee, or mortgage commission of from one to three percent or more of the loan. The fee is a flat charge and is usually paid by the purchaser at the time the transaction is closed. If calculated as a percentage of the loan principal, such fees are spoken of as *points;* for example, a two-percent fee is called *two points.* In addition, the buyer may be charged an assumption fee if he or she assumes the seller's existing financing.

The seller also may be charged fees by a lender. If the buyer finances the purchase with a VA loan, the seller may be required to pay discount points as discussed in Chapter 15. Also, under the terms of some mortgage loans, the seller may be required to pay a prepayment charge or penalty for paying off his or her mortgage loan in advance of its due date.

Tax reserves and insurance reserves (escrows). A *reserve* is a sum of money set aside to be used later for a particular purpose. The mortgage lender usually requires the borrower to establish and maintain a reserve so that the borrower will have sufficient funds to pay general real estate taxes and renew insurance when these items become due.

To set up the reserve, the borrower is required to make a lump-sum payment to the lender when the mortgage money is paid out (usually at the time of closing). The amount first paid into this reserve account should equal at least the earned (used up) portion of both the general real estate taxes and insurance—the amount of taxes or insurance premium for the period *prior* to closing the sale, usually including the date on which the sale is closed. Thereafter, the borrower is required to pay into the reserve an amount equal to one month's portion of the *estimated* general real estate tax and insurance premium as part of the monthly payment made to the mortgage company.

Appraisal fees. Either the seller or the purchaser pays the appraisal fees, depending on who orders the appraisal. When the buyer obtains a mortgage, it is customary for the lender to require an appraisal, which the buyer pays for. A residential mortgage appraisal may cost from $90 to $150.

Survey fees. If the purchaser obtains new mortgage financing, he or she customarily pays the survey fees. In some cases the sales contract may require the seller to furnish a survey.

Prorations

Most closings involve the division of financial responsibility between the buyer and seller for such items as loan interest, taxes, rents, fuel, and utility bills. These allowances are called **prorations.** Prorations are necessary to ensure that expenses are fairly divided between the seller and the buyer. For example, the seller usually owes current taxes that have not been billed; the buyer would want this settled at the closing. In states where taxes must be paid in advance, the seller would be entitled to a rebate at the closing. If the buyer assumes the seller's existing mortgage, the seller usually owes the buyer an allowance for accrued interest through the date of closing.

Accrued items are items to be prorated—such as taxes—that have been earned during the occupancy or ownership of the seller but have not been paid by the seller, and are credited to the purchaser. (*Earned,* as used here, means owed by the seller.) Each accrued item will be paid by the purchaser at some later time, so the seller must pay his or her share (the earned portion) at the closing by giving a credit to the purchaser.

Prepaid items are items to be prorated—such as insurance—that have been prepaid by the seller but not fully earned (not fully used up). They are therefore credits to the seller.

General rules for prorating. The rules or customs governing the computation of prorations for the closing of a real estate sale vary widely from state to state. In many states the real estate boards and the bar association have established closing rules and procedures. In some cases these rules and procedures control closings for the entire state; in others they merely affect closings within a given city, town, or county.

Here are some general rules to guide you in studying the closing procedure and preparing the closing statement:

1. In most states, the seller owns the property on the day of closing, and prorations or apportionments are usually made *to and including the day of closing.* In a few states, however, it is specifically provided that the buyer owns the property on the closing date and that adjustments shall be made as of the day preceding the day on which title is closed.

2. Mortgage interest, general real estate taxes, water taxes, insurance premiums, and similar expenses are usually computed by using *360 days in a year and 30 days in a month.* However, the rules in some areas provide for computing prorations on the basis of the actual number of days in the calendar month of closing. The sales contract may specify which method is to be used.

3. Accrued *general real estate* taxes that are not yet due are usually prorated at the closing. When the amount of the current real estate tax cannot be definitely determined, the proration is usually based on the last obtainable tax bill. *Special assessments* for such municipal improvements as sewers, water mains, or streets are usually paid in annual installments over several years. The municipality usually charges the property owner annual interest on the outstanding balance of future installments. In a sales transaction, the seller pays the current installment and the buyer assumes all future installments. *The special assessment installment is not generally prorated at the closing;* some buyers, however, insist that the seller allow them a credit for the seller's share of the interest to the closing date.

4. *Rents* are usually adjusted on the basis of the *actual* number of days in the month of closing. It is customary for the seller to receive the rents for the day of closing and to pay all expenses for that day. If any rents for the current month are uncollected when the sale is closed, the buyer will often agree by a separate letter to collect the rents if possible and remit the pro rata share to the seller.

5. *Security deposits* made by tenants to cover the last month's rent of the lease or to cover the cost of repairing damage caused by the tenant are generally transferred by the seller to the buyer; some leases may require the tenant's consent to such a transfer of the deposit.

6. Unpaid *wages of building employees* are prorated if the sale is closed between wage payment dates.

7. There is little uniformity in the rules covering *chattels and fixtures.* Each area has established customs that are usually followed. However, the following items are normally considered to be fixtures and are included in the conveyance free and clear of liens, unless there is an agreement otherwise: draperies, shades, blinds, screens, storm doors and windows, plumbing and heating equipment, built-in appliances, and tools. In apartment buildings, the following may also be included: hall carpets, refrigerators, gas and electric stoves, and such garden tools as lawn mowers and hoses.

You should verify these proration rules with the customs in your area.

Accounting for Credits and Charges

The items that must be accounted for in the closing statement fall into two general categories: (1) prorations or other amounts due to either the buyer or seller (credit to) and paid for by the other party (debit to) and (2) expenses or items paid by the seller or buyer (debit only).

The following list shows which items are commonly credited to the buyer, and which to the seller. Other items may be included in such a list, depending upon the customs of your area.

Items Credited to Buyer (debited to seller)	Items Credited to Seller (debited to buyer)
1. buyer's earnest money*	1. sales price*
2. unpaid principal balance of outstanding mortgage being assumed by buyer*	2. prorated premium for unearned (prepaid) portion of fire insurance
3. earned interest on existing assumed mortgage not yet payable (accrued)	3. coal or fuel oil on hand, usually figured at current market price (prepaid)
4. earned portion of general real estate tax not yet due (accrued)	4. insurance and tax reserve (if any) when outstanding mortgage is being assumed by buyer (prepaid)
5. unearned portion of current rent collected in advance	5. refund to seller of prepaid water charge and similar expenses
6. earned janitor's salary (and sometimes vacation allowance)	6. unearned portion of general real estate tax, if paid in advance
7. tenants' security deposits*	
8. purchase-money mortgage (see Chapter 15)	

*These items are not prorated; they are entered in full as listed.

Note that the *buyer's earnest money,* while credited to the buyer, *is not debited to the seller.* The buyer receives a credit because he or she has already paid that amount toward the purchase price; however, under the usual sales contract the money is held by the broker or escrow agent until the settlement, when it will be included as part of the total amount due the seller. Note also that if the seller is paying off an existing loan and the buyer is obtaining a new one, these two items are accounted for with a debit only to the seller for the amount of the payoff and a credit only to the buyer for the amount of the new loan.

Accounting for expenses. Expenses paid out of the closing proceeds are debited only to the party making the payment. Occasionally an expense item—such as an escrow fee, settlement fee, or, in a few areas, transfer tax—may be shared by the buyer and the seller, and each party will be debited for one-half the expense.

The Arithmetic of Prorating

Accurate prorating involves four considerations: (1) what the item being prorated is; (2) whether it is an accrued item that requires the determination of an earned amount; (3) whether it is a prepaid item that requires the unearned amount—a refund to the seller—to be determined; and (4) what arithmetic processes must be used. The information contained in the previous sections will assist in answering the first three questions.

The computation of a proration involves identifying a yearly charge for the item to be prorated, then dividing by 12 to determine a monthly charge for the item. It is usually also necessary to identify a daily charge for the item by dividing the monthly charge by the number of days in the month. These smaller portions are then multiplied by the number of months and/or days in the prorated time period to determine the accrued or unearned amount that will be figured in the settlement.

Using this general principle, there are three basic methods of calculating prorations:

1. The yearly charge is divided by a *360-day year,* or 12 months of 30 days each.
2. The monthly charge is divided by the *actual number of days in the month of closing* to determine the amount.
3. The *yearly charge is divided by 365* to determine the daily charge. Then the actual number of days in the proration period is determined, and this number is multiplied by the daily charge.

In some cases, when a sale is closed on the fifteenth of the month the one-half month's charge is computed by simply dividing the monthly charge by 2.

The final proration figure will vary slightly, depending on which computation method is used. The final figure will also vary according to the number of decimal places to which the division is carried. *All of the computations in this text are computed by carrying the division to three decimal places.* The third decimal place is rounded off to cents only after the final proration figure is determined.

Accrued Items

Consider unpaid real estate taxes, which are an accrued item. When the tax is levied for the calendar year and is payable during that year or in the following year, the accrued portion is for the period from January 1 to the date of closing (or to the day before the closing in states where the sale date is excluded). If the current tax bill has not yet been issued, the parties must agree on an estimated amount based on the previous year's bill and any known changes in assessment or tax levy for the current year.

For example, assume a sale is to be closed on September 17 and current real estate taxes of $1,200 are to be prorated accordingly. The accrued period, then, is 8 months and 17 days. First determine the prorated cost of the real estate tax per month and day:

$$
\begin{array}{cc}
\underline{\quad \$100 \text{ per month}} & \underline{\quad 3.333 \text{ per day}} \\
12)\$1,200 & 30)\$100.000 \\
\text{months} & \text{days}
\end{array}
$$

Next, multiply these figures by the accrued period and add the totals to determine the prorated real estate tax:

$$
\begin{array}{lll}
\$100 & \$\ 3.333 & \$800.000 \\
\underline{\times\ \ 8\ \text{months}} & \underline{\times\ \ \ \ 17\ \text{days}} & \underline{+56.661} \\
\$800 & \$56.661 & \$856.661
\end{array}
$$

Thus, the accrued real estate tax for 8 months and 17 days is *$856.66* (rounded off to two decimal places after the final computation). This amount represents the seller's accrued *earned* tax; it will be a *credit to the buyer* and a *debit to the seller* on the closing statement.

To compute this proration according to the actual number of days in the accrued period, the following method would be used. The accrued period from January 1 to September 17 runs 260 days (January's 31 days plus February's 28 days, and so on). A tax bill of $1,200 ÷ 365 days = $3.288 per day. $3.288 × 260 days = $854.880, or *$854.88.*

In Practice ...   *On state brokers' examinations, tax prorations are usually based on a 30-day month (360-day year) unless specified otherwise in the problem. Note that this may differ with your local customs regarding tax prorations. Many title insurance companies provide proration charts that detail tax factors for each day in the year. To determine a tax proration using one of these charts, you would multiply the factor given for the closing date by the annual real estate tax.*

Prepaid Items   Assume that the water is billed in advance by the city without using a meter. The six months' billing is $8 for the period ending October 31. The sale is to be closed on August 3. Since the water is paid to October 31, the prepaid time must be computed. Using a 30-day basis, the time period is the 27 days left in August plus two full months: $8 ÷ 6 = $1.333 per month. For one day, divide $1.333 by 30, which equals $.044 per day. The prepaid period is two months and 27 days, so:

$$
\begin{array}{ll}
27\ \text{days} \times \$.044 & = \$1.188 \\
2\ \text{months} \times \$1.333 & = \underline{\$2.666} \\
& \ \ \ \$3.854,\ \text{or}\ \$3.85
\end{array}
$$

This is a prepaid item and is *credited to the seller* and *debited to the buyer* on the closing statement.

To figure this on the basis of the actual days in the month of closing, the following process would be used:

$$
\begin{array}{ll}
\$1.333\ \text{per month} \div 31\ \text{days in August} & = \$.043\ \text{per day} \\
\text{August 4 through August 31} & = 28\ \text{days} \\
28\ \text{days} \times \$.043 & = \$1.204 \\
2\ \text{months} \times \$1.333 & = \$2.666 \\
\$1.204 + \$2.666 & = \$3.870,\ \text{or}\ \$3.87
\end{array}
$$

Prorating Prepaid Insurance Premiums   Insurance policies are written for periods of one, three, and five years. The time period covered by an insurance policy includes the date the policy expires. Carefully check the period for which the premium has been paid when you figure insurance premium prorations. In figuring the proration of the insurance premium, you must ascertain the number of future days, months, and years for which the premium has been paid. The formula commonly used for this purpose is as follows (the dates given are examples):

	Years	Months	Days
Premium paid to (April 19, 1986)	1986	4	19
Date of closing (May 24, 1984)	1984	5	24
Number of future years, months, and days for which premium is paid			

Start with the "days" column. When, as in this example, the days on the top line are less than those on the bottom line, borrow one month from the "months" column and increase the "days" by 30 or 31, *using the number of days in the month of closing.* In this case, May has 31 days, so you will borrow 31 to make 50 days. Then subtract 24 days from 50 days and enter 26 days.

Then move to the months. When the number of months on the top line is less than that on the bottom, borrow a year by reducing the "years" by one and adding 12 months to the "months" column. Subtract the months; then subtract the years.

The completed example with all adjustments made would be as follows:

	Years	Months	Days
Premium paid to (April 19, 1986)	1985 ~~1986~~	15 16 ~~4~~	50 ~~19~~
Closing date (May 24, 1984)	1984	5	24
Unearned, or unexpired, period	1	10	26

A mortgage lender who wishes to determine the initial deposit for a borrower to establish an insurance reserve for future insurance renewals must compute the *earned* portion of the insurance premium. Use the same process, except that the closing date is on the top line and the beginning date of the insurance policy is on the bottom line. When borrowing a month and converting it to days in this procedure, use the number of days in the month the insurance began.

	Years	Months	Days
Date of closing	1983 ~~1984~~	17 ~~5~~	24
Beginning date of insurance	1983	6	15
Earned, or expired, period		11	9

In Practice . . .   *Three-year homeowner's insurance policies are no longer common of late, due to the high cost of such coverage. Where such policies do exist, many insurance companies will not allow them to be assumed. The seller will cancel his or her policy and the buyer will take out a new one, both on the closing date. However, most state brokers' exams still include problems dealing with three-year policies to be assumed by the purchaser.*

Sample Closing Statements

As stated previously, there are many possible formats for settlement computations. The remaining portion of this chapter illustrates a sample transaction on two common types of closing statements and on the HUD Uniform Settlement Statement. While the examples are illustrated on preprinted closing forms, this is not necessary. A closer could calculate a settlement on a blank sheet by entering the appropriate items in any acceptable format.

Basic Information of Offer and Sale

John and Joanne Iuro listed their home at 3045 Racine Avenue with the Open Door Real Estate Company. The listing price was $118,500, and possession could be given within two weeks after all parties have signed the contract. Under the terms of the listing agreement, the sellers agreed to pay the broker a commission of 7 percent of the sales price.

On May 18, the Open Door Real Estate Company submitted a contract offer to the Iuros from Brook Redemann, a bachelor. Redemann offered $115,000 and was able to assume the existing mortgage. The Iuros signed the contract on May 29, 1986. Closing was set for June 15, 1986, at the office of the Open Door Real Estate Company. The broker holds earnest money in the amount of $15,000.

The unpaid balance of the Iuros' mortgage as of June 1, 1986 will be $57,700. Payments are $680 per month with interest at 11 percent per annum on the unpaid balance. The Iuros agreed to the assumption of this mortgage if the prospective purchaser could make up the difference in cash. The sellers would not take back a second mortgage.

The sellers submitted evidence of title in the form of a title insurance binder. The cost of this title service was $550, which was paid by the real estate broker on behalf of the sellers. Recording charges of $20 were paid for the recording of two instruments to clear defects in the sellers' title, and state transfer tax stamps in the amount of $115 ($.50 per $500 of sale price or fraction thereof) were affixed to the deed. These amounts were also advanced by the Open Door Real Estate Company on behalf of the sellers. In addition, the sellers must pay an attorney's fee of $400 for preparation of the deed and for legal representation; this amount will be paid from the closing proceeds.

The buyer must pay an attorney's fee of $300 for examination of the title evidence and legal representation, as well as $10 to record the deed. These amounts will also be paid from the closing proceeds.

There is a paid-up insurance policy on the property that will be assumed by the buyer. This policy runs for three years and will expire on March 1, 1988. The premium for this policy was $760.

County real estate taxes for the year 1985, amounting to $1,725, have been paid. According to the contract, general real estate taxes, insurance premiums, and mortgage interest are to be prorated on the basis of 30 days to a month. The mortgage payment due June 1, 1986, has been paid by the sellers. The buyer has agreed to reimburse the sellers for the $825 balance in their tax and reserve account, which is held by the savings and loan association.

Computing the Prorations and Charges

Following are illustrations of the various steps in computing the prorations and other amounts to be included in the settlement.

1. *Closing date*: June 15, 1986

2. *Commission*: 7% × $115,000 (sales price) = *$8,050*

3. *Mortgage interest*:
   11% × $57,700 (principal due after 6/1 payment) = $6,347 interest per year
   $6,347 ÷ 360 days = $17.631 interest per day
   15 days of accrued interest to be paid by the seller
   15 × $17.631 = $264.465, or *$264.46 interest owed by the seller*

4. *Insurance* (paid in advance by seller; buyer will reimburse at closing for unearned portion):
   3-year premium of $760 expires March 1, 1988:
   $760.00 ÷ 3 years = $253.333 per year
   $253.333 ÷ 12 months = $21.111 per month
   $21.111 ÷ 30 days = $.704 per day
   Unearned period:

1987	14	31			
~~1988~~	~~3~~	~~1~~	1 year × $253.333 =	$253.333
1986	6	15	8 months × 21.111 =	$168.888
1	8	16	16 days × $.704 =	$ 11.264
				$433.485 or
				$433.48 buyer owes seller

5. *Real estate taxes* (estimated based on 1985 tax bill of $1,725):
   $1,725.00 ÷ 12 months = $143.75 per month
   $ 143.75 ÷ 30 days = $ 4.792 per day
   The earned period is from January 1, 1986, to and including June 15, 1986, and equals 5 months, 15 days:
   $143.75 × 5 months = $718.750
   $4.792 × 15 days   = $ 71.880
   $790.630, or *$790.63 seller owes buyer*

6. *Transfer tax* ($.50 per $500 of consideration or fraction thereof):
   $115,000 ÷ $500 = 230
   230 × $.50 = *$115.00 transfer tax owed by seller*

Separate Statements for Buyer and Seller

The settlement in figure 23.1 illustrates the closing of the sample transaction with separate closing statements for the buyer (left) and seller (right). Also in use is a similar format (not shown) in which the settlement figures are entered on a single sheet with four columns of figures—the buyer's debits and credits and the seller's debits and credits.

Cash reconciliation. The following tabulation reconciles the cash flow of funds at this closing. The cash received by the broker or closing agent is compared to the cash disbursed. To balance, the receipts must equal the disbursements. This form of tabulation can be used with any closing statement format and is useful in assuring that all items have been accurately entered on the buyer's and seller's statements.

		Receipts	Disbursements
Cash Received:			
Earnest money		$15,000.00	
From buyer to close		42,813.39	
Cash Disbursed:			
Sellers' expenses:			
commission	$8,050.00		
title insurance	550.00		
attorney	400.00		
transfer tax	115.00		
recording	20.00		
	$9,135.00		$9,135.00
Buyers' expenses:			
attorney	$ 300.00		
recording	10.00		
	$310.00		310.00
Balance due sellers:			48,368.39
		$57,813.39	$57,813.39

Single-Statement Closing Format

The statement in figure 23.2 illustrates the same sample transaction with a different closing statement format. This statement is divided into two parts: the division of items between buyer and seller, and the broker's settlement. The upper portion of the statement accounts for those items given by one party to the other—items that in the other format would be credited to one party and debited to the other. As you can see, only the credit is entered; there are no debit entries on this portion of the statement. While the format of this statement is different from that of figure 23.1, the results are the same—the buyer must pay the seller a balance of $42,813.39.

Broker's settlement. Because the broker is the seller's agent, it is customary for the broker to hold the earnest money deposit under the terms of the sales contract until the sale is closed. The bottom portion of this statement, the broker's settlement with the seller (used in many areas of the country), is similar to the cash reconciliation illustrated earlier.

The earnest money received by the broker is entered as a credit to the seller. All of the expenses paid by the broker for the seller are entered as debits. These would include, for example, the cost of the broker's commission, transfer tax, recording fees, and title examination charges.

Various additional items can be included in this type of statement. If, as in the sample transaction, the broker has paid some of the buyer's expenses from the seller's earnest money held by the broker, the seller must collect from the buyer for these expenses. In the closing statement in figure 23.2, note the "credit seller" entries by which the buyer reimburses the seller (attorney's fee and recording fee). If such items are to be included in this form of closing statement, they are entered in the broker's settlement as debits and then reentered in the upper portions as credits to the seller.

Figure 23.1
Separate Statements
for Buyer and Seller

Property Address ___3045 N. Racine___

Seller ___John & Joanne Iuro___   Date of contract ___June 15, 1986___

Buyer ___Brook Redemann___

SETTLEMENT DATE: June 15, 1986	BUYER'S STATEMENT		SELLER'S STATEMENT	
	DEBIT	CREDIT	DEBIT	CREDIT
Purchase Price	115,000.00			115,000.00
Earnest Money Deposit		15,000.00		
First Mortgage Balance		57,700.00	57,700.00	
Interest: 6/1 – 6/15		264.46	269.96	
Real Estate Taxes 1/1 – 6/15		790.63	790.63	
Insurance	433.48			433.48
Tax Escrow	825.00			825.00
Broker's Commission			8,050.00	
Title Insurance			550.00	
Recording Fees	10.00		20.00	
Transfer Tax			115.00	
Attorney's Fees	300.00		400.00	
Subtotals	116,568.48	73,755.09	67,890.09	116,258.48
Due from Buyer to close		42,813.39		
Due to Seller to close			48,368.39	
Totals	$116,568.48	$116,568.48	$116,258.48	$116,258.48

Figure 23.2
Single-Statement
Closing Form

CLOSING STATEMENT-REAL ESTATE	No. 377 FEBRUARY, 1967	GEORGE E. COLE® LEGAL FORMS

CLOSING STATEMENT

PROPERTY __3045 Racine__   BROKER __Open Door Real Estate Co.__

SELLER __John & Joanne Iuro__   ADDRESS __3045 N. Racine__

PURCHASER __Brook Redemann__   ADDRESS __230 Elm__

DATE OF CONTRACT __May 29, 1986__   DATE OF CLOSING __June 15, 1986__

DATE FOR POSSESSION __June 15, 1986__

	CREDIT PURCHASER		CREDIT SELLER	
Purchase Price			$ 115,000	00
Earnest Money	$15,000	00		
First Mortgage	57,700	00		
Interest	264	46		
Second Mortgage				
Interest				
General Taxes 19 85 ($1,725 paid)				
General Taxes 19 85 pro rated from 1/1 to 6/15	790	63		
Special Assessments				
Special Assessments				
Insurance premiums, Unearned (see statement on reverse side)			433	48
Escrow			825	00
Rents from _____ to _____				
Fuel _____ @ $_____ per _____				
Janitor from _____ to _____				
Water Taxes from _____ to _____				
Gas & Light from _____ to _____				
Attorney's Fees - Buyer			300	00
Recording Fees - Buyer			10	00
Check or cash to Balance Due From Buyer	42,813	39		
TOTAL	$116,568	48	$116,568	48

SETTLEMENT

	DEBIT		CREDIT	
Transfer Tax	$ 115	00		
Earnest Money			$15,000	00
Abstract or Guaranty Policy	550	00		
Recording fees - Seller	20	00		
Commission	8,050	00		
Attorney's Fees - $400 seller, $300 Buyer	700	00		
Recording Fees - buyer	10	00		
Balance Due Seller	5,555	00		
Total	$15,000	00	$15,000	00

Accepted   Accepted

_____   _____

Figure 23.3
RESPA Uniform
Settlement Statement

Form Approved OMB NO. 63-R-1501

A. U.S. DEPARTMENT OF HOUSING AND URBAN DEVELOPMENT SETTLEMENT STATEMENT	B. TYPE OF LOAN
	1. ☐ FHA 2. ☐ FMHA 3. ☒ CONV. UNINS. 4. ☐ VA 5. ☐ CONV. INS. 6. FILE NUMBER: 7. LOAN NUMBER: 8. MORT. INS. CASE NO.:

C. NOTE: This form is furnished to give you a statement of actual settlement costs. Amounts paid to and by the settlement agent are shown. Items marked "(p.o.c.)" were paid outside the closing; they are shown here for informational purposes and are not included in the totals.

D. NAME OF BORROWER: Brook Redemann	E. NAME OF SELLER: John & Joanne Iuro	F. NAME OF LENDER: Thrift Federal Savings
G. PROPERTY LOCATION: 3045 N. Racine	H. SETTLEMENT AGENT: Open Door Real Estate Co. PLACE OF SETTLEMENT:	I. SETTLEMENT DATE: June 15, 1986

J. SUMMARY OF BORROWER'S TRANSACTION:		K. SUMMARY OF SELLER'S TRANSACTION:	
100. GROSS AMOUNT DUE FROM BORROWER		400. GROSS AMOUNT DUE TO SELLER	
101. Contract sales price	$115,000.00	401. Contract sales price	$115,000.00
102. Personal property		402. Personal property	
103. Settlement charges to borrower (line 1400)	5,711.60	403.	
104.		404.	
105.		405.	
Adjustments for items paid by seller in advance		*Adjustments for items paid by seller in advance*	
106. City/town taxes to		406. City/town taxes to	
107. County taxes to		407. County taxes to	
108. Assessments to		408. Assessments to	
109. Insurance - 6/15/86 to 3/1/88	433.48	409. Insurance - 6/15/86 to 3/1/88	433.48
110.		410.	
111.		411.	
112.		412.	
120. GROSS AMOUNT DUE FROM BORROWER	$121,145.08	420. GROSS AMOUNT DUE TO SELLER	$115,433.48
200. AMOUNTS PAID BY OR IN BEHALF OF BORROWER		500. REDUCTIONS IN AMOUNT DUE TO SELLER	
201. Deposit or earnest money	15,000.00	501. Excess deposit (see Instructions)	
202. Principal amount of new loan(s)	95,000.00	502. Settlement charges to seller (line 1400)	11,060.00
203. Existing loan(s) taken subject to		503. Existing loan(s) taken subject to	
204.		504. Payoff of first mortgage loan	
205.		505. Payoff of second mortgage loan	56,675.00
206.		506.	
207.		507.	
208.		508.	
209.		509.	
Adjustments for items unpaid by seller		*Adjustments for items unpaid by seller*	
210. City/town taxes to		510. City/town taxes to	
211. County taxes 1/1/86 to 6/15/86	790.63	511. County taxes 1/1/86 to 6/15/86	790.63
212. Assessments to		512. Assessments to	
213.		513.	
214.		514.	
215.		515.	
216.		516.	
217.		517.	
218.		518.	
219.		519.	
220. TOTAL PAID BY/FOR BORROWER	$110,790.63	520. TOTAL REDUCTION AMOUNT DUE SELLER	$68,525.63
300. CASH AT SETTLEMENT FROM OR TO BORROWER		600. CASH AT SETTLEMENT TO OR FROM SELLER	
301. Gross amount due from borrower (line 120)	121,145.08	601. Gross amount due to seller (line 420)	115,433.48
302. Less amounts paid by/for borrower (line 220)	(110,790.63)	602. Less reduction amount due seller (line 520)	(68,525.63)
303. CASH (☒ FROM) (☐ TO) BORROWER	$10,354.45	603. CASH (☒ TO) (☐ FROM) SELLER	$46,907.85

HUD-1 5/76 AS & AS (1322)

U.S. DEPARTMENT OF HOUSING AND URBAN DEVELOPMENT
SETTLEMENT STATEMENT
PAGE 2

L. SETTLEMENT CHARGES		PAID FROM BORROWER'S FUNDS AT SETTLEMENT	PAID FROM SELLER'S FUNDS AT SETTLEMENT
700.	TOTAL SALES/BROKER'S COMMISSION based on price $ 115,000.00 @ 7 % = $8050.00		
	Division of commission (line 700) as follows:		
701.	$ to		
702.	$ to		
703.	Commission paid at Settlement		$8050.00
704.			
800.	ITEMS PAYABLE IN CONNECTION WITH LOAN		
801.	Loan Origination Fee 1 %	$ 1,150.00	
802.	Loan Discount 4 %	1,900.00	1,900.00
803.	Appraisal Fee to Swift Appraisal	125.00	
804.	Credit Report to Acme Credit Bureau	60.00	
805.	Lender's Inspection Fee		
806.	Mortgage Insurance Application Fee to		
807.	Assumption Fee		
808.			
809.			
810.			
811.			
900.	ITEMS REQUIRED BY LENDER TO BE PAID IN ADVANCE		
901.	Interest from 6/15/86 to 7/15/86 @ $ 30.18 /day	905.35	
902.	Mortgage Insurance Premium for mo. to		
903.	Hazard Insurance Premium for yrs. to		
904.	yrs. to		
905.			
1000.	RESERVES DEPOSITED WITH LENDER FOR		
1001.	Hazard insurance mo. @ $ /mo.		
1002.	Mortgage insurance mo. @ $ /mo.		
1003.	City property taxes mo. @ $ /mo.		
1004.	County property taxes 7 mo. @ $ 143.75 /mo.	1,006.25	
1005.	Annual assessments mo. @ $ /mo.		
1006.	mo. @ $ /mo.		
1007.	mo. @ $ /mo.		
1008.	mo. @ $ /mo.		
1100.	TITLE CHARGES		
1101.	Settlement or closing fee to		
1102.	Abstract or title search to		
1103.	Title examination to		
1104.	Title insurance binder to		550.00
1105.	Document preparation to		
1106.	Notary fees to		
1107.	Attorney's fees to	300.00	400.00
	(includes above items No.:)		
1108.	Title insurance to	150.00	
	(includes above items No.:)		
1109.	Lender's coverage $		
1110.	Owner's coverage $		
1111.			
1112.			
1113.			
1200.	GOVERNMENT RECORDING AND TRANSFER CHARGES		
1201.	Recording fees: Deed $ 10.00 ; Mortgage $ 10.00 ; Releases $ 10.00	20.00	10.00
1202.	City/county tax/stamps: Deed $; Mortgage $		
1203.	State tax/stamps: Deed $ 115.00 ; Mortgage $		115.00
1204.			
1205.			
1300.	ADDITIONAL SETTLEMENT CHARGES		
1301.	Survey to	95.00	
1302.	Pest inspection to		35.00
1303.			
1304.			
1305.			
1400.	TOTAL SETTLEMENT CHARGES (enter on lines 103 and 502, Sections J and K)	$ 5,711.60	$ 11,060.00

The Undersigned Acknowledges Receipt of This Settlement Statement and Agrees to the Correctness Thereof.

_____
Buyer

_____
Seller

At the closing, the broker will have ready for delivery to the seller a signed receipt covering the broker's commission and the reimbursement for the listed expenses. The broker will also bring to the closing a check for $5,555.00 payable to the seller for the balance due the seller from the broker. The seller has also received the buyer's check for $42,813.39, making a total of $48,368.39. This is the same total due the seller that is shown in the separate settlement statements in figure 23.1.

When this two-column form of closing statement is used, enough copies are prepared so that the buyer, seller, and broker can each receive one that has been signed by all parties.

RESPA Uniform Settlement Statement

The requirements of the Real Estate Settlement Procedures Act (RESPA) were discussed earlier in this chapter. The Uniform Settlement Statement that appears in figure 23.3 illustrates the sample transaction presented in the preceding pages, *with one change.* In this case, the Iuros (sellers) are paying off their existing mortgage loan at the closing, and Redemann (buyer) is obtaining new financing (thus requiring use of the RESPA form), so a number of new entries and charges must be figured into the settlement.

The sellers' loan payoff is $56,875 ($57,700 less $825 credit for the amount in their tax reserve), and they must pay an additional $10.00 to record the mortgage release, as well as $35.00 for a pest inspection. The buyer's new loan is from Thrift Federal Savings in the amount of $95,000. In connection with this loan, he will be charged $125.00 to have the property appraised by Swift Appraisal and $60.00 for a credit report from the Acme Credit Bureau. In addition, Redemann will be required to pay one month's mortgage interest, $905.35, in advance and to deposit $1,006.25, or 7/12 of the anticipated 1986 county real estate tax (of $1,725) into a tax reserve account. Redemann will have to pay an additional $10.00 to record the mortgage, $150.00 for a mortgagee's title insurance policy to cover the lender's interest in the property, and $95.00 for a survey. The buyer will pay a one-percent loan origination fee, and buyer and sellers will split equally loan discount points of four percent.

The Uniform Settlement Statement is divided into twelve sections. The most important information is included in Sections J, K, and L. The borrower's and seller's summaries (J and K) are very similar to one another and are used like the other formats of closing statements illustrated in this chapter. For example, in Section J, the summary of the borrower's transaction, the buyer-borrower's debits are listed in lines 100 through 112 and totaled on line 120 (gross amount due from borrower). The total of the settlement costs itemized in Section L of the statement is entered on line 103 as one of the buyer's charges. The buyer's credits are listed on lines 201 through 219 and totaled on line 220 (total paid by/for borrower). Then, as with the other statements, the buyer's credits are subtracted from the charges to arrive at the cash due from the borrower to close (line 303).

In Section K, the summary of the seller's transaction, the sellers' credits are entered on lines 400 through 412 and totaled on line 420 (gross amount due to seller). The sellers' debits are entered on lines 501 through 519 and totaled on line 520 (total reduction amount due seller). The total of the sellers' settlement charges is on line 502. Then the debits are subtracted from the credits to arrive at the cash due to the sellers in order to close (line 603).

Section L is a summary of all the settlement charges for the transaction; the buyer's expenses are listed in one column and the sellers' expenses are listed in the other. Note that if an attorney's fee is listed as a lump sum in line 1107, the settlement should list by line number the services that were included in that total fee.

Summary

Closing a sale involves both title procedures and financial matters. The broker, as agent of the seller, should be present at the closing to see that the sale is actually concluded and to account for the earnest money deposit.

The federal *Real Estate Settlement Procedures Act (RESPA)* requires disclosure of all settlement costs when a real estate purchase is financed by a federally related mortgage loan. RESPA requires lenders to use a *Uniform Settlement Statement* to detail the financial particulars of a transaction.

Usually the buyer's attorney examines the title evidence to ensure that the seller's title is acceptable. The gap in time between the date of the abstract or title commitment and the closing date is covered by the seller's *affidavit of title.*

The sale may be closed in *escrow* so that the buyer can be assured of receiving good title as described in the sales contract and the seller can be assured that all funds due him or her are held in cash by the escrow agent.

The actual amount to be paid by the buyer at the closing is computed by preparation of a *closing,* or *settlement, statement.* This lists the sales price, earnest money deposit, and all adjustments and prorations due between buyer and seller. The purpose of this statement is to determine the net amount due the seller at closing. The form is signed by both parties to evidence their approval.

Questions

1. Which of the following is true of real estate closings in most states?

   a. Closings are generally conducted by real estate salespeople.

   b. The buyer usually receives the rents for the day of closing.

   c. The buyer must reimburse the seller for any title evidence provided by the seller.

   d. The seller usually pays the expenses for the day of closing.

2. When an item to be prorated has been earned (or is owing) but has not been paid by the seller:

   I. the amount owed is figured as a credit to the buyer.

   II. the amount owed is figured as a debit to the seller.

      a. I only   c. both I and II
      b. II only   d. neither I nor II

3. When the item to be prorated has been paid by the seller but not fully earned (or used up):

   I. the unused portion is a credit to the seller.

   II. the unused portion is a credit to the buyer.

      a. I only   c. both I and II
      b. II only   d. neither I nor II

4. Certain amounts included in a closing statement are not prorated but are listed at the full amount. Which of the following is always prorated?

   a. state transfer tax

   b. earnest money

   c. the unpaid principal balance of the seller's mortgage assumed by the buyer

   d. interest on the seller's mortgage assumed by the buyer that has accrued since the last interest was paid

5. All encumbrances and liens shown on the report of title, other than those waived or agreed to by the purchaser and listed in the contract, must be removed so that the title can be delivered free and clear. The removal of such encumbrances is the duty of the:

   a. buyer.   c. broker.
   b. seller.   d. title company.

6. Legal title always passes from the seller to the buyer:

   a. on the date of execution of the deed.

   b. when the closing statement has been signed.

   c. when the deed is placed in escrow.

   d. when the deed is delivered.

7. The advantages of closing a real estate sales transaction in escrow include the fact that:

   I. the seller is assured that he or she will receive the buyer's payment for the property.

   II. the buyer is assured that he or she will not become owner unless good title to the property is received.

      a. I only   c. both I and II
      b. II only   d. neither I nor II

8. The closing statement will disclose to the seller:

   I. the amount of money he or she will receive at the closing.

   II. the amount the buyer must bring to the closing.

      a. I only   c. both I and II
      b. II only   d. neither I nor II

9. Which one of the following items is *not* usually prorated between buyer and seller at the closing?

   a. recording charges

   b. general taxes

   c. rents

   d. mortgage interest

Questions 10 through 16 pertain to certain items as they would normally appear on a closing statement.

10. The sales price of the property is a:
    I. credit to the seller.
    II. debit to the buyer.
      a. I only   c. both I and II
      b. II only   d. neither I nor II

11. The earnest money left on deposit with the broker is a:
    a. credit to the seller.
    b. credit to the buyer.
    c. debit to the seller.
    d. debit to the buyer.

12. The principal amount of the purchaser's new mortgage loan is a:
    I. credit to the seller.
    II. debit to the buyer.
      a. I only   c. both I and II
      b. II only   d. neither I nor II

13. Unpaid real estate taxes, water service, scavenger service, janitorial service, and so forth are a:
    I. credit to the buyer.
    II. debit to the seller.
      a. I only   c. both I and II
      b. II only   d. neither I nor II

14. The broker's commission is a:
    I. credit to the buyer.
    II. debit to the seller.
      a. I only   c. both I and II
      b. II only   d. neither I nor II

15. Interest proration on an existing assumed mortgage is a:
    I. credit to the seller.
    II. debit to the buyer.
      a. I only   c. both I and II
      b. II only   d. neither I nor II

16. Fuel oil left in a holding tank on the property is a:
    I. credit to the buyer.
    II. debit to the seller.
      a. I only   c. both I and II
      b. II only   d. neither I nor II

17. The *doctrine of relation back* is most closely associated with which of the following?
    a. escrow   c. prorations
    b. RESPA   d. title evidence

18. The RESPA Uniform Settlement Statement must be used to illustrate all settlement charges:
    a. for every real estate transaction.
    b. for transactions financed by VA and FHA loans only.
    c. for transactions financed by federally related mortgage loans.
    d. for all transactions in which mortgage financing is involved.

19. Which of the following would a lender generally require to be produced at the closing?
    a. title insurance policy
    b. market value appraisal
    c. fire and hazard insurance policy
    d. a and c

20. When a transaction is to be closed in escrow, the seller generally deposits all but which of the following items with the escrow agent before the closing date?
    a. deed to the property
    b. title evidence
    c. estoppel certificate
    d. existing fire and hazard insurance

Real Estate Mathematics Review

Mathematics plays an important role in the real estate business. Math is involved in nearly every aspect of a typical transaction, from the moment a listing agreement is filled out until the final monies are paid out at the closing. In addition, many states' real estate license examinations contain a substantial number of questions that involve math. Knowledge of and proficiency with mathematical equations are thus important, both to acquire a real estate license and to operate in the business itself.

This review is designed to familiarize you with some basic mathematical formulas that are most frequently used in the computations required on state licensing examinations. These same computations are also important in day-to-day real estate transactions. Some of this material has been covered in detail in the text. In these cases, reference is made to the appropriate chapter. If you feel you need additional help in working these problems, you may want to order a copy of *Mastering Real Estate Mathematics,* Fourth Edition, by Ventolo, Allaway and Irby. You will find an order form for this self-instructional text in the back of this book.

Percentages

Many real estate computations are based on the calculation of percentages. A percentage expresses a portion of a whole. For example, 50% means 50 parts of the possible 100 parts that comprise the whole. Percentages greater than 100% contain more than one whole unit. Thus, 163% is one whole and 63 parts of another whole. Remember that a whole is always expressed as 100%.

In problems involving percentages, *the percentage must be converted to either a decimal or a fraction.* To convert a percentage to a decimal, move the decimal two places to the left and drop the percent sign. Thus,

$$60\% = .6 \quad 7\% = .07 \quad 175\% = 1.75$$

To change a percentage to a fraction, place the percentage over 100. For example:

$$50\% = \frac{50}{100} \quad 115\% = \frac{115}{100}$$

These fractions may then be *reduced* to make it easier to work the problem. To reduce a fraction, determine the lowest number by which both numerator and denominator can be evenly divided, and divide each of them by that number. For example:

$$25/100 = 1/4 \text{ (both numbers divided by 25)}$$

$$49/63 = 7/9 \text{ (both numbers divided by 7)}$$

Percentage problems contain three elements: *percentage, total,* and *part.* To determine a specific percentage of a whole, multiply the percentage by the whole. This is illustrated by the following formula:

$$\text{percent} \times \text{whole} = \text{part}$$

$$5\% \times 200 = \mathbf{10}$$

This formula is used in calculating mortgage loan interests, brokers' commissions, loan origination fees, discount points, amount of earnest money deposits, and income on capital investments.

For example: A broker is to receive a 7% commission on the sale of a $100,000 house. What will the broker's commission be?

$$.07 \times \$100,000 = \textbf{\$7,000 broker's commission}$$

A variation, or inversion, of the percentage formula is used to find the total amount when the part and percentage are known:

$$\text{total} = \frac{\text{part}}{\text{percent}}$$

For example: The Masterson Realty Company received a $4,500 commission for the sale of a house. The broker's commission was 6% of the total sales price. What was the total sales price of this house?

$$\frac{\$4,500}{.06} = \textbf{\$75,000 total sales price}$$

This formula is used in computing the total mortgage loan principal still due if the monthly payment and interest rate are known. It is also used to calculate the total sales price when the amount and percentage of commission or earnest money deposit are known, rent due if the monthly payment and interest rate are known, and market value of property if the assessed value and the ratio (percentage) of assessed value to market value are known.

To determine the percentage when the amounts of the part and the total are known:

$$\text{percent} = \frac{\text{part}}{\text{total}}$$

This formula may be used to determine the tax rate when the taxes and assessed value are known, or the commission rate if the sales price and commission amount are known.

Rates

Property taxes, transfer taxes, and insurance premiums are usually expressed as rates. A *rate* is the cost, expressed as the amount of cost per unit. For example, tax might be computed at the rate of $5 per $100 of assessed value in a certain county. The formula for computing rates is:

$$\text{value} \times \text{rate} = \text{total}$$

For example: A house has been assessed at $90,000 and is taxed at an annual rate of $2.50 per $100 assessed valuation. What is the yearly tax?

$$\$90,000 \times \frac{\$2.50}{\$100} = \text{total annual tax}$$

$$\overset{900}{\cancel{\$90,000}} \times \frac{\$2.50}{\underset{1}{\cancel{\$100}}} = \text{total annual tax}$$

$$900 \times \$2.50 = \textbf{\$2,250 total annual tax}$$

See Chapter 10 for a further discussion of tax computations.

Areas and Volumes   People in the real estate profession must know how to compute the area of a parcel of land or figure the amount of living area in a house. To compute the area of a square or rectangular parcel, use the formula:

$$\text{length} \times \text{width} = \text{area}$$

Thus, the area of a rectangular lot that measures 200 feet long by 100 feet wide would be:

$$200' \times 100' = \textbf{20,000 square feet}$$

Area is always expressed in square units. To compute the amount of surface in a triangular-shaped area, use the formula:

$$\text{area} = \tfrac{1}{2} (\text{base} \times \text{height})$$

The base of a triangle is the bottom, the side on which the triangle rests. The height is an imaginary straight line extending from the point of the uppermost angle straight down to the base:

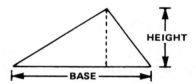

For example: A triangle has a base of 50 feet and a height of 30 feet. What is its area?

$$\tfrac{1}{2} (50' \times 30') = \text{area in square feet}$$

$$\tfrac{1}{2} (1,500 \text{ square feet}) = \textbf{750 square feet}$$

To compute the area of an irregular room or parcel of land, divide the shape into regular rectangles, squares, or triangles. Next, compute the area of each regular figure and add the areas together to obtain the total area.

Example: Compute the area of the hallway shown below:

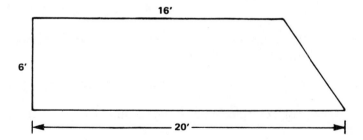

First make a rectangle and a triangle by drawing a single line through the figure as shown here:

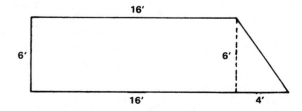

Compute the area of the rectangle:

$$\text{area} = \text{length} \times \text{width} \qquad 16' \times 6' = 96 \text{ sq. ft.}$$

Compute the area of the triangle:

$$\text{area} = \tfrac{1}{2} (\text{base} \times \text{height}) \qquad \tfrac{1}{2}(4' \times 6') = \tfrac{1}{2}(24 \text{ sq. ft.}) = 12 \text{ sq. ft.}$$

Total the two areas:

$$96 + 12 = \textbf{108 square feet in total area}$$

The cubic capacity of an enclosed space is expressed as volume. Volume is used to describe the amount of space in any three-dimensional area. It would be used, for example, in measuring the interior airspace of a room to determine what capacity heating unit is required. The formula for computing cubic or rectangular volume is:

$$\text{volume} = \text{length} \times \text{width} \times \text{height}$$

Volume is always expressed in cubic units.

For example: The bedroom of a house is 12 feet long, 8 feet wide, and has a ceiling height of 8 feet. How many cubic feet does the room enclose?

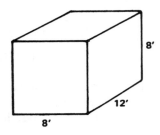

$$8' \times 12' \times 8' = \textbf{768 cubic feet}$$

To compute the volume of a triangular space, such as the airspace in an A-frame house, use the formula:

$$\text{volume} = \tfrac{1}{2} (\text{base} \times \text{height} \times \text{width})$$

For example: What is the volume of airspace in the house shown below?

First, divide the house into two shapes, rectangular and triangular, as shown:

Find the volume of T:

$$\text{volume} = \tfrac{1}{2} (\text{base} \times \text{height} \times \text{width})$$
$$\tfrac{1}{2} (25' \times 10' \times 40') = \tfrac{1}{2} (10,000 \text{ cu. ft.}) = 5,000 \text{ cu. ft.}$$

Find the volume of R:

$$25' \times 40' \times 12' = 12,000 \text{ cubic feet}$$

Total volumes T and R:

$$5,000 + 12,000 = \textbf{17,000 cubic feet of airspace in the house}$$

Cubic measurements of volume are used to compute the construction costs per cubic foot of a building, the amount of airspace being sold in a condominium unit, or the heating and cooling requirements for a building.

Remember that when either area or volume is computed, *all dimensions used must be given in the same unit of measure.* For example, you may not multiply 2 feet by 6 inches to get the area; you have to multiply 2 feet by ½ foot.

Prorations

As discussed in Chapter 23, the proration of taxes, insurance premiums, and other items is customary when a real estate transaction is closed. Questions concerning closing statements generally appear in real estate brokers' examinations. They appear less often in salespersons' exams. Knowledge of the arithmetic of prorations is valuable to all real estate licensees in the course of their business.

When an item is to be prorated, the charge must first be broken down into yearly, monthly, and daily amounts, depending on the type of charge. These smaller amounts are then multiplied by the number of years, months, and days in the pro-rated time period to determine the accrued or unearned amount to be credited or debited at the closing. Depending on local custom, prorations may be made on the basis of a standard 30-day month (360-day year), 365-day year, or the actual number of days in the month of closing.

For example, consider a three-year prepaid insurance policy with a premium of $450. The policy became effective on March 1, 1985; the date of the closing is August 9, 1986. The initial step in determining the unearned amount of the premium that will be credited to the seller at the closing is to figure out the number of years, months, and days not yet used up as of August 9, 1986 as follows:

$$
\begin{array}{ccc}
 & 7 & 15 & 32 \\
198\cancel{8} & \cancel{8} & \cancel{9} \\
\hline
1986 & 8 & 9 \\
\hline
1 & 7 & 23 & \text{or 1 year, 7 months, and 23 days unearned.}
\end{array}
$$

Then the yearly, monthly, and daily breakdowns of the premium amount are determined. (Remember to carry all computations to three decimal places until a final figure is reached, then round off to the nearest penny.) First, divide the premium amount by three to determine the yearly charge:

$$\frac{\$150.000}{3)\$450.00} \text{ yearly premium}$$

Next, divide the yearly charge by 12 to determine the monthly premium:

$$\frac{\$12.500}{12)\$150.000} \text{ monthly premium}$$

Assuming your area computes such charges on the basis of a 30-day month, divide the monthly charge by 30 to arrive at the daily premium:

$$\frac{\$.417}{30)\$12.500} \text{ daily premium}$$

Finally, you must multiply the yearly, monthly, and daily premium amounts by the appropriate number of years, months, and days to determine the unearned amount to be prorated:

$150.000 / 1 year

$12.500
$\times \quad 7$
$87.500 / 7 months

$\quad .417
$\times \quad 23$
$ 9.591 / 23 days

$150.000
   87.500
 +9.591
$247.091, or *$247.09 unearned insurance premium*
            (a credit to the seller and a debit to the buyer)

Similar computations are used to prorate other items, such as real estate taxes and mortgage interest. For a more detailed discussion of closing statement computations, refer to Chapter 23.

Questions

1. Broker Sally Smith, of Happy Valley Realty, recently sold Jack and Jill Hawkins's home for $79,500. Smith charged the Hawkinses a 6½% commission and will pay 30% of that amount to the listing salesperson and 25% to the selling salesperson. What amount of commission will the listing salesperson receive from the Hawkins sale?

   a. $5,167.50   c. $3,617.25
   b. $1,550.25   d. $1,291.87

2. Susan Silber signed an agreement to purchase a condominium apartment from Perry and Marie Morris. The contract stipulated that the Morrises replace the damaged bedroom carpet. The carpet Silber has chosen costs $11.95 per square yard plus $2.50 per square yard for installation. If the bedroom dimensions are as illustrated, how much will the Morrises have to pay for the job?

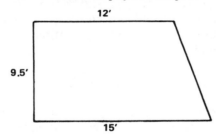

   a. $170.28   c. $205.91
   b. $189.20   d. $228.79

3. Hal Peters, Olive Gamble, Ron Clooney, and Marvin Considine decided to pool their savings and purchase a small apartment building for $125,000. If Peters invested $30,000 and Gamble and Clooney each contributed $35,000, what percentage of ownership was left for Considine?

   a. 20%   c. 28%
   b. 24%   d. 30%

4. Harold Barlow is curious to know how much money his son and daughter-in-law still owe on their mortgage loan. Barlow knows that the interest portion of their last monthly payment was $391.42. If the Barlows are paying interest at the rate of 11½%, what was the outstanding balance of their loan before that last payment was made?

   a. $43,713.00   c. $36,427.50
   b. $40,843.83   d. $34,284.70

5. Nick and Olga Stravinski bought their home on Sabre Lane a year ago for $68,500. Property in their neighborhood is said to be increasing in value at a rate of 12% annually. If this is true, what is the current market value of the Stravinskis' real estate?

   a. $76,720
   b. $77,063
   c. $77,405
   d. none of the above is within $50

6. The DeHavilands' home on Dove Street is valued at $95,000. Property in their area is assessed at 60% of its value, and the local tax rate is $2.85 per hundred. What is the amount of the Dehavilands' monthly taxes?

   a. $1,111.50   c. $111.15
   b. $ 926.30   d. $135.38

7. The Fitzpatricks are planning to construct a patio in their backyard. An illustration of the surface area to be paved appears here. If the cement is to be poured as a 6″ slab, how many cubic feet of cement will be poured into this patio?

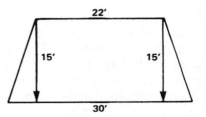

   a. 660 cubic feet   c. 330 cubic feet
   b. 450 cubic feet   d. 195 cubic feet

8. Happy Morgan receives a monthly salary of $500 plus 3% commission on all of his listings that sell and 2.5% on all his sales. None of the listings that Morgan took sold last month, but he received $3,675 in salary and commission. What was the value of the property Morgan sold?

   a. $147,000   c. $122,500
   b. $127,000   d. $105,833

9. The Salvatinis' residence has proved difficult to sell. Salesperson Martha Kelley suggests it might sell faster if they enclose a portion of the backyard with a privacy fence. If the area to be enclosed is as illustrated, how much would the fence cost at $6.95 per linear foot?

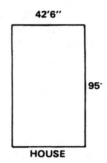

42'6"

95'

HOUSE

   a. $1,911.25   c. $1,615.88
   b. $1,654.10   d. $ 955.63

10. Andrew McTavish leases the 12 apartments in the Overton Arms for a total monthly rental of $4,500. If this figure represents an 8% annual return on McTavish's investment, what was the original cost of the property?

   a. $675,000   c. $54,000
   b. $450,000   d. $56,250

For the following questions regarding closing statement prorations, base your calculations on a 30-day month. Carry all computations to three decimal places until the final solution.

11. A sale is to be closed on March 15, 1986. Real estate taxes for the current year have not been paid; taxes for 1985 amounted to $1,340. What is the amount of the real estate tax proration to be credited to the buyer?

   a. $1,060.84   c. $223.33
   b. $279.16   d. $1,116.60

12. Robert Bell is selling his house to Franklin and Mildred Pierce; the Pierces are assuming Bell's outstanding mortgage, which had an unpaid balance of $58,200 after the last payment on August 1. Interest at 12 percent per annum is paid in advance each month; the sale is to be closed on August 11. What is the amount of mortgage interest proration to be credited to Bell at the closing?

   a. $698.40   c. $213.40
   b. $582.00   d. $368.60

13. Paul Ihlen is selling a home to Ricardo Felski on September 20, 1985. Felski is assuming Ihlen's three-year fire and hazard insurance policy, which is due to expire on May 31, 1986, at the closing. The original cost of the premium was $680. What is the amount of insurance proration that will be charged to Felski at the closing?

   a. $158.04   c. $144.80
   b. $540.87   d. $226.66

14. In a sale of residential property, real estate taxes for the current year amounted to $975 and have already been paid by the seller. The sale is to be closed on October 26; what is the amount of real estate tax proration to be credited the seller?

   a. $173.33   c. $798.96
   b. $162.50   d. $83.96

15. Duncan Pillsbury is buying Emil Nitrate's house, assuming the seller's mortgage. The unpaid balance after the most recent payment (the first of the month) was $61,550. Interest is paid in arrears each month at 13 percent per annum. The sale is to be closed on September 22; what is the amount of mortgage interest proration to be credited to the buyer at the closing?

   a. $666.97   c. $177.82
   b. $488.97   d. $689.01

16. A 100-acre farm is divided into house lots. The streets require one-eighth of the whole farm, and there are 140 lots. How many square feet are there in each lot?

   a. 35,004   c. 27,225
   b. 31,114   d. 43,560

Residential Construction Appendix

The illustrations included in this appendix are designed to introduce the reader to basic residential construction techniques and terminology. Specifically, diagrams depicting various architectural styles, roof designs, roof framing systems, exterior structural walls and framing, and a cutaway view of a typical house—illustrating all major components—are featured.

For a more detailed treatment of these and other important construction techniques and terminology, consult the book *Residential Construction* by William L. Ventolo, Jr., also available from Real Estate Education Company. If this book is not available at your local bookstore, you may order it directly from the publisher. An order form is included at the back of this text.

Figure 1
Architectural Styles

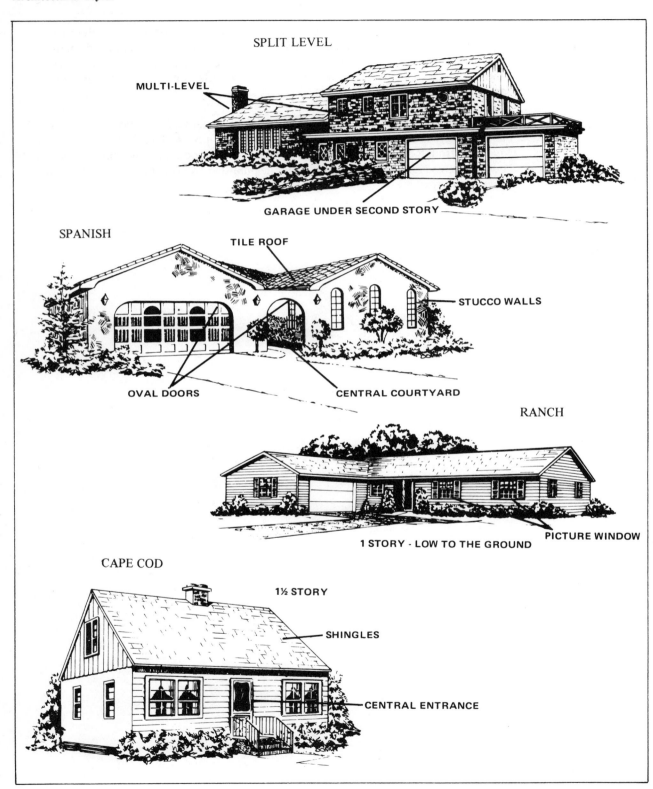

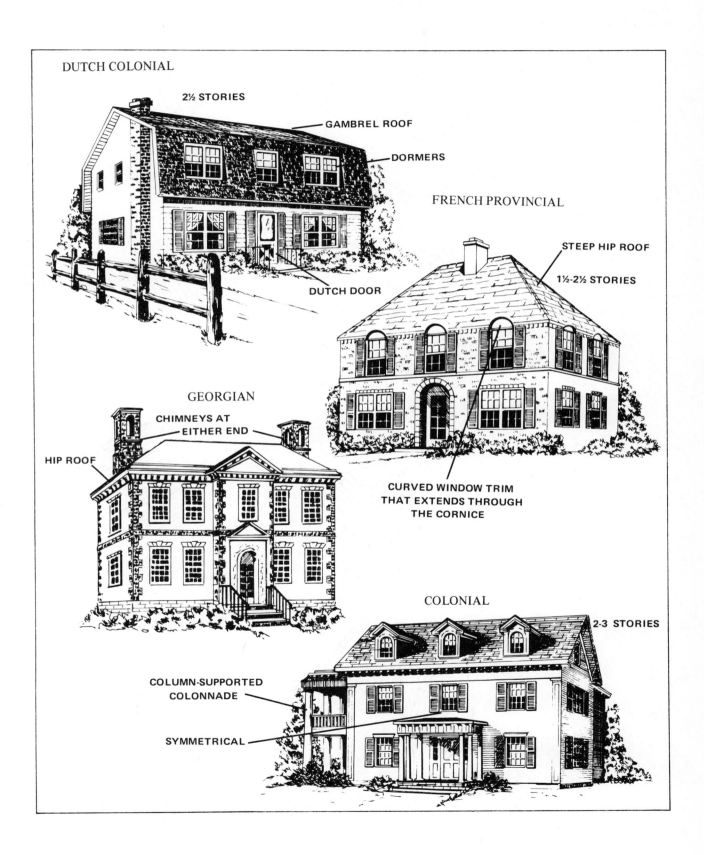

DUTCH COLONIAL

2½ STORIES

GAMBREL ROOF

DORMERS

DUTCH DOOR

FRENCH PROVINCIAL

STEEP HIP ROOF

1½-2½ STORIES

CURVED WINDOW TRIM THAT EXTENDS THROUGH THE CORNICE

GEORGIAN

CHIMNEYS AT EITHER END

HIP ROOF

COLONIAL

2-3 STORIES

COLUMN-SUPPORTED COLONNADE

SYMMETRICAL

Figure 2
Roof Designs

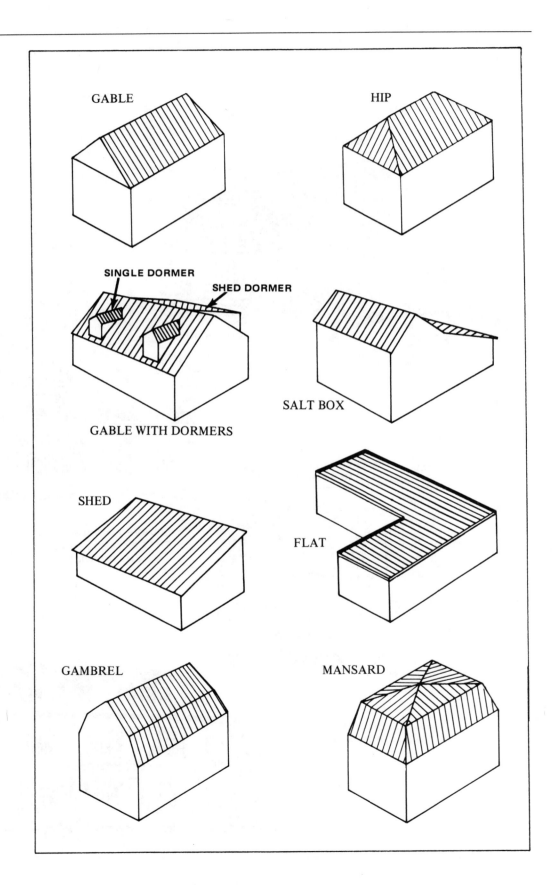

Figure 3
Roof Framing Systems

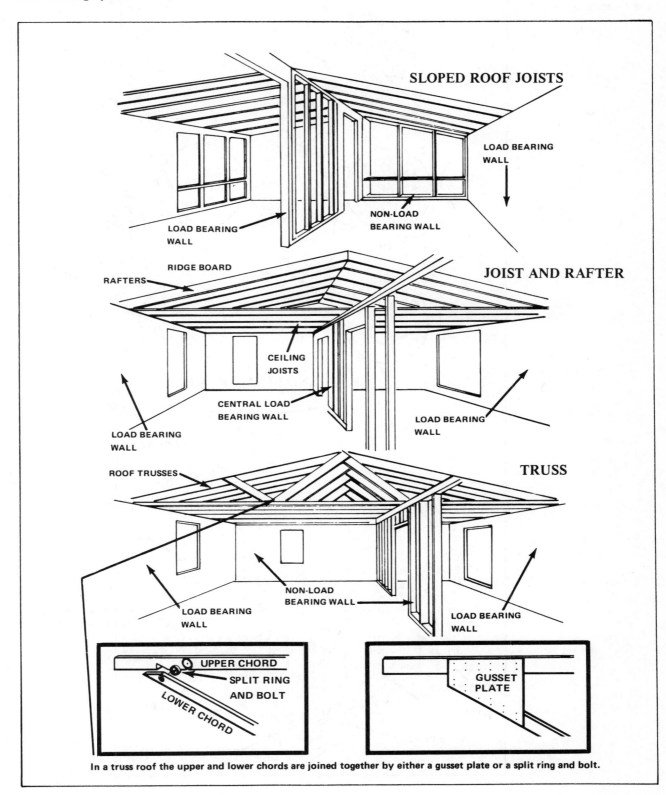

SLOPED ROOF JOISTS

LOAD BEARING
WALL

LOAD BEARING
WALL

NON-LOAD
BEARING WALL

JOIST AND RAFTER

RIDGE BOARD

RAFTERS

CEILING
JOISTS

CENTRAL LOAD
BEARING WALL

LOAD BEARING
WALL

LOAD BEARING
WALL

TRUSS

ROOF TRUSSES

NON-LOAD
BEARING WALL

LOAD BEARING
WALL

LOAD BEARING
WALL

UPPER CHORD

SPLIT RING
AND BOLT

LOWER CHORD

GUSSET
PLATE

In a truss roof the upper and lower chords are joined together by either a gusset plate or a split ring and bolt.

**Figure 4
Exterior Structural Walls
and Framing**

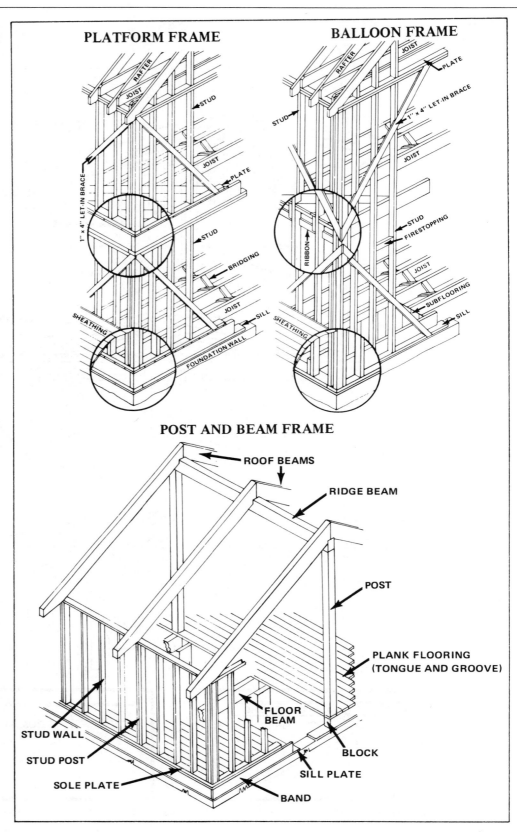

HOUSE DIAGRAM

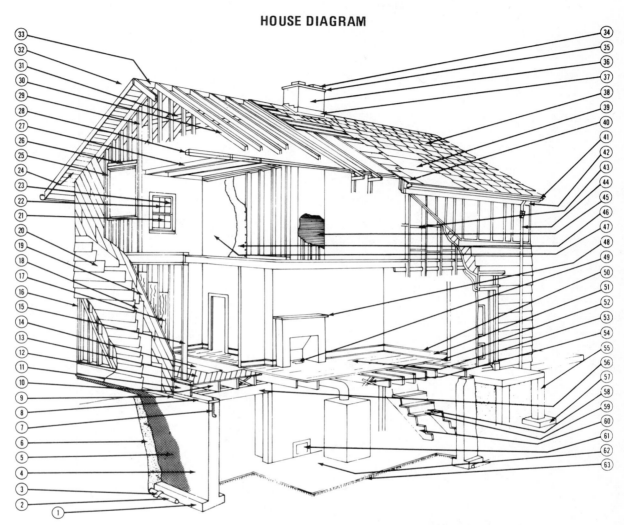

1. FOOTING
2. FOUNDATION DRAIN TILE
3. FELT JOINT COVER
4. FOUNDATION WALL
5. DAMPPROOFING OR WEATHERPROOFING
6. BACKFILL
7. ANCHOR BOLT
8. SILL
9. TERMITE SHIELD
10. FLOOR JOIST
11. BAND OR BOX SILL
12. PLATE
13. SUBFLOORING
14. BUILDING PAPER
15. WALL STUD
16. DOUBLE CORNER STUD
17. INSULATION
18. BUILDING PAPER
19. WALL SHEATHING
20. SIDING
21. MULLION

22. MUNTIN
23. WINDOW SASH
24. EAVE (ROOF PROJECTION)
25. WINDOW JAMB TRIM
26. DOUBLE WINDOW HEADER
27. CEILING JOIST
28. DOUBLE PLATE
29. STUD
30. RAFTERS
31. COLLAR BEAM
32. GABLE END OF ROOF
33. RIDGE BOARD
34. CHIMNEY POTS
35. CHIMNEY CAP
36. CHIMNEY
37. CHIMNEY FLASHING
38. ROOFING SHINGLES
39. ROOFING FELTS
40. ROOF SHEATHING
41. EVE TROUGH OR GUTTER
42. FRIEZE BOARD

43. FIRESTOP
44. DOWNSPOUT
45. LATHS
46. PLASTER BOARD
47. PLASTER FINISH
48. MANTEL
49. ASH DUMP
50. BASE TOP MOULDING
51. BASEBOARD
52. SHOE MOULDING
53. FINISH MOULDING
54. BRIDGING
55. PIER
56. GIRDER
57. FOOTING
58. RISER
59. TREAD
60. STRINGER
61. CLEANOUT DOOR
62. CONCRETE BASEMENT FLOOR
63. CINDER FILL

Glossary of Real Estate Terms

Abstract of title The condensed history of a title to a particular parcel of real estate, consisting of a summary of the original grant and all subsequent conveyances and encumbrances affecting the property and a certification by the abstractor that the history is complete and accurate.

Abstract of title with lawyer's opinion An abstract of title that a lawyer has examined and has certified to be, in his or her opinion, an accurate statement of fact.

Accelerated depreciation A method of calculating for tax purposes the depreciation of income property at a faster rate than would be achieved using the straight-line method. Any depreciation taken in excess of that which would be claimed using the straight-line rate is subject to *recapture* as ordinary income to the extent of gain resulting from the sale. *See also* Straight-line method.

Acceleration clause The clause in a mortgage or trust deed that can be enforced to make the entire debt due immediately if the mortgagor defaults on an installment payment or other covenant.

Accession Acquiring title to additions or improvements to real property as a result of the annexation of fixtures or the accretion of alluvial deposits along the banks of streams.

Accretion The increase or addition of land by the deposit of sand or soil washed up naturally from a river, lake, or sea.

Accrued items On a closing statement, items of expense that are incurred but not yet payable, such as interest on a mortgage loan or taxes on real property.

Acknowledgment A formal declaration made before a duly authorized officer, usually a notary public, by a person who has signed a document.

Acre A measure of land equal to 43,560 square feet; 4,840 square yards; 4,047 square meters; 160 square rods; or 0.4047 hectare.

Actual eviction The result of legal action, originated by a lessor, whereby a defaulted tenant is physically ousted from the rented property pursuant to a court order. *See also* Eviction.

Actual notice Express information or fact; that which is known; direct knowledge.

Adjusted basis *See* Basis.

Ad valorem tax A tax levied according to value; generally used to refer to real estate tax. Also called the *general tax*.

Adverse possession The actual, visible, hostile, notorious, exclusive, and continuous possession of another's land under a claim of title. Possession for a statutory period may be a means of acquiring title.

Affidavit of title A written statement, made under oath by a seller or grantor of real property and acknowledged by a notary public, in which the grantor: (1) identifies him- or herself and indicates marital status; (2) certifies that since the examination of the title on the date of the contracts no defects have occurred in the title; and (3) certifies that he or she is in possession of the property (if applicable).

Agency coupled with an interest An agency relationship in which the agent is given an estate or interest in the subject of the agency (the property).

Agent One who acts or has the power to act for another. A fiduciary relationship is created under the *law of agency* when a property owner, as the principal, executes a listing agreement or management contract authorizing a licensed real estate broker to be his or her agent.

Air lot A designated airspace over a piece of land. An air lot, like surface property, may be transferred.

Air rights The right to use the open space above a property, generally allowing the surface to be used for another purpose.

Alienation The act of transferring property to another. Alienation may be voluntary, such as by gift or sale, or involuntary, as through eminent domain or adverse possession.

Alienation clause The clause in a mortgage or trust deed that states that the balance of the secured debt becomes immediately due and payable at the mortgagee's option if the property is sold by the mortgagor. In effect, this clause prevents the mortgagor from assigning the debt without the mortgagee's approval.

Allodial system A system of land ownership in which land is held free and clear of any rent or service due to the government; commonly contrasted to the feudal system. Land is held under the allodial system in the United States.

Amortized loan A loan in which the principal as well as the interest is payable in monthly or other periodic installments over the term of the loan.

Antitrust laws Laws designed to preserve the free enterprise of the open marketplace by making illegal certain private conspiracies and combinations formed to minimize competition. Violations of antitrust laws in the real estate business generally involve either *price fixing* (brokers conspiring to set fixed compensation rates) or *allocation of customers or markets* (brokers agreeing to limit their areas of trade or dealing to certain areas or properties).

Appraisal An estimate of the quantity, quality, or value of something. The process through which conclusions of property value are obtained; also refers to the report that sets forth the process of estimation and conclusion of value.

Appreciation An increase in the worth or value of a property due to economic or related causes, which may prove to be either temporary or permanent; opposite of depreciation.

Assemblage The combining of two or more adjoining lots into one larger tract in order to increase their total value.

Assessment The imposition of a tax, charge, or levy, usually according to established rates.

Assignment The transfer in writing of interest in a bond, mortgage, lease, or other instrument.

Assumption of mortgage Acquiring title to property on which there is an existing mortgage and agreeing to be personally liable for the terms and conditions of the mortgage, including payments.

Attachment The act of taking a person's property into legal custody by writ or other judicial order in order to hold it available for application to that person's debt to a creditor.

Automatic extension A clause in a listing agreement that states that the agreement will continue automatically for a certain period of time after its expiration date. In many states, use of this clause is discouraged or prohibited.

Avulsion The sudden tearing away of land, as by earthquake, flood, volcanic action, or the sudden change in the course of a stream.

Balloon payment A final payment of a mortgage loan that is considerably larger than the required periodic payments because the loan amount was not fully amortized.

Bargain and sale deed A deed that carries with it no warranties against liens or other encumbrances but that does imply that the grantor has the right to convey title. The grantor may add warranties to the deed at his or her discretion.

Base line One of a set of imaginary lines running east and west and crossing a principal meridian at a definite point, used by surveyors for reference in locating and describing land under the rectangular survey (or government survey) system of property description.

Basis The financial interest that the Internal Revenue Service attributes to an owner of an investment property for the purpose of determining annual depreciation and gain or loss on the sale of the asset. If a property was acquired by purchase, the owner's basis is the cost of the property plus the value of any capital expenditures for improvements to the property, minus any depreciation allowable or actually taken. This new basis is called the *adjusted basis.*

Benchmark A permanent reference mark or point established for use by surveyors in measuring differences in elevation.

Beneficiary 1. The person for whom a trust operates, or in whose behalf the income from a trust estate is drawn. 2. A lender who lends money on real estate and takes back a note and trust deed from the borrower.

Bilateral contract *See* Contract.

Binder An agreement that may accompany an earnest money deposit for the purchase of real property as evidence of the purchaser's good faith and intent to complete the transaction.

Blanket mortgage A mortgage covering more than one parcel of real estate, providing for each parcel's partial release from the mortgage lien upon repayment of a definite portion of the debt.

Blockbusting The illegal practice of inducing homeowners to sell their properties by making representations regarding the entry or prospective entry of minority persons into the neighborhood.

Blue-sky laws Common name for those state and federal laws that regulate the registration and sale of investment securities.

Boot Money or property given to make up any difference in value or equity between two properties in an *exchange.*

Branch office A secondary place of business apart from the principal or main office from which real estate business is conducted. A branch office generally must be run by a licensed real estate broker working on behalf of the broker who operates the principal office.

Breach of contract Violation of any terms or conditions in a contract without legal excuse; for example, failure to make a payment when it is due.

Broker One who acts as an intermediary on behalf of others for a fee or commission.

Brokerage The bringing together of parties interested in making a real estate transaction.

Broker-salesperson A person who has passed the broker's licensing examination but is licensed to work only on behalf of a licensed broker.

Building code An ordinance that specifies minimum standards of construction for buildings in order to protect public safety and health.

Bulk transfer *See* Uniform Commercial Code.

Bundle of legal rights The concept of land ownership that means *ownership of all legal rights to the land*—for example, possession, control within the law, and enjoyment—rather than ownership of the land itself.

Business cycle Upward and downward fluctuations in business activity through the stages of expansion, recession, depression, and revival.

Capital gain Income earned from the sale of an asset. If the asset has been held for a specific period of time (currently six months), the income is a *long-term capital gain*.

Capitalization A mathematical process for estimating the value of a property using a proper rate of return on the investment and the annual net income expected to be produced by the property. The formula is expressed:

$$\frac{\text{Income}}{\text{Rate}} = \text{Value}.$$

Capitalization rate The rate of return a property will produce on the owner's investment.

Cash flow The net spendable income from an investment, determined by deducting all operating and fixed expenses from the gross income. If expenses exceed income, a *negative cash flow* is the result.

Casualty insurance A type of insurance policy that protects a property owner or other person from loss or injury sustained as a result of theft, vandalism, or similar occurrences.

Caveat emptor A Latin phrase meaning "Let the buyer beware."

Certificate of sale The document generally given to a purchaser at a tax foreclosure sale. A certificate of sale does not convey title; generally it is an instrument certifying that the holder received title to the property after the redemption period had passed and that the holder paid the property taxes for that interim period.

Certificate of title A statement of opinion on the status of the title to a parcel of real property based on an examination of specified public records.

Chain of title The succession of conveyances, from some accepted starting point, whereby the present holder of real property derives his or her title.

Chattel *See* Personal property.

Closing statement A detailed cash accounting of a real estate transaction showing all cash received, all charges and credits made, and all cash paid out in the transaction.

Cloud on the title Any document, claim, unreleased lien, or encumbrance that may impair the title to real property or make the title doubtful; usually revealed by a title search and removed by either a quitclaim deed or suit to quiet title.

Clustering The grouping of homesites within a subdivision on smaller lots than normal, with the remaining land used as common areas.

Codicil A supplement or addition to a will, executed with the same formalities as a will, that normally does not revoke the entire will.

Cognovit *See* Confession of judgment clause.

Coinsurance clause A clause in insurance policies covering real property that requires the policyholder to maintain fire insurance coverage generally equal to at least 80 percent of the property's actual replacement cost.

Commingling The illegal act of a real estate broker who mixes the money of other people with his or her own money. By law, brokers are required to maintain a separate *trust account* for other parties' funds held temporarily by the broker.

Commission Payment to a broker for services rendered, such as in the sale or purchase of real property; usually a percentage of the selling price of the property.

Common elements Parts of a property that are necessary or convenient to the existence, maintenance, and safety of a condominium, or are normally in common use by all of the condominium residents. Each condominium owner has an undivided ownership interest in the common elements.

Common law The body of law based on custom, usage, and court decisions.

Community property A system of property ownership based on the theory that each spouse has an equal interest in the property acquired by the efforts of either spouse during marriage. This system stemmed from Germanic tribes and, through Spain, came to the Spanish colonies of North and South America. The system was unknown under English common law.

Comparables Properties listed in an appraisal report that are substantially equivalent to the subject property.

Competent parties People who are recognized by law as being able to contract with others; usually those of legal age and sound mind.

Competitive market analysis A comparison of the prices of recently sold homes that are similar to a listing seller's home in terms of location, style, and amenities. Based on this analysis, a broker or salesperson can help the seller determine a listing price.

Condemnation A judicial or administrative proceeding to exercise the power of eminent domain, through which a government agency takes private property for public use and compensates the owner.

Condition A contingency, qualification, or occurrence upon which an estate or property right is gained or lost.

Condominium The absolute ownership of an apartment or a unit (generally in a multi-unit building) based on a legal description of the airspace the unit actually occupies, plus an undivided interest in the ownership of the common elements, which are owned jointly with the other condominium unit owners. The entire tract of real estate included in a condominium development is called a *parcel,* or *development parcel.* One apartment or space in a condominium building, or a part of a property intended for independent use and having lawful access to a public way, is called a *unit*. Ownership of one unit includes a definite undivided interest in the common elements.

Confession of judgment clause A provision that may be included in notes, leases, and contracts by which the debtor, lessee, or obligor authorizes any attorney to go into court to confess a judgment against him or her for a default in payment. Also called a *cognovit*.

Consideration 1. That which is received by the grantor in exchange for his or her deed. 2. Something of value that induces a person to enter into a contract.

Construction loan *See* Interim financing.

Constructive eviction 1. Actions of the landlord that so materially disturb or impair the tenant's enjoyment of the leased premises that the tenant is effectively forced to move out and terminate the lease without liability for any further rent. 2. A purchaser's inability to obtain clear title.

Constructive notice Notice given to the world by recorded documents. All people are charged with knowledge of such documents and their contents, whether or not they have actually examined them. Possession of property is also considered constructive notice that the person in possession has an interest in the property.

Consummate right The status of the dower or curtesy right when, upon the death of the owning spouse, this right becomes complete or may be completed to become an interest in the real estate.

Contract A legally enforceable promise or set of promises that must be performed and for which, if a breach of the promise occurs, the law provides a remedy. A contract may be either *unilateral*, where only one party is bound to act, or *bilateral*, where all parties to the instrument are legally bound to act as prescribed.

Contract for deed A contract for the sale of real estate wherein the purchase price is paid in periodic installments by the purchaser, who is in possession of the property even though title is retained by the seller until final payment. Also called an *installment contract* or *articles of agreement for warranty deed*.

Conventional loan A loan that is not insured or guaranteed by a government or private source.

Cooperative A residential multi-unit building whose title is held by a trust or corporation that is owned by and operated for the benefit of persons living within the building, who are the beneficial owners of the trust or stockholders of the corporation, each possessing a proprietary lease.

Corporation An entity or organization, created by operation of law, whose rights of doing business are essentially the same as those of an individual. The entity has continuous existence until it is dissolved according to legal procedures.

Correction lines Provisions in the rectangular survey (government survey) system made to compensate for the curvature of the earth's surface. Every fourth township line (at 24-mile intervals) is used as a correction line on which the intervals between the north and south range lines are remeasured and corrected to a full six miles.

Cost approach The process of estimating the value of a property by adding to the estimated land value the appraiser's estimate of the reproduction or replacement cost of the building, less depreciation.

Cost recovery An Internal Revenue Service term for *depreciation*.

Counseling The business of providing people with expert advice on a subject, based on the counselor's extensive, expert knowledge of the subject.

Counteroffer A new offer made as a reply to an offer received. It has the effect of rejecting the original offer, which cannot be accepted thereafter unless revived by the offeror's repeating it.

Covenant A written agreement between two or more parties in which a party or parties pledges to perform or not perform specified acts with regard to property; usually found in such real estate documents as deeds, mortgages, leases, and contracts for deed.

Credit On a closing statement, an amount entered in a person's favor—either an amount the party has paid or an amount for which the party must be reimbursed.

Curtesy A life estate, usually a fractional interest, given by some states to the surviving husband in real estate owned by his deceased wife. Most states have abolished curtesy.

Datum A horizontal plane from which heights and depths are measured.

Debit On a closing statement, an amount charged, that is, an amount that the debited party must pay.

Decedent A person who has died.

Dedication The voluntary transfer of private property by its owner to the public for some public use, such as for streets or schools.

Deed A written instrument that, when executed and delivered, conveys title to or an interest in real estate.

Deed in trust An instrument that grants a trustee full powers to sell, mortgage, and subdivide a parcel of real estate. The beneficiary controls the trustee's use of these powers under the provisions of the trust agreement.

Deed of conveyance The instrument used to reconvey title to a trustor under a trust deed once the debt has been satisfied.

Deed of trust *See* Trust deed.

Deed restrictions Clauses in a deed limiting the future uses of the property. Deed restrictions may impose a vast variety of limitations and conditions—for example, they may limit the density of buildings, dictate the types of structures that can be erected, or prevent buildings from being used for specific purposes or even from being used at all.

Default The nonperformance of a duty, whether arising under a contract or otherwise; failure to meet an obligation when due.

Defeasance clause A clause used in leases and mortgages that cancels a specified right upon the occurrence of a certain condition, such as cancellation of a mortgage upon repayment of the mortgage loan.

Defeasible fee estate An estate in which the holder has a fee simple title that may be divested upon the occurrence or nonoccurrence of a specified event. There are two categories of defeasible fee estates: fee simple determinable and fee simple subject to a condition subsequent.

Deficiency judgment A personal judgment levied against the mortgagor when a foreclosure sale does not produce sufficient funds to pay the mortgage debt in full.

Delinquent taxes Unpaid taxes that are past due.

Demand The amount of goods people are willing and able to buy at a given price; often coupled with *supply*.

Density zoning Zoning ordinances that restrict the maximum average number of houses per acre that may be built within a particular area, generally a subdivision.

Depreciation 1. In appraisal, a loss of value in property due to any cause, including physical deterioration, *functional obsolescence,* and *economic obsolescence.* 2. In real estate investment, an expense deduction for tax purposes taken over the period of ownership of income property.

Descent Acquisition of an estate by inheritance in which an heir succeeds to the property by operation of law.

Determinable fee estate A fee simple estate in which the property automatically reverts to the grantor upon the occurrence of a specified event or condition.

Developer One who constructs buildings on lots and sells them.

Devise A gift of real property by will. The donor is the devisor, and the recipient is the devisee.

Discount points An added loan fee charged by a lender to make the yield on a lower-than-market-value loan competitive with higher-interest loans.

Dominant tenement A property that includes in its ownership the appurtenant right to use an easement over another person's property for a specific purpose.

Dower The legal right or interest, recognized in some states, that a wife acquires in the property her husband held or acquired during their marriage. During the husband's lifetime, the right is only a possibility of an interest; upon his death it can become an interest in land. Dower rights have been modified by law in most states. *See also* Consummate right; Inchoate right.

Dual agency Representing both parties to a transaction. This is unethical unless both parties agree to it, and it is illegal in many states.

Duress Unlawful constraint or action exercised upon a person whereby the person is forced to perform an act against his or her will. A contract entered into under duress is considered voidable.

Earnest money deposit An amount of money, deposited by a buyer under the terms of a contract, that is to be forfeited if the buyer defaults but applied on the purchase price if the sale is closed.

Easement A right to use the land of another for a specific purpose, such as for a right-of-way or utilities; an incorporeal interest in land. An *easement appurtenant* passes with the land when conveyed.

Easement by necessity An easement allowed by law as necessary for the full enjoyment of a parcel of real estate; for example, a right of ingress and egress over a grantor's land.

Easement by prescription An easement acquired by continuous, open, uninterrupted, exclusive, and adverse use of the property for the period of time prescribed by state law.

Easement in gross An easement that is not created for the benefit of any *land* owned by the owner of the easement but that attaches *personally to the easement owner.* For example, a right granted by Eleanor Franks to Joe Fish to use a portion of her property for the rest of his life would be an easement in gross.

Economic obsolescence A loss of value in real property resulting from factors existing outside the property itself. An example of such a factor would be the building of a factory adjacent to an apartment complex.

Emblements Growing crops, such as grapes and corn, that are produced annually through labor and industry; also called *fructus industriales.*

Eminent domain The right of a government or municipal quasi-public body to acquire property for public use through a court action called *condemnation,* in which the court decides that the use is a public use and determines the price or compensation to be paid to the owner.

Employee Someone who works as a direct employee of an employer and has employee status. The employer is obligated to withhold income taxes and social security taxes from the compensation of his or her employees. *See also* Independent contractor.

Employment contract A document evidencing formal employment between employer and employee or between principal and agent. In the real estate business, this generally takes the form of a listing agreement or management agreement.

Enabling acts State legislation that confers zoning powers on municipal governments.

Encroachment A building or some portion of it—a wall or fence for instance—that extends beyond the land of the owner and illegally intrudes upon some land of an adjoining owner or a street or alley.

Encumbrance Any lien—such as a mortgage, tax, or judgment lien; an easement; a restriction on the use of the land, or an outstanding dower right—that may diminish the value of a property.

Equalization The raising or lowering of assessed values for tax purposes in a particular county or taxing district to make them equal to assessments in other counties or districts.

Equalization factor A factor (number) by which the assessed value of a property is multiplied to arrive at a value for the property that is in line with state-wide tax assessments. The *ad valorem tax* would be based upon this adjusted value.

Equitable lien *See* Statutory lien.

Equitable title The interest held by a vendee under a contract for deed or an installment contract; the equitable right to obtain absolute ownership to property when legal title is held in another's name.

Equity The interest or value that an owner has in his or her property over and above any mortgage indebtedness.

Erosion The gradual wearing away of land by water, wind, and general weather conditions; the diminishing of property caused by the elements.

Escheat The reversion of property to the state or county, as provided by state law, in cases where a decedent dies intestate without heirs capable of inheriting or when the property is abandoned.

Escrow The closing of a transaction through a third party called an *escrow agent,* or *escrowee,* who receives certain funds and documents to be delivered upon the performance of certain conditions outlined in the escrow agreement.

Escrow agreement A contract that sets forth the duties of the escrow agent, as well as the requirements and obligations of the parties to the transaction, when a transaction is closed through an escrow.

Estate for years An interest for a certain, exact period of time in property leased for a specified consideration.

Estate from period to period *See* Periodic estate.

Estate in land The degree, quantity, nature, and extent of interest that a person has in real property.

Estate taxes Federal taxes on a decedent's real and personal property.

Estoppel certificate A document in which a borrower certifies the amount he or she owes on a mortgage loan and the rate of interest.

Eviction A legal process to oust a person from possession of real estate.

Evidence of title Proof of ownership of property; is commonly a certificate of title, a title insurance policy, an abstract of title with lawyer's opinion, or a Torrens registration certificate.

Exchange A transaction in which all or part of the consideration is the transfer of *like-kind* property (such as real estate for real estate).

Exclusive-agency listing A listing contract under which the owner appoints a real estate broker as his or her exclusive agent for a designated period of time to sell the property, on the owner's stated terms, for a commission. The owner reserves the right to sell without paying anyone a commission if he or she sells to a prospect who has not been introduced or claimed by the broker.

Exclusive right to sell A listing contract under which the owner appoints a real estate broker as his or her exclusive agent for a designated period of time, to sell the property on the owner's stated terms, and agrees to pay the broker a commission when the property is sold, whether by the broker, the owner, or another broker.

Executed contract A contract in which all parties have fulfilled their promises and thus performed the contract.

Execution The signing and delivery of an instrument. Also, a legal order directing an official to enforce a judgment against the property of a debtor.

Executory contract A contract under which something remains to be done by one or more of the parties.

Expenses Short-term costs, such as minor repairs, regular maintenance, and renting costs, that are deducted from an investment property's income.

Expressed contract An oral or written contract in which the parties state the contract's terms and express their intentions in words.

Fee simple estate The maximum possible estate or right of ownership of real property, continuing forever. Sometimes called a *fee* or *fee simple absolute.*

Feudal system A system of ownership usually associated with precolonial England, in which the king or other sovereign is the source of all rights. The right to possess real property was granted by the sovereign to an individual as a life estate only. Upon the death of the individual, title passed back to the sovereign, not to the decedent's heirs.

FHA loan A loan insured by the Federal Housing Administration and made by an approved lender in accordance with the FHA's regulations.

Fiduciary relationship A relationship of trust and confidence, as between trustee and beneficiary, attorney and client, or principal and agent.

Financing statement *See* Uniform Commercial Code.

Fiscal policy The government's policy in regard to taxation and spending programs. The balance between these two areas determines the amount of money the government will withdraw from or feed into the economy, to try to counter economic peaks and slumps.

Fixture An item of personal property that has been converted to real property by being permanently affixed to the realty.

Foreclosure A legal procedure whereby property used as security for a debt is sold to satisfy the debt in the event of default in payment of the mortgage note or default of other terms in the mortgage document. The foreclosure procedure brings the rights of all parties to a conclusion and passes the title in the mortgaged property to either the holder of the mortgage or a third party who may purchase the realty at the foreclosure sale, free of all encumbrances affecting the property subsequent to the mortgage.

Fraud Deception intended to cause a person to give up property or a lawful right.

Freehold estate An estate in land in which ownership is for an indeterminate length of time, in contrast to a *leasehold estate*.

Functional obsolescence A loss of value to an improvement to real estate arising from functional problems, often caused by age or poor design.

Future interest A person's present right to an interest in real property that will not result in possession or enjoyment until some time in the future, such as a reversion or right of reentry.

Gap A defect in the chain of title of a particular parcel of real estate; a missing document or conveyance that raises doubt as to the present ownership of the land.

General agent One who is authorized by his or her principal to represent the principal in a specific range of matters.

General contractor A construction specialist who enters into a formal construction contract with a landowner or master lessee to construct a real estate building or project. The general contractor often contracts with several *subcontractors* specializing in various aspects of the building process to perform individual jobs.

General lien The right of a creditor to have all of a debtor's property—both real and personal—sold to satisfy a debt.

General partnership *See* Partnership.

General tax *See* Ad valorem tax.

Government lot Fractional sections in the rectangular survey (government survey) system that are less than one quarter-section in area.

Government survey system *See* Rectangular survey system.

Grantee A person who receives a conveyance of real property from the grantor.

Granting clause Words in a deed of conveyance that state the grantor's intention to convey the property at the present time. This clause is generally worded as "convey and warrant," "grant," "grant, bargain, and sell," or the like.

Grantor The person transferring title to or an interest in real property to a grantee.

Gross lease A lease of property under which a landlord pays all property charges regularly incurred through ownership, such as repairs, taxes, insurance, and operating expenses. Most residential leases are gross leases.

Gross rent multiplier A figure used as a multiplier of the gross rental income of a property to produce an estimate of the property's value.

Ground lease A lease of land only, on which the tenant usually owns a building or is required to build his or her own building as specified in the lease. Such leases are usually long-term net leases; the tenant's rights and obligations continue until the lease expires or is terminated through default.

Habendum clause That part of a deed beginning with the words, "to have and to hold," following the granting clause and defining the extent of ownership the grantor is conveying.

Heir One who might inherit or succeed to an interest in land under the state law of descent when the owner dies without leaving a valid will.

Highest and best use That possible use of land that would produce the greatest net income and thereby develop the highest land value.

Holdover tenancy A tenancy whereby a lessee retains possession of leased property after his or her lease has expired, and the landlord, by continuing to accept rent, agrees to the tenant's continued occupancy as defined by state law.

Holographic will A will that is written, dated, and signed in the testator's handwriting but is not witnessed.

Homeowner's insurance policy A standardized package insurance policy that covers a residential real estate owner against financial loss from fire, theft, public liability, and other common risks.

Homestead Land that is owned and occupied as the family home. In many states, a portion of the area or value of this land is protected or exempt from judgments for debts.

Implied contract A contract under which the agreement of the parties is demonstrated by their acts and conduct.

Improvement 1. An improvement *on* land is any structure, usually privately owned, erected on a site to enhance the value of the property—for example, buildings, fences, and driveways. 2. An improvement *to* land is usually a publicly owned structure, such as a curb, sidewalk, street, or sewer.

Inchoate right An incomplete right, often a wife's interest in the land of her husband during his life, which upon his death may become a dower interest.

Income approach The process of estimating the value of an income-producing property by capitalization of the annual net income expected to be produced by the property during its remaining useful life.

Incorporeal right A nonpossessory right in real estate; for example, an easement or right-of-way.

Independent contractor Someone who is retained to perform a certain act but who is subject to the control and direction of another only as to the end result and not as to the way in which he or she performs the act. Unlike an employee, an independent contractor pays for all his or her expenses and social security and income taxes and receives no employee benefits. Many real estate salespeople are independent contractors.

Informed consent exception A provision in many state real estate license laws that permits a broker to represent both buyer and seller to a transaction if he or she has their prior mutual consent to do so.

Inheritance taxes State-imposed taxes on a decedent's real and personal property.

Installment contract *See* Contract for deed.

Installment sale A transaction in which the sales price is paid in two or more installments over two or more years. If the sale meets certain requirements, a taxpayer can postpone reporting such income to future years by paying tax each year only on the proceeds received that year.

Interest A charge made by a lender for the use of money.

Interim financing A short-term loan usually made during the construction phase of a building project (in this case, often referred to as a *construction loan*).

Intestate The condition of a property owner who dies without leaving a valid will. Title to the property will pass to his or her heirs as provided in the state law of descent.

Investment Money directed toward the purchase, improvement, and development of an asset in expectation of income or profits.

Involuntary alienation *See* Alienation.

Irrevocable consent An agreement filed by an out-of-state broker in the state in which he or she wishes to be licensed, stating that suits and actions may be brought against the broker in that state.

Joint tenancy Ownership of real estate between two or more parties who have been named in one conveyance as joint tenants. Upon the death of a joint tenant, his or her interest passes to the surviving joint tenant or tenants by the *right of survivorship*.

Joint venture The joining of two or more people to conduct a specific business enterprise. A joint venture is similar to a partnership in that it must be created by agreement between the parties to share in the losses and profits of the venture. Yet it is unlike a partnership in that the venture is for one specific project only, rather than for a continuing business relationship.

Judgment The formal decision of a court upon the respective rights and claims of the parties to an action or suit. After a judgment has been entered and recorded with the county recorder, it usually becomes a general lien on the property of the defendant.

Junior lien An obligation, such as a second mortgage, that is subordinate in right or lien priority to an existing lien on the same realty.

Laches An equitable doctrine used by courts to bar a legal claim or prevent the assertion of a right because of undue delay or failure to assert the claim or right.

Land The earth's surface, extending downward to the center of the earth and upward infinitely into space.

Land contract *See* Contract for deed.

Last will and testament *See* Will.

Law of agency *See* Agent.

Lease A written or oral contract between a landlord (the lessor) and a tenant (the lessee) that transfers the right to exclusive possession and use of the landlord's real property to the lessee for a specified period of time and for a stated consideration (rent). By state law, leases for longer than a certain period of time (generally one year) must be in writing to be enforceable.

Leasehold estate A tenant's right to occupy real estate during the term of a lease; generally considered to be a personal property interest.

Legacy A disposition of money or personal property by will.

Legal description A description of a specific parcel of real estate complete enough for an independent surveyor to locate and identify it.

Lessee *See* Lease.

Lessor *See* Lease.

Leverage The use of borrowed money to finance the bulk of an investment.

Levy To assess; to seize or collect. To levy a tax is to assess a property and set the rate of taxation. To levy an execution is to officially seize the property of a person in order to satisfy an obligation.

License 1. A privilege or right granted to a person by a state to operate as a real estate broker or salesperson. 2. The revocable permission for a temporary use of land—a personal right that cannot be sold.

Lien A right given by law to certain creditors to have their debt paid out of the property of a defaulting debtor, usually by means of a court sale.

Lien theory Some states' interpretation of a mortgage as being purely a lien on real property. The mortgagee thus has no right of possession, but must foreclose the lien and sell the property, if the mortgagor defaults.

Life estate An interest in real or personal property that is limited in duration to the lifetime of its owner or some other designated person.

Life tenant A person in possession of a life estate.

Like-kind property *See* Exchange.

Limited partnership *See* Partnership.

Liquidity The ability to sell an asset and convert it into cash, at a price close to its true value, in a short period of time.

Lis pendens A recorded legal document giving constructive notice that an action affecting a particular property has been filed in either a state or a federal court.

Listing agreement A contract between a landowner (as principal) and a licensed real estate broker (as agent) by which the broker is employed as agent to sell real estate on the owner's terms within a given time, for which service the landowner agrees to pay a commission.

Listing broker The broker in a multiple-listing situation from whose office a listing agreement is initiated, as opposed to the *selling broker,* from whose office negotiations leading up to a sale are initiated. The listing broker and the selling broker may be the same person. *See also* Multiple listing.

Littoral rights 1. A landowner's claim to use water in large navigable lakes and oceans adjacent to his or her property. 2. The ownership rights to land bordering these bodies of water up to the high-water mark.

Locational obsolescence Reduction in a property's value caused by factors outside the subject property, such as social or environmental forces.

Lot-and-block description A description of real property that identifies a parcel of land by reference to lot and block numbers within a subdivision, as specified on a plat of subdivision duly recorded in the county recorder's office.

Management agreement A contract between the owner of income property and a management firm or individual property manager that outlines the scope of the manager's authority to manage the property.

Market A place where goods can be bought and sold, and a price established.

Marketable title Good or clear title, reasonably free from the risk of litigation over possible defects.

Market comparison approach The process of estimating the value of a property by examining and comparing actual sales of comparable properties.

Market price The actual selling price of a property.

Market value The highest price a ready, willing, and able buyer would pay, and the lowest price a ready, willing, and able seller would accept, neither being under any pressure to act.

Master plan A comprehensive plan to guide the long-term physical development of a particular area.

Mechanic's lien A statutory lien created in favor of contractors, laborers, and materialmen who have performed work or furnished materials in the erection or repair of a building.

Metes-and-bounds description A legal description of a parcel of land that begins at a well-marked point and follows the boundaries, using directions and distances around the tract back to the place of beginning.

Mill One-tenth of one cent. Some states use a mill rate to compute real estate taxes; for example, a rate of 52 mills would be $0.052 tax for each dollar of assessed valuation of a property.

Monetary policy Governmental regulation of the amount of money in circulation through such institutions as the Federal Reserve Board.

Money judgment A court judgment ordering payment of money rather than specific performance of a certain action. *See also* Judgment.

Month-to-month tenancy A periodic tenancy under which the tenant rents for one month at a time. In the absence of a rental agreement (oral or written), a tenancy is generally considered to be month to month.

Monument A fixed natural or artificial object used to establish real estate boundaries for a metes-and-bounds description.

Mortgage A conditional transfer or pledge of real estate as security for the payment of a debt. Also, the document creating a mortgage lien.

Mortgagee A lender in a mortgage loan transaction.

Mortgage lien A lien or charge on the property of a mortgagor that secures the underlying debt obligations.

Mortgagor A borrower who conveys his or her property as security for a loan.

Multiple listing An exclusive listing (an exclusive right to sell or exclusive agency) with the additional authority and obligation on the part of the listing broker to distribute the listing to other brokers in the multiple-listing organization.

Negative cash flow *See* Cash flow.

Negotiable instrument A written instrument that may be transferred by endorsement or delivery. The holder, or payee, may sign the instrument over to another person or, in certain cases, merely deliver it to him or her. The transferee then has the original payee's right to payment.

Net lease A lease requiring the tenant to pay not only rent but also all costs incurred in maintaining the property, including taxes, insurance, utilities, and repairs.

Net listing A listing based on the net price the seller will receive if the property is sold. Under a net listing, the broker is free to offer the property for sale at the highest price he or she can get in order to increase the commission. This type of listing is outlawed in many states.

Nonconforming use A use of property that is permitted to continue after a zoning ordinance prohibiting it has been established for the area.

Nonhomogeneity A lack of uniformity; dissimilarity. Since no two parcels of land are exactly alike, real estate is said to be nonhomogeneous.

Note An instrument of credit given to attest a debt.

Novation Substituting a new obligation for an old one, or substituting new parties to an existing obligation, as when the parties to an agreement accept a new debtor in place of an old one.

Nuncupative will An oral will declared by the testator in his or her final illness, made before witnesses and afterwards reduced to writing.

Offer and acceptance Two essential components of a valid contract; a "meeting of the minds."

Open-end mortgage A mortgage loan that is expandable by increments up to a maximum dollar amount, the full loan being secured by the same original mortgage.

Open listing A listing contract under which the broker's commission is contingent upon the broker's producing a ready, willing, and able buyer before the property is sold by the seller or another broker.

Option An agreement to keep open for a set period an offer to sell or purchase property.

Ostensible agency A form of implied agency relationship created by the actions of the parties involved rather than by written agreement or document.

Package mortgage A method of financing in which the loan that finances the purchase of a home also finances the purchase of certain items of personal property, such as a washer, dryer, refrigerator, stove, and other specified appliances.

Parcel A specific portion of a large tract of real estate; a lot.

Participation financing A mortgage in which the lender participates in the income of the mortgaged venture beyond a fixed return or receives a yield on the loan in addition to the straight interest rate.

Partition The division of cotenants' interests in real property when the parties do not all voluntarily agree to terminate the co-ownership; takes place through court procedures.

Partnership An association of two or more individuals who carry on a continuing business for profit as co-owners. Under the law, a partnership is regarded as a group of individuals rather than as a single entity. A *general partnership* is a typical form of joint venture, in which each general partner shares in the administration, profits, and losses of the operation. A *limited partnership* is a business arrangement whereby the operation is administered by one or more general partners and funded, by and large, by limited or silent partners, who are by law responsible for losses only to the extent of their investments.

Party wall A wall that is located on or at a boundary line between two adjoining parcels of land and is used or is intended to be used by the owners of both properties.

Patent A grant or franchise of land from the United States government.

Percentage lease A lease, commonly used for commercial property, whose rental is based on the tenant's gross sales at the premises; it generally stipulates a base monthly rental plus a percentage of any gross sales above a certain amount.

Periodic estate An interest in leased property that continues from period to period—week to week, month to month, or year to year.

Personal property Items, called *chattels,* that do not fit into the definition of real property; movable objects.

Physical deterioration A reduction in a property's value resulting from a decline in physical condition; can be caused by action of the elements or by ordinary wear and tear.

Planned unit development A planned combination of diverse land uses, such as housing, recreation, and shopping, in one contained development or subdivision.

Plat A map of a town, section, or subdivision indicating the location and boundaries of individual properties.

Plottage The increase in value or utility resulting from the consolidation *(assemblage)* of two or more adjacent lots into one larger lot.

Point A unit of measurement used for various loan charges; one point equals one percent of the amount of the loan. *See also* Discount points.

Point of beginning In a metes-and-bounds legal description, the starting point of the survey, situated in one corner of the parcel; all metes-and-bounds descriptions must follow the boundaries of the parcel back to the point of beginning.

Police power The government's right to impose laws, statutes, and ordinances, including zoning ordinances and building codes, to protect the public health, safety, and welfare.

Power of attorney A written instrument authorizing a person, the *attorney-in-fact,* to act as agent on behalf of another person to the extent indicated in the instrument.

Precedent In law, the requirements established by prior court decisions.

Prepayment penalty A charge imposed on a borrower who pays off the loan principal early. This penalty compensates the lender for interest and other charges that would otherwise be lost.

Price fixing *See* Antitrust laws.

Primary mortgage market *See* Secondary mortgage market.

Principal 1. A sum lent or employed as a fund or investment, as distinguished from its income or profits. 2. The original amount (as in a loan) of the total due and payable at a certain date. 3. A main party to a transaction—the person for whom the agent works.

Principal meridian One of 35 north and south survey lines established and defined as part of the rectangular survey (government survey) system.

Prior appropriation A concept of water ownership in which the landowner's right to use available water is based on a government-administered permit system.

Priority The order of position or time. The priority of liens is generally determined by the chronological order in which the lien documents are recorded; tax liens, however, have priority even over previously recorded liens.

Probate A legal process by which a court determines who will inherit a decedent's property and what the estate's assets are.

Procuring cause The effort that brings about the desired result. Under an open listing, the broker who is the procuring cause of the sale receives the commission.

Progression An appraisal principle that states that, between dissimilar properties, the value of the lesser-quality property is favorably affected by the presence of the better-quality property.

Property manager Someone who manages real estate for another person for compensation. Duties include collecting rents, maintaining the property, and keeping up all accounting.

Prorations Expenses, either prepaid or paid in arrears, that are divided or distributed between buyer and seller at the closing.

Puffing Exaggerated or superlative comments or opinions not made as representations of fact and thus not grounds for misrepresentation.

Pur autre vie For the life of another. A life estate pur autre vie is a life estate that is measured by the life of a person other than the grantee.

Purchase-money mortgage A note secured by a mortgage or trust deed given by a buyer, as mortgagor, to a seller, as mortgagee, as part of the purchase price of the real estate.

Quiet title suit *See* Suit to quiet title.

Quitclaim deed A conveyance by which the grantor transfers whatever interest he or she has in the real estate, without warranties or obligations.

Range A strip of land six miles wide, extending north and south, and numbered east and west according to its distance from the principal meridian in the rectangular survey (government survey) system of land description.

Ready, willing, and able buyer One who is prepared to buy property on the seller's terms and is ready to take positive steps to consummate the transaction.

Real estate Land; a portion of the earth's surface extending downward to the center of the earth and upward infinitely into space, including all things permanently attached thereto, whether by nature or by a person; any and every interest in land.

Real estate broker Any person, partnership, association, or corporation who sells (or offers to sell), buys (or offers to buy), or negotiates the purchase, sale, or exchange of real estate, or who leases (or offers to lease) or rents (or offers to rent) any real estate or the improvements thereon for others and for a compensation or valuable consideration. A real estate broker may not conduct business without a real estate broker's license.

Real estate investment syndicate *See* Syndicate.

Real estate investment trust (REIT) Trust ownership of real estate by a group of at least 100 individuals who purchase certificates of ownership in the trust, which in turn invests the money in real property and distributes the profits back to the investors free of corporate income tax.

Real estate license law State law enacted to protect the public from fraud, dishonesty, and incompetence in the purchase and sale of real estate.

Real property The earth's surface extending downward to the center of the earth and upward into space, including all things permanently attached to it by nature or by people, as well as the interests, benefits, and rights inherent in real estate ownership.

REALTOR® A registered trademark term reserved for the sole use of active members of local REALTOR® boards affiliated with the NATIONAL ASSOCIATION OF REALTORS®.

Recapture *See* Accelerated depreciation.

Reconciliation The final step in the appraisal process, in which the appraiser reconciles the estimates of value received from the market data, cost, and income approaches to arrive at a final estimate of market value for the subject property.

Recording The act of entering or recording documents affecting or conveying interests in real estate in the recorder's office established in each county. Until it is recorded, a deed or mortgage generally is not effective against subsequent purchasers or mortgages.

Recovery fund A fund established in some states from real estate license revenues to cover claims of aggrieved parties who have suffered monetary damage through the actions of a real estate licensee.

Rectangular survey system A system established in 1785 by the federal government, providing for surveying and describing land by reference to principal meridians and base lines.

Redemption The buying back of real estate sold in a tax sale. The defaulted owner is said to have the right of redemption.

Redemption period A period of time established by state law during which a property owner has the right to redeem his or her real estate from a foreclosure or tax sale by paying the sales price, interest, and costs. Many states do not have mortgage redemption laws.

Redlining The illegal practice of a lending institution denying loans or restricting their number for certain areas of a community.

Regression An appraisal principle that states that, between dissimilar properties, the value of the better property is adversely affected by the presence of the lesser-quality property.

Regulation Z Law requiring credit institutions to inform borrowers of the true cost of obtaining credit; commonly called the Truth-in-Lending Act.

Release deed A document, also known as a *deed of reconveyance,* that transfers all rights given a trustee under a trust deed loan back to the grantor after the loan has been fully repaid.

Remainder The remnant of an estate that has been conveyed to take effect and be enjoyed after the termination of a prior estate, such as when an owner conveys a life estate to one party and the remainder to another.

Renegotiable rate mortgage A mortgage loan in which the interest rate may increase or decrease at specified intervals, within certain limits based upon an economic indicator.

Rent A fixed, periodic payment made by a tenant of a property to the owner for possession and use, usually by prior agreement of the parties.

Rent schedule A statement of proposed rental rates, determined by the owner or the property manager or both, based on a building's estimated expenses, market supply and demand, and the owner's long-range goals for the property.

Replacement cost The construction cost at current prices of a property that is not necessarily an exact duplicate of the subject property but serves the same purpose or function as the original.

Reproduction cost The construction cost at current prices of an exact duplicate of the subject property.

Restriction A limitation on the use of real property, generally originated by the owner or subdivider in a deed.

Reversion The remnant of an estate that the grantor holds after he or she has granted a life estate to another person—the estate will return, or revert, to the grantor; also called a *reverter*.

Reversionary interest *See* Reversion.

Reversionary right An owner's right to regain possession of leased property upon termination of the lease agreement.

Right of survivorship *See* Joint tenancy.

Riparian rights An owner's rights in land that borders on or includes a stream, river, or lake. These rights include access to and use of the water.

Sale and leaseback A transaction in which an owner sells his or her improved property and, as part of the same transaction, signs a long-term lease to remain in possession of the premises.

Sales contract A contract containing the complete terms of the agreement between buyer and seller for the sale of a particular parcel or parcels of real estate.

Salesperson A person who performs real estate activities while employed by or associated with a licensed real estate broker.

Satisfaction A document acknowledging the payment of a debt.

Secondary mortgage market A market for the purchase and sale of existing mortgages, designed to provide greater liquidity for mortgages; also called the *secondary money market*. Mortgages are first originated in the *primary mortgage market*.

Section A portion of a township under the rectangular survey (government survey) system. A township is divided into 36 sections, numbered 1 to 36. A section is a square with mile-long sides and an area of one square mile, or 640 acres.

Selling broker *See* Listing broker.

Separate property Under community property law, property owned solely by either spouse before the marriage, or acquired by gift or inheritance after the marriage, or purchased with separate funds after the marriage.

Servient tenement Land on which an easement exists in favor of an adjacent property (called a dominant estate); also called a *servient estate*.

Setback The amount of space local zoning regulations require between a lot line and a building line.

Severalty Ownership of real property by one person only, also called *sole ownership*.

Severance Changing an item or real estate to personal property by detaching it from the land; for example, cutting down a tree.

Shared appreciation mortgage A mortgage loan in which the lender, in exchange for a loan with a favorable interest rate, participates in the profits (if any) the mortgagor receives when the property is eventually sold.

Situs The personal preference of people for one area over another, not necessarily based on objective facts and knowledge.

Sole ownership *See* Severalty.

Special agent One who is authorized by a principal to perform a single act or transaction; a real estate broker is usually a special agent authorized to find a ready, willing, and able buyer for a particular property.

Special assessment A tax or levy customarily imposed against only those specific parcels of real estate that will benefit from a proposed public improvement like a street or sewer.

Special warranty deed A deed in which the grantor warrants, or guarantees, the title only against defects arising during the period of his or her tenure and ownership of the property and not against defects existing before that time, generally using the language, "by, through, or under the grantor but not otherwise."

Specific lien A lien affecting or attaching only to a certain, specific parcel of land or piece of property.

Specific performance suit A legal action brought in a court of equity in special cases to compel a party to carry out the terms of a contract. The basis for an equity court's jurisdiction in breach of a real estate contract is the fact that land is unique and therefore mere legal damages would not adequately compensate the buyer for the seller's breach.

Spot zoning A change in a local zoning ordinance to permit a particular use that is inconsistent with the area's zoning classification. Spot zoning is not favored in the law.

Statute of frauds That part of a state law that requires certain instruments, such as deeds, real estate sales contracts, and certain leases, to be in writing in order to be legally enforceable.

Statute of limitations That law pertaining to the period of time within which certain actions must be brought to court.

Statutory lien A lien imposed on property by statute—a tax lien, for example—in contrast to an *equitable lien,* which arises out of common law.

Steering The illegal practice of channeling home seekers to particular areas, either to maintain the homogeneity of an area or to change the character of an area in order to create a speculative situation.

Straight-line method A method of calculating depreciation for tax purposes, computed by dividing the adjusted basis of a property by the estimated number of years of remaining useful life.

Subcontractor *See* General contractor.

Subdivider One who buys undeveloped land, divides it into smaller, usable lots, and sells the lots to potential users (often *developers*).

Subdivision A tract of land divided by the owner, known as the *subdivider,* into blocks, building lots, and streets according to a recorded subdivision plat, which must comply with local ordinances and regulations.

"Subject to" clause A clause in a deed specifying exceptions and reservations affecting the title.

Subletting The leasing of premises by a lessee to a third party for part of the lessee's remaining term. *See also* Assignment.

Subordination Relegation to a lesser position, usually in respect to a right or security.

Subordination agreement A written agreement between holders of liens on a property that changes the priority of mortgage, judgment, and other liens under certain circumstances.

Subrogation The substitution of one creditor for another, with the substituted person succeeding to the legal rights and claims of the original claimant. Subrogation is used by title insurers to acquire from the injured party rights to sue in order to recover any claims they have paid.

Substitution An appraisal principle that states that the maximum value of a property tends to be set by the cost of purchasing an equally desirable and valuable substitute property, assuming that no costly delay is encountered in making the substitution.

Subsurface rights Ownership rights in a parcel of real estate to the water, minerals, gas, oil, and so forth that lie beneath the surface of the property.

Suit for possession A court suit initiated by a landlord to evict a tenant from leased premises after the tenant has breached one of the terms of the lease or has held possession of the property after the lease's expiration.

Suit to quiet title A court action intended to establish or settle the title to a particular property, especially when there is a cloud on the title.

Supply The amount of goods available in the market to be sold at a given price. The term is often coupled with *demand.*

Surety bond An agreement by an insurance or bonding company to be responsible for certain possible defaults, debts, or obligations contracted for by an insured party; in essence, a policy insuring one's personal and/or financial integrity. In the real estate business, a surety bond is generally used to ensure that a particular project will be completed at a certain date or that a contract will be performed as stated.

Surface rights Ownership rights in a parcel of real estate that are limited to the surface of the property and do not include the air above it (*air rights*) or the minerals below the surface (*subsurface rights*).

Survey The process by which boundaries are measured and land areas are determined; the on-site measurement of lot lines, dimensions, and position of a house on a lot, including the determination of any existing encroachments or easements.

Syndicate A combination of people or firms formed to accomplish a business venture of mutual interest by pooling resources. In a *real estate investment syndicate,* the parties own and/or develop property, with the main profit generally arising from the sale of the property.

Tacking Adding or combining successive periods of continuous occupation of real property by adverse possessors. This concept enables someone who has not been in possession for the entire statutory period to establish a claim of adverse possession.

Taxation The process by which a government or municipal quasi-public body raises monies to fund its operation.

Tax deed An instrument, similar to a certificate of sale, given to a purchaser at a tax sale. *See also* Certificate of sale.

Tax levy *See* Levy.

Tax lien A charge against property created by operation of law. Tax liens and assessments take priority over all other liens.

Tax rate The rate at which real property is taxed in a tax district or county. For example, in a certain county, real property may be taxed at a rate of .056 cents per dollar of assessed valuation.

Tax sale A court-ordered sale of real property to raise money to cover delinquent taxes.

Tax shelter A (legal) means by which an investor may reduce or defer payment of part of his or her federal or state income tax.

Tenancy at sufferance The tenancy of a lessee who lawfully comes into possession of a landlord's real estate but who continues to occupy the premises improperly after his or her lease rights have expired.

Tenancy at will An estate that gives the lessee the right to possession until the estate is terminated by either party; the term of this estate is indefinite.

Tenancy by the entirety The joint ownership, recognized in some states, of property acquired by husband and wife during marriage. Upon the death of one spouse, the survivor becomes the owner of the property.

Tenancy in common A form of co-ownership by which each owner holds an undivided interest in real property as if he or she were sole owner. Each individual owner has the right to partition. Unlike joint tenants, tenants in common have right of inheritance.

Tenant One who holds or possesses lands or tenements by any kind of right or title.

Testate Having made and left a valid will.

Time is of the essence A phrase in a contract that requires the performance of a certain act within a stated period of time.

Title 1. The right to or ownership of land. 2. The evidence of ownership of land.

Title insurance A policy insuring the owner or mortgagee against loss by reason of defects in the title to a parcel of real estate, other than encumbrances, defects, and matters specifically excluded by the policy.

Title theory Some states' interpretation of a mortgage to mean that the lender is the owner of mortgaged land. Upon full payment of the mortgage debt, the borrower becomes the landowner.

Torrens system A method of evidencing title by registration with the proper public authority, generally called the registrar. Named for its founder, Sir Robert Torrens.

Township The principal unit of the rectangular survey (government survey) system. A township is a square with six-mile sides and an area of 36 square miles.

Township line Lines running at six-mile intervals parallel to the base lines in the rectangular survey (government survey) system.

Trade fixtures Articles installed by a tenant under the terms of a lease and removable by the tenant before the lease expires. These remain personal property and are not true fixtures.

Transfer tax Tax stamps required to be affixed to a deed by state and/or local law.

Trust A fiduciary arrangement whereby property is conveyed to a person or institution, called a *trustee,* to be held and administered on behalf of another person, called a *beneficiary.* The one who conveys the trust is called the *trustor.*

Trust account *See* Commingling.

Trust deed An instrument used to create a mortgage lien by which the mortgagor conveys his or her title to a trustee, who holds it as security for the benefit of the note holder (the lender); also called a *deed of trust.*

Trustee *See* Trust.

Trustee's deed A deed executed by a trustee conveying land held in a trust.

Undivided interest *See* Tenancy in common.

Unenforceable contract A contract that has all the elements of a valid contract, yet neither party can sue the other to force performance of it. For example, an unsigned contract is generally unenforceable.

Uniform Commercial Code A codification of commercial law, adopted in most states, that attempts to make uniform all laws relating to commercial transactions, including chattel mortgages and bulk transfers. Security interests in chattels are created by an instrument known as a *security agreement.* To give notice of the security interest, a *financing statement* must be recorded. Article 6 of the code regulates *bulk transfers*—the sale of a business as a whole, including all fixtures, chattels, and merchandise.

Unilateral contract A one-sided contract wherein one party makes a promise in order to induce a second party to do something. The second party is not legally bound to perform; however, if the second party does comply, the first party is obligated to keep the promise.

Unity of ownership The four unities that are traditionally needed to create a joint tenancy—unity of title, time, interest, and possession.

Universal agent One who is empowered by a principal to represent him or her in all matters that can be delegated.

Urban renewal The acquisition of run-down city areas for purposes of redevelopment.

Useful life In real estate investment, the number of years a property will be useful to the investors.

Usury Charging interest at a higher rate than the maximum rate established by state law.

Valid contract A contract that complies with all the essentials of a contract and is binding and enforceable on all parties to it.

VA loan A mortgage loan on approved property made to a qualified veteran by an authorized lender and guaranteed by the Veterans Administration in order to limit the lender's possible loss.

Value The power of a good or service to command other goods in exchange for the present worth of future rights to its income or amenities.

Variable rate mortgage A mortgage loan in which the interest rate may increase or decrease at specified intervals within certain limits, based upon an economic indicator.

Variance Permission obtained from zoning authorities to build a structure or conduct a use that is expressly prohibited by the current zoning laws; an exception from the zoning ordinances.

Vendee A buyer.

Vendor A seller.

Voidable contract A contract that seems to be valid on the surface, but may be rejected or disaffirmed by one or both of the parties.

Void contract A contract that has no legal force or effect because it does not meet the essential elements of a contract.

Voluntary transfer *See* Alienation.

Warranty deed A deed in which the grantor fully warrants good clear title to the premises. Used in most real estate deed transfers, a warranty deed offers the greatest protection of any deed.

Waste An improper use or an abuse of a property by a possessor who holds less than fee ownership, such as a tenant, life tenant, mortgagor, or vendee. Such waste generally impairs the value of the land or the interest of the person holding the title or the reversionary rights.

Will A written document, properly witnessed, providing for the transfer of title to property owned by the deceased, called the *testator*.

Wraparound mortgage A method of refinancing in which the new mortgage is placed in a secondary, or subordinate, position; the new mortgage includes both the unpaid principal balance of the first mortgage and whatever additional sums are advanced by the lender. In essence, it is an additional mortgage in which another lender refinances a borrower by lending an amount over the existing first mortgage amount without disturbing the existence of the first mortgage.

Year-to-year tenancy A periodic tenancy in which rent is collected yearly.

Zoning ordinance An exercise of police power by a municipality to regulate and control the character and use of property.

Answer Key

Answer Key Following are the correct answers to the review questions included in each chapter of the text (except Chapter 14, which has no questions). In parentheses following the correct answers are references to the pages where the question topics are discussed or explained. If you have answered a question incorrectly, be sure to go back to the page or pages noted and restudy the material until you understand the correct answer.

Chapter 1

1. c (4)
2. d (8, 9)
3. c (4)
4. d (4)
5. c (4, 5)
6. d (5)
7. a (5)
8. a (4)
9. b (3)
10. c (3)
11. d (3, 4)
12. c (6)
13. b (5)
14. d (9)
15. b (4)
16. c (5, 6)

Chapter 2

1. b (22)
2. d (17)
3. b (18)
4. c (17)
5. a (19)
6. c (17, 18)
7. d (15, 16)
8. b (16)
9. c (19)
10. d (15)
11. a (18, 19)
12. b (18, 19)
13. c (18, 19)
14. d (16)
15. c (15, 16)
16. a (18)
17. c (19)
18. d (22)
19. d (23)
20. c (18)
21. d (23)
22. c (20)

Chapter 3

1. d (29)
2. a (34)
3. a (30)
4. c (35, 36)
5. a (33)
6. c (32)
7. c (31)
8. d (30)
9. d (31)
10. b (32)
11. d (32, 33)
12. d (31)
13. d (34)

Chapter 4

1. d (44)
2. b (46, 47)
3. b (46)
4. c (45)
5. c (49, 50)
6. a (42)
7. c (44–46)
8. c (44–46)
9. b (50)
10. a (51)
11. c (47)
12. c (49)
13. b (41)
14. a (45)
15. b (45, 46)
16. d (47)
17. c (47)
18. b (47)
19. b (48)
20. d (48)

Chapter 5

1. c (59)
2. a (59–61)
3. d (64)
4. b (64)
5. b (64)
6. c (59, 60)
7. b (62)
8. c (64, 65)
9. a (64, 65)
10. b (57, 58)
11. b (58)
12. c (57)
13. a (58)
14. c (60)
15. b (59)
16. d (62, 63)
17. d (58, 59)
18. c (66)
19. a (57, 58)
20. a (57)

Chapter 6

1. b (73)
2. c (74)
3. b (76)
4. a (73, 74)
5. d (74)
6. c (74, 75)
7. c (76)
8. c (75)
9. d (75)
10. a (76)
11. d (77, 80)
12. d (75, 76)
13. c (76)
14. b (74)
15. d (74, 76)

Chapter 7

1. c (89)
2. b (85)
3. d (93, 95)
4. a (91–92)
5. a (86)
6. b (93)
7. a (89)
8. c (86)
9. d (93)
10. b (89)
11. d (95)
12. a (89)
13. a (93)
14. a (86)
15. c (95)
16. a (86)
17. c (97)
18. d (91–92)

19. c (85)
20. d (91)

Chapter 8

1. d (106)
2. d (105)
3. c (106, 107)
4. b (105)
5. b (112)
6. b (103)
7. d (105)
8. a (110)
9. a (109)
10. d (106, 108)
11. b (105)
12. c (110, 111)
13. b (111)
14. d (112, 113)
15. d (108)
16. b (112, 113)
17. a (109)
18. b (106, 108)
19. c (105)
20. a (108)
21. b (113)
22. b (107)
23. c (108)
24. c (108)
25. a (114)
26. a (112)

Chapter 9

1. b (121)
2. b (125)
3. d (128)
4. d (125)
5. d (121)
6. b (121)
7. a (126)
8. c (125)
9. b (125)
10. b (125)
11. d (125)
12. c (125)
13. b (131)
14. d (131)
15. d (129)
16. c (130)
17. a (125)
18. c (124)
19. d (125)
20. b (131)

Chapter 10

1. d (137)
2. d (144)
3. c (142)
4. b (138)
5. b (143)
6. c (140)
7. c (140)
8. c (140)
9. d (139)
10. c (144, 145)
11. b (144)
12. a (144, 145)
13. c (137)
14. b (138, 139)
15. a (143)
16. c (143)
17. b (140, 142)
18. c (137)
19. d (146)
20. d (146)

Chapter 11

1. d (153)
2. b (163)
3. d (155)
4. a (162)
5. d (153, 154)
6. d (158)
7. b (156)
8. b (157)
9. c (159)
10. b (154)
11. b (155)
12. c (156)
13. a (163)
14. d (164, 165)
15. b (165)
16. d (163)
17. d (157)
18. c (159)
19. b (159)
20. c (162)
21. a (162, 163)
22. b (163)
23. c (164)
24. d (164)
25. b (158)

Chapter 12

1. d (175, 188)
2. a (175)

3. d (176)
4. b (179)
5. d (186)
6. c (177)
7. b (185)
8. a (178, 179)
9. b (179)
10. a (186)
11. a (182)
12. d (183)
13. b (180)
14. a (175)
15. c (187, 188)
16. d (180)
17. b (182)
18. d (183)
19. b (183)
20. d (180, 184)
21. b (187)
22. b (175)
23. d (180)
24. b (180, 183)
25. a (178)

Chapter 13

1. d (197, 198)
2. c (199)
3. c (196)
4. a (197)
5. b (206)
6. c (203, 204)
7. d (196, 197)
8. b (199)
9. d (198)
10. a (198)
11. b (196)
12. a (195)
13. d (203)
14. a (197)
15. c (197, 198)
16. d (195)
17. c (199)
18. b (206)
19. d (197)
20. a (197)

Chapter 15

1. b (242)
2. c (221)
3. a (226)
4. b (248)
5. c (240)
6. c (243)

7. d (241)
8. d (243)
9. c (247)
10. b (247)
11. c (244)
12. c (247, 248)
13. a (219)
14. b (236)
15. b (219, 220)
16. a (224)
17. d (240)
18. a (221)
19. b (237)
20. b (225, 226)
21. b (249)
22. d (249)
23. b (236)
24. d (241)
25. b (227)
26. d (234)

Chapter 16

1. d (257)
2. d (257)
3. c (268)
4. c (268)
5. d (266)
6. a (268)
7. c (257)
8. c (268)
9. a (258)
10. c (266)
11. c (259)
12. d (259)
13. d (259, 263)
14. b (266)
15. b (268)
16. a (264)
17. d (267)
18. d (266, 267)
19. b (265)
20. b (264)

Chapter 17

1. b (284)
2. d (280, 282)
3. d (282)
4. c (284)
5. c (275)
6. c (282)
7. c (275)
8. d (280)
9. c (281)

10. a (280)
11. d (281)
12. c (284)
13. d (282)
14. c (284)
15. c (283)

Chapter 18

1. a (294)
2. c (291)
3. b (294)
4. a (292)
5. d (293)
6. a (293)
7. d (297, 298)
8. c (301)
9. b (297)
10. a (298, 299)
11. c (298, 299)
12. b (295)
13. d (298)
14. a (291)
15. b (298, 299)
16. c (297)
17. b (294)
18. d (294, 295)
19. b (298, 299)
20. a (295)
21. c (299)
22. b (298)

Chapter 19

1. b (315)
2. a (311)
3. c (312)
4. d (312)
5. b (309)
6. a (315)
7. d (310)
8. c (313)
9. c (315)
10. c (310)
11. c (314, 315)
12. c (310)
13. a (315)
14. d (310)
15. b (311)
16. b (312)

Chapter 20

1. b (324)
2. a (321)

3. c (323)
4. b (324)
5. b (325)
6. b (325)
7. d (324)
8. b (324)
9. b (325)
10. d (323, 324)
11. c (322)
12. a (326)
13. b (327)
14. b (321)
15. a (327)
16. d (325)

Chapter 21

1. c (334)
2. a (338)
3. c (342–344)
4. c (337, 338)
5. c (334)
6. d (335)
7. b (339)
8. d (342–344)
9. a (335)
10. a (333)
11. c (335)
12. d (337)
13. c (334, 343)
14. c (338)
15. d (334)

Chapter 22

1. a (349)
2. c (350)
3. c (353)
4. a (355)
5. a (352)
6. d (357)
7. b (351)
8. a (351)
9. c (352)
10. a (353)
11. d (354)
12. d (353)
13. a (350)
14. b (353)
15. c (353, 354)
16. c (356)
17. c (356, 357)
18. a (353)
19. a (355)

Chapter 23

1. d (374)
2. c (373)
3. a (373)
4. d (374)
5. b (370)
6. d (365)

7. c (370)
8. c (371)
9. a (372)
10. c (375)
11. b (375)
12. d (375)
13. c (375)

14. b (375)
15. d (375)
16. d (375)
17. a (371)
18. c (367)
19. d (367)
20. c (370)

Mathematics Review Answer Key

1. $79,500 sale price × 6½% commission =
$79,500 × .065 = $5,167.50, Happy Valley's commission
$5,167.50 × 30% or $5,167.50 × .30 = $1,550.25, listing salesperson's commission

b. $1,550.25

2.

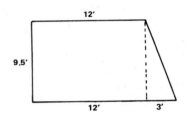

12' × 9.5' = 114 square feet, area of rectangle
½ (3' × 9.5') = ½ (28.5) = 14.25 square feet, area of triangle
114 + 14.25 = 128.25 square feet
To convert square feet to square yards divide by 9:
128.25 ÷ 9 = 14.25 square yards
$11.95 carpet + $2.50 installation = $14.45 cost per square yard
$14.45 × 14.25 square yards = $205.9125 or $205.91

c. $205.91

3. $30,000 Peters + $35,000 Gamble + $35,000 Clooney = $100,000
$125,000 − $100,000 = $25,000, Considine's contribution
$$\frac{part}{total} = percent$$
$25,000 ÷ $125,000 = .20 or 20%

a. 20%

4. $391.42 × 12 = $4,697.04, annual interest
$$\frac{part}{percent} = total$$
$4,697.04 ÷ 11½% or $4,697.04 ÷ .115 = $40,843,826

b. $40,843.83

5. $68,500 × 12% = $68,500 × .12 = $8,220, annual increase in value
$68,500 + $8,220 = $76,720, current market value

a. $76,720

6. $95,000 \times 60\% = \$95,000 \times .60 = \$57,000$, assessed value
Divide by 100 because tax rate is stated per hundred dollars:
$\$57,000 \div 100 = \$570$
$\$570 \times \$2.85 = \$1,624.50$, annual taxes
Divide by 12 to get monthly taxes:
$\$1,624.50 \div 12 = \$135.375$

d. \$135.38

7.

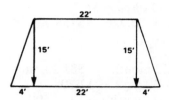

$22' \times 15' = 330$ square feet, area of rectangle
$\frac{1}{2} (4' \times 15') = \frac{1}{2} (60) = 30$ square feet, area of each triangle
$30 \times 2 = 60$ square feet, area of two triangles
$330 + 60 = 390$ square feet, surface area to be paved
$6''$ deep $= \frac{1}{2}$ foot
$390 \times \frac{1}{2} = 195$ cubic feet, cement needed for patio

d. 195 cubic feet

8. $\$3,675 - \$500$ salary $= \$3,175$ commission on sales
$\$3,175 \div 2.5\% = \$3,175 \div .025 = \$127,000$, value of property sold

b. \$127,000

9. two sides of $95'$ plus one side of $42'6''$
$95' \times 2 = 190$ feet
$42'6'' = 42.5$ feet
$190 + 42.5 = 232.5$ linear feet
$232.5 \times \$6.95 = \$1,615.875$

c. \$1,615.88

10. $\$4,500 \times 12 = \$54,000$ annual rental
$\$54,000 \div 8\% = \$54,000 \div .08 = \$675,000$, original cost of property

a. \$675,000

11. $\$1,340 \div 12$ months $= \$111.667/\text{month}$
$\$111.667 \div 30$ days $= \$3.722/\text{day}$
$\$111.667 \times 2$ months $= \$223.334$
$\$3.722 \times 15$ days $= \$55.830$
$\$223.334 + \$55.830 = \$279.164$

b. \$279.16

12. $\$58,200 \times 12\% = \$58,200 \times .12 = \$6,984$
$\$6,984 \div 12$ months $= \$582/\text{month}$
$\$582 \div 30$ days $= \$19.40/\text{day}$
30-day month $- 11$ days $= 19$ days
$\$19.40 \times 19$ days $= \$368.60$

d. \$368.60

13.   1985   17

       1~~986~~   ~~5~~   31   policy expiration date

   − 1985   9   20   closing date

               8   11   = 8 months, 11 days

$680 ÷ 3 years = $226.667/year

$226.667 ÷ 12 months = $18.889/month

$18.889 ÷ 30 days = $ .630/day

$18.889 × 8 months = $151.112

$ .630 × 11 days = $6.926

$151.112 + $6.926 = $158.038

a. $158.04

14. $975 ÷ 12 months = $81.25/month

$81.25 ÷ 30 days = $2.708

$81.25 × 2 months = $162.500

$2.708 × 4 days = $10.832

$162.500 + $10.832 = $173.332

a. $173.33

15. $61,550 × 13% = $61,550 × .13 = $8,001.500

$8,001.500 ÷ 12 months = $666.792/month

$666.792 ÷ 30 days = $22.226/day

$22.226 × 22 days = $488.972

b. $488.97

16. 43,560 sq. ft./acre × 100 acres = 4,356,000 sq. ft.

4,356,000 total sq. ft. × ⅛ = 544,500 sq. ft. for streets

4,356,000 − 544,500 = 3,811,500 sq. ft. for lots

3,811,500 sq. ft. ÷ 140 lots = 27,225 sq. ft./lot

c. 27,225

Index